Cooking
Jewish

Cooking

BY JUDY BART KANCIGOR

Jewish

WORKMAN PUBLISHING · NEW YORK

Library of Congress Cataloging-in-Publication Data is available.

ISBN-13: 978-0-7611-3581-4 (pb)

ISBN-13: 978-0-7611-4452-6 (hc)

Cover and book design by Lisa Hollander

Photographs courtesy of the author, unless otherwise noted with photo and on page 614

Workman books are available at special discounts when purchased in bulk for premiums and sales promotions as well as for fund-raising or educational use. Special editions or book excerpts can be created to specification. For details, contact the Special Sales Director at the address below.

Workman Publishing Company, Inc.

225 Varick Street

New York, NY 10014-4381

www.workman.com

Manufactured in the United States of America

First printing July 2007

10 9 8 7 6 5 4 3 2 1

In Memoriam

In loving memory of
my dad, Jan Bart

My grandparents,
Hinda and Harry
Rabinowitz

Irene Rosenthal

Mac Rosenthal

Sally Bower

Lou Bower

Estelle Robbins

Willy Robbins

Al Robbins

Shirley Robbins

Morris Robbins

Sylvia Robbins

Hilda Robbins

Harold Dubin

With love and gratitude
to my mother,
Lillian Bart

Every daughter
deserves a mother like you!

i'm so farklempt!

Just saying "thank you" doesn't begin to express the overwhelming gratitude I feel toward the hundreds of people who cooked for me, ransacked their photo albums for me, answered my endless questions, and cheered me on (and also humored me through my neurotic obsessions!) during this four-year adventure of expanding *Melting Pot Memories*, my self-published love letter to my family, into the book you have before you.

Thanks first to the Workman family—and they truly are a family—with Peter Workman, the wise and visionary patriarch heading this awesome and talented tribe. To be published at all is a writer's dream; to be published by Workman is an astounding honor. (Steven Raichlen said it best: "Do you realize, Judy, that you've just won the lottery?!!")

To my editor, Suzanne Rafer, respected advisor, savvy collaborator, and sensitive friend: Into your capable hands I entrusted "my baby," and in return you shared your wisdom, experience, compassion, and wit. Thanks for somehow extracting bursts of creativity I never knew were in me, and for letting me break one heck of a lot of rules. Thanks also to Ann ffolliott for your editorial assistance and to Helen Rosner, for answering every request with haste and good cheer. Kudos to production editor Irene Demchyshyn and her proofing elves whose job it is to make me look good. To my copy editor, Kathie Ness, the most detail-oriented person I know, many thanks for saving me from embarrassment. You taught me humility!

To Lisa Hollander, she of the perfect eye, for your brilliant design work. You couldn't have put more heart into this project if it were for your own family. And thanks to your able assistants, Lori Malkin, Dave Riedy, Thea Kennedy, and Kat Millerick. Thanks, too, to Barbara Peragine for all your hard work in getting the design ready for press. And many thanks to Anne Kerman for her great photo help on the cover and Cathy Dorsey for an astounding job on the index.

If a book is published in a forest and no one is there to get out the word, will anybody know about it? Workman's sales team is the best! Many thanks also to my enthusiastic publicity team, especially Ron Longe and Jen Paré Neugeboren. I couldn't be in better hands! And special thanks to Jim Eber (blue-eyes) for making the *shidduch*.

Some things take a village, but this cookbook took the planet! My daily contact with the members of the Jewish Food Mailing List (and its offshoot, Rinaslist) was an invaluable resource. With the click of a mouse, I could lean over my virtual back fence and schmooze with over two thousand Internet neighbors from forty-five countries to solve culinary crises or ask a question about kashrut or Jewish food, cooking history, or traditions. (And you can too! Go to www.jewishfood-list.com.) The information I gleaned from these generous folks could have earned me a degree over the four years I was writing this book—many of them even volunteered to test recipes for me!—but most of all, I treasure the many friendships developed with these giving souls that I've never even met.

While the recipe testers are included in the list below, I would also like to thank Malkie Altman, Wendy Baker, Ruth Baks, Viviane Barzel, Nancy Berry, Dalia Carmel, Kaye Fox, Carolyn C. Gilboa, Susan Green, Naomi Horowitz, Barbara Kaye,

the test of time

◦ ◦ ●

With a thousand recipes to test and retest (whittled down over four years to the 532 that follow) I never could have finished without the help of the many e-mail buddies, relatives, and friends (and friends of friends!) listed below. I'm blown away by your generosity.

Deena Abraham
Carolyn Arnold
Elaine Asa
Sherill Atkins
Tracey Barrett
Gary Bart
Karina Ramos Bart
Lillian Bart
Al Benner
Rita Berlin
Carolyn Blackman
Harriet Botwin
Robin Kancigor Boyko
Teresa Bransky
Heidi Brown
Sandy Calin
Betsy Cheek
Donna Chessen
Ian Choset
Ellyn Clark
Babette Cohen
Brent Cohen
Fredericka Cohen
Leba Cohen
Lilly Kancigor Cohen
Wendy Altman Cohen
Sharon Conway
Cindy Cutler
Linda Daniels
Susan Daoust
Eliane Driessen
Laurence Dubroff
Elena Eder
Monica Engel
Peggy Fallon

Ellen Friedman
Joan Friedman
Glenda Galvan-Garcia
Kim Garden
Ellen Gardner
Doris Gelman
Judy Gelman
Corinne Gibbel
Maury Gibbel
Norene Gilletz
Dede Ginter
Caryn Glasky
Diane Globerman
Lorraine Gold
Susan Goldstein
Debbie Goldwater
Linda Gomberg
Dyan Goodman
Julie Goodman
Linda Gordon
Lois Goren
Marlene Sorosky Gray
Lynn Hamlin
Naomi Horowitz
Jeffrey Janis
Stephanie Kamornick
Shelly Kancigor
Stu Kancigor
Valerie Kanter
Sheilah Kaufman
Joan Kekst
Eva Kilgore
Alyse Kirschen
Barbara Klingsberg
Gloria Kremer

Vicki Krupp
Marylyn Lamstein
Anita Lanner
Jennifer Lerner
Christine Levin
Nancy Levinson
Jessica Levine Levy
Cheryl Liebowitz
Jenna Mackoff
Jodi Orlow Mackoff
Samantha Mackoff
Elyse Mancy
Joyce Marumoto
Susan McNeice
Cathy Mishra
Rene Mosbacher
Cindy Mushet
Marlene Mutzman
Shari Nagy
Taylor Nagy
Helaine Nelson
Jane Peterson
Kathy Pettit
Carla Polakowski
Barbara Queen
Jeanette Ramos
Daryl Robbins
Samra Robbins
Hy Rocklin
Trina Ross
Diane Sachs
Betty Sackler
Virginia Sauer

SueAnn Scheck
Davida Schreiber
Marlene Schwartz-Ehrens
Laura Seligman
Judy Sennesh
Judy Shandling
Barbara Shenson
Pnina Shichor
Joyce Simpson
Valerie Sloane
Carla Small
Judy Sobel
Danielle Solomonic
Suzy Orlow Solomonic
Rachel Stern
Louise Sussman
Barbara Swartz
Hal Taback
Joyce Taback
Raya Tarab
Miriam Van Raalte
Lainy Vinikow
Michael Weisberg
Beth Weisman
Judi Weisman
Joe Werner
Terri Pischoff Wuerthner
Stacey Wilcox
Ariel Wolf
Michelle Wolf
Ronna Wolf
Yehudis Zidele
Debbie Zimmerman

and especially Joanne Rocklin and Brad Kancigor, whose families survived on *Cooking Jewish* experiments for literally months on end, but most of all to Bill Jonke and Sandy Glazier, who took on recipe testing as if their very lives depended on it and without whom I never would have crossed the finish line.

Sharon Kuritsky, Arlene Mathes-Scharf, Marianne Meisels, Jenni Person, Rina Perry, Moshe Reuter, Judy Rin, Judy Sennesh, Sharon Stein, Judy Sobel, Barbara Swasser, Julia Thiele, Liliana Wajnberg, and Maxine Wolfson for their expertise and advice—apologies if I've forgotten anyone!—with a special hug to Brian Mailman, owner and moderator of the list, who continues to astound me with his vast knowledge of cooking and kashrut.

Thanks to the scores of friends, acquaintances, and even strangers who allowed me to turn every party, gathering, chavurah meeting, or temple function I attended during the four years I worked on this book into a recipe-testing event. You welcomed my offerings, whether they matched your menu or not (doesn't everyone eat Pesach in July?), and you and your guests enthusiastically filled out my questionnaires, adding useful critiques. Special thanks to Judi Weisman for organizing a testing party at her condominium's clubhouse for forty-five people.

Scores of other guinea pigs lined up to taste and review my many experiments: The staff and assorted walk-ins at Temple Beth Tikvah, especially Miriam Van Raalte, who tried out my recipes on unwitting attendees of temple Shabbat dinners (they *love* Chicken Stupid!); the staff at the Placentia Public Library where my mother volunteers (they're partial to sweets . . . *any* sweets!); my husband's coworkers, the gang at Hawkeye Development (can't get enough of that Chocolate Chip Mandelbrot); Pnina Shichor, Elaine Asa, and the crew at Bound to Travel (they inhaled the Layered Hummus and Eggplant), and my neighbors, the Bartletts, Bergrens, and Jan Swett (they like it all!).

i learned from the best

Thanks to: Robert Schueller at Melissa's/World Variety Produce, a walking encyclopedia on anything that grows anywhere.

Miriam Morgenstern of *Wine Spectator* and Eitan

Segal at Royal Kedem for teaching me about kosher wine.

Diane Bukatman of For the Love of Food in Reisterstown, Maryland, for the crash course on baking. Your hundreds of e-mails could be a book!

Barbara Shenson, who made a pie-maker out of this "not-a-dough person."

Sandy Calin, for picking up where Aunt Sally left off and teaching me to bake strudel.

Pnina Shichor, for the sufganiyot lessons . . . in your office yet!

Fred Hyde at Poul's Bakery in Tustin, California, for enabling me to resurrect Mama Hinda's challah.

Natalie Haughton, food editor of the *L.A. Daily News*, for the oo's and ah's I get each Passover for my knock-their-socks-off presentation (her idea) of my Apple Matzoh Schalat.

Norman Kolpas for your encouragement. You really get it!

Gershon Padwa, Yehudis Zidele at Kof-K, Arlene Mathes-Scharf at www.kashrut.com, and Rabbi Eliezer Eidlitz at www

.kosherquest.org for keeping me kosher.

Lisa Ekus, media trainer extraordinaire, for readying me for my close-up with flair.

Joyce Marumoto and Taji Marie for bringing my act to Sur La Table.

Rabbi Haim and Elaine Asa, friends and advisors for thirty-five years, for translating the Hebrew street map and answering a gazillion questions.

Steve Rabinowitz (no relation), Barbara Musikar, Gertrude Ogushwitz, and Zvi Shefat, fellow "Slonimers," for providing information about Mama and Papa's birthplace.

Harvey Liss for producing my first website and coining the name Cooking Jewish. Who knew?

Barry Kancigor, Brad Kancigor, Ira Nelson, and Warren Ernst, my able tech support team.

Helaine Nelson, the first one I turn to, since high school, to find a word, check punctuation or grammar, or for an objective opinion.

Edith Goodman and Ann Nanes, I thank you, and my dentist thanks you, for keeping me from breaking my *tzayna* (teeth) over the Yiddish language.

Joanne Rocklin for suggesting that I too could write and inspiring me to find my voice.

Raghavan Iyer, for your shoulders to lean on and knees to knock against.

And to Peggy Fallon, for keeping what passes for my sanity. Your hilarious e-mails are posted on my bulletin board (especially the one that begins "STOP THE INSANITY!"). Without you I would have written this book from a padded cell.

Boundless gratitude and love to Cathy Thomas, my editor at *The Orange County Register* and cherished friend, who took a chance on me, with no experience or training, and handed me a food-writing career. Your evocative descriptions of taste, sight, and smell are

author, author

● ● ●

Each author I've interviewed for my column and articles has taught me something about cooking or Judaism, everything from melting chocolate to the strictures of Passover. Thanks, especially, to the following for your generous help: Tamar Ansh, Rose Levy Beranbaum, Lora Brody, Penny Eisenberg, Peggy Fallon, Susie Fishbein, Gale Gand, Norene Gilletz, Miriyam Glazer, Maggie Glezer, Marcy Goldman, Joyce Goldstein, Marlene Sorosky Gray, Raghavan Iyer, Sheilah Kaufman, Joan Kekst, Levana Kirschenbaum, Elinor Klivans, Alice Medrich, Kitty Morse, Cindy Mushet, Joan Nathan, Terri Pischoff Wuerthner, Amelia Saltzman, Judy Zeidler, and Zell Schulman.

Special thanks to Jennifer Abadi, my Sephardic cooking expert, for my hands-on lesson in borekas, filas, and baklava; to Faye Levy: Who woulda thunk that after you wrote *1,000 Jewish Recipes* anyone could possibly still have questions, but you were always there to answer every one of mine; to Gil Marks, rabbi, historian, and chef, for your inexhaustible knowledge of Jewish law and holiday origins.

And to Sharon Boorstin, author of *Let Us Eat Cake* and *Cookin' for Love,* for convincing the powers-that-be at IACP that I belonged on a panel with you and Ruth Reichl. Thanks, Sharon, for your friendship and for opening the door!

the gold standard to which I can only dream to aspire. Thanks also to Steve Plesa, Helayne Perry, and Nick Koon at the *Register*; Carolyn Blackman at the *Canadian Jewish News;* Amy Klein, Naomi Pfefferman, Howard Blume, and Adam Wills at the *Jewish Journal of Greater Los Angeles;* and Barbara Giasone, Heather McRea, and Bob Ziebell at the *Fullerton News Tribune.* It is such a pleasure to work with all of you!

Thank you to the many Judaica and synagogue gift shops that took a chance on *Melting Pot Memories.* Forgive me for not mentioning them all, but I'm especially grateful to Julie and Shahrokh Ghodsi and Nancy Fox, Golden Dreidle, Newport Beach; Ellen Rose and Tim Fischer, Cook's Library, Los Angeles; Barbara Lang, Audrey's at the Skirball Museum, Los Angeles; Judy Ginsberg, Museum of Tolerance, Los Angeles and Beit Judaica, Agoura Hills; Vicki Flax, Ben Yehuda St., Los Alamitos; Jodi Kinzler, Vroman's, Pasadena; David Cooperman, Shalom House, Woodland Hills. In south Florida: Jeff Gordon, Traditions; Jill Kind, Ahava; and Richard Petrella, Book Fairs with Flair. Bijan Afrah, Chosen Treasures, Atlanta; Barry Greenberg, Brochin's, and Toots Vodovoz, Elijah's Cup, St. Louis Park, Minnesota; Adele Silver, Books & More Book Fairs, Michigan; Karen Adler and Frankie Victor at Scholastic; Tim McGowan at www. books-for-cooks.com; and kisses to Ronni Kaman, The Collector, Merrick, New York (and yes, Ronni, we kept the Cheesecake Bars!).

i sleep around

Thank you to those who opened their guest rooms to me and kept me from being homeless in my travels, shlepping me from hither to yon, wining and dining me, and otherwise serving as my personal escort service: Karina and Gary Bart, Phyllis and Peter Epstein, Lorraine and Michael Gold, Marylyn and Ben Lamstein, Debbie and Ronnie Levine, Carole Orlow, Carolyn Propis, Shirley Robbins, Sheri Simon-Cupkovic, Syble Solomon, Sharon Stein, Janet and Shelly Thaler, and Joyce and Artie Wolf.

the photos!

It's a good thing a picture is worth a thousand words or you'd never be able to lift this book. Thanks to the whole *mishpuchah* for

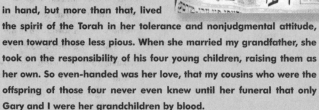

While the pages that follow overflow with tributes to my maternal grandparents, Hinda and Harry Rabinowitz, I would like to say a special thanks to my father's mother, Grandma Ruchel. She was very religious, prayed daily, *siddur* in hand, but more than that, lived the spirit of the Torah in her tolerance and nonjudgmental attitude, even toward those less pious. When she married my grandfather, she took on the responsibility of his four young children, raising them as her own. So even-handed was her love, that my cousins who were the offspring of those four never even knew until her funeral that only Gary and I were her grandchildren by blood.

giving life to this project with their treasured family photos, especially Sheilah and Ed Cohen, Wendy and Brent Cohen, Richard Gardner, Marilyn Dubin, Phyllis and Peter Epstein, David Miller, Rita Miller, Shari Nagy, Linda and Frank Nathan, Bonnie Robbins, Leslie and Marvin Robbins, Laura Seligman, Syble Solomon, Suzy Orlow Solomonic, Joyce Wolf, and a special thanks to Nick Koon.

thank you

To every one of the 303 family members and friends who contributed their recipes and stories (see pages XIV to XVII) to add to the Rabinowitz saga.

To Aunt Sally for your years of cooking with love, your patience with my endless phone calls and questions, your faultless memory, your penchant for saving, and especially your legible handwriting.

To Aunt Estelle, my second mother, for your instant enthusiasm. Even a little heart valve replacement couldn't prevent you from having your cookbook brought to the hospital so you could check off your favorites and give advice.

To Harold Dubin, our family gourmand and my constant advisor. I wore out your copy machine! Everything I asked for was done perfectly and with haste. No one would have enjoyed this cookbook more.

To my "brudda," Gary, who couldn't have taken a greater interest in this book if it were his own, reading every headnote, box, and essay, for your advice, love, and generosity and for finding your angel, Karina.

To my sister-in-law, Karina, who needed to pass the Bar to do my "grunt" work! I bless the day you came into our lives.

To my dad, Jan Bart, for setting the example of integrity and devotion and instilling in me your boundless curiosity and dedication. How you would have loved this project!

To my mother, Lil (Honey), my sounding board, my sous chef, my right arm, my one-woman fan club, my friend. You never say "no"! Without your help every step of the way, I could never have gotten into print.

To my husband, Barry, my high school sweetheart, for willingly tasting your way through this project (at great peril to your cholesterol), for running and shlepping and doing it without complaint, for being the best grandpa ever (in the Papa Harry tradition) and most of all enduring with humor and love my various obsessions, lo, these many years.

To my sons, Stu and Brad, who can count their culinary skills among their many talents, for your unfailing enthusiasm and support and for giving me the daughters I never had—your wonderful wives, Shelly and Tracey—both extraordinary cooks, so very helpful and always willing to give "just one more."

And finally to my grandchildren, Jason, Lauren, Samantha, and Blake, for just being so darn cute! It was Jason's impending birth coinciding with Aunt Estelle's illness that was the catalyst for this project. I wanted to preserve for you and the other *kinderlach* a taste of the miracle that is our family heritage.

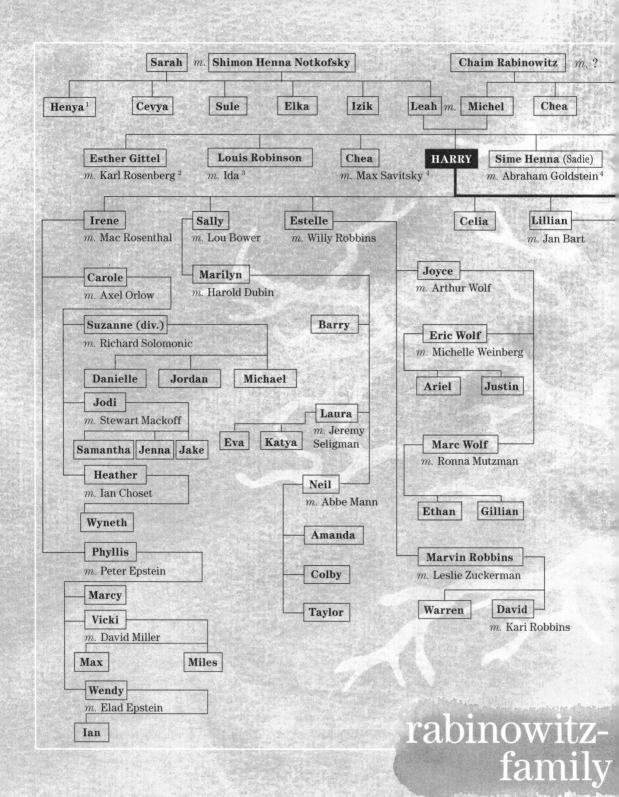

rabinowitz-
family

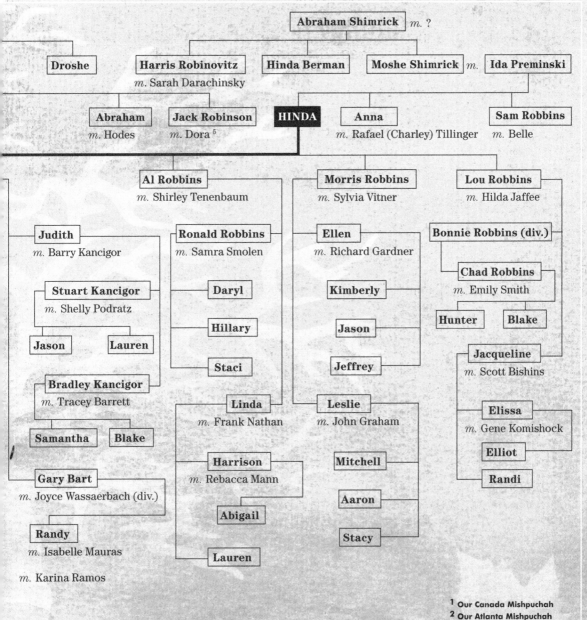

Abraham Shimrick *m.* ?

Droshe

Harris Robinovitz *m.* Sarah Darachinsky

Hinda Berman

Moshe Shimrick *m.* **Ida Preminski**

Abraham *m.* Hodes

Jack Robinson *m.* Dora [5]

HINDA

Anna *m.* Rafael (Charley) Tillinger

Sam Robbins *m.* Belle

Al Robbins *m.* Shirley Tenenbaum

Morris Robbins *m.* Sylvia Vitner

Lou Robbins *m.* Hilda Jaffee

Judith *m.* Barry Kancigor

Stuart Kancigor *m.* Shelly Podratz

Jason   **Lauren**

Bradley Kancigor *m.* Tracey Barrett

Samantha   **Blake**

Gary Bart *m.* Joyce Wassaerbach (div.)

Randy *m.* Isabelle Mauras

m. Karina Ramos

Ronald Robbins *m.* Samra Smolen

Daryl

Hillary

Staci

Linda *m.* Frank Nathan

Harrison *m.* Rebacca Mann

Abigail

Lauren

Ellen *m.* Richard Gardner

Kimberly

Jason

Jeffrey

Leslie *m.* John Graham

Mitchell

Aaron

Stacy

Bonnie Robbins (div.)

Chad Robbins *m.* Emily Smith

Hunter   **Blake**

Jacqueline *m.* Scott Bishins

Elissa *m.* Gene Komishock

Elliot

Randi

shimrick tree

our fabulous family chefs and storytellers

Altman, Blanche
*Wendy Cohen's
grandmother*

Altman, Claire
Juli Altman's wife

Altman, Juli
*Barry Kancigor's
cousin*

Applebaum, Elaine
Hilda Robbins's niece

Barrett, Joan
*Tracey Barrett's
mother*

Barrett, Tracey
Brad Kancigor's wife

Bart, Gary
*Judy Kancigor's
brother*

Bart, Jan
*Judy Kancigor's
father*

Bart, Karina
Gary Bart's wife

Bart, Lillian
Judy Kancigor's mother

Bart, Randy
Gary Bart's son

Bedo, Barbara
*Barbara Itzkowitz's
mother*

Bishins, Jackie
*Hilda Robbins's
daughter*

Bishins, Randi
*Jackie Robbins's
daughter*

Bower, Lou
*Sally Bower's
husband*

Bower, Mirtza
Lou Bower's mother

Bower, Sally
*Lillian Bart's
sister*

Boyko, Robin Kancigor
*Barry Kancigor's
cousin*

Boyko, Sophie
*Robin Boyko's
mother-in-law*

Cahn, Leah
*Samra Robbins's
grandmother*

Capler, Rose
*Rebecca Nathan's
grandmother*

Carlson, Vi
*Shelly Kancigor's
great-aunt*

Choset, Arlyne
*Heather Orlow-Choset's
mother-in-law*

Choset, Erica *Heather
Orlow-Choset's
sister-in-law*

Ciomei, Lisa
*Samra Robbins's
cousin*

Cohen, Brent
*Wendy Altman
Cohen's husband*

Cohen, Ed
Sally Cohen's son

Cohen, Esther
*Brent Cohen's
grandmother*

Cohen, Lilly Kancigor
*Barry Kancigor's
cousin*

Cohen, Sally
*Harry Rabinowitz's
niece*

Cohen, Sheilah
Ed Cohen's wife

Cohen, Wendy Altman
*Juli Altman's
daughter*

Crane, Jack
*Sadie Goldstein's
grandson*

Dubin, Abbe
Neil Dubin's wife

Dubin, Barry
Marilyn Dubin's son

Dubin, Harold
*Marilyn Dubin's
husband*

Dubin, Marilyn
*Sally Bower's
daughter*

Dubin, Neil
Marilyn Dubin's son

Einsbruch, Janice
Hilda Robbins's niece

Engel-Padwa, Malka
Gershon Padwa's aunt

Epstein, Marcy
*Phyllis Epstein's
daughter*

Epstein, Nava
*Wendy Epstein's
mother-in-law*

Epstein, Peter
*Phyllis Epstein's
husband*

Epstein, Phyllis
*Irene Rosenthal's
daughter*

Epstein, Trude
Peter Epstein's mother

Epstein, Wendy
*Phyllis Epstein's
daughter*

Feltingoff, Arlene
*Honorary Rabinowitz
(my best friend)*

Frank, Barb
*Shelly Kancigor's
aunt*

Frank, Robin
*Hilda Robbins's
niece*

Frank, Tom
*Shelly Kancigor's
uncle*

Frankel, Isabelle
Jan Bart's sister

Friedman, Essie
Jan Bart's sister

Fritkin, Sera
*Michelle Gullion's
grandmother*

Gardner, Ellen
*Sylvia Robbins's
daughter*

Gardner, Jason
Ellen Gardner's son

Gardner, Jeffrey
Ellen Gardner's son

Gardner, Kimberly
*Ellen Gardner's
daughter*

Gold, Lorraine
*Michael Gold's
wife*

Gold, Michael
*Judy Kancigor's
cousin*

Goldman, Bea
*Edith Kancigor's
cousin*

Goldstein, Sadie
*Harry Rabinowitz's
sister*

Moreno, Victoria
  Ketty Moreno's
  daughter
Musikar, Barbara
  Barry Kancigor's
  cousin
Mutzman, Marlene
  Ronna Wolf's mother
Nagy, Shari
  Marylyn Lamstein's
  daughter
Nagy, Taylor
  Shari Nagy's
  daughter
Nathan, Frank
  Linda Nathan's
  husband
Nathan, Harrison
  Linda Nathan's son
Nathan, Lauren
  Linda Nathan's
  daughter
Nathan, Linda
  Shirley Robbins's
  daughter
Nelson, Gerry
  Barry Kancigor's
  cousin
Orlow, Axel
  Carole Orlow's
  ex-husband
Orlow, Carole
  Irene Rosenthal's
  daughter
Orlow, Mady
  Axel Orlow's mother
Orlow-Choset, Heather
  Carole Orlow's
  daughter
Padwa, Gershon
  Barry Kancigor's
  cousin
Padwa, Ruchi
  Gershon Padwa's wife

Pincus, Beth
  Laura Seligman's
  sister-in-law
Podratz, Diane
  Shelly Kancigor's
  mother
Rabinowitz, Harry
  Judy Kancigor's
  grandfather
Rabinowitz, Hinda
  Judy Kancigor's
  grandmother
Riebe, Ilo
  Shelly Kancigor's
  grandmother
Robbins, Belle
  Hinda Rabinowitz's
  sister-in-law
Robbins, Bonnie
  Hilda Robbins's
  daughter
Robbins, Chad
  Bonnie Robbins's
  son
Robbins, Daryl
  Samra Robbins's
  daughter
Robbins, Emily
  Chad Robbins's
  wife
Robbins, Estelle
  Lillian Bart's sister
Robbins, Hilda
  Lou Robbins's wife
Robbins, Hillary
  Samra Robbins's
  daughter
Robbins, Kari
  Leslie Robbins's
  daughter-in-law
Robbins, Leslie
  Marvin Robbins's wife
Robbins, Lou
  Lillian Bart's brother

Robbins, Marvin
  Estelle Robbins's son
Robbins, Ronald
  Shirley Robbins's son
Robbins, Samra
  Ronald Robbins's wife
Robbins, Shirley
  Lillian Bart's sister-
  in-law
Robbins, Staci
  Samra Robbins's
  daughter
Robbins, Sylvia
  Lillian Bart's sister-
  in-law
Robbins, Warren
  Leslie Robbins's son
Rosenberg, Lena
  Harry Rabinowitz's
  sister Esther Gittel's
  husband's second
  wife
Rosenblum, Rose
  Alice Weiss's mother
Rosenthal, Irene
  Lillian Bart's sister
Schulte, Diane
  Shelly Kancigor's
  brother's mother-in-
  law
Seligman, Eva
  Laura Seligman's
  daughter
Seligman, Jeremy
  Laura Seligman's
  husband
Seligman, Laura
  Marilyn Dubin's
  daugher
Seligman, Robert
  Jeremy Seligman's
  father
Selmanowitz, Louis
  Livia Straus's father

Silberman, Nancy Gimpel
  Syble Solomon's
  sister-in-law
Simpson, Joyce
  Randy Bart's mother
Simpson, Lorraine
  Joyce Simpson's
  mother-in-law
Skolberg, Mary
  Shelly Kancigor's
  aunt
Smolen, Claire
  Samra Robbins's
  mother
Solomon, Allison Miller
  David Miller's sister
Solomon, Lil
  Syble Solomon's
  mother
Solomon, Syble
  Sadie Goldstein's
  granddaughter
Solomonic, Suzy Orlow
  Carole Orlow's
  daughter
Starrett, Marilyn
  Wendy Cohen's cousin
Straus, Barbara
  Judy Kancigor's
  cousin
Straus, Livia
  Judy Kancigor's
  cousin
Strausser, Ruchel
  Jan Bart's mother
Swartz, Inez
  Marilyn Dubin's
  sister-in-law
Tenenbaum, Mary
  Shirley Robbins's
  mother
Tillinger, Anna
  Hinda Rabinowitz's
  sister

Trinkler, Myra
*Stewart Mackoff's
aunt*
Vitner, Fanny
*Sylvia Robbins's
mother*
Vitner, Joanne
*Sylvia Robbins's
sister-in-law*
Wallach, Miriam
*Judy Kancigor's
cousin*

Warady, Barbara
*Brent Cohen's
cousin*
Weiser, Mollie
*David Miller's
grandmother*
Weiss, Alice
*Sylvia Robbins's
cousin*
Weiss, Marian
*Judy Kancigor's
cousin*

Wolf, Ariel
*Michelle and
Eric Wolf's
daughter*
Wolf, Arthur
*Joyce Wolf's
husband*
Wolf, Eric
Joyce Wolf's son
Wolf, Joyce
*Estelle Robbins's
daughter*

Wolf, Marc
Joyce Wolf's son
Wolf, Michelle
Eric Wolf's wife
Wolf, Ronna
Marc Wolf's wife
Zimmerman, Debbie
*Lorraine Gold's
daughter*
Zuckerman, Selma
*Leslie Robbins's
mother*

friends of the family

Aaron, Sylvia
Asa, Elaine
Atkins, Sherill
Baker, Wendy
Berlin, Rita
Bukatman, Diane
Cappel, Claire
Cohen, Babette
Cohen, Carol
Creighton, Chris
Cullen, Jonathan
Dana, Kathi
Dymond, Carolyn
Feltingoff, Brett
Fenster Family
Fouathia, Zoulikha
Freedman, Eleanor
Freilich, Diana
Friedman, Joan
Frohling, Kerry
Giambastiani, Scott
Giannone, Cathy
Gilboa, Carolyn C.
Goldberg, Janette
Goldstein, Anna

Gomberg, Linda
Goodman, Bernice
Goren, Lois
Graham, Rosie
Greenberg, Marilyn
Grob, Tracy
Hakim, Harvey
Hakim, Melissa
Hamenahem, Yuval
Hasson, Malca Luzia
Herzog, Lena
Horenstein, Barbara
Kaplowitz, Steve
Kaufman, Sheilah
Kay, Sally
Kellich, Wanda
Ketover, Barbara
Kirschenbaum, Corrinne
Klingsberg, Barbara
Kolodkin, Judy
Kravetz, Shayna
Kremer, Gloria
Levin, Ruth
Levy, Jintil
Levy, Rachel

Levy, Sydell
Lewis, Eileen
Lichtman, Jeff
Magnan, Sue
McGlawn, Steve
Mishra, Cathy
Mitrani, Rachel
Modelevsky, Loretta
Morett, Ben
Morris, Paul
Nachawati, Susan
Nelson, Max
Nodiff, Sarah Dolgin
Patterson, Brian
Porter, Michael
Quast, Linda
Reinstein, June
Reytan, Rosa
Rocklin, Adele
Rocklin, Joanne
Rosen, Barbara
Rosen, Chuck
Rousso, Gladys
Rubin, Deb
Rubin, Dorothy

Rubin, Helen
Sachs, Cole
Sackler, Betty
Schnee, Marilyn
Schneider, Amy
Schreiber, Marilyn
Sennesh, Judy
Shenson, Barbara
Shichor, Pnina
Silverberg, Eric
Sobel, Judy
Solomon, Dori
Swartz, Sylvan
Taback, Hal
Taback, Joyce
Tarab, Raya
Thacker, Carolyn
Wallach, Anna
Weisman, Judi
Weiss, David
Zeidler, Judy
Zubi, Guner

contents

introduction: recipe for a cookbook XXI

So I'm sitting minding my own business, and I'm thinking, I know. I'll collect my aunts' recipes and put them in a book. So look what happened! Meet the family, each with a recipe and a story to tell. You're gonna need a scorecard. (The photos will help.)

b'raysheet: in the beginning XXIX

Back in Slonim, first they liked us, then they hated us—Papa Harry said, "Enough already!" How my grandparents set down roots in the Promised Land, and from there sprang the whole *mishpuchah*.

cooking kosher XLVI

To play the game you gotta know the rules. If you're observant, you know all this stuff already. If not, here's a quick course in separating the meat from the dairy.

appetizers 3

A little nosh before the main event. Not "little" like the French with their dainty *amuse-bouches*. Not *that* little. And why just one? Have a knish and borekas and some chopped liver too. And a little hummus would be good. And try the eggplant. Hummus *with* the eggplant. M-m-m-m.

soups 61

I don't care what you say—my mother's chicken soup really *is* better than your mother's. Better than anybody's. But it doesn't stop there. Carrot, Mushroom Barley, Roasted Beet Borscht, lentil . . . and Shiitake Mushroom Matzoh Balls to go with them all! Soups from the Old World and soups from the New.

salads 93

You peel, you chop, and then you crunch. From Mandarin to Indian to Israeli, Korean, and Thai—I mean the salads, not the people. They're Jewish. Well, some of them are Israeli. Oh, you get the idea.

meats 127

You're thinking, Jewish cookbook—brisket. (Not that there's anything wrong with that!) We've got four, not counting two for the cholents, and darn proud of it! But there's also Moroccan Spicy Apricot Lamb

Shanks, Hazelnut Crusted Rack of Lamb, Osso Buco, Spanish Short Rib Stew. . . . Go ahead. Browse.

poultry

oasted with fennel, baked with cherries and chili sauce, stir-fried with walnuts, grilled with mustard and herbs—if it clucks you'll find it here. And no part of the chicken—or turkey or hen—is ever wasted.

fish

here's more than herring and gefilte in this chapter. Okay, lox too. Okay, herring and gefilte are in appetizers, and lox is in breakfast. But the other fish are here, like salmon five ways to Sunday and sea bass and halibut and mahi-mahi and . . .

vegetables

hey didn't eat 'em in Slonim, but we're in this country now. Flash-roasted asparagus. Portobello wrap. Southwestern Tsimmes in Chile Pockets. Triple Corn Pudding to die for. Spinach-Stuffed Squash. So be good and eat your veggies. Dessert is coming in just 130 pages.

potatoes, noodles, rice, and grains

ou want comfort? I'll give you comfort: Three kinds of latkes, a dozen noodle kugels, pirogen (potato and cheese), mamaliga, shlishkes, stuffings, sweet potatoes—with marshmallows, sure, but also with pecans or honey-orange glaze. And these they call side dishes?

breads

ou don't have to be Jewish to love challah. But put away the knife and tear off a piece. Unless you're making a French toast casserole or challah chips. Then you can use the knife. And if you don't have a bread machine, get one for the pita. You'll thank me. (If you're looking for onion rolls, pretzels, biscuits, and scones, they're in here too.)

breakfast

he most important meal of the day. Well, the most fun. Try the Hoppel-Poppel or blintzes or Apple-Cinnamon Pancakes or—wait! Caramel French Toast—no! Apple and Cheese-Stuffed French Toast. Oh, I can't make up my mind! You pick. Surprise me.

cakes

ow we're talking. Everything sweet and yummy. Old-fashioned Apple Cake. Chocolate, chocolate, chocolate. Peach, orange, and honey-orange sponge. Five kinds of cheesecake. And did I mention chocolate? Coffee cakes. Pound cake. Aunt Sally's Red, White, and Blue. Cut me just a sliver. Well, maybe a little bigger than that. Oh, give me that knife!

pies and pastries

ow a dough phobic found joy and happiness learning to make pie crust. (And if I can do it, you can too!) Now to fill it: towering apple topped with walnut

crunch, rhubarb, pecan, lemon meringue, Key lime with mountains of whipped cream . . . and baklava, strudel (and I'm not talking with filo—that would be cheating—I mean the real deal).

cookies

Jews invented cookies. At least dunking cookies. Okay, at least baking them by the dozens. Mandelbrot, rugelach, kichel, chocolate chip. Brownies, hamantaschen, New York Black & Whites. Rolled out, dropped, spread into bars, boiled in honey . . . that would be the taiglach, but promise me you'll be careful. That honey is hot! (Don't make me tell you twice.)

desserts and candy

In case there aren't enough sweets already, here's a fourth chapter. (Some people have a sweet tooth, but we have sweet teeth, every one of them.) You'll need a spoon: soufflé, flan, trifle, chocolate mousse, tiramisù, puddings, custard . . . you know, all that sweet, slippery, wobbly, and jiggly stuff. Oh, and candy too. Just 'cuz.

passover

Leave it to the Jews to take a board of matzoh and fashion a feast. Restrictions? Hah! We wait all year for this stuff. Yemenite Haroset Truffles, kugels savory and sweet, Sephardic Chicken, Mom's Killer Brisket with Tsimmes. And the sweets! Chocolate Fudge Pecan Pie, meringues, sponge cakes aplenty . . . we invented the term "I'm stuffed."

drinks

A woozy little dink of a chapter. But thirst-quenching. (This family is more likely to crowd the Viennese table than an open bar!) Yet several stalwarts save us from total abstinence with their Sea Breeze, Margarita, French 75. . . . Then there's my husband's Egg Cream and malted. You'll have a glass of tea, a cup of coffee—it'll be fine.

conversion tables

No, silly, not that kind of conversion. You know, metric and cups to quarts and all that good stuff you can't remember from geometry . . . or was it algebra?

who's who

Did I mention you were gonna need a scorecard? For the photo montages you'll want to know the players. Take notes. There'll be a test later.

credits

Here's a list of the professional photographers and cookbook authors who so generously allowed me to use their work.

index

You're so busy you can't just sit there and read? Suit yourself. You'll look it up and you'll find it. But don't complain to me if you miss something.

recipe for a cookbook

Before Food TV, even before cookbooks, our foremothers were *shiterein* cooks. Who needs to measure? You throw in a little of this and a little of that, and a wonderful dish emerges. Far from haphazard, it's a style born of experience, confidence, instinct, and skill.

You don't have to be Jewish to be a *shiterein* cook. Throughout history little girls have watched their mothers, grandmas, and aunts and learned just how much water to add to the dough, how long to knead it, and how long to bake it.

My grandmother, Mama Hinda, was a *shiterein* cook. She didn't need a recipe to tell her how much sugar to add to the applesauce she made with apples from our backyard tree, or how much farina went into the ground beef fat she got from the kosher butcher for her kishka. She never wrote down her recipes, and if not

shiterein (yiddish):
v. to add an unspecified amount **adj.** describing one who cooks from experience and touch without recipes or measuring

for Aunt Sally, who memorialized them in a notebook, we wouldn't have them either.

When pinned down, the *shiterein* cook may provide somewhat quirky measurements and instructions. As Sam Levenson writes in his memoir *In One Era & Out the Other:*

"How much flour do you use, Ma?"

"What do you mean, how much do I use?"

"I mean a cup, a half cup . . .?"

"What do you need cups for? You use your head."

"Okay. So how many eggs?"

"Not too many."

"How much sugar?"

"Not too much."

"How much salt?"

"Not too salty."

"How much water?"

"A mouthful."

"What? Okay. So how long do I leave it in the oven?"

"It shouldn't burn."

In compiling recipes for this cookbook, I encountered the following variations on the same theme:

"A glass flour" or
"A gluzzela" (little glass)

"An eggshell water"

"2 cents yeast"

"A nice piece of veal"

"Beat the eggs good"

"If too sweet, next time add less sugar"

"Till it smells good"

"Until it's just right"

and of course, the ever popular: *"Cook until done."*

I love this one from my friend Amy Schneider's mother-in-law, Dora: "First you put water up to the screws in the pot." But my personal favorite is from my friend Shayna Kravetz's mother, Rebbitzen Shoshanna Kravetz of Winnipeg, whose recipe for Iced Fruit Torte begins: "Six months ago you put cherries to soak in brandy."

Perhaps you'll note herein a rather eclectic assortment of recipes. The contributors to this cookbook range in age from four to ninety-four and represent many different eras and cuisines. Cholent resides very comfortably between the same covers as boeuf bourguignon; gefilte fish and horseradish-crusted salmon; kreplach and shiitake mushroom matzoh balls. The old recipes are a window into a world, a reflection of a way of life. Through them we learn Jewish history—and it doesn't hurt that they're tasty too!

Note: This is not the definitive book on authentic Jewish cooking. This is a slice of life, as it were, a portrait of one family, warts and all, how we live and how we cook. So if we put ketchup in our *fassoulias*, go ahead and roll your eyes, but don't knock it till you try it!

In a way what follows is a *shiterein* cookbook. Over 200 family members contributed more than 500 recipes, but they also sent in stories, letters, photos, poems, drawings, documents, Russian history, maps—a little of this, a little of that, until we *shitereined* the saga of the Rabinowitz clan for all to taste and, hopefully, enjoy.

Aunt Irene, about 1923.

getting started

I began this project in 1996, when my dear Aunt Estelle was facing a heart valve replacement and we were counting the months for our Jason to be born. Our first grandchild—is there a greater joy?—was about to enter our world and my second mother was slipping away. Eager anticipation and dire dread waged war in my mind, as Time marched inexorably on. If only, like Jim Croce, "I could save time in a bottle."

As Aunt Estelle's condition worsened, Aunt Sally was moving into assisted living, Aunt Hilda was on dialysis, and Aunt Irene didn't know who I was when I called. That's when it hit me. One generation was leaving; another generation was coming. How would my new grandchild know the history of our family? Would he hear the stories? Would he ever taste all the wonderful food so wrapped in memories of love? I thought, if only I could reach my arms across the generations and somehow pass on to this child a taste of the legacy that had been bequeathed to me.

I decided that I would be a conduit and pass along Aunt Estelle's essence to the great-great-nephew that she would never hold. And because I love my family and because I love food, I decided to write a family cookbook. But it would be more than a cookbook, I envisioned. It would hold precious old photos of our family and the Russian town my grandparents had left almost a century before, some of the documents and maps I had collected fifteen years earlier when my hobby/obsession was genealogy, an updated family tree, and most important, as many stories as I could gather.

I would try to tell, with laughter and with love, the history of our family from the shtetl to the suburbs. And I'd do it where Jewish families always gather, of course—in the kitchen!

So I sent letters to my Rabinowitz aunts, my first cousins, and their adult children, asking them for their signature recipes and for stories. The response was overwhelming! In-laws of in-laws begged to be in the cookbook, and my answer was a resounding "yes!" Anyone related to the Rabinowitzes by blood or marriage was eagerly wel-

comed, which meant I would include my dad's family and my husband Barry's family as well. My little project was growing. I called the book *Melting Pot Memories* and planned to self-publish it for my family and friends. By print time 156 family members were included (not to mention some talented friends who slipped in through the back door).

Early in the process I enrolled in a cookbook-writing seminar at UCLA given by food writer and cookbook author Norman Kolpas. The class was gathered in a huge lecture hall, and Norman began by asking us each to stand and state our project. Everyone in the room was either a chef, a food writer, a caterer, or a restaurateur. When it was my turn, I was very intimidated, and I mumbled, "Oh, I'm just writing a family cookbook." Norman got very serious, pointed a finger at me for emphasis, and said, "What you are doing is very important. Don't let anything stop you." I remembered those words as I plowed along, but I still thought of my

Aunt Estelle, 1950s.

project as basically a recipe book, never imagining that anyone outside of my family and loyal friends would ever see it.

The first recipe I tested was Mama Hinda's Passover Nut Cake (page 571), which our family had not seen in decades. When it came out of the oven, I broke off a piece and put it in my mother's mouth. "Ma, is this it?" I asked. I was astonished to see her eyes widen and then brim with tears! What memories flooded her mind she did not reveal, but at that moment I knew that Norman Kolpas was right. *What I was doing was very important.*

Unlike a photo or even a video, a treasured recipe, passed down from mother to daughter for who knows how long, summons the past with all five senses, revealing a slice of our

Evolution of a Jewish Cookbook

GENERATION 1: 1907. Mama Hinda steps off boat, baby Ida (Irene) in tow. Under that babushka lies the hope for a new life, the determination that her children will be educated and will succeed, and centuries of inbred passion to nurture her family. She feeds them without a cookbook. Her recipes are "in her head," and despite improving financial circumstances, she continues to produce the familiar delicacies of the shtetl. She needs few tools. A *yahrtzeit* glass is her measuring cup, a hand chopper her Cuisinart. Her ingredients are simple, the food delicious: potatoes, bread, chicken fat, every conceivable innard and organ. Cholesterol is a far-off future scientific enigma, like moon landings and DNA. She lives to be ninety-one, her husband eighty-nine.

Papa and Mama, 1940s.

GENERATION 2: Her children, the "Magnificent 7" grow up on the kishka and kreplach of Mama's kosher kitchen. They speak English, thrive in the *goldena medina*, fulfill their parents' dreams, hear no hoofbeats of Cossack horses. The Old Country is rarely mentioned—they are Americans!

When they marry and have families, the women continue to cook the Old World favorites in their spanking new, modern kitchens while embracing innovations like sliced bread and Jell-O. Jewish cookbooks, if they use them, now preserve for posterity the blintzes and borscht. Sometimes they measure; more often they don't. Mama's "handful" is still a universal symbol, her *shiterein* (a little of this, a little of that) still the method of choice. They've begun clipping recipes from *Ladies' Home Journal*, and when they exchange them with friends, they always append the word "enjoy!" They don't apologize for the animal fat and sugar content, as their children guiltily will. Food is still to be relished, a bounty to bestow on their families with love.

My brother, Gary, with cousins Carole and Bonnie.

GENERATION 3: If, like me, you grow up with Mama and Papa living upstairs, you wake up and smell the challah! Your children will not. Kishka you see in New York delis and at Bar Mitzvahs. Your mother probably doesn't make it; you won't either. Your children may never taste it; their children won't know what it is. You grow up in the land of plenty, with meat accompanying those potatoes. Later in your own kitchen you take to the casserole, the cake mix, instant potatoes, all things "new and improved." Your company table still jiggles with Jell-O. Mama's chicken soup simmers, but you've discovered Manischewitz Matzoh Ball Mix. Dieting begins to overtake pleasure in the culinary consciousness of your generation, and you wonder what Mama Hinda was thinking, rendering all that chicken fat. You still cook "the good stuff," but save it for company. As a generation you venerate the written word and respect the wonders of science. Your shelves bulge with cookbooks, but you're branching out. The quiche replaces the knish.

The Magnificent 7. Standing: Al (holding Gigi), Lou, Morris, Irene, Lillian; seated: Estelle, Sally.

GENERATION 4: Comes the sexual revolution, and the shock waves reverberate even unto the kitchen. Boys whose daddies had no inkling or interest in how food miraculously appeared on the table each night are now joining their working wives in cutting and chopping and searing and sautéing. Jewish cookbooks of the day, if couples have one, feature Nouvelle *Yiddishkeit:* terrines of gefilte, cilantro-laden latkes, and low-fat renditions of the old classics. They're just as likely to get a recipe

off the Internet as from a cookbook, and they attack the mysteries of torching a crème brûlée with the same marvelous intensity they apply to their jobs and everything else in their hectic lives.

My sons, Stu and Brad, and their wives, Shelly and Tracey.

GENERATION 5: The babies have babies, and, oh, are they thriving. Their mothers are so much smarter than we ever were! They are nourished in kitchens steeped with the latest nutritional know-how. Will they ever crimp a kreplach or pan-fry a pirogen? Hang on to this cookbook. Who knows? Maybe they will. Enjoy!

Ethan Wolf and Justin Wolf, 2004.

ancestors' life, a cuisine borne by ingenious Jewish women within the confines of both kashrut and poverty. While the Czar and his family dined in opulent splendor on only the finest cuts, back in the shtetls our ancestors devised ways to feed their families well on what the royal family probably threw away. (And we all know what happened to *them!*)

To my great fortune, Aunt Estelle and Aunt Sally opened their hearts and their kitchens, contributing their complete cookbooks—Aunt Estelle's reading much like a diary, food samples dotting the well-worn pages, and Aunt Sally's containing meticulously hand-copied recipes, opening with her epigraph that tells it all: "From the Kitchen of Sally Bower with Love."

Taking a huge gamble, I printed 500 copies of *Melting Pot Memories,* secretly fearing that Barry would kill me, because we'd be stepping over those boxes in the garage for the rest of our lives. But

somehow word spread and strangers began ordering copies (causing my son Brad to ponder, "Why are people reading about our family?"). All the books were gone in six weeks. I reprinted another thousand. Suddenly I was in the book business.

That fall I was asked to speak at an ORT new membership brunch. Before I knew it I was crisscrossing the country, speaking at synagogues, churches, and organizations about the Rabinowitz family saga and the importance of preserving memories.

I began writing a food column for the *Fullerton News Tribune;* then Cathy Thomas, food editor of *The Orange County Register,* asked me to start writing Jewish holiday feature stories. Soon I was teaching Jewish cooking classes for Sur La Table (where I freely admit I was not trained at La Varenne) and found myself, a new grandmother, with a new career.

I kept reprinting, happily adding each new grandchild —Lauren, Samantha, and Blake—to join Jason on our family tree. By 2003 I had sold 9,000 copies of *Melting Pot Memories* (the final tally grew to 11,000 by the time the last printing sold out) when Sharon Boorstin, author of *Let Us Eat Cake* and *Cookin' for Love*, asked me to join her panel in Montreal at the International Association of Culinary Professionals yearly conference on the subject of "The Memoir Cookbook." The third panelist was to be Ruth Reichl (*Comfort me with Apples*, *Tender at the Bone, Garlic and Sapphires*), editor in chief of *Gourmet* magazine! The room was packed. It never dawned on me that there would be publishers in the audience, but after

> " A treasured recipe, passed down from mother to daughter for who knows how long, summons the past with all five senses, revealing a slice of our ancestors' life. . . . "

Sadly, Aunt Estelle, Aunt Irene, and Aunt Hilda did not live to see the finished book. But Aunt Sally, our family Julia Child, took bows until the day she died at age ninety-four. While my mother and her sisters were all great cooks, Aunt Irene also worked (she was an executive secretary for a large advertising firm), Aunt Estelle also sewed (for her family as well as in her thriving business), and my mother had her music (her honeyed contralto, and her on-again, off-again singing career). Aunt Sally's kingdom, however, was the kitchen, and in it she reigned supreme.

Her memory was impeccable. In the years I worked on the cookbook, I think I spoke more with Aunt Sally than I had in my whole life till then. She willingly dispensed cooking wisdom right up until just days before she died. A typical call might go like this:

"Aunt Sally, you didn't write down whether you greased the pan. When you baked your cakes, did you grease the pan?"

"Ask me which cake, and I'll tell you whether I greased the pan."

For Passover 2001, food editor Deborah S. Hartz of the *South Florida Sun Sentinel,* with photographer in tow, interviewed Aunt Sally for a story about *Melting Pot Memories,* catapulting her to instant celebrity status among her fellows at the Morse Geriatric Center. After reciting from memory a litany of goodies she used to prepare for the holiday, she was quoted as saying, "I'll be cooking in my dreams tonight."

the presentation, representatives from Workman approached me about publishing an expanded version of *Melting Pot Memories*, the results of which you have before you. (Just don't drop it on your toe!)

I thought *Melting Pot Memories* was a recipe book with stories. What others seemed to see was a storybook with recipes. Now strangers all across the country know that my mother wrote book reports for her brothers and that her identical twin brothers used to take tests for each other. People began talking to me about my aunts and my mother by name, as if they were characters in a novel. "I have pictures just like those in my drawer," "Your aunts look so glamorous," "Your Uncle Al looks just like my grandfather" and—cross my heart—"Is your Uncle Morris alive and is he available?" (No, unfortunately, to both.)

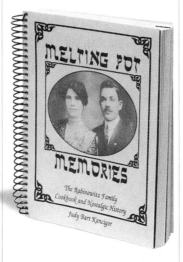

Jews and non-Jews alike seemed to connect with the nostalgia and with the immigrant experience, a universal theme that cuts through all religions and nationalities.

"The onion rolls are just like my mother-in-law used to make. My husband wept when I made them," one woman told me. People have mentioned that certain recipes (the Detroit and Minnesota salads come to mind) have become their signatures. One woman called to order a book because her neighbor walked in with the Ice Cream Strudel and said, "You've got to taste this."

What did I want the children to inherit besides Aunt Sally's apple cake and Aunt Irene's kugel? I wanted them to know the stories, know where they came from, know their history.

With thousands of cookbooks out there, why were some people who long ago turned their kitchens into planters reading *Melting Pot Memories* like a novel? Perhaps the answer lies in an anonymous quotation my ex-sister-in-law found (and if we knew who said it, we would tell you!):

It is the grandmother who is responsible for the continuance of culture. The ancestral stories that she relates to her grandchildren feed the generations to come.

We *bubbes* (grandmas) —and *zaydes* (grandpas) too!—feed the generations to come, but not just with food.

For as long as I can remember I have always loved old things. My mother knows that the quickest way for her to move a tchotchke from her house to my house is for her to tell me that it's old. Even faster if she tells me that it belonged to my grandmother, and faster still if she tells me my grandmother brought it with her from the Old Country.

I grew up in a two-family house with my grandparents living upstairs. My favorite pastime was sitting on the glider on our front porch with my grandpa, my Papa Harry, listening to his stories. My favorite and his, of course, was the saga of his coming to America. Papa Harry had been drafted into the Czar's army—conscription for Jewish lads in those days was twenty-five years! The Czar put Papa Harry on a horse, and, as he used to love to tell us, the army went this-away and Papa Harry went that-away!

Because my grandparents lived upstairs, everyone who came to visit them was familiar to me, and I grew up listening to their stories too. The Rabinowitz family is huge! My mother and her sisters were inseparable, and all of us cousins were raised together. When we converted the old movies of my childhood to video and my kids watched it for the first time, they gasped, "What, did you live with your cousins?" They couldn't conceive of the way we were raised—the tumult, the constant companionship, the hovering aunties, always on hand for love and advice (and, yes, an occasional attitude adjustment too).

I started this project as a tribute to *my* family, but as the recipes and remembrances poured in, it soon morphed into a tribute to others' mamas, grandmas, *imas*, *omas*, and *nonas* as well. Like a well-worn snapshot, it captures a moment in time, a legacy to pass along as we each create our own traditions. Like our family, this cookbook is inclusive, reaching out to embrace in-laws of in-laws in an ever-widening circle of the extended Rabinowitz *mishpuchah*, and like our family, it is big and boisterous, filled with laughter and love.

mishpuchah: Oh, so much more than the English word "family." Includes cousins (all degrees) and in-laws (even their cousins and in-laws) and of course *machatunim* (a word for which there is no English equivalent), meaning your children's in-laws, who with the breaking of a glass automatically join your *mishpuchah*.

b'raysheet

In the Beginning

Our story begins halfway around the world in Slonim, where Mama Hinda and Papa Harry were born, in Grodno *Gubernia* (province), located presently in the independent state of Belarus. The name itself means "lowland"; it lies in a valley of meadows surrounded by rolling hills covered with forests, a beautiful landscape some call "Slonim Switzerland." Here the Scara and Isa rivers meet, which in Mama and Papa's day made it a favorite vacation destination.

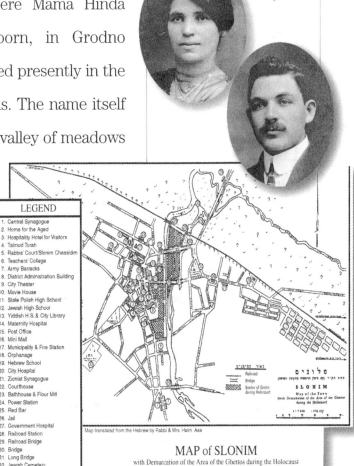

Mama Hinda and Papa Harry, 1914.

LEGEND

1. Central Synagogue
2. Home for the Aged
3. Hospitality Hotel for Visitors
4. Talmud Torah
5. Rabbis' Court/Slonim Chassidim
6. Teachers' College
7. Army Barracks
8. District Administration Building
9. City Theater
10. Movie House
11. State Polish High School
12. Jewish High School
13. Yiddish H.S. & City Library
14. Maternity Hospital
15. Post Office
16. Mini Mall
17. Municipality & Fire Station
18. Orphanage
19. Hebrew School
20. City Hospital
21. Zionist Synagogue
22. Courthouse
23. Bathhouse & Flour Mill
24. Power Station
25. Red Bar
26. Jail
27. Government Hospital
28. Railroad Station
29. Railroad Bridge
30. Bridge
31. Long Bridge
32. Jewish Cemetery
33. Scara River

Railroad
Bridge
Border of Ghetto during Holocaust

SLONIM
Map of the Town
(with Demarkation of the Area of the Ghettos during the Holocaust)

Map translated from the Hebrew by Rabbi & Mrs. Haim Asa

MAP of SLONIM
with Demarcation of the Area of the Ghettos during the Holocaust

Old map with location of Slonim, Mama and Papa's birthplace; modern map inset.

a special tax. In 1642 the Great Synagogue, a magnificent stone structure, was erected; it served as the center of Jewish religious and social life and was spared from destruction during World War II because of its use as a landmark for aerial navigation. After the war it was used for several decades as a warehouse, then lay empty in sad disrepair until 2001, when the East European Jewish Heritage Project announced plans to restore this historic monument. Sadly, due to lack of funds, little has been done to accomplish this.

For centuries the fortunes of the Jews of Russia and Poland in general, and Slonim in particular, rose and fell with the prevailing political climate. Russian persecution by the armies of Stephen Czarniecki is recorded in Slonim in 1660. By the end of the seventeenth century the Jews of Slonim were trading in wheat and timber, wealthy merchants traveling to the Leipzig fairs, others earning a living in contracting, manufacturing alcoholic beverages, and crafts.

As wars were fought and won and borders changed, Slonim became part of Poland-Lithuania in 1316, fell within Russia in 1795, reverted to Poland after World War I, and then after World War II became part of the Byelorussian Soviet Socialist Republic (White Russia) until the breakup of the Soviet Union in 1991.

Although Jews had lived throughout Russia for centuries, the first documentary evidence of a Jewish community in Slonim dates back to the 1500s when it was mentioned as one of the communities exempt from

The second half of the eighteenth century brought prosperity to the Jewish community of Slonim with the help of Count Mikhail Kazimir Oginski (1728–1800). Oginski, Polish composer, author, and poet, and elder of the town, established a printing office and financed and built a theater, a palace, and the Oginski Canal, a great boon to industry and trade in the area. When Slonim managed to repel the advancing Russian army in 1764, the twenty-sixth of Sivan was commemorated as the day of deliverance by the community.

of the newcomers were Jews, and Catherine, wishing to confine them, created what became known as the Pale of Settlement for the Jews to live in, an imaginary border stretching from Latvia to the Crimean peninsula in what was once part of Poland. For the next 150 years most of Europe's Jews lived in little towns and villages (shtetls) and a few crowded cities within the Pale, forced to pay high taxes and forbidden to travel without permission to attend Russian schools.

Czar Nicholas I, who assumed power in 1825, hoped to unify Russia and attempted to hasten the breakdown of separate nationalistic groups within his kingdom. He disbanded the *Kahal* (organ of Jewish community self-government), setting up special schools to assimilate the children and pressuring conversion to Christianity. Conditions improved somewhat under the more liberal rule of Czar Alexander II, but Alexander III used the now millions of Jews living

the pale of settlement

ש hen Russia annexed Poland in 1795, the Jews of Poland fell under the rule of the German-born Czarina Catherine the Great, who welcomed Germans to immigrate to Russia. Many

Roman Vishniac
At the market, ca. 1935–38
© Mara Vishniac Kohn, courtesy the
International Center of Photography

under his rule as convenient scapegoats for government failures; he even blamed them for the 1881 assassination of his father. Pogroms (from "destruction" in Russian), or peasant revolts, aimed at the Jews with the tacit approval of authority, occurred throughout Russia. With the expulsions from nearby villages, the Jewish population of Slonim swelled, and in 1897 Jewish workers there began to organize in trade unions and political organizations.

Between anti-Semitic attacks, the Jews of Slonim were engaged in wholesale trading in timber, furs, and hides; in transport and supplying the army; in the manufacture of agricultural

> *Slonim was not built according to a plan. Its old narrow streets and alleys turn and twist, uphill and down, sometimes growing wider when least expected. . . .*
>
> *Before the Nazi destruction Slonim had a Jewish Quarter—the old courtyard with the Great Synagogue in the center . . . encircled by a dozen Study Houses. . . . Near the Great Synagogue sprawled the 'Old Marketplace,' full of butcher shops, herring stalls, flour stores, and the workshops of various Jewish craftsmen. Always there was a din there: Jewish women with big baskets on their shoulders, porters, coachmen, peasants, buyers and sellers. . . . And wherever you looked you saw friendly Jews always busy and absorbed in the pursuit of earning a livelihood.*
>
> *Directly outside the synagogue courtyard, between the Tailors Synagogue and the Slaughterhouse, the street led uphill to 'The Mountain,' a densely populated working-class neighborhood where, in a dozen crooked, narrow little streets the Jewish poor huddled together in their crowded little homes.*
>
> **—THE DESTRUCTION OF SLONIM JEWRY BY NACHUM ALPERT, translated from the Yiddish by Max Rosenfeld**

machinery, matches, woolen scarves, curtains, yeast, and Jewish ritual articles; and were employed in iron foundries, tanneries, saw mills, brick kilns, and steam mills. In fact, in 1826 the first textile factory in Slonim was founded by a Jew.

Roman Vishniac
Noon, ca. 1935–38
© Mara Vishniac Kohn,
courtesy the International
Center of Photography

Papa Harry often told us stories about a great fire in Slonim. Indeed, in 1881 anti-Jewish hooligans set fire to the town, and much of it was destroyed. By 1885, after considerable restoration, the situation had improved, and a railroad line was constructed through Slonim from Baranovich to Volkovysk. The end of the nineteenth century brought new roads and the expansion of industry, but conditions worsened for Jews, who, forbidden to settle in large cities, crowded further into the shtetls. The Kishinev pogrom and other attacks in 1903 to 1904 and the Bialystok pogrom in 1906 made life in Slonim intolerable for Jews, and great waves of immigration to America and elsewhere began. Between 1890 and 1914 nearly two million Jews fled the Russian empire, although many idealistic youth chose to remain and fight.

By 1885, when Papa Harry and Mama Hinda were born, there were over four million Jews living in the Pale. Papa's father, Michel, had a tannery as well as a large fruit orchard in Slonim. Michel's father, Chaim, was from Gerdev, ten miles away, where he had a ranch. Papa's mother, Leah (Notkofsky or Notkovich), died of a lung ailment around 1915. (My mother, Lillian, is named for her.) Michel remarried, but nothing is known of the second wife. Because the Rabinowitz name is so common (it means "son of a rabbi"—every family likes to think there is one in the family tree!), it has been very difficult to find addi-

tional information about our ancestors.

We know even less about Mama Hinda's family. Her father, Moshe Shimrick, died in 1921, practically on the eve of his emigration to America. (Uncle Morris was named for him.) His tomb-

stone tells us he was son of Abraham (for whom Uncle Al was named) and refers to him as "teacher" or perhaps "pious one," but we do not know his occupation for sure. Mama's mother, Ida, died young (Aunt Irene was named for her), and as a young girl Mama took on the care of the family, including her sister, Anna, and seven-year-old brother, Sam.

Mama and Papa married in 1905 on *Shabbos nuch Shavuos* (the Sabbath after Shavuos). They were both twenty years old, and it was not an arranged marriage. Trained as a carpenter, Papa Harry worked in a stair factory, sometimes traveling to other towns by horse and wagon to do cabinetwork. Mama and Papa lived in their own home by the river.

With the outbreak of the Russo-Japanese war in 1904, Slonim became the mobilization center for northwest Russia. The Jews of Slonim, seeking protection against the hooligans now in their midst, bargained with the City Commander and paid 2,000 rubles for the services of fifty Cossacks and two officers.

In this climate Papa Harry was drafted into the Czar's army, and he knew it was time to go. Using the forged papers of his brother-in-law, Max Savitsky, he boarded the vessel S.S. *Zeeland* in Antwerp, Belgium, on February 12, 1906, arriving ten days later at Ellis Island. A pregnant Mama Hinda

Above: Moshe Shimrick, Mama Hinda's father.

Papa Harry and Mama Hinda, just married, 1905. He looks like a Bar Mitzvah boy and she looks like his mother in her sheitel (wig).

Mama's little brother, Sam.

outbreak of World War II in 1939. Slonim was home to an important branch of Hasidim, the Slonimer Dynasty, and there were synagogues, Jewish schools *(yeshivot)*, Jewish sport clubs and youth organizations, a Yiddish quarterly, and a Yiddish weekly, the *Slonimer Vort*. Slonim was also the birthplace of the father of Roman Vishniac, world-famous photographer and chronicler of Jewish life in prewar Eastern Europe, some of whose photos of the town are reproduced here.

Slonim was captured by the Germans on June 25, 1941, and in December Jews from surrounding towns were crowded into a ghetto established in the Zhabinka district (cross-hatched area on the map, page XXIX). In all about 35,000 Jews were executed in Slonim during the Holocaust, including those refugees. By the time Soviet forces took Slonim on July 10, 1944, only 80 Jews remained. Some who had managed to escape to the forests formed a partisan unit, an active Jewish underground; among them was Papa's cousin, Chaim (Hy) Savitsky, who lost his leg in the fight. (It was Hy's father who had given Papa Harry his papers to flee to America.) In 1984 I visited Hy at his home in Union, New Jersey, and he supplied many of the names on our family tree and details of our family history.

waited until he would make enough money to send for her—which he did in 1907, when Mama, nine-month-old Irene, and Mama's little brother, Sam, joined him in New York. (Papa's brother Louis, who later wound up in St. Louis, was not so fortunate and spent two years in a Japanese prison camp.)

Back in Slonim, despite pogroms and Polish repression (Slonim having reverted to Poland after World War I) and the growing tide of Nazi anti-Semitism, Jewish life continued until the

The S.S. Zeeland carried Papa to America in 1906. Inset: Papa Harry, 1930s.

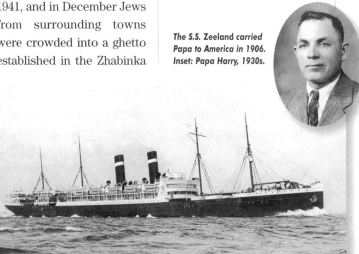

Roman Vishniac, *Jewish street, ca. 1935–38*, © Mara Vishniac Kohn, courtesy the International Center of Photography

from slonim to suburbia

ש hen Papa Harry arrived in America, he was greeted by *landsleit* (fellow townsmen). Like thousands of other immigrants of the time, he bonded most in the confusing, new land with others from his own shtetl, and eventually he joined the Slonimer Branch of the Workmen's Circle. These *landsmenshaften* were part social club, part benevolent society, and there were as many of them as there were shtetls in Europe. After World War II many *landsleit* societies published memorial (*yiskor*) books to commemorate those lost in the Holocaust and to preserve the Jewish history of their towns. These books are treasure troves for genealogists or anyone interested in the Jewish history of an area, and the Slonim memorial book, *Pinkas Slonim*, is no exception. Written in Hebrew and Yiddish, it is four volumes long, filled with photos, and can be found in many research libraries.

Like so many eager immigrants, Papa Harry, proud to be an American, adopted July 4th as his birthday. Trained as a carpenter, he went right to work. As a boarder on the Lower East Side of New York—we're not sure with whom—he slept in the bed of a night-shift worker who used the same bed by day. He saved every penny and quickly had enough to send for Mama Hinda. Nine-month-old Ida (Irene), who had never seen her Papa, was afraid of him

Left: Mama and Papa with Irene, Estelle, and Sally, 1914. **Right:** Daughter Celia, who died at 15 months in 1916.

Before the Depression Papa went into the construction business with his partners, Mr. Litwin and Mr. Ditkoff. A horse fitted with a bucket in back, pulled by a man in front, helped dig the foundations—it must have been a slow excavation process! The family then moved to a succession of houses—whatever Papa couldn't sell they moved into.

at first. We can only imagine what that reunion was like!

The family soon grew: Next Sarah (Sally), then Esther (Estelle), baby Celia (born with a hole in her heart, she contracted whooping cough and died at fifteen months), then my mother, Lillian. Would Papa ever get a son! Finally Abraham (Al) arrived, followed by the twins, Morris and Lou.

On September 12, 1921, Papa Harry, at age thirty-six, became a U.S. citizen. The family was then living in their first house, a two-family home on Williams Avenue in Brooklyn, where

Papa conducted his stair-building business in the large unfinished basement. There he had his equipment and a single burner, which he used to heat up the glue. During Passover Mama Hinda would use that burner downstairs to make cereal for the baby twins, so as not to bring *chometz* into the kitchen. The house had a large back porch and a brass railing in front; every Thursday, cleaning day in preparation for *Shabbos*, the older girls had to scrub that railing with Bon Ami.

Uncle Al, with King.

> *Mama would hide the cookies, but our dog, King, could always be counted on to find them. We'd say, 'King, get the cookies,' and he would sniff them out of the treadle of the sewing machine or wherever she had hidden them.*
>
> **—SALLY BOWER**

Finally Papa built a one-family house especially for his brood on East 40th Street in Brooklyn, a beautiful home with combed ceilings, fine detailed moldings, and a beautiful wooden staircase. There they had a finished basement with a cold-storage room where Mama kept eggs by the case for Passover. In summer she would cook dinner down there to keep the house cool. Every Monday night Mama would make white fish with boiled potatoes and carrots, which of course she cooked downstairs so as not to smell up the house.

Sally and Estelle shared one bedroom; Al, Morris, and Lou had another; and Irene and Lillian shared another. There was a big peach tree in the backyard, and Mama Hinda made peach pie, peach cake, and peach sauce. She made her own noodles and baked her own challah for *Shabbos*. During the week they ate a black bread they called health bread. To save a little money she bought day-old pumpernickel, and she flicked her own chickens (removed the pin feathers) to save three cents apiece.

As was the custom, on *Erev* Yom Kippur (Yom Kippur eve) a live chicken was waved over the heads of the children three times, a custom known as *kapores*. The chicken was thought to absorb all sins. It was then taken to the *shochet* (ritual butcher) to be slaughtered and served for the holiday dinner.

Pesach brought a frenzy of cleaning and preparation. Fresh fish waiting to be "gefilted" swam in the bathtub. Glasses were soaked for three days and silver buried outside with hot coals for purification. The house was cleaned from top to bottom, and any

recipe for tumult

1. Take one young husband with ripe young wife,

2. Fill with desire and knead for a son.

3. Add one tiny daughter, repeat 3X.

4. Crush hope well after each addition.

5. Expectations rising, at long last a son!

6. Results so delicious, double the batch.

Mama and Papa with the Magnificent 7: Estelle, Irene, Sally, Lillian, Al, Morris, and Lou.

remaining crumbs of *chometz* were searched out by Papa and the children with a feather and burned.

As in most struggling, large families of the time, there was little disposable income for toys. Mama Hinda made dolls for the girls with Turkish towels tied with a ribbon. She even made them twins. Of course, there was always a baby carriage in the house for the towel dolls. The children played hopscotch and stickball, and Aunt Sally remembers riding one skate, because she shared the pair with Irene.

Mama sewed clothes for the family—for the older girls, dresses with embroidery around the collars and beautiful smocking. But as the family expanded and times grew lean, she had little time for sewing, and they took in boarders to make ends meet. By then Estelle, who had learned to sew from Mama's sister, Aunt Anna, was sewing for herself and Lillian and whoever needed something.

During the Depression Papa took work wherever he could find it. When he'd give Mama money for the household, he would say, "Take this. Who knows what I'll be able to give you next week." With Irene's help, they got by. She had landed a good job as an executive in an advertising firm and turned over her salary to Mama each week. (Irene also was Lillian's "angel," nurturing her singing talents by taking her to concerts and paying the

Papa Harry's candy store on Utica near Carrol in Brooklyn. That's Uncle Willy at the soda fountain and my mom (left) behind the candy counter, about 1933.

catskill capers

For a few summers before the Depression the family would spend a month in Mountaindale in the Catskills. An enterprising farmer had taken a deposit for his farmhouse retreat, a series of *kuchaleins* (Yiddish for "cook alone") where families could vacation and escape the city heat, each doing their own cooking in a community kitchen.

Picture Mama and Papa and the seven Rabinowitz children off for vacation in Papa Harry's smashing Studebaker (complete with crystal vases with artificial flowers on the side panels). A vehicle designed for six easily accommodates the Rabinowitz brood, because Papa Harry has constructed a wooden bench in front of the backseat. (Of course, seat belts and car seats have not been invented, air conditioning not even imagined!) All the luggage is strapped to the running board outside with ropes, and off they go. The drive to the mountains is horrendous! The roads are poor and the traffic impossible. Finally after nearly eight hours of huffing and puffing up the hills, they arrive at the farmhouse, and Mama Hinda is not pleased. The photo the farmer had shown her must have been taken fifty years earlier. The place is sadly neglected and far below Mama Hinda's exacting standards of cleanliness, so Papa Harry leaves them all there and runs to locate a hotel, which turns out to be Purlin's Farmhouse, clean and kosher, offering three meals a day.

Purlin's has cows and chickens, the eggs deliciously fresh, and the milk served warm right from the udder. Meals are served family-style, herring being a prominent selection—either schmaltz herring or pickled herring, with fried herring as a special treat on Sundays. Tomatoes, cucumbers, and all sorts of vegetables from the garden are served at the table. There is one bathroom on the floor, shared by a few families, and Mama Hinda washes the clothes outdoors on a big tin washboard and hangs them to dry in the sun. Days are spent playing outdoors, mainly running after the tiny twins. Papa Harry, like other working husbands, makes the grueling commute on weekends.

Before the Depression, Mama and Papa and their brood of seven would spend summers in the mountains—a pleasant respite from the city heat.

three dollars each for her singing lessons.)

When the construction business dried up, for a short time Papa Harry had a candy store on Utica Avenue in Brooklyn. Estelle was the bookkeeper, and Lillian would open the store with Papa at six before school. His partner was Uncle Willy, who joined our family as a boarder and soon fell in love with Aunt Estelle.

Even in lean times the long-awaited sons brought no end of merriment to the Rabinowitz household. Their teachers were not amused. When the principal would call, the older girls, more conversant in English than their parents and not wishing to "trouble" them, would appear at school. Once when Al got in trouble the principal asked Lil, "How do I know you're really his sister?" As proof she showed him her front teeth. "See? We both have the same gap!"

On a dare Lou once took a math final for his twin, Morris. When he could not find a seat, the teacher invited him to sit at her desk! Although his heart was pounding, he landed Morris a 98. Sometimes the confusion worked the other way, however. Once when Morris got a "licking" for something Lou had done, he was told, "That's for next time."

The age gap between Lil and Estelle divided the children into two groups, the three older girls and then Lil and the boys. Whenever Lil wanted to go to the movies with friends, she always had to take the twins. (Al, the oldest son, was of course "excused.") To wangle the precious dime admission, Lillian would sing to Papa this little ditty she composed:

> *Zekelah, zekelah,*
> *effen zich uf.*
> *Lilleh darf gayn*
> *tzu de muvis.*
>
> *(Little sac, little sac,*
> *open up.*
> *Lil needs to go*
> *to the movies.)*

Aunt Sally and Uncle Lou, 1931. Papa paid a wad for this one. (My parents were married in a basement. There was no gown . . . or even a photographer!)

It's hard to imagine Mama Hinda keeping her immaculate home with all the havoc those boys could wreak (not to mention their assorted friends, one of whom dropped a hammer on Mama's glass buffet top). To them her mangle iron was a galloping horse. Of course it broke, and they didn't admit their guilt until they were in the army.

For the next few years Papa managed to feed the family by taking carpentry work wherever he could find it. Then, with the outbreak of World War II, he put his talents to work at the Brooklyn

> *Papa Harry had his own 'still' in the basement where he made homemade wine and beer. One day we heard a loud 'pop, pop, pop!' It sounded like machine guns going off. When we went downstairs to investigate, all the taps from the beer had blown off!*
>
> **—LOU ROBBINS**

Navy Yard, while Mama Hinda rolled bandages for the Red Cross and his boys served their country: Al, a captain in Germany, Morris, seeing plenty of action in France (in the "foxes' holes,"

as Papa put it), and Lou, fighting the mosquitoes in Florida.

After the war, the construction boom found Papa Harry again building homes, one of which was a cozy two-family house in Belle Harbor, New York (you guessed it—he couldn't sell it!), which my family moved into in 1948, Mama and Papa taking the upstairs apartment, where, to my great fortune, they lived out the rest of their lives, never more than a flight of stairs away from a little girl with a skinned knee, a case of the challah munchies, or just in need of an extra hug.

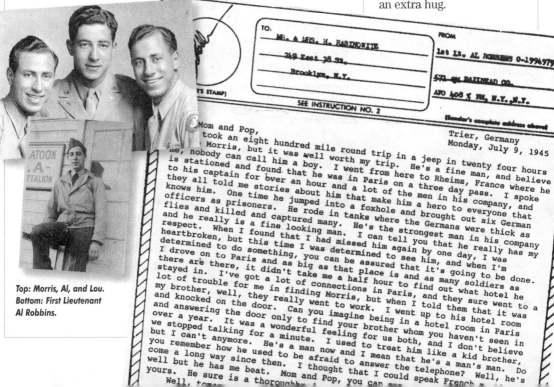

Top: Morris, Al, and Lou.
Bottom: First Lieutenant Al Robbins.

TO:
MR. & MRS. H. RABINOWITZ
249 East 98 St.
Brooklyn, N.Y.

FROM
1st Lt. AL ROBBINS O-1994979
573 ... BATTHEAD CO.
APO 408 % PM, N.Y., N.Y.

SEE INSTRUCTION NO. 2

Trier, Germany
Monday, July 9, 1945

Mom and Pop,
took an eight hundred mile round trip in a jeep in twenty four hours Morris, but it was well worth my trip. He's a fine man, and believe me, nobody can call him a boy. I went from here to Rheims, France where he is stationed and found that he was in Paris on a three day pass. I spoke to his captain for over an hour and a lot of the men in his company. They all told me stories about him that make him a hero to everyone that knows him. One time he jumped into a foxhole and brought out six German officers as prisoners. He rode in tanks where the Germans were thick as flies and killed and captured many. He's the strongest man in his company and he really is a fine looking man. I can tell you that he really has my respect. When I found that I had missed him again by one day, I was heartbroken, but this time I was determined to see him, and when I'm determined to do something, you can be assured that it's going to be done. I drove on to Paris and as big as that place is and as many soldiers as there are there, it didn't take me a half hour to find out what hotel he stayed in. I've got a lot of connections in Paris, and they sure went to a lot of trouble for me in finding Morris, but when I told them that it was my brother, well, they really went to work. I went up to his hotel room and knocked on the door only to find your brother whom you haven't seen in over a year. It was a wonderful feeling for us both, and I don't believe we stopped talking for a minute. I used to treat him like a kid brother, but I can't anymore. He's a man now and I mean that he's a man's man. Do you remember how he used to be afraid to answer the telephone? Well, he's come a long way since then. I thought that I could speak French well but he has me beat. Mom and Pop, you can ...
yours. He sure is a thoroughb...
Well, to...

mama hinda 1885–1975

—excerpted from her eulogy by Judy Bart Kancigor

y memories are filled with her: the smell of *Shabbos*, the annual arrival of her beautiful roses, the *simchas*, the parties, and always Mama in the midst of it all, beaming like a queen, with her children, her grandchildren, and great-grandchildren around her. Her family was her life, as anyone who ever visited knows well. Her walls and tabletops spilled with pictures of the children, the joy of her life, and even though in later years she may have had to run through three or four names before she landed on *your* husband's, she loved them all as her own. The word *in-law* never existed in the Rabinowitz lexicon. Her heart was big enough to include them all.

I was so lucky to have been touched by her. Mama and Papa were an inseparable part of my childhood. I can't think of Hanukkah without thinking of running upstairs to light candles with Mama and Papa. Smelling her incredible challah, Gary and I needed no prodding to recite *Shabbos* blessings with them.

How can I ever forget the Mama of yesteryear who, rather than invade the privacy of the "downstairs-ikas," always walked all the way around the house to knock at our door when she wanted to come in, how she would sit for hours painstakingly copying English letters into her notebook. And, oh, the blaring arguments with Papa! The "*Oy*, Yishel!" How she was teased by that man!

I remember Mama, the *balabusteh*, the pride she took in her home, how she beamed when my father sang, how she primped, how she fussed. Whoever heard of a woman her age taking such pride! Did the shoes match? Did they cover her bad toe? Was the dress length all right? And how can I ever forget the way she would always ask me timidly, "Judelah, dahlink, can you fix *meine* hair?"

And at *simcha* after *simcha*, when it would be their turn to march down the aisle, there they would stand, a truly beautiful couple, Papa in his rented tux, dapper at any age, and radiant Mama at his side, wearing yet another one of Aunt Estelle's magnificent creations. Vanity? Maybe, but that's what kept her young. Once as a teenager I appeared upstairs wearing the latest rage, fishnet stockings. She stared for a while and asked, "Judelah, dahlink, tell me, is that for dressy or for sporty?"

Yet it was more than mere vanity. The woman had about her a sense of pride and dignity. For so many years she withstood unbelievable pain. Yet when I'd ask her, "Mama, how do you feel?" her answer was always "vunderful." She was an anachronism. In our alienated age when people are always asking why, Mama never asked why. She didn't need to find herself, to seek outlets for self-expression, to question her role or search for fulfillment. Some may say what a lucky woman to have lived so long. I say, what a lucky woman to have lived so well.

papa harry 1885–1979
—excerpted from his eulogy by Gary Bart

I come from a good mold—from Papa. Much of what I am today I owe to him. Who was Harry Rabinowitz from Slonim? A father who worked hard for his children, a grandfather who delighted in his offspring, a husband for sixty-eight years, a friend who was always ready to help with a hammer. I used to love to listen to his stories about the old times in Russia, in Brooklyn.

I treasure my childhood memories. Papa put my first bicycle together and taught me how to ride it, running after the bike to keep me up. He even rode it himself! In the summer we painted the little white picket fence together, and Mama screamed at us for dripping paint. Papa took me for haircuts, "with a twenty-five cent tip," he used to say proudly.

In his lifetime he had seen the world move from the horse and buggy into the atomic age, but nothing shocked him. He was always up on the news, preferring a good documentary to what he called Mama Hinda's *shpillen und tantzen* (singing and dancing), although they both loved Perreh Komo and Ed Solomon. When we got our first little Dumont TV, he scratched his head but let me watch my Farmer Brown cartoons.

When he took a rare breather between running to fix things in our house or someone else's, we'd sit on the porch together and watch the world go by. He used to love to polish my shoes, and I used to love to watch him work. He was so happy when he had a project to do. Sometimes I'd try to help or imitate him, but I would only lose his tools. I'd say, "What are you doing, Papa?" and he'd stop and look at me and say, "Gary, vat I do you can never do."

I watched him as he built with skill a breakfront, a closet, a built-in TV. He was always moving, usually two steps at a time. I saw the tear and gleam in his eyes as he listened to my father's words as each family member came up to light a candle at his and Mama's fiftieth anniversary party. I saw as he came alive on Sundays when the house was filled with relatives, especially the children, the grandchildren, and later the great-grandchildren.

I heard him listen to a very loud Yiddish radio station (my personal alarm clock) and saw him beam when my father was singing. If it was to be done with a yarmulke Papa was there, reciting the blessings over the challah at every *simcha*. I learned the seasons when Papa would say early one morning, "Come, Gary, let's put up the awning" or "let's cover the air conditioner." I watched as he proudly would show off a gift someone he loved gave him, a good bottle of schnapps or a box of cigars.

Papa cared. When I would come back home to visit he would ask, "But Gary, are you happy? That's the most important thing." I am fortunate. Some people don't have grandparents. Even fewer get to live and grow up with them.

Mom

I'm waiting in my car for my mom (Lillian) to emerge from the library, where she volunteers once a week. Since she stopped driving, I now transport her the mile and a half back to her home. The mist on the windshield brings to mind another rainy day over forty years ago. I was newly married and teaching English at Lafayette High School in Brooklyn. Home was an apartment a subway ride north. The subway station was two blocks away. As I exited the building, buckets of rain poured from the heavens, but there, across the street, was my mom's Oldsmobile. "Just because you're married, that doesn't mean you should get wet," she declared as I gratefully opened the door.

My mother is the most reliable person I know. When I was in high school, she knew the names of all my classmates, which came in handy in case of party crashers. If she didn't recognize your name, you didn't get in. She read every paper I ever wrote. Now she reads every column and story. But her comments are hardly "critiques." (She thinks I hang the moon every night.)

Her teachers knew early that Mom had a special gift—her gorgeous contralto voice. In high school she sang with New York's All-City Chorus under the direction of famed composer and director Peter Wilhousky. (He was still there when I tried out. He promised me I would have a lovely voice once it matured. We're still waiting.) Her singing coach, Miss Stone, encouraged her to audition for Radio City Music Hall before conductor Erno Rape, and she became a soloist, earning the astounding sum of forty dollars a week! Her career was taking off.

It was at Miss Stone's studio that she became acquainted with another rising star, Jan Bart. They began singing duets together, and as Mom loves to tell it, they were offered a job that was too good to refuse, singing together for the summer in the Catskills, so they got married and went.

Once Gary and I came along, Mom quit working to devote herself full-time to her family. She did have her own radio show, however, interviewing the likes of Jimmy Stewart and Lena Horne. She even interviewed Jan Bart. When she complimented him on his fine singing skills, he said, "Do you say that to all your husbands?"

After I got married and Gary went off to college, Mom resumed her singing career and traveled with my dad for six glorious years until his death in 1971. Growing up as Lillian and Jan Bart's daughter—can you imagine how special that was? Life was a perpetual seat on the dais. My parents' lives were a love song. How he adored her!

—*Judy Bart Kancigor*

JAN BART sings in yiddish

Fiddler on the Roof IN PERSON with Lillian Bart

קאָנג. בני יעקב צמח צדק
CONG. BNEI JACOB ZEMACH ZEDEK
391 Avon Ave.   Cor. 13th St.   Newark, N. J.

דער וואונדער קינד פון ניו יאָרק
חזן שלום-קע שטרוים
וועט דאוונען
פרייטאָג אבענד שבת פּרײה
MAY 12 - 13, 1933
פרשה אמור
25 סענט   מאָריס

Dad

rial skills, conducting High Holiday services at the Riverside Plaza Hotel each fall and Passover services at Green's, Stevensville, Young's Gap, and the Windsor Hotel in the Catskills. His many recordings include *Yinglish*, old Yiddish melodies sung in English, and *Fiddler on the Roof* in Yiddish. There wasn't a family *simcha* that he and my mother, Lillian, didn't sing for. He officiated as cantor at just about every family wedding. He wrote individual anniversary songs for each occasion and sang "When did she get to be a beauty?" for every wedding and "When did he grow to be so tall?" for every Bar Mitzvah.

My father was very passionate in everything he touched. Even his stamp collections were world famous. He started the Judaica Historical Philatelic Society and was flown to Israel several times to judge stamp shows. Despite all his accomplishments he was truly a family man, traveling through the night, if necessary, rather than sleep in a hotel, just to get home to his family.

—Gary Bart

Singer, entertainer, raconteur, my dad, Jan Bart, was a prominent Jewish performer who bridged the gap between the rich music of European Jewry and American musical tastes.

He was born in Sambor, Poland (now Ukraine), and his family owned a bakery. As a child, he would stand on a stool and sing to the customers. By age eleven, he had already become a cantor. At sixteen he wanted to compete on the *Major Bowes Amateur Hour* radio show, the *American Idol* of its day. When he could not get an appointment, he went to the offices, found a piano, and accompanied himself to an aria from *Pagliacci*. Major Bowes [shown above] was so taken with his voice that he changed the following Sunday's schedule to put him on. He won the contest and toured the country with Major

Bowes, supporting his family during the Depression. From there he went on to appear in nightclubs, cabarets, and theaters. He was a regular on Yiddish radio shows, including *Yiddish Swing* and *The American-Jewish Caravan of Stars* and had his own *Jan Bart Show* on radio and TV.

When Israel became a state in 1948, he truly found his calling, working tirelessly for Israel bonds throughout the world.

As gifted a singer as he was, he was an even better fund-raiser. At Israel bond rallies, he always doubled and tripled the expected return. By his death at age fifty-two in 1971, he had raised more money for Israel bonds than any other entertainer.

Throughout his life he continued to use his canto-

cooking kosher

I am not an expert on kashrut. I don't even play one on TV. Fortunately I've made many friends who are! Special thanks to Rabbi Eliezer Eidlitz at www.kosherquest.org, Arlene Mathes-Scharf of www.kashrut.com, and Brian Mailman, Wendy Baker, and members of the Jewish Food List (www.jewishfoodlist.com) for answering my endless questions. I continue to learn from all of them.

The contributors to this cookbook range in observance from Barry's ultra-orthodox cousins in Antwerp, Belgium, to those who married into our family and who are not even Jewish, much less kosher. I have tried my best to conform the recipes to the kosher laws, but if you spot an error, the responsibility is all mine and does not reflect on any of the knowledgeable experts who so generously helped me.

The rabbis have been debating many aspects of the kosher laws for centuries. Orthodox Jews follow stricter guidelines than conservatives do. Some laws are different in Israel than they are in the U.S. Different communities observe different rules, so it's best to consult your own rabbinical authority on matters of question.

Generally speaking, the kosher laws are as follows:

- Only animals that have cloven hooves and chew their cud—such as cattle, sheep, goats, and deer—are permitted.

- Only fish that have fins and scales are permitted. Shellfish is forbidden.

- Only birds that do not scavenge—such as chicken, geese, ducks, and turkeys—are permitted.

- Rodents, reptiles, amphibians, and insects are forbidden.

- Any product derived from forbidden animals, such as their milk, eggs, fat, or organs, is forbidden.

- Permitted animals and birds must be slaughtered humanely according to Jewish law.

- The blood of mammals and birds is forbidden. Some blood is drained during slaughter, the remainder by salting or broiling. An egg that contains a blood spot is forbidden.

- The sciatic nerve and its adjoining blood vessels, as well as a kind of fat known as *chelev*, which surrounds the vital organs and the liver, are forbidden. Because removal of the sciatic nerve is time-

The recipes have been marked M for meat, D for dairy, and P for pareve, as of this writing. (Note that some supermarket brands contain ingredients that are pareve one year and dairy the next.)

consuming, most American slaughterers sell the hind quarters to nonkosher butchers.

- Meat (*fleishig* in Yiddish) and dairy (*milchig*) foods must be separated, as must anything they come in contact with, such as utensils, pots, pans, plates, flatware, dishwashers, dishpans, even drying towels.

- Foods that contain neither meat nor dairy ingredients are pareve (neutral) and may be eaten with anything.

- All fruits, grains, and vegetables in their natural state are kosher and pareve.

- Grape products, such as wine and grape juice, must be certified kosher (see box, page 596).

- Store-bought prepackaged foods must be

identified by a *hechsher* (a symbol from a reputable rabbinical certifying agency).

- Some communities follow the tradition of not mixing fish and meat on the same plate and will use a non-fish Worcestershire sauce product in meat dishes.

nondairy substitutes

Because the laws of kashrut demand that dairy products and meat cannot be mixed, kosher cooks are always on the lookout for pareve (neutral) ingredients to use with meat

meals. When cooking with meat, some kosher cooks will substitute oil, nondairy margarine, or shortening for butter. Instead of milk, cream, sour cream, and cheese, they will substitute nondairy creamer, nondiary sour cream, soy products (such as soy milk, cream, sour cream, or cheese, and tofu and its derivatives), or coconut milk. They will use vegetarian meat substitutes with dairy meals.

gelatin

When gelatin was introduced commercially in the eighteenth century, the controversy arose

The name Jell-O was first registered in 1897 by Pearle B. Wait, setting off an entertaining revolution that would last for decades. According to Lynne Belluscio, curator of the LeRoy [New York] Historical Society, by 1902 recipe booklets were distributed en masse, illustrated by artists such as Norman Rockwell. Certainly by the '40s and '50s no company table was complete without a platter of shimmering, quivering gelatin, filled with everything from pineapple to cucumbers to fish and beyond. Every *balabusteh* had a stash of favorite recipes and owned several molds in all sorts of fancy shapes and sizes. I fondly remember at family get-togethers there would be at least two or three Jell-O molds on the groaning board, served both as salads and as dessert.

among Orthodox Jews as to its kashrut and pareve status. Despite the claim that the meat by-products used in its production undergo a chemical change rendering it neutral, it was not accepted by them as kosher. In fact, my mother reports that Mama Hinda never used it (although by the next generation, the aunties who kept kosher did). The more observant use Kojel, which was released in 1933, and other vegetable- or fish-based products. All work differently from each other and from Jell-O, so it is difficult to convert recipes between them.

The controversy continues to this day. The major Orthodox certifying agencies do not accept animal-based gelatin as being kosher, while, according to *How to Keep Kosher* by Lisë Stern: "The Conservative ruling, based on Isaac Klein's 1969 Responsum, is that all gelatin is acceptable." While Ms. Stern follows this statement with personal reservations, I have chosen to comply with the conservative decision, and you will find several recipes containing gelatin here.

Please know that it is not my intention to offend more observant readers (or even family members!).

salt & pepper

You don't have to be kosher or even Jewish to use kosher salt, which most chefs prefer to table salt. Most of the recipes in this book were tested using kosher salt. (I use fine sea salt or table salt for baking.) If you do use table salt where I have indicated kosher salt, you will need *about* half the amount given. (Remember that kosher meat has already been salted.) Salt is such an important ingredient— too little and even the best recipe falls flat, too much and it is inedible. Yet one's preference for salt is such a personal thing. Let your taste buds be your guide.

Freshly ground black pepper is preferred to pre-ground. Instead of a pepper mill I use my Peppermate (www.peppermate.com), which has a convenient container for catching the ground pepper so you can measure it.

vegetable oil

Except where olive oil or other oil is specifically stated, I have specified vegetable oil for its neutral taste and high burn point. My personal preference is canola oil, which is low in saturated fats as well as economical.

vanilla

Use pure vanilla extract and not imitation vanilla. For Passover substitutions see page 564.

A few recipes call for **sour salt**, used in days of yore by kosher cooks who had limited access to citrus fruit. It is available today in kosher markets or even on your grocer's shelf. Pure citric acid, it is a souring agent, not a salt, and imparts a sour taste with no citrus undertones. Today citrus fruits are readily available, and many cooks prefer using lemon juice for this purpose. I have even seen recipes calling for sauerkraut as an alternative. Be judicious in using sour salt, however. Once you've added too much, it's hard to unring the bell.

Cooking
Jewish

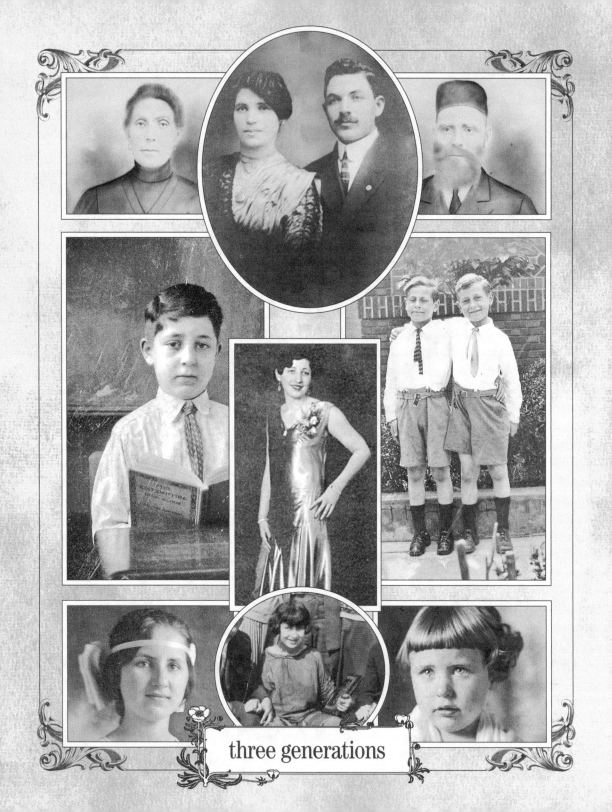

three generations

appetizers

forshpeis — a foretaste

In radio they call it "dead air time"—those dreaded seconds of unplanned silence that seem like hours. In broadcasting every moment must be filled with sound. As I remember the family gatherings of my youth, there was a similar avoidance of "dead food time." The moment you crossed the threshold you would immediately be invited to have "a little something." God forbid one should faint from hunger while awaiting dinner! I call it the three-minute rule: A guest must get something to eat within the first three minutes of arrival or it's a *shandah* (shame) on the host or hostess. "Come in. Give me your coat. Have a knish."

> *"Come in. Give me your coat. Have a knish."*

The "sandwich generation," 1914-style. Mama Hinda and Papa Harry (top center), with the parents they left behind in Slonim and the children they raised in America. Who's who on page 613.

3

Cooking at
Sur La Table.

When I started teaching cooking classes at Sur La Table, I was cautioned to be sure the students had something to sample within the first forty-five minutes of class. Obviously they didn't know with whom they were dealing. In my classes students partake of "a little something" as soon as they arrive. God forbid they should faint from hunger during *my* demonstration!

As a child, I looked forward to Aunt Irene's Sweetbreads (it's in Meats, page 164), her signature *forshpeis*. At Aunt Sally's we'd always expect Kreplach in Marinara Sauce, and no one could make Gefilte Fish better than Aunt Estelle. My mother's Sautéed Liver in Patty Shells was her standard first course.

Whether it's a tiny nibble to crunch, like Bruschetta or Toasted Pita Triangles, something to dip them into, like Tzatziki, Hummus, Baba Ghanoush, or Caponata, or more elaborate preparations to be passed on a tray, served family-style from a bowl or platter, or individually plated at the table, *forshpeis* is meant to whet the appetite (as if our appetites needed whetting!), a delicious preview of the feast to come.

Think of this chapter as the *forshpeis* of those that follow, in which young and old family members, in-laws of in-laws, introduce themselves with their signature palate-teasers. You'll find starters right out of the shtetl, such as Chopped Liver, Chopped Herring, and Potato Pletzels; Sephardic finger food, such as Bouraks, Filas, and Borekas; easy-to-throw-together openers such as Saucy Salami Crisps, Chiles Rellenos Quiche, and Parmesan Crisps; and more labor intensive (but, oh, so worth it) creations like Stuffed Mushrooms with Salmon Mousse, Potato Knishes, and Greek Spinach Pie.

Need an elegant meal starter? Try Mushrooms in Mini Croustades, Salmon Mousse, or Baked Brie en Croûte. Looking for a just-kickin'-back, pass-the-paper-napkins, down-home crowd pleaser? Go for the Chicken Wings, Sweet-and-Sour Meatballs, or Zucchini Fritters.

So let me introduce you to my family. Sit back. Put your feet up. Listen to their stories. And while you're at it, have a little something.

Left: My classic pose by an open oven door.
Below: Baking with my granddaughters
Samantha and Lauren, 2004.

it's a g thing toffee walnuts

from Gary Bart

I happened to be testing Rita's Special Kugel (page 292) the day before my sister-in-law Karina's birthday party. Not realizing the party was catered, I brought it, but no problem—caterer Cathy Giannone of It's a G Thing Caterers generously made room for it on the buffet. While we were eating, my brother, Gary, speared a candied walnut from Cathy's outrageous salad and said, "Can you believe how good these are? You should put them in the kugel!" I said, "Get me the recipe and I will!"

These are the richest, crunchiest caramelized walnuts that ever graced a salad . . . or a kugel! But there's never enough for either one, because the snackers get to them first. You can try this recipe with pecans or other nuts as well. **MAKES 1 3/4 CUPS** [D]

1/2 cup (packed) dark brown sugar

1 1/2 cups walnut pieces

3 tablespoons butter

1. Spread 1/4 cup of the brown sugar on a baking pan and set aside.

2. Heat a large skillet (do not use nonstick) over medium heat. Add the walnuts and toast, stirring with a wooden spoon, until they are fragrant and just beginning to

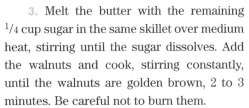

Gary in front of the Dumont, early '50s.

brown, 5 to 6 minutes. Remove the toasted nuts to a clean plate and set aside. Wipe out the pan.

3. Melt the butter with the remaining 1/4 cup sugar in the same skillet over medium heat, stirring until the sugar dissolves. Add the walnuts and cook, stirring constantly, until the walnuts are golden brown, 2 to 3 minutes. Be careful not to burn them.

4. Remove the candied walnuts with a slotted spoon and roll them in the brown sugar on the baking sheet, covering them completely on all sides. Allow them to cool. Store them in an airtight container for up to 5 days.

Note: For easy cleanup, reheat the pan and the caramel will come right off.

toasted pita triangles

from Samra Robbins

No matter what else is on the menu, these crispy bites always draw the biggest crowd. Yes, you can freeze them, but don't count on leftovers. These are habit-forming nibbles all by themselves, and super scoopers for hummus or a dip. **MAKES 96 TO 128 TRIANGLES** [D]

1 package (14 to 16 ounces) pita bread
  (6 to 8 breads)
1¹/₂ cups regular or light mayonnaise
¹/₂ cup freshly grated Parmesan cheese
¹/₃ cup dried minced onions
Garlic salt, for sprinkling on top

1. Preheat the oven to 375°F.

2. Separate each pita into two layers.

3. Combine the mayonnaise, Parmesan cheese, and onions in a bowl, and mix well. Spread a thin layer of the mixture over the inside of each pita half. Cut each half into 8 triangles.

4. Place the triangles in a single layer on an ungreased baking sheet, and sprinkle with garlic salt. Bake until browned, 10 to 12 minutes. Watch carefully, as they burn very easily. You may have to remove some before the others are done.

5. Let the triangles cool completely, and then store them in an airtight container for up to 1 week.

Note: These can be frozen: Lay the triangles in a single layer on a baking sheet and freeze them; then transfer them to plastic freezer bags. When you are ready to serve them, warm them on a baking sheet in a preheated 325°F oven for 5 to 7 minutes.

parmesan crisps

from Arlene Feltingoff

Arlene's husband and mine, the two Barrys, became best friends in third grade. They practically lived in each other's houses, went with each other on family vacations, and were as inseparable as twins. When they both married, happily Arlene and I became best friends too. When Barry F. died, he left a hole in our lives as wide as the country that separates us. Our grandson Blake is named for "Uncle" Barry, and our prayer is that he will grow up with Barry's integrity, loyalty, lust for life, and wit. (His sense of direction wouldn't be bad either.) Our friendship surely redefines "family," so in these pages Arlene is dubbed an honorary Rabinowitz.

There's always that one person you call first with good news or bad, and for me it is Arlene. Often a recipe is exchanged as well, and these tangy, lacy wafers are one of my favorites. Try them as a snack, or serve them instead of croutons in soup or salad. For the best flavor, Arlene always springs for real Parmigiano-Reggiano. When there's only one ingredient, use the best!

MAKES ABOUT 2 DOZEN

Left: My husband, Barry (center), with pals Richie Propis and Barry Feltingoff. Right: The two Barrys—Kancigor and Feltingoff.

8 ounces Parmesan cheese, in 1 piece—that's it!

1. Preheat the oven to 350°F. Line a baking sheet with parchment paper.

2. Grate the cheese and arrange 1 tablespoon mounds 2 inches apart on the prepared baking sheet.

3. Bake just until the cheese melts and turns golden, about 6 minutes. Do not overbake, or the flavor will turn bitter. Using a metal spatula, transfer the crisps, as soon as possible, to a wire rack. Let them cool completely; then store them, the layers separated with waxed paper, in an airtight container for 2 to 3 days.

baked brie en croûte

from Tracey Barrett

Sunday's "post-game celebration" after Brad and Tracey's wedding reception was a festive affair catered by Royal Event Gourmet Catering. This baked Brie was the hit of the party, and Tracey liked it so much, she convinced caterer Steve McGlawn to give her the recipe. Even if you can't duplicate Steve's gorgeous presentation of cascading leaves, this appetizer will bring "wows" from your guests. By the way, Steve says that the trick to getting the leaves to adhere is to brush the egg wash very lightly over the shapes, not letting it get too close to the edges, so they will rise properly. This is a treat with or without the leaves. Serve it with sliced French baguettes or fancy crackers. **SERVES 15 TO 20**   **D**

3 cups (packed) fresh basil leaves
    (about 2 generous bunches)
15 large cloves garlic
¹/₂ cup extra-virgin olive oil
1 cup oil-packed sun-dried tomatoes,
    cut into julienne strips and patted dry
Kosher (coarse) salt and freshly ground
    black pepper to taste
1 wheel (2 pounds) Brie cheese
2 sheets frozen puff pastry dough,
    such as Pepperidge Farm, thawed
    according to the package directions
Egg wash: 1 large egg lightly beaten with
    1 tablespoon water

1. Combine the basil, garlic, and olive oil in a food processor or blender, and process to form a thick, smooth paste. Stir in the sun-dried tomatoes, and season with salt and pepper. Spread the mixture evenly over the top of the wheel of Brie.

2. Unfold the puff pastry sheets onto a lightly floured surface. Pinch the longer edges of the two sheets together to form one large rectangle, and roll it out to form a rectangle measuring approximately 14 × 18 inches. Place the wheel of cheese in the center of the pastry sheet, and wrap the dough up and over the Brie to enclose it completely. Pinch the pastry together to seal it, and trim off the excess. Place the Brie, seam side down, on a baking sheet.

3. If you feel creative, cut out decorative

shapes from the trimmed dough, using a knife or a cookie cutter. Brush the underside of the decorations lightly with the egg wash, and arrange them on top of the pastry-wrapped Brie. Be careful not to twist or tug the dough, or the pastry layers will rise unevenly. Cover the remaining egg wash with plastic wrap and refrigerate it until you are ready to use it again.

4. Cover the Brie with plastic wrap and refrigerate it for at least 30 minutes or up to 24 hours; the longer you chill it, the crisper and more puffed the pastry will be.

5. When you are ready to bake the Brie, brush the entire surface with the remaining egg wash. Bake until the pastry is golden brown, about 30 minutes. Allow the baked Brie to stand for 40 to 60 minutes before serving, to allow the cheese to firm up. Serve warm or at room temperature.

> *Officials in Paris had refugees watch cowboy movies to teach them English. When my father [Sol, right with wife, Isabelle] wired his brother Sioma and asked him his size so he could send him clothes, Sioma wired back, 'I'm as tall as Gary Cooper and as wide as Wallace Beery.' When he got off the boat with Aunt Anda, my emaciated Uncle Sioma was wearing thick cord wrapped around his pants four times to hold them up and more cord around the folded-up hems of his pants. He wasn't as tall as Gary Cooper, and for sure he wasn't as wide as Wallace Beery.* —MARYLYN LAMSTEIN

sheilah kaufman's
smoked salmon cheesecake

from Marylyn Lamstein

marylyn found this elegant appetizer in Sheilah Kaufman's *Simply Irresistible: Easy, Elegant, Fearless, Fussless Recipes*. It can be served warm, at room temperature, or cold. Spread it on bagels, bread, crackers, or even fresh vegetables. *The Boston Globe* called the recipe "rich and delightful" when they reviewed my self-published book *Melting Pot Memories*.

SERVES 10 TO 14 **D**

Solid vegetable shortening or vegetable
  cooking spray
1 tablespoon vegetable oil
1/2 cup minced onion
3 packages (8 ounces each) cream cheese,
  at room temperature
4 large eggs, at room temperature
1/4 cup half-and-half
1/4 cup chopped fresh dill, or 2 tablespoons
  dried dill
4 ounces Swiss cheese, grated
8 ounces smoked Nova Scotia salmon,
  diced

1. Preheat the oven to 300°F. Grease a 9-inch springform pan with shortening or cooking spray. Wrap a sheet of aluminum foil around the outside of the bottom and about two-thirds of the way up the sides of the pan (this will prevent any leakage while baking).

2. Heat the oil in a small saucepan over medium heat. Add the onion and cook until soft and golden, about 4 minutes. Allow to cool slightly.

3. Meanwhile, place the cream cheese, eggs, and half-and-half in a mixing bowl and cream with an electric mixer on medium speed until well blended.

4. Add the sautéed onion, dill, Swiss cheese, and salmon to the cream cheese

"*I was three when my father, Nathan, died in 1943, leaving my mother, Anda [right, with husband, Sioma], a very young widow. Her sister and brother-in-law, Aunt Isabelle and Uncle Sol, invited us to live with them. Sol's parents and two sisters had been killed in Skole (Poland) in 1941 by the Nazis. In 1947, Sol received the astonishing news that his brother, Sioma, was alive and living in a displaced persons camp in Austria. Uncle Sol had his brother brought to Paris for rehabilitation and asked my mother to meet him there and marry him, if she chose, and bring him to America. They fell instantly in love, and their marriage lasted until my mother's death, 40 years later.* —MARYLYN LAMSTEIN*"

mixture, and mix on low speed or with a spatula until all the ingredients are incorporated.

5. Pour the mixture into the prepared pan, smoothing it out to form an even layer. Place the filled springform pan in a baking pan that's large enough to hold it comfortably. Carefully pour boiling water into the baking pan to reach halfway up the sides of the springform pan. Bake for 45 minutes; then turn off the oven and leave the cheesecake in the oven until it is thoroughly cooled, 1 to 2 hours.

6. Store the cheesecake, covered with plastic wrap and then wrapped in aluminum foil, in the refrigerator for up to 5 days. Or freeze it, wrapped well in plastic wrap and then in foil, for up to 2 months; thaw it overnight in the refrigerator before removing the plastic wrap and serving.

7. Remove the springform sides just before serving.

sally kay's tzatziki dip

from Brad Kancigor

Sally—Brad's friend and former coworker—adds chopped olives to this traditional Greek dip. Drained yogurt, known as "yogurt cheese," becomes thicker and thicker the longer you drain it. After 24 hours it has a consistency somewhere between sour cream and cream cheese. Some people like to save the drained whey as a nutritious substitute for water in other dishes.

Surround the bowl of tzatziki with pita bread, or better yet, with Samra's Toasted Pita Triangles (page 5). **MAKES ABOUT 3½ CUPS**　　　　　**D**

2 cups plain yogurt (see Note)

2 cucumbers, peeled, seeded, and finely chopped

Kosher (coarse) salt

8 Kalamata olives, pitted and finely chopped

1 clove garlic, crushed

2 teaspoons extra-virgin olive oil

1 teaspoon fresh lemon juice, or to taste

1 tablespoon finely chopped fresh dill, or 1 teaspoon dried dill

¼ teaspoon ground cumin, or to taste

Kosher (coarse) salt and freshly ground pepper, preferably white, to taste

Paprika, for garnish (optional)

1. Line a strainer with cheesecloth or ink-free paper towels and place it over a bowl. Pour the yogurt into the strainer, cover, and refrigerate for 12 to 24 hours. Discard the liquid in the bowl or reserve it for another use.

2. Place the chopped cucumber in a bowl, sprinkle it generously with kosher salt, mix well, and allow to stand for 30 minutes. Then rinse the cucumber in cold water and drain it on ink-free paper towels. Squeeze it in additional paper towels until quite dry.

3. Combine the drained yogurt, chopped cucumbers, and all the remaining ingredients (except the paprika) in a bowl and mix well. Refrigerate for at least 2 hours. (The mixture is best used within a day, but it'll keep for up to 1 week.)

4. When you are ready to serve the tzatziki, transfer it to a serving bowl and sprinkle with paprika if you like.

Note: You can use nonfat, low-fat, or full-fat yogurt for this dish, but make sure the brand you use doesn't contain gelatin, which clings to the whey and prevents it from draining off.

If you want to use the whey, it will keep in the refrigerator for 2 weeks, or in the freezer for 2 months.

Mom and grandson Brad during his college days.

vegetarian chopped "liver"

If you were stranded on a desert island and could take only one vegetarian chopped liver with you, which one would you pick? Well, I couldn't decide either, so I offered all three at a party. My taste testers were evenly divided, so you'll just have to try them (maybe not all on the same day, however) and see for yourself. This delicious appetizer mimics the color and texture of chopped liver by combining nuts with green beans or lentils or peas, but is meat-free and adored by liver-lovers and -haters alike.

bea goldman's

My mother-in-law's cousin Bea uses fresh green beans and sautés the onions v-e-r-y slowly for that grandmotherly taste and rich flavor. **MAKES 3 1/3 CUPS** P

1 pound fresh green beans, trimmed

1/4 cup vegetable oil

1 large onion, chopped

1/2 cup walnuts, toasted (see box, page 17) and chopped

2 large eggs, hard-cooked and coarsely chopped

1 teaspoon kosher (coarse) salt, or to taste

1/4 teaspoon freshly ground black pepper, or to taste

1. Bring a saucepan of water to a boil, add the green beans, and simmer, uncovered, until they are cooked but still crisp, 3 to 4 minutes. (Or you can steam the beans in a steamer basket over simmering water for 3 to 5 minutes.) Drain the beans well and set them aside on ink-free paper towels to dry.

2. Heat the oil in a medium-size saucepan over medium-low heat. Add the onion and cook slowly, stirring occasionally, until very soft and golden brown, 20 to 30 minutes. Allow to cool.

3. Combine the cooked green beans, cooled sautéed onion, walnuts, eggs, salt, and pepper in a food processor and pulse just until blended.

4. Cover and refrigerate for at least 2 hours, or up to 3 days.

steve kaplowitz's

from Judy Bart Kancigor

I met Steve when I was doing a cooking demonstration at the Palo Alto Jewish street festival called "To Life!" He opened my *Melting Pot Memories* and turned immediately to the vegetarian chopped livers. "Mine is better," he announced. "So where's the recipe?" I countered. (I love a challenge.) He sent it, and when I saw peanut butter, I was hooked! This is Steve's adaptation of the dish served at the old Ratner's Dairy Restaurant on Manhattan's Lower East Side. Lentils, substantial and meaty but bland by themselves, are the perfect backdrop for the rich peanuty/garlicky flavors. This dish has become my substitute for sticking my finger in the peanut butter jar, and now when friends assign me the appetizers for a potluck, they'll often say, "And bring that peanut butter liver thing."

Serve it with crackers or cocktail rye as a schmear, or on lettuce with a radish garnish as an appetizer. It also makes a great sandwich. **MAKES 6 CUPS**   **P**

1¹/₂ cups (10 ounces) green lentils

2 bay leaves

3 large onions (8 ounces each), chopped

6 tablespoons olive oil

3 large cloves garlic, crushed

2 tablespoons smooth peanut butter

1¹/₄ teaspoons kosher (coarse) salt, plus more
    to taste

¹/₂ teaspoon freshly ground black pepper,
    plus more to taste

3 large eggs, hard-cooked and coarsely
    chopped

1. Prepare the lentils: Bring 6 cups water to a boil in a medium-size saucepan. Add the lentils and bay leaves, and reduce the heat to a simmer. Cover the pan, leaving the lid slightly askew, and simmer until the lentils are tender, 15 to 20 minutes. (An option here is to use a pareve "chicken-flavor consommé" powder to flavor the cooking liquid. Osem, from Israel, makes a good one. If using, adjust the salt accordingly.) When the lentils are done, remove the bay leaves and allow the lentils to cool in the cooking liquid. When cool, drain, reserving the liquid.

2. Set aside about ¹/₂ cup chopped onions. Heat the oil in a large skillet over low heat. Add the remaining chopped onions and cook until they are a rich, dark brown—this may take 20 minutes or more. The key here is to cook the onions slowly—this is where they will develop the flavor needed to carry this dish. When the onions are dark brown, add the crushed garlic and cook a few minutes more. Allow to cool.

3. Place the cooled lentils, the cooled onion mixture, the peanut butter, the reserved ¹/₂ cup raw onion, the 1¹/₄ teaspoons salt, and the ¹/₂ teaspoon pepper in a food processor and pulse. You are looking for a mixture with some texture, not a smooth paste. Transfer the mixture to a bowl and if it is too stiff, stir in some of the reserved lentil cooking liquid. Fold in the eggs, and add salt and pepper to taste.

4. Chill, covered with plastic wrap, for at least 4 hours to allow the flavors to meld.

My cooking demonstration at the Palo Alto Jewish street festival, as my mother handles book sales (with a little help from Samantha) in the rear.

jackie bishins's

Cousin Jackie's version is the one I remember from Aunt Hilda's beautiful parties. The peas have to be Le Sueur, she says, and do make it somewhat sweeter than the others. No wonder I love it!
MAKES 4 CUPS [P]

3 tablespoons vegetable oil

1 large Spanish or other sweet onion, chopped

2 cans (15 ounces each) Le Sueur peas, drained

3/4 cup chopped walnuts, toasted (see box, page 17)

12 saltine crackers, or more to taste, crushed by hand

1 teaspoon kosher (coarse) salt, or to taste

1/4 teaspoon freshly ground black pepper, or to taste

1. Heat the oil in a medium-size skillet over medium heat. Add the onion and cook until soft and golden, 10 to 15 minutes. Allow to cool.

2. Combine the cooled sautéed onion and all the remaining ingredients in a food processor and pulse just until blended. Add more crushed crackers if you like a thicker consistency, but keep in mind that the mixture will become firmer as it chills.

3. Cover and refrigerate for at least 2 hours, or up to 3 days.

malca's baba ghanoush
(eggplant with tahini)

from Wendy Altman Cohen

Wendy's Israeli friend Malca Luzia Hasson is pleased to share some authentic Middle Eastern recipes with us—but she is quick to point out that Israel itself has become a melting pot, her own Sephardic family cooking the matzoh balls of Eastern Europe and her Ashkenazi neighbors enjoying dishes like this one. Serve the Baba Ghanoush with pita bread (page 335). **MAKES ABOUT 1 1/2 CUPS** [P]

1 eggplant (1 to 1 1/4 pounds)

1/2 cup tahini (sesame seed paste)

Juice of 1 lemon (about 3 tablespoons), or to taste

1 clove garlic, crushed

1 1/2 teaspoons kosher (coarse) salt, or to taste

Paprika, for garnish

1. Preheat the oven to 350°F, or preheat an indoor or outdoor grill to medium heat.

2. If you are cooking the eggplant in the oven, place it on an aluminum foil–lined baking sheet and roast until tender, about 1 hour. If you are grilling it, grill it slowly on all sides until the skin is charred and the eggplant is soft. Set the eggplant aside until it is cool enough to handle. Then scoop out the flesh, chop it fine, and place it in a bowl.

3. Combine the tahini, lemon juice, garlic, and 3 tablespoons water in a food processor. Process until a soft, creamy paste is formed; if it is too thick, add more water, 1 teaspoon at a time, through the feed tube while the processor is running. Mix this with the eggplant. Taste, and add lemon juice and salt as desired.

4. Garnish with paprika, and serve at room temperature. The Baba Ghanoush will keep, covered, in the refrigerator for up to 1 week.

Jackie and Scott Bishins.

a word (or two) about eggplant

• • •

Roasted eggplant is such a popular ingredient among our Sephardic *mishpuchah* (extended family) but how can one vegetable cause so much controversy!

My contributors are divided on the method of roasting. Some favor grilling; some use the oven (but their oven temperatures differ); some prefer the gas flame of a stovetop. Feel free to use any method you like to obtain the creamy flesh necessary for any of these recipes.

And here's a tip: I have found that it's easier to scoop out the flesh with a serrated grapefruit spoon than to try to peel a slippery roasted eggplant—and you get more flesh this way too. In fact, so strongly do I recommend this procedure that although all the contributed eggplant recipes said to "peel the skin," I've taken the liberty of changing the directions to "scoop out the flesh."

eggplant dip

from Jackie Bishins

my husband, Barry, claims he doesn't like eggplant. Sure, he likes eggplant parmigiana, but in that dish the eggplant is just a delivery system for the fried crust and cheese. I've stopped making announcements. My new philosophy on such matters is: "Don't ask, don't tell." Eggplant is such a chameleon anyway. Unless it's served sliced, you often never even know it's there. This appetizer is tasty, like a tangy eggplant salsa, and—another secret—low-fat!

Serve the dip with a crisp scoop: crackers, pita, bagel chips, raw veggies . . .

MAKES ABOUT 4 CUPS　　　　　**P**

1 eggplant (about 1 pound)

1 green bell pepper, stemmed, seeded, and coarsely chopped

2 large or 3 small plum tomatoes

1 jar (12 ounces) mild salsa

1 medium-size onion, coarsely chopped

2 to 3 tablespoons balsamic vinegar, or to taste

1 tablespoon olive oil

$^1/_2$ package (about $2^1/_4$ teaspoons) Good Seasons Italian dressing mix

$^1/_4$ teaspoon garlic powder, or to taste

2 teaspoons dried basil, or to taste

$^1/_2$ teaspoon kosher (coarse) salt, or to taste

$^1/_8$ teaspoon freshly ground black pepper, or to taste

1. Preheat the oven to 350°F. Cover a rimmed baking sheet or a baking pan with aluminum foil.

2. Prick the eggplant in several places with a fork or skewer, place it on the prepared baking sheet, and roast until it is soft and tender, about 1 hour. Set it aside to cool.

3. When the eggplant is cool enough to handle, cut it in half lengthwise. Scoop out the flesh, and discard the skin. Chop the flesh well. Transfer the flesh to a colander or strainer and let it drain for about 1 hour.

4. Combine the bell pepper, tomatoes, salsa, and onion in a food processor and pulse 10 to 15 times, until mixed but still chunky.

5. Transfer the mixture to a bowl and stir in the chopped eggplant, vinegar, olive oil, Italian dressing mix, garlic powder, basil, salt, and pepper. Cover and refrigerate until serving time.

Top: Jackie struts her stuff at a costume ball on a cruise ship, about 1962. Bottom: Jackie, about 1954.

rosie graham's eggplant appetizer

from Victoria Moreno

This is wonderful as an hors d'oeuvre, scooped up in wedges of pita bread (a bit messy—you'll want to lick your fingers). You can also leave the slices whole and serve it as an appetizer at the table. **SERVES 6 TO 8** **D**

FOR THE EGGPLANT

1 eggplant (1 to 1 1/4 pounds)
About 1/2 cup olive oil, for frying
3 ounces feta cheese, crumbled,
    or more to taste
3 cloves garlic, finely chopped

FOR THE DRESSING

2 tablespoons balsamic vinegar
1/4 cup olive oil
1/2 teaspoon sugar
1/4 teaspoon kosher (coarse) salt,
    or to taste
Freshly ground black pepper to taste

1/2 bunch cilantro, leaves and stems,
    chopped (1/4 cup)

1. Cut the eggplant into 1/4-inch-thick slices.

" *Rosie is a Sephardic woman I met in Israel. When she visited me in California several years ago, she taught me how to prepare this savory dish, which brings applause whenever I serve it. I remember with sweet affection our experience in the kitchen, sharing recipes and discovering a connection that transcends time and geography.*

—VICTORIA MORENO "

layered hummus and eggplant

with roasted garlic & pine nuts

from Judy Bart Kancigor

I've often heard chefs say they created a recipe in a dream, but I never believed it until it happened to me. I had prepared both the Israeli Hummus and Rosie Graham's Eggplant Appetizer for a party, and that night, as I slept, the two merged into one. After making a few adjustments in the two recipes, I tried it out on a cooking class, and students have told me that it has become a staple in their entertaining repertoire. Don't let the fresh chickpeas and roasted garlic intimidate you. For an easier version, prepare the Israeli Hummus on page 18 (or you can even use store-bought). The appearance is smashing and the combination of flavors, seductive. **SERVES 10 OR MORE** P

2 eggplants (1 to 1¹/₄ pounds each)

¹/₂ to ³/₄ cup olive oil

Hummus with Roasted Garlic (recipe follows)

Double recipe Rosie Graham's dressing (page 15)

¹/₂ bunch cilantro or flat-leaf parsley, chopped (¹/₄ cup)

¹/₃ cup pine nuts, toasted (see box, facing page)

About 8 pita breads, cut into wedges

2. Heat 1 to 2 tablespoons oil in a large, heavy frying pan over medium-high heat (use just enough oil to cover the bottom of the pan). Add the eggplant, in batches, and fry on both sides until it is cooked, brown, and slightly crisp, about 5 minutes per side. Drain on ink-free paper towels. Continue cooking the eggplant, adding more oil as needed. (The eggplant slices will absorb as much oil as you give them, but then they'll just get soggy. They will brown using a lesser amount, so add oil judiciously with each batch. Just be sure not to crowd the slices.)

3. Arrange the eggplant in a single layer on a large serving platter, and sprinkle with the feta cheese and garlic.

4. Prepare the dressing: Whisk the vinegar into the olive oil in a small bowl. Add the sugar, salt, and pepper, and mix well. Pour the dressing over the eggplant and top with the chopped cilantro. For the best flavor, let the dressed eggplant slices stand, covered, at room temperature for 1 hour or longer.

5. For communal scooping with wedges of pita bread, cut each slice into bite-size portions. Or, if you are serving it separately as a first course, leave the slices whole.

1. Prepare the eggplant according to the directions on page 13, Steps 1 and 2.

2. Coarsely chop the drained eggplant, and transfer it to a bowl.

3. Whisk the dressing, pour about 6 tablespoons of it over the eggplant, and stir. (If you like more dressing, go ahead and use it, but I find this is enough. Reserve the remainder for use as a salad dressing.) For the best flavor, let the dressed eggplant slices stand, covered, at room temperature for 1 hour or longer.

4. To assemble: Spread the hummus evenly on a large, flat decorative platter. Spread the chopped eggplant to within about 1 inch of the edge of the hummus. Sprinkle with the cilantro and toasted pine nuts. Serve with torn or cut pita bread for scooping.

toast thy nuts!

If you asked me to suggest just one simple thing you could do to improve your cooking, it would be to toast nuts. It doesn't take very long, and the difference it makes in your salads, pastas, cookies, and cakes is amazing. There is just no comparison. Untoasted nuts are like a limp handshake—lifeless and dull, all form and no substance. Toasting them brings out their intoxicating, aromatic oils—which you will smell as they perfume your kitchen—and yields a deeper, more intense flavor and crunch. Conduct your own taste test and see.

TO TOAST NUTS:

1. Preheat the oven to 350°F.

2. Spread the nuts in a single layer in an ungreased baking pan. Bake, shaking the pan and stirring occasionally, moving the nuts from the outside in, until they are fragrant and lightly browned, 5 to 10 minutes, depending on their size. Whole nutmeats take longer to toast than smaller pieces. Watch carefully, as nuts can turn from golden brown to black in a matter of seconds. Pine nuts, small in size and with a high oil content, take even less time—3 to 5 minutes—and should be stirred more often and watched very carefully.

3. As soon as they are toasted, transfer the nuts to a plate to stop the cooking, and allow to cool.

TO TOAST SEEDS:

1. Heat a skillet over medium-high heat.

2. Add the seeds in a single layer and toast, shaking the pan or stirring, until they are fragrant and lightly browned, 15 seconds to 1 minute.

3. Transfer the seeds to a plate and allow to cool.

■ Hot toasted nuts may seem soft, but they will become firm as they cool.

■ If you intend to chop the nuts after toasting them, allow them to cool completely first.

■ When a recipe calls for chopped nuts, I prefer to toast them whole or in large pieces first and then chop them. Chopped pieces burn more easily than whole nuts. If you do toast chopped nuts, shake them in a strainer first to eliminate the "crumbs," which will burn quickly.

■ The seductive aroma will tempt you to taste, but be careful. Nuts that feel cool on the outside may conceal hot oils within.

■ Store toasted nuts in an airtight container in a cool, dry place. They will keep for 1 to 2 weeks at room temperature and up to 6 months in the freezer.

■ In baking, unless the recipe calls for nuts to be sprinkled on top, where they will be exposed to the oven's heat, I always toast them before adding them to the batter.

hummus with roasted garlic

○ ◑ ●

hen I interviewed Faye Levy about her cookbook *A Feast from the Mideast*, she told me that her favorite hummus place is an Arab restaurant in Israel where it is made fresh from dried chickpeas. So great is the turnover that it is served warm! I couldn't get the image out of my head and had to try it. Sure, it's a little more work, but it's worth it. The roasted garlic is my own innovation and makes this hummus a standout. **MAKES ABOUT 2 CUPS** Ⓟ

1 cup dried chickpeas

2 teaspoons kosher (coarse) salt, or more to taste

1 head garlic

1 tablespoon plus ¹/₄ cup vegetable oil

¹/₂ cup tahini (sesame seed paste)

3 to 4 tablespoons fresh lemon juice, or to taste

1 teaspoon ground cumin

¹/₈ teaspoon white pepper

¹/₈ teaspoon cayenne pepper

1. Place the chickpeas in a bowl, add 4 cups water, and soak overnight.

2. Drain the chickpeas, transfer them to a medium-size saucepan, and cover generously with fresh water. Bring to a boil. Then reduce the heat and simmer, covered, for 2 hours. In the last 10 minutes stir in 1 teaspoon of the salt. Drain the chickpeas, reserving about ¹/₂ cup of the liquid.

3. Meanwhile, preheat the oven to 400°F.

4. Slice off the top of the garlic head so that all the cloves are exposed. Place the garlic on a square of aluminum foil, and pour the 1 tablespoon oil over the exposed cloves. Twist the foil tight, and roast for 40 minutes. Open the foil and let the garlic cool for 5 to 10 minutes.

5. Place 1¹/₂ cups of the cooked chickpeas in a food processor, and add the tahini, remaining ¹/₄ cup oil, 2 tablespoons of the reserved chickpea cooking liquid, the lemon juice, remaining 1 teaspoon salt, and the cumin, white pepper, and cayenne pepper. When it is cool enough to handle, squeeze the roasted garlic out of the cloves and add it to the other ingredients. Process until smooth. If the mixture is too thick, add either more lemon juice or more chickpea cooking water—enough to reach the desired consistency. For a chunkier texture (my preference), add an extra ¹/₂ cup chickpeas and pulse once or twice. Adjust the seasonings. Use any remaining chickpeas in salad or soup.

6. The hummus will keep, covered, in the refrigerator for up to 1 week.

israeli hummus

from Tracey Barrett

racey based this recipe on one she found in Lora Brody's *Cooking with Memories*. You know how you find one appetizer that becomes your signature? This is Tracey's. Best served with pita bread, especially homemade if you have the time (see page 335). **MAKES 2 CUPS** **P**

1 can (15 ounces) chickpeas, drained

$^1/_2$ cup tahini (sesame seed paste)

$^1/_4$ cup vegetable oil

$^1/_4$ cup fresh lemon juice, or to taste

2 large cloves garlic, crushed

1 teaspoon ground cumin

1 to 1$^1/_2$ teaspoons kosher (coarse) salt,
    or to taste

$^1/_4$ teaspoon white pepper

$^1/_8$ teaspoon cayenne pepper

Combine all the ingredients in a food processor, add $^1/_2$ cup water, and process until smooth. Transfer to a bowl, cover, and refrigerate until ready to serve (it will keep for about 1 week).

caponata
with pine nuts and capers

from Laura Seligman

aura adapted this recipe from one in Gina Williams and Michele Pedraita's cookbook, *From Our Kitchen Counter*. I demonstrated it in my cooking classes, and it was unanimously pronounced a winner. Just the right amount of sweetness offsets the puckery capers and olives in this vibrant appetizer. Serve it on crackers or as a dip with raw vegetables. **SERVES 8 TO 10** **P**

Laura in her college days, 1973. If her father had known she hitched rides, he would not have been amused.

6 tablespoons olive oil

2 eggplants (about 1 pound each),
    cut into $^1/_2$-inch dice

3 medium-size onions, chopped

3 ribs celery, diced

3 large cloves garlic, minced

1 can (28 ounces) Italian peeled tomatoes,
    drained and coarsely chopped

$^1/_3$ cup red wine vinegar

2 tablespoons sugar

$^1/_4$ cup pine nuts, toasted (see box, page 17)

$^1/_2$ cup pitted green olives, sliced

$^1/_3$ cup capers, drained and rinsed

$^1/_4$ teaspoon red pepper flakes

Kosher (coarse) salt to taste

Freshly ground black pepper to taste

1. Preheat the oven to 375°F. Coat two baking sheets with 2 tablespoons of the olive oil each.

2. Place half the chopped eggplant on each baking sheet and roast until it starts to brown, about 10 minutes. Transfer the eggplant to a medium-size bowl.

3. Heat the remaining 2 tablespoons olive oil in a large skillet over medium heat. Add the onions and celery and cook, stirring, until the vegetables are soft and lightly browned, about 10 minutes. Add the garlic and cook, stirring, for 1 minute more. Then add the tomatoes, reduce the heat, and cover the skillet. Simmer, stirring occasionally, until the celery is tender, about 10 minutes.

4. Stir the vinegar and sugar together in a small bowl. Add this to the onion-tomato mixture. Stir in the eggplant. Continue simmering, covered, stirring occasionally, until all the vegetables are tender, about 20 minutes. Allow to cool to room temperature. (The mixture can be made to this point up to 3 days ahead. Cover and refrigerate. Return to room temperature before continuing.)

5. When you are ready to serve the caponata, stir in the pine nuts, olives, capers, red pepper flakes, salt, and black pepper.

My daughter-in-law Shelly and my son Stu in a rare tuxedo sighting.

bruschetta
with tomatoes and garlic

from Shelly Kancigor

It's summer in Minnesota, and the tomato plants are as high as an elephant's eye. (So is the corn, but that's another chapter.) Shelly doesn't wait for company. While the tomatoes are sweet, she and Stu enjoy them practically every day, just as they do the fleeting warm weather. **MAKES ABOUT 16**　**P** or **D**

Vegetable cooking spray
6 large cloves garlic, coarsely chopped
¹/₂ teaspoon kosher (coarse) salt
1 loaf (16 ounces) Italian bread
Olive oil, for brushing the bread
3 large ripe tomatoes, seeded, chopped, and drained
3 tablespoons olive oil
2 tablespoons balsamic vinegar
16 fresh basil leaves, cut into thin slivers (chiffonade)
¹/₂ teaspoon dried oregano, or to taste
¹/₄ teaspoon ground cumin
¹/₄ teaspoon cayenne or freshly ground black pepper, or to taste
About ¹/₄ cup Parmesan cheese (optional)

1. Preheat the oven to 350°F. Grease a baking pan with cooking spray.

2. Combine the garlic and ¹/₄ teaspoon of the salt on a cutting board, and finely

chop them together. (The coarse salt helps to break down the garlic.)

3. Cut the bread into ³/4- to 1-inch-thick slices. Brush one side of each slice with olive oil, and distribute the chopped garlic evenly over the slices. Place the bread slices in the prepared dish and bake in the oven until toasted, 5 to 10 minutes.

4. Meanwhile, combine the chopped tomatoes, olive oil, vinegar, basil, oregano, cumin, remaining ¹/4 teaspoon salt, and pepper in a bowl. Mix well.

5. Arrange the toasted bread on a serving plate. Using a slotted spoon, spread the tomato mixture over the toast. Sprinkle with the Parmesan cheese, if using, and serve immediately.

with challah. Every family has its own method of preparing shashooka (not to be confused with shakshooka, a popular brunch or lunch meal in Israel, in which a "nest" is burrowed into the pepper-tomato mixture for an egg, which cooks over very low heat). Usually, bell peppers and tomatoes are grilled and peeled—although Abbe uses canned tomatoes as a shortcut. Some people add tomato paste, a sprinkle of vinegar, and/or a variety of spices. The mixture is simmered and reduced to an almost spreadable consistency. I have combined all three recipes for my favorite iteration and like to serve it, as Abbe does, with pita wedges for scooping or as a topping over steak. Leftovers turn even the most ho-hum sandwich into a smashing tour de force. **MAKES ABOUT 5 CUPS** **P**

shashooka

from Regine Jaffee, Martine Mann, Abbe Dubin

oth Regine and Martine, who have never met—Regine is cousin Bonnie and Jackie's cousin and Martine is cousin Abbe's sister-in-law— were born in Morocco and make this traditional salad of roasted peppers and tomatoes. Known also as salade cuite (cooked salad) or salade poivrons (pepper salad), it commonly appears on the colorful *meze* (appetizer) display for the Friday evening meal or Shabbat lunch, served

**3 red bell peppers (Abbe and Martine), or
   3 green (Regine), or 2 red and 1 green (me)**
**5 cans (28 ounces each) peeled tomatoes,
   drained well**
3 large cloves garlic
¹/4 teaspoon kosher (coarse) salt, or to taste
¹/4 cup vegetable oil
1 teaspoon good-quality paprika
¹/8 to ¹/4 teaspoon cayenne pepper, or to taste
Small pinch of red pepper flakes

1. Preheat the oven to 400°F. Line a rimmed baking sheet or a baking pan with aluminum foil.

2. Place the peppers on the baking sheet and roast, turning them occasionally, until they are soft and tender and charred on all sides, about 45 minutes. Place the peppers

Cousin Neil Dubin and his harem—wife, Abbe, and daughters Amanda, Colby, and Taylor, 1999.

stuffed mushrooms

with salmon mousse

from Judy Bart Kancigor

A few years ago, I was asked to do a book signing at a Planned Parenthood "Taste Of" event. The best dish among all the offerings was stuffed mushrooms, presented by a local restaurant. They weren't about to give out the recipe, but after much experimentation I came up with this version. When I served it the next time the kids came to town, my daughter-in-law Tracey went wild! **MAKES 18 TO 24**   **D** or **P**

18 ounces fresh salmon fillet, cut into pieces

3 large eggs

1 1/2 teaspoons kosher (coarse) salt

1/8 teaspoon freshly ground black pepper

3/4 cup heavy (whipping) cream or half-and-half
    or soy cream or nondairy creamer

1/4 cup chopped flat-leaf parsley

2 teaspoons chopped fresh tarragon,
    or 1 teaspoon dried

18 to 24 large mushrooms

Balsamic Reduction (recipe follows)

1. Place the salmon in a food processor and process until smooth. Add the eggs, salt, and pepper, and pulse just to combine, scraping the bowl down as necessary. With the processor running, gradually add the cream

in a brown paper bag, close it tight, and set it aside for about 15 minutes (this will allow for easy peeling later).

3. Meanwhile, chop the tomatoes into small pieces and drain them again.

4. Combine the garlic and 1/4 teaspoon coarse salt on a cutting board, and finely chop them together. (The coarse salt helps to break down the garlic.)

5. Combine all the ingredients except the bell peppers in a large saucepan, cover, and simmer, stirring often, until the tomatoes are very soft, about 1 hour.

6. Meanwhile, when the peppers have cooled, remove them from the paper bag and peel off and discard the skin. Remove and discard the veins and seeds. Cut the peppers from top to bottom into thin slices, and then cut the slices into thirds.

7. Add the roasted peppers to the cooked tomato mixture, cover the pan, and simmer until the mixture is thick, about 15 minutes. (If the mixture is too watery, simmer uncovered.) Serve at room temperature.

through the feed tube. Transfer the mixture to a medium-size bowl. Stir in the parsley and tarragon, cover with plastic wrap, and refrigerate.

2. Preheat the oven to 350°F.

3. Remove and discard the mushroom stems (or save them for another use). Clean the mushroom caps with a damp cloth, and dry them well. Scrape out the gills (a serrated grapefruit spoon works well for this task), leaving a nice well for the mousse.

4. Pour the Balsamic Reduction into a 13 × 9-inch glass baking dish. Arrange the mushrooms in a single layer in the dish. (If the mushrooms are too large to fit in the dish, use a smaller dish for the overflow. As the mushrooms shrink during cooking, you can then transfer them to the 13 × 9-inch dish.) Fill the mushrooms with the mousse. Bake, basting every 10 minutes, until the mousse feels firm to the touch, 20 to 30 minutes.

5. Serve hot, with the pan sauce. (If the sauce appears too thin because of the moisture exuded by the mushrooms, pour it into

My sister-in-law Karina helps me stuff the mushrooms.

a saucepan and reduce it over medium heat for 5 to 15 minutes, until you get the desired consistency.)

balsamic reduction

This sauce is easy, and the proportions of the ingredients are not etched in stone. At first the vinegar kicks back like a .22-caliber rifle, but as you reduce it, it mellows out. Feel free to add stock and/or wine and reduce it further. **MAKES 1¼ TO 1½ CUPS**   **D** or **P**

2 tablespoons butter or nondairy margarine
½ cup finely chopped shallots (about 8 large)
1 clove garlic, crushed
½ cup balsamic vinegar
3 cups vegetable broth (fresh, canned, or made
    with bouillon cubes)
1½ cups dry white wine
2 teaspoons fresh rosemary, chopped,
    or 1 teaspoon dried, crushed
1 teaspoon chopped fresh thyme, or
    ½ teaspoon dried
1 teaspoon sugar, or to taste (optional)
Kosher (coarse) salt, to taste

1. Melt the butter in a medium-size saucepan over medium heat. Add the shallots and cook until soft, about 3 minutes. Add the garlic and cook, stirring, for 1 minute. Then add the vinegar, broth, wine, rosemary, and thyme. Raise the heat to medium-high and cook, stirring occasionally, until reduced to 1¼ to 1½ cups, 30 to 40 minutes.

2. Add the sugar, if using, and salt to taste, and remove from the heat. (This can be prepared a day or two ahead and stored in the refrigerator. I even freeze it.)

mushrooms in mini croustades

from Joan Kalish

These tartlets are quite rich and elegant, yet surprisingly easy to make. A croustade is an edible container; the term describes anything from hollowed-out loaves of bread holding soup to these dainty, crispy cups. **MAKES 24** **D**

FOR THE CROUSTADES
About 2 tablespoons butter, at room temperature
24 thin slices white bread

FOR THE FILLING
4 tablespoons (¹/₂ stick) unsalted butter
3 tablespoons finely minced shallots
(about 3 large)
8 ounces button mushrooms, finely minced
2 tablespoons all-purpose flour
1 cup heavy (whipping) cream
¹/₂ teaspoon fresh lemon juice
1 tablespoon finely chopped flat-leaf parsley,
plus more for garnish
1 tablespoon finely chopped chives
¹/₈ teaspoon cayenne pepper
¹/₂ teaspoon kosher (coarse) salt, or to taste
2 tablespoons freshly grated Parmesan cheese

> "When Aunt Joanie died, the rabbi asked her children, Lisa and Louis, to describe their mother in one word. 'Perfect,' said Lisa without hesitation. What a tribute to this wonderful lady, who was such a major influence in my life. Her world was her family and friends. She was an inspired cook who dished out love as generously as she did her gourmet creations. Aunt Joanie was more like a sister to me than an aunt. From the time I was little, she lived in our home. She had the sofa in the porch room of our two-bedroom, one-bathroom house, Nannie living right behind us. I thought it was paradise! I was raised with so much love that I have nothing to say at cocktail parties—not a bad way to grow up!
> **—SAMRA ROBBINS**"

1. Preheat the oven to 400°F.

2. Prepare the croustades: Grease 24 mini muffin cups well with the butter. Cut 24 rounds out of the bread slices with a 3-inch cookie cutter. (If you have one that's fluted, they will be even prettier.) Press the rounds gently into the buttered muffin cups. Toast the rounds in the oven until lightly browned, 8 to 11 minutes (watch carefully so they don't burn).

3. Remove the croustades from the muffin cups and let them cool on a wire rack before filling them. The croustades can be made ahead and frozen in plastic freezer bags for up to 1 month.

4. Prepare the filling: Melt the butter in a large skillet over medium heat. Add the shallots and cook, stirring constantly, until they are soft but not browned, 3 to 4 minutes. Stir in the mushrooms and cook until they give

up their liquid and it cooks away, about 10 minutes.

5. Remove the skillet from the heat and whisk in the flour. Then whisk in the cream, return the skillet to the heat, and bring to a boil. Simmer, covered, until very thick, about 2 minutes. Remove from the heat. Stir in the lemon juice, parsley, chives, cayenne, and salt. Transfer the mixture to a bowl and set it aside to cool. (The filling can be made ahead to this point and refrigerated, covered, for a day or two.)

6. Reduce the oven temperature to 350°F.

7. Fill the croustades with the cooled mushroom filling. Place them on an ungreased rimmed baking sheet and sprinkle with the Parmesan cheese. Bake until they are hot and the cheese has melted, 8 to 10 minutes (watch carefully). Garnish with additional chopped parsley, and serve immediately.

potato knishes

from Judy Bart Kancigor

This recipe was adapted from one by radio personality Arthur Schwartz, and I'll go to my grave believing that if my daughter-in-law Shelly hesitated for one minute about marrying Stu, it was my knishes that pushed her over the edge. These are the rich, oniony knishes of yesteryear. The key is in the very slow cooking of the onions, spread out in two skillets so they fry properly. (I call them Jewish onions.) If the smell transports you back to your grandma's apartment, you're there.

You will find this dough very forgiving and easy to work with. Freezing the knish rolls makes them much easier to cut, and it's so convenient just to reach in the freezer for as many rolls as you need. The potato filling is also great for shepherd's pie (page 144), potato blintzes (page 275), or even alone, baked in a casserole dish. And for something really different, try the Potato Blintz Soufflé (page 278). **MAKES ABOUT 90 (6 LOGS)** **P**

FOR THE DOUGH

2 large eggs

1/2 cup vegetable oil

1/2 cup warm water

1 teaspoon kosher (coarse) salt

1 teaspoon baking powder

3 cups all-purpose flour

FOR THE FILLING

1 cup vegetable oil

2 pounds onions, diced

5 pounds baking potatoes, peeled and cut into quarters

2 egg whites, lightly beaten

1 cup instant mashed potatoes

1 tablespoon plus 1 teaspoon kosher (coarse) salt

3/4 teaspoon white pepper, or to taste

Solid vegetable shortening or vegetable cooking spray

Yolks of 2 large eggs

3 tablespoons vegetable oil

1. Prepare the dough: Combine the eggs, oil, warm water, salt, and baking powder in a bowl, and beat with an electric mixer on medium speed until well combined. Reduce the speed to low and add 2 cups of the flour, 1 cup at a time, mixing well and scraping the bowl down after each addition. Using your hands, knead in the last cup of flour, a little at a time, until the dough is pliable and smooth. Wrap the dough in plastic wrap and refrigerate for at least 15 minutes or up to 8 hours.

2. Prepare the filling: Divide the oil between two large skillets and place them over medium-low heat. Add the onions to the two skillets and cook, stirring occasionally, until they are very soft and golden brown, 20 to 30 minutes.

3. Meanwhile, bring a large pot of water to a boil. Add the potatoes and simmer until tender, about 30 minutes. (Testing with a skewer, rather than a fork, will prevent them from breaking up.) Drain the potatoes, discarding the water, and return them to the pot over medium heat. Heat, stirring, for a minute or two to dry them out a bit. Then transfer the potatoes to a very large mixing bowl.

4. Add the sautéed onions (including the oil), egg whites, instant mashed potatoes, salt, and white pepper to the mixing bowl. Using a hand masher, mash the potato-onion mixture thoroughly. Set it aside to cool.

5. Cut the chilled dough into 6 equal parts. Roll out 1 piece of dough on a board to form a rectangle measuring about 8 × 14 inches (if it sticks, lightly flour the board; keep the remaining dough covered.) Place one sixth of the filling in a narrow strip along one long edge of the dough, about $1/2$ inch in from the edge. Fold in $1/2$ inch of both short sides, and roll up the log. The whole log (about 13 inches long) can then be stretched to the length of the baking pan you are going to use. Repeat with the remaining dough and filling. Place the logs on a baking sheet, cover with aluminum foil, and freeze (to facilitate cutting) until solid, 2 to 3 hours. When they are solidly frozen, wrap each log in plastic wrap and then in foil, and freeze.

6. About 2 hours before serving time, grease a baking sheet with shortening or cooking spray. Place as many of the frozen logs as you wish to use, seam side down, on the prepared baking sheet. (Each log will yield about 15 knishes.) Let them thaw until you can *just* get a knife through them, about 30 minutes. Then cut each log, *without* cutting through the bottom layer of dough, into 1- to $1^1/2$-inch-wide slices, keeping the log together. (This will make it easier to cut them into individual knishes later while keeping the log together for baking.) Let the logs thaw completely.

7. Preheat the oven to 375°F.

8. Whisk the egg yolks and oil together in a bowl, and brush the tops of the knish logs with this mixture. Bake until golden brown, about 45 minutes. Cut into individual knishes, following the lines precut in Step 6. Serve hot.

Barry and me—our first New Year's Eve together.

fenster family sweet potato knishes

from Laura Seligman

Katya Seligman's Bat Mitzvah brings back special memories. As luck would have it for Katya, the first edition of our family cookbook, *Melting Pot Memories*, had been delivered just a few weeks before, and since the whole family would be gathered in Rochester, New York, for the event, Katya generously shared a little of the limelight with me by allowing me to distribute the long-awaited books to the family on Friday evening after services.

Harold Dubin with granddaughter Katya Seligman.

Co-officiating with Katya on her special day was Jason Fenster, celebrating his Bar Mitzvah. Both families were treated to these wonderful knishes, made by Jason's dad and younger brother Aaron, at the kiddush luncheon on Saturday. Much to our delight, the Fensters passed the recipe on to Laura, Katya's mother. **MAKES ABOUT 60 (4 LOGS)** Ⓟ

4 large sweet potatoes (4 pounds total)

2 to 2¹/₂ cups all-purpose flour

1 large egg, lightly beaten

¹/₄ cup plus 2 tablespoons vegetable oil

3 teaspoons kosher (coarse) salt

1 to 2 tablespoons sugar, or to taste

1 teaspoon ground cinnamon, or to taste

¹/₄ teaspoon freshly ground black pepper, or to taste

Solid vegetable shortening or vegetable cooking spray

Yolk of 1 large egg

1. Scrub the sweet potatoes thoroughly. Cut off the ends, but do not peel them. Place the sweet potatoes in a large saucepan, add water to cover, and bring to a boil. Simmer until tender, 40 to 50 minutes. (Testing with a skewer, rather than a fork, will prevent them from breaking up.)

2. Meanwhile, prepare the dough: Place 2 cups of the flour in a bowl and make a well in it. Add the egg, ¹/₂ cup water, the ¹/₄ cup oil, and 1 teaspoon of the salt to the well and mix with a fork, incorporating the flour until the mass comes together in a ball. Knead by hand, adding more flour as necessary, until the dough is pliable, smooth, and slightly tacky. (To do this, I start out in the bowl, then move the dough to a board.) Divide the dough into 4 portions, form them into balls, cover, and set aside to rest for 10 to 15 minutes.

3. Prepare the filling: Drain the cooked sweet potatoes and allow them to cool a bit. When they are cool enough to handle, peel off the skin. Combine the sweet potatoes, sugar, remaining 2 teaspoons salt, cinnamon, and pepper in a bowl, and mash thoroughly.

4. Roll out 1 ball of dough on a board (if it sticks, lightly flour the board) to form a rectangle measuring about 8 × 14 inches. Place a quarter of the filling in a narrow strip along one long edge of the dough, about 1/2 inch in from the edge. Fold in 1/2 inch of both short ends of the dough, and roll the dough and filling up into a log. The whole log (about 13 inches long) can then be stretched to the length of the baking pan you are going to use. Repeat with the remaining dough and filling. Place the logs on a baking sheet, cover with aluminum foil, and freeze until solid (to facilitate cutting), 2 to 3 hours. When they are solidly frozen, wrap each log in plastic wrap and then in foil, and freeze.

5. About 2 hours before serving time, grease a baking sheet with shortening or cooking spray. Place as many of the frozen logs as you wish to use, seam side down, on the prepared baking sheet. (Each log will yield about 15 knishes.) Let them thaw until you can *just* get a knife through them. Then cut each log, *without* cutting through the bottom layer of dough, into 1- to 1½-inch-wide slices, keeping the log together. (This will make it easier to cut them into individual knishes later while keeping the log together for baking.) Let the logs thaw completely.

6. Preheat the oven to 350°F.

7. Whisk the egg yolk and remaining 2 tablespoons oil together in a bowl, and brush the tops of the knish logs with this mixture. Bake until golden brown, 45 to 60 minutes. Cut into individual knishes, following the lines precut in Step 5. Serve hot.

sally's potato pletzels

from Harold Dubin, Fanny Gordon

Pletzel, from the Yiddish word for "little plate," usually refers to a flat onion roll, but Aunt Sally called these little potato pillows with their rich liver filling pletzels too. (Her instructions say to "flatten like a pletzel.") Her son-in-law, Harold, the proud recipient of her handwritten cookbook, filled his retirement days with re-creating her specialties. This was a particular favorite. Fanny made the same dish, but she called them "liver knishes." What's in a name? A pletzel by any other name would taste as heavenly.

MAKES 32　　　　　　　　　**M**

1/4 cup vegetable oil, chicken fat, or nondairy
　　margarine
2 large onions, diced
8 ounces liver (any kind)
2½ teaspoons kosher (coarse) salt, or to taste
3 cups mashed potatoes
2 large eggs, beaten
6 tablespoons plus 1/2 cup matzoh meal
1/4 teaspoon pepper, preferably white, or to taste
Vegetable oil, for frying

1. Heat the 1/4 cup oil in a large skillet over medium-low heat. Add the onions and cook, stirring occasionally, until they are very soft and golden, 20 to 30 minutes. Allow them to cool.

2. Meanwhile, preheat the broiler.

3. Place the liver on a rack in a broiler pan and broil on both sides just until no pink remains, about 3 minutes per side, depending on the thickness of the liver; be careful not to overcook it. Allow the liver to cool slightly. When it is cool enough to handle, remove and discard any gristle. Allow the liver to cool completely.

4. Place the liver and half of the cooked onions (including half the oil) in a meat grinder (preferred) or food processor, and grind or pulse just until ground. Do not over-process. Add $1/2$ teaspoon of the salt, or more to taste. Set the mixture aside.

5. Place the mashed potatoes in a large bowl, and add the remaining onions (including the oil), the eggs, and the 6 tablespoons matzoh meal. Mash well, and add the remaining 2 teaspoons salt and the pepper. Taste (see Notes), and add more salt and pepper if needed.

6. To form the pletzels, place the remaining $1/2$ cup matzoh meal on a flat plate. Dust your hands with some of the matzoh meal, and roll 2 tablespoons of the potato mixture into a ball. Use your finger to make a depression in the ball, and place 1 tablespoon of the liver filling in the depression. Cover the filling completely with the potato mixture, reroll the pletzel into a ball, and then flatten it to about $3/4$ inch thick. Dip the flattened pletzel into the matzoh meal. Repeat until all the potato and liver mixtures are used up.

7. To fry the pletzels (alas, the preferred method), pour vegetable oil to a depth of about $1/2$ inch in a large skillet, and heat over medium to medium-high heat. Fry the plet-zels in gently bubbling oil, turning them once, until they are brown and crisp on both sides, 5 to 6 minutes altogether. (Alternatively, bake the pletzels in a well-greased baking pan in a preheated 375°F oven until browned and crisp on both sides, about 15 minutes per side.) Serve immediately.

Notes: To taste the potato mixture, or any mixture containing raw eggs, microwave a tablespoon or so until the egg is cooked, 5 to 15 seconds; then taste.

Pletzels are best served at once, but they can be held, covered, in the refrigerator for up to 3 days and then reheated in a preheated 325°F oven for about 15 minutes.

Harold regaling Barry and me, 1983.

zucchini fritters

from Wendy Altman Cohen

I tested these for our Super Bowl 2004 party, and everyone was so busy fighting over them, we all missed Janet Jackson's big reveal! These fritters puff up into all sorts of odd shapes and disappear as quickly as they are fried. **MAKES ABOUT 48**

1¹/₄ to 1¹/₂ pounds zucchini, unpeeled,
   finely grated

1 cup all-purpose flour

1¹/₂ teaspoons baking powder

2 teaspoons sugar

2 teaspoons plus a pinch of kosher
   (coarse) salt

2 large eggs, separated

¹/₃ cup milk, preferably whole milk

1 tablespoon butter or margarine, melted

Vegetable oil or solid vegetable shortening,
   for deep-frying

¹/₃ cup freshly grated Parmesan cheese

1. Spread the grated zucchini on ink-free paper towels to drain.

2. Stir the flour, baking powder, sugar, and the 2 teaspoons salt together in a large bowl.

3. Beat the egg yolks well in a separate bowl. Stir in the milk and melted butter.

4. Beat the egg whites with an electric mixer on medium-high speed until foamy. Add the pinch of salt, increase the speed to high, and beat until stiff peaks form.

5. Stir the egg yolk mixture and the drained zucchini into the flour mixture. Carefully fold in the beaten egg whites.

6. Pour oil to a depth of 1 to 2 inches in a deep-fryer or a large, deep frying pan. Heat the oil to about 375°F.

7. Carefully drop the batter, 1 tablespoon at a time, into the hot oil. (Do not crowd the pan, or the temperature of the oil will decrease and the fritters will be soggy.) Fry, turning once, until golden brown all over, about 3 minutes. As they are cooked, use a slotted spoon to transfer the fritters to ink-free paper towels to drain. Continue frying until all the batter is used.

8. To serve, shake the fritters in a paper bag with the Parmesan cheese. Serve hot.

Variation: Instead of the Parmesan cheese, serve the fritters with your favorite ranch or blue cheese dressing.

artichoke spread

from Samra Robbins

Remember this one? Like my clutch bags from the '60s, if you hold on to things long enough, eventually they do come back! This oldie-but-goodie has aged well, waiting to be rediscovered by a whole new generation. Serve it on crackers or party rye bread. **SERVES 8—OR AS SAMRA SAYS, 1 GARY (MY BROTHER) AND 1 RONALD (HER HUSBAND)** D

1 cup regular or light mayonnaise

1 cup freshly grated Parmesan cheese

1 jar (6 ounces) marinated artichoke hearts,
   drained and shredded

Dash of garlic powder

Dash of Tabasco sauce

¹/₄ cup plain dry bread crumbs

Paprika, for garnish (optional)

1. Preheat the oven to 350°F.

2. Combine the mayonnaise, Parmesan cheese, artichoke hearts, garlic powder, and Tabasco sauce in a medium-size bowl, and mix well. Transfer the mixture to a 9-inch pie plate, and spread it out evenly. Sprinkle the bread crumbs on top. Sprinkle with paprika, if using.

3. Bake until browned and bubbly, about 30 minutes. Serve warm.

My brother, Gary, with kissin' cousin Ronald Robbins.

greek spinach pie

from Rita Miller

The traditional Greek spinach pie called spanakopita has become very popular all over the globe, even among people who have never thrown a plate or even liked Anthony Quinn. The cheese and spinach filling sandwiched in a flaky pastry makes an irresistible appetizer. Serve larger squares for brunch. If you prefer a thicker layer of filo, use two or three sheets for each layer.

MAKES 25 APPETIZER OR 6 BRUNCH PORTIONS ▣

Solid vegetable shortening or vegetable cooking spray

FOR THE FILLING
1 tablespoon vegetable oil
1/2 cup sliced scallions (white and green parts)
1/2 teaspoon dried dill
1 box (10 ounces) frozen spinach, thawed, well drained, and squeezed as dry as possible
4 tablespoons (1/2 stick) butter
1/4 cup all-purpose flour
1/2 teaspoon kosher (coarse) salt
1 1/2 cups milk, preferably whole milk
1 cup cream-style cottage cheese
1/2 cup crumbled feta cheese
1/4 teaspoon baking powder
2 large eggs, beaten

FOR THE PASTRY
2 sheets (about 16 inches square) frozen filo dough, thawed according to the package directions
2 tablespoons butter, melted

1. Preheat the oven to 325°F. Grease an 8-inch square baking pan with shortening or cooking spray.

2. Heat the oil in a medium-size skillet over medium heat. Add the scallions and the dill, and cook until soft, about 4 minutes.

3. Add the spinach to the skillet and cook just to heat it through, about 1 minute. Remove and keep warm.

4. Melt the butter in a large saucepan over medium heat. Whisk in the flour and salt. Add the milk all at once, stirring. Cook, stirring, until the mixture thickens and

bubbles, about 2 minutes. Then cook, stirring, for 1 minute more. Remove the pan from the heat.

5. Stir the cheeses, spinach mixture, and baking powder into the white sauce.

6. Stir $^1/_4$ to $^1/_2$ cup of the hot mixture into the eggs, and return the egg mixture to the saucepan. Mix well.

7. Brush half of 1 sheet of filo dough with some of the melted butter, and fold the sheet in half. Butter half of the dough rectangle, and fold it in half again, forming an 8-inch square. Butter the top of the square. Place the folded square in the prepared baking pan. Cover the filo with the spinach mixture. Butter and fold the remaining filo sheet as before, and place the square over the filling. Tuck in the edges. Butter the top.

8. Bake until the pie is set and browned, 35 to 48 minutes. Let it stand for 10 minutes before cutting into squares and serving.

Variation: If you want a thicker layer of filo, use up to 3 sheets each for the top and bottom pastry. Melt an extra amount of butter, and butter each layer before folding, as described.

Rita shares a dance with her son David.

june reinstein's chiles rellenos quiche

from Judy Bart Kancigor

I have been serving this dish as an appetizer or brunch buffet item since my friend June gave it to me twenty-five years ago, and it has never lost its appeal. What could be easier? Just whiz the batter in the blender, mix in the cheese, chiles, and melted butter, and bake. If you have any, the leftovers are fine reheated for breakfast. **MAKES 36 APPETIZER OR 18 BRUNCH PORTIONS**　**D**

Butter, for greasing the pan
10 large eggs
1 pint cottage cheese
1 teaspoon baking powder
1 teaspoon kosher (coarse) salt
10 drops Tabasco sauce
$^1/_2$ cup all-purpose flour
1 pound Monterey Jack cheese, shredded
1 can (7 ounces) diced green chiles, undrained
8 tablespoons (1 stick) butter, melted

1. Preheat the oven to 400°F. Butter a 13 × 9-inch glass baking pan.

2. Combine the eggs, cottage cheese, baking powder, salt, Tabasco, and flour in a blender, and whirl until smooth.

3. Combine the Jack cheese, chiles (and their liquid), and melted butter in a large

bowl. Add the cottage cheese mixture and mix together lightly.

4. Pour the mixture into the prepared baking pan and bake for 15 minutes. Then reduce the heat to 350°F and bake until golden brown, set, and puffy, 25 to 30 minutes.

5. Cut into squares or rectangles, and serve hot.

spinach and cheese frittata

from Ketty Moreno

Ketty brings an international flair to the kitchen. Her parents fled their home in Smyrna, Turkey, because of religious oppression and settled in Cairo, where she was born. Then, when she was fourteen, the family moved to Paris, where she later met her husband, Robert. Ketty and Robert married in the Philippines, resided in Paris, and then moved to Spain, where they lived for a couple of years during the Spanish Civil War before emigrating to the U.S. Her cooking reflects her rich Sephardic heritage. This frittata serves double duty as a standout appetizer or brunch dish. Feel free to use any combination of your favorite cheeses. **MAKES 36 APPETIZER OR 12 LUNCH OR BRUNCH PORTIONS** **D**

Solid vegetable shortening or vegetable cooking spray
2 tablespoons olive oil
2 tablespoons butter
1 large onion, chopped
8 ounces button mushrooms, sliced
10 large eggs
1/2 cup ricotta cheese
1 bag (6 ounces) prewashed fresh baby spinach, or 1 box (10 ounces) frozen leaf spinach, thawed
3 cups grated cheese (see Note)
1/4 cup matzoh meal
1 teaspoon kosher (coarse) salt, or to taste
1/4 teaspoon pepper, preferably white, or to taste

1. Preheat the oven to 350°F. Lightly grease a 13 × 9-inch glass baking dish with shortening or cooking spray.

2. Heat the oil and butter in a large skillet over medium heat. Add the onion and cook until soft, about 10 minutes. Then add the mushrooms, raise the heat to medium-high, and cook, stirring often, until the mushrooms are tender and have exuded their moisture, about 5 minutes. Set aside.

3. Mix the eggs with the ricotta in a large bowl. (This is accomplished more easily if you add the first 3 or 4 eggs one at a time.)

4. If you are using fresh spinach (and I highly recommend you do), coarsely chop it. If using frozen, drain it very well and coarsely chop it.

5. Add the onion-mushroom mixture, grated cheese, spinach, and matzoh meal to the egg mixture. Mix well, and pour into the prepared baking dish. Bake until set and

golden, 30 to 40 minutes. (Watch the bottom of the dish—you don't want it to burn.) Cut into squares and serve hot.

Note: Ketty uses a mixture of kasseri, sharp Cheddar, Parmesan, and feta.

eggplant frittata

from Ketty Moreno

According to Matthew Goodman (the "Food Maven") in a series he wrote for the *Forward* on the Jews of Spain, egg casseroles with vegetables and cheese were originally prepared on top of the stove—hence the name fritadas, meaning "fried" (frittatas in Italian). Today they are usually baked, and roasted eggplant with its characteristic smoky earthiness, is a natural—and yummy—choice in the Sephardic kitchen. Claudia Roden includes a Tunisian version called a marcoude, a popular appetizer of eggs, eggplant, and onions made without cheese, in *The Book of Jewish Food*, which, like Ketty's, may be served hot or at room temperature. But don't think of frittatas as only an hors d'oeuvre. This one would be a hit on your brunch menu too. **MAKES 36 APPETIZER OR 12 BRUNCH PORTIONS** Ⓓ

Solid vegetable shortening or vegetable cooking spray

2 eggplants (1 pound each)

2 tablespoons vegetable oil

2 tablespoons unsalted butter

1 large onion, finely chopped

10 large eggs

2 cups grated Romano cheese

1 cup freshly grated Parmesan cheese

¹/₂ cup ricotta cheese

¹/₂ cup fresh bread crumbs

¹/₂ cup chopped flat-leaf parsley

Pinch of sugar

Up to ¹/₂ teaspoon kosher (coarse) salt, to taste

1. Preheat the oven to 350°F. Lightly grease a 13 × 9-inch glass baking dish with shortening or cooking spray, and set it aside.

2. Prick the eggplants in several places with a fork or skewer, and roast them according to the directions on page 13, Step 2. When they are cool enough to handle, cut them in half lengthwise. Scoop out the flesh, and discard the skin. Chop the flesh well. Transfer the flesh to a fine-mesh strainer or a colander lined with cheesecloth, and allow the excess liquid to drain off for about 15 minutes.

3. Meanwhile, heat the oil and butter together in a large skillet over medium heat until the butter melts. Add the onion and cook, stirring occasionally, until soft but not browned, about 10 minutes. Set aside.

4. Beat the eggs in a large bowl. Add the drained eggplant, all three cheeses, bread crumbs, parsley, sugar, and salt, and mix thoroughly. Stir in the sautéed onion with the oil and butter from the skillet.

5. Transfer the mixture to the prepared baking dish and bake, uncovered, until set and golden brown, about 40 minutes. Cut into squares and serve hot.

potato-cheese borekas

from Ketty Moreno

Borekas can be sweet or savory and are sometimes made with puff pastry. There are as many fillings as there are cooks willing to make them.

These irresistible turnovers are to our Sephardic *mishpuchah* what knishes are to us—that familiar, comforting, yet habit-forming starter that guests never seem to tire of. Until I tested this recipe, I had never even seen them. Fortunately, Syrian cookbook author Jennifer Abadi *(A Fistful of Lentils)* offered to demonstrate making them for me on

Ketty with great-granddaughter Rachel.

a recent visit to L.A. I borrowed cousin Wendy Cohen's nearby kitchen—she wasn't even home!—for a lesson in Sephardic pastry making that I will never forget. When Wendy returned from work, a tray of assorted borekas and filas awaited her. What a dinner! **MAKES ABOUT 60** **D**

Solid vegetable shortening, vegetable cooking spray, or parchment paper

FOR THE FILLING
1 large white potato
3 large eggs, lightly beaten
1¹/₂ cups grated cheese (see Notes)
¹/₄ teaspoon kosher (coarse) salt, or to taste

FOR THE DOUGH
About 4¹/₂ cups all-purpose flour
1¹/₄ teaspoons kosher (coarse) salt
³/₄ cup vegetable oil
4 tablespoons (¹/₂ stick) unsalted butter, melted and cooled to room temperature

FOR THE TOPPING
1 large egg, beaten
Grated Parmesan cheese

1. Preheat the oven to 350°F. Grease several baking sheets with shortening or cooking spray, or better yet, line them with parchment paper.

2. Prepare the filling: Scrub the potato well and rinse it. Place it in a saucepan, add water to cover, and bring to a boil. Reduce the heat and cook until the potato is very soft and can be pierced with a skewer, about 30 minutes. When the potato is done, strain it, reserving the cooking water. Refrigerate the cooking water (you'll be using it for the dough).

3. When the potato is cool enough to handle, peel it and mash with a ricer or hand masher until very soft and creamy. Place $1/2$ cup of the mashed potato in a medium-size bowl. (Reserve the remainder for another use.) Add the eggs, cheese, and salt. Stir well to combine, and set aside.

4. Prepare the dough: Stir 4 cups of the flour and the salt together in a large bowl. Add the oil, melted butter, and $3/4$ cup of the cooled, strained potato water. Stir with a wooden spoon until the dough comes together. Form the dough into a ball, using your hands, and place it on a clean, dry surface. Knead just until all the ingredients are evenly combined (flour the work surface if necessary). The dough should feel soft and wet, but not too sticky to handle. If it is, incorporate the remaining flour, a tablespoon at a time, until it is no longer sticky.

5. Roll the dough out until it is very thin, $1/8$ inch thick or slightly less (lightly flour your work surface if necessary). Using the rim of a glass or a 3-inch cookie cutter, cut out a round of dough. (It is better to fill each round as it is cut, rather than to cut out all the rounds and then fill them.) If the dough round shrinks immediately, stretch it with a rolling pin. Place 1 level teaspoon of the filling on the center of the dough round. Fold the round of dough in half to form a half-moon. Pinch the edges together and crimp them with a fork. Repeat with the remaining dough and filling.

6. Place the pastries on the prepared baking sheets. Brush the top of each boreka liberally with beaten egg, and sprinkle with Parmesan cheese. Bake until lightly golden, 25 to 30 minutes. Serve hot or at room temperature.

Note: Ketty uses a combination of grated Parmesan and kasseri or fontina.

Variations: Borekas can also be filled with meat (see Filas with Meat, page 40, or Bourak, page 38). When preparing the dough, use cold water instead of the potato water, margarine instead of the butter, and omit the cheese topping.

nona rosa reytan's spinach & cheese borekitas

from Arlene Feltingoff

Moreno family lore tells of an uncle who was a blind musician in a *mikvah* (ritual bath) in Smyrna, Turkey. The family always wondered . . . was he really blind?

When Arlene's daughter, Melissa and son-in-law Harvey, returned from Florida after visiting Harvey's Nona Rosa, they spoke so wistfully and

> Before the war, my grandparents lived in the city of Alexandroupolis in Greece. When the Nazis came, they fled with my Aunt Rachel, who was three at the time, to the island of Evia to go into hiding, taking Christian names. They had been very wealthy and rented the biggest house in the village (Ahladi). When the German officers came one night to the village, they demanded to be fed and more or less relax at the nicest house. The mayor, who knew my family was Jewish, begged my grandparents to accommodate them. My grandfather immediately rolled up a mattress and took off for the mountains! The Greeks did not circumcise, and if anyone would betray them, they would be sent to the camps or be killed on the spot. My grandmother, Nona Rosa, cooked for them. Fortunately everything went well, and my grandfather later returned when he felt it was safe. My mother was born there at the end of the war.
>
> —HARVEY HAKIM

longingly about her borekitas that Arlene had to get the recipe for this old Greek family favorite. Perhaps it's the Olympian influence, but Nona Rosa's borekitas ("little borekas") seem to be the same size as borekas elsewhere. Whatever size you make them, my friend Jennifer Abadi gave me a terrific shortcut: Instead of rolling the dough and cutting out rounds, she divides the dough equally into little balls and rolls out each ball. (In fact, this dough is so pliable, you may be able to push the balls into rounds without a rolling pin.) Now, why didn't I think of that! **MAKES 48**

Solid vegetable shortening, vegetable cooking spray, or parchment paper

FOR THE FILLING

1 box (10 ounces) frozen chopped spinach, thawed, very well drained, and squeezed as dry as possible
2 large eggs, beaten
1 package (7.5 ounces) farmer cheese, crumbled
2 tablespoons crumbled feta cheese
$^1/_4$ to 1 teaspoon kosher (coarse) salt, to taste
$^1/_4$ teaspoon freshly ground black pepper, or to taste

FOR THE DOUGH

$^1/_2$ cup vegetable oil
$^1/_2$ cup ice water
$^1/_2$ teaspoon kosher (coarse) salt
2 cups all-purpose flour

FOR THE TOPPING

Yolks of 2 large eggs, lightly beaten

1. Preheat the oven to 400°F. Lightly grease several baking sheets with shortening or cooking spray, or better yet, line them with parchment paper.

2. Combine all the filling ingredients in a bowl and mix well. Set aside.

3. Prepare the dough: Mix the oil, ice water, and salt with a fork in a large bowl. Add the flour all at once, and combine with the same fork (no kneading is necessary). Bring the dough together with your hands to create a very soft ball. On a clean surface or countertop, roll the dough into a ball and cut it into quarters as evenly as you can. Keeping the remaining dough covered with plastic wrap,

use your hands to roll 1 quarter into a long, even sausage shape. Cut it into 12 pieces.

4. Using your hands, roll each piece of dough into a ball. Roll (or even pat) each ball out to form a very thin round, $2^1/2$ to 3 inches in diameter. Place 1 heaping teaspoon of the filling in the center of the round and spread it to within $1/2$ inch of the edge. Wet the edges with a little water, fold the dough in half to form a half-moon, and crimp the edges with a fork to seal them. Place the filled borekitas on one of the prepared baking sheets.

5. Repeat with the remaining quarters of the dough, forming it into a sausage shape, cutting, rolling, filling, and sealing, until all the dough and filling is used.

6. Brush the tops of the borekitas with the beaten egg yolk. Bake until lightly browned, 12 to 14 minutes. Serve immediately.

Note: You can really save time by using the assembly-line method: Roll out 12 small balls of dough at a time. Spread the filling on all 12. Fold the 12, then crimp them. Bake these while working on the next 12. If the phone doesn't ring, you'll be done in 30 minutes.

bourak

from Phyllis Epstein

Cousin Phyllis toiled for many years in the U.N. as a member of the Hospitality Committee under the Office of Protocol, which assists in helping our foreign friends assimilate into our culture and country. In our family we like to say that she is the cousin in charge of world peace. Through the years many of the ambassadors, delegates, and their wives have become valued friends, joining the Epsteins for their lavish seders and dinners. Here is the recipe for a Middle Eastern specialty given to Phyllis by Zoulikha Fouathia, wife of an Algerian diplomat. **MAKES 50**   Ⓜ

FOR THE FILLING
1/4 cup vegetable oil

2 medium-size onions, chopped

2 1/4 pounds ground beef

1 1/2 teaspoons ground cinnamon

1/2 teaspoon ground ginger

Generous pinch of saffron threads

2 teaspoons kosher (coarse) salt,
*   or to taste*

6 large eggs, beaten

1 bunch cilantro, finely chopped (1/2 cup)

1 bunch curly-leaf parsley, finely chopped
*   (1/2 cup)*

50 pareve spring roll sheets

Whites of 2 eggs, beaten

Vegetable oil, for deep-frying

2 to 3 lemons, cut into wedges

1. Prepare the filling: Heat the oil in a large skillet over medium heat. Add the onions and cook until soft, about 10 minutes. Add the beef, cinnamon, ginger, saffron, and 1 teaspoon of the salt. Raise the heat to medium-high and cook until the beef

is completely browned, about 5 minutes. Then add the eggs, cilantro, and parsley, and cook, stirring constantly, for 1 minute. Add the remaining 1 teaspoon salt, or to taste. Remove the skillet from the heat and allow the mixture to cool somewhat.

2. Fold a spring roll sheet in half, and place 2 tablespoons of the filling in a sausage shape about 1 inch in from the short edge. Start rolling the sheet up, tightening it as you roll, into a cigar shape. When you get about a third of the way up, tuck in the side edges to contain the filling. Finish rolling, and then seal the edge closed by brushing it, inside and out, with the beaten egg white. Set aside, and repeat until all the rolls are formed in this fashion.

3. Pour oil to a depth of 1 to 2 inches in a deep-fryer or a large, heavy skillet, and heat it to 370°F. Place 1 roll in the hot oil to test the temperature; the oil should be bubbling very slightly. Fry the rolls, 3 to 4 rolls at a time, until browned all over, about 3 minutes altogether. Do not crowd them, or the temperature of the oil will drop and the bouraks will be soggy. Drain on ink-free paper towels.

4. Serve immediately, with lemon wedges alongside.

Aunt Irene and Phyllis, late '70s.

kreplach
with marinara

from Sally Bower

Of course Aunt Sally served these meat-filled dumplings in chicken soup—anyone could do that! But her signature appetizer was kreplach in marinara sauce, served on a platter with little toothpicks. And heaven help the child who sloshed sauce on her divan. While we were always invited to her parties, we were frequently shown the door to "get some fresh air." Aunt Sally was a firm believer in fresh air—rain, snow, or shine—and just when the adult conversation would get interesting, she would consider the state of our health. Cousin Joyce used to grumble, as we'd struggle with our galoshes, "Oh, Aunt Sally and her outside business!"

MAKES 3 TO 4 DOZEN M

Kosher (coarse) salt
¹/₂ recipe Kreplach with St. Louis Dough and Belle Harbor Filling (page 67), fresh or frozen
1 recipe Homemade Marinara Sauce (page 152)

1. Bring a large pot of lightly salted water to a boil. Drop the kreplach, one at a time, into the boiling water and cook, stirring occasionally, until the dough is al dente, 20 to 25 minutes (you'll have to do this in batches).

2. Meanwhile, bring the pasta sauce to a boil in a large pot. Reduce the heat to a simmer.

3. Add the kreplach to the pasta sauce and simmer, covered, until heated through, about 5 minutes.

Note: If you want to prepare these ahead, boil the kreplach as described in Step 1. Then drain them and let them cool to room temperature. Spray them with vegetable cooking spray to keep them from sticking together, cover, and refrigerate for up to 1 day.

filas
with meat

from Ketty Moreno

All around the Mediterranean, cooks make some version of these yummy little pies with filo dough. My friend Amy Kremer tells me her Greek ya-ya (grandmother) used to make her own filo, which she would roll out on an oilcloth. She didn't have a rolling pin that was long enough, so she would use a roller from a pull-down window shade and roll the filo as thin as tissue paper. Few go through this laborious process today, when frozen filo is available. Just be sure to keep the unused portion covered, as it dries out easily.

When Ketty, who was close to ninety at the time, sent me this recipe, she sent along a sheet of tracing paper, cut to size and folded into triangles "like a flag," to make sure I understood how to form them.

MAKES ABOUT 40　　　　　　**M**

FOR THE FILLING
2 tablespoons vegetable oil
1 small onion, chopped
1 pound ground beef
1 large egg, lightly beaten
¹/₄ cup pine nuts, toasted (see box, page 17)
¹/₄ cup flat-leaf parsley leaves, finely chopped
¹/₂ teaspoon kosher (coarse) salt, or to taste
Freshly ground black pepper to taste

Solid vegetable shortening, vegetable cooking spray, or parchment paper

FOR THE DOUGH
8 ounces frozen filo dough, thawed according to the package directions
³/₄ cup olive oil
1 large egg, lightly beaten
Sesame seeds, for sprinkling on top

1. Prepare the filling: Heat the oil in a large skillet over medium heat. Add the onion and cook until soft and golden, about 7 minutes. Add the meat and cook, stirring constantly, until browned, about 5 minutes. Then add the egg, pine nuts, parsley, salt, and pepper. Mix well and set aside.

2. Preheat the oven to 350°F. Lightly grease several baking sheets with shortening or cooking spray, or better yet, line them with parchment paper. Set them aside.

3. Unroll the filo dough onto a cool,

clean, dry surface. If the filo is not precut, cut it into 4 equal rectangles (see Notes). Place 1 sheet of filo on your work surface with the longer edge facing you. Cover the remaining sheets with a slightly damp (not soaking) towel to keep them moist. Carefully brush the left half of the rectangle with oil. Pick up the right side of the sheet and fold it in half to meet the left side. Brush the left side with oil and fold in half again. Now you have a vertical 4-layer sheet before you. Brush the top with oil.

4. Place a scant tablespoon of filling at the lower left-hand corner, about $1/2$ inch in from the edge (see Notes). Pick up the lower right corner and bring it over the filling to meet the left edge of the dough, creating a triangle. Tuck the unfilled $1/2$-inch left margin over, and then fold the triangle of filling, as tightly as possible, to the end of the folded sheet as you would fold a flag. Tuck any unfilled portion of the filo dough into the filled triangle.

5. Repeat with the remaining filling and filo dough.

6. Lightly brush the folded filo packets with oil and then with beaten egg. Sprinkle them lightly with sesame seeds. Arrange the filas on the prepared baking sheets and bake until they are golden brown, 25 to 30 minutes. Serve immediately.

Notes: Some precut filo dough comes in rectangles measuring approximately 9×14 inches, which makes it perfect for assembling baklava (page 452) in a 13×9-inch pan. But different brands of filo come in different sizes, so for these filas you may need to use more or less filling, depending on the size of the rectangles you get.

If you prefer larger filas, use 2 sheets of filo, brushing each sheet with oil before stacking them one on top of the other. Then fold the dough into thirds instead of fourths.

Variations: Use either of the borekas fillings—potato-cheese (page 35) or spinach and cheese (page 36)—for the filas.

not exactly russian piroshki

from Stu Kancigor

my son Stu learned to make these easy, meaty morsels in his seventh-grade cooking class.

Okay, you're thinking, Excuse me? Hoisin sauce in piroshki? I'd love to tell you these piroshki were created by a little-known ancient Jewish sect on the Russo-Chinese border, but I'd be lying. Actually, Russians use sour cream in their meat pies, which explains why our fore-mothers in the shtetls never picked up this recipe. Sure, there are nondairy sour cream substitutes, but I found that hoisin gives them much more flavor. The dough is a no-brainer and would work beautifully for an easy version of the borekas or filas.

MAKES ABOUT 48   Ⓜ

FOR THE FILLING

1¹/₄ cups chopped beef

2 tablespoons vegetable oil

¹/₄ cup chopped onion

1 clove garlic, crushed

3 tablespoons hoisin sauce

1 teaspoon ground ginger

1 teaspoon kosher (coarse) salt,
*   or to taste*

¹/₈ teaspoon freshly ground black
*   pepper, or to taste*

Sure Stu likes to cook, but I'd be lying if I said there wasn't other stuff he'd rather do.

FOR THE DOUGH

1¹/₂ cups pareve biscuit mix

Solid vegetable shortening or vegetable
*   cooking spray*

All-purpose flour

Egg wash: 1 egg beaten with
*   2 tablespoons water*

1. Prepare the filling: Place the beef in a large skillet. Turn the heat under the skillet to medium-high and cook the beef, breaking it up with a spatula or fork, until no trace of pink remains, about 4 minutes. Using a slotted spoon, transfer the meat to a medium-size bowl and set it aside.

2. Heat the oil in the same skillet over medium heat. Add the onion and cook, stirring often, until soft, about 4 minutes. Add the garlic and continue cooking, stirring constantly, for about 1 minute. Return the browned beef to the skillet and stir in the hoisin sauce, ginger, salt, and pepper. Cook for 1 minute or so to blend the flavors. Return the mixture to the bowl and allow it to cool.

3. Prepare the dough: Using a fork, stir the biscuit mix and ²/₃ cup water together in a bowl. The dough should cling together and clean the sides of the bowl. Add more water, 1 tablespoon at a time, if necessary.

4. Preheat the oven to 425°F. Lightly grease several baking sheets with shortening or cooking spray.

5. Sprinkle a board with flour. Roll the dough in the flour to lightly coat it. Then knead the dough 10 to 12 times by folding it in half, pressing down with the heels of your hands, turning the dough a quarter turn, and repeating. (This will make the dough flaky.) Roll or pat the dough out very thin (¹/₁₆ inch) and cut out 3-inch rounds with a glass, cookie cutter, or biscuit cutter.

6. Fill each round of dough with a scant tablespoon of the meat filling. Fold it in half, and crimp the edges with a fork or pinch them closed. If any edges refuse to stick, wet them lightly with water and then crimp or pinch.

7. Place the filled pastries on the prepared baking sheets. Lightly brush the tops with the egg wash, and cut a small slit in the top of each pastry with a sharp knife so the steam can escape. Bake until golden brown, about 8 minutes. Serve hot.

savory steamed dumplings

from Shelly Kancigor

Shelly got this recipe from a coworker in her BJ (before Jason) days, when she was employed at a fast-paced L.A. advertising agency. Now that she's doing the most important work there is—raising my grandchildren!—her focus groups are attended by eight- and ten-year-olds, her photo shoots take place at Little League games and school plays, and deadlines mean homework due tomorrow. As you wrap the wonton skins around the filling, leave some of the meat exposed. (Think mini cupcakes sitting in fluted paper liners.) And don't crowd the steamer. Make sure they don't touch each other, or they will stick together. **MAKES ABOUT 32** Ⓜ

2 tablespoons hoisin sauce

1 teaspoon cornstarch

$^1/_2$ cup finely chopped baby bok choy

$^1/_4$ cup finely chopped shiitake mushroom caps

$^1/_4$ cup shredded carrot

$^1/_4$ cup finely chopped water chestnuts

$^1/_4$ cup thinly sliced scallions (white and green parts)

$^1/_2$ jalapeño pepper, seeded and finely chopped

3 tablespoons chopped cilantro or flat-leaf parsley

2 teaspoons grated fresh ginger

$^1/_4$ teaspoon kosher (coarse) salt

12 ounces lean ground turkey or beef

About 32 pareve wonton wrappers

Lettuce or cabbage leaves, for lining the rack

Vegetable cooking spray

Soy Dipping Sauce (recipe follows)

1. Stir the hoisin sauce and cornstarch together in a large bowl. Add the bok choy, mushrooms, carrot, water chestnuts, scallions, jalapeño pepper, cilantro, ginger, and salt. Mix well. Add the ground turkey and combine thoroughly.

2. Place 1 tablespoon of the filling in the center of each wonton skin. Pinch the skin up and around the filling, leaving the meat exposed on top.

3. Fit a steamer or a large Dutch oven with a rack. Fill with water nearly up to the rack, but not touching. Lay lettuce leaves over the rack, and spray them with vegetable cooking spray. (This will keep the dumplings from sticking or falling through the rack while cooking.) Place the dumplings in a single layer, open side up, on the leaves. You may have to do this in batches; refrigerate any dumplings that do not fit on the rack.

4. Steam the dumplings, covered, over gently boiling water until the meat is thoroughly cooked (no visible pink color), 16 to 18 minutes. Happily, you are the cook and get to conduct this test. (Calories don't count when tasting for scientific purposes.)

5. Serve hot, with Soy Dipping Sauce.

soy dipping sauce

● ● ●

hili oil is very spicy, so use more or less to your taste. **MAKES** ⅔ **CUP** P

¹⁄₃ cup rice vinegar

¹⁄₃ cup reduced-sodium soy sauce

2 drops chili oil

2 scallions (white part only), thinly sliced

Combine the rice vinegar, soy sauce, and chili oil in a small serving bowl. Sprinkle with the scallion slices.

sweet-and-sour meatballs

from Sally Bower

y popular demand! When I announced my cookbook project to my family, one of the most frequent requests I received was "Be sure and get Aunt Sally's Sweet-and-Sour Meatballs." Her original instructions called for frying the meatballs in fat. By broiling them we get the same nice crust and leave the fat behind. Serve them with toothpicks or as a main dish over rice or noodles. **SERVES 6 TO 8** M

FOR THE MEATBALLS

2 handfuls (1¹⁄₂ cups) corn flakes, crushed
  by hand

2 pounds ground beef

2 large eggs, beaten

1¹⁄₂ teaspoons kosher (coarse) salt

¹⁄₂ teaspoon freshly ground black pepper

FOR THE SAUCE

¹⁄₄ cup vegetable oil

2 large onions, chopped

2 cans (15 ounces each) tomato sauce

1 can (20 ounces) pineapple tidbits,
  undrained

³⁄₄ cup golden raisins

3 to 4 tablespoons dark brown sugar,
  or to taste

Grated zest of 1 lemon

Juice of 1 lemon, or to taste

¹⁄₂ teaspoon kosher (coarse) salt,
  or to taste

Freshly ground black pepper
  to taste

1. Preheat the broiler, with a rack placed about 8 inches from the heat source.

2. Prepare the meatballs: Combine the crushed cornflakes with ¹⁄₂ cup water in a small bowl, and set aside to soak for a minute or two. Then crumble the soaked cornflakes into a large bowl. Add the meat, eggs, salt, and pepper, and mix well. Using your hands, form the mixture into balls about 1¹⁄₄ inches in diameter. Place them in a 13 × 9-inch glass baking pan.

3. Broil the meatballs until a brown crust begins to form, about 10 minutes. Then turn them over and broil on the other side until

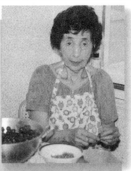

browned, about 5 minutes more. Remove from the broiler and set aside.

4. While the meatballs are browning, prepare the sauce: Heat the oil in a Dutch oven or other large, heavy, ovenproof pot over medium heat. Add the onions and cook until they are golden brown, about 10 minutes. Then stir in the tomato sauce, pineapple tidbits with their juice, 2 pineapple cans of water, and the raisins, brown sugar, lemon zest, and lemon juice.

5. Preheat the oven to 275°F.

6. Using a slotted spoon, add the browned meatballs to the sauce and bake, uncovered, for 2½ hours. No basting is necessary.

7. Add the salt, if needed, and pepper to taste. Serve hot.

Notes: This dish can be prepared a day or two ahead and refrigerated. It also freezes well.

saucy salami crisps

from Bonnie Robbins

I don't know how she does it, but Bonnie is famous for finding the easiest, best-tasting recipes. These crispy snacks are perfect for watching the game. The last time I made them, my then four-year-old granddaughter, Samantha, gobbled them up by the handful, and they were gone before the end of the first quarter. **SERVES 6**

1 whole kosher salami (12 ounces)
²/₃ cup Chinese duck sauce, such as
   Saucy Susan

1. Preheat the oven to 350°F.

2. Place the salami on a disposable oven tray and cut it into ½-inch-thick slices *without* slicing all the way through (cut about three quarters of the way down), so that the salami remains whole.

3. Spoon the duck sauce liberally between the slices and over the top, and

bake for 30 minutes. Then fan the salami out, forming a circle, so more surface is exposed. Baste, and continue baking until crisp, 30 to 60 minutes.

4. Slice the salami all the way through and cut each slice into 4 wedges. If you like them even crisper, bake the wedges for about 15 minutes more.

5. Serve hot with toothpicks.

sautéed liver in patty shells

from Lillian Bart

When I was a child, my mother's company dinners always began with sautéed liver, her signature first course (her *only* first course, but that's another story). As Sharon Boorstin points out in *Let Us Eat Cake*, when women in the '50s perfected a recipe, they stuck to it. Their company menus rarely varied. They even served the same dishes to each other. It must have been an easier time.

My mom hadn't made this dish in probably forty years, and we spent a glorious afternoon re-creating her original and reminiscing about her elegant formal table set with her Wedgwood china and Francis I silver service. At five years old I was a chubby little ballet student who couldn't bring her toes to the barre, but I knew which fork went where and how to fold a napkin.

Those who put liver at the top of their "do not try on pain of death" list have undoubtedly experienced only overcooked shoe liver—I mean leather—and probably nothing I could say would convince them otherwise. But those folks have already turned the page, leaving just the rest of us here with mouths watering at the thought of that rich, delicate meat in this beefy sherry sauce.

The laws of kashrut prescribe that liver, an organ meat, be broiled so that no blood remains. The broiling time will vary depending on the thickness of the liver and the distance from the heat source. Watch carefully so that you don't overcook it. The broiled liver need only be warmed in the sauce before serving. **SERVES 6** Ⓜ

1 box (10 ounces) frozen pareve patty shells
(6 shells)
1 pound fresh beef liver
Kosher (coarse) salt and freshly ground
black pepper to taste
Garlic powder
3 tablespoons olive oil
1 medium-size onion, finely chopped
1 rib celery, finely chopped
8 ounces white mushrooms, thinly sliced
1 large clove garlic, crushed
1¼ cups reduced-sodium beef broth
¼ cup dry sherry or white wine
½ teaspoon dried thyme leaves
1 can (8 ounces) water chestnuts,
drained and sliced
1 cup frozen baby peas, thawed
2 tablespoons cornstarch
2 tablespoons reduced-sodium soy sauce

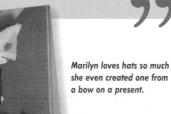

Marilyn loves hats so much she even created one from a bow on a present.

1. Bake the patty shells according to the package instructions. Set them aside.

2. Preheat the broiler.

3. Season the liver lightly with salt, pepper, and garlic powder, and place it on a rack in a broiler pan. Broil on both sides just until no pink remains, about 3 minutes per side. Be careful not to overcook it. Discard the juices and trim off any skin or gristle. Cut the liver into bite-size chunks and set it aside.

4. Heat the oil in a large skillet over medium heat. Add the onion and celery, and cook until starting to soften, about 5 minutes. Add the mushrooms and garlic and cook until the mushrooms are tender, 5 to 7 minutes more. Add the broth, sherry, and thyme, and bring to a boil. Then reduce the heat, cover the skillet, and simmer, stirring occasionally, for 4 minutes. Add the liver and continue cooking for it to absorb the flavors, about 1 minute more. Stir in the water chestnuts and peas.

5. Mix the cornstarch with the soy sauce, and add this to the skillet. Cook, stirring, until the sauce thickens, about 1 minute. Add salt and pepper to taste. (The soy sauce contains sodium, the liver was salted before broiling, and the beef broth will contain some salt, so little if any salt may be needed.)

6. Fill the baked patty shells with the liver mixture, allowing some to run down the sides, and serve immediately.

aunt anna's cream puffs

from Anna Tillinger

mama Hinda's sister, Anna, was a dear, sweet lady. She was the one who taught Aunt Estelle to sew, starting her on a lifetime of creativity. All Mama's daughters used this versatile recipe for appetizers—filling the puffs with liver and mushrooms (facing page) or sweetbreads (page 164)—as well as for an endless array of desserts. **MAKES 1 DOZEN LARGE OR 2 DOZEN SMALL PUFFS**   **M** or **D** or **P**

Solid vegetable shortening, butter, margarine,
or vegetable cooking spray
8 tablespoons (1 stick) unsalted butter or
margarine, or ¹/₂ cup solid vegetable
shortening or chicken fat (depending on your
filling: dairy, pareve, or meat)
1 cup cold water
¹/₄ teaspoon kosher (coarse) salt
1 cup all-purpose flour
4 large eggs

1. Preheat the oven to 425°F. Lightly grease 12 standard or 24 mini muffin cups with shortening, butter, margarine, or vegetable cooking spray. (If the muffin tin is a nonstick one, you can skip this.)

2. Bring the butter, water, and salt to a boil in a medium-size saucepan. Remove the pan from the heat and add the flour all at once, mixing well with a wooden spoon until the mixture is thick and smooth and comes away from the sides of the pan. Allow it to cool for about 10 minutes.

3. Transfer the batter to the bowl of an electric mixer and beat in the eggs, one at a time, beating until smooth after each addition. Place a spoonful of batter in each muffin cup and bake until the puffs are golden brown, dry, and crisp on the outside, 20 to 25 minutes for small and 25 to 30 minutes for large.

4. Remove the muffin tin from the oven.

Prick each cream puff with a skewer to allow the steam to escape. Shut off the heat and return the cream puffs to the oven to dry them out further, 5 to 10 minutes. Cool on a wire rack before filling.

5. To fill the cream puffs, cut off the tops and fill with the desired filling. (Add the filling as close to serving time as possible so the puffs don't get soggy.) Replace the tops, if you like, and serve.

Notes: If you prefer a free-form look, you can pipe or spoon the batter onto a greased, parchment-lined or nonstick baking sheet.

Use the puffs within a day, or freeze them.

Mama Hinda (right) with her sister Anna, about 1920.

gehachte leber
(chopped liver)

from Lillian Bart

The French have pâté; we have chopped liver. There are as many variations as there were hairs on

Papa Harry's head (well, at least when he was young!). Arguments have raged for centuries—which is best: beef liver? calves' liver? chicken livers? Who's got time for such philosophical discussions? Some say you can't make chopped liver without chicken fat. I've made a satisfactory version with all chicken livers and no fat at all. Aunt Sally's handwritten recipe called for 3 pounds broiled calves' liver, 10 large eggs, fried onions, and chicken fat. My mother-in-law, Edith, used to serve it with chicken fat and radishes.

This version is my mother's and my personal favorite. My mother uses a hand-powered meat grinder which she attaches to the stepladder that Papa Harry made for this purpose. Though she still regrets leaving her heart-shaped living room chairs in Belle Harbor when she moved to California, there was no question about taking the chopped liver stepladder. And, yes, it is in her will as my *yerusheh* (inheritance), so my brother, Gary, can take this as official notice: Hands off.

While a meat grinder ensures the proper consistency, a food processor is second best (although Aunt Sally would disagree). Just pulse it and don't let the mixture get too well blended. Kosher cooks broil liver to drain out the blood, but even if you're not kosher (or even Jewish), broiling ensures that only the liver and none of the "gook" (a highly technical culinary term) finds its way into the dish. **SERVES AT LEAST 12 (UNLESS OUR FRIEND JACK IS ON THE GUEST LIST)** Ⓜ

3 tablespoons nondairy margarine

1 tablespoon vegetable oil

2 medium-size onions, coarsely chopped, plus

* $1/2$ medium-size onion, coarsely chopped*

1 pound chicken livers

1 pound beef liver

6 large eggs, hard-cooked

Kosher (coarse) salt and black pepper to taste

1. Heat the margarine and oil together in a medium-size saucepan over medium heat. Add the 2 chopped onions and cook until soft and golden, 10 to 15 minutes. Remove from the heat, allow to cool, and then refrigerate.

2. Preheat the broiler.

3. Place the chicken and beef livers on a rack in a broiler pan and broil on both sides just until no pink remains, about 3 minutes per side for the chicken livers, and 3 to 5 minutes per side for the beef. Be careful not to overcook them, or they'll dry out. Allow the livers to cool, then refrigerate.

4. Combine the cooled onions and livers with the hard-cooked eggs and the remaining raw onion in a hand grinder or a food processor. Grind until well blended but not too smooth. Add salt and pepper to taste.

Notes: Use fresh liver. Defrosted frozen liver exudes moisture, making the finished product dry.

It's important to refrigerate the cooked livers and onions before grinding the mixture. If you grind it warm, it may turn sour.

Chopped liver is an ephemeral treat. Eat it within 3 days. (If you use chicken fat, make it 2 days. Trust me—I know this from bitter experience.)

chicken wings 1890

from Marilyn Dubin

It's probably safe to say that more Milani 1890 French salad dressing has been slathered over chicken than has ever touched a lettuce leaf. Scores of recipes have evolved over the years pairing its pungent taste with something sweet: cranberry sauce, duck sauce, ketchup, or jam. This retro version still pleases. Just don't skimp on the napkins.

MAKES 40 TO 50   M

Vegetable cooking spray

4 to 5 pounds chicken wings or
  drumettes

1 bottle (8 ounces) French dressing,
  such as Milani 1890

1 envelope dehydrated onion soup mix

1 can (16 ounces) whole-berry
  cranberry sauce

1. Preheat the oven to 350°F. Spray a very large baking pan (about 17 × 11 inches) with vegetable cooking spray, or line it with heavy-duty aluminum foil and spray the foil.

2. If you are using chicken wings, cut off and discard the tips. Cut the wings in half at the joint. Arrange the wings or drumettes in a single layer in the prepared pan.

3. Mix the dressing, soup mix, and cranberry sauce in a medium-size bowl. Pour this over the chicken and bake, turning and basting occasionally, until crisp, about 1¼ hours.

4. Serve hot.

chicken fingers
with orange apricot sauce

from Shirley Robbins

Here chicken fingers move off the kiddy menu and grow up, although no kids we tried them on had any complaints. The sauce also elicits applause when it is poured over boneless, skinless chicken breasts and baked for about 30 minutes in a preheated 350°F oven.

MAKES 16 TO 20   M

1 cup all-purpose flour, plus extra for dusting
  the chicken

3/4 cup (1/2 can) light beer

1 teaspoon paprika

1 teaspoon kosher (coarse) salt

Vegetable oil, for deep-frying

1 pound boneless, skinless chicken breasts,
  cut into "fingers," or 1 pound chicken
  "tenders"

Orange Apricot Sauce (recipe follows)

1. Combine the 1 cup flour, beer, paprika, and salt in a bowl, and stir to form a smooth paste.

" My dad [Al] met my mom [Shirley] on a blind date in 1940. He was working in Atlanta and staying with relatives. My mom took him to a Purim Ball. She always said what a great first date it was, because that night she was named Queen Esther. (We still have the cup. It's a little tarnished, but . . .) They dated for a few months and then eloped to North Carolina. My mom was only seventeen, and they just couldn't wait. Later that year, when they were visiting Mama and Papa in New York, Mama walked in on them at night, so of course they had to tell her they were married. Unbelievably, she kept the secret, and the following year they had a real wedding. They didn't tell anyone until their fifteenth wedding anniversary that it was really their sixteenth.
                                —LINDA NATHAN "

orange apricot sauce

MAKES ABOUT 1 1/2 CUPS   🅿

2/3 *cup orange marmalade*
1/3 *cup apricot preserves*
1/3 *cup orange juice*
1 *teaspoon ground ginger*
1/2 *teaspoon curry powder*
1/4 *teaspoon kosher (coarse) salt*
1/8 *teaspoon freshly ground black pepper*

Combine all the ingredients in a small saucepan over medium heat, and heat until the marmalade and preserves melt. Transfer the sauce to a serving bowl, and serve warm.

2. Pour vegetable oil to a depth of 2 to 3 inches into a heavy pot, and heat it to 365°F. If you use a small pot, you'll need less oil, but you'll be able to fry only a small quantity at a time. Use a larger pot and you'll get it done more quickly, but you'll have to use a lot of oil. (The key is not to allow the temperature of the oil to drop, or you'll get a soggy result, so do not crowd the pot.)

3. Spread some flour on a plate and roll the chicken fingers in it. Shake off the excess flour, and dip the chicken into the batter. Fry in the hot oil until cooked through and golden, 2 to 3 minutes. Transfer the chicken to a plate lined with ink-free paper towels, and drain.

4. Serve hot, with the Orange Apricot Sauce for dipping.

gefilte fish

from Estelle Robbins, Sally Bower

The serving of gefilte fish has been a Sabbath tradition since the Middle Ages—fish being seen by Jewish mystics as signaling the coming of the Messiah. Fish was expensive in Europe, and the recipe was developed as an economical way to stretch it so that every family member could get a taste. It became a particularly traditional Sabbath dish, made on Friday because to remove the flesh from the bone was viewed by the devout as "work."

The word *gefilte* is actually German for "stuffed." The original recipe called for seasoned, ground boned fish mixed with eggs and fillers, such as vegetables and crumbs, which was then stuffed back into the fish skin and cooked. Over the centuries the skin was eliminated, with cooks shaping the mixture into balls or patties and poaching them.

Canned or bottled gefilte fish, while convenient, cannot compare to authentic homemade. Its preparation need not be daunting. Preground fish is available at kosher food markets, or (although Aunt Sally vehemently disagrees) the food processor does the job easily. A good Litvak (see page 117), Aunt Estelle emphatically crossed out the teaspoon of sugar in the original recipe. (It must have been written by a Galitzianer.)

The best gefilte fish is made from whitefish, pike, and a little carp—but maybe I think so because I come from New York, where all are readily available. You go ahead and try whatever firm white fish swims near you. The carp adds flavor, but Aunt Estelle warned to use it sparingly, as the less carp used, the whiter the finished product. For a more elegant presentation, Aunt Estelle and Aunt Sally always discarded the well-worn carrots after cooking the fish and steamed an additional batch separately, sliced on the diagonal, to serve on the side. **MAKES 32 TO 36** **P**

> *Friday night dinners at my grandmother's home hold some of the best memories of my life. The last thing a teenager wants to do is hang out with family on a Friday night, but there would always be time to go out with friends later—and they can attest to this, because Grandma Estelle's phone number is still in their phone books. She was the glue that made the sum of our family greater than the individual parts.*
>
> —MARC WOLF

TO FLAVOR THE COOKING LIQUID

Fish bones, fish heads, and skin from the
   fish used
5 large onions, quartered
4 large carrots, cut into 2-inch-thick slices
4 ribs celery, cut into 2-inch-thick slices
2 tablespoons kosher (coarse) salt
$^1\!/_2$ teaspoon freshly ground black pepper

FOR THE FISH

3 pounds whitefish
2 pounds yellow pike
1 small piece (about 4 ounces) carp
2 medium-size onions, grated
4 large eggs, beaten
2 tablespoons matzoh meal
$2^1\!/_2$ tablespoons kosher (coarse) salt, or to taste
$1^1\!/_4$ teaspoons freshly ground black pepper,
   or to taste

FOR SERVING

Lettuce leaves
Cooked carrots, thinly sliced on the diagonal
Lou Bower's Horseradish for the Holidays
   (recipe follows)
Matzoh or challah

1. Bring 5 quarts of water to a boil in a 12- or 16-quart pot.

2. Place the fish bones, heads, and skin in the boiling water, and add the onions, carrots, celery, salt, and pepper. Simmer for about 1 hour.

3. Meanwhile, finely grind the whitefish, pike, and carp (or ask your fish man to do it for you). Alternatively, divide the fish into 3 batches and pulse in a food processor until ground.

4. Thoroughly combine the ground fish with the onions, eggs, matzoh meal (see Notes), salt, and pepper. Add about 1 cup water $1/4$ cup at a time, to form a soft but manageable mixture, and combine thoroughly. Cover and refrigerate until the broth is ready.

5. Wet your hands and, using a rounded $1/3$ cup of the fish mixture at a time, form the mixture into ovals. One at a time, place each oval on a wet plate and slide it gently into the boiling water.

6. Simmer, partially covered, for $1^1/2$ hours, adding more boiling water as needed. Occasionally push the ovals below the water level, as they tend to rise to the top.

7. Allow the gefilte fish and broth to cool to room temperature. Store the fish in its cooking liquid, covered, in the refrigerator. (Leftover cooking liquid can be frozen for 1 month. It makes a nice fish stock.)

8. Using a slotted spoon, transfer the chilled gefilte fish to a bed of lettuce. Arrange the carrot slices alongside. Pass the horseradish and matzoh.

Notes: Aunt Sally used a small piece of challah, ground with the fish, instead of matzoh meal.

To taste the raw fish mixture, microwave a tablespoon or so until the egg and fish are cooked, 5 to 15 seconds; then taste.

lou bower's horseradish for the holidays

from Harold Dubin

Despite Harold's grim warnings and instructions (Steps 1 and 2 are his, verbatim—he did have a good time with this one), you won't require a sinus transplant when preparing fresh horseradish—unless you remove the lid of the food processor, and lean directly over it to turn on the

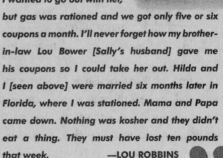

" When I was in the service during World War II, my sister Sally fixed me up with her friend Ethel's daughter, Hilda. Of course I wanted to go out with her, but gas was rationed and we got only five or six coupons a month. I'll never forget how my brother-in-law Lou Bower [Sally's husband] gave me his coupons so I could take her out. Hilda and I [seen above] were married six months later in Florida, where I was stationed. Mama and Papa came down. Nothing was kosher and they didn't eat a thing. They must have lost ten pounds that week. **—LOU ROBBINS** "

light. The hardest part is peeling the stubborn horseradish root! When that's done, it's a simple matter to whiz the ingredients and fill little jars to give to friends or freeze for future use. Once you've tasted the fresh, you'll never go back to store-bought.

MAKES ABOUT 3½ CUPS

1 pound horseradish root, peeled and cleaned

1 can (16 ounces) sliced beets, undrained

1 tablespoon kosher (coarse) salt, or to taste

3 tablespoons sugar, or to taste

¼ cup distilled white vinegar or red wine vinegar

1. Open all kitchen windows.

2. Remove all flowers and plants from the kitchen.

3. Cut the horseradish root into 1-inch pieces and process them in a food processor until uniformly shredded. Add the beets with their liquid, salt, sugar, and vinegar, and process until the mixture is finely chopped and well mixed. Add up to ¼ cup water, until it

reaches the desired consistency. Do not over-process or the mass will liquefy.

4. Serve with gefilte fish (but you knew that), any fish at all, brisket, or—my personal favorite—boiled chicken.

salmon gefilte fish

from Judy Bart Kancigor

For years I denied myself gefilte fish at holiday time because my kids would turn up their noses. Then I created a variation of Marlene Sorosky's recipe from *Fast and Festive Meals for the Jewish Holidays*, using all salmon and baking the fish as individual "muffins." Good thing I made enough for seconds! It makes a lovely presentation on a bed of greens, surrounded with thinly sliced cucumber, a few grape tomatoes, and Uncle Lou's horseradish (page 53).

MAKES 24 P

Aunt Sally, Gary, me, and Uncle Lou in Florida.

Vegetable cooking spray

2 medium-size onions, cut into chunks

5 medium-size carrots, cut into 1-inch pieces

2 ribs celery, cut into 1-inch pieces

1 cup curly-leaf parsley leaves

3 pounds skinless salmon, cut into 2-inch pieces

3 large eggs

1/2 cup vegetable oil

1/4 cup sugar, or to taste

2 teaspoons kosher (coarse) salt, or to taste

2 teaspoons freshly ground black pepper,
    or to taste

1. Preheat the oven to 350°F. Spray 24 standard muffin cups.

2. Place the onions in a food processor and pulse until they are minced. Transfer the onions to a very large bowl.

3. Process the carrots, celery, and parsley together until ground. Add to the onions.

4. Process about two thirds of the salmon, adding 1 piece at a time through the feed tube, until ground. Add the processed salmon to the onion mixture.

5. Process the remaining salmon, adding it through the feed tube. Then add the eggs, oil, sugar, salt, and pepper, and process until well blended. Add this mixture to the onion-salmon mixture, and combine well.

6. Divide the salmon mixture evenly among the prepared muffin cups. Bake until the top feels set when touched, 25 to 30 minutes. Let the fish cool in the muffin cups; then unmold.

Note: Remove from the refrigerator about 30 minutes before serving.

adele rocklin's pickled salmon

from Lillian Bart

A dele made the best pickled salmon and shared the recipe with my mom one summer evening when our two families met for our annual picnic dinner at the Hollywood Bowl. While strains of Shostakovich vibrated through the air, visions of pickled salmon danced in Mom's head. It's been one of her favorites ever since.

Simmering the salmon briefly gives the pickling process a head start. It then "cooks" (or pickles) in a zippy marinade for a few days in the refrigerator. **SERVES 8 TO 10**   P

2/3 cup distilled white vinegar

2 pounds skinless baby salmon fillets
    or regular salmon fillets cut
    into pieces

1 to 2 large onions, sliced

1/4 cup chili sauce or ketchup

1/4 cup sugar

1 tablespoon pickling spices

1/4 teaspoon kosher (coarse) salt

1. Bring the vinegar and 2/3 cup water to a boil in a pot that is large enough to hold the salmon in a single layer. Reduce the heat to barely a simmer, add the salmon and half the onions, and cook, uncovered, for 5 minutes.

2. Transfer the salmon and the cooked onions to a container (reserve the liquid). Add the remaining (uncooked) onions.

3. Combine the reserved hot liquid with the chili sauce, sugar, pickling spices, and salt in a bowl, and pour over the salmon. Cover and refrigerate for at least 2 days.

4. When you are ready to serve it, cut the salmon into smaller pieces. Serve with the onions and some of the pickling liquid. The salmon will keep for at least a week after it is pickled.

ruth levin's mock herring salad

from Zena Kaplan

ity the poor herring. The staple of our ancestors in Eastern Europe, where it was plentiful—and therefore, for the impoverished, the only reliable source of protein—is now reduced to being the butt of Borscht Belt humor.

What's green, hangs on the wall, and whistles?

A herring.

A herring is green?

OK, it's not green.

Since when does a herring hang on the wall?

All right, it doesn't hang.

And what kind of herring whistles?

Nu, so it doesn't whistle!

Then there's all that flap about a red herring. How's a fish supposed to keep up its reputation? If herring for you is the fish Jews love to hate, try this salad instead. It's delicious as an appetizer served with crackers for scooping, on a bed of lettuce as a first course, or even in a sandwich.

MAKES 3¾ CUPS　　　　　　　　**P**

2 cans (3.75 ounces each) sardines in
*　　soybean oil, drained*
4 large eggs, hard-cooked
1 medium-size crisp apple, peeled, cored,
*　　and finely chopped*
1 medium-size onion, finely chopped
1¹/₂ cups cider vinegar
¹/₂ cup sugar
4 slices (1 ounce each) bread (preferably challah)
About ¹/₄ cup regular or light mayonnaise
1¹/₂ tablespoons fresh lemon juice, or to taste
Kosher (coarse) salt and freshly ground
*　　black pepper, to taste (optional)*

1. Mash the sardines and eggs together in a bowl. Stir in the apple and onion.

2. Combine the vinegar and sugar in another bowl. Tear up the bread and immerse it in the vinegar mixture. Stir until it is thoroughly saturated. Then transfer the bread to a strainer and squeeze out as much liquid as you can, using a fork or the back of a spoon. Mash the soaked bread into the sardine mixture.

3. Add the mayonnaise (more or less than ¹/₄ cup, depending on how creamy you

like it), lemon juice, and salt and pepper if using. Stir thoroughly.

4. Serve cold, preferably the same day it is made. The salad will keep, covered and refrigerated, for up to 3 days.

louis selmanowitz's
chopped herring

from Livia Straus

L ivia's father, Louis Selmanowitz, became head of the Kashrut Division of the Department of Agriculture of the State of New York in 1954. His father, Rabbi Abraham Isaac Zelmanowitz, a Rosh Yeshiva at Yeshiva University and the leader of the American Gerer Hasidic community, had been instrumental in starting the department. **SERVES ABOUT 6** 📭

2 salted herrings, filleted

1 small white onion, chopped

1 large tart apple, peeled and finely chopped

2 tablespoons distilled white vinegar

1 large egg, hard-cooked and mashed

1/8 teaspoon freshly ground black pepper

Romaine lettuce, for serving

Grated hard-cooked egg and finely chopped onion, for garnish

Plain crackers, for serving

1. Soak the herrings in cold water to cover for 24 hours. Then rinse them well and grind them by hand.

" In his original capacity as a field inspector for the department in the 1940s and '50s, my father [Louis with wife, Ethel] would visit the growing Catskill hotels and kosher restaurants. Grossinger's, Concord, Pine View, Pioneer, Shmulke Bernstein's, and Lou G. Siegel's were on his regular route. He would return from these trips with recipes, like his chopped herring, which then became favorites at family events and synagogue kiddushim. —LIVIA STRAUS "

2. Combine the ground herring, onion, apple, vinegar, egg, and pepper in a bowl, and mix thoroughly.

3. Spoon the mixture onto a platter lined with romaine lettuce leaves, and garnish with grated egg and chopped onion.

4. To serve, schmear on plain crackers.

joanne rocklin's
chopped herring
appetizer

from Judy Bart Kancigor

T here are never any leftovers when I serve this piquant appetizer. My friend Joanne always makes people guess what it is. Herring is one of those foods that people who've never even tried it are sure they hate. My feeling is, why tell them in the first place? I'm not thinking the Alpo scene from *The Prince of Tides*, but more Julia Child's famous quote: "You're in the kitchen alone . . ." Serve the herring in a bowl, with crackers or rye bread alongside. **MAKES ABOUT 4 CUPS** **P**

1 jar (12 ounces) herring in wine sauce, undrained
1 small red onion, chopped
1 small green bell pepper, stemmed, seeded, and chopped
1 can (4.25 ounces) chopped black olives, drained
1 jar (6 ounces) marinated artichokes, drained and chopped
1 jar (12 ounces) chili sauce

Cut the herring into bite-size pieces, and place them in a bowl. Add the herring liquid and the onion, bell pepper, olives, artichokes, and chili sauce. Stir to mix. Refrigerate, covered, for at least 24 hours.

easy salmon mousse

from David Kooperman

David's mousse was the hit of a recent tasting party, garnering more recipe requests than anything else on the menu. How can something this easy taste so good? Double or triple the recipe for a larger crowd. **SERVES 6, OR MORE AS PART OF A BUFFET** **D**

1 can (8 ounces) red salmon, drained and flaked
1 package (8 ounces) cream cheese, at room temperature
1 tablespoon fresh lemon juice
1/2 cup sour cream
Chopped chives, for garnish
Lettuce leaves, for serving

1. Combine the salmon, cream cheese, and lemon juice in a bowl, and mix thoroughly. Cover and refrigerate for 1 hour.
2. Form the salmon mixture into a flattened mound (or if you're creative, a fish shape). Cover it with the sour cream, and garnish with chives. Serve on a bed of lettuce.

salmon mousse

from Phyllis Epstein

Cousin Phyllis likes to serve this light and delicate dish as an hors d'oeuvre, first course, or addition to a summer buffet. We like it any time of year. **SERVES ABOUT 10** **D**

2 envelopes unflavored gelatin
1 cup cold water
1 cup regular or light mayonnaise
1 cup regular or light sour cream

2 tablespoons fresh lemon juice

2 tablespoons chopped fresh dill,
    or 2 teaspoons dried dill

1 tablespoon white horseradish

1 tablespoon Worcestershire sauce

Vegetable cooking spray

1 can (14.5 ounces) best-quality red salmon,
    drained and flaked

1 cup chopped peeled seeded cucumber

2 scallions (white and green parts), finely
    chopped

1¹/₂ teaspoons kosher (coarse) salt,
    or to taste

¹/₈ teaspoon Tabasco sauce, or to taste

1 cucumber, peeled and very thinly sliced,
    for garnish

1. Stir the gelatin into the water in a small saucepan. Place the pan over low heat and warm the mixture, stirring, until the gelatin is thoroughly dissolved; do not let it boil. Let the mixture cool to room temperature.

2. Combine the mayonnaise, sour cream, lemon juice, dill, horseradish, and Worcestershire sauce together in a bowl. Whisk in the cooled gelatin mixture, and chill in the refrigerator until slightly thickened, about 20 minutes.

3. Spray a 5-cup mold with vegetable cooking spray. (If you have a fish-shaped mold, all the better.)

4. Fold the salmon, chopped cucumber, scallions, salt, and Tabasco sauce into the thickened mayonnaise mixture, and spoon it into the prepared mold. Chill in the refrigerator until firm, at least 3 hours.

5. To unmold the mousse, fill a large bowl (or the sink) with hot water. Dip the mold into the hot water—carefully, so no water splashes on the contents—for about 2 seconds, and then remove it quickly. Shake the mold from side to side. If the mousse does not loosen, repeat, holding the mold in the water for only 1 second. Invert a serving dish over the mold and holding them together, turn them over. Lift off the mold.

6. Decorate the mousse with wafer-thin cucumber slices, overlapping slightly, and serve.

I gave a friend a recipe.
My intentions were sincere.

Her baby drank up all the milk,
so she used a can of beer.

She didn't have the cornflake crumbs,
so made them out of bread.

She had no cream of tartar,
used tartar sauce instead.

She stirred it with a spoon because
her mixer's on the blink.

She couldn't find a bowl,
so she used the kitchen sink.

She forgot to set the timer,
so the smoke detector wailed,

And now she says I am to blame
for the recipe that failed.

going places

soups

Soup—a course as metaphor. Nourishment and comfort in a bowl.

The word is almost a symbol for food itself. So pervasive is the concept, that our language is steeped with soup idioms. A facility to feed the hungry and poor is a "soup kitchen." A revved-up car is "souped up." If it has it all, it's "from soup to nuts." A real cinch is "as easy as duck soup." When you're in the thick of it, you're "in the soup." And what's the standard example given to distinguish a *schlemiel* from a *schlimazel*? A schlemiel is one who spills his soup; a schlimazel is the person he spills it on.

Soup is mysterious, deep, and alluring—think witch's brew and blinding fog—the giver of life

"Dig in. Slurping is optional."

The Rabinowitz movers and shakers. We get around! Who's who on page 613.

from whence we come, the prehistoric primordial soup. And don't even get me started on the whole *Chicken Soup for the Soul* series. No wonder, when dinner is ready, whether the meal includes soup or not, the cook exclaims, "Soup's on!"

In grandma's day soup might be a meal, as she stretched her meager allotment of meat, poultry, or fish (if she had any) to feed her hungry family. Say the word *soup* and instantly that tummy-warmer from childhood comes to mind: The steaming bowl of tomato soup

my mother fed me when I was sick. Holiday dinners with Aunt Irene's matzoh balls or Aunt Sally's kreplach. Aunt Estelle's vegetable soup, a veritable garden in a bowl, with no less than (count 'em) twenty-one ingredients. My mother's incredible chicken soup.

Soup can be a first course or a full meal. If it's stick-to-the-ribs you're after, try Paul's Mushroom Barley, Aunt Myra's Sweet and Sour Cabbage, Tanta Sadie's Lima Bean, or Diane's Potato Soup. You'll find Old World favorites here—chicken soup and borscht—and vegetable potages of every kind from carrot to squash to an elegant French Onion Soup Quintet.

So grab a spoon, put a napkin in your collar, and dig in. Slurping is optional.

From top: Jake Mackoff enjoying his grandma's (Irene) kreplach. David mans the stockpot. The author off to an early start.

lil's four immutable laws for chicken soup

1. Even if you're not Jewish, you must use kosher chickens. The jury is still out on why they taste so much better. Is it the method of killing? The freshness? The salting? The blessing? Who knows, but there really is a difference. (*Note:* Kosher chickens are salted, so watch that shaker!)

2. Pack it in! Oh, does my mother laugh when she sees recipes for chicken soup calling for 3 carrots and 2 ribs of celery. Use as much chicken and vegetables as you can pack into your pot, or conversely, use as little water as possible, to produce the most intense flavor. Resist the temptation to get a little more soup by adding a little more water.

3. You must use fresh dill, and lots of it.

4. After cooking, reserve the carrots to be sliced into the soup later. Then squeeze the remaining vegetables well through a strainer for extra flavor.

chicken soup
(jewish penicillin)

from Lillian Bart

Open letter to my cousins: Many of you claimed that your mother's chicken soup is the best. My mother's made the final cut for two reasons. First of all, this cookbook was *my* idea, and when you write *your* cookbook, you can say *your* mother's is the best! Second, I am including it because it really is the best, and anyone who disagrees either has never had my mother's chicken soup or is congenitally taste-bud challenged. It is dark golden in color, intensely flavorful, and, in short, an elixir of the gods. I hoard the leftovers to use on special occasions in recipes calling for chicken stock (the real secret of my stuffing and gravy). You see, my mother adheres to the "if some is good, more is better" school of cooking. While this theory usually spells disaster in the kitchen (notably in her meat loaf!), it is the method of choice in making chicken soup. And this is one case where the method is as important as the ingredients.

While her exact ingredients vary as the mood hits her, here is her recipe from a typical day. Serve the soup with matzoh balls and lokshen (thin noodles), or on Passover with mandlen (soup nuts). **MAKES ABOUT 3 QUARTS** Ⓜ

2 chickens (3¹/₂ to 4 pounds each) with giblets (no liver), quartered

2 pounds carrots (yes, 2 pounds, not 2 carrots)

2 large onions, cut in half

5 large ribs celery with leaves, cut in half

2 large parsnips

1 small sweet potato (6 ounces), cut in half

1 turnip (6 ounces), cut in half

1 rutabaga (6 ounces), cut in half

1 small celery root, cut in half (optional)

¹/₂ large green bell pepper, stemmed and seeded

¹/₂ large yellow pepper, stemmed and seeded

2 large bunches dill, coarsely chopped (about 1¹/₂ cups)

¹/₂ bunch curly-leaf parsley (about ¹/₄ cup)

3 cloves garlic

Kosher (coarse) salt and freshly ground black pepper to taste

Chopped dill, for serving (optional)

Photo by Ana Venega

Mom, the cover girl, on page 1 of The Orange County Register's food section, March 4, 2002.

63

1. Place the chicken in a 16-quart stockpot and add water to barely cover. Bring just to the boiling point. Then reduce the heat to a simmer and skim off the foam that rises to the top. Add all the remaining ingredients (except the optional chopped dill) and only enough water to come within about two thirds of the height of the vegetables in the pot. (Most recipes will tell you to add water to cover. Do not do this! You want elixir of the gods or weak tea? As the soup cooks, the vegetables will shrink and will be covered soon enough. Eight to 10 cups of water total is plenty for this highly flavorful brew.) Simmer, covered, until the chicken is cooked through, about $1^{1}/_{2}$ hours.

2. Remove the chicken and about half the carrots from the pot, and set them aside.

3. Strain the soup through a fine-mesh strainer into another pot or container, pressing on the vegetables to extract all the flavor. Scrape the underside of the strainer with a rubber spatula and add the pulp to the soup. Discard the fibrous vegetable membranes that remain in the strainer. If you're fussy about clarity (and we're not), you can strain it again through a fine tea strainer, but there goes some of the flavor. Cover the soup and refrigerate overnight.

4. When you are ready to serve the soup, scoop the congealed fat off the surface and discard it. Reheat, adding more dill if desired (and we do). Slice the reserved carrots, add them to the soup, and serve.

P.S. If you think this chicken soup is controversial, wait till you get to the kugels and mandelbrot!

P.P.S. Actual message on my answering machine from my friend Diane Weiss in New Jersey after I sent her a copy of *Melting Pot Memories:* "Judy? I just made your mother's chicken soup, and my whole family is standing around the pot slurping with a straw!"

and what about the chicken?

● ● ●

When the chicken is cold, cut some into half-inch cubes to serve in the soup as a first course, or serve chicken quarters in the soup with matzoh balls, lokshen, and carrots for a steaming and bracing one-pot dinner. Mom and I are big fans of boiled chicken served hot or cold, preferably with Uncle Lou's horseradish (page 53), and have no trouble "using up" the leftover chicken for meals until it's gone. Not everyone, however, enjoys plain boiled chicken served *au naturel,* even prepared in a brew as flavorful as Mom's. Cube or shred the chicken, and heat it in your favorite sauce. My family loves my Almost Homemade Pasta Sauce (page 152), or try Abbe's Homemade Marinara Sauce (page 152), Stew's Ten-Minute Marinara Sauce (page 153), or your own favorite sauce, store-bought or homemade, and serve it over pasta, rice, or couscous. Add it to stuffed baked potatoes, tacos, pizza . . . the possibilities are endless. Grind some to make chicken kreplach instead of beef (page 67). Cubed and served cold, this dill-drenched chicken turns a tossed salad into a meal, or mix it with mayonnaise for chicken salad (but you already knew that).

aunt estelle's chicken soup
from Estelle Robbins

● ● ● ● ●

A shopping list found in Aunt Estelle's cookbook gives a nostalgic variation on the chicken soup theme. Many say using only the dark meat imparts a richer flavor to the soup. After much research I finally solved the *petrushka* mystery—they're parsley roots. "Knob celery" I assume is celery root, but what she meant by "roots" will just have to remain one of those mysteries of life.

Aunt Estelle's recipe book is part recipes, part journal, part manual for the *kinder*. Her knaidel instructions read like a memoir of quantity cooking:

25 bottom chicken quarters	11 onions
2 pieces flanken	5 bunches carrots
From 20 chickens, giblets	3 roots
10 wings	3 petrushkas
8 pulkas	Garlic
2 bunches celery	2 packages dill
	knob celery

"I bought 4 boxes matzoh ball mix, 2 packages in each box. I used 3 pots. In my big white pot I put in 2 boxes. Then my heavy pot on top of stove 1 box, 2 packages and another heavy pot, 1 box, 2 packages. You must put in oil; otherwise it breaks. I got 60 knaidels from 4 boxes. Don't put salt in pot. The knaidels have enough salt."

knaidlach
(matzoh balls)

from Irene Rosenthal

The world is divided into those who love floaters and those who love sinkers. While the delicate floaters are favored by matzoh ball mavens everywhere, I am a closet sinker-lover, which is the way my father's mother, Grandma Ruchel, made them. Which is not to say I haven't gobbled with gusto a floater or two in my day. Aunt Irene's are definitely floaters. Some say club soda makes for a lighter knaidel. Cooking them longer will make them lighter too.

MAKES ABOUT 8 LARGE OR 16 SMALL BALLS   **M** or **P**

2 tablespoons melted chicken fat, melted shortening, or vegetable oil
2 large eggs, lightly beaten
1/2 cup matzoh meal
1 teaspoon kosher salt
1 teaspoon baking powder (see Note)
2 tablespoons club soda, chicken broth, or water

1. Blend the fat and eggs together in a small bowl. Add the matzoh meal, salt, and baking powder and blend well. Add the club soda and mix thoroughly. Cover and refrigerate until the mixture is firm, at least 1 hour.

2. Bring a large pot of water to a boil, and lightly salt it.

3. Using wet hands, form the mixture into balls (2 tablespoons each for 2-inch knaidlach, 1 tablespoon for 1^1/$_2$-inch), and carefully drop them into the boiling water. Do not crowd the pot. Cover the pot and cook at a slow, steady boil (not a hard boil) until soft, 30 to 40 minutes.

4. Remove the knaidlach with a slotted spoon, and serve in soup.

Note: For Passover use kosher-for-Passover baking powder. If none is available, it may be omitted.

In my earliest memories, Mama 'Reen [in photo with Marcy] enters my house, after walking several blocks and taking several buses, carrying four or five heavy shopping bags full of home-made foods and lifts them weightlessly as she approaches me for a great big kiss. In those bags, which she methodically recycles, are tubs of her magnificent matzoh ball soup, her famous baked kreplach, indescribable and velvety chopped liver, tasty stuffed cabbage, and the world's best chocolate chip mandelbrot. She always catered to each individual taste: soft, fluffy matzoh balls for my mom and dad, hard ones for me and my sisters, cheese kreplach, meat kreplach, large and bite-size stuffed cabbage, and any permutation in between just to make us happy. No one could compete with Mama 'Reen's generosity and her endless, selfless need to feed. I am ever so grateful that I had, loved, and was loved by Mama 'Reen. **—MARCY EPSTEIN**

shiitake mushroom matzoh balls

from Judy Bart Kancigor

ℶ either of my daughters-in-law ever liked matzoh balls until I came up with this recipe. I doctored up plain old matzoh ball mix—and a fine product it is!—with shiitake mushrooms and scallions for a shtetl favorite with an Asian twist. (Not surprising. Jews have had a long love affair with Chinese food!) Go ahead and double or even triple the recipe (and you may have to!), but be careful not to crowd the pot when you are cooking them. **MAKES 24 TO 30 GOLF-BALL-SIZE BALLS** Ⓜ or Ⓟ

^{1}/$_4$ cup melted chicken fat or vegetable oil

4 scallions, white and half the green part, thinly sliced

3 ounces shiitake mushrooms, stems discarded, finely chopped (1 to 1^1/$_2$ cups)

1 envelope matzoh ball mix, such as Manischewitz

^{1}/$_2$ cup matzoh meal

4 large eggs, lightly beaten

2 tablespoons finely chopped flat-leaf parsley

1 teaspoon kosher (coarse) salt

^{1}/$_8$ teaspoon white pepper

1 teaspoon baking powder (see Notes)

2 tablespoons club soda, chicken broth, or water

1. Heat the chicken fat in a medium-size saucepan over medium heat. Add the scallions and mushrooms and cook, stirring often, until the mushrooms are soft, about 5 minutes. Set aside.

2. Combine the matzoh ball mix with the matzoh meal in a medium-size bowl. Add the eggs and mix well. Stir in the mushroom mixture (with the oil), parsley, salt, white pepper, and baking powder. Add the club soda and mix thoroughly. Cover and refrigerate until firm, at least 1 hour.

3. Bring a large pot of water to a boil and lightly salt it.

4. Form the mixture into balls that are a little larger than a marble, wetting your hands if necessary to keep them from sticking. Drop the balls into the boiling water and cook, covered, at a slow, steady boil (not a hard boil) until tender, about 30 minutes (depending on the size of the balls).

5. Carefully remove the matzoh balls with a slotted spoon, and serve in soup.

My grandson Blake, the matzoh ball maven.

Notes: For Passover use kosher-for-Passover baking powder, or if unavailable, it may be omitted.

You will find that after cooking these matzoh balls, the cooking liquid is so flavorful, it is almost a soup in itself, particularly if you have used chicken fat. I use this broth instead of water in soups and stews and for cooking rice.

Alternate serving suggestion: Allow the matzoh balls to cool somewhat. Cut into bite-size pieces to be eaten by hand. Offer several whole for throwing. Serve my mother's Chicken Soup (page 63) lukewarm on the side in a sippy cup.

kreplach
with st. louis dough and belle harbor filling

from Sally Cohen, Sally Bower

Kreplach, savory meat-filled dumplings, go together with chicken soup like meatballs and spaghetti, apples and Brown Betty, Sacco and Vanzetti . . . you get the idea. But few cooks have the patience or skill to make them at home. Pity.

I remember as a young bride trying to make kreplach in our Parsippany, New Jersey, apartment. I don't remember where I got the recipe, but the little dumplings exploded in the boiling water—and with them my confidence. That experience created a fear of all things rolled—a dough phobia, if you will—that spilled over to pie crusts and pastries of all sorts and lasted more than thirty years. "I'm just not a dough person," I would lament . . . until testing recipes for this cookbook forced me to face my fears (and without a support group yet).

> *My mother [Sally Cohen] began dating my father Harry [shown in photo with Sally] in 1932 at the height of the Depression. Neither had a job, and they couldn't afford to get married. One Saturday my grandfather announced that the family was moving to Detroit. My folks panicked. The next morning they went to a small town in southern Missouri and got married by a justice of the peace. They gave a phony address so nothing would show up in the St. Louis paper. When they got back on Sunday afternoon, my grandfather again brought up the subject of moving to Detroit. At that point my grandmother said, 'No, we aren't, and that's the end of it.' Two years later my folks were married by a rabbi in front of the whole family. They never told anyone about their having eloped until their fortieth anniversary. No one knew—not their parents, brothers, or sisters. When my mother died they had been married sixty-five years. I have never known anyone who could keep a secret that long.* —ED COHEN

This is a wonderful dough—a very pliant, elastic, and forgiving little lump, as fun to knead as Silly Putty. If you can roll out sugar cookies, you can do this. The food processor cuts out all the work. And as for the filling, next time you make brisket, measure out some slices for kreplach and freeze them until the mood hits. I think kreplach-making parties should become pre-holiday family affairs, the way tamale-making parties are in the Mexican-American community.

The two Sallys, first cousins who never met in life, had very similar recipes. I prefer one's dough and the other's filling. I don't think either would mind meeting like this. **MAKES 6 TO 8 DOZEN, DEPENDING ON THE THICKNESS OF THE DOUGH** Ⓜ

FOR SALLY COHEN'S DOUGH
2 large eggs, beaten
1 teaspoon kosher (coarse) salt
About 1¹/₄ cups all-purpose flour

FOR SALLY BOWER'S FILLING
¹/₄ cup vegetable oil or chicken fat
2 large onions (1 pound total), chopped
8 ounces cooked beef brisket or stew meat, thinly sliced or chopped (1¹/₃ cups firmly packed)
¹/₄ teaspoon kosher (coarse) salt, or to taste
¹/₈ teaspoon freshly ground black pepper, or to taste
1 large egg

Kosher (coarse) salt
Vegetable cooking spray

1. Prepare the dough: Mix the eggs, salt, and 6 tablespoons water in a medium-size bowl with enough of the flour to make a soft, elastic, and slightly tacky dough. Knead well, adding more flour if necessary. (To prepare the dough using a food processor, process the ingredients until the dough comes

Aunt Sally (Bower) and me.

together in a ball, about 20 seconds. The dough should feel tacky, but it should not stick to your hands.) Gather the dough into a roughly rectangular shape, cover it with plastic wrap, and allow it to rest for 20 minutes.

2. Meanwhile, prepare the filling: Heat the oil in a large skillet over low heat. Add the onions and cook, stirring occasionally, until they are very soft and golden, 20 to 30 minutes.

3. Pulse the beef in a food processor until shredded. Add the sautéed onions (with the oil), salt, pepper, and egg. Pulse just until combined, scraping the bowl down if necessary.

4. Cut the ball of dough in half. Cover one half so it doesn't dry out, and roll the other half out on a lightly floured pastry board to form a 1/16-inch-thick rectangle. Cut the dough into 2-inch squares, and place 1 level teaspoon of the filling on each square. Wet two adjacent edges of each square, dry your hand, and fold the dampened sides over, forming into a triangle. Pinch the edges tightly. Allow them to rest and dry for about 5 minutes.

5. Bring a large pot of water to a boil and lightly salt it. Drop the kreplach, one at a time, into the boiling water and cook, uncovered, until the dough is al dente, 20 to 25 minutes. (You'll have to do this in batches; do not crowd the pot.) Stir from time to time so they do not stick together.

6. Drain the kreplach and let them cool to room temperature. Spray them with vegetable cooking spray to keep them from sticking together, cover, and refrigerate for up to 1 day.

Note: If you should have filling left over, cover it tightly and freeze it. The next time you make meatballs or meat loaf, throw it in.

next door grill's chicken tortilla soup

from Shelly Kancigor

When my son Stu and daughter-in-law Shelly lived here in Southern California, they came to love Mexican food, and one of their favorite dishes was the Chicken Tortilla Soup at Next Door Grill. After they moved to

Minnesota, I interviewed chef David Weiss for my column and requested this recipe, which he had developed as his final exam in culinary school. Shelly made some slight changes to the original, and now she and Stu can enjoy it in Minnesota. (So maybe getting the recipe for them wasn't such a good idea. Just kidding!)

Feel free to modify the spiciness to your liking. Some say that the heat is in the veins; others believe that it's released when you cut into the chile, so the more you chop, the spicier it gets. The best advice is to experiment and see what your heat comfort level is. The oil from the chiles can do the same number on your hands as they do on your throat, so after handling them, rub your hands with lemon juice and wash them several times in warm, soapy water. And remember, if anticipation of eating this dish brings tears to your eyes, this would not be a good time to wipe them. **SERVES 8** Ⓜ

Shelly shakes it up at my nephew Ross's Bar Mitzvah, 1993.

1 tablespoon canola oil

1 large onion, diced

4 ribs celery, diced

3 large carrots, diced

2 cloves garlic, chopped

3 tablespoons ground cumin

4 serrano chiles, seeded and diced

2 quarts homemade chicken stock (page 63)
    or low-sodium boxed or canned broth

1 can (14.5 ounces) diced tomatoes, undrained

4 boneless, skinless chicken breasts
    (8 ounces each), cut into $^1/_2$-inch cubes

Kosher (coarse) salt and freshly ground
    black pepper to taste

2 corn tortillas, cut in strips and deep-fried,
    or store-bought tortilla chips

1 bunch cilantro, chopped ($^1/_2$ cup packed)

2 Hass avocados, chopped

$^1/_2$ cup nondairy sour cream

1 bunch (6 to 8) scallions, white and
    green parts, sliced

1. Heat the oil in an 8-quart soup pot over medium heat. Add the onion, celery, and carrots and cook, stirring often, until the carrots are soft and the onion is translucent, about 7 minutes.

2. Add the garlic and cumin and cook, stirring constantly, for about 2 minutes. Then add the chiles and cook for 2 minutes more. Add the chicken stock, tomatoes, and chicken, and bring to a boil. Reduce the heat and simmer, covered, until the chicken is cooked through and the flavors have blended, 20 to 30 minutes. Add salt and pepper to taste.

3. To serve, crush the tortillas and place some, with the chopped cilantro and

chopped avocado, in the bottom of each bowl. Ladle the soup over these ingredients and top with a dollop of nondairy sour cream, a sprinkling of scallions, and a few more tortilla chips.

paul's mushroom barley soup

from Harold Dubin

Harold adapted this recipe from one given to him by his friend Paul Morris. Paul's cooking and baking talents are legendary, and he and Harold shared recipes as well as an enduring friendship. In his retirement Harold became quite the chef and, after years of being the thin one in the family, developed the requisite middle-aged pot—much to the delight of my mother, who still reeled from his wondering, often and aloud, why overweight people can't just stop eating.

I prefer meaty boneless short ribs for this dish, but I always add 2 pounds or so of marrowbones to make up for bone loss. The dried mushrooms and their soaking liquid add an incredible earthy flavor. The phrase "stick to the ribs" (maybe "stick to the hips"!) was invented for this soup. Paul's version was so thick that a spoon

could stand up in it. This iteration, still thick and hearty, is perfect for those blustery winter days. (Oh, will these California winters never cease?) **SERVES 12**　Ⓜ

1 ounce dried mushrooms, preferably shiitake
Boiling water
1/3 cup all-purpose flour
3 pounds boneless beef stew meat or flanken,
*　or a combination, trimmed of visible fat*
2 tablespoons vegetable oil
2 beef marrowbones (optional)
1/2 to 1 bunch dill
1/2 to 1 bunch curly-leaf parsley
1 1/4 cups pearled barley, rinsed and
*　picked over*
1 1/4 cups dried baby lima beans, rinsed
*　and picked over*
1 envelope dehydrated onion soup mix
3 medium-size carrots, thinly sliced
2 medium-size yellow or white potatoes,
*　cut into 1/2-inch cubes*
2 ribs celery, sliced
2 tablespoons garlic powder, or to taste
Freshly ground black pepper to taste
Beef bouillon powder or salt, or a combination,
*　to taste*
8 ounces fresh white mushrooms, thinly sliced

1. Place the mushrooms in a heatproof bowl and add boiling water to cover (you may have to weight them down with a smaller bowl or dish). Soak until very soft, at least 1 hour.

2. Place the flour in a large bowl and dust the meat lightly with it, shaking off any excess.

3. Heat the oil in a Dutch oven or other large, heavy pot over medium-high heat, and

brown the meat on all sides, about 8 minutes altogether. (You will probably have to do this in batches.)

4. Return the meat to the pot, add the marrowbones if using, and add water to cover. Bring to a boil. Reduce the heat to a simmer and remove the foam, if any (a tea strainer is handy for this).

5. Cut the dill and parsley into 2-inch lengths and tie them up in a cheesecloth bag. Add this to the pot along with the barley, lima beans, soup mix, carrots, potatoes, celery, garlic powder, and pepper. Simmer, covered, stirring occasionally, for 2 hours. Add water and bouillon powder or salt as needed.

6. Strain the dried mushrooms, reserving the soaking liquid. Then strain the soaking liquid through a cheesecloth-lined strainer to remove the grit. Add the strained liquid to the soup. Cut the mushrooms into very thin slices and add them to the soup; if you used dried shiitakes, cut off the stems, wrap them in a cheesecloth bundle, and add them too.

7. Add the fresh mushrooms to the soup, cover the pot, and simmer, stirring occasionally, until the meat is very tender, 30 to 60 minutes more.

> " A chance meeting with my aunt at a recent family reunion produced this recipe from my childhood—and along with it memories of Passover dinners gone by when Aunt Myra used to serve this tasty soup as an alternative to the usual chicken soup. It is now standard Mackoff, Solomonic, and Orlow fare for holiday or Shabbat dinners. "
>
> —STEWART MACKOFF

8. Remove the meat and cut it into bite-size chunks, trimming off any fat. Return the meat to the pot and correct the seasonings. The soup will get thicker on standing, so add more water if you like. Remove the cheesecloth bundles before serving.

Note: This soup freezes well.

myra trinkler's sweet-and-sour cabbage soup

from Stewart Mackoff

It's not a mistake—you can substitute sauerkraut or lemon juice for the sour salt. Serve this with challah for dipping, if you like. **SERVES 6 TO 8** Ⓜ

3 to 5 pounds flanken or brisket

2 tablespoons vegetable oil

2 large Spanish onions, chopped

2 cans (28 ounces each) crushed tomatoes in puree

1 to 2 tablespoons sour salt (see box, page XLVIII),
    1 cup prepared sauerkraut, or $^1/_2$ cup fresh
    lemon juice, or to taste

$^1/_4$ cup (packed) dark brown sugar, or to taste

2 teaspoons chopped fresh ginger

2 bay leaves

2 teaspoons kosher (coarse) salt, or to taste

$^1/_2$ teaspoon freshly ground black pepper,
    or to taste

1 large cabbage, coarsely chopped

1. Place the flanken in a large pot, add water to cover, and bring to a boil. Boil for 15 minutes.

2. Meanwhile, heat the oil in a Dutch oven or other large, heavy saucepan over medium heat. Add the onions and cook, stirring occasionally, until soft, about 10 minutes. Stir in the tomatoes. Fill one of the tomato cans with water, and pour it into the pot.

3. Remove the flanken from the boiling water and add it to the Dutch oven. Cover, and simmer for 1 hour.

4. Stir in the sour salt, brown sugar, ginger, bay leaves, salt, and pepper. Add the cabbage and cook until the meat is tender, about 1 hour more. Correct the seasonings.

5. Remove the meat and cut it into bite-size pieces. Return the meat to the pot, and serve hot.

Note: This soup tastes even better the next day.

21-ingredient vegetable soup

from Estelle Robbins

Aunt Estelle made an incredible vegetable soup, which she would give away in huge jars to family and friends. She always cooked in super-large quantities, an enormous undertaking involving two or three pots, but after I sent her a 16-quart stockpot, things really got out of hand! With this farmers' market in a bowl—no snap to prepare—it was always a treat to be on the receiving end. The following recipe, believe it or not, is half the original. **MAKES AT LEAST 8 QUARTS**
P

8 ounces dried baby lima beans, rinsed and
    picked over (see Note)
3 cloves garlic
1 large leek, thoroughly cleaned, white part
    chopped, green part reserved
1 bunch dill, trimmed and coarsely chopped
    (1 cup packed)
1 package (6 ounces) dehydrated vegetable
    soup mix, such as Manischewitz
1 small celery root
1 medium-size rutabaga
4 ounces pearled barley, rinsed and picked over
4 ounces dried split peas, rinsed and picked over
1 very large sweet onion, chopped
2 pounds carrots, thinly sliced
3 cups chopped celery
1 green bell pepper, stemmed, seeded, and
    chopped
1 red bell pepper, stemmed, seeded, and
    chopped
2 parsnips, thinly sliced
1 eggplant (1 pound), cut into $^1/_2$-inch dice
1 large sweet potato (1 pound), cut into
    $^1/_2$-inch dice
2 tablespoons kosher (coarse) salt, or to taste
$^3/_4$ teaspoon freshly ground black pepper,
    or to taste
2 medium-size zucchini, thinly sliced
1 box (10 ounces) frozen French-cut green beans
1 box (10 ounces) frozen corn kernels
1 box (10 ounces) frozen peas

1. Place the lima beans in a small saucepan and add water to cover. Bring to a boil. Then reduce the heat, cover the pan, and simmer for 2 minutes. Remove the pan from the heat and allow the lima beans to steam, covered, for at least 1 hour.

2. Meanwhile, tie the garlic, green portion of the leek, and chopped dill in a cheesecloth bag.

3. Combine the soup mix (beans only—set aside the flavoring packet) with 5 quarts water in a large (at least 12-quart) stockpot. Add the celery root, rutabaga, and cheesecloth packet, and bring to a boil. Reduce the heat and simmer, covered, for 30 minutes.

4. Drain the lima beans and add them to the stockpot. Stir in the barley, split peas, onion, carrots, celery, bell peppers, parsnips, eggplant, sweet potato, 1 tablespoon of the salt, and $1/2$ teaspoon of the pepper. Bring back to a boil. Then reduce the heat and simmer, covered, for 15 minutes.

5. Add the zucchini and continue to simmer, covered, for 40 minutes more.

6. Stir the frozen vegetables into the soup, along with the flavoring packet from the soup mix. Bring back to a boil. Then reduce the heat and simmer, covered, until the vegetables are cooked to your liking, about 10 minutes. Add the remaining 1 tablespoon salt and $1/4$ teaspoon pepper, or to taste. Remove the celery root, rutabaga, and cheesecloth packet before serving.

Variation: Although Aunt Estelle never did this, I like to use my immersion blender to puree the soup just a tad—not into a smooth blend, but just to thicken it, leaving lots of chunky vegetables. If you don't have an immersion blender, you can puree a few cups of the soup in a blender, then stir the puree back into the soup. Just remember to allow the soup to cool a bit before blending—to avoid burning yourself and having it overflow in your blender.

Notes: Aunt Estelle used large lima beans, which she simmered for 5 minutes, drained, and skinned. I don't know about you, but I put skinning lima beans right up there with skinning hazelnuts: a time-consuming, thankless job, unless you can recruit some little kids (five- to eight-year-olds find this particularly amusing) to skin the beans by squeezing the slippery little suckers. Absent such assistance, I use baby lima beans, with their thinner skins, and don't bother with the skinning. If I see a few skins floating on top, I just scoop them up and discard them.

This soup freezes well.

lentil vegetable soup

from Syble Solomon

Lentils do not have to be soaked before they are cooked. They'll become tender in 45 minutes or so, but Syble likes to simmer the soup longer to cook the vegetables down for a thicker potage. I take it one step further and use my immersion blender for just a few seconds to produce an even thicker blend, just as Barry likes it. It's especially delicious with Shiitake Mushroom Matzoh Balls (page 66), as I learned the first time I made it for Shabbat dinner with friends. **SERVES 4 TO 6** **M** or **P**

1 cup lentils, picked over, rinsed, and drained

4 to 6 cups homemade chicken stock (page 63) or vegetable stock or low-sodium boxed or canned broth

1 can (15 ounces) diced tomatoes, undrained

$^1/_2$ cup chopped onion

$^1/_2$ cup thinly sliced celery

$^1/_2$ cup thinly sliced carrots

1 bay leaf

$^1/_2$ teaspoon garlic powder

1 teaspoon kosher (coarse) salt, or to taste

$^1/_8$ teaspoon freshly ground black pepper, or to taste

Combine all the ingredients (using 4 cups of stock) in a large saucepan, and bring to a boil. Then reduce the heat, cover, and simmer, stirring occasionally, for 2 hours. Add more stock as needed, depending on how thick you like it. Serve hot.

Harry and Miriam Levine, just married, 1939.

roasted beet borscht

from Miriam Levine

נ o "Jewish" food gets more ribbing than borscht, that ever-present beet soup on the shtetl table. They even named a whole "Belt" after it. Yet, with the exception of chicken soup, it is probably the most beloved Old World favorite. Served hot or cold, with meat or without, sweet or sweet-and-sour, thick or thin— the varieties are endless. Miriam serves her sweet-and-sour version cold, topped with sour cream and a hot potato. **SERVES 4 TO 6** **D** or **P**

$1^1/_2$ pounds fresh beets

2 tablespoons butter or nondairy margarine

1 medium-size onion, finely chopped

2 ribs celery, finely chopped

3 tablespoons sugar, or more to taste

Juice of 1 lemon (about 3 tablespoons), or more to taste

$1^1/_2$ teaspoons kosher (coarse) salt, or to taste

Freshly ground black pepper to taste

6 small boiling potatoes

Regular or nondairy sour cream, for garnish

2 tablespoons finely chopped dill, for garnish

1. Preheat the oven to 375°F.

2. Wash the beets well and trim off the greens, leaving 1 inch of stem. Wrap them individually in aluminum foil. Place them on a baking sheet and roast until tender, 1 to 1¹/₂ hours, depending on the size.

3. Remove the foil packets from the oven, and when the beets are cool enough to handle, peel off the skins. (Those disposable plastic gloves that food handlers wear really come in handy here to prevent being caught red-handed.) Coarsely grate the beets and set them aside.

4. Melt the butter in a medium-size saucepan over medium heat. Add the onion and celery, and cook, stirring occasionally, until soft and golden, about 8 minutes.

5. Add the beets and 1 quart water to the pan. Stir in the sugar, lemon juice, salt, and pepper. Bring to a boil. Then reduce the heat, cover the pan, and simmer for 20 minutes.

6. Using a slotted spoon, transfer 2 to 3 cups of the vegetables to a blender, leaving some in the pot for texture. Process until smooth. (Or use an immersion blender until the mixture has the desired consistency.) Return the pureed mixture to the pan, taste, and adjust the sugar, lemon juice, salt, and pepper as needed. Let cool to room temperature, and then cover and refrigerate until thoroughly chilled, about 2 hours.

7. Shortly before you are ready to serve the borscht, boil or steam the potatoes until tender, about 15 minutes.

8. Serve the borscht cold, each serving topped with a hot potato, a dollop of sour cream, and a sprinkling of fresh dill.

sally's chicken kuftelas
(patties) in borscht

from Harold Dubin

They say something must be at least a hundred years old to be an antique. This old Russian recipe, in which ground chicken patties are briefly fried and then simmered in an easy-to-prepare borscht, certainly qualifies. Aunt Sally, who died in 2003 at ninety-four, got this old family recipe from her mother-in-law, Mirtza Bower (who had been a caterer in Russia), so you do the math.

In his retirement, Aunt Sally's son-in-law, Harold, trawled through her handwritten cookbook and tried every recipe. You've heard of people teaching themselves to cook by starting on page 1 of Julia Child's *The Art of French Cooking* and working their way to the end? Aunt Sally's cookbook was Harold's *Art of Jewish Cooking*, but he liked to do his own thing too, as you can see from the note (see box, facing page) he sent me shortly

Aunt Sally with her grandchildren, Barry and Laura, about 1959.

before he died. He must have been multiplying the recipe many times to freeze for later. **SERVES 8** ⓜ

FOR THE BORSCHT

1/4 cup vegetable oil

2 large onions, chopped

2 cans (15 ounces each) sliced beets, undrained

1/4 cup plus 3 tablespoons sugar

5 tablespoons fresh lemon juice

1 1/2 teaspoons kosher (coarse) salt

FOR THE PATTIES

1 1/4 pounds skinless, boneless chicken breasts

1 1/2 ounces challah, cubed (about 1 cup)

2 large eggs, lightly beaten

1/2 cup matzoh meal

3/4 teaspoon kosher (coarse) salt

1/8 teaspoon freshly ground black pepper

Vegetable oil, for frying

1. Prepare the borscht: Heat the oil in a Dutch oven or other large, heavy pot over medium heat. Add the onions and cook, stirring occasionally, until they are soft but not browned, about 15 minutes. Remove half of the onions and set them aside to cool.

2. Add the beets and their juice to the remaining sautéed onions in the pot. Stir in 2 beet cans of water, 1/4 cup of the sugar, 3 tablespoons of the lemon juice, and 1 teaspoon of the salt. Bring to a boil. Then reduce the heat, cover, and simmer while you prepare the patties.

3. Prepare the patties: Grind the chicken, challah, and reserved cooled sautéed onions in a grinder if you have one. If not, use a food processor, but be careful not to chop the mixture too fine. Add the eggs, 1 tablespoon of the matzoh meal, the salt, and the pepper, and blend thoroughly.

4. Pour oil to a depth of 1/4 inch in a large skillet and heat it over medium-high heat. Form the ground chicken mixture into patties about 2 inches in diameter and 3/4 inch thick. Dust each patty lightly in the remaining matzoh meal. Fry the patties, a few at a time, in the oil until beginning to brown, about 3 minutes on each side.

5. Slip the fried patties into the borscht and continue to simmer, covered, for about 1 hour. After 30 minutes or so, start tasting the borscht and add the remaining 3 tablespoons sugar, remaining 2 tablespoons lemon juice, and remaining 1/2 teaspoon salt—or to taste.

6. Divide the patties among individual soup bowls, ladle the hot borscht over them, and serve.

Mama and Papa's prized first grandchild, Marilyn, with Aunt Sally and Uncle Lou.

> "When I make kuftelas, I buy a 5- to 6-pound chicken. I use all the white and dark meat for the patties and put the chicken bones into the beet soup. The bones add a flavor that makes the soup as good as the patties. Of course, the bones are delicious too. I make sure to leave some meat on the bones. —HAROLD DUBIN"

my father's daughter

To the world Jan Bart was the star of stage, screen, and song. To me he was just "Daddy." As an infant I fell asleep to "Go to Sleep, My Pretty One," a lullaby he wrote especially for me, which I sang to my own babies and now sing to my grandchildren. By the time I got out of first grade, he had introduced me to Sophie Tucker, let me watch from the catwalk as he appeared with Milton Berle, and gotten my brother and me cameos in the cornball Yiddish film/review *Catskill Honeymoon*.

get the twenty dollars!"—but I never acquired the necessary proficiency, although I did a mean "Country Gardens" with my brother, Gary, on the trumpet. I'd be practicing in the basement, my mother thirty feet away in her sewing room, my dad next door in his office, "playing" with his stamps. I'd hit a wrong note, and in stereo I'd hear, "B *flat*!"

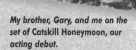

My brother, Gary, and me on the set of Catskill Honeymoon, our acting debut.

In other homes, children doing their homework while mom and dad entertained friends in the basement might be interrupted by sounds of "Gin" or "Touchdown." I did mine to the strains of "Bei Mir Bist Du Shayn" or "Tum-Balalaika." And speaking of strains, I took piano lessons, not weekly from a visiting teacher, but twice a week at the Harbor Conservatory of Music. My father wanted so for me to accompany him on stage—"Why shouldn't YOU

While other kids went to picnics with their parents on Sundays, we went to "the program" (WEVD's *American-Jewish Caravan of Stars* radio show). While my parents rehearsed with the Barry Sisters, Molly Picon, Mickey Katz, and the like, Gary and I played with the microphones, then watched the live performance from the wings.

carried away that he pledged a hundred dollars—he was seven!)

Dad lived to see his grandchildren, and nothing gave him more pleasure. From the time Barry and I married

dozen. How much more than all your time can they take up?" I like to think that somewhere in that concert in the sky his great-grandchildren touch his heart too.

Borscht Belt Standup

"Two men go into a restaurant. One orders borscht, and the other orders pea soup. When the waiter returns with the order, he gives one the borscht and the other potato soup.

'I ordered pea soup,' says the one who ordered pea soup.

'And what's wrong with the potato soup?' asks the waiter.

The man tastes the potato soup, and sure enough, he likes it. 'Boy, that certainly is delicious potato soup. Here, Sam, taste it,' and gives his friend a taste of the potato.

'Boy, you're right. That certainly is wonderful potato soup,' and the man who ordered borscht turns to the waiter and asks, 'Why didn't you bring me potato too?' Says the waiter, 'Did you order pea soup?'"

—Jan Bart, circa 1940

"While other kids went to picnics . . . we went to WEVD's American-Jewish Caravan of Stars radio show."

At home my father's jokes were of the corny, punny variety, but he must have saved the good stuff for the audience. As I sat off-stage at my first Israel Bond rally, he got some extra laughs because the half of the audience that could see me was laughing at me cracking up. (At Gary's first bond rally, he got so

he nudged, "So *nu*?" and no sooner was our Stuart born then that became, "If you can make children like this, you should have a

Left: WEVD Conductor-composer Abe Ellstein giving me musical pointers. Right: Dad and me.

carrot soup

from Wendy Epstein

One of the great benefits of being my mother's daughter (aside from her handicapped parking sticker and usefulness in getting me into the carpool lane) is the fact that when she makes her chicken soup, she makes tons of it, and thus vats of the stuff perpetually loll about in both our freezers, ready to super-infuse recipes like this one. So sorry, Wendy, but here I have to side with Mama Irene. Homemade chicken stock makes this great soup even greater—but go ahead and use canned if that's all you've got. With canned it's superb; with homemade it's sublime.

SERVES 4 TO 6　　　　　　　　　**M**

1 quart homemade chicken stock
　　(page 63) or low-sodium boxed
　　or canned broth
1¹/₂ pounds carrots, chopped
2 large onions, chopped
2 teaspoons kosher (coarse) salt, or to taste
Freshly ground black pepper to taste
1 cup nondairy sour cream
¹/₂ bunch fresh dill, trimmed
　　and finely chopped
　　(¹/₂ cup packed)
Sugar to taste (optional)

1. Bring the stock to a boil in a large saucepan. Reduce the heat to a simmer and add the carrots, onions,

> *Mom and I spent many a winter's day preparing this soup for the family. It was 'our' recipe and brings back memories of our time together. And it's easy too, because although my grandma, Mama Irene, would disapprove, we use canned broth.*
>
> **—WENDY EPSTEIN**

1 teaspoon of the salt (of course the Epsteins use Flavolin—page 129—but the rest of us have to content ourselves with salt), and pepper. Simmer, covered, until the vegetables are soft, 20 to 25 minutes.

2. Puree the soup, in small batches, in a blender. (It is best to allow the soup to cool first if you have time. Otherwise, make sure the blender lid is on securely and that you cover it with a kitchen towel to avoid scalding your palms. You can avoid this problem by using an immersion blender, my second-favorite implement, next to my microplane.) The soup can be made a day or two ahead up to this point and refrigerated. Return the soup to the pan, leaving about 1 cup in the blender.

3. Add the sour cream to the blender and process until smooth. Return this mixture to the pan, and stir in the

Wendy (top right) at cousin Heather's (bottom right) bridal shower tea. Hats required.

dill. Heat, but don't boil. Add the remaining 1 teaspoon salt, pepper to taste, and sugar if using, and serve.

Dairy version: Use vegetable broth instead of chicken broth, and sour cream or plain yogurt instead of nondairy sour cream.

french onion soup quintet

from Judy Bart Kancigor

After visiting Quebec when we were first married, Barry and I longed for the baked onion soup, oozing with cheese, that we fell in love with there. For years I experimented for a way to mimic the rich, hearty undertone of beef broth, the usual ingredient, to use in a dairy soup. Then I hit upon dried shiitake mushrooms: Their earthy, satisfying flavor more than compensates for any lack of beef. And every time I made it, I threw in different onions—leeks, red onions, shallots, scallions—along with the standard issue, like different instruments harmonizing in a quintet. (Really, though, any combination of onions will do—just measure out 6 cups packed.) This soup is my boys' absolute favorite; whenever they came home from college, it was always their first choice for a welcome-home dinner. **SERVES 6**   **D**

1 ounce dried shiitake mushrooms
Boiling water
1 medium-size onion, unpeeled but washed well, cut in half (optional; see Note)
1 large leek, white part thinly sliced, green part reserved
1 large bunch (about 8) scallions, white part thinly sliced, green part reserved
5 sprigs fresh thyme, or 1/2 teaspoon dried thyme leaves
8 tablespoons (1 stick) butter
1 large onion, thinly sliced (2 cups)
1 cup thinly sliced red onion
4 ounces shallots, thinly sliced (1 cup)
1 cup dry sherry
1 envelope dehydrated onion soup mix
1 1/2 teaspoons Worcestershire sauce
1 1/2 teaspoons kosher (coarse) salt, or to taste
1/4 teaspoon freshly ground black pepper, or to taste

FOR THE TOPPING
6 slices (3/4 inch thick) Italian or French bread, trimmed to fit the tops of 6 individual crocks
Butter
8 ounces shredded mozzarella cheese
4 ounces freshly grated Parmesan cheese (1 1/3 cups)

1. Place the shiitake mushrooms in a heatproof bowl and add boiling water to cover (you may have to weight them down with a smaller bowl or dish). Soak until very soft, at least 1 hour.

2. Strain the mushrooms, reserving the soaking liquid. Then strain the soaking liquid through a cheesecloth-lined strainer into a large measuring cup to remove any grit. Add

enough water to equal 6 cups total, and set aside.

3. Tie the mushrooms and the unpeeled onion halves, if using, in a cheesecloth bag, and set it aside. Tie the green part of the leeks, green part of the scallions, and fresh thyme sprigs, if using, in another cheesecloth bag, and set it aside.

4. Melt the butter in a large saucepan or stockpot over medium heat. Add the sliced onion, sliced leek, red onion, and shallots, and cook, stirring often, for 10 minutes. Then add the sliced scallions and continue cooking, stirring often, until they are very soft, about 5 minutes more.

5. Add $1/2$ cup of the sherry to the onion mixture and stir for a few seconds, until most of the alcohol has burned off. Stir in the reserved mushroom soaking liquid and the onion soup mix, Worcestershire sauce, salt, dried thyme (if not using fresh), and pepper. Submerge the reserved cheesecloth packets in the mixture and bring just to a boil. Reduce the heat and simmer, covered, for 15 minutes.

6. Add the remaining $1/2$ cup sherry, cover, and simmer for 30 minutes.

7. Set the soup aside and remove the cheesecloth packets. Let them cool slightly. When they are cool enough to handle, squeeze them through a strainer over the pot to extract all the liquid, and discard them (or if you're like me, save the onions and mushrooms in the refrigerator for another use, forget about them for a few weeks, *and then* throw them away when they start getting fuzzy). Taste, and add salt and pepper if necessary. The soup can be made a day or two ahead up to this point. You can even freeze all or part of it for several months.

8. When you are ready to serve the soup, preheat the oven to 350°F.

9. Spread the slices of bread lightly with butter, and toast them in a toaster oven. Ladle the soup into individual ovenproof crocks set on a baking sheet (for easy handling). Place a piece of toast on top of each serving. Distribute the cheeses evenly over the toast, and bake until the cheese melts, about 15 minutes.

10. Preheat the broiler. Place the baking sheet under the broiler and cook until the cheese is lightly browned, 1 to 2 minutes. Serve immediately.

Note: You're wondering about the whole unpeeled onion, aren't you? The onion skin makes the soup darker, and of course the extra onion just makes the soup that much more flavorful.

lilly gutman's tomato soup

from Susan Levy

I can't eat tomato soup without thinking of Stella Dallas. When I got sick as a little girl, my mother always gave me not the chicken soup you would expect, but tomato soup. To keep me company, she would bring her ironing board and radio into my room, and we'd listen to the soaps as she starched and pressed. Day after day, as Stella sacrificed all for her daughter's happiness, so my mother fed me tomato soup, nourished me with her humor and love, and got me well.

When Grandma Lilly (my niece Jessica's husband Josh's grandmother) and her family lived in Forest Hills, New York, they had an Italian gardener who had his own vegetable garden and would bring her the biggest, juiciest tomatoes. He knew how much Lilly loved to cook and would bring her a constant supply. Lilly became famous for her tomato soup, a family favorite made with those sweet and luscious tomatoes and plenty of onions, slowly sautéed and caramelized. She used to strain the tomato mixture, pushing with the back of a spoon until only the skin was left in the strainer. (A food mill will also accomplish this feat.) She must have had a lot of patience (and a lot of time!). Call me a philistine, but what's a little tomato skin? I don't worry about it, since I use my immersion blender—which I prefer to a standing blender for this purpose because it gives me more control (not to mention how much safer it is in blending hot ingredients). The result is a slightly chunky, more "homey" mixture, rather than a smooth puree. Of course, if you like it smooth, use your blender. (Or if you want to strain and push, be my guest!)

The gardener is long gone, and these days Lilly's daughter Susan combs the farmers' market for ripe tomatoes at the peak of the season. **SERVES 3 OR 4**　Ⓜ

2 tablespoons olive oil

2 tablespoons nondairy margarine

3 large onions, chopped

2 pounds ripe tomatoes, chopped

1 scant teaspoon sugar, or to taste

³/₄ teaspoon kosher (coarse) salt,
*   or more if needed*

³/₄ cup homemade chicken stock
*   (page 63) or beef stock or boxed*
*   or low-sodium canned chicken*
*   or beef broth*

Nondairy sour cream, for garnish
*   (optional)*

1. Heat the olive oil and margarine in a medium-size saucepan over medium heat until the margarine melts. Add the onions and cook until they are soft and golden, about 20 minutes.

2. Add the tomatoes, sugar (Lilly's secret ingredient), salt, and stock. Cover the pan and simmer for about 30 minutes. The tomatoes should have given up all their juices; if there is not enough liquid, add a little water.

3. Whiz the soup with an immersion blender until it reaches the desired consistency. (Or use a standing blender, but be careful: Make sure the top is on securely and that you cover it with a kitchen towel to avoid scalding your palms.) Add more salt if needed, and water if you prefer a thinner soup.

4. Pour the soup into individual bowls. For an extra fillip, spoon a dollop of nondairy sour cream onto each serving.

gazpacho

from Lorraine Gold

The summer between our freshman and sophomore years of college, I got married and my best friend, Helaine, went off to Europe. Or to put it another way, she went to Paris and I went to Flatbush Avenue. When Helaine returned, she invited a bunch of friends to lunch and made gazpacho, the chilled and refreshing summery soup she re-created from her memories of Spain. So when cousin Lorraine gave me this recipe, Helaine was the first one I thought of to try it. The avocado garnish is Helaine's idea, and Lorraine heartily approves.

SERVES 8 TO 10   P

1¹/₂ cups canned tomato juice

¹/₂ cup olive oil

¹/₂ cup red wine vinegar

3 large eggs, lightly beaten (optional; see Note)

6 large ripe tomatoes, cored and coarsely chopped, juices reserved

2 red bell peppers, stemmed, seeded, and coarsely chopped

2 medium-size onions, coarsely chopped

2 large cucumbers, peeled, seeded, and coarsely chopped

¹/₂ cup chopped dill or chives

¹/₂ teaspoon kosher (coarse) salt

Freshly ground black pepper to taste

1 Hass avocado, chopped, for garnish (optional)

1. Combine the tomato juice, oil, vinegar, eggs if using, and juice from the tomatoes in a large bowl, and whisk to blend.

2. Working with small batches, place the tomatoes, peppers, onions, and cucumbers in a blender and process by pulsing. Leave the vegetables slightly chunky. As you prepare them, add each batch to the tomato juice mixture. (You could also do this in one batch in a food processor—just be careful not to overprocess.)

3. Stir in the dill, salt, and pepper. Cover and chill for several hours.

4. Serve in chilled bowls, garnished with the avocado if using.

Note: When using raw eggs, buy only farm-fresh eggs that have been kept under refrigeration. Or the eggs can be omitted. For a more traditional way to thicken the soup, add a slice or two of crusty bread to the blender and process it with the vegetables.

sadie goldstein's lima bean soup

from Lil Solomon

I'm one of the few cousins who remembers Tanta Sadie, Papa Harry's sister, because we lived in a two-family house with Mama and Papa upstairs, so I got to meet everyone who came to see them and listen to their stories. Tanta Sadie lit up a room when she visited, with her red-rouged cheeks, large, jangling earrings, and twinkly eyes. She was famous for her soups, which granddaughter Syble says she simmered all day. A couple of hours does it for me. At that point the potatoes have fallen apart, thickening the soup without added flour, and little specks of carrots brighten the dish. **SERVES 6 TO 8**   **D** or **P**

1 package (16 ounces) dried baby lima beans, rinsed and picked over

2 to 3 tablespoons butter or vegetable oil

1 large onion, chopped

2 medium-size potatoes, cut into $^1/_2$-inch dice

3 large carrots, thinly sliced

2 ribs celery, chopped

1 tablespoon kosher (coarse) salt, or to taste

$^1/_4$ teaspoon pepper, preferably white, or to taste

My mother's cousin Lil Solomon at age 19 (left) and at 9 (below) in 1942.

Tanta Sadie

"Visiting Grandma Sadie every summer in Coney Island was my first exposure to steam rooms, and I was shocked to see all these older women more or less wrapped in towels, totally comfortable visiting and chatting with each other. We could barely keep up with her when we walked on the boardwalk. She was so energetic and never tired! Every week we would watch the fireworks together and walk her back to her apartment, leaving her to her summer friends and her summer life.

—SYBLE SOLOMON"

1. Combine the lima beans with 6 to 8 cups water (enough to cover them) in a medium-size saucepan and bring to a boil. Reduce the heat, cover the pan, and simmer for 2 minutes. Then remove the pan from the heat and allow the beans to sit in the water for 1 hour.

2. Melt the butter in a large saucepan over medium heat. Add the onion and cook until soft and golden, 10 to 15 minutes.

3. Drain the lima beans and add them to the onion, along with the potatoes, carrots, and celery. Add water to cover and bring to a boil. Then reduce the heat and simmer, covered, stirring occasionally, until the soup is as smooth or as chunky as you like, $1^1/_2$ to $2^1/_2$ hours, or even more if you choose.

4. Add salt and pepper to taste. If the soup is too thick, add more water. If it is too thin, cook uncovered to reduce it. Serve hot.

escarole and salami bean soup

from Jack Crane

This soup is Jack's twist on the Italian classic fagioli (beans) con scarola (escarole). If you can't find escarole, you can substitute Swiss chard. Jack, like his grandmother Sadie, likes to cook his soup for hours, creating a thicker and more uniform brew. My family prefers the twenty-minute version, in which the ingredients are more identifiable. It's entirely up to you. **SERVES 8** Ⓜ

4 tablespoons olive oil

8 ounces salami, cut into ¹/₂-inch cubes

8 ounces turkey sausage, cut into ¹/₂-inch cubes

1 medium-size onion, chopped

6 cloves garlic, coarsely chopped

1 large Savoy cabbage, cut into 1-inch-wide
    slices

2 medium-size heads escarole, cut into
    1-inch-wide slices

2 cans (14.5 ounces each) low-sodium chicken
    broth, or 3¹/₂ cups homemade chicken stock
    (page 63), plus more if desired

2 cans (15 to 20 ounces each) cannellini beans,
    drained and rinsed

1¹/₄ teaspoons kosher (coarse) salt, or to taste

¹/₄ teaspoon freshly ground black pepper,
    or to taste

"On Sunday mornings my brother Mike and I would wait to meet our stately dressed Grandma Sadie and Grandpa Abe at the bus stop, which was located next to White Tower Hamburgers. While we waited, Mike and I could just see the hamburger grilling table. Noses on glass, we ogled with envy the unattainable treyfe morsels being browned, turned, and served—often to kids like us.

Grandma Sadie, the matriarch, her gigantic pot on a coal-fired cast-iron stove, ladled her soup for visitors from a pot that never emptied. The flavors were superb, the taste always the same, the directions simple and pointed: 'Ess, kinderlach, ess.' ('Eat, children, eat.') Probably most reflective of her indomitable spirit is my memory of her dragging herself out of bed after cancer surgery, despite my mother's protests, with her coin box to collect for the Pioneer Women.

—JACK CRANE"

Above right: Jack and daughter Stacey, 1989.

1. Heat 1 tablespoon of the oil in a large, heavy soup pot over medium-high heat. Add the salami and turkey sausage and cook until browned, about 3 minutes. Transfer the meat to a plate and set aside.

2. In the same pot, heat the remaining 3 tablespoons oil over medium heat. Add the onion and cook until soft and golden, about 15 minutes. Add the garlic and cook 1 minute more.

3. Add the cabbage and escarole and

cook, stirring continuously, until the greens are wilted, 5 to 8 minutes.

4. Return the meat to the pot. Add the broth, beans, salt, and pepper. Simmer, covered, for about 20 minutes—longer if you like a thicker soup.

eggplant and parsnip soup

from Judy Bart Kancigor

I came up with this recipe when I had an eggplant in my fridge and some parsnips left over after making my mother's chicken. I am a roasted-vegetable addict. Roasting brings out the sugars in everything from broccoli to carrots, but roasted parsnips are my all-time favorite.

SERVES 5 OR 6

Vegetable cooking spray

1 large eggplant (1 to 1¹/₄ pounds)

1 pound parsnips, cut into ³/₄-inch-thick rounds

2 tablespoons olive oil

1 tablespoon nondairy margarine

2 leeks (about 1 pound), white part only, thickly sliced and well washed

2 large cloves garlic, crushed

5¹/₄ to 7 cups homemade vegetable stock or chicken stock (page 63) or low-sodium boxed or canned broth

1¹/₂ teaspoons kosher (coarse) salt, or to taste

¹/₂ teaspoon freshly ground black pepper, or to taste

1. Preheat the oven to 450°F. Line a baking sheet with aluminum foil and spray it with vegetable cooking spray.

2. Place the whole eggplant and the parsnip chunks on the prepared baking sheet and roast, turning once, until the eggplant is soft and the parsnips are tender and browned, 30 to 35 minutes. (See those nice, skinny, now very crisp parsnip tips? Go ahead and nibble—just a little perk for your efforts.)

3. Meanwhile, heat the oil and margarine in a large saucepan over medium-low heat until the margarine has melted. Add the leeks and cook, stirring occasionally, until they are soft, about 10 minutes. Add the garlic and cook, stirring, for about 1 minute more.

4. When it is cool enough to handle, slice the eggplant lengthwise and coarsely chop it (skin and all). Combine the eggplant and the roasted parsnips in a food processor and process until well combined, about 45 seconds. No need to be too obsessive here—you're going to get another crack at it.

5. Add the pureed eggplant mixture to the cooked leeks, and stir in 5¹/₄ cups of the chicken broth. Simmer, covered, for 20 minutes. Then process the mixture again in the food processor, in three batches. (This will require using a large bowl to place the processed soup in. Yes, another thing for you to wash, but trust me, you'll be washing your whole kitchen if you try to process the entire mixture at once. Liquids that come over the top of the blade of a food processor will overflow, a bitter lesson I learned the hard way . . . and in my daughter-in-law's kitchen, yet!)

6. Return the mixture to the pot, and if you find it too thick (and we don't), add more chicken broth. Add the salt and pepper, and serve.

cathy mcgill's pumpkin soup

from Kelly McGill-Barrett

שe moved from New York to California in 1971, and most of the time I never look back, but on holidays I long for those noisy, hectic family celebrations. I miss the crowds! So no wonder I was doubly thrilled when my daughter-in-law Tracey's brother Tyler and his wife, Kelly, announced they'd be moving to L.A. for Tyler to do his residency. More family! For four wonderful years we got to add an extra leaf to the dining room table as they joined our holiday celebrations, and I got to ply CARE packages to another busy, grateful young couple. One Thanksgiving Kelly brought pumpkin soup, a recipe her mom had gotten in a cooking class long before.

All good things come to an end, they say. Tyler and Kelly have moved back East to start a new life. As I write this, it's October, and what passes for fall in Southern California is upon us. Summer's last gasp—Yom Kippur's stifling heat having come and gone, right on schedule—has given way to autumn's crisp days and cooler nights. This morning Tyler e-mailed photos of their new baby, and instantly I craved pumpkin soup. This creamy, comforting brew with a touch of thyme simmers on the stove. Barry will be pleased tonight.

SERVES 4　　　　　　**D** or **M** or **P**

2 tablespoons butter or nondairy margarine

1 tablespoon olive oil

1 large onion, chopped

1 large or 2 small cloves garlic, chopped

*2 cans (14 ounces each) vegetable broth or
low-sodium chicken broth*

1 can (15 to 16 ounces) pumpkin puree

*1 1/2 teaspoons fresh thyme leaves, or
1/2 teaspoon dried*

1/2 teaspoon kosher (coarse) salt, or to taste

*1/4 teaspoon freshly ground black pepper,
or to taste*

*1/2 cup half-and-half or soy cream or nondairy
creamer*

1. Heat the butter with the olive oil in a medium-size saucepan over medium-low or low heat. Add the onion and cook, stirring occasionally, until very soft and golden, 20 to 25 minutes. Then add the garlic, raise the heat to medium, and cook, stirring, for 1 minute longer.

2. Combine the sautéed onion mixture, 1 can of the broth, and the pumpkin in a food processor or blender, and puree until smooth.

3. Return the mixture to the pan and add the remaining 1 can broth, the thyme, and the salt and pepper. Heat thoroughly. Stir in the half-and-half and heat, but do not boil. Serve hot.

cathy mishra's roasted pepper—squash soup

from Tracey Barrett

This flavorful soup from Tracey's friend Cathy marries sweet and savory with an aromatic accent of cumin and cinnamon. Use jarred red peppers (without vinegar) or roast your own.

SERVES 5 TO 6   **D** or **M** or **P**

2 pounds butternut squash, cut in half
   lengthwise and seeded (see Note)

3 tablespoons butter or nondairy margarine

2 medium-size onions, coarsely chopped

1 clove garlic, crushed

1 cup roasted red peppers, drained

1 large sweet apple, peeled, cored,
   and cut into eighths

1 cup apple juice

2 to 3 cups vegetable broth or homemade
   chicken stock (page 63) or low-sodium
   boxed or canned broth

1 teaspoon dried thyme leaves

1 teaspoon ground cumin

1/4 teaspoon ground cinnamon

1/8 to 1/4 teaspoon cayenne pepper

2 teaspoons kosher (coarse) salt,
   or to taste

1 to 2 teaspoons sugar (optional)

1 cup half-and-half or soy cream or
   nondairy creamer

1. Preheat the oven to 400°F.

2. Place the squash halves, cut side down, in a 13 × 9-inch baking pan. Add water to a depth of 1/2 inch to the pan and bake, uncovered, until the squash is very tender, about 45 minutes. Remove and allow to cool.

3. Meanwhile, melt the butter in a large saucepan over medium heat. Add the onions and cook, stirring occasionally, until they are soft and beginning to brown, about 12 minutes. (Reduce the heat to medium-low if necessary to prevent burning.) Add the garlic and cook, stirring constantly, for about 1 minute more. Set aside.

4. When the squash is cool enough to handle, peel it and place the flesh in a food processor. Add the sautéed onion mixture (hold on to the saucepan, unwashed—you'll be using it again) and the roasted peppers, apple wedges, and apple juice. Puree until smooth. Transfer the puree to the saucepan and add 2 cups of the broth. Stir in the thyme, cumin, cinnamon, cayenne pepper, salt, and sugar if using. Cover and simmer, stirring occasionally, for about 10 minutes. Then add the half-and-half or creamer and heat gently. Do not let it boil. If the soup is too thick, add some of the remaining broth until it has the desired consistency. Add more salt, cayenne, or sugar, if needed, and serve.

Note: Butternut squash is deliciously sweet, but it is very hard to cut when it is raw. Here's a trick: Poke several holes in the squash with a skewer (so that it doesn't burst), and microwave it on high power for 5 minutes. If it is still tough and hard to cut, rotate the

Tracey with her friend Kathy at Tracey's baby shower, 2000.

squash and microwave again on high power for 3 minutes more. At this point you should be able to cut it easily. (If not, microwave again for 2 minutes.) When it is cool enough to handle, cut the squash in half and remove the seeds. (A grapefruit spoon is great for this purpose.) Then bake it in the oven as described, reducing the time to 25 minutes.

diane podratz's potato soup

from Shelly Kancigor

y daughter-in-law Shelly's Minnesotan family thinks of the potato as a food group unto itself. Through the years her mother's hearty, satisfying soup has enlivened many a blustery winter's day. My editor at *The Canadian Jewish News*, Carolyn Blackman, who volunteered to test soup recipes for me (winter blusters there too—what a surprise), reports that she has substituted 2% milk for the cream and gotten rave reviews, even from the pickiest youngsters. **SERVES 8**   **D** or **M** or **P**

8 tablespoons (1 stick) butter, or nondairy margarine
$^1/_2$ large onion, thinly sliced
4 carrots, thinly sliced
3 ribs celery, thinly sliced
5 vegetable or chicken bouillon cubes
7 medium-size potatoes ($2^1/_4$ to $2^1/_2$ pounds total), thinly sliced
3 cups half-and-half, soy cream, or nondairy creamer
2 tablespoons chopped flat-leaf parsley
2 teaspoons kosher (coarse) salt, or to taste
$^1/_4$ teaspoon fresh ground black pepper, or to taste
$^1/_2$ teaspoon cayenne pepper, or to taste
$^1/_4$ teaspoon mace, or to taste
$^1/_2$ cup dry white wine
Chopped chives, for garnish

1. Melt the butter in a large saucepan or stockpot over medium-low heat. Add the onion, carrots, and celery, and cook until quite soft, about 15 minutes. Using a slotted spoon, transfer the vegetables to a bowl and set aside.

2. Add 5 cups water, the bouillon cubes, and the potatoes to the saucepan and simmer, covered, for 40 minutes.

3. Return the sautéed vegetables to the pan and simmer for 15 minutes more. Then add the half-and-half, parsley, salt, pepper, cayenne, and mace and heat slowly. (Careful, it burns easily.) Stir in the wine and heat through (do not let it boil).

4. Ladle the soup into bowls, top with chopped chives, and serve.

Note: Do not store in aluminum.

grandma ethel jaffee's
manhattan
fish chowder

from Robin Frank

Ethel's soup is everything a chowder should be: loaded with vegetables and chunks of fish. She always made lots so guests could take a jar home. Manhattan chowder is tomato based, as opposed to New England chowder, which is cream based. To prepare this dish as a main course meal-in-a-bowl, double the amount of fish and adjust the seasonings accordingly. Serve it with soda or oyster crackers, or with fresh French bread.

MAKES ABOUT 5 QUARTS   **M** or **P**

8 ounces smoked turkey or soy sausage,
    finely diced
1 tablespoon vegetable oil, if needed
1 large onion, chopped
2 cans (28 ounces each) crushed tomatoes
    in puree
6 chicken or vegetable bouillon packets
    or cubes, or 2 tablespoons chicken
    or vegetable bouillon powder
1 pound carrots, cut into ¼-inch-thick rounds
8 ounces fresh green beans, cut into
    1-inch pieces
4 medium-size potatoes, cut into
    ½-inch dice
2 parsnips, cut into ¼-inch-thick rounds
2 ribs celery with tender leaves, sliced

3 tablespoons chopped fresh thyme,
    or 1 tablespoon dried, or to taste
Kosher (coarse) salt and freshly ground black
    pepper to taste
2 pounds firm fish, such as cod, red snapper,
    rockfish, grouper, sea bass, halibut,
    or pompano, cut into 1-inch chunks
8 ounces frozen peas, thawed
½ cup chopped flat-leaf parsley

1. Heat an 8- or 10-quart soup pot over medium-high heat. Add the sausage and sauté until soft, about 2 minutes, adding the oil if necessary (some sausages have a higher fat content than others). Reduce the heat to medium, add the onion, and cook, stirring often, until it is soft and golden, about 7 minutes.

2. Add the tomatoes and 2 tomato cans of water. Stir in the bouillon, carrots, and green beans, and bring to a boil. Reduce the heat and simmer, covered, for 10 minutes.

3. Add the potatoes, parsnips, celery, thyme, and salt and pepper, and continue to simmer for 15 minutes more.

4. Add the fish and simmer until it is opaque and flakes easily, about 15 minutes. Add the peas and simmer for a minute or so, just to warm them through. Stir in the parsley. Correct the seasonings and serve steaming hot.

Aunt Sally (left) and
Uncle Lou with Ethel
in Florida, late '40s.

the magnificent 7

salads

The only salad I ever remember Mama Hinda serving consisted of individual leaves of iceberg lettuce decorated with tomato and cucumber slices—radishes sometimes added for a flight of fancy—and served with Milani 1890, Russian dressing, or oil and vinegar. Fresh vegetables were hardly a staple in the shtetl, but my forward-thinking grandmother, eager to learn and assimilate, quickly adapted to American customs.

As I was growing up, my diet-conscious mother always served a salad before dinner—more to fill us up, I suspect, than for its nutritive value! Through the years my daily salad habit has morphed into practically an addiction. I've never met a salad I didn't like.

"That palette of vibrant color, that gosh darn chompability!"

Mama and Papa's seven children (my mom and her siblings) then and . . . well, then. Who's who on page 613.

That palette of vibrant color, that endless variety of fresh tastes and textures, that gosh darn chompability! But keep your 12-step programs. This is one habit I have no intention of breaking.

With my mother the sous-chef paring and slicing at my side, we gnawed our way through this chapter. Signature salads contributed by others have become our signatures too. Minnesota Salad is now our first choice for a chicken salad lunch. I've brought Samra's Detroit Salad to more potlucks than I can count. Linda's Sunshine Salad brings a burst of summer to my buffets.

I love surprises, don't you? Give me frizzled ginger crisps and raspberries on a bed of greens or that extra crunch of caramelized pecans.

Choose international salads from far and near—Malca's Tabbouleh, Romanian Eggplant Salad, Turkish Cacik—as well as unusual versions of Korean, Thai, Indian, and Israeli salads that may not be authentic, but you'll get no complaints.

So think of your salad bowl as your own little field of dreams. And as the voice commands Kevin Costner in the movie of the same name, "Build it, and they will come."

the scoop on salad

■ Choose the freshest greens and vegetables, and use them within a day or two of purchase. Lettuce should be torn rather than sliced with a knife, to prevent browning.

■ If you haven't gotten around to purchasing a salad spinner, what are you waiting for? There's nothing worse than soggy salad, and think of the money you'll save on paper towels. Make sure your greens are really dry before adding the dressing and other ingredients. Remember how oil and water don't mix? Dressing will not cling properly to wet vegetables.

■ If your salads taste flat, tossing with a light sprinkling of salt and pepper will really perk them up. Think about it: The dressing contains some salt and pepper, but it gets spread over a lot of other stuff. (I'd like to take credit for this brilliant observation, but would you believe, after more years of cooking than I'd like to admit, my daughter-in-law Tracey was the one who pointed this out to me.) I don't find this necessary if the salad contains cheese or olives or other salty ingredients, but that's up to you.

■ In general, vinaigrettes containing fresh ingredients—such as onion, garlic, or herbs—taste best when prepared no more than 1 day ahead. However, leftovers will keep in the refrigerator: for 7 to 10 days if the dressing is made with vinegar, 4 to 6 days if it is made with fresh lemon or lime juice. Vinaigrettes that contain no fresh ingredients will keep even longer—2 to 3 weeks.

■ Opinions vary widely as to the amount of dressing to use. Some people ladle that stuff out like soup. I prefer the lightest of coatings. Therefore I've suggested tossing the salads with enough dressing to lightly coat (split infinitive notwithstanding). You can then serve any remaining dressing in a sauceboat or bowl for the soup—I mean dressing—lovers. If you have slathered on too much—and who likes to be overdressed?—invert a saucer on the bottom of the salad bowl and pile your salad on top of the saucer. Any excess dressing will drain off. Dress your salads immediately before serving to keep the veggies crisp, and chomp away!

mandarin tossed salad

from Shelly Kancigor

This is Barry's favorite salad, and our daughter-in-law, Shelly, makes sure to serve it at least once every time we visit. We love the crunch of the caramelized almonds and celery. Shelly prefers romaine, but use any lettuce you like. **SERVES 4**　　　**P**

FOR THE CARAMELIZED ALMONDS

1/4 cup sliced almonds

2 tablespoons sugar

FOR THE DRESSING

1/4 cup vegetable oil

2 tablespoons white wine vinegar

2 tablespoons sugar

1/2 teaspoon kosher (coarse) salt, or to taste

Freshly ground black pepper to taste

FOR THE SALAD

1 head romaine lettuce, rinsed, dried, and torn

1 cup chopped celery

1 can (11 ounces) mandarin oranges, drained

2 scallions, white and green parts, sliced

1 tablespoon chopped parsley

1. Caramelize the almonds: Heat a small or medium-size skillet (do not use nonstick) over medium heat. Add the almonds and cook, stirring constantly with a wooden spoon, until they are lightly toasted, about 45 seconds. Add the sugar and cook, stirring constantly, until it dissolves, 20 to 30 seconds. Remove the skillet from the heat and continue stirring until the almonds are lightly browned, 20 to 30 seconds more. Watch carefully, as they burn easily. Remove the caramelized almonds from the skillet and allow them to cool on aluminum foil. When they are cool enough to handle, separate them as best you can. (The almonds can be prepared a day ahead. Store in an airtight container in a cool, dry place.)

2. Combine all the dressing ingredients in a screw-top jar. Cover, and shake well.

3. Immediately before serving, toss the lettuce and celery in a large bowl. Add the oranges, scallions, parsley, and dressing, and toss gently. Top with the caramelized almonds.

Note: After caramelizing the almonds, soak the skillet in warm, soapy water for 10 minutes. The sugar will come off easily.

pear and walnut salad

from Beth Pincus

Just when we bid adieu to the last melon, peach, and berry of summer, in comes fall's luscious consolation, the pear. Pick firm but sweet pears to cozy up to the toasted walnuts for a lively contrast in textures. **SERVES 4**　　　**D**

FOR THE DRESSING

¹/₂ cup regular or light mayonnaise

¹/₂ cup sugar or equivalent artificial sweetener,
or to taste

¹/₄ cup nonfat, low-fat, or regular milk

2 tablespoons distilled white vinegar

2 teaspoons poppy seeds

FOR THE SALAD

1 head romaine lettuce, rinsed, dried, and torn

3 pears, cored and sliced

³/₄ cup walnut pieces, toasted (see box, page 17)

1. Whisk all the dressing ingredients together in a bowl or jar. (The dressing can be prepared up to 2 days ahead and kept covered in the refrigerator. Let it return to room temperature before using.)

2. Immediately before serving, place the lettuce in a large bowl. Add the pear slices, walnuts, and enough of the dressing to lightly coat. Serve any extra dressing in a boat or bowl on the side.

cranberry, pecan, and feta salad

from Ellen Gardner

Dried fruit, toasted nuts, and cheese are my very favorite salad toppings—ya got yer sweetness, yer crunch, and yer tang. Add the pungent kick of basil and I am in heaven. I use purple basil when I can find it for an extra flavor blast. **SERVES 8**　　　　　**D**

FOR THE CARAMELIZED PECANS

1 cup pecans

¹/₄ cup sugar

FOR THE BASIL VINAIGRETTE

¹/₄ cup white wine vinegar or sherry vinegar

1 shallot, finely chopped

1 tablespoon finely chopped basil leaves

1 tablespoon sugar

³/₄ teaspoon kosher (coarse) salt, or to taste

Freshly ground black pepper to taste

¹/₂ cup olive oil

FOR THE SALAD

14 to 16 ounces fancy mixed salad greens,
rinsed and dried

¹/₂ large cucumber, peeled and thinly sliced

¹/₂ cup thinly sliced red onion
(separated into rings)

1 Granny Smith apple, peeled, cored,
and thinly sliced

1 container (about 3.5 ounces) crumbled
feta cheese

¹/₂ cup dried cranberries

1. Caramelize the pecans: Heat a medium-size skillet (do not use nonstick) over medium heat. Add the pecans and cook, stirring constantly with a wooden spoon, until they are lightly toasted, about 2 minutes. Add the sugar and cook, stirring constantly, until it dissolves and the pecans are coated, about 3 minutes more. If the skillet starts to smoke, remove it from the heat

and continue stirring until all the sugar is dissolved. Remove the candied pecans from the skillet and allow them to cool on aluminum foil. When they are cool enough to handle, separate them. (The pecans can be prepared a day ahead. Store in an airtight container in a cool, dry place.)

2. Prepare the Basil Vinaigrette: Whisk the vinegar, shallot, basil, sugar, salt, and pepper together in a bowl. Slowly pour in the oil in a thin stream while continuing to whisk. Whisk until thick. (This can be made a day or two ahead and refrigerated. Bring to room temperature before serving.)

3. Immediately before serving, combine all the salad ingredients in a bowl, and toss with enough of the vinaigrette to lightly coat. Top with the caramelized pecans. Serve any extra dressing in a boat or bowl on the side.

Note: After caramelizing the pecans, soak the skillet in warm, soapy water for 10 minutes, and the hardened sugar will come off easily.

mango and avocado salad

from Hillary Robbins

Cousin Hillary reports that this salad is zooming all over Chicago. (No wonder they call it the Windy City.) Slice the avocado as close to serving time as possible; tossing it with a bit of the dressing prevents it from turning brown.

SERVES 4 TO 6 Ⓟ

FOR THE HONEY DRESSING
1/4 cup vegetable oil
1/4 cup regular or light mayonnaise
1/4 cup honey
2 tablespoons cider vinegar
1 tablespoon Dijon mustard

FOR THE SALAD
1 head romaine lettuce, rinsed, dried,
 and torn
1 red bell pepper, stemmed, seeded,
 and cut into 1/4-inch-wide strips,
 strips cut in half
1/2 English (hothouse) cucumber, thinly sliced
1/4 cup dried cranberries
1/4 cup sliced almonds, toasted
 (see box, page 17)
1 mango, cut into 1/2-inch cubes
2 avocados, preferably Hass, cut into
 1/4-inch-thick slices

1. Whisk all the dressing ingredients together in a bowl.

2. Immediately before serving, gently toss the lettuce, bell pepper strips, and cucumber slices in a large bowl. Add the cranberries,

Staci, Hillary, and Daryl Robbins, daughters of Samra and Ronald Robbins.

almonds, and mango cubes, and toss gently with enough dressing to lightly coat.

3. In a small bowl, gently toss the avocado slices with a tablespoon or so of the remaining dressing. Arrange the avocado slices on top of the salad. Serve any extra dressing in a boat or bowl on the side.

detroit salad

from Samra Robbins

I was once asked to bring samples to feed a hundred people for a "Taste of Passover" event at a local synagogue. I was the only presenter who was not a caterer. I brought my Apple Matzoh Schalat (page 556), made into individual cupcakes, and Samra's Detroit Salad. Using the same irresistible dressing, I substituted a few ingredients and turned it into coleslaw (see the variation), and I have to say I drew the largest crowd. There was nary a shred of cabbage left. People were milling around sipping leftover dressing from plastic spoons! **SERVES 6**   **D**

FOR THE DRESSING

1 cup vegetable oil

³/₄ cup sugar

¹/₃ cup red wine vinegar

1 tablespoon prepared mustard

1 tablespoon grated onion

1¹/₂ tablespoons poppy seeds

Dash of kosher (coarse) salt, or to taste

FOR THE SALAD

1 large head romaine lettuce, rinsed, dried, and torn

2 tart apples, such as Granny Smith, cored, thinly sliced, slices cut in half

8 ounces fresh button mushrooms, sliced

8 ounces Swiss cheese, cut into ¹/₄-inch cubes

1 cup cashews (salted or unsalted)

1. Combine all the dressing ingredients in a blender and process until well mixed. (The dressing can be made ahead and refrigerated, covered. Allow it to come to room temperature before tossing with the salad.)

2. Combine all the salad ingredients in a large bowl. Immediately before serving, toss the salad with enough of the dressing to lightly coat. Serve any extra dressing in a boat or bowl on the side.

Variation: To prepare coleslaw for a crowd, substitute sliced almonds for the cashews, shredded cheese for the cubed, and a 16-ounce package of shredded coleslaw mix for the romaine. Double or triple as needed.

raspberry salad
with ginger crisps

from Barbara Straus

Parties at cooking schools are becoming very popular and, oh, so much fun. Barbara got this recipe at a friend's birthday bash that was held at L'Académie de Cuisine in Bethesda, Maryland, where chef Brian Patterson served this unique salad. The finest shreds of fresh ginger are quickly fried and then perched atop baby salad greens, crowned with sweet raspberries. **SERVES 4**　**P**

FOR THE GINGER CRISPS

Oil for deep-frying

2 to 3 ounces fresh ginger, cut into thin
  julienne strips ($^1/_4$ cup)

Kosher (coarse) salt to taste

FOR THE RASPBERRY VINAIGRETTE

$^1/_4$ cup raspberry vinegar

2 tablespoons hoisin sauce

$^1/_2$ cup fresh or frozen raspberries

$^1/_2$ cup canola oil

Kosher (coarse) salt and black pepper
  to taste

2 tablespoons chopped fresh herbs,
  such as basil, tarragon, thyme,
  or even mint (optional)

FOR THE SALAD

6 cups mesclun greens, rinsed and dried

1 cup fresh raspberries

1. Prepare the Ginger Crisps: Pour oil to a depth of about 2 inches in a small saucepan and heat it to 350°F (the oil will shimmer when it is hot enough). In small batches, drop the ginger julienne into the hot oil and fry until golden brown, about 1 minute. Drain, and season lightly with salt. Serve the ginger crisps within 1 hour of making them.

2. Prepare the Raspberry Vinaigrette: Combine the vinegar, hoisin sauce, and raspberries in a mixer bowl, and blend with an electric mixer on medium speed. With the mixer running, add the oil in a thin stream. Strain the dressing through a fine-mesh strainer into another bowl or jar. Add salt and pepper, and stir in the fresh herbs if using.

3. When you are ready to serve the salad, toss the greens with enough of the dressing to lightly coat. Garnish with the raspberries and fried ginger crisps. Serve any extra dressing in a boat or bowl on the side.

sunshine salad

from Linda Nathan

This bright, citrusy salad was cousin Linda's cure for the winter blues all those years when she and Frank were living in Cincinnati. Now that they've moved to Tampa, sunshine is at her door year-round, but this sunny salad is still a favorite. I brought it to my friend Joanne's housewarming, and it was the most popular dish there. **SERVES AT LEAST 8**　**D**

Cousin Linda Nathan, happy to be a resident of the Sunshine State (despite the hurricanes their first year!).

FOR THE POPPY SEED DRESSING

$1/2$ cup regular or light mayonnaise

$1/4$ cup regular or light sour cream

$1/4$ cup orange juice concentrate

$1/4$ cup fresh lemon juice

2 teaspoons poppy seeds

$1/2$ teaspoon pure vanilla extract

2 teaspoons sugar, or to taste

1 teaspoon kosher (coarse) salt, or to taste

$1/4$ teaspoon freshly ground black pepper,
   or to taste

FOR THE SALAD

1 head green curly-leaf or Bibb lettuce,
   rinsed, dried, and torn

2 to 3 cups shredded red cabbage

1 can (5 ounces) water chestnuts, drained
   and sliced (see Note)

1 can (15 ounces) mandarin oranges, well drained

$1/2$ cup pecans, toasted (see box, page 17)

2 to 3 ounces banana chips, lightly crushed

$1/2$ cup raisins

$1/2$ cup sweetened flaked coconut

2 tablespoons roasted sunflower seeds
   (salted or unsalted)

1. Combine all the dressing ingredients in a blender, and process until smooth.

2. Immediately before serving, gently toss the lettuce and cabbage in a large bowl. Toss with the remaining ingredients and enough of the dressing to lightly coat. Serve any extra dressing in a boat or bowl on the side.

Note: Canned water chestnuts are available presliced, but I find the slices too thick and prefer to buy them whole and slice them myself.

israeli warm wild mushroom salad

from Judy Bart Kancigor

Our favorite restaurant in Tel Aviv was Picasso, where they served this wonderful salad. We liked it so much, we went back there every night. We asked the chef for the recipe, and guess what—he said no! Here is my attempt to re-create it. To taste the original, call your travel agent. **SERVES 6**　**P**

3 tablespoons olive oil

1 tablespoon dark sesame oil

1 pound mixed mushrooms (see Note),
   sliced

2 tablespoons dry red wine

1 tablespoon rice vinegar

1 tablespoon reduced-sodium soy sauce

Kosher (coarse) salt and freshly ground
   black pepper to taste

6 cups torn butter lettuce

$1/2$ cup walnut pieces, toasted
   (see box, page 17)

2 tablespoons sunflower seeds, toasted
   (see box, page 17)

2 tablespoons sesame seeds, toasted
   (see box, page 17)

1 bunch fresh basil, leaves cut into thin
   slivers (about $1/2$ cup packed)

Fronds from 1 fennel bulb, chopped

1. Combine 1½ tablespoons of the olive oil and 1½ teaspoons of the sesame oil in a wok or a large skillet over medium-high heat. Add half of the mushrooms and cook until they are tender and have released their juices, about 5 minutes. Do not crowd the skillet, or the mushrooms will steam and not brown. (For portobellos cook 2 minutes more. For oyster mushrooms cook 2 minutes less.) Transfer the mushrooms to a baking pan and spread them out in a single layer so they don't steam.

2. Repeat with the remaining 1½ tablespoons olive oil, 1½ teaspoons sesame oil, and mushrooms. Transfer them to the baking pan.

3. Remove the skillet from the heat (for safety's sake), and stir in the wine, vinegar, and soy sauce. Deglaze the skillet, scraping up all the crusty brown bits. Add salt and pepper to taste.

4. Immediately before serving, pour the warm wine mixture over the lettuce in a salad bowl. Add the sautéed mushrooms, walnuts, sunflower seeds, sesame seeds, basil, and fennel fronds. Toss, and serve.

Note: Choose three or more varieties, such as shiitake, portobello, cremini, oyster, chanterelle, and porcini. If using shiitake and/or oyster mushrooms, remove the stems and save them for stock.

israeli salad: a bit of history

The pioneers of the first and second aliyah (waves of immigration) worked, when they could get work, with the Arabs, in Turkish Palestine. They earned the same as or less than the Arabs, and, like them, had no crockery or utensils. Vegetables and pita were the most affordable food, so with the one available knife, they diced the vegetables into one bowl, and used the pita to eat the salad. By the time I lived there (from 1953), we had advanced to one knife per table and one plate, spoon, and fork per person. By then, we grew our own food. We imported only Jews, not things. We didn't have much—a bed, maybe a wardrobe, perhaps a chair in our rooms, and the communal dining room. We no longer rationed vegetables, just meat, butter, and such, and our salads were wonderful. In season, we used cucumber, green pepper, tomatoes, radishes, and onions, all diced, usually in equal amounts, and olives, pitted and sliced. It was all mixed together with a tiny bit of olive oil and salt and pepper. Most also added in the portion of protein: one slice of yellow cheese or two small sardines or half a hard-boiled egg, also diced. It stretched a little further that way. We ate it with a fork and a piece of bread (European-style).

At my wedding, right after the Sinai Campaign, we had one fried egg and a little mountain of Israeli salad per person. At the time, there were over 1,000,000 Jews in Israel (including 400,000 Holocaust survivors and victims of persecutions in Arab countries), and not half a dozen privately owned automobiles.

The next time you eat an Israeli salad, remember that it built a homeland and nourished a people. All different, but all eating that same salad.

—CAROLYN C. GILBOA

israeli chopped vegetable salad

from Nava Epstein

Chopped salad is popular all over Israel, and there are as many variations as there are Israelis. The classic calls for tomatoes, cucumbers, and some form of onion with a splash of lemon juice and oil. I love this one, with the crunch of toasted seeds, the explosion of fresh herbs, and the briny, rich addition of feta cheese. Cousin Wendy says her mother-in-law, Nava, instructed her to chop the vegetables quite small—$1/4$ inch is common, but Wendy makes them even tinier for her husband, Elad. **SERVES 6** 🇩

FOR THE DRESSING
Juice of 1 lemon (about 3 tablespoons)
5 tablespoons olive oil
1 teaspoon sugar, or to taste (optional)
$1^1/2$ teaspoons kosher (coarse) salt, or to taste
$1/4$ teaspoon freshly ground black pepper,
    or to taste

FOR THE SALAD
3 cucumbers, peeled, seeded, and chopped
3 tomatoes, seeded and chopped
1 red bell pepper, stemmed, seeded, and
    chopped
1 large carrot, grated
2 scallions, white and green parts, finely sliced
2 tablespoons chopped flat-leaf parsley

2 tablespoons chopped oregano
2 tablespoons chopped cilantro
2 tablespoons chopped mint
4 ounces feta, Bulgarian feta, or other salted
    cheese, crumbled
2 tablespoons pumpkin seeds, toasted
    (see box, page 17)
2 tablespoons sunflower seeds, toasted
    (see box, page 17)
2 tablespoons pine nuts, toasted
    (see box, page 17)
Kosher (coarse) salt and freshly ground black
    pepper to taste (optional)

1. Whisk all the dressing ingredients together in a large bowl.

2. Add the vegetables, herbs, and feta, and mix thoroughly.

3. Immediately before serving, add the toasted pumpkin seeds, sunflower seeds, and pine nuts and toss well. Taste, and add salt and pepper if necessary. Serve with a slotted spoon.

lorraine simpson's indian spinach salad

from Joyce Simpson

Joyce says her mother-in-law's sweet and spicy salad always steals the show. Adjust the hot sauce to your taste—none at all for your most timid guests or pour it on for the red-hot lovers. Although the chutney, curry, and peanuts are probably responsible for this salad's name, my friend Raghavan Iyer, author of *The Turmeric Trail*, tells me no self-respecting Indian would call this an Indian salad. He says there are no green salads or vinaigrettes in Indian cuisine. "Salads" are usually accompaniments or condiments, based on vegetables or fruit.

SERVES 6 🄿

Joyce's mother-in-law, Lorraine, and that's Joyce's husband, Bob, in the high chair, 1944.

FOR THE DRESSING

¹/₂ cup white wine vinegar

²/₃ cup vegetable oil

3 tablespoons chopped chutney (any type)

1 teaspoon dry mustard

2 teaspoons curry powder

¹/₄ teaspoon hot pepper sauce, or to taste (optional)

¹/₂ teaspoon kosher (coarse) salt, or to taste

FOR THE SALAD

9 cups baby spinach leaves, rinsed and dried

¹/₂ cup finely sliced scallions, white and green parts

2 large crisp apples, cored and thinly sliced

²/₃ cup dry-roasted peanuts

¹/₂ cup golden raisins

3 tablespoons sesame seeds, toasted (see box, page 17)

1. Whisk all the dressing ingredients together in a bowl.

2. Immediately before serving, toss the spinach and scallions in a large bowl.

3. Reserve about one fourth of the apple slices, nuts, raisins, and sesame seeds for garnish. Toss the remainder with the spinach mixture and enough of the dressing to lightly coat.

4. Top the salad with the reserved apples, nuts, raisins, and sesame seeds. Serve any extra dressing in a boat or bowl on the side.

sue magnan's korean salad

from Linda Nathan

Linda's friend Sue got this recipe from a long-forgotten Korean restaurant in Cincinnati. Linda reports it is her kids' favorite. "For Harrison to eat spinach is amazing," she told me. "The only vegetable he likes is French fries!" **SERVES 6** 🄿

FOR THE KOREAN DRESSING

1 cup vegetable oil

³/₄ cup sugar

¹/₃ cup ketchup

¹/₂ teaspoon kosher (coarse) salt, or to taste

¹/₄ cup distilled white vinegar

2 teaspoons Worcestershire sauce

1 small onion, diced

FOR THE SALAD

9 cups baby spinach leaves, rinsed and dried

1 can (16 ounces) bean sprouts, drained and
    rinsed

1 large can (8 ounces) whole water chestnuts,
    drained and sliced (see Note on page 100)

2 large eggs, hard-cooked and chopped

1. Combine all the dressing ingredients in a blender and process until smooth.

2. Immediately before serving, toss the spinach and the bean sprouts in a large bowl. Add the water chestnuts, chopped eggs, and enough of the dressing to lightly coat. Toss gently.

hal taback's no lettuce salad

from Lillian Bart

When most of your family is on one coast and you're on the other, friends become family. Over the years we've shared holidays and *simchas* with the Tabacks . . . and recipes too!

This wonderful salad is a staple at the splendid holiday dinners put on by the Tabacks. Pretty red cabbage leaves are filled with a colorful array of vegetables. Hal never makes it the same way twice, so the list below is just a suggestion. Any other items that you can think of can be added. The only rule is ix-nay on the ettuce-lay. My mom added the jicama, and she prefers making it with a balsamic vinaigrette—use store-bought or substitute balsamic for the white wine vinegar in Ellen's Basil Vinaigrette on page 96.

SERVES 10 TO 12　　　　**D** or **P**

4 cups shredded red cabbage (about 1 pound)

¹/₂ English (hothouse) cucumber, thinly sliced,
    slices cut in half

2 medium-size carrots, thinly sliced

8 ounces snow peas, strings removed,
    sliced in thirds diagonally

2 cups cherry and/or grape tomatoes,
    various shapes, colors, and sizes,
    halved if large

1 can (14 ounces) hearts of palm, drained and
    thinly sliced, or 2 jars (6¹/₂ ounces each)
    marinated artichoke hearts, drained and
    sliced

2 cups diced bell peppers of various colors
    (about 3 large halves)

1 cup diced jicama

8 to 10 radishes, thinly sliced

1 bunch (6 to 8) scallions, white part only,
    thinly sliced

1 container (4 to 5 ounces) crumbled feta
    cheese, or 2 eggs, hard-cooked and
    mashed (either is optional)

¹/₂ cup sliced green olives

¹/₂ cup blueberries (optional)

¹/₂ cup pine nuts, toasted (see box, page 17)

¹/₂ cup pistachios, toasted (see box, page 17)

²/₃ cup dried cranberries

Balsamic vinaigrette (see headnote)

10 to 12 whole red cabbage leaves
    for serving

1. Combine the shredded cabbage, cucumber, carrots, snow peas, tomatoes, hearts of palm, bell peppers, jicama, and radishes in a large bowl, and toss to mix.

2. Immediately before serving, add the scallions, feta if using, olives, blueberries if using, pine nuts, pistachios, and cranberries. Toss well. Add enough of the vinaigrette to lightly coat, and toss again.

3. Place a red cabbage leaf on each plate, and spoon the salad onto the leaves. Serve immediately.

Mom and Eric.

> When Ariel was just a little baby, Grandma 'Stelle (or Grandma Cupcake, as Ariel used to call her) and Great-Aunt Lil babysat while we went out to eat. When we came back to Grandma 'Stelle's, there was Ariel on the bed with Aunt Lil massaging one of her tiny, little feet and Grandma massaging the other tiny foot. The baby was cooing, and Aunt Lil said, 'Such beautiful feet. No corns, no bunions, no calluses, and they smell good too!'
>
> —ERIC WOLF

claremont salad

from Bobbi Mackoff

The Claremont Diner in Montclair, New Jersey, for decades a popular hangout, was, alas, torn down and is now the site of a car dealership. Bobbi lives not far away, but you didn't need to live nearby to know the Claremont—we used to go there from Long Island! The diner is best remembered for its signature salad. Best remembered, that is, until it was used, shortly before its demise, by HBO for filming a few sequences of *The Sopranos*.

SERVES 12 **P**

2¹/₂ cups distilled white vinegar

1¹/₂ cups sugar

³/₄ cup vegetable oil

²/₃ cup cold water

3 tablespoons kosher (coarse) salt

1 large head cabbage (about 4 pounds),
    shredded

2 cucumbers, peeled and thinly sliced

2 green bell peppers, stemmed, seeded, and
    thinly sliced

1 large onion, thinly sliced, slices separated
    into rings

2 carrots, thinly sliced

2 garlic cloves, speared on toothpicks

1. Combine the vinegar, sugar, oil, and water in a large bowl and mix thoroughly.

2. Add all the remaining ingredients and

marinate, covered, for 3 days in the refrigerator, stirring the salad each day.

3. Pick out the garlic before serving. Transfer, using a slotted spoon, to a serving dish and serve.

creamy coleslaw

from Hilda Robbins

Aunt Hilda preferred shredding her own cabbage and carrots to buying the ready mixes, but if you're in a hurry, use three 8-ounce bags of shredded coleslaw mix. **SERVES 8 TO 10**   D

FOR THE SALAD

1 medium-size cabbage (about 3 pounds), cored

2 green or red bell peppers, or 1 of each, stemmed and seeded (optional)

3 to 4 medium-size carrots

FOR THE DRESSING

1 cup regular or light mayonnaise

$1/4$ cup regular or light sour cream

2 tablespoons cider vinegar

1 tablespoon sugar

1 teaspoon dry mustard

$1^1/2$ teaspoons kosher (coarse) salt, or more to taste

$1/4$ teaspoon freshly ground black pepper

thousand island dressing

from Hilda Robbins

● ● ●

Aunt Hilda used chili sauce rather than ketchup for this thick dressing. It is the only one I can picture poured over a big hunk of iceberg lettuce. Some say that around 1923 the chef of the Drake Hotel in Chicago first made the salad and was inspired to name it after the islands he had recently visited. Others contend that the original recipe was created in the Thousand Islands town of Clayton, New York, by Sylvia LaLonde, whose husband, George, a fishing guide, would serve it to his patrons. **MAKES 1$1/2$ CUPS**   P

1 cup regular or light mayonnaise

$1/2$ cup chili sauce

1 tablespoon sweet pickle relish

1 tablespoon grated onion

1 teaspoon paprika

1 teaspoon dry mustard

Whisk the mayonnaise and chili sauce together in a bowl. Add the remaining ingredients and combine well. Covered and refrigerated, this dressing will keep for up to 2 weeks.

1. Shred the cabbage, and the bell peppers if using, by hand or in a food processor. Transfer the shredded cabbage and peppers to a large bowl.

2. Shred the carrots by hand or in the processor with the shredding disk, and add them to the cabbage mixture.

3. Whisk all the dressing ingredients together in a bowl. Add the dressing to the shredded vegetables and mix thoroughly. Refrigerate, covered, for at least 1 hour, or as long as 24 hours, before serving.

old-fashioned potato salad

from Ilo Riebe

Shelly's Grandma Ilo's potato salad is rich and creamy and serves a crowd. Of course, she grows her own potatoes. **SERVES 12 TO 16** [D]

5 pounds red or white waxy potatoes

1 cup sugar

4 teaspoons all-purpose flour

1 heaping teaspoon dry mustard

About 3 teaspoons kosher (coarse) salt

4 large eggs, beaten

3/4 cup distilled white vinegar

1 cup mayonnaise, regular or light

1/2 cup heavy (whipping) cream

3 ribs celery, chopped

1 bunch (about 12) radishes,
*   thinly sliced*

1 medium-size sweet onion, finely
*   chopped*

1 tomato, chopped (optional)

3 large eggs, hard-cooked and
*   chopped*

Freshly ground black pepper to taste

1. Bring a pot of lightly salted water to a boil. Add the potatoes and cook just until tender, about 30 minutes, depending on their size. (Test with a thin skewer or a cake tester rather than a fork, and you won't break the potatoes apart.) Remove the potatoes as they are done. Drain, and let them cool.

2. Meanwhile, combine the sugar, flour, mustard, and 1/4 teaspoon of the salt in the top of a double boiler. Stir in the eggs and vinegar, and cook over simmering water, stirring constantly, until thick, about 10 minutes. Remove from the heat and allow to cool. (This slow heating and stirring should prevent the eggs from scrambling, but if perchance you see white specks, no problem: Just strain the sauce.)

3. Whisk the mayonnaise and cream together in a medium-size bowl until smooth; then refrigerate.

4. When the potatoes have cooled, thinly slice them into a large bowl. Add the celery, radishes, onion, tomato if using, hard-cooked eggs, 2 1/2 teaspoons of the salt, and pepper.

> " In 1945 I was on furlough, and Hilda and I took the train from Pratt, Kansas, where I was stationed, back home to New York. The train was from the Civil War—no water, no bathroom, no food, and freezing cold. When we stopped in Chicago, of course Hilda ran out and got us food. We were sitting facing all these hungry soldiers and sailors, eating. By the time we got to Newark, people were burning the cushions to warm up. The trip took 48 hours. We were a mess!
> **—LOU ROBBINS** "

5. Stir the cooled sauce into the mayonnaise mixture, and add this dressing to the potato mixture. Add salt and pepper to taste. Mix together gently but thoroughly, and chill for at least 2 hours, or as long as 24 hours.

6. Remove the salad from the refrigerator 15 to 30 minutes before serving.

Shelly and Grandma Ilo.

" Grandma Ilo's potato salad is always expected at family gatherings. She used to send an ice-cream-pail-full with Grandpa for his fishing weekends at the cabin in rural northern Minnesota. My grandma adds ¹/₂ cup of whipping cream to everything she makes! —SHELLY KANCIGOR "

minnesota salad

from Diane Podratz

Called Fuji salad elsewhere, this is the yummy, crunchy salad we first tasted at the gift-opening lunch hosted by the Podratzes for their daughter Shelly and my son Stu during their wedding weekend. To retain its crispness, be sure to wait until the last minute to toss in the almonds, noodles, and dressing. Leftovers, if you have any, are great added to a stir-fry. This is my absolute favorite recipe for Chinese chicken salad; check out the first variation. **SERVES 8 TO 10**　　　　　**P**

FOR THE DRESSING

¹/₄ cup rice vinegar

2 tablespoons canola oil

2 tablespoons dark sesame oil

1¹/₂ tablespoons confectioners' sugar

Flavoring packet from ramen mix
    (see below)

FOR THE SALAD

Dry noodles from 1 package (3 ounces)
    Oriental-flavor ramen mix

1 package (16 ounces) coleslaw mix

1 bunch (6 to 8) scallions, white and
    most of the green part,
    thinly sliced

1 cup Chinese snow peas, strings removed,
    sliced in thirds diagonally

³/₄ cup slivered almonds, toasted
    (see box, page 17)

1. Combine all the dressing ingredients in a screw-top jar. Cover, and shake well.

2. Place the ramen noodles in a resealable plastic bag, seal it tightly, and crush them with a rolling pin. Set aside.

3. Combine the coleslaw mix, scallions, and snow peas in a large bowl. Toss to mix.

4. Immediately before serving, add the almonds, crushed ramen noodles, and dressing to the salad. Toss well, and serve.

Variations:

Chinese Chicken Salad: Add 4 cooked chicken breast halves (preferably marinated in a Chinese-style marinade), cut into 1-inch chunks.

Double-Crunch Topping: In Zena Kaplan's variation (from her friend Bernice Goodman) on our Minnesota Salad, the crunchies get a sunburn (she *is* from the South, you know). The noodles, almonds, and sunflower seeds (and lots of 'em) are toasted in butter and sprinkled on at the last moment for the ultimate gnaw. Combine 2 packages (3 ounces each) ramen noodles (any flavor), crushed, $^{1}/_{2}$ cup sliced almonds, $^{1}/_{2}$ cup sunflower seeds (salted or unsalted), and 4 tablespoons ($^{1}/_{2}$ stick) melted butter or margarine in a bowl. Arrange the mixture in a single layer on a baking sheet and toast in a preheated 350°F oven, shaking the baking sheet occasionally, just until golden brown, about 10 minutes. Watch carefully after 5 minutes, as the mixture burns easily. Transfer the topping to a bowl and allow to cool before serving.

malca's tabbouleh

from Wendy Altman Cohen

This salad, which is so common in Israel, has caught on here as well. It is especially delightful in the summer, when tomatoes are at their sweet, juicy peak and the parsley and mint are snappy fresh (not to mention what they do for your breath!). **SERVES 4 TO 6**　　**P**

$^{1}/_{2}$ **cup fine bulgur**

$^{1}/_{2}$ **cup (packed) chopped flat-leaf parsley leaves**

1 bunch (6 to 8) scallions, white and green parts, chopped

2 medium-size tomatoes, peeled, seeded, and cut into $^{1}/_{4}$-inch dice

2 medium-size cucumbers, peeled, seeded, and cut into $^{1}/_{4}$-inch dice

Juice of 1 lemon (about 3 tablespoons), or to taste

2 tablespoons olive oil

1$^{1}/_{2}$ teaspoons kosher (coarse) salt, or to taste

$^{1}/_{4}$ teaspoon freshly ground black pepper, or to taste

1 tablespoon finely chopped mint leaves

1. Prepare the bulgur according to the package directions (see Note). Fluff the grains with a fork, and allow to cool completely.

2. Mix the bulgur with all the remaining ingredients in a large bowl. Toss well, and allow to sit for 1 hour at room temperature before serving.

Note: If you buy your bulgur loose from a bin, here are the cooking instructions: Combine the bulgur with 1$^{1}/_{2}$ cups water and $^{1}/_{2}$ teaspoon salt in a medium-size saucepan and bring to a boil. Reduce the heat, cover the pan, and simmer until tender and the water is completely absorbed, 20 to 25 minutes.

Remove the pan from the heat and let it stand for 10 minutes. Then fluff the grains with a fork and allow the bulgur to cool completely.

barbara rosen's israeli couscous salad

from Judy Bart Kancigor

I first tasted this colorful salad at a bridal shower and had to have the recipe. Couscous is not a grain, but actually a pasta, and if you've tried only the fine-grained variety, you're in for a treat. Israeli couscous boasts larger, tapioca-size toasted rounds that have a chewy, almost buttery texture, the perfect backdrop for the crisp vegetables, toasted pine nuts, and refreshing citrus dressing. **SERVES 6 TO 8**

P

Mom, Gary, and me, 1949.

FOR THE SALAD

1 package (8 ounces) toasted Israeli couscous

1 teaspoon olive oil

Kosher (coarse) salt

1 or 2 medium-size carrots, cut into $^1/_4$-inch dice

1 red or yellow bell pepper, stemmed, seeded, and cut into $^1/_4$-inch dice

1 cup frozen peas, thawed and drained

$^1/_2$ cup chopped red onion

$^2/_3$ cup diced dried dates, snipped dried apricots, or raisins

$^1/_2$ cup pine nuts, toasted (see box, page 17)

$^1/_4$ cup chopped cilantro or mint

Freshly ground black pepper, to taste

FOR THE DRESSING

$^1/_2$ cup olive oil

$^1/_4$ cup fresh lemon juice

3 tablespoons orange juice

$^1/_2$ teaspoon ground cinnamon

1 teaspoon kosher (coarse) salt, or to taste

Freshly ground black pepper, to taste

1. Prepare the couscous: Combine the couscous, oil, and 1 teaspoon salt with $2^1/_4$ cups water in a large saucepan and bring to a boil. Reduce the heat to a simmer, cover, and cook until tender and the water is completely absorbed, 8 to 10 minutes, stirring occasionally. Remove the pan from the heat and fluff the couscous with a fork. Transfer the couscous to a large bowl to cool. Stir occasionally to separate the grains.

2. Combine the cooled couscous with the remaining salad ingredients.

3. Whisk all the dressing ingredients together in a bowl. Pour the dressing over the salad and toss well. Add more salt and

pepper if needed. Cover and chill for at least 2 hours or overnight.

4. Remove the salad from the refrigerator 30 minutes before serving.

kerry frohling's thai vegetable salad

from Judy Bart Kancigor

The indisputable favorite of our annual Labor Day block party is this dish, brought by my neighbor Kerry, who "reverse-engineered" it from one featured at a popular local restaurant. I've been to that restaurant. Kerry's is better! The natural peanut butter seems to work better than the stabilized kind, he advises. **SERVES 10 TO 12** **P**

1/2 head romaine lettuce, rinsed, dried,
*   and shredded*
1 cup small uncooked broccoli florets
1/2 cup chopped scallions (white and green parts)
4 cups cooked brown rice
1 medium-size uncooked zucchini, chopped
1/2 cup salted or unsalted roasted peanuts
1/2 cup raisins
1/2 cup crispy rice noodles or chow mein noodles
Thai Dressing (recipe follows)
Canned baby corn, drained, for garnish
*   (optional)*
Thin red bell pepper strips, for garnish (optional)

1. Combine the lettuce, broccoli, and scallions in a large salad bowl, and toss. Refrigerate, covered, if not serving right away.

2. Immediately before serving, add the rice, zucchini, peanuts, raisins, noodles, and Thai Dressing. Toss well. Garnish with the baby corn and/or red bell pepper strips if desired.

thai dressing

The cooked peanut butter dressing is just the ticket for the brown rice and crunchies. **MAKES ABOUT 1 1/2 CUPS** **P**

1 cup cold water
6 tablespoons white wine vinegar
2 tablespoons soy sauce
1/4 cup honey
1 tablespoon cornstarch
3 tablespoons natural peanut butter
2 tablespoons chopped cilantro, mint,
*   or flat-leaf parsley*
2 cloves garlic, crushed
1/2 teaspoon red pepper flakes
Kosher (coarse) salt to taste (optional)

1. Combine the water, vinegar, soy sauce, honey, and cornstarch in a medium-size saucepan off the heat. Stir until the cornstarch has dissolved. Then bring the mixture to a boil, reduce the heat to medium, and cook, stirring constantly, until it thickens, 1 to 2 minutes. Remove from the heat.

2. Whisk in the peanut butter until

Me and Mom at the surprise 25th anniversary party Gary, Barry, and I threw my parents.

smooth. Add the cilantro, garlic, red pepper flakes, and salt if using. Stir until well combined, and allow to cool to room temperature before using.

moroccan carrot salad

from Regine Jaffee

ש hen I heard cousins Bonnie and Jackie had a Moroccan cousin on their mother's side, I jumped at the chance to call her and beg for recipes. This one came just in time for Rosh Hashanah and was such a hit that I had to give the recipe to all present. While this salad would be wonderful as part of a *meze* spread at any time of the year, carrots are especially appropriate for this holiday—both for their sweetness, symbolizing the wish for a sweet new year, and for the shape of the carrot "coins," symbolizing the wish for prosperity. As Phyllis Glazer and Miriyam Glazer point out in *The Essential Book of Jewish Festival Cooking*, the Yiddish word for carrots, *merren*, also means "increased," so we wish for "increased" health and prosperity at this time. **SERVES 6 TO 8** **P**

1 pound carrots, cut into ¹/₄-inch-thick rounds

3 tablespoons olive oil

3 to 4 tablespoons fresh lemon juice

1 large clove garlic, crushed

¹/₄ teaspoon ground cumin

¹/₄ teaspoon good-quality paprika

1 teaspoon kosher (coarse) salt, or to taste

¹/₈ teaspoon freshly ground black pepper, or to taste

1 teaspoon sugar, or to taste (optional)

2 tablespoons chopped flat-leaf parsley or mint, or a combination

1. Prepare a bowl of ice water and set it aside. Bring a saucepan of salted water to a boil, add the carrots, and cook until crisp-tender, about 5 minutes. Drain the carrots and submerge them in the ice water to cool. Then drain again, and set aside.

2. Whisk the olive oil, lemon juice, garlic, cumin, paprika, salt, pepper, and sugar together in a medium-size bowl. Add the cooled carrots, and toss. Taste, and add more salt and pepper if necessary. Let the salad sit for at least 1 hour before serving, for the flavors to blend.

3. Mix the parsley into the salad, and serve.

baked eggplant salad

from Bea Goldman

The caramelized onions and peppers contribute a lovely sweetness to this dish, without any added sugar. Use red, green, or yellow peppers or all three for extra color. Serve this as a salad or first course, or as a dip with crackers or pita chips. **MAKES 2½ TO 3 CUPS** 🅿

1 eggplant (about 1¼ pounds)
3 tablespoons vegetable oil
1 large onion, diced
1 cup diced bell peppers
3 large eggs, hard-cooked and chopped
1 teaspoon fresh lemon juice
¾ teaspoon kosher (coarse) salt, or to taste
¼ teaspoon freshly ground black pepper,
   or to taste

1. Preheat the oven to 425°F. Cover a rimmed baking sheet or baking pan with aluminum foil.

2. Prick the eggplant in several places with a fork or skewer, and place it on the prepared baking sheet. Roast until it is soft and tender, about 40 minutes. Set the eggplant aside to cool slightly.

3. Meanwhile, heat the oil in a large skillet over medium-low heat. Add the onion and peppers and cook slowly, stirring occasionally, until the onion is very soft and golden, about 20 minutes. Allow to cool.

4. When the eggplant is cool enough to handle, cut it in half lengthwise. Scoop out the pulp, and discard the skin. Chop the pulp well and transfer it to a strainer. Allow it to drain for about 1 hour.

5. Combine the chopped eggplant, sautéed onion and peppers, hard-cooked eggs, lemon juice, salt, and pepper in a bowl. Stir well. (This can be made a day ahead; cover and refrigerate.) Serve at room temperature.

romanian eggplant salad

from Becky Green

Although Barry's Grandma Becky was born in Odessa, her heritage was Romanian. She frequently made this salad, charring the eggplant and peppers one at a time over a gas flame. Then she would weight them down to extract excess liquid. I find it simpler to roast them in a hot oven. Serve it as a salad, as Grandma Becky did—on a bed of lettuce with sliced tomatoes and

Barry's grandparents walking down the aisle at our wedding. From left: Rose and Ben Kancigor and Becky Green.

challah or matzoh. It also makes a great dip, with crackers or pita bread for scooping. **SERVES 4 TO 5** **P**

1 eggplant (about 1¹/₄ pounds)
2 red bell peppers
1 green bell pepper
¹/₂ cup finely chopped sweet onion
1 large clove garlic, crushed
3 tablespoons vegetable oil
3 tablespoons red wine vinegar
1¹/₄ teaspoons kosher (coarse) salt, or to taste
Freshly ground black pepper to taste

1. Preheat the oven to 425°F.
2. Prick the eggplant in several places with a skewer or fork. Place the eggplant and the peppers on a baking sheet and roast, turning them often, until they are soft and blackened on all sides, about 40 minutes. Carefully transfer the peppers to a paper bag, close it tightly, and allow to cool. Allow the eggplant to cool on a dish or plate.
3. When the eggplant is cool enough to handle, slice it in half lengthwise. Scoop out the flesh and discard the skin. Transfer the eggplant flesh to a strainer or colander set over a bowl.
4. When the peppers have cooled, remove them from the paper bag and peel off the skin. Remove and discard the stems, seeds, and inner membranes. Transfer the peeled peppers to the strainer. Place a piece of waxed paper over the vegetables in the strainer, and push with your hand to squeeze out the excess liquid. Discard the liquid or reserve it for another use, such as in soups or stews.

5. Place the eggplant, peppers, onion, and garlic on a chopping board, and chop them together. Transfer to a bowl, add all the remaining ingredients, and mix thoroughly. Cover, and marinate in the refrigerator for at least 24 hours. Serve at room temperature.

cacik
(cucumber salad)
with minty yogurt sauce

from Phyllis Epstein

Phyllis received this recipe from Guner Zubi, the Turkish-born wife of a former Libyan diplomat with the United Nations, who wrote: "This salad is very refreshing, especially on hot summer days. Cacik [pronounced 'jah-jik'], should have a subtle tang or sharpness." Although Turkish cooks think of cacik as a salad, they also serve it as a cold summer soup in a frosted bowl with an ice cube or two. Salting and draining the cucumbers prevents them from becoming watery in the finished dish. **SERVES 4 TO 6** **D**

1 English (hothouse) cucumber,
    or 2 regular cucumbers
Kosher (coarse) salt
2 cups plain yogurt
1 to 2 teaspoons crushed garlic
2 tablespoons extra-virgin olive oil
2 tablespoons crushed dried mint leaves
Fresh mint leaves, for garnish

1. If you are using regular cucumbers, peel them, cut them in half lengthwise, and remove the seeds. Grate the cucumber(s) coarsely into a colander. Sprinkle generously with salt, and allow to stand for 15 to 20 minutes. Rinse off the salt and let drain.

2. Combine the yogurt, garlic, olive oil, dried mint, and salt to taste in a bowl, and whisk until smooth and creamy.

3. Pat the cucumbers dry, and combine them with the yogurt sauce. Taste and adjust the salt. Cover, and chill for at least 1 hour.

4. Serve garnished with fresh mint leaves.

> *Every summer Marilyn would invite me to visitors day at her beach club. She'd pick me up in her Lincoln Continental. It had a stereo and air conditioning! I thought I died and went to heaven.* **—JUDY BART KANCIGOR**

eileen lewis's molded egg salad

from Marilyn Dubin

The late comedian Paul Lynde used to say that his idea of lunch was a jar of mayonnaise and a spoon. If you're nodding your head, this one's for you. Plain old egg salad with mayonnaise (especially if it's Hellmann's or Best Foods) is a hard act to follow. Let's face it—who doesn't love it? But here it gets a fashion makeover with little flecks of pimento and relish. This is a lovely dish for lunch or brunch, served with thin slices of rye bread. I've even served it as an appetizer, with crackers for scooping. **SERVES 6 TO 8** **P**

Vegetable cooking spray
1 envelope unflavored gelatin
1/4 cup cold water
1/2 cup boiling water
1 cup regular or light mayonnaise
2 teaspoons fresh lemon juice
10 large eggs, hard-cooked and chopped
1/2 cup finely diced celery
1/2 cup finely diced sweet onion
1 jar (4 ounces) chopped pimentos, well drained
2 tablespoons sweet pickle relish, well drained
1 teaspoon kosher (coarse) salt, or to taste
*1/4 teaspoon freshly ground black pepper,
      or to taste*
Leaf lettuce, for serving
Cherry tomatoes, for serving

1. Spray a 6-cup mold with vegetable cooking spray.

2. Dissolve the gelatin in the cold water in a large bowl, stirring until smooth. Stir in the boiling water. Allow to cool to room temperature.

3. Whisk the mayonnaise and lemon juice into the cooled gelatin mixture until smooth.

4. Stir in the chopped eggs, celery, onion, pimentos, relish, salt, and pepper. Transfer

the mixture to the prepared mold and refrigerate it, covered, for at least 4 hours or as long as overnight.

5. Unmold the salad onto a decorative platter. Surround it with the lettuce and cherry tomatoes, and serve.

Note: For help unmolding the salad, see page 59, Step 5.

Debbie and me in 1978 watching our husbands turn green on the roller coaster (my kids ate it up).

> *I met Eileen at a party when we were all young marrieds living in Woodmere [Long Island]. She was quite attractive, and the next day [my husband] Harold put Neil in the carriage and said, 'I think I'll go walk over to the Lewises'.' Harold never walked a baby in his life! I said, 'Wait a minute. I'll get my hat. I'm coming with you!' And we've been the best of friends for forty-six years.*
>
> **—MARILYN DUBIN**

anna goldstein's egg salad and mushrooms

from Debbie Levine

Anna Goldstein, my sister-in-law Debbie's friend's mother, coincidentally figured prominently in my childhood. For many years she worked at Dottie's, our legendary neighborhood appetizing store, where nearly every Sunday my mother would go to pick up bagels and lox. For parties the menu was expanded to include platters of herring, whitefish, and Dottie's signature salmon salad. I've never tasted the likes of it since. How I wish I had asked Anna for the recipe! Next best is her egg salad. The secret is in the very slow cooking of the onions.

SERVES 6　　　　　　　　　　　**P**

3 tablespoons olive oil
1 large Spanish onion, diced
8 ounces white mushrooms, sliced
6 large eggs, hard-cooked and chopped
Kosher (coarse) salt and freshly ground black pepper to taste

1. Heat the oil in a large skillet over medium or medium-low heat. Add the onion and cook slowly, stirring occasionally, until very soft and golden, 20 to 30 minutes.

2. Add the mushrooms, raise the heat to medium, and cook until they have reduced in size and their liquid has evaporated, about 6 minutes. Remove the skillet from the heat

and allow the vegetables to cool to room temperature. Chop fine.

3. Combine the chopped onion mixture and the eggs in a bowl, and season with salt and pepper. Cover and refrigerate for at least 1 hour.

4. Remove the salad from the refrigerator 30 minutes before serving.

Galitzianers vs. Litvaks

• • •

A Galitzianer is a Jew who hailed from Galitzia, corresponding roughly to southern Poland, as opposed to a Litvak, who hailed from northern Poland or Lithuania.

So much for the geography lesson. The sociology is a lot more interesting. You think the Hatfields and McCoys had *tsurris*? To the Litvaks, who considered themselves intellectual and refined, Galitzianers were untrustworthy, materialistic, and cunning, and—worse yet— they put sugar in their gefilte fish! So when my Galitzianer father, at that time a nightclub and vaudeville singer, came to court my Litvak mother (yes, alas, I am the product of a mixed marriage), Papa Harry was not impressed. "An actor?" he asked. (Or as he pronounced it, "Un ac-tayr?") Don't know if Mama Hinda was more concerned about how her daughter would fare with a husband in show business or about the prospect of being served sweetened gefilte fish by the future in-laws.

molded cucumber salad for fish

from Sally Bower

Aunt Sally created this dish as a tart accompaniment to fish. And tart it is (not that there's anything wrong with that!)—cucumbers are suspended in a shimmering mold for a puckery palate cleanser that goes swimmingly with any cold fish, from gefilte to salmon.

I have to admit that I added the sugar and pineapple, but then again, I'm half Galitzianer (see box, left)! Let your own palate be your guide as to how sweet or tart you want it to be. **SERVES 12** **P**

2 cups boiling water

2 boxes (3 ounces each) lemon-flavored gelatin

1 envelope unflavored gelatin dissolved in $^1/_2$ cup cold water

$^3/_4$ to 1 cup distilled white vinegar

2 teaspoons sugar (optional)

$^1/_2$ teaspoon kosher (coarse) salt

1 can (8 ounces) crushed pineapple packed in juice, drained, juice reserved (optional)

Vegetable cooking spray

$1^1/_2$ English (hothouse) cucumbers, thinly sliced

1 to 2 bunches (6 to 12) scallions, white part only, sliced

1. Pour the boiling water over the lemon gelatin in a large heatproof bowl, and stir until smooth. Add the dissolved unflavored gelatin and stir until smooth. Stir in ³/₄ cup of the vinegar, the sugar if using, and the salt.

2. Now taste, and add either the remaining ¹/₄ cup vinegar (if you'd like it more tart), ¹/₄ cup water (if it's just about right), or ¹/₄ cup of the reserved pineapple juice (if you'd like it sweeter). Chill until thickened (drawing a spoon through the gelatin leaves a definite impression), about 3 hours (start checking after 2).

3. Lightly grease a 6-cup mold with vegetable cooking spray.

4. Stir the cucumbers, scallions, and crushed pineapple, if using, into the thickened gelatin. Pour the mixture into the prepared mold and refrigerate until set, at least 3 hours or overnight.

5. Unmold (see page 59) and serve with fish.

sweet dill pickles

from Ilo Riebe

For Ilo's famous crunchy pickles, an old family recipe, she uses the tiniest cucumbers, which her husband, Wilmer, had developed over the years, cultivating a hybrid from a hybrid of his own plants. Good luck finding them! They are our favorite of Ilo's garden creations. We fight over the smallest ones, which are under an inch long. **MAKES 5 QUARTS** **P**

¹/₂ cup salt

1¹/₂ cups sugar

2¹/₂ cups distilled white vinegar

10 sprigs fresh dill

About 10 pounds small pickling cucumbers

5 cloves garlic

1. Pour 5 cups water into a large saucepan and stir in the salt, sugar, and vinegar. Bring to a boil.

2. Place 1 dill sprig in the bottom of each of 5 sterile hot quart canning jars. Divide the pickles among the jars, and pour the hot brine over them. Top each jar with another dill sprig. Add 1 garlic clove to each jar, and then seal according to the manufacturer's directions.

> *Dear Judy,*
>
> *The garden is all in again. Yes, we grow our own cucumbers, dill, and garlic. The weather has been so cold here. I have tomato plants that are over two feet tall. They want ground, but it's been too cold to set them out as yet. I plant them from seed into pots. Wilmer has planted peas, onions, cucumbers, corn, beets, and radishes in the garden.*
>
> *I sure enjoyed Passover that one year at your house and I sure would like to come again.*
>
> *Love, Ilo*

esrog eingemacht
from Gershon Padwa

● ● ● ● ●

Some years ago, a young man in Antwerp, Belgium, e-mailed me after finding my name on www.jewishgen.org, requesting information about the Padwa family (my husband Barry's Grandma Rose's illustrious ancestry, which can trace its roots all the way back to the great rabbi Rashi—we're talking the 11th century here!). From the first e-mail I could tell that he was ultra-Orthodox and knew that he would be especially thrilled to receive the nine pages of genealogical charts I had of his family. (It turned out that his great-great-grandmother and Barry's great-great-grandfather were sister and brother.) Through the years, with many e-mails across the ocean, we have shared recipes, delighted in each other's *simchas*, and developed a treasured friendship. Gershon sends me pictures of his beautiful family—including his wife, Ruchi (see her Rosh Hashanah Honey Cookies, page 484), and at last count 12 children—and has immeasurably enriched my knowledge of Jewish customs and lore.

Eingemacht loosely means "worked in" in Yiddish and refers to a mixture that is tossed all together (see Beet Eingemacht, page 546). The esrog (citron) looks like a large lemon and is used on Sukkot, the Jewish Thanksgiving, along with the lulov (palm branch) for a special blessing and ceremony.

Gershon and Ruchi Padwa, with their kids, at son Tulli's Bar Mitzvah, 2004 (baby Malki came later).

From: Gershon Padwa
To: judy@cookingjewish.com
Date: Wednesday, January 7, 2004 10:04 a.m.
Subject: Esrog Eingemacht

Hello Judy—

You asked about the esrog eingemacht. My father always told us that his grandmother, who was from a very famous family (she was a granddaughter of the Belzer rebbe and of the Dizertchover rebbe) used to make esrog eingemacht, and every Shabbos after Kiddush she used to eat a spoonful of it and I do it too.

First one takes the esrog from Succos, and then one searches in the neighborhood for anybody who doesn't need theirs. (I also have one or two that I hang up in my succah.) The esrogim are then soaked for four weeks in water, and every day the water has to be changed. After that you slice the fruit into thin slices and bring them to a boil five times in plain water, changing the water each time. Once that is done, you put the slices into a pot with sliced apple equal in amount to the esrog and water, so that everything is generously covered. Then add enough sugar so that the water is really syrupy and a tablespoon of vanilla sugar for each sliced esrog. You leave it on a slow flame for a few hours. (You have to taste it the whole time and add sugar if it is too bitter. It will be, trust me.) Turn it off when the apple is completely unrecognizable and the esrog is soft but not falling to pieces.

This gets eaten the first time on Tu b'shvat [literally, the fifteenth of the month of Shevat, celebrated as the new year for trees], and then, as I said, the rest gets eaten by the spoonful once a week, Shabbos by kiddush. Hope that helps.

Bye,
Gershon

sun dills

from My G&R Family

hen I decided to self-publish *Melting Pot Memories* for my family, I selected G&R Publishing. Through the years, over the course of eight printings, Kathi Dana and her wonderful staff became family to me, holding my hand through many changes, tolerating my obsessiveness with humor and patience, and generally doing their darnedest to please me. Kathi and I became friends as we exchanged recipes and commiserated on the challenges of long-distance grandparenting. Her dill pickles, made without vinegar, have become my family's favorite. Four days in the summer sun in Southern California produces an all-sour dill you'd swear came out of a New York deli barrel. Taste and adjust for your own climate. **MAKES 1 GALLON** Ⓟ

About 4 pounds kirby cucumbers

1 medium-size onion, cut into ¹/₄-inch-thick slices

1 to 2 bunches fresh dill sprigs (1 to 2 cups)

6 cloves garlic, large ones cut in half

1 or 2 dried red chile peppers (optional)

6 tablespoons kosher (coarse) salt (see Note)

1 thick slice rye bread

1. Pack the cucumbers, onion slices, dill, garlic, and chile pepper, if using, in a gallon glass jar, distributing the vegetables and flavorings throughout.

2. Combine the salt and about 2 cups water in a bowl or large measuring cup, and stir until the salt has dissolved. Pour this into the jar. Fill the jar with water.

3. Wrap the rye bread in cheesecloth and place it on top, making sure the bread is completely submerged. Cover the jar with plastic wrap. Set a plastic lid on top, and place a rock on it (to keep the bugs out). Leave the jar in the sun for 4 days.

4. Squeeze the bread and remove it. Store the pickles, in the jar, in the refrigerator. They will stay crisp for 3 to 4 weeks if

can-can, anyone?

kay, I'll admit it: I don't can, won't can, refuse to can. If you do, I respect you, admire you, will even eat your home-canned goodies. It's me I don't trust! If I screw up a recipe, all you'll get is a lousy meal. But if I screw up the canning . . . sorry, I have enough guilt in my life. I'm not discouraging you from trying; it's just not for me. (That is not to say I won't make pickles, however. A jar is in my fridge as we speak. Mine just has a shorter shelf life.)

People have been "putting up" pickles, jams, peaches, and the like for centuries. Trouble is, some of the recipes are centuries old too—not just the ingredients, but the method as well. The National Center for Home Food Preservation tells me that instructions and warnings have changed recently. The latest information is included with the seals sold for canning, but no one who has been canning for years ever reads them. Whether you're an experienced canner or a novice, please read the instructions or send for the latest USDA "Complete Guide to Home Canning."

sliced, at least 2 months if unsliced. After that, they will start to soften.

Note: Do not use iodized salt for pickles and preserved vegetables, which may discolor them and make them mushy.

pickled peppers
from Estelle Robbins

Don't know about Peter Piper, but Aunt Estelle made a mean pickled pepper. These tickle-your-tongue sweet-and-sour beauties in a rainbow of colors pick up your spirits just to look at them, not to mention what they do for your sandwich. **MAKES 4 PINTS** Ⓟ

3 pounds (about 6 large) green, red, orange,
    yellow, purple, or any color bell peppers
2¹/₂ cups distilled white vinegar
1¹/₄ cups sugar
1 tablespoon pickling spices, wrapped in a
    cheesecloth bundle
8 cloves garlic
4 teaspoons vegetable oil
2 teaspoons kosher (coarse) salt

1. Stem and seed the peppers, removing all the white membranes. Cut the peppers into ¹/₂- to ³/₄-inch-wide strips. Set them aside.

2. Pour 2¹/₂ cups water into a large saucepan. Add the vinegar, sugar, and pickling spices, and bring to a boil. Reduce the

> *Aunt Estelle was like a second mother to me. She and my mother were inseparable and were always sewing together—for themselves, for Mama Hinda, and for cousin Joyce and me. If we got fresh, we'd get it in stereo. As she'd be fitting me, Aunt Estelle would threaten (pins hanging out of the side of her mouth, which amazingly she never swallowed), 'Judy, if you don't watch out, I'll put the bust in the back!'*
> **—JUDY BART KANCIGOR**

Aunt Estelle, my mom (Lillian), and Aunt Sally on holiday in the Catskills.

heat and simmer, covered, for 5 minutes. Add the peppers and bring the water back to a boil. Reduce the heat and simmer for another minute or so, just to slightly wilt the peppers.

3. Pack the peppers, with the vinegar solution, in 4 clean 1-pint canning jars, adding 2 garlic cloves, 1 teaspoon oil, and ¹/₂ teaspoon salt to each. (Discard the spice bundle.) Cover the jars and refrigerate. The peppers will be ready in about 5 days—although I have to admit I start nibbling in about 3—and will last 2 to 3 weeks in the refrigerator.

Note: To seal the peppers in the jars for a longer shelf life, use only sterile hot jars. Pour the hot vinegar mixture over the peppers to within $1/2$ inch of the top, covering the peppers completely, cap the jars, and process according to the manufacturer's instructions.

pickled beets

from Ilo Riebe

I have never had a green thumb. Plants have been known to expire in paroxysms of dread in the arms of guests at my front door, rather than face the inevitable prospect of a slow, torturous demise under my care. So I gasp with awe at those who pick their salad from their own backyard while mine is picked from a grocer's stall. My daughter-in-law Shelly's grandma Ilo, the consummate gardener, couldn't tell us how many pounds of beets to buy for her wonderful pickled beets because if she needs more, she just goes out back and digs them up. **MAKES 6 PINTS** P

About 6 pounds fresh beets, weighed with greens
3 cups distilled white vinegar
2 cups sugar
*2 tablespoons pickling spices, tied in a
   cheesecloth bundle*

1. Wash the beets thoroughly and trim the tops to within 3 inches. Do not trim the roots. Place the beets in a large pot and add water to cover. Bring to a boil and cook until tender, 20 minutes to 1 hour, depending on their size. As they are done, remove the beets with a slotted spoon and set them aside to cool. When they are cool enough to handle, slip off the skins. Slice or dice the beets.

2. Meanwhile, bring the vinegar, sugar, 1 cup water, and the pickling spices to a boil in a medium-size saucepan. Reduce the heat and simmer, covered, for about 15 minutes. Remove the pickling spices.

3. Pack the beets into 6 sterile hot 1-pint canning jars. Pour the hot vinegar mixture over them to within $1/2$ inch of the top, covering the beets completely, cap the jars, and process according to the manufacturer's directions.

the too hot tamales cranberry salsa

from Judy Bart Kancigor

For years at Thanksgiving I experimented with different cranberry sauce recipes, only to hear from my family, "Why can't you just buy that jellied stuff in the can?" That is, until I stumbled upon this zippy salsa from Mary Sue Milliken and Susan Feniger, which I found in a brochure at a Whole Foods market. With some adaptation, it has been my Thanksgiving staple ever since. While the Too Hot Tamales, as they were known on the Food Network, prefer to use the cranberries raw, I cook them, so my version is really a cross between a salsa and cranberry sauce.

Before I mix in the cilantro, I set aside a little dish of the salsa for my mother, who can't stand the herb. I've read that for some people who lack a certain enzyme, cilantro tastes like soap. Thank heavens I inherited that enzyme from my father, because I could bathe in the stuff. I buy it weekly and chop it into every salad I eat.

MAKES ABOUT 5 CUPS   P

1 cup sugar

1 pound fresh cranberries

3 Granny Smith apples, peeled and diced

3 oranges, seeded and diced

2 teaspoons grated orange zest

1 bunch cilantro, chopped (¹/2 cup)

4 serrano chiles, seeded and diced

1 bunch (6 to 8) scallions, white part only, chopped

1. Combine the sugar and 1 cup water in a medium-size saucepan, and stir to dissolve the sugar. Add the cranberries and bring to a boil. Reduce the heat and boil gently until the berries pop open and most of the liquid has evaporated, 5 to 10 minutes. Using a spoon, smash any unpopped berries against the side of the pan. Remove the pan from the heat and allow to cool for 30 minutes.

2. Combine the cooled cranberries with all the remaining ingredients in a large bowl, and toss to mix. This salsa can be prepared 6 to 8 hours in advance and refrigerated, but serve it at room temperature.

almond cranberry sauce

from Phyllis Epstein

Every family has a favorite cranberry sauce to look forward to for Thanksgiving. This is signature Epstein fare: Cranberries team up with pineapple and mandarin oranges with a jolt of amaretto. Almonds and Italian cookies give it a surprise crunch. **MAKES AT LEAST 4 CUPS**   P

1 can (16 ounces) whole-berry cranberry sauce

1 cup applesauce

1 can (11 ounces) mandarin oranges, chopped and well drained on paper towels

1 can (8 ounces) pineapple tidbits or crushed pineapple, well drained on paper towels

3 tablespoons Amaretto liqueur

1 tablespoon pure almond extract

1 to 2 pinches salt, or to taste

³/4 cup slivered almonds, toasted (see box, page 17) and chopped

³/4 cup finely crushed amaretti or other hard almond-flavored cookies, such as biscotti

> When I married Peter and first started cooking, he taught me that everything on the plate should have a different flavor. You don't just put, say, garlic on everything (like my mother did! Her only flavorings were garlic powder, onion powder, paprika, and G. Washington Beef Broth, and she used them on everything, bless her soul). So carrots may have dill, another vegetable will have thyme—every accompaniment will have a different flavor. I love almonds, and my Almond Cranberry Sauce more than satisfies my almond flavor quota for Thanksgiving. But in deference to Peter, there wouldn't be almonds in anything else on the plate.
> **—PHYLLIS EPSTEIN**

1. Mix the cranberry sauce, applesauce, mandarin oranges, pineapple, Amaretto, almond extract, and salt in a bowl. (The mixture can be made a day ahead up to this point.) Cover and refrigerate until ready to serve.

2. Immediately before serving, stir in the almonds and cookie crumbs.

Relaxing at the beach is not quite the same for Jessica and Josh since Hayden has come along.

roasted corn and mango salsa

from Jessica Levine Levy

Lazy afternoons in the Hamptons bring my niece Jessica, husband Josh, and any number of friends into the kitchen, where everyone throws something into the pot. Sometimes the results are stupendous; sometimes it's tossed and they head for town to eat. This salsa was one of their more successful creations. Thank goodness someone was taking notes. **MAKES ABOUT 6½ CUPS** **P**

4 ears corn (preferably speckled), shucked
2 tablespoons olive oil
1 can (about 15 ounces) black beans, drained and rinsed
½ cup chopped red onion
1 red bell pepper, stemmed, seeded, and chopped
2 mangos, diced
1 bunch cilantro, chopped (½ cup)
¼ cup balsamic vinegar
1 teaspoon salt, or to taste
Freshly ground black pepper to taste

1. Preheat the oven to 500°F, or preheat a barbecue grill to high.

2. Brush the corn with the olive oil (or use your hands), and place the ears in a bak-

ing pan. Roast in the oven, turning the ears occasionally, until they are browned on all sides, about 20 minutes. (Alternatively, roast the ears on the grill for about 10 minutes.) Allow the roasted corn to cool.

3. When it is cool enough to handle, slice the kernels off the cobs with a sharp knife. Mix the kernels with all the remaining ingredients in a large bowl. Allow the salsa to stand for at least 1 hour before serving. (It is best eaten the day it is made.) Serve at room temperature.

pear compote

from Tracey Barrett

The second best thing about visiting "the kids" in Northern California (okay, a very pale second to the joy the grandkids give us) is shopping at Draeger's, which to call it a supermarket is like calling Tiffany's a trinket store. Tracey adapted this recipe from one she got at a cooking class that she took with award-winning chef Scott Giambastiani of Draeger's fine restaurant, Viognier. More a chutney than a compote, this savory yet sweet mixture pairs well with chicken, turkey, or duck. **MAKES ABOUT 3 CUPS**
P or **D**

2 tablespoons nondairy margarine or butter
$^1/_4$ cup finely chopped shallots (about 3 large)
$^1/_4$ cup cider vinegar

$^1/_4$ cup sugar
1 tablespoon minced ginger
1 tablespoon yellow mustard seeds
Pinch of red pepper flakes
Pinch of salt
2 pounds ripe Bartlett pears, peeled, cored, quartered, and thinly sliced crosswise
$^2/_3$ cup golden raisins (4 ounces)

1. Melt the margarine in a medium-size saucepan over medium heat. Add the shallots and cook, stirring often, until the shallots are soft and translucent, 2 to 3 minutes.

2. Add the vinegar, sugar, ginger, mustard seeds, pepper flakes, and salt, and stir to dissolve the sugar. Bring to a boil over medium-high heat and add the pears. Reduce the heat to a gentle boil and cook uncovered, stirring often, until the pears are quite soft and the pungent vinegar loses some of its "kick," about 30 minutes. If the mixture starts to become too concentrated, cover the pan while cooking. Serve chilled or at room temperature. The compote will keep frozen for 3 months.

Brad and Tracey. Who doesn't love a cook?

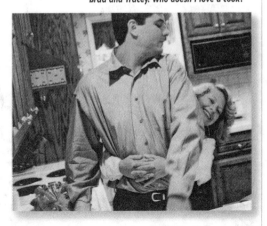

let's dance!

meats

In the 1980s a diminutive octogenarian named Clara Peller made advertising history with three words: "Where's the beef?" A century earlier any shtetl dweller could have come up with the same one-liner.

For the impoverished peasants of Eastern Europe, meat was an infrequent luxury. Little wonder that after coming to America and achieving success, first-generation Jews in that pre-cholesterol-conscious era reveled in the land of plenty and embraced their hard-won briskets and chops.

When I was growing up, every dinner plate held the holy triumvirate: meat, starch, vegetable. Okay, maybe we'd have chicken once in a while, but my dad was a carnivore.

"Brisket recipes abound."

At every simcha toes are tappin'. Who's who on page 613.

When he was in town, meat was a given. Only when he was traveling did my mother change the menu to something more exotic: salad with canned salmon, fish chowder, or, our personal favorite, salami and eggs.

For company my mother had a single menu: roast beef, new potatoes, and her colorful mélange of steamed fresh vegetables. She didn't do anything special to the roast except buy the best—that is, if you don't count her uncanny ability to time the thing perfectly. To this day, she has only to feel the weight of the roast in her hand and she can tell you, to the minute, exactly how long to cook it. I prefer Gracie Allen's method: Take one large roast beef and one small roast beef and put them in the oven. When the little one burns, the big one is done.

My son Brad makes the roasts in our family now. When he and Tracey do the holidays, we've come to expect his signature Roast Beef with Cabernet Reduction. (The propensity must have skipped a generation. When you're married to someone who prefers his meat burnt, you tend to braise.)

Because kosher cuts of meat come from the fore section of the animal and not from the more tender (and more expensive) rear, most Jewish recipes favor slow cooking, which tenderizes the meat and makes it succulent, infusing delicious flavors along with the braising liquid. Brisket recipes abound, and

every family has a favorite. Four made the cut for this chapter: my mother-in-law Edie's Pot Roast (my husband's favorite), a zippy Russian brisket with red potatoes, Abbe's Easy Brisket for Every Holiday (and we do mean easy), and Veal Brisket from Marilyn Dubin.

When it comes to slow cooking, no dish has a longer history or more exemplifies Jewish cooking than cholent, the Sabbath stew mentioned in the Talmud. Because Jews are not permitted to cook on the Sabbath, this mixture of meat, grains, potatoes, and/or vegetables is started before sundown on Friday and served for lunch after shul. Back in the shtetl the dish would be brought to a communal oven to be cooked. Every Jewish community has a version—in fact, it is believed that the French cassoulet was derived from this early recipe, one of the few foods that can truly be called Jewish. You'll find two favorites here.

Above: My mother-in-law, Edith, cooking with daughter Debbie, 1970s. Suzy Solomonic preparing for Shabbat dinner. Left: Brad checking on Mom and me. Opposite: David Miller (Vicki's husband), the family grill guy.

flavolin: a spicy story

Peter Epstein, our family spice king, tells a harrowing tale of the birth of First Spice. His parents, Felix and Trude Epstein, escaped Germany with his four-year-old sister, literally as the door was closing behind them. They sojourned for a year in Holland while awaiting a visa (learning English while they were there), and after bribing a secretary with a box of chocolates, boarded the last ship to leave Holland for America, Trude five months pregnant with Peter.

In Germany Felix had worked for Raps & Co. Kulmbach, a pharmaceutical house that also sold herbs. Spices were a natural outgrowth, and Felix had become their leading salesman, generating 2,000 accounts. Once safely in New York, he found a job selling waxed paper to butchers, many of whom were German and welcomed a compatriot. He soon began selling them spices as well, creating mixtures at night in the bathtub of the family's Washington Heights apartment. At one point, when Felix needed $50 to pay the rent, he offered cousin Axel's father, David Orlow, a 50 percent partnership in return. "Here's the fifty dollars," said David, "but no thanks. I didn't come to America to stand in a kitchen mixing spices!"

Through trial and error Felix modified the formulas to suit American taste and standards of uniformity and sterility. Flavolin, a flavor enhancer, evolved as the signature seasoning of First Spice, and the rest, as they say, is history. Oh, you want the recipe? Sorry, it's a trade secret!

Today First Spice, with offices in New York, San Francisco, and Toronto, does research and development for food processing companies as well as selling them ingredients for manufacture. Now the third generation of Epsteins has joined the company: Vicki is vice-president, Marcy is director of R&D, and Wendy is legal counsel.

Stuffed cabbage, whether served as a main dish or an appetizer, typifies Eastern European cooking and has been a favorite for generations. Aunt Sally elevated its preparation to an art form, but if you're pressed for time, try Aunt Irene's Easy "Unstuffed" Cabbage or cousin Bonnie's Easier Still version.

In this chapter you'll find slow-cooked stews from around the world: Beef Gulyas with sauerkraut from Hungary; Lamb Stew with Prunes and Moroccan Spicy Apricot Lamb Shanks from the Mediterranean; Italian dishes such as a succulent veal roast, a meat loaf scented with lemon and parsley, Osso Buco, Veal Marengo, cousin Eric's grand concoction of meatballs, sausage, and chicken, and several mouth-watering pasta sauces; as well as good ole' American finger-lickin' ribs, roasted or barbecued, three in all.

From Italian Meat Loaf to Hazelnut-Crusted Rack of Lamb, for family meals or elegant company dinners, here's the beef (and the lamb and the veal . . .).

roast beef
with cabernet reduction

from Brad Kancigor

y son Brad handles holiday dinners with flair. His favorite (and
ours) is his celebratory roast
smothered in a deep, rich wine reduction.
In selecting a wine, the old adage applies:
If you wouldn't drink it, don't use it.

SERVES 8 TO 10   **M**

3 to 4 tablespoons olive oil

1 large onion, chopped

6 large shallots, chopped

2 large cloves garlic, finely chopped

3$^{1}/_{2}$ cups beef broth (see box, page 137)

1$^{1}/_{2}$ cups Cabernet Sauvignon

1 bouquet garni (see Note)

1 tablespoon tomato paste

1 tablespoon Dijon mustard

1 boneless beef roast (4 to 5 pounds)

Kosher (coarse) salt and freshly
   ground black pepper to taste

1 tablespoon nondairy margarine

1 tablespoon all-purpose flour

1. Heat 3 tablespoons of the oil in
a large skillet over medium-high heat. Add
the onion and shallots and cook, stirring
constantly, until they are very soft and
golden, about 9 minutes. Add the garlic and
continue cooking, stirring constantly, for 1
minute. Remove the skillet from the heat,
and using a slotted spoon, transfer the veg-

etables to a bowl. Set it aside. No need to
wash the skillet.

2. Combine the broth, Cabernet, and
bouquet garni in a medium-size saucepan
over medium-high heat, and bring to a boil.
Cook until the mixture is reduced by half, 25
to 30 minutes. Remove the pan from the heat.
Discard the bouquet garni, and whisk in the
tomato paste and mustard. Set the Cabernet
reduction aside.

3. Meanwhile, preheat the oven to
375°F.

4. Pat the beef dry with paper towels, and
sprinkle salt and pepper all over it. Place the
large skillet over medium-high heat. If there
is a layer of fat on the beef, do not add more
olive oil to the skillet. If there is no fat on the
beef, add the remaining 1 tablespoon oil. Add
the beef to the skillet and brown it on all sides
(fat side first, if there is one), 6 to 8 minutes.

5. Transfer the beef to a roasting pan.
Add about $^{1}/_{4}$ cup of the Cabernet reduction
to the skillet and deglaze it over medium heat,
scraping up any browned bits. Pour this mixture back into the remaining reduction and
set it aside again. Don't wash that skillet yet.

6. Roast the beef until a meat thermometer inserted in the center reads 125°F for
rare or 130° to 135°F for medium-rare, 50 to
75 minutes, depending on the shape of the
roast. Remove the roast from the pan, cover
it loosely with aluminum foil, and allow it to
rest for 10 minutes before carving.

7. Meanwhile, remove as much fat from
the roasting pan as you can, with either a
spoon or a fat separator. Place the roasting
pan over medium-high heat (you may want to
use two burners), and add about $^{1}/_{2}$ cup of the

Cabernet reduction. Deglaze the pan, scraping up any browned bits. Return this mixture to the remaining Cabernet reduction.

8. Melt the margarine in the large skillet over medium-high heat. Whisk in the flour until completely incorporated. Gradually add the Cabernet reduction and the reserved onion mixture, and simmer until the sauce thickens, about 2 minutes. Add salt and pepper to taste.

9. To serve, spoon some sauce on each plate, top with a slice of beef, and pass the remaining sauce. (Okay, *now* you can wash that skillet!)

Note: To prepare the bouquet garni, tie 4 large sprigs parsley, 3 sprigs thyme, 2 sprigs rosemary, 1 bay leaf, and 3 black peppercorns in a square of cheesecloth, forming a packet.

chinese pepper steak

from Marcy Epstein

This was one of Marcy's favorite meat dishes when she was growing up, especially for its sweet, peppery smells and flavors. Her mom (Phyllis) prepared it often upon request, she says, and added a lot of fresh and colorful vegetables. Have all your ingredients chopped and ready before you begin to stir-fry.

SERVES 4 TO 6　　　　M

peeling tomatoes

To peel tomatoes: Fill a bowl with ice water and set it aside. Bring a medium-size pot of water to a boil. Using a slotted spoon, plunge the tomatoes, one at a time, into the boiling water and hold them there for 5 to 10 seconds—just until the skin loosens a bit. Remove the tomatoes from the water and plunge them into the ice bath. When they have cooled a bit, remove the stems and slip off the skin.

2 tablespoons olive oil

12 ounces button mushrooms, sliced

1 clove garlic, crushed

1 teaspoon grated fresh ginger

1 teaspoon kosher (coarse) salt

$^1/_2$ teaspoon freshly ground black pepper

$^1/_2$ to 1 teaspoon paprika

1 pound beef flank steak, cut into thin diagonal slices (see Note)

$^1/_4$ cup reduced-sodium soy sauce

$^1/_2$ teaspoon sugar

2 cups fresh bean sprouts

2 medium-size tomatoes, peeled (see box above), seeded, and coarsely chopped

2 green or red bell peppers, stemmed, seeded, and cut into $^1/_2$-inch-wide slices

$^1/_2$ cup slivered almonds, toasted (see box, page 17)

1 tablespoon cornstarch mixed with 2 tablespoons cold water

Hot steamed rice, for serving

3 scallions (white part only), thinly sliced

1. Heat the oil in a large skillet over medium heat. Add the mushrooms, garlic, ginger, salt, and pepper, and cook until the

mushrooms are tender, about 10 minutes. Using a slotted spoon, transfer the mushroom mixture to a plate. Raise the heat under the skillet to medium high.

2. Sprinkle the paprika over the meat slices, add them to the skillet, and sauté until lightly browned, 1 to 2 minutes. Then reduce the heat to medium and add the soy sauce and sugar. Cook, covered, until the meat is cooked through, about 2 minutes. Remove the meat and cover to keep it warm.

3. Add the bean sprouts, tomatoes, and peppers to the skillet. Raise the heat to medium high, cover, and cook for 3 minutes. Then return the meat and the mushrooms to the skillet, and stir in the almonds and the cornstarch mixture. Cook, stirring, until the sauce thickens, about 1 minute.

4. Serve over steamed rice, sprinkled with the scallions.

Note: Kosher "flank steak" is cut from the shoulder. Putting it in the freezer for 15 minutes makes it easier to cut it into thin slices.

edie's pot roast

from Edith Kancigor

This is it: Barry's favorite pot roast. No one makes it like my mother-in-law! When she would come to California for a visit, he would beg me, "Watch her!" I would buy the same meat I always use, and Edie would prepare it using my pot (my own mother's Magnalite), and it would be perfect. Yet when I'd try to duplicate it, I would come really close but never quite attain her signature rich, brown crust. The secret, she says, is in the browning. Maybe she has a more loving touch. No one but Barry has ever noticed the difference, however, and this hearty meal, prepared with the most mundane of ingredients, is unbeatable. Because the meat is sliced at midpoint and finishes cooking in the gravy, every piece is tender and moist and doesn't fall apart when sliced. Note that pot roast always tastes best the next day. Cook the meat on day 1, the potatoes on day 2. **SERVES 4 TO 6** Ⓜ

3 to 3¹/₂ pounds top of the rib or first-cut beef brisket (see Notes)
About 5 cups boiling water (see Notes)
1 tablespoon vegetable oil
1 large onion, chopped
1 large clove garlic, crushed, or a liberal sprinkling of garlic powder
1 envelope dehydrated onion soup mix
Kosher (coarse) salt and freshly ground black pepper to taste
3 medium-size russet potatoes, peeled and cut into ¹/₂-inch chunks

1. Pat the meat dry with paper towels. (Wet meat will not brown properly.)

2. Have the boiling water ready.

3. Heat the oil in a Dutch oven or other large, heavy pot over medium heat. Add the meat and sear it on all sides for 5 minutes per side. Raise the heat to medium-high and keep turning and searing, almost burning the

meat, for 15 to 20 minutes more, adding up to 1¹/₂ cups boiling water little by little as necessary to keep it from sticking. (If the water is not boiling, it will cool off the meat, and it won't brown properly; see Notes.) The meat will exude juices during this process. When the meat is thoroughly browned, remove it from the pot and set it aside. Stir the onion and garlic into the juices in the pot. Reduce the heat to medium and cook until the onion is soft, about 5 minutes.

4. Return the meat to the pot, and add enough boiling water to barely cover (about 3 cups). Stir in the onion soup mix and simmer, covered, for 1³/₄ to 2 hours; the meat should be not quite done (firm but getting there). Add salt and pepper if needed.

5. Transfer the meat to a cutting board and allow it to cool slightly. Remove all visible fat, and cut the meat into ¹/₂-inch-thick slices. Return the sliced meat to the pot and simmer, covered, until tender, about 1 hour.

6. Refrigerate the meat, in its juices, overnight.

7. The next day, remove any congealed fat from the meat and juices. Place the potatoes and the juices in a Dutch oven or other large, heavy pot. Add only enough water to make enough gravy. Cover the pot and simmer until the potatoes can be pierced with a skewer (so as not to break them), about 20 minutes. Add salt and pepper to taste.

8. Carefully return the sliced meat to the pot and simmer until it is hot, about 5 minutes more.

My mother-in-law, Edie, in my kitchen, her signature pot roast in my mother's Magnalite pot (right), about 1992.

9. Serve the pot roast hot, with the potatoes, spooning the gravy over the meat. (The leftovers make a great sandwich, hot or cold, the next day.)

Notes: Edie's preference for this dish is top of the rib, a cut that is not available in all parts of the country. Brisket is second best.

You probably won't use all 1¹/₂ cups boiling water for the browning, but have it ready. Keep reheating it in a saucepan or the microwave, if necessary, so it is always very hot.

gramma sera fritkin's russian brisket

from Michelle Gullion

Brisket is a cut of beef requiring slow cooking; pot roast is what you make with it (or with other cuts). What makes this version Russian is unclear (I doubt they had chili sauce in Minsk!). Here brisket is marinated in lemon juice, which tenderizes it and provides the tart backdrop for the sweet and tangy chili sauce that comes later. **SERVES 8 TO 10**

Ⓜ

About 4^1/$_2$ pounds first-cut beef brisket

Juice of 6 lemons

Freshly ground black pepper to taste

Garlic powder to taste

2 envelopes dehydrated onion soup mix

3 tablespoons dark or light brown sugar

1 bottle (12 ounces) chili sauce, such as Heinz

1 head garlic, cloves separated and peeled

About 2 pounds very small red potatoes

1. Place the brisket in a large glass baking dish or in a resealable plastic bag, and add the lemon juice. Cover the dish with plastic wrap or seal the bag, and marinate, turning the meat occasionally, in the refrigerator for 24 hours.

2. Preheat the oven to 350°F.

3. Rinse the lemon juice from the meat, and sprinkle both sides of the meat liberally with pepper and garlic powder. Place the brisket, fat side up, in a large roasting pan.

4. Pour water to a depth of about 1 inch around the meat, and sprinkle 1 envelope of the onion soup mix, brown sugar, three fourths of the chili sauce, and the garlic over the meat. Cover the pan tightly with aluminum foil and roast for 2^1/$_2$ hours.

5. Add ^{1}/$_2$ cup water to the remaining chili sauce in the jar, shake, and stir this mixture into the liquid in the roasting pan. Add some of the remaining soup mix to taste. Add the potatoes and baste with the liquid. Roast, uncovered, until the potatoes are fork-tender and caramelized, 1 hour. The liquid will reduce to a rich, caramelized sauce. If it becomes too thick, stir in hot water, ^{1}/$_4$ cup at a time, until it reaches the desired consistency.

6. Remove the meat from the pan, slice it diagonally across the grain, and serve with the potatoes and sauce.

easy brisket for every holiday

from Abbe Dubin

Cousin Neil heads up a harem: He and his wife, Abbe, have three daughters—Amanda, Colby, and Taylor. Even the two Maltese are females. Yet a man's gotta eat what a man's gotta eat, and the ladies (not to mention the very spoiled dogs!) love this hearty dish—as do their guests, who never num-

" Some of my dearest memories of my Gramma [Sara Fritkin, in photo] surround the Passovers at her small apartment. We could smell the aroma of her brisket all the way down the hall. How her face would light up when she saw I had brought friends! To this day there is always room at her table for one more. **—MICHELLE GULLION** "

ber less than thirty for holiday meals. And what could be easier than this brisket, especially since it's prepared a day ahead. According to Neil, it's best served with kasha (see page 316). **SERVES 8 TO 10** Ⓜ

4 to 5 pounds first-cut beef brisket

¹/₂ cup ketchup

1 envelope dehydrated onion soup mix

6 ounces (¹/₂ can) Coca-Cola

1. Preheat the oven to 375°F.

2. Place the brisket, fat side down, in a 13 × 9-inch baking pan (or one large enough to hold it) and add water to a depth of about 1 inch. Spread the ketchup evenly over the meat, using a spatula or a spoon. Sprinkle the soup mix over the ketchup, and use the spatula or spoon to press it into the ketchup. Pour the Coca-Cola around the meat. Cover the pan tightly with aluminum foil.

3. Bake until tender. The time will vary according to the thickness of the meat and your preference: Start checking after 2¹/₂ hours. Three to 3¹/₂ hours usually does it for me, although Abbe's family likes it really falling apart, and she's been known to cook it for as long as 5 hours. (I like to remove the foil and roast the brisket uncovered for the last 20 minutes or so.)

4. Remove the pan from the oven and allow to cool. Then transfer the brisket and sauce to a nonreactive dish or container, cover, and refrigerate.

5. The next day, remove and discard the fat that has congealed on top of the sauce as well as the layer of fat on the meat. Slice the meat against the grain. Strain the sauce. Arrange the meat in a Dutch oven or other large, heavy pot, add the gravy, and simmer until hot.

6. Serve hot, passing any extra gravy in a sauceboat.

grandma ruchel strausser's cholent

from Isabelle Frankel

I f we called it cassoulet, would you try it? Cholent was created by observant Jews, who are forbidden to cook on the Sabbath. Started before sundown on Friday, it is ready for lunch on Shabbos. Ironically, this dish—which was designed so mothers would *not* work—can actually help today's *working* mothers serve a hearty dinner by working its own magic in a slow cooker in the same eight hours they are out of the house.

Any fresh vegetable, grain, and/or beans can be added to cholent; any meat, chicken, or none at all. "Use your imagination!" instructed my Aunt Isabelle, who was still making her mother's (my Grandma Ruchel's) cholent when she was in her eighties. My friend Linda Nelson says her own Russian Grandma Ruchel (Rudman) made cholent with flanken, lots of garlic, onions, and yellow butter beans and cooked it until it was thick enough to spread on challah, which is how they used to eat it. **SERVES AN ARMY** Ⓜ

³/₄ *cup dried baby lima beans, rinsed and*
   picked over
³/₄ *cup dried kidney beans, rinsed and*
   picked over
³/₄ *cup dried yellow split peas, rinsed and*
   picked over
³/₄ *cup dried lentils, rinsed and picked over*
4 *pounds beef flanken or brisket, or*
   a combination
2 *large onions, chopped*
3 *medium-size (about 1 pound) russet potatoes,*
   peeled and cut into 1-inch cubes
2 *cloves garlic, crushed*
1 *tablespoon kosher (coarse) salt, or to taste*
1 *teaspoon good-quality paprika*
¹/₂ *teaspoon freshly ground black pepper,*
   or to taste
2 *cups dry red wine*

1. Combine the lima beans and kidney beans in a large bowl, and add water to cover (about 4 quarts). Set aside to soak overnight.

2. Preheat the oven to 350°F. Drain and rinse the beans.

3. Combine the beans, split peas, lentils, meat, and all the remaining ingredients in a Dutch oven or other large, heavy, ovenproof pot. Add water to cover. Bake, covered, for 1¹/₂ hours.

4. Reduce the oven temperature to 250°F and continue cooking, covered, for 10 to 24 hours. (The longer it cooks, the thicker the mixture will be.) An hour or two before serv-ing, check for seasoning and add salt and pepper if needed. If you like a thicker cholent, uncover the pot and finish cooking. If it is too thick, add some water, re-cover the pot, and continue cooking.

5. Spoon the cholent onto plates, and serve.

Some of the Strausser clan (my dad's family) gathered for Brad and Tracey's engagement party, 1994. Front: Marylyn Lamstein, Aunt Isabelle Frankel, Jonathan Lamstein. Rear: Debbie Zimmerman, Shari Nagy, Matthew Lamstein, Ronnie Kaufman, Josh Jacobson, me, Jerry Kraus.

had-to-try-it cholent

from Judy Bart Kancigor

The old shtetl fare is actually making a comeback—cholent cookoffs, like chili cookoffs, are springing up all over the country. I listened to Aunt Isabelle and used my imagination (or rather, used what I had in the house) for this version. I thin the leftovers with some beef stock to make a delicious soup, much to my husband's delight. **SERVES SAME ARMY, DIFFERENT REGIMENT**　M

2 to 3 pounds first-cut beef brisket

1 cellophane package (12 ounces) bean
　　soup mix with seasoning packet, such as
　　Manischewitz Four Bean or Hearty Bean

1¹/₄ cups pearled barley, rinsed

5 small potatoes, quartered

2 large onions, chopped

8 ounces baby carrots

2 ribs celery, cut into ¹/₄-inch-thick slices

5 parsnips, cut into ¹/₄-inch-thick slices

10 cloves garlic, sliced

¹/₄ cup chopped flat-leaf parsley

¹/₄ cup prepared barbecue sauce

2 tablespoons honey

3 bay leaves

2 cups dry red wine

Kosher (coarse) salt and freshly ground black
　　pepper to taste

1. Preheat the oven to 350°F.

2. Arrange all the ingredients in a Dutch oven or other large, heavy, ovenproof pot. Add water to cover, cover the pot, and bake for 1¹/₂ hours.

3. Reduce the oven temperature to 250°F and continue cooking, covered, for 10 to 24 hours. (The longer it cooks, the thicker the mixture will be.) An hour or two before serving, check for seasoning and add salt and pepper if needed. If you like a thicker cholent, uncover the pot and finish cooking.

If it is too thick, add some water, re-cover the pot, and continue cooking.

4. Spoon the cholent onto plates, and serve.

beef broth

You can use prepared beef broth in the box (preferred) or in the can in any of the recipes calling for it. To make your own:

Roast meaty beef bones and add them instead of chicken to my mother's Chicken Soup recipe (page 63; the dill is optional). Simmer very gently for 2 to 3 hours. Strain the vegetables as described. Refrigerate overnight; then skim the congealed fat from the surface. Freeze in 1- or 2-cup containers for use in other recipes.

easy boeuf bourguignon

from Claire Altman

After my son Brad tested this recipe, he had two questions: "Who is Claire Altman?"—her husband and my husband are second cousins once removed—and "What other recipes did she give you?" Claire's Boeuf Bourguignon is an easy version of the classic, with all the flavor of the original. In choosing a wine, select one that you would like to drink. The frozen pearl onions are a big time-saver, but go ahead and use fresh mushrooms and potatoes if you prefer. (And Brad does.) **SERVES 6**　　**Ⓜ**

3 to 4 tablespoons olive oil

2 pounds lean beef stew meat, cut into 1-inch
　　cubes, patted dry

3 to 4 medium-size onions, chopped

3 to 4 cloves garlic, crushed

1 shot glass (3 tablespoons) cognac (optional)

2 cups red Burgundy wine

2 tablespoons kosher "bacon" bits

1 tablespoon dried parsley flakes, or
　　2 tablespoons finely chopped flat-leaf
　　parsley

1 teaspoon dried thyme leaves

1 bay leaf

1 1/2 teaspoons kosher (coarse) salt, or to taste

1/4 to 1/2 teaspoon freshly ground black pepper

1 bag (10 ounces) frozen pearl onions,
　　thawed

2 cans (16 ounces each) small peeled
　　potatoes, drained

1 can (7 ounces) whole button mushrooms,
　　drained

2 tablespoons cornstarch

2 tablespoons cold water

1. Heat 2 tablespoons of the oil in a Dutch oven or other large, heavy pot over medium-high heat. Add the beef, in batches, and brown it well on all sides, about 4 minutes per batch. Do not crowd the pot. Remove the beef and set it aside.

2. Add the remaining 1 or 2 tablespoons of oil to the pot, if needed for cooking the onions. Add the chopped onions and cook over medium heat, stirring often, until they are soft and golden, about 7 minutes. Add the garlic and cook for 1 minute more. Then add the cognac, if using. Remove the pot from the heat and, making sure it is away from anything flammable, ignite the cognac, preferably with a long-handled barbecue lighter. (This will burn off most of the alcohol.)

3. Return the pot to the stove and add the beef, wine, "bacon" bits, parsley, thyme, bay leaf, salt, and pepper. Bring to a boil. Then reduce the heat, cover the pot, and simmer, stirring occasionally, until the beef is tender, about 1 1/2 hours. (However, a longer simmering in the wine, say another hour or so, renders it that much more tender and delicious.)

4. Add the pearl onions, potatoes, and mushrooms, and simmer, covered, for 15 minutes.

5. Mix the cornstarch with the cold water, and add this to the sauce (see Notes). Stir until thickened, 1 to 2 minutes (you may not need all of the cornstarch mixture).

6. Spoon the Boeuf Bourguignon onto dinner plates, making sure each person gets some onions, potatoes, and mushrooms along with the meat.

Notes: If you are using fresh mushrooms instead of canned, more of the cornstarch mixture may be needed, because mushrooms exude moisture.

If you are using fresh potatoes, cut 1 1/2 pounds potatoes into 1-inch cubes and add them after the beef has cooked for 1 1/4 hours.

beef and carrot tsimmes

with "gonif" knaidel

from Sally Cohen

W hen Papa Harry came to America, he settled in New York. His brother Jack went to Detroit, and another brother, Louis, landed in St. Louis (both brothers changed their name to Robinson.) Oddly, the three brothers, who looked so much alike, rarely saw each other. When I did my genealogical research in the early 1980s, I found Sally Cohen, a first cousin my mother never even knew she had. Her son Ed told me that Sally had been known as the cook in her family and sent me some of her handwritten recipes.

One of Sally's specialties was her carrot tsimmes, which she would prepare in a pressure cooker, an implement I vowed never to own when, at age nine, I watched my mother scrape liver off the kitchen ceiling. A lot has happened since I was nine. Spacecraft have rocketed to Mars, the human genome has been mapped, and I'm sure in all that time someone has worked the kinks out of the pressure cooker. But you'll forgive me if I pass and present my stovetop version of Sally's carrot tsimmes instead.

The crown on Sally's tsimmes was her knaidel (matzoh ball) topping. You could use it on your own favorite tsimmes recipe as well. Covering the tsimmes, it picks up its flavors and is therefore sometimes referred to as a *gonif* (thief) knaidel.

SERVES 6 TO 8   Ⓜ

FOR THE TSIMMES

2 pounds boneless beef chuck,
*   cut into 1¹/₂-inch cubes*
1 to 2 tablespoons vegetable oil
1 large onion, chopped
3 cups reduced-sodium beef broth
*   (see box, page 137)*
¹/₂ cup (packed) dark brown sugar
3 tablespoons all-purpose flour
¹/₂ cup cold water
3 pounds carrots, coarsely shredded
1 cup raisins (optional)
Kosher (coarse) salt and freshly ground
*   black pepper to taste*
"Gonif" Knaidel for Tsimmes
*   (recipe follows)*

1. Pat the beef very dry with paper towels. Heat 1 tablespoon of the oil in a Dutch oven or other large, heavy, ovenproof pot over medium-high heat. Add the beef and cook until browned, about 4 minutes. Remove the browned beef with a slotted spoon.

2. Add the remaining 1 tablespoon oil if necessary (depending on how lean the meat is), and add the onion. Cook over medium heat, stirring occasionally, until soft, about 5 minutes. Return the meat to the pot and add the beef broth. Cover, and simmer for 1 hour.

3. Combine the brown sugar, flour, and cold water in a bowl and whisk until no

specks of white remain. Stir this mixture into the beef. Add the carrots, raisins if using, and salt and pepper. Cover and continue simmering until the meat is tender, 1 to 1 1/2 hours.

4. Toward the end of the simmering time, prepare the knaidel batter (see recipe that follows).

5. Preheat the oven to 325°F.

6. Before placing the knaidel on the tsimmes, check that the tsimmes is soupy, as the knaidel will absorb some of the sauce. (If it is too dry, add some boiling water. No need to correct the seasonings, as the tsimmes will reduce again while the knaidel cooks.)

7. Using a large spoon, carefully drop the batter onto the hot tsimmes, covering as much of it as possible. Cover the pot and bake until the topping is firm, about 45 minutes.

8. Serve the tsimmes with a wedge of knaidel on top.

Note: For another meat and carrot tsimmes, see page 547.

"gonif" knaidel

This knaidel topping is so good, it's a shame to save it just for tsimmes. My personal favorite—don't laugh, now—is atop Phyllis's vegetarian chili (page 241)! Use it over any saucy stew. Unlike other knaidel toppings, which are more like stiff loaves, this one is really like a fluffy knaidel and just may be the best reason to lay away some gribenes. **SERVES 6 TO 8** Ⓜ

1/4 cup chicken fat or canola oil

1 cup very finely chopped onion

4 large eggs

1/2 cup homemade chicken stock (page 63) or low-sodium boxed or canned broth

1/4 cup gribenes (page 173; optional)

1 teaspoon kosher (coarse) salt, or to taste

Pinch of white pepper, or to taste

3/4 cup matzoh meal

1. Heat the fat in a medium-size saucepan over medium heat. Add the onion and cook until it is soft and beginning to turn brown, about 6 minutes. Set it aside to cool.

2. Using a fork, beat the eggs in a large bowl. Add the cooled onion with all the fat, the chicken stock, gribenes if using, salt, and white pepper, and mix very well. Then add the matzoh meal and mix thoroughly to form a batter. Cook following Steps 5 to 8 in the main recipe.

Sally Cohen (2nd from left) with sisters Rose and Kate, parents, Ida and Louis Robinson, and brothers Sam and Dave, about 1920.

beef gulyas

from Alice Weiss

Traditional Hungarian fare from Aunt Sylvia's cousin, this is goulash with tangy sauerkraut. Plain old paprika just won't do here—get yourself a tin of sweet Hungarian paprika, which is so much more flavorful. We prefer to go heavy on the caraway seeds, but add as much (or as little) as you like.

SERVES 6 **M**

**$^1/_4$ cup vegetable oil, chicken fat, or
   solid vegetable shortening**

3 large onions, chopped

3 large cloves garlic, crushed

**2$^1/_2$ to 3 pounds beef stew meat, cut into
   1$^1/_2$-inch cubes and patted dry**

**2 to 3 tablespoons sweet Hungarian
   paprika**

1 to 2 tablespoons caraway seeds

1 can (28 ounces) crushed tomatoes in puree

1 pound sauerkraut, rinsed well and drained

**1$^3/_4$ cups homemade chicken stock
   (page 63) , or 1 can (14$^1/_2$ ounces)
   low-sodium chicken broth**

2 teaspoons dried dill

1$^1/_2$ teaspoons kosher (coarse) salt, or to taste

**$^1/_2$ teaspoon freshly ground black pepper,
   or to taste**

Hot cooked wide noodles, for serving

1. Heat the oil in a Dutch oven or other large, heavy pot over medium heat. Add the onions and cook, stirring occasionally, until soft, about 10 minutes. Stir in the garlic and cook, stirring constantly, for about 1 minute more.

2. Add the beef and brown it well on all sides along with the onions, about 10 minutes.

3. Stir in the paprika and caraway seeds, mixing well. Add the tomatoes, sauerkraut, chicken broth, dill, 1 teaspoon of the salt, and $^1/_4$ teaspoon of the pepper. Simmer, covered, for 1$^1/_2$ hours.

4. Add the remaining $^1/_2$ teaspoon salt and $^1/_4$ teaspoon pepper, cover, and continue cooking until the beef is tender, 30 to 60 minutes.

5. Serve the goulash over hot noodles.

lena herzog's spanish short rib stew

from Gary Bart

When my brother, Gary, left for Latvia to produce the movie *Invincible*, I asked him to bring back a recipe. I'm thinking authentic fare from the land of our forefathers. What does he come home with? A Spanish recipe from writer-director Werner Herzog's wife. Well, it's delicious anyway—brings to mind a flamenco rather than a kazatski— and trust me, our forefathers never dined like this!

Lena's original recipe was for oxtail stew. For a kosher version, I took my cue from Anya von Bremzen, author of *The New Spanish Table*, who suggests short ribs as an alternative to her own oxtail stew. This dish, called rabo de toro in Spain, is popular in Andalusia, she says, where it is particularly savored the day after a bullfight. Like most braised dishes, it will benefit from a day of rest. Cook it a day ahead, refrigerate, and then skim off the fat before rewarming and serving. **SERVES 6** Ⓜ

Left: Werner Herzog (center) directs Gary Bart (left) in Invincible, the story of the Jewish folk hero Zishe Breitbart (see page 475) played by Juoko Ahola (right). Right: Breitbart poster, about 1920.

About 3 tablespoons all-purpose flour

About 5 pounds beef short ribs

4 tablespoons olive oil

2 medium-size onions, chopped

3 medium-size leeks, chopped and well rinsed

4 medium-size carrots, cut into $1/8$-inch-thick rounds

3 large cloves garlic, chopped

6 to 8 ounces smoked turkey sausage, diced

1 teaspoon good-quality sweet paprika (preferably Spanish)

1 can (about 14.5 ounces) stewed tomatoes, chopped, juices reserved

2 cups dry red wine

$1/2$ to 1 cup beef broth (see box, page 137)

$1/4$ cup brandy

$1/2$ teaspoon dried thyme leaves

$1/4$ teaspoon ground marjoram

1 to 2 teaspoons kosher (coarse) salt

$1/4$ to $1/2$ teaspoon freshly ground black pepper

2 or 3 bay leaves

1. Spread the flour on a baking sheet and roll the short ribs in it to lightly dust them. Shake off any excess.

2. Heat 2 tablespoons of the oil in a Dutch oven or other large, heavy pot over medium-high heat. Add the short ribs in batches and brown well on all sides, about 9 minutes per batch. Transfer the ribs to a platter and set it aside.

3. Heat the remaining 2 tablespoons oil in the Dutch oven over medium heat. Add the onions, leeks, and carrots, and cook, stirring occasionally, until they are starting to soften, about 5 minutes. Add the garlic and cook, stirring, for 1 minute. Then add the turkey sausage and continue cooking, stirring often, until the sausage is browned, about 5 minutes more. Stir in the paprika.

4. Add the tomatoes, wine, $1/2$ cup of the beef broth, and the brandy. Stir in the thyme, marjoram, 1 teaspoon of the salt, and $1/4$ teaspoon of the pepper. Add the bay leaves. Return the short ribs, with their juices, to the pot and, if necessary, add the remaining $1/2$ cup beef broth to barely cover the meat. Cover and simmer, stirring occasionally,

until the meat is very tender and practically falling off the bone, about 3 hours. If you prefer a thicker stew, uncover the pot for the last 30 minutes of cooking. Add the remaining 1 teaspoon salt and $^1/_4$ teaspoon pepper, if needed. Allow the stew to cool somewhat and then refrigerate it, covered, for a day.

5. When you are ready to serve the stew, skim off the fat and reheat it.

short ribs
with mop sauce

from Joan Kalish

Texans make this dish in batches so large that they use a mop to swab the sauce on the ribs. No mopping here, though. What could be easier than braising the ribs in a foil pouch until tender, leaving them to bathe in their own luscious juices, and then broiling them briefly to a lip-smacking crispness? If you'd like some dipping sauce for the finished ribs, double the sauce ingredients and reserve half to be warmed separately and served on the side. Either way, have plenty of napkins handy. **SERVES 6** **M**

$^1/_4$ **cup dark corn syrup**

$^1/_4$ **cup ketchup**

$^1/_4$ **cup cider vinegar**

$^1/_4$ **cup Worcestershire sauce**

2 tablespoons vegetable oil

2 tablespoons prepared mustard

2 teaspoons instant coffee granules

1 teaspoon kosher (coarse) salt

$^1/_4$ **teaspoon freshly ground black pepper**

$^1/_8$ **teaspoon hot pepper sauce**

About 6 pounds beef short ribs

1. Combine all the ingredients except the ribs in a large bowl, and whisk to blend. Dip the short ribs in the sauce, turning them to coat well. Cover and refrigerate, turning the ribs occasionally, for 4 to 24 hours.

2. Preheat the oven to 400°F. Line a large baking pan with heavy-duty aluminum foil.

3. Transfer the ribs and sauce to the prepared pan and arrange them in a single layer. Cover the baking pan tightly with aluminum foil and bake for 1 hour.

4. Wearing oven mitts, *very carefully* open the foil to release the steam. Baste the ribs with the pan juices, and turn them over. Cover the pan again and continue baking until the ribs are very tender, 30 to 60 minutes. Remove the pan from the oven, uncover it, and allow to cool somewhat. (The dish can be prepared a day ahead up to this point; refrigerate, covered.)

5. When you are ready to serve the ribs, preheat the broiler. Set an oven rack about 8 inches below the heat source.

6. Remove the layer of fat from the short ribs. Turn the ribs and baste them with the pan juices.

7. Broil the ribs until they are brown and crisp on one side, about 10 minutes. Turn and broil on the other side, about 3 minutes more. Serve hot, and pass the extra sauce if using.

barbecued ribs
with pineapple

from Claire Smolen

Claire sometimes substitutes pre-served kumquats for the pineapple in this succulent dish. The ribs are first roasted to give off their fat, then slow-cooked in a tantalizing sauce, and finally marinated overnight before they are finished the next day. Choose long, meaty ribs, and dig in. **SERVES 4 TO 6** Ⓜ

About 5 pounds lean, meaty long beef ribs
1 cup light molasses
1 cup ketchup
1 cup chopped onions
Grated zest of 1 orange
Juice of 1 orange ($^1/_3$ to $^1/_2$ cup)
2 tablespoons nondairy margarine
2 tablespoons distilled white vinegar
1 tablespoon vegetable oil
6 whole cloves
2 cloves garlic, minced
1 teaspoon prepared mustard
1 teaspoon Worcestershire sauce
$^1/_2$ teaspoon Tabasco sauce
$^1/_2$ teaspoon kosher (coarse) salt
$^1/_2$ teaspoon freshly ground black pepper
1 can (20 ounces) pineapple chunks,
   drained

1. Preheat the oven to 325°F. Line a large, shallow, open pan with heavy-duty aluminum foil.

2. Place the ribs in the prepared pan, cover it with foil, and roast for 30 minutes. Then pour off the fat and continue roasting, covered, for another 45 minutes.

3. Meanwhile, prepare the sauce: Combine all the remaining ingredients except the pineapple in a medium-size saucepan over medium heat, and simmer for 5 minutes. Set the sauce aside.

4. Pour off all the fat from the ribs, and cover them with the sauce. Continue to roast the ribs, uncovered, basting often, until tender, very brown, and glazed, about 45 minutes.

5. Toss the pineapple with the sauce and ribs in the roasting pan. Cool, then cover the pan with aluminum foil, and refrigerate overnight.

6. Preheat the oven to 325°F.

7. Discard any congealed fat in the pan. Roast, covered, until the ribs are hot and tender, about 1 hour. If you like them extra-crispy, uncover the pan for the last 15 minutes. Serve hot.

grandma estelle's
shepherd's pie

from Joyce Wolf

I had to ask. "Joyce, why do you jab the meat pie with a fork before baking?" "I don't know," she answered. "My mother told me to do it. When your mother tells you to do something, you do it."

After Aunt Estelle died, Joyce took over Friday night dinners. This dish was always the favorite of grandsons Eric, Marc, Warren, and David, and with all those growing boys at the table, Aunt Estelle usually made two. The "boys" are now men, but they've never outgrown it. Joyce swears she follows her mother's recipe exactly, but Eric usually complains, "I like the way Grandma used to make it. Yours is too neat!" **SERVES 6 TO 8** **M**

FOR THE MASHED POTATO LAYER

¹/₂ cup vegetable oil

2 large onions (1¹/₄ pounds total)

3 pounds russet potatoes, peeled and
cut into 1¹/₂-inch chunks

Kosher (coarse) salt

¹/₄ teaspoon freshly ground black pepper,
or to taste

FOR THE MEAT LAYER

3 slices white bread

1 large onion, finely chopped

3 pounds ground beef

2 large eggs, beaten

3 cloves garlic, crushed

2 teaspoons kosher (coarse) salt

Freshly ground black pepper to taste

1. Prepare the mashed potato layer: Heat the oil in a very large skillet over medium-low heat. Add the onions and cook slowly, stirring occasionally, until very soft and golden, 30 to 40 minutes.

2. Meanwhile, place the potatoes in a large pot, add water to cover, lightly salt it, and bring to a boil. Reduce the heat and

Aunt Estelle with Joyce and Marvin, 1948.

The greatest compliment ever paid me (at least when it comes to cooking!) came from Aunt Irene, Aunt Sally, and Aunt Estelle when they flew to California in 1978 for my son Stu's Bar Mitzvah weekend. *They all asked me* for my potato knish recipe! The potato filling became Aunt Estelle's topping for her Shepherd's Pie, but she preferred a smoother mixture and would process the sautéed onions in a blender before adding them to the mashed potatoes. Personally, I like the little specks of onion, but the choice is yours.

gently boil the potatoes until tender, 20 to 30 minutes. Drain the potatoes and put them through a ricer (preferred) or hand-mash them.

3. Strain the onions, reserving the oil. Puree the strained onions in a blender, and combine the puree with the mashed potatoes. Add about 2 teaspoons salt and the pepper, and set aside.

4. Preheat the oven to 350°F.

5. Prepare the meat layer: Place the bread in a shallow bowl, add water to cover, and soak for 1 or 2 minutes. Then drain the bread, and using your hands, squeeze out the excess water. Crumble the bread into bits in a large bowl. Add the onion, ground beef, eggs, garlic, salt, and pepper, and mix together.

6. Spread about one third of the mashed potato mixture over the bottom of a 13 × 9-inch baking pan. Pat the meat mixture evenly over the potatoes; then cover it with

the remaining mashed potatoes. Jab all over with a fork. (Don't ask why.) Brush lightly with the reserved oil, and bake until the meat is cooked through and the potatoes are golden brown, about 1$^1/4$ hours. Cut into squares and serve hot.

Variation: This dish can be made using your own favorite meat loaf and/or mashed potato recipe.

italian meat loaf

from Suzy Orlow Solomonic

nlike the meat loaf I grew up on, this one is a ketchup-free zone. Here the flavors of garlic, lemon juice, and parsley sing in perfect harmony.

SERVES 8 TO 10   M

1 pound ground beef

1 pound ground veal

1 pound ground lamb

$^1/2$ cup finely chopped onion

$^1/2$ cup Italian-flavored dry bread crumbs

2 large eggs, beaten

$^1/4$ cup fresh lemon juice

3 tablespoons finely chopped flat-leaf parsley

1 tablespoon chopped garlic

2 teaspoons kosher (coarse) salt

2 teaspoons olive oil

1$^1/4$ cups homemade chicken stock (page 63) or
    low-sodium boxed or canned broth

A
t our table everyone always wants the end piece, so I devised a plan to satisfy all. After the meat loaf mixture is thoroughly combined, I shape it into a long log, then bring the ends of the log together to form a ring. (It looks like a big bagel.) Now each person gets a nice crusty slice, and everyone is happy. (Well, at least about the meat loaf.)

1. Preheat the oven to 350°F.

2. Combine all the ingredients except the chicken stock in a bowl, and mix together. Place the mixture in a 13 × 9-inch baking pan and shape it into a loaf, leaving at least 1$^1/2$ inches of space on all sides for proper browning. Pour $^1/4$ cup of the chicken stock over the loaf.

3. Bake, basting with $^1/4$ cup of the stock every 20 minutes, until the loaf is brown and firm, about 1$^1/2$ hours. A meat thermometer should register 160°F.

4. Remove the pan from the oven, cover it loosely with aluminum foil, and allow the meat loaf to rest for at least 5 minutes before slicing. Serve hot or at room temperature.

stuffed cabbage

from Marilyn Dubin

ven into her nineties, Aunt Sally worked with Marilyn to make the stuffed cabbage for their large family gatherings, each roll lovingly shaped. In fact, everything from Aunt

Sally's kitchen always looked as good as it tasted. Her maxim: "When you're cooking, you can't do anything else at the same time." I always think of that when I'm cooking and the phone keeps ringing and I can't remember if I've added the salt.

MAKES ABOUT 36 ROLLS Ⓜ

2 large green cabbages, cored

FOR THE MEAT MIXTURE

3 pounds ground beef

1 medium-size onion, finely chopped (¹/₂ cup)

1 cup soft (stale) challah crumbs

2 large eggs, beaten

2 teaspoons kosher (coarse) salt

¹/₂ teaspoon freshly ground black pepper

2 teaspoons fresh lemon juice

FOR THE SAUCE

2 cups chopped onions

1 can (28 ounces) chopped tomatoes, undrained

1 can (6 ounces) tomato paste

5 to 9 tablespoons fresh lemon juice to taste

3 tablespoons granulated sugar

3 to 4 tablespoons dark brown sugar to taste

2 to 4 tablespoons honey, or to taste

2 to 3¹/₂ teaspoons kosher (coarse) salt to taste

¹/₂ teaspoon freshly ground black pepper,
    or to taste

1. Three days prior to serving, wrap the cabbages in plastic wrap or seal them in plastic bags, and freeze them (this will soften the leaves). The night before you plan to make the stuffed cabbage, set them on the kitchen counter to thaw. When they have thawed, separate the leaves. (This is much easier than boiling them, but if you're pressed for time, steam the cabbages over boiling water until the leaves are soft, 50 to 60 minutes. When they are cool enough to handle, separate the leaves.)

2. Place the separated leaves on clean Turkish towels (Aunt Sally's preference) or on paper towels to dry.

3. Combine all the ingredients for the meat mixture in a large bowl, and mix well. Depending on the size of the cabbage leaf, spoon 1 or 2 tablespoons of the meat mixture onto the root end. Roll the cabbage leaf up from the bottom, covering the meat. Tuck in the sides of the leaf and continue rolling, forming a fairly tight cylinder. Larger leaves can be cut in half; trim and reserve any hard pieces. Repeat until all the meat mixture is used, placing the rolls, seam side down, on a large platter or a baking sheet. You will undoubtedly have a lot of cabbage left over, but this is better than running out, and it will be used in the sauce later.

4. Chop the leftover cabbage pieces, measure out 3 cups, and put it in a Dutch oven or other large, heavy pot. Stir in the onions, chopped tomatoes with their liquid, and the tomato paste. Add 5 tablespoons of the lemon juice, the granulated sugar, 3 tablespoons of the brown sugar, 2 tablespoons of the honey, 2 teaspoons of the salt, and the pepper, and stir to mix. (Think of these flavorings as merely the rough sketch of your sauce, which will later develop into a fully rendered canvas.) Arrange the stuffed cabbage rolls, seam side down, on top of the sauce (there will be more than 1 layer of rolls), and cover the pot.

5. Place the pot over medium-high heat and bring to a boil. Reduce the heat and

simmer for 2 hours. Then, using a slotted spoon, transfer the cabbage rolls to an oven-proof serving dish (a 17 × 11-inch dish should hold them all in one layer, or use several smaller ones if you intend to freeze some).

6. Taste the sauce and add the remaining 4 tablespoons lemon juice, 1 tablespoon brown sugar, 2 tablespoons honey, and 1^1/2 teaspoons salt—or more or less, according to your preference. (If, like me, you weren't as diligent as Aunt Sally in drying the cabbage leaves, you may find that the sauce is a little too thin at this stage. With the rolls safely tucked into the serving dish, it is a simple matter to reduce the sauce by simmering it for a few minutes while you are executing your final taste test.)

7. Pour the sauce over the stuffed cabbage rolls, and allow to cool. Then cover the dish with plastic wrap and refrigerate for a day or two (see Notes).

8. When you are ready to serve the cabbage rolls, bring them to room temperature.

9. Preheat the oven to 350°F.

10. Reheat the cabbage rolls, covered, until piping hot, 30 to 45 minutes

Notes: Aunt Sally gradually added the extra lemon juice, brown sugar, honey, and salt during the 2 hours of cooking, she and Marilyn in frequent consultation as they tasted the sauce. She wouldn't approve of my method, but I just don't have their patience.

To freeze the cabbage rolls, cover the dish tightly with heavy-duty aluminum foil and freeze for up to 6 weeks. Thaw and then reheat, covered, in a preheated 350°F oven until piping hot, 30 to 40 minutes.

marilyn greenberg's
easy "unstuffed" cabbage

from Irene Rosenthal

Here meatballs and chopped cabbage recall the classic with much less of the actual work. Aunt Irene's version produces a gravy-like sauce that is thick, rich, and sweet without being cloying. Serve this over rice or noodles.

SERVES 6　　　　　　　　Ⓜ

FOR THE MEATBALLS

1^1/2 pounds ground beef

^{1}/4 cup cooked rice

1 tablespoon dark brown sugar

2 teaspoons fresh lemon juice

1 tablespoon ketchup

^{1}/2 teaspoon kosher (coarse) salt

FOR THE SAUCE

2 tablespoons vegetable oil

1 large onion, finely chopped

1 can (10^3/4 ounces) condensed
　　tomato soup

^{1}/4 cup fresh lemon juice, or to taste

^{1}/2 cup (packed) dark brown sugar

^{1}/2 teaspoon kosher (coarse) salt,
　　or to taste

Freshly ground black pepper, to taste

1 small green cabbage (about 1^1/2 pounds),
　　cored and shredded

3 gingersnaps, crushed

Aunt Irene and Uncle Mac, out on the town, early '40s.

1. Combine all the ingredients for the meatballs in a large bowl, and mix well. Set the mixture aside.

2. Prepare the sauce: Heat the oil in a large pot over medium heat. Add the onion and cook until soft and golden, about 10 minutes. Then add the soup, 1$^{1}/_{2}$ soup cans of water, and the lemon juice, brown sugar, salt, and pepper. Mix well, and stir in the shredded cabbage and crushed gingersnaps.

3. Using your hands, form the meat mixture into balls about 1$^{1}/_{4}$ inches in diameter and add them to the sauce. Cover the pot, and simmer over medium heat for 30 minutes.

4. Meanwhile, preheat the oven to 350°F.

5. Transfer the meatballs and sauce to a 13 × 9-inch glass baking dish. Cover the dish and bake for 1$^{1}/_{2}$ hours.

6. Spoon the meatballs and sauce over hot rice or noodles, and serve.

Notes: This dish can be prepared a day or two ahead and refrigerated. It also freezes well.

You can also make mini meatballs and serve them as an appetizer for a party.

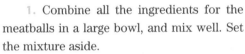

easier still "unstuffed" cabbage

from Bonnie Robbins

Cousin Bonnie favors easy recipes that taste great. After all, who's got time to roll and fold when grandsons Hunter and Blake want to play?

Chili sauce and grape jelly—mundane ingredients by themselves—may seem a wacky combo to some, but if you were around in the '60s, you'll remember this hot-sweet blend bursting on the scene in dozens of recipes at about the same time Neil Armstrong landed on the moon. One small step for the cook, one giant leap for the family.

These meatballs in their piquant sauce can be prepared alone, without the chopped cabbage, if you like. **SERVES 4** M

FOR THE MEATBALLS

1 slice white bread

1 pound ground beef

1 egg, beaten

³/₄ teaspoon kosher (coarse) salt

¹/₄ teaspoon freshly ground
    black pepper

1 teaspoon garlic powder

FOR THE SAUCE

1 bottle (12 ounces) chili sauce

1 jar (10 ounces) grape jelly

1 small green cabbage
    (about 1 pound), cored and
    chopped

Hot cooked rice or noodles,
    for serving

1. Prepare the meatballs: Tear the bread into pieces and combine it with ¹/₄ cup water in a small bowl. Let soak for a minute or two. Then crumble the soaked bread into a bowl. Add all the remaining ingredients and mix well. Set aside.

2. Prepare the sauce: Combine the chili sauce and grape jelly in a large saucepan, and heat over medium heat until the jelly dissolves.

3. Using your hands, form the meat mixture into balls about 1¹/₄ inches in diameter, drop them and the cabbage into the sauce, cover the pan, and simmer for 45 minutes.

4. Spoon the meatballs and sauce over hot rice or noodles, and serve.

Notes: This dish can be prepared a day or two ahead and refrigerated. It also freezes well.

Cousin Bonnie and my brother, Gary, who were in Mrs. Schlicter's class together. If not for Bonnie, he never would have survived.

You can also make mini meatballs, with or without the cabbage, and serve them as an appetizer for a party.

italian meatball stew
with chicken and sausage

from Eric Wolf

ucky Michelle: Hubby Eric loves to cook, and when he cooks, he *really* cooks! If you're going to mess up your kitchen anyway, you might as well get a few meals out of it, and Michelle reports that on a cold winter night it is such a treat to defrost a portion of Eric's special Italian stew, boil up some spaghetti, and *voilà* . . . I mean *ecco*! Dinner!

SERVES ABOUT 16   Ⓜ

FOR THE MEATBALLS

3 pounds ground beef

2 cups fresh bread crumbs

2 large eggs, beaten

1/4 cup chopped flat-leaf parsley

2 teaspoons kosher (coarse) salt

1/2 teaspoon freshly ground black pepper

FOR THE CHICKEN AND SAUSAGE

1 chicken (3 1/2 to 4 pounds), cut into
*   8 to 10 pieces*

Kosher (coarse) salt to taste

Freshly ground black pepper to taste

Paprika to taste

2 to 3 tablespoons olive oil

1 pound turkey sausage, preferably spicy,
*   cut into 1 1/2-inch chunks*

1 large (12 ounces) sweet onion, chopped

1 small head garlic, cloves separated,
*   peeled, and chopped*

5 cans (28 ounces each) crushed tomatoes in
*   puree*

2 tablespoons dried oregano

1 bunch fresh basil leaves, cut into thin slivers
*   (chiffonade; about 1/2 cup packed)*

3 tablespoons sugar, or to taste

1 pound skinless, boneless chicken breasts,
*   cut into 3/4-inch-wide slices*

1. Preheat the broiler, with a rack placed about 8 inches from the heat source.

2. Combine all the meatball ingredients in a large bowl, and mix well. Using your hands, form the mixture into balls a little larger than golf balls. Place them on a rack in a broiling pan, and broil on both sides until lightly browned, about 5 minutes per side. Set the meatballs aside. Leave the broiler on.

3. Sprinkle the chicken parts with salt, pepper, and paprika. Place them, skin side up, on a rack in a broiling pan and broil on the same oven rack until the fat drips off and the skin blisters, 8 to 10 minutes. Turn and brown on the other side, 2 to 3 minutes. (The drumsticks and wings may take a few minutes longer.) Set the chicken aside.

4. Heat 1 tablespoon of the oil in a very large pot over medium-high heat and brown the sausage on all sides, about 4 minutes. Remove with a slotted spoon and set aside.

5. Add 1 or 2 tablespoons of the oil (if the sausage was very lean) to the pot and cook the onion over medium heat, stirring occasionally, until soft, about 10 minutes. Add the garlic and cook, stirring constantly, for about 1 minute more. Then stir in the tomatoes, oregano, half the basil, and the sugar. Season with salt and pepper. Return the meatballs, chicken pieces, and sausage to the pot, and stir. Simmer, covered, stirring occasionally, until the chicken is cooked through and the flavors come together, 1 to 1 1/4 hours.

6. Add the chicken breast slices and cook, covered, for 20 minutes. (If you prefer a thicker sauce, cook uncovered.) Stir in the remaining basil, and serve.

Aunt Estelle's first grandchild, Eric Wolf, with his wife, Michelle. My aunt and mother had seven grandsons between them.

homemade marinara sauce
with meatballs . . . or not

from Abbe Dubin

A bbe cooks this sauce for hours and hours. I prefer an hour and a half because I like my sauce chunky, but you be the judge. As meatballs and spaghetti is one of Barry's favorite dishes, I freeze individual servings for an easy last-minute meal. This recipe makes enough sauce for about 1½ pounds of pasta.

SERVES 6 TO 8   **P** or **M**

2 tablespoons olive oil

1 large onion, chopped

4 large cloves garlic, chopped

3 cans (28 ounces each) crushed tomatoes

10 large leaves fresh basil, cut into thin slivers
   (chiffonade)

1 tablespoon sugar, or to taste

1½ teaspoons kosher (coarse) salt, or to taste

¼ teaspoon freshly ground black pepper,
   or to taste

½ recipe Italian Meat Loaf mixture (page 146),
   uncooked, or your favorite using 1½ to 2
   pounds ground meat (optional)

1. Heat the oil in a large saucepan over medium-high heat. Add the onion and cook, stirring occasionally, until soft and golden, about 7 minutes. Add the garlic and cook, stirring constantly, for another 30 seconds or so.

Then stir in the tomatoes, half the basil, and the sugar, salt, and pepper. Cover the pan and simmer, stirring occasionally, for 1½ to 2 hours (or longer if you like a smoother sauce).

2. Meanwhile, if you are using the meatballs, form the meat loaf mixture into 2-inch balls. After the sauce has cooked for 30 minutes, drop them into it. Let them cook without stirring until they have firmed up a bit, about 30 minutes. Then stir gently and continue cooking in the sauce for another 30 to 60 minutes.

3. Taste the sauce, and adjust the seasonings if necessary. Just before serving, stir in the remaining basil.

almost homemade pasta sauce

from Judy Bart Kancigor

W hen vegetable meets oil in hot oven, it's pure animal (or rather vegetarian) attraction. Nothing beats the taste of roasted vegetables—roasting concentrates the sugars and imparts a flavor you cannot achieve any other way. I tend to go easy on the oil, but feel free to use a little more for a glossier look and an even richer taste. Use your favorite spaghetti sauce right from the jar. (We like the spicy red pepper variety.)

Use this sauce over chicken, fish, meatballs, or your favorite Italian dish. **MAKES ABOUT 3½ CUPS (ENOUGH FOR 1 POUND OF PASTA)** 🄿 or 🄼

Vegetable cooking spray
1½ pounds plum tomatoes
1 large onion, quartered
2 large carrots, quartered
1 red or green bell pepper (or half of each),
*   stemmed, seeded, and cut in half*
1 jalapeño pepper, cut in half, seeded,
*   and deveined (optional)*
6 cloves garlic
1 tablespoon olive oil
2 cups prepared spaghetti sauce
1 tablespoon sugar, or to taste (optional)
1 teaspoon Italian seasoning, or to taste
1½ teaspoons kosher (coarse) salt, or to taste
Freshly ground black pepper to taste

1. Preheat the oven to 375°F. Line a roasting pan or a rimmed baking sheet with aluminum foil and spray it with vegetable cooking spray.

2. Combine the tomatoes, onion, carrots, bell pepper, jalapeño if using, and garlic in the prepared pan. Sprinkle the olive oil over the vegetables and toss to mix. Place the pan in the oven and roast, stirring occasionally, until the vegetables are soft and beginning to brown on all sides, about 45 minutes. Don't be alarmed if they get mushy, because they'll go in the blender later. You'll know you're there when the carrots are tender.

3. Transfer the vegetables and the exuded juices, in small batches, to a blender and puree. (Hot ingredients let off a lot of steam in the blender, so be careful to close the lid tightly. As an extra precaution, cover the lid with a kitchen towel. Burnt palms are no fun.)

4. Transfer the puree to a medium-size saucepan, and add the prepared spaghetti sauce. Stir in the sugar, if using, Italian seasoning, salt, and pepper. Cover and bring to a boil. Then reduce the heat and simmer for 30 minutes. If you like a thicker sauce, uncover the pan and simmer further until the sauce has reduced to the desired consistency. Use immediately, or freeze for up to 3 months.

ten-minute marinara sauce

from Stewart Mackoff

This fresh, chunky sauce cooks up in no time, ready to serve over chicken, veal, fish, meatballs, or alone with pasta. **MAKES 3½ CUPS (ENOUGH FOR 1 POUND OF PASTA)** 🄿

1 tablespoon olive oil
1 small onion, finely chopped
4 cloves garlic, thinly sliced
1 can (28 ounces) crushed tomatoes
2 tablespoons chopped fresh basil, or
*   2 teaspoons dried*
1 teaspoon dried oregano
Pinch of red pepper flakes, or to taste
¼ teaspoon kosher (coarse) salt, or to taste
Freshly ground black pepper to taste

1. Heat the oil in a large skillet over medium-high heat. Add the onion and cook, stirring occasionally, until soft, about 4 minutes. Add the garlic and cook, stirring constantly, for 30 seconds more.

2. Stir in the tomatoes, basil, oregano, red pepper flakes, salt, and pepper. Simmer, partially covered, for 5 minutes.

3. Serve immediately.

tongue polonaise

from Irene Rosenthal

If you attended Bar Mitzvahs in the 1950s, you probably saw some permutation of this recipe on the buffet table. Tongue has fallen out of favor in the intervening decades, except on sandwiches in kosher delis, and even then it's ordered only by people old enough to remember that era. Personally, I adore it, and not just because I'm nostalgic about the '50s. Tongue has a soft, creamy texture and rich taste that is difficult to compare

Sally, Estelle, Marilyn, and Irene at my nephew Randy's Bar Mitzvah, 1983.

to anything else. Still not convinced? Try this sauce on corned beef or even brisket—but you're missing one of life's little pleasures if you forgo the tongue. **SERVES 8 TO 10; MAKES 4 CUPS SAUCE** Ⓜ

1 pickled beef tongue (about 4 pounds)

1 can (20 ounces) pineapple chunks, drained

1 cup canned pitted black cherries, drained and chopped

¹/₄ cup golden raisins

1 jar (10 ounces) orange marmalade

2 cups orange juice

¹/₂ cup (packed) light or dark brown sugar

¹/₄ cup distilled white vinegar

Juice of 1 lemon (about 3 tablespoons)

¹/₂ teaspoon dry mustard

10 gingersnaps, crushed

¹/₄ teaspoon kosher (coarse) salt, or to taste

> *Mama Irene's love and her devotion to keeping the family together, to helping us achieve our goals, and to educating our minds will live on. Ahead of her time, she stands out in our family for her belief in female power and strength—that all women, through education and commitment, can achieve whatever they set their minds to. She set a great example with her charitable ways, always finding an extra seat for anyone who needed a place to eat for the holidays and donating her time to Jewish and community causes. Even though she always said 'Life is hard,' she never complained. If you asked how she was doing, the most she ever said was 'I'm doing.' Her unbridled spirit and love will always be a part of us.*
>
> **—WENDY EPSTEIN**

lung and liver kugel
from Sally Bower

◦ ◦ ●

Like the dinosaur and the dodo bird, this kugel, alas, is extinct. Cousin Peter informs me that lung is no longer sold in the United States because of health considerations. Aunt Sally's recipe is included here, verbatim, for sentimental reasons only. Do not try this at home!

1 lb liver broiled
2 lbs lung. Stew with about 2 lbs onions.

Grind or chop lung and liver and onions. Add beaten eggs (about 10), salt, pepper and a little matzoh meal, about 2 or 3 tablespoons. Grease pan (large). Line bottom of pan with large blintz dough. Then pour in above ingredients and cover with another blintz (a few of them). Dot top with oil or fat and bake about 1 hour. Then cut squares and serve hot. (Very good.) Served like a kugel.

---

1. Prepare the tongue according to the package directions.

2. Combine all the remaining ingredients in a large saucepan and bring to a boil. Add the tongue, then reduce the heat and simmer, uncovered, for 30 minutes.

3. Slice the tongue and serve it warm, layered with the sauce.

grandma ruchel's pitcha
(calves' foot jelly)

from Isabelle Frankel

my Aunt Isabelle remembers this standard shtetl fare from my father's mother, Grandma Ruchel. Some people used beef bones, but Grandma preferred calves' feet, which were simmered with onions and garlic for hours, producing a gelatinous substance when cooled. She served each portion chilled with the egg in the center, or sometimes hot with lots of challah to mop up the juices. Maybe not the stuff of gourmet dreams, but our inventive foremothers could suck protein from a stone to keep starvation at bay. My friend Marci Klein thinks good pitcha must be covered with a thin film of soot, as her mother always cooled it on the fire escape. **SERVES 1 SHTETL FAMILY, WITH OR WITHOUT BOARDERS** ▣

6 pieces calves' feet
2 large Bermuda onions, chopped
8 cloves garlic, chopped
Kosher (coarse) salt and freshly ground black pepper to taste
2 large eggs, hard-cooked

When my parents would go away, Grandma Ruchel would come to stay with us. She would always bring her own chicken, soup, and meatballs in glass jars. She would put an asbestos pad on top of two of the stove burners and would light the burners on Friday before Shabbos so that she could warm up her food. When she would sit across the kitchen table from me and daven [pray], I would mimic her lip movements, but she never got angry. In fact, it would make her smile. Although she was very observant, she was always tolerant and accepting of what we did.
—MICHAEL GOLD

Grandma Ruchel never played favorites. All of her grandchildren were special. Here she is with my cousin Jerry Kraus, about 1952.

1. Buy the calves' feet from a kosher butcher who will cut them into 3-inch pieces for you. Make sure they keep the marrow intact. Scrub the feet well and then soak them in cold water to cover for 1 hour. Drain.

2. Place the onions, garlic, and salt and pepper in a 6- to 8-quart pot. Add the calves' feet, cover with fresh water, and bring to a boil. Skim off the foam that rises to the top. Reduce the heat and simmer until the flesh is pulling away from the bone, 3 to 4 hours.

3. Remove the meat to cool, and chop it fine. Strain the liquid into a glass dish and stir in the chopped meat. Set aside to cool for about 1 hour (fire escape optional).

4. Slice the hard-cooked eggs and arrange them on top. Chill until firm, about 3 hours.

veal brisket

from Marilyn Dubin

Sure, you can try this recipe with beef, but Marilyn prefers veal. Veal brisket is juicier, has a milder flavor, and is more tender than beef, she says—the better to receive the tangy sauce.

SERVES 6 TO 8 Ⓜ

1 tablespoon vegetable oil
3 to 4 pounds veal brisket
1 large onion, chopped
2 cloves garlic, chopped
1/2 cup ketchup
1/2 cup chili sauce
1/4 cup steak sauce

1. Heat the oil in a Dutch oven or other large, heavy pot over medium-high heat. Add the veal and brown it on both sides, about 10 minutes altogether. Remove the brisket from the pot.

2. Add the onion to the pot and cook until soft and golden, about 7 minutes. Add the garlic and cook for 1 minute more. Then stir in the ketchup, chili sauce, steak sauce, and 1/2 cup water. Return the veal to the pot and simmer, covered, until quite tender, about 2 hours.

3. Cut the brisket diagonally across the grain into thin slices, and serve with the sauce.

Note: If you make this a day ahead and then refrigerate the brisket in the sauce, the meat will be easier to slice and tastier too: Remove the chilled brisket from the sauce, slice it diagonally, and then combine the slices and sauce in a Dutch oven or other large, heavy pot. Reheat the brisket slices in the sauce, and serve.

yuval hamenahem's roasted veal
with dried apricots

from Rachel Humphrey

For their fifteen minutes of fame, Rachel and her family were chosen to be on The Learning Channel's hit show *Trading Spaces: Family*. You know the one: Two families trade houses for two days and work with a designer on each other's rooms, often to the delight (but sometimes to the dismay) of the homeowners. Since the families keep kosher, the shoot was catered by a local kosher market owned by the Hamenahem family.

The Hamenahems generously shared a few of their favorite recipes with Rachel, who especially loves this veal roast for Shabbat dinner. Slow braising coaxes the herb-infused, honeyed flavor from the fork-tender meat, and the slices look festive dotted with apricots. **SERVES 5 TO 6** **M**

2¹/₂ pounds veal shoulder roast

Kosher (coarse) salt to taste

Freshly ground black pepper to taste

3 to 5 tablespoons olive oil

1 medium-size onion, chopped

4 cloves garlic, crushed

1 cup dry red wine

1 cup veal stock or beef broth (see box, page 137)

1 bouquet garni (see Notes)

6 tablespoons honey

2 tablespoons prepared mustard

2 tablespoons light or dark brown sugar

20 dried apricots

1. Season the veal on all sides with salt and pepper. Heat 3 tablespoons of the oil in a Dutch oven or other large, heavy pot over medium-high heat, and brown the meat on all sides, 10 to 15 minutes altogether. Remove the veal.

2. Reduce the heat to medium and add 1 or 2 tablespoons of the remaining oil, as needed, to cook the onion. Add the onion and cook, stirring occasionally, until soft and golden, about 5 minutes. Add the garlic and cook, stirring constantly, for 1 minute more. Add the wine and deglaze the pot, scraping up all the brown bits. Then stir in the stock, bouquet garni, honey, mustard, and brown sugar. Return the veal to the pot and bring to a boil. Reduce the heat, cover the pot, and simmer for 30 minutes, turning the meat every 10 minutes.

> **When the Trading Spaces scout came out to visit our houses, my neighbor, Amy, and I were informed that the network would cater all the meals during the taping period. As both houses keep kosher, we politely requested that the caterer be kosher, and the network asked us to select one. We chose our favorite, Westville Kosher Market in Woodbridge, Connecticut, owned by the Hamenahems. The Hamenahems outdid themselves and provided nine of the best meals we'd ever had! They prepared classic kosher, Jewish soul foods, and everyone was very impressed. Some, including Hildi, the designer, wanted to know more about what it means to 'keep kosher.' The cast and crew all voted that they should get kosher meals at every shoot. Considering that they are on the road ten out of every twelve days, this was quite a compliment.**
> —RACHEL HUMPHREY

3. Stir in the dried apricots, and season with 1 teaspoon salt if necessary. Continue simmering, turning it occasionally, until the veal is very tender, 30 to 40 minutes.

4. Remove the veal and let it rest, covered, for 5 minutes.

5. Meanwhile, simmer the sauce to reduce it slightly.

6. Slice the veal and return the slices to the pot. Stir to distribute the sauce, and serve.

Notes: To prepare the bouquet garni, tie 5 large sprigs parsley, 3 sprigs thyme, 2 sprigs rosemary, and 5 black peppercorns in a square of cheesecloth, forming a packet.

If you prefer a thicker sauce, mix 2 tablespoons cornstarch with 2 tablespoons cold water and add this before returning the veal slices to the pot. Heat until thickened.

northern italian veal roast

from Holly Grippo

olly's husband, Joe, taught her how to cook the Italian dishes he grew up on. This simple roast veal was a Grippo family favorite. While there are more elaborate preparations, the slow cooking in this recipe produces a tender and succulent roast. Holly likes to serve this over a bed of fusilli pasta. **SERVES 6 TO 8** **M**

3 to 4 pounds veal neck roast

Kosher (coarse) salt to taste

Freshly ground black pepper to taste

2 to 4 tablespoons olive oil

3 large onions, coarsely chopped

2 ribs celery, cut into $1/2$-inch-thick slices

3 cloves garlic, chopped

8 ounces turkey sausage, diced

1 cup homemade chicken stock (page 63) or low-sodium boxed or canned broth

1 cup dry white wine

2 tablespoons all-purpose flour

2 tablespoons cold water

Holly and Joe Grippo.

I brought an Italian into the Robbins family, and I hope I can bring a little Italian to the cookbook.
—HOLLY GRIPPO

ring, until the sauce has thickened, about 2 minutes. Slice the veal, and spoon the sauce over it.

stuffed breast of veal

from Marilyn Dubin

My glamorous cousin Marilyn at her son Barry's Bar Mitzvah, 1965.

1. Dry the veal well and season it generously all over with salt and pepper. Heat 2 tablespoons of the oil in a Dutch oven or other large, heavy pot over medium-high heat. Brown the veal on all sides, 10 to 15 minutes altogether. Remove it from the pot.

2. Heat the remaining 2 tablespoons oil, if needed, for cooking the vegetables, over medium heat. Add the onions, celery, and garlic, and cook, stirring occasionally, until they are starting to soften, about 5 minutes. Then add the turkey sausage and continue cooking, stirring often, until the sausage is well browned, 5 to 10 minutes more.

3. Push the vegetables and sausage to the sides of the pot and place the veal in the center. Add the chicken stock and wine, and bring to a boil. Reduce the heat and simmer, partially covered, until the veal is very tender, about 2 hours.

4. Remove the veal from the pot and set it aside, covered, to keep warm.

5. Combine the flour and cold water in a small dish, and add this to the pot. Cook, stir-

Once a familiar holiday dish, breast of veal has gotten expensive and can be difficult to find. It's worth the splurge, however. Look for a thick breast and ask the butcher to make a pocket in it. While the Dubins love chicken livers in the stuffing (as do I), if that's not your cup of tea, you can either omit them or substitute diced turkey sausage that you brown along with the onions and celery.

SERVES 4 TO 6

FOR THE STUFFING

3 tablespoons vegetable oil

2 medium-size onions, finely chopped

2 ribs celery, finely chopped

8 ounces white mushrooms, thinly sliced

2 cloves garlic, crushed

6 to 8 ounces chicken livers (optional)

Kosher (coarse) salt and freshly ground
    black pepper, to taste

1 stale challah (1 pound), crusts removed
    (see Note), bread torn into small pieces

1/4 cup chopped flat-leaf parsley

1 teaspoon dried basil

1/8 teaspoon ground dried sage

1/8 teaspoon ground dried marjoram

About 1/2 cup homemade chicken stock
    (page 63) or low-sodium boxed
    or canned broth

FOR THE SAUCE

1/2 cup Chinese duck sauce, such as
    Saucy Susan

1/2 cup ketchup

1/4 cup grainy Dijon mustard

FOR THE VEAL

1 breast of veal (4 pounds) with a pocket

3 medium-size onions, sliced

4 carrots, cut diagonally into 1/4-inch-thick slices

6 cloves garlic, coarsely chopped

1. Prepare the stuffing: Heat the oil in a large skillet over medium heat. Add the onions and celery and cook, stirring occasionally, until soft, about 7 minutes. Add the mushrooms and garlic and cook, stirring often, until the mushrooms are tender and have released their juice, about 10 minutes.

2. Meanwhile, if you are using the chicken livers, preheat the broiler, with the broiler rack about 8 inches from the heat source. Lightly season the chicken livers with salt and pepper, and broil them on both sides just until no pink remains, about 3 minutes—don't overcook them. Chop the chicken livers.

3. Combine the chicken livers, if using, the challah, the sautéed vegetables, and the parsley, basil, sage, and marjoram in a bowl. Stir in just enough of the chicken stock to moisten the mixture. Add salt and pepper to taste. Set the stuffing aside.

4. Prepare the sauce: Mix the duck sauce, ketchup, and mustard together in a bowl, and set it aside.

5. Preheat the oven to 350°F.

6. Rub the inside of the veal pocket with some of the sauce. Fill the pocket with the stuffing mixture, and close the opening with skewers. (Any leftover stuffing can be placed in a greased baking pan and baked along with the veal during the last 30 to 40 minutes of cooking.)

7. Cover the bottom of a large roasting pan with the sliced onions and carrots, and sprinkle the garlic over them. Place the veal on top of the vegetables and rub the remaining sauce over both sides of the meat. Roast, covered, for 1½ hours. Then uncover and continue roasting until tender and brown, about 1 hour more.

8. To serve, slice between the ribs.

Note: Don't throw away those challah crusts: Make challah chips instead. Cut the crusts off with a serrated knife and divide them into chip-size pieces. Grease or spray a baking sheet with vegetable cooking spray, and arrange the crusts on it in a single layer. Spray the crusts with vegetable cooking spray, sprinkle with garlic powder, seasoned salt, and grated Parmesan cheese if you're serving dairy, and bake in a preheated 350°F oven until crisp, 5 minutes or so (longer for thicker crusts). Remove the chips as they brown. Store in an airtight container for up to 1 week.

osso buco

from Joe Grippo

This is another extremely flavorful Italian preparation from Joe's family. If you think Osso Buco is only a rare restaurant splurge, you'll be surprised to see how easy it is to prepare at home. Be sure to ask your butcher for meaty shanks.

SERVES 4 TO 8 Ⓜ

FOR THE VEAL

1 cup all-purpose flour
Kosher (coarse) salt and freshly ground black
    pepper to taste
8 bone-in veal shanks, each approximately
    2 inches thick
3 to 4 tablespoons olive oil
3 to 4 tablespoons nondairy margarine
1 large onion, coarsely chopped
2 large cloves garlic, chopped
$1/2$ teaspoon dried basil

$1/2$ teaspoon dried oregano
1 cup dry white wine
1 can (28 ounces) Italian plum tomatoes,
    drained and chopped
1 cup homemade chicken stock (page 63) or
    low-sodium boxed or canned broth

FOR THE RICE

1 cup long-grain white rice
$2^1/4$ cups homemade chicken stock (page 63) or
    low-sodium boxed or canned broth
Pinch of saffron threads, crushed

FOR THE GREMOLATA

$3/4$ cup chopped flat-leaf parsley
Grated zest of 1 lemon

1. Preheat the oven to 350°F.

2. Combine the flour, $1^1/2$ teaspoons salt, and $1/2$ teaspoon pepper in a plastic bag. Shake well to combine. Dry the veal shanks well and toss them, one at a time, in the seasoned flour in the bag.

3. Heat 2 tablespoons of the oil and 2 tablespoons of the margarine in a large skillet over medium-high heat. Add the veal shanks and brown them well on all sides, 10 to 15 minutes (you may have to do this in batches). Transfer the cooked veal to a paper-towel-lined plate.

4. Lower the heat to medium and heat the remaining 1 to 2 tablespoons oil and 1 to 2 tablespoons margarine, as needed, to cook the onion. Add the onion and cook, stirring occasionally, until soft, about 10 minutes. Add the garlic, basil, and oregano and cook, stirring constantly, for about 1 minute more. Then add the wine and cook for a minute or

two to reduce it somewhat, scraping up any brown bits that may have stuck to the pan. Add the tomatoes, chicken stock, and salt and pepper to taste. Cook, stirring often, until the flavors come together, about 5 minutes.

5. Place the veal shanks in a large roasting pan and cover with the tomato mixture. Roast, covered, turning and basting them occasionally, until tender, about 1¹/₂ hours. Then uncover and continue roasting until they are very tender, with the meat almost falling off the bone, about 20 minutes more.

6. Meanwhile, prepare the rice: Bring the rice, chicken stock, and saffron to a boil in a medium-size saucepan. Reduce the heat to low and cook, covered, until the rice is tender and the liquid has been absorbed, about 20 minutes. Fluff with a fork.

7. For the gremolata, combine the parsley and lemon zest. To serve, arrange the veal on top of the rice and garnish with the gremolata.

Note: Gremolata is a traditional accompaniment to Osso Buco.

hungarian veal goulash

from Lilly Gutman

my niece Jessica's grandma-in-law, Lilly, made all her Hungarian dishes with fresh tomatoes. When choosing between the out-of-season "faux" variety (you know, those shiny, tasteless red balls they display in the produce section instead of the toy aisle) and canned, I'll take the canned any day. Use a good-quality sweet Hungarian paprika, to your liking. **SERVES 6**   **M**

2 to 4 tablespoons vegetable oil
2 pounds boneless veal stew meat,
*   cut into 1¹/₂-inch cubes*
2 large onions, chopped
5 medium-size tomatoes, diced, or 2 cans
*   (16 ounces each) crushed tomatoes*
1 can (14¹/₂ ounces) low-sodium chicken
*   broth or 1³/₄ cups homemade (page 63) or*
*   low-sodium boxed chicken stock*
2 to 4 tablespoons sweet Hungarian
*   paprika*
1 tablespoon caraway seeds
1 teaspoon kosher (coarse) salt, or to taste
Hot cooked wide noodles, for serving

1. Heat 1 tablespoon of the oil in a large, heavy pot over medium-high heat. Add the veal, in batches, and brown it on all sides, 3 to 4 minutes altogether, adding another tablespoon of oil if needed. Remove the veal chunks as they brown. Cover to keep them warm.

2. Reduce the heat to medium and add the remaining 1 to 2 tablespoons oil, as needed, to cook the onions. Add the onions and cook, stirring often, until soft, about 10 minutes. Add the tomatoes and cook, stirring, for a minute or two, just to break them up. Then stir in the chicken broth, paprika, caraway seeds, and salt. Simmer, covered, for 20 minutes.

3. Return the browned veal to the pot and simmer, covered, until tender, about 1 hour. Serve over noodles.

veal marengo

from Suzy Orlow-Solomonic

Every Friday night the entire Orlow family gets together for Shabbat dinner. The children help recite the blessings. When it's Suzy's turn to host, she likes to serve this dish because the whole family loves it. It's easy, yet fancy enough for company. Beef can be substituted for the veal. **SERVES 6 TO 8** **M**

2 tablespoons nondairy margarine

8 ounces white mushrooms, sliced

1/4 cup all-purpose flour

2 1/2 pounds boneless veal stew meat,
   cut into 1 1/2-inch cubes

3 to 4 tablespoons olive oil

2 cups pearl onions, peeled (see Note),
   or 2 medium-size onions, coarsely
   chopped

2 cloves garlic, crushed

1 can (28 ounces) crushed tomatoes

1 cup homemade chicken stock (page 63) or
   low-sodium boxed or canned broth

1 cup dry white wine, preferably Bordeaux

1 teaspoon dried thyme leaves

Kosher (coarse) salt and freshly ground
   black pepper to taste

Hot cooked noodles or rice, for serving

1. Melt the margarine in a Dutch oven or other large, heavy pot over medium heat. Add the mushrooms and cook until they are tender and have released their juice, 8 to 10 minutes. Remove the mushrooms and set them aside.

2. Place the flour in a large bowl. Dry the veal well and dredge it in the flour, shaking off any excess. Heat 3 tablespoons of the oil in the same pot over medium-high heat. Add the veal, in batches, and cook until the chunks are browned all over, 3 to 4 minutes altogether, adding the last tablespoon of oil if needed. Remove the veal chunks as they brown, and set them aside.

3. Reduce the heat to medium and add the onions. Cook, stirring often, until they are soft, about 5 minutes. Stir in the garlic and cook for 1 minute more. Then stir in the tomatoes, chicken stock, wine, thyme, and salt and pepper.

4. Return the browned veal to the pot and simmer, covered, until the meat is tender, 1 to 1 1/2 hours. Return the reserved cooked mushrooms to the pot during the last 15 minutes of cooking. Serve over noodles or rice.

Note: For an easy way to peel pearl onions, I do as Julia Child recommends: Drop them into rapidly boiling water and boil for about 10 seconds. Drain, and rinse under cold water. Slice off the itsiest bit of the tips and root ends so as not to disturb the layers, and the outer skin will peel right off.

Sometimes it's veal and sometimes it's chicken, but every Shabbat Suzy's family gets together.

sweetbreads
with peas and carrots

from Irene Rosenthal

Aunt Irene's sweetbreads were as much a part of my childhood as piano lessons and metal roller skates. Neither sweet nor bread, they are actually the pancreas and the thymus glands. If you can get past thoughts of anatomy, they are delicious and delicate. Look for those that are white, plump, and firm. Sweetbreads are very perishable, so prepare them within a day of purchase. They are traditionally served with peas, but Aunt Irene always served peas and carrots. **SERVES 4** **Ⓜ**

1¹/₂ to 2 pounds veal sweetbreads

2 tablespoons fresh lemon juice

4 tablespoons vegetable oil

1 medium-size onion, diced

1 rib celery, chopped

4 ounces white mushrooms, sliced

1 cup frozen peas and carrots, thawed

Kosher (coarse) salt and freshly ground
*   black pepper to taste*

1. Soak the sweetbreads in cold water to cover for 2 hours, changing the water once.

2. Drain the sweetbreads and place them in a medium-size saucepan. Add fresh water to cover and bring to a boil. Stir in the lemon juice, reduce the heat, and simmer for 20 minutes.

3. Meanwhile, prepare a large bowl of ice water.

4. Using a slotted spoon, transfer the sweetbreads to the ice water. When they are cool enough to handle, remove any loose membranes. Cut them into bite-size chunks and pat them dry. Set them aside.

5. Heat 2 tablespoons of the oil in a large saucepan over medium heat. Add the onion and celery and cook until soft, about 7 minutes. Add the mushrooms and cook until tender, about 10 minutes more. Remove the vegetables from the pan and set them aside.

6. Heat the remaining 2 tablespoons oil in the pan over medium-high heat, and cook the sweetbreads until brown on both sides, about 5 minutes total. Return the cooked vegetables to the pan, add the peas and carrots, and cook just to warm through, 1 minute or so. Add salt and pepper to taste, and serve immediately.

hazelnut-crusted rack of lamb
with cherry wine sauce

from Joan Kalish

most people eat rack of lamb only when dining out, but it's really simple to prepare at home. My friend Linda Gomberg says that the hazelnut topping is so divine, you don't need the cherry sauce—but as a firm believer in more is more, I think this is one lily I prefer to gild. **SERVES 4**　　　　**M**

FOR THE LAMB

2 lamb rib racks (8 ribs each)

3 to 4 tablespoons coarse-grain
　　Dijon mustard

¹/₃ cup plain dry bread crumbs

¹/₃ cup hazelnuts, skin removed and
　　finely chopped (see Note, page 403)

¹/₄ cup flat-leaf parsley leaves,
　　finely chopped

1 teaspoon dried thyme leaves

¹/₂ teaspoon freshly ground black pepper

¹/₄ teaspoon kosher (coarse) salt

FOR THE CHERRY WINE SAUCE

²/₃ cup dry red wine

¹/₃ cup beef broth (see box, page 137)

3 tablespoons honey

¹/₂ teaspoon dried thyme leaves

¹/₄ teaspoon dry mustard

¹/₄ teaspoon kosher (coarse) salt

2 teaspoons cornstarch

2 tablespoons balsamic vinegar

1 can (16¹/₂ ounces) pitted dark cherries,
　　drained

1. Preheat the oven to 400°F.

2. Place the lamb racks in a roasting pan, fat side up. Spread the mustard over them.

3. Combine the bread crumbs, hazelnuts, parsley, thyme, pepper, and salt in a bowl, and stir well. Pat this mixture evenly over the racks.

4. Roast for 10 minutes. Then cover the exposed bones with strips of aluminum foil (to prevent burning), reduce the oven temperature to 375°F, and roast for 30 minutes for medium-rare.

5. Meanwhile, prepare the sauce: Combine the wine, broth, honey, thyme, mustard, and salt in a heavy saucepan and bring to a boil. Reduce the heat and boil gently for 5 minutes.

6. Combine the cornstarch and vinegar in a bowl, and add this to the wine mixture. Bring it back to a boil. Then reduce the heat and boil gently until thick, about 1 minute. Stir in the cherries.

7. Let the ribs sit for 5 minutes, covered, before carving. Separate the ribs by slicing between them, and serve. Pass the Cherry Wine Sauce.

moroccan spicy apricot lamb shanks

from Victoria Moreno

While brisket and roast chicken are standard fare for our holiday dinners, our Sephardic *mishpuchah* dines on dishes like this tender, spicy lamb, which was adapted from Molly O'Neill's take on a recipe by superchef Alain Ducasse.

When I interviewed Wolfgang Puck about his seders at Spago, he told me that if he had been born Jewish, he would have liked to have been born Sephardic because of the cuisine. I know what he means! I love the pungent Moroccan spice mixture and usually make extra to save for flavoring other dishes, such as Sephardic Chicken with Olives and Honey (page 549). The wine is an untraditional addition and would never be used in a Moroccan kitchen. Interestingly, cookbook author Joyce Goldstein told me that Jews in Moslem countries, despite the fact that they do not share their neighbors' prohibition against drinking wine, traditionally do not use it in cooking either. Purists may substitute additional chicken broth for the wine. For proper browning, be sure the meat is thoroughly dry and the oil is hot enough. **SERVES 4**
M

4 lamb shanks (about 1 pound each),
  visible fat removed
Kosher (coarse) salt to taste
2 tablespoons olive oil
2 medium-size onions, chopped
2 to 3 tablespoons coarsely chopped
  garlic
1 cup dry red wine
1³/₄ cups homemade chicken stock
  (page 63), or 1 can (14¹/₂ ounces)
  low-sodium chicken broth
2 tablespoons Moroccan Spice Mix
  (recipe follows)
1 cup dried apricots
Freshly ground black pepper to taste

1. Preheat the oven to 350°F.

2. Dry the lamb shanks well with paper towels, then season them all over with salt.

3. Heat 1 tablespoon of the olive oil in a Dutch oven or other large, heavy, ovenproof pot over medium-high heat. Add the shanks and brown them on all sides, about 15 minutes altogether. Remove the shanks and set them aside.

4. Add the remaining 1 tablespoon oil to the pot, if necessary (you will need it if you have been diligent in removing all the visible fat from the lamb), reduce the heat to medium, and cook the onions until they are soft, about 10 minutes. Add the garlic and cook, stirring, for 1 minute more. Remove the pot from the heat. Stir in the wine and deglaze the pot, scraping up all the crusty brown bits. Stir in the chicken stock and the Moroccan Spice Mix. Return the lamb shanks to the pot.

5. Place the pot in the oven and roast, covered, turning and basting the shanks frequently, for about 1 hour.

6. Add the apricots and continue roasting, covered, until the meat is very soft, about 1¹/₂ hours more.

7. Transfer the shanks to a platter and keep warm. Remove as much fat as possible from the sauce, using a spoon or a fat separator. Season the sauce with salt and pepper to taste.

8. Spoon the sauce over the lamb shanks and serve, passing any extra sauce in a sauceboat.

Note: This dish tastes even better the next day and freezes well.

moroccan spice mix

⊙ ⊙ ⊙

MAKES ABOUT 4 TABLESPOONS

2 thin cinnamon sticks (about 3 inches each),
    broken into pieces
2 teaspoons black peppercorns
2 teaspoons fennel seeds
1 teaspoon coriander seeds
1 teaspoon ground ginger
1/2 teaspoon whole cloves
1/2 teaspoon ground nutmeg, or a sliver of
    whole nutmeg
1/2 teaspoon cumin seeds
1/2 teaspoon ground cardamom, or seeds from
    6 cardamom pods
1/2 teaspoon ground allspice

Combine the spices in a spice grinder or coffee mill and grind until fine and well mixed.

hamenahem's lamb shanks
in an aubergine blanket

from Rachel Humphrey

Another *wow!* presentation from the *Trading Spaces* kosher caterer (see box, page 158). Here lamb shanks are braised with artichoke hearts and potatoes in a delectable sauce and then tucked under an eggplant blanket for a final roast in the oven. **SERVES 4** Ⓜ

1 medium-size eggplant, peeled and cut into
    1/2-inch-thick slices
Kosher (coarse) salt
1/4 cup potato starch
4 lamb shanks (about 1 pound each),
    visible fat removed
Grated zest of 1 large lemon
About 6 tablespoons vegetable oil
2 large or 4 medium-size red or white boiling
    potatoes, cut into 1/2-inch-thick slices
3 shallots, chopped
3 cloves garlic, chopped
About 21/2 cups beef broth (see box, page 137)
1 box (10 ounces) frozen artichoke hearts,
    thawed
Juice of 1 large lemon
1/4 cup sugar
1/2 teaspoon ground cardamom
Pinch of ground turmeric
1/4 teaspoon freshly ground black pepper,
    or to taste

1. Spread the eggplant slices out on a baking sheet and sprinkle them with kosher salt. Allow to stand for 1 hour.

2. Pat the eggplant slices dry with paper towels (see box, page 168). Spread the potato starch on a plate and dredge the eggplant slices in it, coating both sides and shaking off any excess. Set the eggplant aside.

3. Dry the lamb shanks very well with paper towels. Press the lemon zest all over them.

4. Heat 1 tablespoon of the oil in a Dutch oven or other large, heavy, ovenproof pot over medium-high heat. Add the shanks and brown on all sides, about 15 minutes altogether. Transfer them to a plate and set aside.

5. Reduce the heat to medium, add the potato slices, and brown on both sides, about 7 minutes per side. Set them aside.

6. Heat another 1 tablespoon of the oil, if needed, over medium heat and cook the shallots and garlic until softened, about 2 minutes. Using a slotted spoon, transfer them to a plate and set aside.

7. Heat 1 tablespoon more of the remaining oil over medium-high heat. Lightly brown the coated eggplant slices on both sides, in batches, adding more oil as needed. Transfer the eggplant to a plate and set aside.

8. Add $1/2$ cup of the broth to the pot and deglaze it, scraping all the brown bits. Return the lamb shanks, potatoes, and shallot mixture to the pot. Add the artichoke hearts, lemon juice, sugar, cardamom, turmeric, pepper, and 1 teaspoon salt, along with enough of the remaining broth to barely cover the shanks. Bring to a boil. Then reduce the heat, cover the pot, and simmer, turning the shanks occasionally, until they are tender, about $1^1/4$ hours.

9. Meanwhile, preheat the oven to 375°F.

10. Remove the pot from the heat. Distribute the potato slices around the edge of the pot. Place the reserved eggplant slices on top of the lamb shanks. If your pot is wide enough, arrange the potato slices peeking through the sauce so they can brown further. Transfer the pot to the oven and roast, uncovered, until the shanks are very tender and the meat is pulling away from the bone, about 30 minutes.

11. To serve, place each lamb shank on a dinner plate and spoon some sauce over it. Surround it with potatoes and top it with an eggplant blanket.

Photo by Daniel Ottenstein

Rachel Humphrey and husband, Jeffrey, at son Daniel's Bar Mitzvah, 2007.

My indefatigable recipe tester Sandy Glazier saw a great tip for frying eggplant on an episode of *America's Test Kitchen* (PBS) the day before she tried this dish. After salting the eggplant slices and letting them stand for an hour, place them in a strainer to drain for 1 hour. Then wrap each slice in 3 layers of paper towels, place it on the counter, and press down with the palm of your hand. A lot more moisture will be eliminated, and you will need a lot less oil to brown the slices.

algerian lamb stew
with prunes

from Phyllis Epstein

Another traditional Mediterranean recipe from Phyllis's friend Zoulikha Fouathia. In Algeria this lamb stew would probably be prepared in a *tagine*, an earthenware casserole with a distinctive cone-shaped lid. Saffron, while expensive, really makes the dish. Just be sure you are getting the real thing: Look for deep red threads. Your mama was right: You get what you pay for. The good news is that saffron lasts for years when stored in a tightly closed container away from the light—and it takes only a few threads to contribute its special flavor. **SERVES 6** Ⓜ

FOR THE LAMB

2 to 4 tablespoons olive or vegetable oil
2¹/₄ pounds boneless lamb (or beef)
stew meat, cut into 1¹/₂-inch
chunks
3 medium-size onions, chopped
2 cloves garlic, chopped
¹/₂ teaspoon ground ginger
Kosher (coarse) salt
Pinch of saffron threads
¹/₃ cup honey
¹/₂ teaspoon ground cinnamon
1 pound pitted dried prunes

FOR THE COUSCOUS

2¹/₂ cups homemade chicken stock (page 63) or
low-sodium boxed or canned broth
Pinch of kosher (coarse) salt
2 teaspoons olive or vegetable oil
2 cups couscous

¹/₂ cup sliced almonds, toasted (see box, page 17)
¹/₄ cup sesame seeds, toasted (see box, page 17)

1. Heat 2 tablespoons of the oil in a Dutch oven or other large, heavy pot over medium-high heat. Add the meat, in batches, and brown it on all sides, 3 to 5 minutes per batch. Set the meat aside.

2. Add the remaining 1 to 2 tablespoons oil to the pot if needed to cook the onions. Add the onions and cook until soft, about 5 minutes. Add the garlic and cook for 30 seconds more. Return the meat to the pot and add the ginger, ¹/₂ teaspoon salt, and enough water to barely cover. Bring to a boil. Crush the saffron with your fingers and add it to the boiling liquid. Lower the heat, cover the pot, and simmer for 1 hour.

3. Add the honey and cinnamon and simmer, covered, for 10 to 15 minutes. Then stir in the prunes and simmer until the meat is tender, 10 to 15 minutes more.

4. Meanwhile, prepare the couscous: Bring the chicken stock to a boil in a medium-size saucepan. Add the salt and the oil, and stir in the couscous. Boil for 1 minute. Then remove the pot from the heat, cover it, and let it stand for 5 minutes. Fluff the couscous with a fork.

5. Serve the stew over the couscous, and garnish with the almonds and sesame seeds.

coming of age

poultry

When the taste testers of the prestigious *Cooks Illustrated* magazine conducted a study to determine the tastiest chicken, Empire kosher took top honors. Yes, kosher beat free-range, beat organic, beat all-natural. But why?

The testers concluded that both the method of slaughter and the soaking and salting process, in accordance with Jewish law, ensure the highest-quality bird, with home brining of the other contenders an acceptable second.

My experience with *Melting Pot Memories* leads me to suspect that many readers of this book may not even be Jewish, much less

"Kosher cooks have always used every part of the chicken."

Today he is a man; today she is a woman. Bar and Bat Mitzvahs—joyous celebrations. Who's who on page 613.

kosher. Those of you who have never tasted kosher poultry will be surprised to find it so much fresher and less fowl-tasting than the bird you are used to. And you don't have to show your Bar or Bat Mitzvah certificate at the door to buy at a kosher market, either. Empire chickens are even sold frozen in many supermarkets. But remember, kosher chickens are salted, so adjust your favorite recipes accordingly.

It's easy to understand why chicken plays such an important role in Jewish cuisine. In the shtetls of Eastern Europe, it was far more common than beef. Cheaper and easier to raise than cattle, which require an expanse of land for grazing, chickens are also much easier to butcher—and they provide eggs as well.

Aunt Sally remembered Mama Hinda plucking the chicken's pinfeathers herself to save the three cents that the butcher charged for this service. She also recalled the family practicing a custom known as *kapores*: On the eve of Yom Kippur, a live chicken was waved over their heads to pass along any transgressions to the unwitting bird. (Of course my mother, who is *much* younger than Aunt Sally, recalls no such thing.)

With centuries of thrift passed along in the genes, kosher cooks have always used every part of the chicken. The liver becomes a delicious spread (page 48), the neck and giblets find their way into a fricassee or gravy,

Top: My niece Jessica, about 1987. Bottom: My friend Barbara Klingsberg and I prepare the chicken for our Cooking Pleasures photo shoot.

Photo by Nick Koon

the backbone emboldens soup, and even the fat becomes that elixir called schmaltz (chicken fat), which when rendered with bits of skin, yields the precious gribenes (cracklings).

Our family members have adopted and adapted dishes from around the globe: Italian Chicken Cacciatore (my husband's personal favorite), Arroz con Pollo from Cuba, Chicken Biryani perfumed with Indian spices, Spicy Roasted Chicken with exotic Thai flavors, Hungarian Chicken Paprikash, Asian Chicken Stir-Fry with Walnuts, and more. You'll find retro dishes that never fail to please, like Coq au Vin, Chicken Kiev, and Chicken Marsala, and of course my good luck charm, Aunt Hilda's Cherry Chili Chicken. Our Herb-Roasted Garlic Chicken on a bed of fennel and shallots is an elegant choice for company, but you'll want to serve it for family dinners too. Looking for a kid-pleaser? Honey's Crumby Chicken always had my kids licking their plates (and fingers). Since cousin Barry gave me his recipe for Orange-Mustard Grilled Chicken, I've been making it almost every week.

With chicken recipes galore, not to mention a Cornish hen, four turkeys, and a sausage (sorry, no partridge—and no pear tree, for that matter) this chapter will have you clucking!

schmaltz and gribenes

from Hinda Rabinowitz

About 1½ pounds (3 cups) chicken fat and skin (trimmed of meat), cut into fine pieces (see Note)

1 medium-size onion, chopped

Kosher (coarse) salt

mama Hinda rendered her own schmaltz (chicken fat) to use in cooking. The by-product, gribenes (skin cracklings), was the Pringles of her day, fought over and devoured by the children. An old Yiddish proverb goes *"Meshugeneh genz, meshugeneh gribenes"*—"crazy geese, crazy cracklings" (or "Like parents, like children").

A while ago I removed from the freezer what I thought was a large bag of boneless, skinless chicken breasts. When it had defrosted, I discovered that they were chicken breasts all right, but not skinless. So I removed all the skin and fat, and when I was through, there was a huge mound of the stuff. Mama Hinda's frying pan happened to be in the sink. I looked at that mound and I looked at that frying pan, and I was seized by an irresistible urge to render. I communed with Mama Hinda all afternoon as the smell of slow-cooked onions percolating in chicken fat perfumed my kitchen.

There is nothing sacred about the proportions here. C'mon—who's gonna weigh or measure fat? I freeze the fat and loose skin, and when I have a nice pile and the mood hits, I render away. **MAKES ABOUT 1½ CUPS SCHMALTZ; ABOUT 1 CUP GRIBENES** Ⓜ

1. Pour 2 tablespoons water in a large, heavy skillet, then add the chicken fat and skin. (The steam from the water as it evaporates will prevent the skin from burning when it comes in contact with the hot pan.) Bring to a boil, then reduce the heat and simmer, uncovered, stirring often to prevent sticking, until all the fat has rendered, about 20 minutes.

2. Add the onion and continue simmering until the skin and onion are brown and crisp, 20 to 30 minutes. As the onion and skin begin to brown, stir more often to prevent the skin pieces from sticking to the pan.

3. Remove the skillet from the heat and for safety's sake, allow the mixture to cool to lukewarm in the skillet. (If you're not going to listen to me, at least warm the jars before you pour the hot fat into them.)

4. Strain the schmaltz through a fine-mesh strainer into clean glass jars, and cover the jars tightly. Don't be alarmed if there are tiny dark particles that sink to the bottom. The schmaltz will keep in the refrigerator for several weeks and in the freezer for months. Use the fat in place

Mama Hinda and me in Florida, 1946 (Uncle Lou Bower behind). Mama brought her kosher pots for the three-month stay.

of oil for frying anything from onions to liver—and especially in place of oil for matzoh balls.

5. Drain the gribenes on paper towels and sprinkle with salt to taste. Serve the gribenes plain as a snack or schmeared on bread, or use it in chopped liver, matzoh balls, or mashed potatoes.

Note: It is *much* easier to cut poultry skin with kitchen shears than with even the sharpest knife. Be sure the skin is finely cut. Larger pieces take too long to brown and the onions could burn.

corrinne's mock schmaltz

from Judy Bart Kancigor

This healthier version of the artery-clogging classic comes from the South African Women's Zionist Organization *International Goodwill Cookbook*, given to me by my "keyboard pal," Corrinne Kirshenbaum of Johannesburg, where it is considered a staple. This pareve (neutral) substitute for chicken fat can be used both with dairy meals and as an alternative to chicken fat with meat meals. The slow-cooked onions and carrots infuse the mixture with a hearty, almost schmaltz-like flavor that vegetarians will appreciate as well. **MAKES 2½ CUPS** Ⓟ

1¼ cups solid vegetable shortening
1¼ cups vegetable oil
1 large (8 ounces) onion, chopped
1 cup finely grated carrots

1. Combine the shortening, oil, onion, and carrots in a medium-size, heavy saucepan over medium-high heat, and melt the shortening. Reduce the heat to a gentle boil and cook, stirring occasionally, until the onions are soft and very lightly browned, about 30 minutes.

2. Remove the pan from the heat and for safety's sake, allow the mixture to cool to lukewarm in the pan. (If you're not going to listen to me, at least warm the jars before you pour the hot fat into them.)

3. Strain the mixture through a fine-mesh strainer into clean glass jars, and cover the jars tightly. The mock schmaltz will keep in the refrigerator for several weeks and in the freezer for months. (Refrigerate the mock schmaltz before freezing it. If the mixture separates slightly, stir, and then freeze.)

herb-roasted garlic chicken

from Julie Gullion

Here classic roast chicken gets the spa treatment: an herbal wrap inside and out. Put off by the price of shallots? Grab an onion. But if you've never tried fennel, this is a great place to start.

SERVES 4 Ⓜ

1 chicken (about 4 pounds), rinsed inside and
    out and patted dry

1 small bunch thyme sprigs

1 small bunch rosemary sprigs

1 small bunch sage sprigs

10 cloves garlic

1 teaspoon kosher (coarse) salt

¹/₄ teaspoon freshly ground black pepper

Juice of 1 lemon

16 shallots, coarsely chopped

1 head fennel, fronds removed, bulb coarsely
    chopped

¹/₂ cup dry white wine

1. Preheat the oven to 400°F.

2. Finely chop enough of the thyme, rosemary, and sage leaves to equal 1 tablespoon of each. Crush enough of the garlic to equal 1 tablespoon. Mix the chopped herbs and crushed garlic with the salt, pepper, and 1 tablespoon of the lemon juice. Carefully lift the skin of the chicken and spread about half the herb mixture under it. Rub the remaining herb mixture all over the skin. Put half of the remaining herb sprigs inside the chicken, along with about a third of the chopped shallots.

3. Combine the remaining shallots, garlic, herb sprigs, lemon juice, and the fennel in a roasting pan. Spread the mixture over the bottom, and place the chicken on top. Roast for 10 minutes. Then pour the wine over the chicken and continue roasting, basting often, until the juices run clear when pierced with a fork and the drumsticks move easily, about 1 hour. (A meat thermometer inserted in the thickest part—without touching the bone—should read 165°F.)

4. Remove the pan from the oven and allow the chicken to rest, covered, for 5 to 10 minutes before carving. Serve with the vegetables.

Note: For crisper skin on the underside of the chicken, begin roasting with the chicken positioned breast side down. After 30 minutes, carefully turn the chicken over and finish roasting.

spicy roasted chicken

from Miriam Wallach

ש hen Heshy retired, he and Miriam began taking cooking classes at the Institute of Culinary Education in New York City. This sweet and tangy dish

Photo by
Daniel Ottenstein

My proud cousin
Miriam with
grandson Daniel
Humphrey at
his Bar Mitzvah,
2007.

from chef Richard Ruben has become their favorite. I love the bold Indonesian flavors in the creamy marinade. Coconut milk is an underused ingredient in the kosher kitchen and is perfect here. **SERVES 4 TO 8** Ⓜ

1 medium-size onion, coarsely chopped

2 anchovy fillets

2 cloves garlic

2 tablespoons soy sauce

1 tablespoon fresh lemon juice

¹/₂ cup coconut milk

2 whole star anise, ground (see Note)

1 teaspoon sambal (chili paste, available at Southeast Asian markets; Huy Fong is one kosher brand)

¹/₂ teaspoon mustard seeds, preferably black

¹/₂ teaspoon freshly ground black pepper

¹/₄ teaspoon ground mace

3 to 4 pounds chicken pieces, or 8 boneless, skinless chicken breast halves, rinsed and patted dry

1. Combine the onion, anchovies, garlic, soy sauce, and lemon juice in a blender and process until very smooth. Add the coconut milk, star anise, sambal, mustard seeds, pepper, and mace, and process to combine well. Place the chicken pieces in a bowl or a resealable plastic bag, and pour the marinade over them. Cover the bowl, or seal the bag, and marinate in the refrigerator for 8 to 24 hours, turning occasionally.

2. Preheat the oven to 375°F.

3. Transfer the chicken and marinade to a baking pan and roast, basting occasionally, until cooked through, 45 to 60 minutes for chicken pieces, 25 to 30 minutes for bone-less, skinless breasts. (Alternatively, you can discard the marinade and grill the chicken over a very hot grill, turning it frequently.)

4. Serve the chicken hot, at room temperature, or even cold in a salad.

Note: To grind star anise (or any whole spices), use an electric coffee grinder. They're relatively inexpensive, and one whiff as it works its magic will prove the value of your investment. Just make sure you use a separate grinder for your coffee. To clean the grinder, grind bread or raw rice in it, and discard.

mahogany chicken
with figs and cranberries

from Lisa Ciomei, Wendy Altman Cohen

I combined two recipes, using figs and cranberries, my favorite dried fruits, which go well with chicken, basted in this glorious sauce. But any dried fruit, such as apricots, cherries, or prunes— or a combination— can be substituted. **SERVES 4** Ⓜ

Wendy and her Grandma Blanche, early '90s.

1 chicken (3¹/₂ to 4 pounds), cut into 8 pieces,
  rinsed and patted dry
Kosher (coarse) salt and freshly ground
  black pepper
³/₄ cup orange marmalade
¹/₄ cup finely chopped shallots or onion
2 cloves garlic, crushed, or ¹/₄ teaspoon
  garlic powder
1 teaspoon grated fresh ginger, or ¹/₂ teaspoon
  ground ginger
¹/₂ cup orange juice
¹/₄ cup prepared barbecue sauce
4 ounces dried Black Mission figs, stems
  removed, sliced in half (see Note)
2 ounces sweetened dried cranberries
  (¹/₂ cup; see Note)
Hot cooked rice or couscous, for serving

1. Preheat the oven to 375°F.

2. Sprinkle both sides of the chicken pieces with salt and pepper, and place them, skin side up, in a 13 × 9-inch baking pan.

3. Combine the marmalade with the shallots, garlic, and ginger in a bowl, and spread this mixture over the chicken. Roast, uncovered, for 25 minutes.

4. Transfer the chicken to a platter (reduce the oven temperature to 350°F), and carefully pour the hot liquid from the baking pan into a medium-size saucepan. Using a spoon or a fat separator, remove as much fat as you can from the top of the liquid. Add the orange juice and barbecue sauce to the pan, and bring to a boil. Cook until the sauce is reduced by about half, about 8 minutes.

5. Return the chicken to the baking pan, and distribute the figs and cranberries around it. Baste the chicken with the sauce and return it to the oven. Roast, basting often, until the chicken is cooked through and golden brown, about 25 minutes more.

6. Serve hot, smothered in the sauce and warm fruit, over rice or couscous.

Note: If the dried fruit is not soft, add it to the reducing sauce in Step 4 for the last minute or so, rather than waiting until Step 5.

honey's crumby chicken

from Lillian Bart

This dish was my kids' favorite when eating at Honey's (my mom's) house. The name was their idea. Kids' food, yes, but so far no one has outgrown it. Honey finds the prepared cornflake crumbs too fine and likes to process her own so the chicken has a "crumbier" texture.

SERVES 4   Ⓜ

2 tablespoons nondairy margarine, melted
About 10 cups cornflakes
3 large eggs, beaten
1 teaspoon kosher (coarse) salt
1 teaspoon garlic powder
2 teaspoons paprika
¹/₄ teaspoon freshly ground black pepper
¹/₃ cup all-purpose flour
1 chicken (3 to 4 pounds), cut into 8 pieces,
  rinsed and patted dry

> Everyone calls my grandma [Lil] 'Honey.' My friends think that's her name. I have such wonderful childhood memories of being with her— Honey wasn't just my grandmother; she was my best friend. We'd go out to dinner and movies together, and I loved to spend the night at Honey's house. I even kept a bike there. She is just so much fun to be around. Even today, for no apparent reason, she will break out in song, a trait we notice in our daughter, Samantha. We're keeping our fingers crossed that she has inherited the singing gene from Honey and Poppy. (Stay tuned.)
>
> —BRAD KANCIGOR

1. Preheat the oven to 350°F. Line a baking pan with heavy-duty aluminum foil, and spread the melted margarine evenly over the foil.

2. Place the cornflakes in a food processor and process to form coarse crumbs. Set them aside in a shallow bowl or plate.

3. Beat the eggs, salt, garlic powder, paprika, and pepper together in a large shallow bowl. Place the flour in a resealable plastic bag or on a plate.

4. Coat each piece of chicken with flour, shaking off the excess. Then dip them in the egg mixture, and finally in the cornflake crumbs. (If you keep one hand for dry and one hand for wet, the crumbs won't get soggy.) Press the crumbs firmly onto the chicken, so it is coated all over.

5. Place the chicken pieces in the prepared baking pan and bake, turning them halfway through the cooking, until they are cooked through and the skin is nice and crisp, about 1 hour. Serve hot, cold, or at room temperature.

hawaiian chicken

from Claire Smolen

Claire and her sister, Joan Kalish (whose recipes also appear in these pages), belonged to a gourmet group that was an Atlanta institution for thirty-eight years. Calling themselves the "Gour-Menschen," the five talented couples included an artist, a professional chef, a writer, and an opera singer. Every other month they would pull the name of a country or region out of a jar, and then the research would begin. The elaborate menus, decorations, photos, movies—and more recently videos—of their gastronomic excursions around the globe could fill attics. The hardest part, Claire told me, was selecting a date: They would not meet unless all ten of them could be there, and alas, when Joanie died (followed two years later by her husband, Murray), the group, while remaining close, never met again as Gour-Menschen.

Over the years they had tasted some pretty exotic fare. Not every dish was a hit, however. Claire remembers making a bean dish with mousseline sauce that absolutely reeked. "How can I bring this?" she asked Perry. "Take it," he said, "so if we ever visit that country we'll know what not to order."

One of the more successful dishes from the Gour-Menschen's virtual travels was Claire's Hawaiian Chicken, with its sweet tropical flavors and crunchy almond topping. **SERVES 8** **Ⓜ**

Vegetable cooking spray
2 chickens (3 to 3¹/₂ pounds each),
*   each cut into 8 pieces, rinsed and*
*   patted dry*
About 2 tablespoons vegetable oil
Kosher (coarse) salt and freshly ground
*   black pepper to taste*
Paprika to taste
1 cup (packed) light brown sugar
2 tablespoons distilled white vinegar
6 tablespoons grainy Dijon mustard
1 can (8 ounces) crushed pineapple,
*   undrained*
¹/₂ cup sliced almonds

1. Preheat the broiler. Spray a broiler rack with vegetable cooking spray.

2. Rub both sides of the chicken pieces with the oil, and then sprinkle salt, pepper, and paprika all over them. Place the chicken on the prepared rack in a broiler pan, and broil on both sides until the skin is brown and crisp, 7 to 10 minutes per side.

3. Meanwhile, combine the brown sugar, vinegar, mustard, and pineapple, with its juice, in a bowl.

4. Remove the chicken from the broiler. Line a large baking pan with heavy-duty aluminum foil, and arrange the chicken in it.

5. Preheat the oven to 350°F.

6. Measure out ¹/₂ cup of the brown sugar mixture and set it aside. Spoon the remaining mixture over the chicken pieces and bake, basting often, for 40 minutes.

7. Stir the almonds into the reserved mixture, and spoon it over the chicken. Continue baking until the chicken is cooked through and the topping is crispy, 5 to 10 minutes more. Serve hot.

chicken cacciatore

from Lilly Kancigor Cohen

illy got this recipe years ago from a coworker who came from a large Italian family. My husband, Barry, who loves Italian

Barry's cousin, Lilly, at daughter Halley's Bat Mitzvah. It's hard to believe that when I met Lilly, she was four.

food so much that he's sure there must be Italians in his family tree—he likes to think the Padwa side of his family actually came from Padua—proclaimed this his favorite of all the chicken dishes here and pouted when I nailed it the first time. "Don't you want to test it again?" he begged. **SERVES 4**　Ⓜ

3 tablespoons all-purpose flour

1 teaspoon kosher (coarse) salt,
    or to taste

1/4 teaspoon freshly ground black pepper,
    or to taste

1 chicken (3¹/2 to 4 pounds), cut
    into 8 pieces, rinsed and patted
    dry

2 to 3 tablespoons olive oil

3/4 cup chopped shallots or onions,
    or a combination

1 tablespoon nondairy margarine

3 large cloves garlic, finely chopped

1/3 cup finely chopped flat-leaf parsley

3/4 cup dry white wine

1 can (6 ounces) tomato paste

1³/4 cups homemade chicken stock
    (page 63) or low-sodium
    boxed or canned broth

1 bay leaf

2 teaspoons dried basil

1 teaspoon dried oregano

1/2 teaspoon dried thyme leaves

1/4 teaspoon ground marjoram

12 ounces white mushrooms,
    sliced

1. Combine the flour, salt, and pepper in a bowl or a resealable plastic bag, and dredge the chicken, 1 or 2 pieces at a time, in this mixture. Shake off the excess flour and set the chicken pieces aside.

2. Heat 2 tablespoons of the oil in a large skillet over medium-high heat until it is quite hot but not smoking. Add the chicken and cook until golden brown on both sides, 3 to 4 minutes per side, adding the third tablespoon of oil if necessary. Transfer the chicken to a plate.

3. Add the shallots to the skillet and cook until soft, about 4 minutes. Add the margarine, garlic, and parsley, and cook, stirring constantly, for 1 minute more.

4. Remove the skillet from the heat, add the wine, and scrape up the brown bits from the bottom of the pan. Return the skillet to the heat and stir in the tomato paste, chicken stock, bay leaf, basil, oregano, thyme, and marjoram. Bring to a boil.

5. Return the chicken to the skillet and reduce the heat. Simmer, covered, basting and turning the chicken pieces occasionally, until they are cooked through, tender, and moist, about 40 minutes. (If the breasts finish cooking before the thighs, remove them and keep them covered until the thighs are cooked through.)

6. Remove the chicken and cover it with aluminum foil to keep warm. Add the mushrooms to the skillet and cook, uncovered, over medium-high heat, stirring often, until they are tender, about 10 minutes. Add salt and pepper to taste.

7. Return the chicken to the skillet and heat it through. Serve immediately, spooning the sauce over the chicken.

indian chicken

from Gary Bart

my brother, Gary, loves Indian cooking and is an ardent follower of Madhur Jaffrey. Here he combines some of her favorite ingredients and techniques in this highly flavored dish that no one region could ever claim. I am having a little, er, family disagreement with my brother on the issue of skin removal, however. When I tested his recipe, rewrote it, and e-mailed it back to him, his response included the following subject line: YOU HAVE TO LEAVE SKIN ON JUDY OTHERWISE FEH. Yet according to Jaffrey, in Indian cuisine the skin is usually removed—and I couldn't agree more when it comes to this dish. It is decidedly *not feh* this way, in my opinion, but I'll leave the choice to you. One word of caution: Be careful when using turmeric. If the sauce splashes, you'll be wearing it forever. And if you think you don't like dates, I have one word for you: Medjool!

Gary suggests serving this over saffron rice flavored with cumin and currants, with your favorite chutney alongside.

SERVES 4 Ⓜ

1 chicken (3¹/₂ to 4 pounds), cut into 8 pieces, rinsed and patted dry

2 teaspoons ground cumin

2 teaspoons ground turmeric

1 teaspoon ground ginger

1 teaspoon ground cardamom

1 medium-size onion, coarsely chopped

¹/₃ cup slivered almonds

5 cloves garlic

¹/₂ cup homemade chicken stock (page 63) or low-sodium boxed or canned broth

2 to 4 tablespoons vegetable oil

1 medium-size onion, thinly sliced

¹/₃ cup fresh lemon juice

1 teaspoon sea salt or kosher (coarse) salt, or to taste

¹/₈ to ¹/₂ teaspoon cayenne pepper

8 Medjool dates, sliced (optional)

1. Remove the skin (or not—see the headnote) from the chicken pieces. Set the chicken aside.

2. Stir the cumin, turmeric, ginger, and cardamom together in a bowl, and set aside.

3. Combine the chopped onion, almonds, garlic, and chicken stock in a blender or food processor, and process until smooth. Set the mixture aside.

4. Heat the oil in a large skillet over medium-high heat until it is quite

My brother, Gary, and me in front of our house in Belle Harbor. Times were good. There was a new Hudson in the driveway every year.

hot but not smoking. Add the chicken pieces, in batches, and cook until browned on both sides, 3 to 4 minutes per side. Remove the chicken and set it aside. Discard all but 2 tablespoons of the oil in the skillet.

5. Return the skillet to the heat and when the oil is hot, add the reserved spice mixture all at once. Stir-fry for a few seconds. Then reduce the heat to medium, add the sliced onions, and cook until soft, about 4 minutes. Stir in the reserved onion/almond mixture and the lemon juice, salt, and cayenne. Heat until bubbling. Return the chicken pieces to the skillet and simmer, covered, stirring occasionally, until they are cooked through, 30 to 40 minutes. Add the dates, if using, during the last 10 minutes of cooking. Serve hot, spooning the sauce over the chicken.

chicken paprikash

from Carole Orlow

The essential ingredient in paprikash, as any Hungarian cook will tell you, is the paprika. Some like it sweet, some like it hot, but the important thing is that there really is a difference between good-quality Hungarian paprika and that red stuff our mothers sprinkled over chicken for color. While sour cream was an essential part of this dish for their non-Jewish neighbors, kosher cooks in Hungary, of course, omitted it. **SERVES 4 Ⓜ**

1 chicken (3¹/₂ to 4 pounds), cut into 8 pieces, rinsed and patted dry
Kosher (coarse) salt to taste
Freshly ground black pepper to taste
Garlic powder to taste
Dried oregano to taste
Sweet or hot Hungarian paprika
4 tablespoons olive oil
2 medium-size onions, finely chopped
2 to 3 cloves garlic, crushed
1 can (28 ounces) whole tomatoes, coarsely chopped, juices reserved
1 can (6 ounces) tomato paste
¹/₄ teaspoon red pepper flakes
2 large green bell peppers, stemmed, seeded, and chopped
1 pound white mushrooms, sliced
1 cup nondairy sour cream (optional)
Hot cooked egg noodles, for serving

1. Season the chicken on both sides lightly with salt. Then lightly sprinkle pepper, garlic powder, and oregano over the chicken. Finally, season with the paprika—very liberally if using sweet, a light sprinkling if using hot. Set the chicken aside.

2. Heat 2 tablespoons of the oil in a Dutch oven or other large, heavy pot over medium heat. Add the onions and cook until

Cousin Carole, early '50s. She always made all her own clothes. In high school she won a national contest designing a costume for Maria Callas, who wore it as Carmen at the Met.

soft, about 5 minutes. Add the garlic, cook, stirring, for 1 minute more, and then transfer the onions and garlic to a plate.

3. Raise the heat to medium-high and add the remaining 2 tablespoons oil to the pot. When the oil is quite hot but not smoking, add the chicken pieces and brown them on both sides, 3 to 4 minutes per side.

4. Remove the chicken from the pot. Stir the tomatoes with all their juices, tomato paste, the reserved onion/garlic mixture, and the red pepper flakes into the pot. Return the chicken to the pot, making sure to cover all the pieces with the sauce. Simmer, covered, for 30 minutes. Add salt and pepper to taste.

5. Add the bell peppers and mushrooms and continue to simmer, covered, until the chicken is cooked through, 20 to 30 minutes.

6. Just before serving, remove the chicken from the pot and keep it warm. Add the sour cream, if using, to the sauce and heat it over medium-low heat, being careful not to let it boil. Serve hot, spooning the sauce over the chicken and noodles.

easy coq au vin

from Claire Altman

When the chicken hits the bottle, no one cries "fowl," least of all the diners. Here Claire uses some of the same techniques as in her Easy Boeuf Bourguignon (page 137) and garners the same applause. The frozen pearl onions are a time-saver. Use fresh potatoes instead of canned, if you prefer. Or you can skip the potatoes altogether and serve this over rice or couscous. **SERVES 4** **M**

2 to 3 tablespoons olive oil
1 chicken (3 1/2 to 4 pounds), cut into 8 pieces, rinsed and patted dry
1 can (7 ounces) whole mushrooms, drained, or 8 ounces fresh white mushrooms, sliced
1/4 cup kosher "bacon" bits
2 cloves garlic, crushed
2 cups dry red wine
1/2 teaspoon onion powder
1/2 teaspoon garlic powder
2 bay leaves
1/4 teaspoon dried thyme leaves
1 tablespoon chopped fresh parsley, or 1 teaspoon dried parsley flakes
1/2 teaspoon crushed dried rosemary
1 1/2 teaspoons kosher (coarse) salt, or to taste
Freshly ground black pepper to taste
1 bag (10 ounces) frozen pearl onions, thawed
2 cans (15 ounces each) baby new potatoes, or 1 1/2 pounds fresh boiling potatoes, cut into 1-inch cubes (optional)
Paprika to taste
2 tablespoons cornstarch
2 tablespoons cold water

1. Preheat the oven to 350°F.

2. Heat 2 tablespoons of the oil in a Dutch oven or other large, heavy, ovenproof

pot over medium-high heat until it is quite hot but not smoking. Add the chicken and cook until browned on both sides, about 4 minutes per side, adding the remaining 1 tablespoon oil if needed. Remove the chicken from the pot and set it aside. Discard all but 1 tablespoon of the oil in the pot (leave the crusty chicken bits).

3. Add the mushrooms to the pot and cook until tender, about 5 minutes. Add the imitation bacon bits and the garlic, and cook, stirring, for 1 minute more.

4. Remove the pot from the heat and pour in the wine. Deglaze the pan, scraping up all the brown bits. Return the pot to the heat, add the onion powder, garlic powder, bay leaves, thyme, parsley, rosemary, 1 teaspoon of the salt, and pepper to taste. Bring just to a boil.

5. Return the chicken to the pot, and snuggle it into the wine sauce. Add the onions, and the potatoes if using, and sprinkle everything liberally with paprika. Transfer the pot to the oven and bake, uncovered, basting occasionally, until the chicken is cooked through, about 1 hour.

6. Remove the chicken from the pot, cover, and keep warm. Taste the sauce, and add the remaining 1/2 teaspoon salt and more pepper if needed. Combine the cornstarch and the cold water in a bowl or cup. Bring the sauce to a simmer and pour in half of the cornstarch mixture. Stir until thickened, about 1 minute. If you desire a thicker sauce, repeat with the remaining cornstarch. Serve hot, spooning the sauce over the chicken.

> My mother-in-law, Jintil [second from right in the photo], was a very gentle person, as her name implies. Still, she was a sharp businesswoman who assisted her husband in his dry goods store, which they ran on a sugar plantation in the countryside of Cuba. As Sephardic Jews who spoke Ladino, they had emigrated from Turkey to a Spanish-speaking country, and she always dreamed of the time when they would move to Havana. Sadly, in 1962, just as she was about to achieve her dream, Castro's ascendancy dashed it, and they were lucky to get on a flight to the U.S. They left with only the clothing on their backs. Even my mother-in-law's wedding band was snipped off at the airport. My father-in-law had a small attaché case of photos, which was opened, the photos unceremoniously dumped, and returned to him empty. When he commented to the official, 'You may as well keep the case,' the official responded, 'One more word and I keep you, too.'
> —SYDELL LEVY

jintil levy's arroz con pollo

from Marian Weiss

My cousin Marian's friend Sydell Levy remembers her mother-in-law, Jintil, grinding spices in a mortar for her version of this traditional Cuban dish. **SERVES 8**   Ⓜ

FOR THE CHICKEN AND MARINADE

**2 chickens (3 to 4 pounds each), each cut into
    8 pieces, rinsed and patted dry**

**2 tablespoons coarsely chopped garlic
    (3 to 5 large cloves)**

¹/₄ teaspoon kosher (coarse) salt

2 tablespoons distilled white vinegar

¹/₂ cup fresh lemon juice

¹/₈ teaspoon ground cumin

FOR THE ARROZ CON POLLO

**1¹/₂ cups homemade chicken stock
    (page 63) or low-sodium boxed
    or canned broth**

Small pinch of saffron threads

2 to 3 tablespoons olive oil

1 large onion, chopped

1 can (15 ounces) tomato sauce

**1 cup dry white wine, Sauternes, sherry,
    or beer**

¹/₄ teaspoon poultry seasoning

¹/₄ teaspoon freshly ground black pepper

¹/₄ teaspoon ground oregano

¹/₄ teaspoon ground cumin

¹/₄ teaspoon kosher (coarse) salt

¹/₄ teaspoon garlic salt

¹/₄ teaspoon onion salt

Dash of cayenne pepper

¹/₂ cup small green olives, undrained

**1 jar (4 ounces) chopped red pimentos,
    undrained, or ¹/₂ cup bottled roasted red
    peppers, chopped, undrained**

**1 can (8 ounces) petit pois or sweet peas,
    undrained**

2 cups long-grain white rice

1. Remove all visible fat, and any hanging or loose skin, from the chicken pieces.

Place the chicken in a resealable plastic bag (preferred) or a bowl.

2. Prepare the marinade: Finely chop the garlic and the salt together. Combine the garlic/salt mixture with the vinegar, lemon juice, and cumin in a small bowl, and pour the marinade over the chicken. Seal the bag, or cover the bowl, and marinate for 2 to 6 hours in the refrigerator, turning the pieces occasionally.

3. Bring the chicken stock to a boil in the microwave or in a small saucepan. Crush the saffron with your fingers and drop it into the hot stock. Let it steep while you prepare the remaining ingredients.

4. Heat 2 tablespoons of the oil in a Dutch oven or other large, heavy pot over medium heat. Add the onions and a few tablespoons of the tomato sauce, and cook until soft, about 4 minutes.

5. Drain the chicken, discarding the marinade. Add the chicken pieces, with any garlic clinging to them, to the pot and cook over medium-high heat for 3 minutes on each side. (You will probably need to do this in batches. If necessary, heat the remaining 1 tablespoon oil in the pot for the second batch of chicken.) The chicken will not really brown, as it has been marinating in a liquid, but it will darken because of the tomato sauce and onions. Remove the chicken, and if you like (and I do), pour off some of the fat.

6. Add the remaining tomato sauce, the saffron-infused chicken stock, and the wine to the pot. Stir in the poultry seasoning, pepper, oregano, cumin, salt, garlic salt, onion salt, and cayenne. Add 1 tablespoon of the liquid from the olives, 1 tablespoon of the

liquid from the pimentos, and the liquid from the peas. Return the chicken to the pot and bring to a boil. Reduce the heat, cover the pot, and simmer, turning and basting the chicken occasionally, for 40 minutes. (You want to make sure that all the chicken pieces have had a turn bathing in the liquid.)

7. Remove the chicken from the pot and stir in the rice and olives. Return the chicken and simmer, covered, until the rice is tender, about 25 minutes. If the liquid is not fully absorbed, take the pot off the heat and set it aside, covered, for 10 minutes or so. Stir in the peas and let them warm for a minute or two.

8. Spoon the rice and chicken onto a warm platter, scatter the pimentos over the top, and serve.

cherry chili chicken

from Hilda Robbins

For some it's a rabbit's foot. For others it's a lucky penny. For me it's Cherry Chili Chicken.

My lucky recipe was Aunt Hilda's specialty, her decades-old signature dish, eagerly anticipated by all (although she just called it "holiday chicken"—I always was a sucker for alliteration). Sweet yet zippy, pretty plump cherries peeking through the piquant sauce, Aunt Hilda's holiday chicken ushered in countless New Years,

> " Hilda and I were married in 1945. I was stationed in Pratt, Kansas. Decent apartments were hard to find, and we took anything we could get. Our landlady used to kill her own chickens. We would ask her, 'Could you please wait until we leave before you kill the chickens?' 'Oh, sure,' she'd say, and as we were walking away we'd hear 'EEP!' and that was the end of another chicken. One time she offered Hilda one of her chickens. Hilda asked her, 'How come your chickens are so white? How do you clean them so well?' Her secret? She used Borax!
>
> **—LOU ROBBINS** "

heralded scores of birthdays, and graced many a holiday table.

When the self-published *Melting Pot Memories* first came out, I noticed a very strange thing. Everyone who told me they were trying the recipes seemed to start with the same one. How odd is that! You guessed it—it was the now renamed Cherry Chili Chicken. Then four food editors who featured my book in their various publications also selected the Cherry Chili Chicken to highlight their holiday stories. So forgive me if I attribute magical powers to this recipe!

But where did it come from, I wondered. After much research, I found a similar recipe called Chicken Jubilee in that fifties classic, long out of print, called *Thoughts for Buffets*. Did Aunt Hilda own that book? Cousins Bonnie and Jackie don't remember it. We'll never know.

SERVES 8

³/₄ **cup raisins**

1 can (16¹/₂ ounces) pitted black cherries, undrained

2 large onions, thinly sliced

2 chickens (3 to 4 pounds), each cut into 8 pieces, rinsed and patted dry

Garlic powder to taste

Paprika to taste

Kosher (coarse) salt and freshly ground black pepper to taste

2 to 4 tablespoons vegetable oil

1 cup dry sherry or white wine

2 bottles (12 ounces each) chili sauce, such as Heinz

¹/₃ cup (packed) dark brown sugar

1. Put the raisins in a small bowl and pour the juice from the canned cherries over them. Set aside.

2. Preheat the oven to 350°F. Scatter the onion slices over the bottom of a large baking pan or roasting pan. Set the pan aside.

3. Season the chicken with garlic powder, paprika, and salt and pepper.

4. Heat 1 tablespoon of the oil in a large skillet over medium-high heat until it is quite hot but not smoking. Add the chicken, in batches, and cook until browned on both sides, 3 to 4 minutes per side, adding the remaining oil 1 tablespoon at a time, if needed. As the chicken pieces brown, arrange them, skin side up, on top of the onions in the baking pan.

5. Remove the skillet from the heat and discard all the oil. Add ¹/₂ cup of the sherry to the skillet and scrape up all the brown bits. Stir in the chili sauce, brown sugar, ¹/₄ cup water, and the plumped raisins with the cherry juice. Bring the mixture to a boil, and then pour it over the chicken. Roast, uncovered, basting occasionally, for 25 minutes.

6. Pour the remaining ¹/₂ cup sherry around the chicken, distribute the cherries throughout the pan, and baste. Roast, basting occasionally, until cooked through, 20 to 30 minutes.

7. Transfer the chicken to a warm serving platter and cover to keep warm. Strain the liquid into a medium-size saucepan, reserving the solids. Bring the strained sauce to a boil over medium-high heat and boil until reduced by about one third, or until thick, 8 to 10 minutes (longer if you like a thicker sauce).

8. Spoon the onions, cherries, and raisins over the chicken, and pass the sauce.

Optional dipping sauce for latkes: For Hanukkah—and do we really have to wait for this holiday to have latkes?—use the warm reduction as a dipping sauce, a nice change from applesauce. Even if you're not serving Cherry Chili Chicken, you can create a sauce that's almost as good. Slice the cherries and combine them with their liquid, the raisins, wine, chili sauce, and brown sugar in a medium saucepan. Reduce this mixture over medium-high heat until it's as thick as you like it, about 20 minutes.

Aunt Hilda and my mom, Lillian, at Stu and Shelly's wedding, 1988. Shelly's family learned the hora and we learned the polka.

chicken fricassee

from Lillian Bart

My favorite dish on cold winter nights was my mom's fricassee: chicken practically falling off the bone, plenty of giblets for me and my dad to fight over, necks to suck clean, and carrots and meatballs poking through the tomato gravy. She'd serve it like soup, in big bowls, with plenty of challah for dunking. Her secret is that she removes the skin before cooking. Frankly, our family has never been a great fan of chicken with flaccid skin. If we're gonna eat skin, it better be crisp!

But wait! Are you sure you want to throw out that skin and fat? I freeze it, and when I'm feeling particularly nostalgic and am missing Mama Hinda, I take out her old frying pan and make Schmaltz and Gribenes (page 173). I freeze that too, and when the holidays roll around, my matzoh balls are incredible! C'mon—once or twice a year won't kill us. **SERVES 8 TO 10** Ⓜ

FOR THE MEATBALLS

2 pounds ground beef

2 large eggs

2 slices challah, torn into small pieces

1 envelope dehydrated onion soup mix

$^1/_4$ cup ketchup

FOR THE FRICASSEE

2 tablespoons vegetable oil

2 medium-size (1 pound) onions, chopped

2 ribs celery, chopped

1 green bell pepper, stemmed, seeded, and chopped

3 cloves garlic, crushed

2 pounds chicken giblets and necks (no liver), skin removed

1 can (28 ounces) crushed tomatoes

1 can (15 ounces) tomato sauce

1 cup homemade chicken stock (page 63) or low-sodium boxed or canned broth

3 bay leaves

Kosher (coarse) salt to taste

Freshly ground black pepper to taste

1 chicken (3 to 3$^1/_2$ pounds), cut into 8 pieces, skin and fat removed, rinsed and patted dry

3 medium-size carrots, cut into $^1/_2$-inch-thick slices

Mom and me, circa 1952. Note my dog tag from the "duck and cover" days.

1. Prepare the meatball mixture: Combine all the meatball ingredients in a bowl and mix well. Cover and refrigerate until ready to use.

2. Heat the oil in a Dutch oven or other large, heavy pot over medium heat. Add the onions, celery, and bell pepper, and cook until the onions are soft and golden but not brown, about 8 minutes. Add the garlic and cook, stirring, for 1 minute more.

3. Add the giblets, crushed tomatoes, tomato sauce, chicken stock, bay leaves, 1 teaspoon of the salt, and pepper to taste.

Bring to a boil. Then reduce the heat and simmer, covered, for 1 hour.

4. Add the chicken pieces and simmer, covered, for 20 minutes more.

5. Form the meatball mixture into balls about 1½ inches in diameter and carefully add them to the pot. Add the carrots and simmer, partially covered, until the meatballs and chicken are cooked through, about 30 minutes. Add the remaining 1 teaspoon salt and pepper to taste, if needed, and serve.

chicken veracruz

from Brad Kancigor

y son Brad became quite the chef when I was working on this book, gladly testing recipes for me. He created his own version of Chicken Veracruz after watching Rick Bayliss on TV. Brad and Tracey use thighs for this recipe, which they find to be juicier than breasts, but feel free to use breasts, or a combination, if you prefer. (I know. You're wondering, hey, Brad, where are the olives and capers? He and Tracey don't like 'em, but if this recipe leaves you brine-deprived, add 2 tablespoons capers and 1 cup sliced green olives with the chicken stock.) Serve on a bed of rice. **SERVES 6** M

2 fresh mild green chiles, such as Anaheim,
    pasilla, or poblano

2 red bell peppers

5 medium-size plum tomatoes

2 to 3 tablespoons vegetable oil

12 chicken thighs, rinsed and patted dry

2 large onions, finely chopped

3 cloves garlic, crushed

1 cup dry red wine

1 cup homemade chicken stock (page 63)
    or low-sodium boxed or canned broth

$^1/_2$ teaspoon ground cumin

1 teaspoon kosher (coarse) salt, or to taste

$^1/_4$ teaspoon freshly ground black pepper

$^1/_4$ cup cilantro leaves, chopped

1. Preheat the broiler.

2. Place the chiles, bell peppers, and tomatoes in a roasting pan. Broil, turning them, until they are blackened all over, about 10 minutes. Then place them in a paper bag, close the bag, and set them aside until cool, at least 15 minutes.

3. Meanwhile, preheat the oven to 350°F.

4. Remove the blackened vegetables from the bag and slip off the skins. Remove the stems, veins and seeds from the chiles and bell peppers. Transfer the chiles, bell peppers, and tomatoes to a food processor, and process until pureed. (Alternatively, press them through a food mill.) Set aside.

5. Heat 2 tablespoons of the oil in a large ovenproof skillet over medium-high heat. Add the chicken and cook until browned all over, about 3 minutes per side, adding the remaining 1 tablespoon oil if needed. Remove the chicken and set aside.

6. Drain all but 2 tablespoons oil from the skillet, place it over medium heat, and add the onions. Cook until they are soft and golden, about 10 minutes. Then add the garlic and cook, stirring constantly, for 1 minute more.

7. Remove the skillet from the heat and add the wine. Deglaze the pan, scraping up the crusty brown bits. Return the skillet to the heat and cook until the mixture has reduced slightly, about 5 minutes. Add the stock, the pureed chile mixture, and the cumin, salt, and pepper. Return the chicken to the skillet. Cover, and transfer the skillet to the oven. Bake until the chicken is cooked through, about 45 minutes.

8. Sprinkle the cilantro over the chicken, and serve hot.

My son Brad at home in
the kitchen.

baked sesame chicken

from Suzy Orlow Solomonic

Suzy is always looking for easy recipes for Shabbat dinners—ones that can be thrown together Friday night after work. This one pleases the kids as well as the adults. Serve it over rice. **SERVES 6 TO 8** [M]

FOR THE MARINADE

2 tablespoons vegetable oil

2 tablespoons toasted sesame oil

$1/4$ cup soy sauce

3 tablespoons sesame seeds

2 tablespoons dry white wine

1 clove garlic, crushed

1 small onion, coarsely chopped

2 teaspoons light or dark brown sugar

1 teaspoon chili powder

1 teaspoon grated fresh ginger,

    or $1/2$ teaspoon ground

6 to 8 boneless, skinless chicken breast halves

    (each 6 to 8 ounces), rinsed and patted dry

2 to 3 tablespoons sesame seeds

1. Combine all the marinade ingredients in a blender, and process until smooth.

2. Place the chicken in a large bowl, a nonreactive baking dish, or a resealable plastic bag, and pour the marinade over it. Cover (or seal) and refrigerate for 6 to 24 hours, turning the chicken occasionally.

3. When you are ready to cook the chicken, preheat the oven to 350°F. Line a 13 × 9-inch baking pan with heavy-duty aluminum foil.

4. Pour the chicken and marinade into the prepared pan, arranging the chicken in a single layer. Sprinkle the sesame seeds over the chicken. Bake until the chicken is cooked through and the sesame seeds are golden, 25 to 30 minutes. Serve hot.

crispy sesame seed chicken

from Erica Choset

This tasty, crispy chicken from cousin Heather's new sister-in-law can be prepared using whole chicken breast halves, or with breast meat cut into nuggets (see Note) for decidedly un-fast-food-like chicken nuggets. **SERVES 6** [M]

Solid vegetable shortening or vegetable cooking

    spray, for greasing the baking pan

FOR THE EGG MIXTURE

2 large eggs

2 tablespoons soy sauce

FOR THE DRY MIXTURE

1 cup Italian-flavored dry bread crumbs

$1/4$ cup sesame seeds

1 teaspoon paprika

$1/2$ teaspoon garlic powder

$1/2$ teaspoon kosher (coarse) salt

$1/2$ teaspoon freshly ground black pepper

FOR THE CHICKEN

$3/4$ cup all-purpose flour

6 large boneless, skinless chicken breast halves

    (each about 8 ounces), rinsed and patted dry

FOR THE SAUCE

1 jar (12 ounces) apricot preserves

1 clove garlic, crushed

2 teaspoons soy sauce

1. Preheat the oven to 350°F. Lightly grease a baking pan.

2. Prepare the egg mixture: Lightly beat the eggs, soy sauce, and 2 tablespoons water in a bowl. Set it aside.

3. Prepare the dry mixture: Combine the bread crumbs, sesame seeds, paprika, garlic powder, salt, and pepper in a bowl, and mix well. Set it aside.

4. Place the flour in a shallow bowl. Dip each piece of chicken in the flour, then in the egg mixture, then in the dry mixture. Arrange the chicken in the prepared baking pan, and bake, turning once, until the chicken is crisp and cooked through, about 35 minutes.

5. Meanwhile, prepare the sauce: Heat the preserves, garlic, soy sauce, and 1/2 cup water in a small saucepan over medium-low heat until the preserves have melted and the sauce is hot.

6. To serve, spoon the apricot sauce over the chicken, or pass it separately.

Note: To prepare crispy chicken nuggets, cut the breasts into 1 1/2-inch cubes. Coat them with the flour, egg mixture, and dry mixture as described. Pour vegetable oil to a depth of about 1/2 inch in a large, heavy saucepan and place it over medium to medium-high heat. Cook the chicken in the oil, turning the nuggets once, for about 7 minutes altogether. Remove with tongs or a slotted spoon. (If the pieces are thick, you may want to finish them in a preheated 350°F oven for 5 minutes or so.)

chicken stupid!

from Shirley Robbins

Just a few months before Aunt Shirley's sudden death, I had a speaking engagement in Atlanta and stayed with her for a few days. Through the years I had seen her only for family *simchas* (celebrations), and we had never really spent much time together, just the two of us. I will always treasure those few days, window-shopping at Judith Leiber, lunching at her favorite grill, and gossiping over late evening tea. (And yes, she told me who said "Chicken, stupid" and swore me to secrecy. My lips are sealed, so don't even ask.)

Aunt Shirley was known in our family as the first responder. No sooner was an invitation received then her response card was in the mail. So it was no surprise that when I sent out the first letter to my family begging for recipes, hers was the first

Many years ago I invited a new bride-and-groom-to-be to meet the family. When I served this dish, the groom said to his bride, 'What is it?' She said, 'Chicken, stupid!' and it has remained that ever since. (And in case you're wondering, yes, they're still married!)

—SHIRLEY ROBBINS

to arrive. (In fairness, I have to add that cousin Joyce's arrived on the same day.)

This was Aunt Shirley's special-occasion dish, and no occasion is as special as the *machatunim* dinner, when families of the bride and groom get to bond before the wedding. The chicken breasts are coated in flour, baked until golden and crisp, and then covered in a voluptuous mushroom sauce. No sharp edges. No controversial spices. And if all goes well, by dessert both families, satisfied and content with the meal and with each other, proclaim the happy couple a match made in heaven.

SERVES 8   Ⓜ

FOR THE CHICKEN

8 tablespoons (1 stick) nondairy margarine, melted and cooled

¹/₂ cup all-purpose flour

1 teaspoon kosher (coarse) salt

¹/₄ teaspoon freshly ground black pepper

1 teaspoon paprika

8 large chicken breast halves (with skin and bone, each about 10 ounces), rinsed and patted dry

FOR THE SAUCE

2 tablespoons nondairy margarine

8 ounces white mushrooms, thinly sliced

¹/₄ cup finely chopped onion

2 tablespoons all-purpose flour

¹/₂ cup soy or other nondairy creamer

¹/₂ cup nondairy sour cream

¹/₂ teaspoon kosher (coarse) salt, or to taste

¹/₈ to ¹/₄ teaspoon freshly ground black pepper to taste

1. Preheat the oven to 325°F.

2. Pour the melted margarine into a shallow bowl.

3. Place the flour, salt, pepper, and paprika in a resealable plastic bag, seal the bag, and toss to mix. Add the chicken breasts, 1 or 2 at a time, seal the bag again, and toss to coat them with the flour.

4. Shake off any excess flour and roll the chicken in the melted margarine. Arrange the chicken, skin side up, in a single layer in a large baking pan and bake until golden, about 30 minutes. Then turn and bake until golden on the other side, about 30 minutes.

5. Meanwhile, prepare the sauce: Melt the margarine in a large skillet over medium-high heat. Add the mushrooms and onion and cook until soft, 4 to 5 minutes. Reduce the heat to low, cover the skillet, and cook, stirring occasionally, for 10 minutes. Add the flour and stir until smooth. Then add the creamer, sour cream, salt, and pepper. Heat very slowly, stirring constantly. Do not allow it to boil.

6. Arrange the chicken on a platter and pour the sauce over it. Serve immediately.

baked chicken florentine

from Sylvia Robbins

שׁ hen Uncle Morris and Aunt Sylvia would come to town from Atlanta, he would regale the children with war stories. Well, in fairness, so would Uncle Lou and Uncle Al, but only Uncle Morris's were true!

Florentine, meaning "in the style of Florence, Italy," refers to a dish served on a bed of spinach. In Aunt Sylvia's version the spinach is tossed with the noodles in a creamy tarragon sauce, then topped with sautéed chicken breasts. **SERVES 6** Ⓜ

6 boneless, skinless chicken breast halves
   (each 6 to 8 ounces),
   rinsed and patted dry
Paprika to taste
Kosher (coarse) salt and
   freshly ground black
   pepper to taste
2 tablespoons nondairy
   margarine
1¹/₂ cups nondairy
   creamer
1 envelope dehydrated
   onion soup mix
¹/₂ cup dry white wine
2 tablespoons Dijon mustard
2 teaspoons dried tarragon leaves
12 ounces egg noodles
¹/₂ cup mayonnaise
1 box (10 ounces) frozen chopped spinach,
   thawed and well drained

1. Sprinkle the chicken lightly with paprika, salt, and pepper.

2. Melt the margarine in a large skillet over medium heat. Add the chicken and brown on both sides, about 8 minutes altogether. Remove the chicken and set aside.

3. Whisk the nondairy creamer, soup mix,

A man is only as strong as his love for his family, and our grandpa, Morris Robbins, was as strong a man as has ever lived. His family filled his life with a zest for living that only his gregarious nature could equal. Decorated for bravery in World War II, he helped liberate the death camps in Germany. He was a terrific grandpa who gave of himself unconditionally. It is with great honor, love, respect, and admiration that we remember the man we all loved so much.

—THE GRAHAM AND GARDNER KIDS

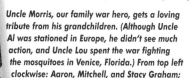

Uncle Morris, our family war hero, gets a loving tribute from his grandchildren. (Although Uncle Al was stationed in Europe, he didn't see much action, and Uncle Lou spent the war fighting the mosquitoes in Venice, Florida.) From top left clockwise: Aaron, Mitchell, and Stacy Graham; Kimberly, Jason, and (center) Jeffrey Gardner.

wine, mustard, and tarragon into the skillet. Return the chicken to the skillet, cover, and simmer until the chicken is tender and cooked through, about 20 minutes.

4. Meanwhile, cook the noodles according to the package directions, and drain.

5. When the chicken is cooked through, remove it from the skillet and cover to keep warm. Whisk the mayonnaise into the sauce. Add salt and pepper to taste. Remove about ³/₄ cup of the sauce and set it aside. Stir the spinach into the remaining sauce, combine well, and cook to heat through, 1 minute. Toss the spinach mixture with the noodles.

6. Serve the chicken on top of the noodles, spooning the reserved sauce over the chicken.

my chicken marbella

from Judy Bart Kancigor

my version of the *Silver Palate* classic. Because my kids can live without olives, prunes, and capers, I use artichokes, apricots, and sun-dried tomatoes. And boneless, skinless chicken breasts really soak up the delicious marinade. **SERVES 12 TO 18** **Ⓜ**

FOR THE MARINADE

1 head garlic, cloves separated and crushed

2 jars (6.5 ounces each) marinated artichoke
    hearts, drained

$1/2$ cup drained oil-packed sun-dried tomatoes,
    cut into julienne strips

$1/2$ cup red wine vinegar

$1/2$ cup olive oil

$1 1/2$ cups dried apricots, larger ones snipped
    in half

1 tablespoon dried basil

1 tablespoon dried oregano

6 bay leaves

2 teaspoons kosher (coarse) salt, or to taste

Freshly ground black pepper to taste

FOR THE CHICKEN

12 to 18 ($5 1/2$ to $6 1/2$ pounds) boneless, skinless
    chicken breast halves, rinsed and patted dry

1 cup (packed) dark brown sugar

1 cup dry white wine

$1/4$ cup cilantro or flat-leaf parsley leaves,
    finely chopped

1. Combine all the marinade ingredients in a bowl and stir well.

2. Place the chicken breasts in a very large nonreactive bowl or dish, and pour the marinade over them. Marinate, covered, in the refrigerator overnight.

3. Preheat the oven to 350°F.

4. Arrange the chicken breasts in a single layer in a 17 × 11-inch baking pan, and spoon the marinade over them. Sprinkle the brown sugar over the chicken breasts and pour the wine around them. Bake, uncovered, basting frequently, until the chicken is cooked through, about 45 minutes. Sprinkle with the cilantro, and serve.

orange-mustard grilled chicken

from Barry Dubin

Here's an easy chicken dish with a sunny, robust orange-mustard flavor. Its lovely golden color is dappled with specks of green herbs and mustard seeds. Of course it can be baked or

Cousin Barry Dubin. And, no, his last name is not really Gibb, although he's been stopped on the street more than once for his autograph.

broiled, but grilling gives it a smokiness that adds a nice counterpoint to the herbs. **SERVES 4 TO 6** ☐ **M**

FOR THE MARINADE

¹/₄ cup grainy mustard

¹/₄ cup Dijon mustard

¹/₄ cup orange juice

¹/₂ teaspoon grated orange zest

2 tablespoons chopped fresh tarragon, mint, thyme, basil, or dill, or any combination

1 tablespoon balsamic vinegar

1 tablespoon olive oil

¹/₂ teaspoon kosher (coarse) salt, or to taste

¹/₄ teaspoon freshly ground black pepper

Vegetable cooking spray, for greasing the rack

4 to 6 boneless, skinless chicken breast halves (each 6 to 8 ounces), rinsed and patted dry

1. Combine all the marinade ingredients in a bowl and mix well. Place the chicken breasts in a resealable plastic bag or nonreactive baking dish, and pour the marinade over them. Marinate, sealed or covered, in the refrigerator for 6 to 24 hours, turning the chicken occasionally.

2. Grease a barbecue grill rack. Preheat the grill to medium.

3. Drain the chicken, and grill it on each side until cooked through, 7 to 10 minutes total. (To create the distinctive crosshatch marks, rotate the chicken 90 degrees halfway through the cooking on each side.) Allow to rest, covered, for 5 minutes before serving.

4. Serve hot, at room temperature, or even cold the next day, in a salad or sandwich.

golden curry chicken

from Barbara Warady

Probably no flavoring strikes more fear in the uninitiated than curry. A needless worry. Used judiciously, curry spikes this easy, zingy sauce and makes the mouth sing. Try a teaspoonful and see. Use more if you dare (and I do). You'll want to serve this over rice—the better to appreciate the sauce. **SERVES 8** **M**

Solid vegetable shortening or vegetable cooking spray, for greasing the baking pan

8 boneless, skinless chicken breast halves (each 6 to 8 ounces), rinsed and patted dry

4 tablespoons nondairy margarine

¹/₃ cup honey

¹/₄ cup Dijon mustard

2 tablespoons dry mustard

1 small clove garlic, crushed

2 teaspoons fresh lemon juice

1 to 2 teaspoons curry powder to taste

¹/₂ to 1 teaspoon kosher (coarse) salt to taste

1. Preheat the oven to 350°F. Grease a 13 × 9-inch nonreactive baking pan.

2. Arrange the chicken breasts in a single layer in the prepared baking pan.

3. Melt the margarine in a small saucepan over medium heat. Whisk in the honey, mustard, dry mustard, garlic, lemon juice, curry powder, and salt, stirring until smooth.

4. Pour the sauce over the chicken. Cover the baking pan with aluminum foil and bake for 10 minutes. Then uncover and baste with the sauce. Continue baking, uncovered, basting occasionally, until the chicken is cooked through, 15 to 20 minutes. Serve hot.

chicken with artichokes

from Juli Altman

This recipe is fancy enough for company, yet easy enough for everyday dinners. The chicken is simmered in a piquant wine sauce that marries well with the artichoke hearts and capers. Serve over fettuccine. **SERVES 4**   **M**

4 boneless, skinless chicken breast halves
   (each about 6 ounces), rinsed and patted dry
Kosher (coarse) salt and freshly ground black
   pepper
$1/3$ cup all-purpose flour
2 tablespoons olive oil
1 cup homemade chicken stock (page 63) or
   low-sodium boxed or canned broth
$1/4$ cup dry white wine
1 tablespoon fresh lemon juice
2 teaspoons Worcestershire sauce
$1/2$ teaspoon dried oregano
1 can (14 ounces) artichoke hearts, drained,
   rinsed, and quartered
2 tablespoons capers, drained

1. Sprinkle the chicken lightly with salt and pepper. Place the flour in a shallow bowl, and coat the chicken in it, shaking off any excess.

2. Heat the oil in a large skillet over medium-high heat until it is quite hot but not smoking. Add the chicken, in two batches without crowding, and cook until browned on both sides, about 4 minutes per side. Remove the chicken and cover it with aluminum foil to keep warm.

3. Add the stock, wine, lemon juice, Worcestershire sauce, and oregano to the skillet and bring to a boil, scraping up the brown bits that have stuck to the bottom. Return the chicken to the skillet and add the artichoke hearts and capers. Reduce the heat and simmer, covered, until the chicken is cooked through, 10 to 15 minutes. Serve hot, spooning the sauce over the chicken.

chicken kiev

from Marc Wolf

I doubt that our ancestors dined on Chicken Kiev in Kiev. In fact, they weren't making it in Kiev at all. French chef Nicolas Appert is generally credited with its creation: pounded boneless chicken breasts rolled around cold flavored butter (kosher cooks of course substitute nondairy margarine) and then breaded and fried. The butter (or margarine) melts during cooking and bursts

> My specialty, which I served to Ronna [in photo with Marc] on our second dinner date. I also made it for her mother's birthday the first time we met. I'm not saying it's why Ronna said yes, but . . . **—MARC WOLF**

joyfully from the center when you cut into the chicken. The name was coined by a New York restaurateur to please his Russian customers. Marc serves this dish with chicken-flavored rice pilaf and fresh green beans with pimento. **SERVES 8** Ⓜ

Vegetable cooking spray, for greasing the baking pan

4 large eggs, beaten

1¹/₂ cups Italian-seasoned dry bread crumbs

8 boneless, skinless chicken breast halves (6 to 8 ounces each), rinsed and patted dry, pounded thin

Garlic powder to taste

Dried oregano to taste

Dried parsley flakes to taste

Dried basil to taste

¹/₄ cup olive oil

4 tablespoons (¹/₂ stick) cold nondairy margarine

3 cloves garlic, crushed

Paprika to taste

Freshly ground black pepper to taste

1. Preheat the oven to 350°F. Grease a 13 × 9-inch baking pan.

2. Place the eggs and the bread crumbs in separate shallow bowls. Stir the garlic powder, oregano, parsley, and basil into the bread crumbs. Dip the chicken breasts into the egg, then in the bread crumb mixture, coating both sides well. Reserve the remaining eggs and bread crumb mixture.

3. Place 1 teaspoon of the olive oil, 1¹/₂ teaspoons of the margarine, and a little crushed garlic on the center of each chicken breast. Fold the chicken around the ingredients and roll it up, making sure the margarine is completely covered. Fasten the rolls with kitchen string, skewers, or wooden toothpicks. Dip each rolled breast into the remaining egg and then in the remaining crumbs. Sprinkle paprika and pepper over the rolls.

4. Place the chicken in the prepared baking pan and bake until golden and cooked through, 20 minutes. Serve immediately.

lois goren's lemon chicken

from Judy Bart Kancigor

my friend Lois got this recipe from a long-gone Chinese restaurant in Youngstown, Ohio, which claimed to have invented it. It was actually their version of Lee Lum's chicken from Pearl's restaurant in New York, popularized by Craig Claiborne in the '70s. When Lois was first married, it was her dinner party dish . . . her *only* dish. She served it so often and exclusively that it became a neighborhood joke. The chicken is irresistibly crisp, in a sweet and sour lemony sauce just this side of puckery. Barry says he wishes we'd known Lois back then! **SERVES 6 TO 8** Ⓜ

FOR THE CHICKEN AND MARINADE

6 to 8 boneless, skinless chicken breast halves (each 6 to 8 ounces), rinsed and patted dry

¹/₄ cup soy sauce

2 tablespoons toasted sesame oil

¹/₄ cup gin or vodka

FOR THE SAUCE

1 cup homemade chicken stock (page 63) or low-sodium boxed or canned broth

³/₄ cup sugar

¹/₂ cup mirin (Japanese rice wine), or ¹/₂ cup dry sherry plus 4 teaspoons sugar

Juice of 2 large lemons (6 tablespoons)

Grated zest of 2 lemons (2 tablespoons)

¹/₂ teaspoon kosher (coarse) salt, or to taste

FOR COOKING AND SERVING

Whites of 3 large eggs

1 cup rice flour

Peanut or vegetable oil, for frying

4 medium-size carrots, cut into thin matchsticks

1 green or red bell pepper, stemmed, seeded, and very thinly sliced

1 bunch (6 to 8) scallions, white part only, cut into thin rounds

1 can (8 ounces) crushed pineapple, undrained

2 tablespoons cornstarch mixed with 2 tablespoons cold water

2 teaspoons lemon extract

Hot steamed rice, for serving

1. Lightly pound the thickest part of the chicken breasts, just to even them out somewhat.

2. Combine the soy sauce, sesame oil, and gin in a bowl. Place the chicken breasts in a resealable plastic bag, pour the marinade over them, and seal the bag. Marinate in the refrigerator, turning the breasts occasionally, for 6 to 24 hours.

3. Prepare the sauce: Combine the stock, sugar, mirin, lemon juice, lemon zest, and salt in a medium-size saucepan and bring to a boil. Cover and remove from the heat. Set aside.

4. Whisk the egg whites in a bowl until fluffy. Place the rice flour in a shallow bowl. Drain the chicken, discarding the marinade. Dip the chicken breasts in the egg whites and then in the flour, coating them completely. Shake off any excess flour.

5. Pour oil into a large skillet to a depth of about ¹/₂ inch, and heat it over medium-high heat. When the oil is very hot but not smoking, add the chicken breasts gradually (to keep the temperature of the oil constant) and fry them, in batches, without crowding, until they are crisp and golden brown on both sides, and cooked through, 8 to 10 minutes total (the time depends on the thickness of the chicken; see Note). As the chicken breasts are finished, drain them on paper towels and keep them warm in a 200°F oven.

6. While the chicken is cooking, add the carrots to the reserved sauce and bring to a boil; boil gently for 2 minutes. Add the pepper slices, scallions, and pineapple with its juice. Continue cooking until the vegetables are tender but still crunchy, about 2 minutes.

Stir the cornstarch mixture into the sauce and cook, stirring, until the sauce thickens, about 1 minute. Stir in the lemon extract.

7. Serve the chicken over steamed rice, and spoon the sauce over it.

Note: To tell if it's done, insert a sharp knife into the thickest part of a chicken breast. There should be no trace of pink in the center.

marilyn schreiber's chicken marsala

from Leslie Robbins

Cousin Leslie met her friend Marilyn about thirteen years ago, when Marilyn started teaching at the same school in Queens as Leslie. Leslie says she gets all her best recipes from Marilyn, who is a divine cook.

The rich, smoky flavor of marsala wine adds depth to the sauce in this popular dish, which decades ago was considered the height of elegance and was always found on the best restaurant menus. Over the years the restaurants have moved on, but it's still one of Leslie and Marvin's favorite dishes. **SERVES 4** **M**

1/2 cup all-purpose flour

1 teaspoon garlic powder

1/2 teaspoon freshly ground black pepper

2 large eggs, beaten

1 pound chicken cutlets (thinly sliced chicken breasts), rinsed and patted dry

4 tablespoons olive oil

8 ounces white mushrooms, sliced

2 chicken bouillon cubes

1 cup boiling water

1/2 cup marsala wine

1/4 cup flat-leaf parsley leaves, chopped

1. Preheat the oven to 350°F.

2. Mix the flour, garlic powder, and pepper together in a shallow bowl. Place the eggs in another bowl.

3. Dip the chicken cutlets in the seasoned flour, and shake off any excess. Then dip them in the egg, and then again in the flour.

4. Heat 1 tablespoon of the oil (or 2, if you can fit 2 cutlets without crowding) in a large skillet over medium-high heat until it is quite hot but not smoking. Add a cutlet (or 2) and brown on both sides until golden, about 4 minutes altogether. Repeat with the remaining oil and cutlets, transferring the cutlets to a shallow baking pan as they are done.

5. Add the mushrooms to the skillet and cook until they have released their juices and are tender, about 10 minutes. Dissolve the bouillon cubes in the boiling water and add the mixture to the skillet, along with the marsala and parsley. Simmer until reduced somewhat and sauce-like, 1 to 2 minutes.

6. Pour the sauce over the chicken cutlets, place the pan in the oven, and bake

until the chicken is cooked through, about 15 minutes.

7. Serve hot, with any extra sauce spooned over the chicken.

taal's chicken biryani

from The Second Wednesday Book Club

O ur book club meets every month for dinner and discussion, with the menu inspired by the book we have read. I have to admit that on more than one occasion we have selected a book based on the cuisine involved. Our group has certainly had our thirty minutes of fame: fifteen when *Cooking Pleasures* magazine visited and featured us in their February 2004 issue, and another fifteen when we landed in *The Book Club Cookbook* with this recipe that I provided to authors Judy Gelman and Vicki Levy Krupp. It comes from our favorite Indian restaurant, Taal, in Orange County, California, where we dined as we discussed *A Fine Balance* by Rohinton Mistry. **SERVES 6 TO 8** Ⓜ

FOR THE CHICKEN

2 tablespoons corn oil

2 large onions, chopped

1 tablespoon minced fresh ginger

2 teaspoons minced garlic (about 4 cloves)

**2 large tomatoes, seeded and diced, or 2 cans
 (15 ounces each) diced tomatoes, drained**

2 teaspoons garam masala (see Note)

2 teaspoons ground coriander

2 teaspoons ground cumin

2 teaspoons cayenne pepper

1¹/₂ teaspoons kosher (coarse) salt

**1¹/₂ pounds skinless, boneless chicken
 breasts, rinsed, patted dry, and cut
 into 1-inch cubes**

FOR THE RICE

2 teaspoons cumin seeds

4 bay leaves

¹/₂ teaspoon kosher (coarse) salt

1 teaspoon corn oil

2 cups basmati rice

FOR THE GARNISH

¹/₄ cup golden raisins

¹/₄ cup cilantro leaves, coarsely chopped

¹/₄ cup mint leaves, coarsely chopped

My friends and fellow bookworms Linda Gomberg and Diane Sachs join me in preparing the spread for our Cooking Pleasures photo shoot.

Photo by Nick Koon

Here's to friendship and fancy feasts! Ivy Johnson, me, Linda Gomberg, Judi Weisman.

Photo by Nick Koon

chicken stir-fry
with walnuts

from Leslie Graham

The secret to stir-frying is to have all the ingredients prepped and measured out before you begin—what the French call *mise en place*. Once that's done, the cooking happens quickly. The vegetables should be nice and crisp—have the family at the table so you can serve this immediately. (If you like your stir-fry over rice, steam the rice first and keep it warm while you stir-fry the chicken and vegetables.) **SERVES 4 TO 6**   **M**

1 tablespoon cornstarch

1¹/2 pounds skinless, boneless chicken breast, rinsed, patted dry, and cut into 1-inch cubes

¹/4 cup homemade chicken stock (page 63) or low-sodium boxed or canned broth

3 tablespoons soy sauce

2 tablespoons mirin (Japanese rice wine), or 2 tablespoons dry sherry plus 1 teaspoon sugar

1 teaspoon grated fresh ginger

¹/4 to ¹/2 teaspoon red pepper flakes to taste

1 medium-size green or red bell pepper, stemmed, seeded, and cut into 1-inch wide strips

3 to 4 tablespoons peanut or vegetable oil

6 scallions, white and green parts, cut diagonally into 1-inch-long pieces

1. Prepare the chicken: Heat the oil in a large skillet over medium heat. Add the onions and cook until they are beginning to soften, about 5 minutes. Add the ginger, garlic, and tomatoes, and cook for 2 minutes. Stir in the garam masala, coriander, cumin, cayenne pepper, and salt. Add the chicken and cook, stirring occasionally, until it is cooked through but still tender, 15 to 20 minutes.

2. Meanwhile, prepare the rice: Bring 3¹/2 cups water to a boil in a medium-size saucepan. Add the cumin seeds, bay leaves, salt, and oil. Stir in the rice. Cover, reduce the heat, and simmer until the rice is tender and the liquid has been absorbed, 15 to 20 minutes.

3. Combine the chicken and rice (discard the bay leaves) in a large serving bowl, and toss to mix. Garnish with the raisins, cilantro, and mint. Serve hot.

Note: Garam masala is a mixture of dry-roasted, ground spices. There are many variations, but most include cumin, cardamom, cinnamon, cloves, black pepper, and other spices. You can find commercially prepared garam masala at Indian and specialty markets or even some supermarkets.

2 cups (6 ounces) chopped baby bok choy

1 cup walnut halves

Hot steamed rice, for serving (optional)

1. Place the cornstarch in a bowl or in a resealable plastic bag, add the chicken cubes, and toss or shake to coat them with the cornstarch.

2. Stir the stock, soy sauce, mirin, ginger, and red pepper flakes together in a bowl, and set aside.

3. Cut the bell pepper strips in half crosswise.

4. Heat 1 tablespoon of the oil in a wok or a large skillet until it is quite hot but not smoking. Add the bell peppers and scallions, and stir-fry until tender but crisp, about 2 minutes. Transfer the vegetables to a bowl.

5. Add 1 tablespoon of the oil to the wok and stir-fry the bok choy until it is tender but crisp, about 1 minute. Transfer it to the bowl.

6. If necessary, heat about 1 teaspoon of the oil in the wok. Add the walnuts and stir-fry until golden, about 1 minute. Add them to the bowl.

7. Heat another tablespoon of the oil in the wok and add half of the chicken cubes. Stir-fry until cooked through, 2 to 3 minutes. Transfer the chicken to a plate. Repeat with the remaining chicken, adding oil if needed.

8. Return all the chicken to the wok. Stir in the stock mixture and cook until bubbly and thick, about 1 minute. Then return the vegetables and walnuts to the wok, and stir. Cover and cook for 1 minute. Serve immediately, over steamed rice if you like.

peanut chicken
in 15 minutes flat

from Marilyn Starrett

hen I posted this recipe on the Jewish Food List, who knew that I would set off an international cooking riot? Kudos were e-mailed back and forth from South Africa to Sydney to Sacramento. That's when I discovered that people really do like easy! (Although list member Diana Freilich wrote that she likes the sauce so much she pours it over chicken parts to be baked the traditional way.) Think your microwave is just for reheating? Think again. Yes, you can use it to cook raw chicken, at least in this dish. It really works. Time it!

Serve this over rice or noodles.

SERVES 4   Ⓜ

1 onion, finely chopped

1 clove garlic, crushed

¹/₄ cup chunky peanut butter

¹/₂ cup homemade chicken stock (page 63) or low-sodium boxed or canned broth

¹/₄ cup honey

2 teaspoons Dijon mustard

1 tablespoon curry powder

Pinch of ground cardamom

Dash of Tabasco or other hot pepper sauce

4 boneless, skinless chicken breast halves (6 to 8 ounces each), rinsed, patted dry, and cut into 1¹/₂-inch cubes

1. Combine the onion and garlic in a 1½-quart microwave-safe dish and microwave, uncovered, on high power for 2 minutes.

2. Stir in the peanut butter, chicken stock, honey, mustard, curry powder, cardamom, and Tabasco. Add the chicken cubes. Microwave, uncovered, on high power for 6 minutes.

3. Stir, and microwave on high power until the chicken is cooked through, another 6 minutes. Serve hot.

heart-healthy jambalaya

from Debbie Zimmerman

Debbie and hubby Matt met as students at Tulane in New Orleans, where they fell in love with each other—and with Cajun food. They devised this healthier, yet satisfying variation of the classic, which called for tons of lard and andouille sausage.

SERVES 4 TO 5   Ⓜ

Matthew and Debbie
Zimmerman at their wedding
rehearsal dinner, 1996.

Vegetable cooking spray, for greasing
　the baking pan
2 tablespoons olive oil
8 ounces smoked turkey sausage
　(preferably spicy), cut into
　¼-inch-thick slices
1 pound boneless, skinless chicken breasts,
　rinsed, patted dry, and cut into
　1-inch cubes
1 teaspoon dried thyme leaves
½ teaspoon white pepper
½ teaspoon freshly ground black pepper
Pinch of ground sage
Pinch of cayenne pepper, or to taste
Pinch red pepper flakes (optional)
1½ cups chopped onions
1½ cups chopped celery
1 large green or red bell pepper,
　stemmed, seeded, and chopped
1½ tablespoons minced garlic
½ cup tomato sauce
1 cup chopped peeled tomatoes
　(canned or fresh)
2 bay leaves
2½ cups homemade chicken stock
　(page 63) or low-sodium boxed
　or canned broth
　1¼ cups rice
　1½ teaspoons kosher (coarse) salt
　Hot pepper sauce, such as
　　Tabasco, for serving

1. Preheat the oven to 350°F. Spray a 13 × 9-inch baking pan.

2. Heat the olive oil in a large skillet over medium-high heat. Add the sausage and brown it on both sides, about 1 minute. Transfer the sausage

to a plate. Add the chicken to the skillet and brown it briefly, about 1 minute.

3. Add the thyme, white pepper, black pepper, sage, cayenne, and red pepper flakes if using. Cook for 1 minute. Then add the onions, celery, bell pepper, and garlic, and cook over medium heat until soft, about 5 minutes. Stir in the tomato sauce and cook for 1 minute. Add the tomatoes and bay leaves, and continue cooking for the flavors to combine, 3 to 5 minutes. Remove the skillet from the heat.

4. Return the sausage to the skillet, and stir in the chicken stock, rice, and salt. Transfer the entire mixture to the prepared baking pan, cover it with aluminum foil, and bake until the rice is tender and the liquid has been absorbed, about 1 hour.

5. Serve hot, and pass the hot pepper sauce.

spaghetti à la bradley

from Stu Kancigor

As a teenager, my son Brad invented this dish: pasta in a creamy sauce with leftover vegetables and chicken. He never made it the same way twice. Now, no matter who's cooking or what they throw in, we always call it Spaghetti à la Bradley. **SERVES 6** Ⓜ

> *My brother created this dish when we were in junior high, using spaghetti and any leftovers he could find. These days he's busy working on his wine reduction sauce, but I'm still making his signature creation. Here's my new, improved version. Warning: If you're out of garlic, do not use a whole jar of the bottled stuff—as I learned the first time I cooked dinner for my in-laws!* **—STU KANCIGOR**

1 teaspoon plus 2 tablespoons olive oil
*8 ounces smoked turkey sausage, cut into
    ¹/₄-inch dice*
*1¹/₂ pounds boneless, skinless chicken breasts,
    rinsed, patted dry, and cut into ³/₄-inch
    chunks*
Seasoned salt
1 large onion, chopped
8 ounces white mushrooms, sliced
2 cloves garlic, crushed
12 ounces penne pasta
1¹/₂ tablespoons all-purpose flour
1 cup soy cream or other nondairy creamer
*¹/₂ to ³/₄ cup homemade chicken stock (page 63)
    or low-sodium boxed or canned broth*
¹/₄ cup oil-packed sun-dried tomatoes, drained
1 cup frozen peas, thawed

1. Heat the 1 teaspoon oil in a large skillet over medium-high heat. Add the sausage and brown it all over, about 4 minutes. Transfer the sausage to a bowl.

2. Sprinkle the chicken lightly all over with seasoned salt. Add the 2 tablespoons oil to the skillet and cook the chicken over medium-high heat, stirring constantly, until it is cooked through, about 5 minutes. Remove

Stu and Brad Kancigor in 1988 and in 1973.

egg foo bower

from Harold Dubin

ש hile Harold was always a great dancer, he didn't begin his cooking career until he was retired, using his mother-in-law's (Aunt Sally Bower's) handwritten cookbook as his guide. This dish was his own creation, however. This is not your Chinese restaurant egg foo yong, which is more like an omelet dotted with extras. Harold's is literally loaded with "stuff"—marinated chicken, crisp stir-fried veggies—but then, Harold always was a generous soul. **SERVES 4** Ⓜ

Some of the most wonderful memories I have of my father [Harold Dubin, right] revolve around dancing. When I was a little girl I used to get a kick hearing about how he met my mother on a blind date and took her dancing, impressing her that he was King of the Mambo. I watched my parents dance with such grace all my life. To me they were Ginger Rogers and Fred Astaire, with a little Jackie Gleason and George Burns thrown in. I first learned to dance by standing on my father's feet, and at every wedding and Bar and Bat Mitzvah I had at least one special dance with the King of the Mambo.
—LAURA SELIGMAN

the chicken with a slotted spoon, leaving the oil in the skillet, and add it to the sausage.

3. Add the onion to the skillet and cook over medium heat, stirring occasionally, until soft, about 5 minutes. Add the mushrooms and garlic and cook until the mushrooms have released their juice and are tender, about 10 minutes more.

4. Meanwhile, bring a pot of water to a boil and cook the penne pasta until al dente, about 12 minutes.

5. Add the flour to the skillet, stirring until no traces of white remain. Then add the soy cream and $1/2$ cup of the chicken stock, and scrape up any brown bits in the skillet. Heat, stirring, until the mixture has thickened, 2 to 3 minutes. Return the sausage and chicken to the skillet, and add the sun-dried tomatoes and peas. Warm just to heat through. If the mixture is too thick, add more chicken stock.

6. Drain the pasta, toss it with the chicken mixture, and serve.

FOR THE MARINADE AND CHICKEN

1 tablespoon hoisin sauce

1 tablespoon ketchup

1 tablespoon low-sodium soy sauce

1 tablespoon dry sherry

1 clove garlic, minced

2 teaspoons grated fresh ginger (optional)

1 pound boneless, skinless chicken breasts,
rinsed, patted dry, and cut into $^1/_2$-inch dice

FOR THE OMELET AND SAUCE

2 tablespoons vegetable oil, plus more
for frying

1 green bell pepper, stemmed, seeded,
and cut into $^1/_4$-inch dice

1 medium-size onion, chopped

8 ounces fresh bean sprouts, or 1 can
(about 16 ounces) bean sprouts, rinsed
and drained

1 cup homemade chicken stock
(page 63) or low-sodium boxed
or canned broth

2 tablespoons reduced-sodium soy sauce

1$^1/_2$ teaspoons sugar, or to taste

1 tablespoon cornstarch

$^1/_8$ teaspoon Chinese five-spice powder
(optional)

2 tablespoons cold water

6 large eggs

$^1/_2$ teaspoon kosher (coarse) salt, or to taste

$^1/_8$ teaspoon freshly ground black pepper,
or to taste

1. Prepare the marinade: Combine the hoisin sauce, ketchup, soy sauce, sherry, garlic, and ginger in a bowl and stir well. Stir in the chicken, cover the bowl, and marinate in the refrigerator for 2 to 4 hours.

2. When you are ready to cook the eggs, heat 1 tablespoon of the oil in a large skillet over medium-high heat. Add the bell pepper and onion, and stir-fry until tender but still crisp, 2 minutes. Stir in the bean sprouts and stir-fry for a few seconds more. Remove the vegetables from the skillet and set them aside to cool.

3. Heat the remaining 1 tablespoon oil in the same skillet over medium-high heat. Drain the chicken and add it to the skillet. Sauté, stirring constantly, until cooked through, about 4 minutes. Using a slotted spoon, remove the chicken from the skillet and set it aside to cool.

4. Combine the chicken stock, soy sauce, and sugar in a small saucepan and bring to a boil. Combine the cornstarch and Chinese five-spice powder, if using, in a small bowl. Add the cold water and stir until smooth. Stir the cornstarch mixture into the broth mixture and heat, stirring, until thickened, about 1 minute. Remove the sauce from the heat and keep it warm.

5. Whisk the eggs, salt, and pepper together in a bowl. Add the cooked chicken and sautéed vegetables, and mix well.

6. Pour oil to a depth of about $^1/_8$ inch in the skillet, and heat over medium-high heat. Pour half of the egg mixture into the hot oil, distributing the ingredients evenly, and cook until the omelet is golden brown on the bottom, about 2 minutes. Flip the omelet over and cook until it is golden brown on the other side, about 2 minutes. (If you have trouble flipping this super-loaded omelet, cut it in half, or even in quarters, with a spatula and flip each portion. It won't be as neat

that way, but no one will care.) Remove the omelet from the skillet and keep it warm while you repeat with the remaining half, adding more oil to the skillet if needed. Serve warm, covered with the sauce.

apricot-glazed cornish hens

from Barbara Straus

This is Barbara's favorite holiday dish, and it has become a real crowd-pleaser in our family as well. The hens are seasoned, roasted, spread with a perky sauce, then roasted some more until crisp. For proper browning, give the little darlings plenty of legroom. Because a Cornish hen has less meat on the bone than a chicken, one hen usually feeds one person. But there will always be a nibbler or two (well, maybe in *your* family) who will want just a half. **SERVES 6 TO 12** Ⓜ

FOR THE CORNISH HENS
Vegetable cooking spray
6 Cornish hens (about 2 pounds each), rinsed inside and out and patted dry
1 teaspoon kosher (coarse) salt
1/4 teaspoon freshly ground black pepper
1/4 teaspoon dried thyme leaves, crushed
8 tablespoons (1 stick) nondairy margarine, melted

FOR THE SAUCE
2 tablespoons nondairy margarine
1 medium-size onion, finely chopped
1 tablespoon all-purpose flour
1 tablespoon sugar
2 teaspoons curry powder
2 teaspoons chicken bouillon powder
1 cup apricot preserves
1 tablespoon fresh lemon juice

1. Preheat the oven to 375°F. Line one or two roasting pans with heavy-duty aluminum foil, and spray them with vegetable cooking spray.

2. Combine the salt, pepper, and thyme in a bowl, and rub 1/4 teaspoon of the mixture into the cavity of each hen. Place the hens in the prepared roasting pans, breast side down; do not crowd them. Brush melted margarine all over the hens. Roast, uncovered, for 30 minutes. Baste them with melted margarine, turn them over, and roast, basting once or twice, for another 30 minutes.

3. Meanwhile, prepare the sauce: Melt the margarine in a skillet over medium heat, and add the onion. Cook until soft and golden, about 10 minutes. Blend in the flour, sugar, curry powder, and bouillon powder. Cook, stirring, until bubbly. Then stir in the apricot preserves and lemon juice, and cook until the preserves melt. Set the sauce aside.

4. Carefully drain most of the fat from the roasting pan, and spoon half of the apricot sauce over the hens. Roast for 10 minutes. Turn the hens over, spoon the remainder of the sauce over the hens, and roast for

10 minutes more. (For even crispier birds, turn the birds back over, breast side up, and roast for another 10 minutes, basting with the pan juices.) Serve hot.

roast turkey

from Karina Ramos Bart

m y sister-in-law, Karina, made this superb turkey for Thanksgiving dinner. She roasted it at a high temperature—425°F—yielding a beautifully browned bird without basting. Determined to do the Norman Rockwell thing, Gary watched a how-to video on carving technique and did the honors with flair. Kosher turkeys are already salted—no brining is necessary—and yield tender, juicy slices. Or so I hear. I've never eaten nice, neat slices in my life! Just give me the carcass and I'm a happy camper. Want gravy? See the next recipe. **SERVES 10 TO 14** Ⓜ

Pupik

Gizzards (the muscular pouch used by fowl to grind their food) In humans, belly button (as in "Her skirt was so short it came up to her pupik")

1 whole turkey (13 to 15 pounds), pin feathers and giblets removed, rinsed and patted dry
6 tablespoons (³/4 stick) nondairy margarine, at room temperature, or vegetable oil
Kosher (coarse) salt to taste
Freshly ground black pepper to taste
Paprika to taste
1 medium-size onion, quartered
1 rib celery, quartered
1 orange, quartered
1 lemon, quartered
4 sprigs rosemary
4 sprigs thyme

1. Preheat the oven to 425°F.

2. Rub the turkey evenly inside and outside with the margarine, and sprinkle it lightly inside and outside with salt and pepper. Sprinkle paprika over the outside. Place the onion, celery, orange, and lemon quarters in the cavity with the rosemary and thyme sprigs. Tie the legs together and tuck the wing tips under the wings. Place the turkey on a roasting pan, breast side up.

3. Place the turkey in the oven and roast for 30 minutes. Then cover the breast with aluminum foil and roast for 1 hour more.

4. Rotate the roasting pan front to back, and continue roasting until a meat thermometer inserted into the thickest part of the thigh registers 170°F, 40 minutes to 1¹/4 hours, depending on the size of the bird. Remove the foil for the last 20 minutes or so of roasting.

5. Remove the turkey from the oven and let stand, loosely covered with foil, for 20 minutes before carving.

nearly no-fat turkey gravy

from Judy Bart Kancigor

This triple reduction process replaces the fat, and no one will ever know. Feel free to use any vegetables you like—fennel, leeks, shallots, turnips—as each imparts a different flavor. If you've been storing chicken giblets and necks in the freezer, as I do, thaw some and throw them in. Homemade chicken stock is really the secret here, especially if it's my mother's), which makes the gravy so rich, you'd swear it contained a stick of butter. If you like giblets in your gravy, chop and add them. You'll never see them in my gravy, however, because I love giblets so much that I shamelessly hoard them for myself. My father and I used to wrestle for the *pupiks* (see page 209), a practice I never encouraged in my own children, who thankfully never developed a taste for them. **MAKES ABOUT 2½ CUPS, MORE WHEN THE PAN JUICES ARE ADDED** M

My son Brad is our family carver. (My husband and I have an arrangement—I stay out of his woodshop, and he stays out of my kitchen.)

Giblets and neck (no liver) from 1 turkey

Giblets and necks from 3 to 4 chickens (optional)

1 large onion, coarsely chopped

3 large carrots, cut into 1-inch-thick slices

2 ribs celery, cut into 1-inch-thick slices

1 parsnip, cut into 1-inch-thick slices

1 large clove garlic, coarsely chopped

4 cups homemade chicken stock (preferably my mother's, page 63) or reduced-sodium boxed or canned broth (only in a pinch)

½ cup dry sherry or dry white wine

½ bunch curly-leaf parsley (about ½ cup sprigs)

1 small bunch dill (about ½ cup sprigs)

Kosher (coarse) salt and freshly ground black pepper, to taste (optional, and added only at the very end)

1. While the turkey is roasting, rinse the giblets and neck, and the chicken giblets and necks if using, and place them in a large (preferably nonstick) saucepan. Add the onion, carrots, celery, parsnip, garlic, and ½ cup of the chicken stock. Boil uncovered over high heat, stirring often, until the stock has evaporated and the vegetables and giblets brown and stick to the pan, 15 to 25 minutes. Repeat this process twice more, using ½ cup of the stock each time and scraping to release the browned bits. This should take 4 to 5 minutes each time.

2. Remove the pan from the heat and stir in the wine. Deglaze the pan, scraping up all the crusty

brown bits. Return the pan to the heat and add the remaining stock and the parsley and dill. Simmer, covered, until the giblets are very tender. Depending on their size, this will take 2 to 3 hours.

3. Remove the giblets, and if you wish to add them to the gravy or your stuffing (don't even think about it if you've invited me), chop them and set them aside. Strain the stock through a strainer, pressing hard on the vegetables to extract as much liquid as possible. Scrape the underside of the strainer and add the strained vegetables to the stock; discard the remaining pulp. Stir the chopped giblets into the gravy if you wish.

4. The gravy can be served at this point. Or, for an even richer gravy, while the cooked turkey is resting, remove as much fat from the pan juices as possible, using a turkey baster or a fat separator. Strain the defatted juices into the gravy (a nice rule of thumb is about one-third pan juices to two-thirds vegetable gravy).

5. Add salt and pepper—but only if necessary. (Reducing the stock three times concentrates the salt. The pan juices will contain salt from the turkey as well. If the gravy is too salty, dilute it with water or wine.)

Note: The vegetable particles released from the underside of the strainer thicken the gravy. If you prefer a smoother gravy, puree it, in batches, in a blender with a tightly covered lid. If you prefer it even thicker, mix 2 tablespoons cornstarch with 2 tablespoons cold water, and add only enough to achieve the desired thickness. Heat over medium heat until thickened, about 1 minute.

turkey breast pinwheels
with spinach & mushroom stuffing

from Judy Bart Kancigor

Inspired by Sara Moulton's demonstration on the Food Network, I developed this eye-catcher: turkey slices wrapped around a colorful spinach stuffing, bathed in a rich balsamic sauce. Braising keeps the turkey moist and tender. Ask the butcher to bone the turkey breast for you. (But be sure you keep the bones for soup.) **SERVES 12 TO 14** Ⓜ

*1 turkey breast (6 to 7 pounds), skin on,
   boned and split in half*
*Kosher (coarse) salt and freshly ground black
   pepper*
*1 recipe Spinach and Wild Mushroom Medley
   (page 258)*
About 4 tablespoons olive oil
*6 cups homemade chicken stock (page 63) or
   low-sodium boxed or canned broth*
1 bouquet garni (see Note)
1 recipe Balsamic Reduction (page 23)

1. Remove the tenderloin fillets from both turkey breast halves. Slice each fillet in half lengthwise. Remove any tendons or silver skin from the turkey with a sharp knife. (This is the toughest part of the

preparation, but worth it. Just grab hold of a piece, carefully slide a sharp knife down its length, and pull it out without tearing the meat.) Butterfly only the thickest part of each breast half (run the knife horizontally through the meat), leaving the meat attached, so that each breast is approximately uniform in thickness. No need to pound.

2. Open up one of the butterflied turkey breasts on a double layer of cheesecloth, skin side down. Sprinkle it lightly with salt and pepper. Spread one fourth of the Spinach and Wild Mushroom Medley over the turkey breast to within 1 inch of the edge. Place 2 fillet halves evenly on top of the stuffing, lengthwise. Cover with another one fourth of the stuffing.

3. Arrange the filled breast half lengthwise in front of you, and roll it away from you, forming a cylinder. Enclose the rolled breast tightly in the cheesecloth. Tie the ends with string.

4. Repeat the process, filling and rolling the remaining turkey breast.

5. Preheat the oven to 350°F.

6. Dry the turkey rolls with paper towels. Heat the oil in a large Dutch oven or large roasting pan over medium heat, and brown the cheesecloth-wrapped turkey breasts on all sides, about 5 minutes altogether.

7. Add the stock and bouquet garni to the pan, cover it tightly, and transfer it to the oven. Roast, basting occasionally, for 30 minutes.

8. Turn the turkey rolls over, cover, and continue roasting until the juices run clear when the meat is pricked with a fork and the internal temperature is 165°F, 30 to 45 minutes.

9. Allow the turkey breasts to rest, covered with aluminum foil, for at least 5 minutes. Then remove the cheesecloth and the turkey skin, and slice each roll into rounds. Serve with the Balsamic Reduction.

Note: To prepare the bouquet garni, tie 6 thyme sprigs, 2 large rosemary sprigs, and 10 sage leaves in a square of cheesecloth, forming a packet.

After raising two sons, at last we got daughters! Here I am in all my glory with Tracey and Shelly.

poached turkey breast
with basil-mint vinaigrette

from Syble Solomon

Tanta Sadie's granddaughter, Syble, got this recipe during a cooking class given at a gourmet market in Greensboro, North Carolina. It makes a lovely luncheon dish: delicate poached turkey breast slices with a sprightly vinaigrette bursting with fresh herbs. **SERVES 6** Ⓜ

1 boneless, skinless turkey breast half
　(about 2 pounds)
2 cups dry white wine
2 tablespoons chicken base (see Note)
3 sprigs flat-leaf parsley
1 clove garlic
Basil-Mint Vinaigrette (recipe follows)

1. Place the turkey in a saucepan that is just large enough to accommodate it. Add the wine, chicken base, parsley, garlic, and enough water to barely cover the turkey. Remove the turkey and bring the contents in the saucepan to a boil. Then reduce the heat, return the turkey breast to the saucepan, cover the pan, and simmer slowly until cooked through, about 1 hour. (Do not boil.)

2. Remove the pan from the heat and allow the turkey to cool in the broth.

3. When it is cool, remove the turkey from the broth and refrigerate it, wrapped in plastic wrap, until you're ready to serve it.

4. Slice the turkey to the desired thickness and arrange the slices on a platter. Drizzle with some of the vinaigrette, and serve the extra on the side.

Note: Chicken base is a chicken-flavored seasoning paste, sold in jars.

basil-mint vinaigrette

You can also try this fresh and lively vinaigrette on a salad. Although regular (dark) balsamic vinegar tastes fine in this preparation, the dressing will be more attractive if you use the white or mango variety. **MAKES ABOUT 1¼ CUPS**

1 cup fresh basil leaves
1 cup fresh spearmint, orange mint,
　or lemon mint leaves
2 cloves garlic
1/2 cup pine nuts, toasted (see box, page 17)
2 tablespoons frozen orange juice concentrate,
　thawed
1/2 cup extra-virgin olive oil
1 tablespoon white or mango balsamic vinegar
Kosher (coarse) salt and freshly ground pepper
　to taste

1. Combine the basil, mint, garlic, and pine nuts in a food processor and purée until smooth.

2. Add the orange juice concentrate, oil, vinegar, and salt and pepper and process until well combined. Refrigerate until ready to serve.

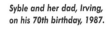

Syble and her dad, Irving,
on his 70th birthday, 1987.

jonathan cullen's bobotie

from Brent Cohen

Brent's grandparents, Esther and Joe Cohen, and the brood.

Bobotie is a traditional South African meat pie that is usually made with lamb or beef. Every South African cook has a favorite recipe. The Dutch, who monopolized the spice trade in the seventeenth century, established a settlement at Capetown, and Indian cuisine blossomed there as ships passed through en route between Indian Ocean ports and the Netherlands. Brent's South African friend Jonathan likes to use ground turkey for this recipe, which is a bit fruitier than most versions. While non-Jewish South Africans use milk and eggs for the custard topping, their kosher neighbors omit it. Brent substitutes coconut milk, a delicious alternative. **SERVES 6**　Ⓜ

2 tablespoons olive oil

1 large sweet onion, chopped

1 clove garlic, crushed

1¼ to 1½ pounds ground turkey
　(see Note)

1 to 3 teaspoons curry powder

Kosher (coarse) salt and freshly ground
　black pepper to taste

1 cup diced packaged dried fruit medley

3 large eggs

1 cup coconut milk

1. Preheat the oven to 350°F.

2. Heat the oil in a large skillet over medium heat. Add the onions and cook until soft, about 4 minutes. Add the garlic and cook, stirring, for about 30 seconds more.

3. Add the turkey and sprinkle 1 teaspoon of the curry powder over it. Cook, breaking up the turkey with the back of a spoon, until no pink remains, 3 to 4 minutes. Stir in another teaspoon of curry powder, if desired (and we do), and the salt and pepper. Add the dried fruit and cook, stirring, for about 1 minute.

4. Transfer the turkey mixture to an 8-inch square baking pan. Whisk the eggs, coconut milk, and remaining 1 teaspoon curry powder together in a bowl. Pour this over the turkey mixture and bake until set, about 30 minutes. Cut into squares and serve.

Note: You could just as easily make this dish with the traditional ground lamb or beef.

lazy sunday one-pan sausage dinner

from Leslie Robbins

It's a chilly winter Sunday and the guys are watching football. Who feels like cooking? Leslie loves to throw this dish together on those lazy days when it's all you can do to get through the Sunday *New York Times*. The cooking time will vary according to the thickness of the sausage (Leslie's butcher's are really thick) and on how dry or crisp you like it. In the Robbins house, that means *really* crisp. Leslie sometimes uses veal sausage, and she says it is yummy, too, with cut-up chicken in combination with the sausage or alone. **SERVES 6**   **M**

1 tablespoon olive oil, for greasing
   the baking pan
2 pounds uncooked kosher turkey or
   chicken sausage
4 medium-size russet potatoes,
   cut into ¹/₂-inch-thick slices
2 red bell peppers, stemmed, seeded,
   and cut into ¹/₂-inch-wide slices
2 green bell peppers, stemmed, seeded,
   and cut into ¹/₂-inch-wide slices
2 medium-size onions, cut into
   ¹/₄-inch-thick slices
2 tablespoons minced garlic
   (about 4 large cloves)
2 cans (8 ounces each) tomato sauce
1 tablespoon dried basil
1 tablespoon dried oregano
Kosher (coarse) salt and freshly ground
   black pepper to taste

1. Preheat the oven to 400°F. Grease a 17 × 11-inch baking pan. (Leslie uses a throwaway pan for easier cleanup.)

2. Scatter the sausages, potatoes, bell peppers, onions, and garlic in the prepared baking pan. Mix the tomato sauce with the basil and oregano. Pour evenly over all. Bake, turning the mixture occasionally, for 1¹/₂ to 2 hours, depending on how dry or crisp you like it. Season with salt and pepper to taste. Serve hot.

Aunt Estelle and Aunt Sally with cousin Marvin (Leslie's husband) and me.

FAMILY PORTRAITS OF FORWARD READERS לעזער

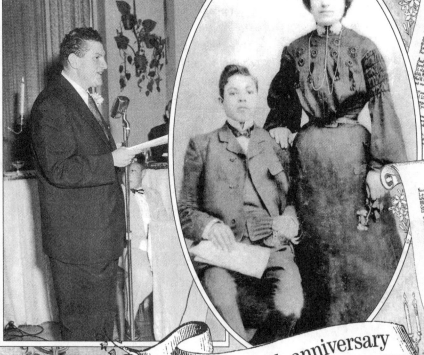

the 50th anniversary

fish

The Israelites couldn't get out of Egypt fast enough, but as they wandered in the desert, they sure missed the cuisine. Even manna gets old after forty years. As they sat around torturing themselves with memories of the delicacies they left behind, what did they miss most?

We remember the fish, which we did eat in Egypt freely, the cucumbers, and the melons, and the leeks, and the onions, and the garlic.
—NUMBERS 11:5

Now, fast forward a couple of thousand years, and if there was one source of protein that our ancestors in the shtetl could be said to have eaten "freely"—well, at least cheaply—it was herring. According to John Cooper in

"Herring is not about to go away any time soon."

Mama and Papa beaming at their golden anniversary with their seven children and their spouses, thirteen grandchildren, and two great-grandchildren around them. Who's who on page 613.

Eat and Be Satisfied, herring and "sours," such as pickled cucumbers, were the only appetizers eaten daily by our Eastern European ancestors living in the Pale. And while the Jewish appetizer repertoire has certainly broadened since that time, herring is not about to go away anytime soon. You'll find Chopped Herring—both the real, old-fashioned variety and a 21st-century version—as well as Herring Salad, and even Mock Herring Salad, in the Appetizers chapter.

And while we're on the subject of what's *not* in this chapter, what discussion of fish and Jewish cuisine would be complete without mentioning gefilte fish, which you can also find in the Appetizers chapter. If you're turning up your nose, my guess is your gefilte fish experience has been limited to the bottled variety—fine, if you're into sacrificing delight for convenience.

The tradition of serving fish on the Sabbath goes back to the mystical teachings of the Talmud, which profess that the eating of fish will usher in the Messianic Age. No wonder it became an important component of the Sabbath meal.

Aunt Sally remembered, when she was a child, live fish swimming in the bathtub waiting to be *gefilted*. By the time I came along, Mama Hinda was buying her fish from the neighborhood fishmonger. My mother could be sent on an errand to Waldbaum's for matzoh meal or salt, but the selection of fish was Mama's domain. Were the eyes clear? Was the skin shiny and the flesh firm? Most important, could the candidate pass her rigid sniff test? I can still hear the *chuck-chuck-chuck-swoop* of Mama Hinda's ancient hand chopper against her wooden bowl as she prepared the gefilte fish for Friday night. And lucky for us living downstairs that she made lots—what better lunch for Shabbos, with Uncle Lou's chrain (horseradish) on the side.

While fish was most often served as an appetizer by Mama Hinda—and hardly at all by my mother—once the cholesterol police invaded the kitchens, it became a popular meal as well. Our family has a definite predilection for salmon, whether baked en papillote (in parchment paper), grilled, broiled, poached, or encrusted with horseradish and pistachios.

But salmon is not the only fish in the sea, so grill some halibut, as my daughter-in-law Shelly does, or try cousin Phyllis's Bran-Crusted Fish Fillets—like grown-up fish sticks, low in calories and high in crunch. And speaking of calories, my daughter-in-law Tracey's Easy Low-Fat Orange Roughy has been our satisfying, guilt-free staple for years.

You won't need to fish for compliments if you serve Baked Mahi Mahi with

Stu Kancigor, hunter-gatherer.

Mushroom Duxelles, an extravagant entrée bathed in a Mushroom-Pepper Cream Sauce, or Asian-inspired Rice Paper–Wrapped Sea Bass. Cousin Abbe's sister-in-law Martine's Moroccan Fish with Chickpeas, scented with cumin and saffron, is a Sephardic Sabbath dish we like to serve any day of the week. My mother's Fish Chowder Dinner in a Bowl is a comforting throwback to my childhood. And while we're waxing nostalgic, here you'll find two tuna casseroles straight out of the '50s as well as an award-winning sardine sandwich from cousin Laura's father-in-law, Bob Seligman—it took third place in the National Restaurant Association contest in 1956.

I think the old saw about guests and fish stinking after three days is too generous—at least when it comes to the fish. I like to do as Mama Hinda did: cook it and serve it the day it is bought. When Barry and I lived in our first house on Long Island, I used to send him to the Freeport pier for fresh fish, or we'd drive out to Montauk and make a day of it. Fish that fresh practically jumps out of the sea onto your plate. These days, for me and for many contributors to this chapter—from Allentown to Manhattan to Cincinnati—it's a long walk to the beach. But today's fish are sophisticated travelers, quickly packed on ice or flash-frozen if need be, and flying first class to a fishmonger near you. Which only goes to prove that great fish cooks are everywhere!

Fish-filled Sunday brunch for Mom's surprise 85th birthday party.

salmon en papillote
with parsley rice pilaf

from Tracey Barrett

Tracey learned to prepare this dish during a Wellesley alumnae event, a cooking demonstration by renowned Bay Area chef Barbara Shenson, who teaches hands-on cooking classes through her company, A Recipe for Success. Barbara is also a chef-instructor for DACOR, a major kitchen appliances company, in their South San Francisco showroom. Baking in parchment is a wonderful method that allows the fish to cook in its own juices. Because paper does not conduct heat very well, the oven temperature is high in order for the heat to penetrate the paper and cook the fish. The presentation is dramatic, as the packages puff up during the cooking. (But be careful when opening the package—the released steam is really *hot*.) **SERVES 6**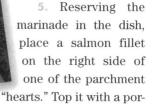

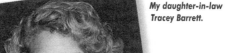

My daughter-in-law Tracey Barrett.

FOR THE MARINADE

¹/₄ cup soy sauce

2 tablespoons dry sherry

1 tablespoon rice vinegar

1 tablespoon light brown sugar

1 clove garlic, crushed

1 teaspoon grated fresh ginger

¹/₂ teaspoon Chinese five-spice powder

FOR THE FISH

6 center-cut salmon fillets (6 ounces each)

Vegetable oil

4 scallions, white and green parts,
    cut into fine julienne

Kosher (coarse) salt and freshly ground
    black pepper to taste

Parsley Rice Pilaf (recipe follows)

1. Preheat the oven to 450°F.

2. Combine all the marinade ingredients in a bowl, and stir well.

3. Arrange the salmon in a single layer in a nonreactive dish. Pour the marinade over the salmon, and refrigerate for 10 to 30 minutes.

4. While the salmon is marinating, cut 6 pieces of cooking parchment into 15 × 12-inch rectangles. Fold each piece in half like a book, and trim the edges to form a half-heart shape. Open the parchment to form a full heart shape. Lightly brush each "heart" with oil.

5. Reserving the marinade in the dish, place a salmon fillet on the right side of one of the parchment "hearts." Top it with a portion of the julienned scallions, and sprinkle lightly with salt and pepper. Fold the parchment over the fish so the cut edges meet. Starting at the top, fold the edges over twice so that the package is completely sealed. Repeat with the remaining salmon and parchment. Place the packages on a baking sheet, and bake until cooked through, 10 minutes.

6. While the fish is baking, pour the reserved marinade into a small saucepan. Bring it to a boil, reduce the heat, and simmer for 5 minutes.

7. When the fish is done, remove the baking sheet from the oven and allow the papillotes to rest for 2 to 3 minutes. Then carefully slit them open and transfer the fish and scallions to dinner plates. (Or transfer the puffed-up packages to a platter, bring it to the table, and then carefully slit the papillotes open after your guests have been duly impressed.)

8. Lightly drizzle the sauce over the salmon, and serve with the pilaf alongside.

parsley rice pilaf

SERVES 6

3 tablespoons olive oil

1 small onion, finely diced

2 cups basmati rice

4 cups homemade chicken stock
(page 63) or low-sodium boxed
or canned broth

1 teaspoon kosher (coarse) salt

2 teaspoons grated lemon zest

2 tablespoons chopped parsley

1. Heat the oil in a medium-size saucepan over medium heat. Add the onion and cook, stirring occasionally, until soft, about 5 minutes. Add the rice and cook, stirring constantly, until it is lightly browned, 1 to 2 minutes. Add the stock and salt, and bring the mixture to a boil. Reduce the heat, cover the pot, and simmer until the rice is tender, about 20 minutes.

2. Fluff the rice with a fork. Remove the pot from the heat and let it stand, covered, for 10 minutes.

3. Stir in the lemon zest and parsley, and serve.

deb rubin's firecracker salmon

from Brad Kancigor

My mother's friend Dorothy Rubin loves to cook and frequently sends me recipes. Not long ago, my son Brad was visiting and noticed Dorothy's latest pile on my counter. This salmon recipe from her daughter Deb caught his eye and he took it home to try. Even Samantha, just four years old when she first tasted it, loves the sweet, zippy flavor of this fish, which can be grilled, broiled, or baked. Brad recommends using salmon with the skin on if you intend to grill it. He likes to grill it skin side down for three fourths of the cooking time and then flip it over for the remainder.

SERVES 4 TO 6　　　P

Kitchens are for cuddling too. Brad and Tracey, 1994.

Samantha, a flower girl at great-uncle Gary's marriage to Karina.

FOR THE MARINADE

¹/3 cup balsamic vinegar

¹/3 cup ketchup

¹/3 cup (packed) light brown sugar

1 tablespoon grated fresh ginger, or

  1¹/2 teaspoons ground ginger

1 tablespoon chopped flat-leaf parsley

3 cloves garlic, crushed

¹/4 teaspoon kosher (coarse) salt, or

  to taste

¹/4 teaspoon freshly ground black pepper,

  or to taste

Vegetable cooking spray

2 pounds salmon fillet, in 1 piece,

  skin on

1. Combine all the marinade ingredients in a medium-size bowl, and stir well.

2. Place the salmon in a nonreactive dish, such as a glass baking pan, and pour the marinade over it. Marinate, covered, turning the salmon once, in the refrigerator for 1 to 3 hours.

3. Preheat a barbecue grill to medium, with a rack set about 4 inches from the heat source. Spray both sides of the grill rack with vegetable cooking spray.

4. Spoon the marinade over the salmon and transfer it to the grill. Cook, turning once, until cooked through, 3 to 5 minutes per side. Do not overcook it (see Note).

5. Remove the salmon from the grill and place it on a baking sheet or cutting board. Slice it into individual pieces. Using a spatula, transfer the pieces to dinner plates, leaving the skin behind. Serve immediately.

Note: Suggested cooking times for salmon depend on the thickness of the fish and how you like it. For my husband, Barry, burnt to a crisp is just about right. For our friend Ira Nelson, anything more than a brief wave over an open flame is too much. Fish is usually considered done if it appears opaque when flaked. But go tell that to a sushi lover (or Ira).

Variations: If you are using the broiler, place the salmon on an oiled rack in a broiler pan and broil it 4 inches from the heat source as described.

If you prefer to bake it, line a baking dish with aluminum foil and bake the fish, covered, in a preheated 350°F oven for about 20 minutes.

oven-poached salmon

from Livia Straus

Poached salmon is delicious served hot, cold, or at room temperature. A mélange of vegetables poach along with the fish for this colorful, fresh, and lively presentation. Just be sure to seal the packets tightly. Then put some good crusty bread on the table and you've got a great meal. **SERVES 6 TO 8**   **D** or **P**

Years ago cousin Phyllis gave me a great tip: With fish, of course, the fresher the better. But if the fish is more than a day old or has been previously frozen, soak it in whole milk in a resealable plastic bag or a nonreactive baking dish for 30 minutes, refrigerated. Then drain (magic—no fishy smell!) and cook.

Canola oil or vegetable cooking spray,
    for greasing the baking pan
2¹/₂ to 3 pounds salmon fillet, in 1 piece
1 tablespoon butter or nondairy margarine,
    melted
1 large red onion, thinly sliced
1 large green bell pepper, stemmed,
    seeded, and thinly sliced
1 large red bell pepper, stemmed, seeded,
    and thinly sliced
1 medium-size yellow crookneck squash,
    thinly sliced
2 large carrots, thinly sliced
4 scallions, white and green parts,
    thinly sliced
¹/₂ cup dry white wine
3 tablespoons Dijon mustard
Juice of 1 lemon
1 tablespoon fresh oregano leaves,
    or 1 teaspoon dried
1 tablespoon slivered fresh basil leaves,
    or 1 teaspoon dried
¹/₂ teaspoon kosher (coarse) salt
¹/₂ teaspoon freshly ground black pepper
1 bunch (²/₃ to ³/₄ ounce) fresh
    dill sprigs

1. Preheat the oven to 375°F. Grease a large baking pan with fairly high sides. Line the pan with a piece of heavy-duty alumi-num foil or cooking parchment that is long enough to enclose the fish.

2. Brush both sides of the salmon fillet with the melted butter. Scatter half the onion, bell peppers, squash, carrots, and scallions in the prepared pan, and place the salmon on top of the vegetables.

3. Whisk the wine, mustard, lemon juice, oregano, basil, salt, and pepper together in a bowl, and pour the mixture over the salmon. Arrange the dill on top of the salmon, and scatter the remaining vegetables over it.

4. Wrap the foil around the fish and vegetables, folding the edges twice so it forms a tight seal. Bake until the fish is cooked through, about 35 minutes.

5. Remove the pan from the oven and carefully open the foil. Cut the salmon into individual pieces and transfer them to dinner plates. Spoon some of the vegetables alongside each portion, and serve.

salmon croquettes

from Harold Dubin

In his retirement Harold filled four loose-leaf notebooks with recipes and meticulous notes. His salmon croquettes were a favorite with the kids as well as the grownups. By the way, my nutritionist, Natalie Nankin, recommends eating the bones in canned salmon—they mash easily and are a great source of calcium.

MAKES ABOUT 10   **D** or **P**

2 tablespoons canola oil, plus extra for
   frying
1 medium-size onion, chopped
1 can (14.5 ounces) salmon, undrained
3 large eggs, lightly beaten
1/4 cup matzoh meal
1 teaspoon fresh lemon juice
1/2 teaspoon kosher (coarse) salt, or to taste
Dash of freshly ground black pepper, or to taste
Butter or nondairy margarine, for frying

1. Heat the 2 tablespoons oil in a medium-size skillet over medium-low heat. Add the onion and cook until very soft, 10 to 12 minutes.

2. Remove as much of the salmon skin as possible. Mash the salmon in a bowl, and blend in the sautéed onion, beaten eggs, matzoh meal, lemon juice, salt, and pepper.

3. Heat 1 tablespoon butter and 1 tablespoon oil in the same skillet over medium-high heat. Using 1/4 cup of the mixture per patty, drop the batter into the pan and flatten each patty to 3 to 4 inches wide. (You will need to do this in batches.) Fry the patties until they are golden brown on one side, about 3 minutes. Reduce the heat to medium, turn the patties over, and continue cooking until golden brown on the other side and cooked through, about 4 minutes more.

4. Repeat with the remaining batter, heating equal amounts of butter and oil as necessary for frying.

5. Drain on paper towels and serve hot.

horseradish-crusted salmon

from Arlene Feltingoff

This has to be my all-time favorite of Arlene's contributions to my repertoire—she learned it in a local cooking class. It is a company crowd-pleaser, and when a synagogue that has invited me to speak at a dinner or luncheon asks me which of my recipes to serve, I usually suggest Arlene's salmon. Everything can be measured and prepared in advance, but keep the bread crumbs, nuts, and oil separate. Then mix them with the remaining ingredients just before you are ready to bake the salmon, so the topping doesn't get soggy. **SERVES 6 TO 8**   **P**

Vegetable cooking spray, for greasing the
   baking pan
2 1/2 to 3 pounds skinless salmon fillet,
   in 1 piece
1 1/2 cups panko bread crumbs (see Note)
3/4 cup chopped unsalted pistachios or
   pecans
1 bottle (5 to 6 ounces) white horseradish
   (not creamed), drained and squeezed dry
1/4 cup finely chopped shallots
1 clove garlic, crushed
1/2 teaspoon grated lemon zest
1/4 cup chopped fresh dill
1/4 teaspoon fennel seeds, lightly crushed
1/4 teaspoon red pepper flakes
1 tablespoon olive oil

1. Preheat the oven to 350°F. Spray a 13 × 9-inch nonreactive baking pan.

2. Place the salmon in the prepared pan. Combine all the remaining ingredients in a bowl and mix well. Press this mixture evenly over the salmon. Bake, uncovered, until cooked through, 20 to 30 minutes.

3. Transfer the salmon to a platter, using two spatulas. Cut it into individual slices, and serve.

Note: Panko bread crumbs are coarser in texture than ordinary bread crumbs and stay crisp longer.

rice paper–wrapped sea bass

from Tracey Barrett

m y daughter-in-law Tracey reports that this dish, from Jacques Pepin's *Happy Cooking*, is Brad's favorite, and it has become one of ours too. She likes to use sea bass instead of Jacques's haddock, and I've also prepared it with salmon. The rice paper disks are available in Asian markets and soften easily in water. The fish steaks are sautéed in their edible wraps and are served with a delightful shallot and soy sauce. (I often double the sauce so I can freeze half for next time.)

SERVES 4　　　　　　　　　**P**

FOR THE SEA BASS

4 Vietnamese rice paper disks (each 8¹/₂ inches in diameter)

1 teaspoon finely chopped tarragon

¹/₂ teaspoon kosher (coarse) salt

¹/₂ teaspoon freshly ground black pepper

4 pieces sea bass (1 inch thick, about 7 ounces each)

FOR THE SAUCE

2 large shallots, finely chopped (3 tablespoons)

2 tablespoons chopped chives

1 large clove garlic, crushed

3 tablespoons rice vinegar

¹/₄ cup reduced-sodium soy sauce

1 teaspoon sugar

¹/₄ teaspoon Tabasco sauce

1 tablespoon canola oil

1. Soak the rice paper disks in water in a shallow baking pan until soft, about 5 minutes. (You want them flexible, but not so soft that they become mushy or tear.) Drain off the water.

2. Mix the tarragon, salt, and pepper in a bowl, and sprinkle this mixture on both sides of the fish. Place each portion of seasoned fish in the center of a softened rice paper disk. Fold the paper around the fish to enclose it securely. (The fish packets can be held in a single layer, covered, in the refrigerator, for up to 4 hours.)

3. Mix all the sauce ingredients together in a bowl. Cover, and set aside until serving time.

4. Heat the oil in a large nonstick skillet over medium heat. Sauté the fish packets, seam side down, for 2 minutes. Turn the

packets over and cook, covered this time, for 2 minutes. Set the skillet aside, still covered, and let the fish steam until cooked through, about 4 minutes.

5. Heat the sauce in a small saucepan, but do not let it boil.

6. To serve, drizzle the sauce over and around the fish packets. Instruct your guests to slice right through the packet and eat the rice paper along with the fish.

baked mahi mahi
with mushroom duxelles

from Jonathan and Jill Lamstein

In just a few short years Jonathan and Jill's business, Josh's Place, has grown—by word of mouth alone—from a small café on Manhattan's Upper West Side to one of the tri-state area's lead-

Jonathan and Jill Lamstein, my busy cousins, with four children and a successful catering business.

ing strictly kosher catering establishments. This is an elegant dish—very showy, with a creamy, voluptuous, peppery sauce. And sure, you could just slather the mushroom mixture onto the fish if you like, but using the plastic wrap is a chef's trick that helps it adhere better and makes for a lovelier presentation. **SERVES 6**

FOR THE MAHI MAHI

6 mahi mahi fillets (5 to 6 ounces each)
Kosher (coarse) salt and freshly ground black pepper to taste
Sweet paprika to taste

FOR THE MUSHROOM DUXELLES

2 tablespoons butter
8 ounces medium-size white mushrooms, trimmed and cut into quarters
1/2 red bell pepper, stemmed, seeded, and chopped
1/2 green bell pepper, stemmed, seeded, and chopped
2 large shallots, finely chopped
3 cloves garlic, finely chopped
1 tablespoon fresh rosemary, finely chopped
1 tablespoon fresh thyme, finely chopped
3/4 teaspoon kosher (coarse) salt, or to taste
Freshly ground black pepper to taste
1/2 cup dry white wine
3 tablespoons plain dry bread crumbs

2 tablespoons dry white wine
1/2 medium-size red onion, thinly sliced
Mushroom-Pepper Cream Sauce (recipe follows)

1. Sprinkle the mahi mahi fillets with salt, pepper, and paprika to taste. Cover and refrigerate while preparing the duxelles.

2. Prepare the mushroom duxelles: Melt the butter in a large skillet over medium-high heat. When the foam subsides, add the mushrooms, bell peppers, and shallots. Sauté, stirring often, until the mushrooms begin to release moisture, about 4 minutes. Then add the garlic, rosemary, and thyme, and cook, stirring often, until the vegetables are soft, about 4 minutes more. Season with the salt and pepper. Add the $1/2$ cup wine and cook until the liquid has evaporated, 3 to 4 minutes. Then stir in the bread crumbs, and transfer the mixture to a food processor. Allow it to cool. (This is the time to prepare the sauce if you haven't done so ahead.)

3. Blend the cooled mushroom mixture in the processor until it forms a thick paste.

4. Preheat the oven to 350°F.

5. Pour the 2 tablespoons wine into a 13 × 9-inch nonreactive baking pan, and arrange the red onion slices in the pan.

6. Cut a piece of plastic wrap at least twice the size of a fish fillet, and place it on a work surface. Spoon one sixth (about 3 tablespoons) of the mushroom mixture onto the center of the plastic wrap. Fold the plastic wrap around it and mold the mixture into a rectangular shape roughly the size of the portion of mahi mahi. Open the plastic wrap and place a mahi mahi fillet, top side down, on the mushroom rectangle. Scrape away any excess mushroom mixture, and then place the mahi mahi, top side up, in the prepared baking pan. Peel off the plastic wrap. The mushroom layer should remain on the fish.

7. Repeat for each mahi mahi fillet.

8. Bake, uncovered, just until the duxelles start to develop a crust, about 15 minutes. Watch that they do not burn. Rotate the pan, cover it, and continue baking until the fish is cooked through, 5 to 10 minutes more, depending on the thickness of the fillets.

9. To serve, pour some cream sauce on a plate, arrange the fish on top of it, and cover with additional sauce.

mushroom-pepper cream sauce

Heavy cream infused with veggies, herbs, and pepper is reduced for this seductive sauce that can top other fish or vegetable dishes as well. **MAKES ABOUT 1 2/3 CUPS**   **D**

4 tablespoons (1/2 stick) butter

8 ounces white mushrooms, thinly sliced

1/2 medium-size red onion, chopped

1/2 cup diced zucchini

1/4 cup diced yellow crookneck squash

1/4 cup diced carrot

2 cloves garlic, finely chopped

2 cups heavy (whipping) cream

1 tablespoon fresh rosemary, finely chopped

1 tablespoon fresh thyme, finely chopped

1 teaspoon kosher (coarse) salt, or to taste

1 tablespoon black peppercorns, cracked (see Notes)

1. Melt 2 tablespoons of the butter in a large skillet over medium heat. When the foam subsides, add the mushrooms and sauté until tender, about 5 minutes. Remove the mushrooms and set them aside.

2. Melt the remaining 2 tablespoons butter in the same skillet over medium heat. When the foam subsides, add the onion, zucchini, yellow squash, carrot, and garlic. Sauté, stirring often, until soft, 4 to 5 minutes.

3. Add the cream, rosemary, thyme, salt, and pepper, and bring the mixture to a boil. Once the cream reaches the boiling point, maintain a rolling boil, stirring constantly, for 7 minutes to thicken the sauce. Then remove the skillet from the heat and pass the mixture through a fine-mesh strainer into a bowl. Press hard with the back of a spoon to extract all the liquid and strained vegetables.

4. Return the cream sauce to the skillet and add the reserved mushrooms. Bring the sauce to a boil; then reduce the heat and simmer for 2 minutes to blend the flavors. Add salt if needed.

Notes: Do not grind the peppercorns. Place them in a resealable plastic bag and smash them with a mallet or rolling pin, just to crack them.

This sauce can be prepared up to 1 day ahead. Cover and refrigerate. Reheat gently just before serving.

My daughter-in-law Shelly.

grilled halibut
with basil

from Shelly Kancigor

For years I avoided halibut, thinking it was too dry—which it can be when it is overcooked. However, whisked off the grill at the moment it's done, halibut's mild flavor is perfect for this fragrant preparation. **SERVES 4**   **P**

1/4 **cup olive oil, plus extra for oiling the grill**
1/4 **cup dry white wine**
2 **tablespoons Dijon mustard**
2 **tablespoons fresh lemon juice**
2 **cloves garlic, crushed**
1 **cup (loosely packed) fresh basil leaves, cut into thin slivers (chiffonade)**
4 **halibut steaks (8 ounces each)**

1. Whisk the oil, wine, mustard, lemon juice, and garlic together in a bowl until smooth. Stir in the basil. Place the fish in a nonreactive baking pan and pour the marinade over it. Cover and refrigerate, turning the fish occasionally, for 2 to 3 hours.

2. Preheat a barbecue grill. Oil the grill rack.

3. Remove the halibut steaks from the marinade and discard the marinade. Grill the fish until cooked through, about 6 minutes on each side. Serve immediately.

bran-crusted fish fillets

from Phyllis Epstein

A spa is Phyllis's favorite vacation destination. At the Greenhouse in Arlington, Texas, she and daughter Vicki enjoyed this yummy, crusty fish and begged chef Leopoldo Gonzalez for the recipe. The fish sticks you loved as a child are all grown up now, and at 227 calories per serving, go ahead and enjoy!

SERVES 6 P

FOR THE MARINADE

2 shallots, minced

2 tablespoons teriyaki sauce

2 tablespoons snipped basil

2 cloves garlic, minced

1 tablespoon chopped cilantro

1 teaspoon grated fresh ginger

FOR THE FISH

6 boneless fish fillets, such as cod,
    sole, flounder, orange roughy,
    haddock, whiting, perch, or tilapia
    (4 ounces each)

Vegetable cooking spray

1 cup bran flakes cereal, crushed

1/4 cup chopped pecans

1/3 cup plain dry bread crumbs

1/2 teaspoon freshly ground black pepper

1/3 cup all-purpose flour

2 large eggs, lightly beaten

1. Mix all the marinade ingredients together in a bowl. Place the fish in a non-reactive baking dish and pour the marinade over it. Cover and refrigerate for 3 hours.

2. Preheat the oven to 450°F. Spray a baking sheet with vegetable cooking spray.

3. Combine the bran flakes, pecans, bread crumbs, and pepper in a food processor and process until well mixed. Place the mixture in a plate or shallow bowl. Place the flour in a second plate or shallow bowl, and the beaten eggs in a third.

4. Drain the fish, discarding the marinade, and pat the fillets dry. Dip each fillet in the flour, then in the egg, and finally in the bran flakes mixture, making sure you cover them completely. Lightly spray both sides of the breaded fish fillets with vegetable cooking spray.

5. Place the fish on the prepared baking sheet and bake until golden brown and crisp, about 8 minutes. (The time will vary according to the thickness of the fillets.) Turn the fish over and bake for about 7 minutes. The crust should be golden brown and crisp, and the fish cooked through. Serve immediately.

> " When I was growing up, I lived only four blocks from Mama and Papa and visited often. Every Thursday was 'hair day,' when I would arrive with my rollers and spray for Mama's coif du jour. No matter where I had put my pocketbook, when I got home, I always found my wallet stuffed with coins and sometimes small bills. (When I got married, I told Papa that I didn't need any money, but the practice continued.)
> —**PHYLLIS EPSTEIN** "

easy low-fat orange roughy

from Tracey Barrett

Until the 1970s, no one had even heard of this versatile fish from New Zealand. In my house orange roughy has become a staple and appears almost as frequently as chicken. Even though there are only two of us at home now, I usually make the whole batch because I love it cold for lunch too. And I often triple the topping mixture so I can have some to use as a dill sauce for other fish, such as salmon. **SERVES 6** D

Vegetable cooking spray
¹/₂ cup low-fat or fat-free mayonnaise
2 teaspoons fresh lemon juice
2 teaspoons Dijon mustard
1 tablespoon chopped fresh dill,
    or 1¹/₂ teaspoons dried
6 orange roughy fillets (6 to 8 ounces each)
2 tablespoons grated Parmesan cheese

1. Preheat the oven to 375°F. Spray a 13 × 9-inch baking pan with vegetable cooking spray.

2. Combine the mayonnaise, lemon juice, mustard, and dill in a bowl, and mix well.

3. Place the fillets in the prepared pan and spread the mayonnaise mixture liberally over them. Sprinkle with the cheese. Bake until the fish is cooked through, about 10 minutes. (The cooking time depends on the thickness of the fish, which can vary widely.)

4. Preheat the broiler.

5. Place the baking pan under the broiler and cook until the topping is crisp, about 1 minute. Serve immediately.

broiled lemon sole
with vegetables

from Marcy Epstein

This quick meal takes about 15 minutes to prepare. Marcy uses precut, prewashed vegetables. She likes to serve it with seven-grain bread. **SERVES 4** D or P

1¹/₂ tablespoons butter or nondairy
    margarine
1 cup dry white wine
About 1 rounded teaspoon all-purpose
    seasoning for fish, or more to taste
2 tablespoons fresh lemon juice, or more
    to taste
4 lemon sole fillets (6 ounces each)
4 teaspoons Italian-flavored dry bread crumbs
4 cups cut-up vegetables, such as peppers,
    mushrooms, broccoli, or carrots, or
    a mixture
Kosher (coarse) salt and freshly ground
    black pepper to taste (optional)

Abbe Dubin and Marcy Epstein at Katya Seligman's Bat Mitzvah, 1999.

1. Preheat the broiler.

2. Place the butter, wine, fish seasoning, and lemon juice in a medium-size saucepan and bring to a boil. Reduce the mixture by about one third, about 5 minutes. Set it aside.

3. Arrange the fish in a single layer in a 13 × 9-inch baking pan (or a disposable broiling pan, as Marcy does). Pour the sauce over the fish and sprinkle with the bread crumbs. Don't wash that saucepan yet—just set it aside.

4. Broil the fish until it is cooked through and the top is brown and crispy, about 5 minutes, depending on the thickness of the fillets and the distance from the heat source.

> "Because I do not have much time to prepare the kinds of meals my mother used to make, I compensate by broiling fish, which takes a fraction of the time it would to bake.
> —MARCY EPSTEIN

5. Meanwhile, place the vegetables and 2 tablespoons of the sauce in a microwave-safe dish and microwave on high power until crisp-tender, 3 to 5 minutes. Leave the vegetables, covered, in the microwave until the fish is done.

6. When the fish is done, remove it with a slotted spatula to a plate. Strain the drippings into the set-aside saucepan and taste. Add lemon juice and salt and pepper if needed.

7. To serve, drizzle with half of the drippings. Arrange the vegetables next to the fish, and pour the remaining drippings over them.

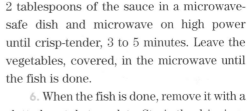

moroccan fish with chickpeas

from Martine Mann

Cousin Abbe's sister-in-law Martine was born in Meknes, Morocco, and emigrated to Israel with her family when she was eight. In Morocco this fish is traditionally served for Friday night dinner. For the sauce, tomatoes are very slowly simmered with lots of cilantro. "Without cilantro, fish is not fish," Martine instructed. Thinner fillets will cook in eight minutes or so, thicker steaks in about fifteen, but longer simmering in this flavorful sauce doesn't seem to hurt. In Martine's family cumin is served in a shaker at the table, like salt, she told me. I love its flavor in this fish, which has become a favorite in my house too. **SERVES 4**　**P**

FOR THE FISH AND MARINADE

2 tablespoons fresh lemon juice

1¹/₂ to 2 pounds salmon, tilapia, or
　other fish fillets of choice (see Note)

White pepper to taste

Good-quality paprika, preferably Spanish,
　to taste

FOR THE SAUCE

5 ripe medium-size tomatoes,
　peeled (see box, page 131)

2 tablespoons olive oil

³/₄ cup chopped cilantro

3 cloves garlic, chopped

1 teaspoon good-quality paprika,
　preferably Spanish

1 teaspoon ground cumin

Pinch of saffron threads

1 teaspoon kosher (coarse) salt, or to taste

1 teaspoon sugar, or to taste (optional)

White pepper to taste

1 can (15 ounces) chickpeas, drained
　and rinsed

1. Place the lemon juice in a 13 × 9-inch nonreactive baking pan, and dip the fish in it, coating both sides. Sprinkle both sides of the fish with white pepper and paprika, and set it aside to marinate.

2. Meanwhile, prepare the sauce: Chop the peeled tomatoes, reserving their juice, and place them, with their juice, in a large deep skillet. Add the oil, cilantro, garlic, paprika, cumin, saffron, and salt. Cover the pan and simmer slowly until the tomatoes are very soft, about 40 minutes. Add the fish and continue simmering until it is cooked through, 8 to 15 minutes more, depending on its thickness. Add the sugar if using, and season with white pepper. Add more salt if needed.

3. Arrange the chickpeas around the fish and continue cooking for a minute or so, just to heat through.

4. Serve the fish hot or at room temperature, spooning the sauce and chickpeas on top.

Note: Just about any fish can be used. Martine's favorites are salmon and tilapia. Cod, striped bass, whiting, red snapper, orange roughy, and ocean perch are other possibilities.

pan-grilled tuna
with tomato & parsley sauce

from Phyllis Epstein

This is a quick and easy way to prepare a meaty fish like tuna. Phyllis also uses this method to cook halibut or cod. I love the sauce, which I occasionally prepare on its own to serve over omelets, vegetables, or pasta. **SERVES 4**　**P**

3 tablespoons olive oil

1 large Spanish or other sweet onion, chopped

6 cloves garlic, minced

1 1/2 pounds tuna steaks, at least
    1 inch thick

2 cups chopped fresh tomatoes, or 1 can
    (28 ounces) whole tomatoes, chopped
    and drained

3 tablespoons tomato paste

1 cup dry white wine or vermouth

2 to 3 tablespoons red wine vinegar or
    balsamic vinegar, or to taste

2 teaspoons sugar, or to taste (optional)

1 teaspoon kosher (coarse) salt, or to taste

Freshly ground black pepper to taste

1/4 cup flat-leaf parsley leaves, chopped

1. Heat the oil in a large skillet over medium heat. Add the onion and cook until soft and golden, about 10 minutes. Then add the garlic and cook, stirring, for 1 minute more. Remove the onion mixture from the skillet and set aside.

2. Raise the heat to medium-high and when the skillet is hot, add the tuna. Sear it for 3 to 4 minutes. Then turn it over and sear on the other side for 2 to 3 minutes. Set the tuna aside.

3. Return the sautéed onion mixture to the skillet and stir in the tomatoes, tomato paste, wine, vinegar, sugar if using, salt, and pepper. Simmer, uncovered, until thick and blended, 6 to 8 minutes.

4. Add the seared tuna and cook just to warm it for rare, longer if you like your tuna a little more done (but be aware that tuna is better when served rare and is tough and dry when cooked through).

5. Just before serving, stir in the chopped parsley. Serve hot.

fish chowder dinner in a bowl

from Lillian Bart

My mother used to prepare this one-dish dinner for us when my father, a devout meat-eater, was on the road. I still think of fish as a "when the cat's away" treat, and we "mice" would lick the bowl. **SERVES 4**   **D**

2 tablespoons olive oil

1 large onion, chopped

1/2 green bell pepper, stemmed, seeded,
    and chopped

1/2 red bell pepper, stemmed, seeded, and
    chopped

2 cups vegetable stock or water

2 large potatoes, cut into 1-inch chunks

2 teaspoons dried basil

1 teaspoon kosher (coarse) salt, or to taste

1/4 teaspoon freshly ground black pepper,
    or to taste

1 1/2 pounds cod, tilapia, or haddock fillets,
    cut into 1 1/2-inch cubes

1 can (15 1/4 ounces) corn kernels, undrained

1 can (12 ounces) regular, low-fat, or
    nonfat evaporated milk

1. Heat the oil in a large saucepan over medium heat. Add the onion and bell peppers, and cook until soft, about 10 minutes.

2. Add the stock. Stir in the potatoes, basil, salt, and pepper, and bring to a boil. Reduce the heat and simmer, covered, for 15 minutes.

3. Place the fish on top of the potatoes and simmer, covered, until the potatoes are tender and the fish is cooked through, about 10 minutes. Then stir in the corn, with its liquid, and the evaporated milk. Taste, and add more salt and pepper if needed. Cover the pan and heat the chowder slowly. Do not let it boil. Serve immediately, in large bowls.

angel hair pescatore

from Emily Robbins

 mily uses both fresh and canned tomatoes for this outstanding sauce. But here's the real secret: apple juice! She and husband Chad are health-conscious cooks—notice, there's only two tablespoons of oil in the dish. I tested her recipe right before a visit to son Brad and daughter-in-law Tracey (who am I kidding—more importantly, the grandkids!) and it was so good, I called and said I was bringing dinner. (I usually get on a plane with more food than clothes!) We substituted grilled chicken for the seafood and served it over penne, and even Samantha, four years old at the time, quite the pasta cognoscente, pronounced it a major yum. **SERVES 6**   **P**

2 tablespoons olive oil

²/₃ cup chopped onions

4 cloves garlic, finely chopped

¹/₂ cup apple juice

4 large plum tomatoes, chopped

2 cans (16 ounces each) Italian-style
    chopped tomatoes

1 tablespoon slivered fresh basil,
    or 1 teaspoon dried

¹/₄ teaspoon dried thyme leaves

¹/₄ teaspoon dried oregano

Kosher (coarse) salt and freshly ground
    black pepper to taste

¹/₂ to 1 can (8 ounces) tomato sauce
    (optional)

1 pound angel hair pasta

1 pound kosher imitation seafood

1. Heat the oil in a large skillet over medium heat. Add the onions and cook, stirring often, until softened, about 4 minutes. Add the garlic and cook, stirring constantly, for about 30 seconds more.

2. Reduce the heat, stir in the apple juice, and simmer, uncovered, for 15 minutes. Then add the fresh and canned tomatoes, basil, thyme, oregano, $1/2$ teaspoon salt, and pepper to taste. Simmer, covered, until the sauce is as chunky or as smooth as you like, about 1 hour for my family, 2 hours for Emily's. If you like a thicker sauce, stir in the tomato sauce. Taste, and add more salt and pepper if needed.

3. Bring a large pot of salted water to a boil.

4. Add the pasta to the boiling water and cook until al dente, 4 minutes.

5. While the pasta is cooking, stir the imitation seafood into the sauce and heat it through.

6. Drain the pasta, divide it among six dinner plates, and spoon some of the tomato-seafood sauce over each portion.

tuna noodle casserole

from Lauren Nathan

This recipe brings back fond memories of evenings Lauren shared with her mom, just the two of them. When her dad had to work late and her brother, Harrison, was away at school, they would make tuna noodle casserole. Lauren says the original recipe claimed to make six to eight servings, but "I'd say four for us!"

SERVES 4   D

Vegetable oil, for greasing the casserole
8 ounces medium egg noodles, cooked
*   according to the package directions*
*   and drained*
2 cans (6$1/4$ ounces each) solid white
*   oil-packed tuna, well drained*
1$1/2$ cups sour cream
$1/4$ cup whole or low-fat milk
1 can (3 ounces) sliced mushrooms,
*   drained*
1$1/2$ teaspoons kosher (coarse) salt
$1/4$ teaspoon freshly ground black pepper
$1/4$ cup plain dry bread crumbs
$1/4$ cup grated Parmesan cheese
2 tablespoons butter or nondairy margarine,
*   melted*
Paprika to taste

1. Preheat the oven to 350°F. Grease a 2-quart casserole.

2. Combine the noodles, tuna, sour cream, milk, mushrooms, salt, and pepper in a bowl, breaking up the tuna into small chunks. Pour into the prepared casserole.

3. Mix the bread crumbs, cheese, and butter in a small bowl, and distribute the mixture evenly over the casserole. Sprinkle with paprika. Bake, uncovered, until bubbly, 35 to 40 minutes. Serve hot.

Variation: Marlene Mutzman adds 1 cup frozen peas, thawed, and $1/2$ cup shredded Cheddar cheese to her casserole mixture.

barbara ketover's tuna fish casserole

from Sally Bower

Can't you just hear Alan Freed spinning those 45s? Nothing says the '50s like Tuna Fish Casserole. Canned creamed soup came along just as families moved to the suburbs, where it surely found itself in more casseroles than soup tureens. Aunt Sally got this recipe from Marilyn's friend Barbara. She served it for her ladies' luncheons, on her good china with her cloth napkins.

SERVES 6 TO 8 🄳

Vegetable oil, for greasing the
   baking pan
3 cans (10³/₄ ounces each) condensed
   cream of mushroom soup
1 cup whole or low-fat milk
3 cans (6¹/₄ ounces each) solid white
   water-packed tuna, drained
2¹/₂ cups diced celery
1 can (16 ounces) bean sprouts,
   drained
1 can (8 ounces) sliced water chestnuts,
   drained
³/₄ cup cashews (salted or unsalted),
   coarsely chopped
¹/₂ cup finely chopped onion
3 cans (5 ounces each) Chinese chow mein
   noodles

> 66 *Barbara and I met in college. One weekend she invited me to the bungalow colony in Arverne [Long Island], where her family was spending the summer. When her future mother-in-law met me, she said, 'Have I got a boy for you!' and gave my number to the son of a friend. When Barbara found out, she pleaded with me, 'Marilyn, don't go out with Harold. He'll break your heart.' I said, 'Oh, Barbara, it's only a date. I'm not marrying him!' Six weeks later we were engaged.*
> **—MARILYN DUBIN** 99

Harold Dubin, former heartbreaker.

1. Preheat the oven to 325°F. Grease a 2-quart baking pan.

2. Combine the soup and milk in a large bowl. Add the tuna, in chunks rather than flaked. Stir in the celery, bean sprouts, water chestnuts, cashews, onion, and half of the Chinese noodles.

3. Transfer the mixture to the prepared baking pan, and bake for 20 minutes. Top with the remaining Chinese noodles and continue baking until piping hot, about 10 minutes more.

4. Serve hot, with or without your finest linens.

jim dandy sandwich

from Bob Seligman

ob's award-winning sandwich was named for Jim Abramson, a steady customer at Bob's tiny Newark, New Jersey, eatery in the '50s, who, according to the *Newark Sunday News,* requested something different. Bob concocted this sandwich on the spot, and when he asked him how he liked it, Jim replied, "Just dandy!" **SERVES 1**

3 slices dark pumpernickel bread

Mayonnaise

1 can (3³/4 ounces) boneless, skinless brisling
    sardines, mashed

Dash of fresh lemon juice

3 thin slices red onion

1 large egg, hard-cooked and sliced

2 tablespoons drained creamy coleslaw

2 slices Swiss cheese

1 large lettuce leaf

2 thin slices tomato

1. Spread 1 slice of pumpernickel lightly with mayonnaise. Cover it evenly with the sardines and sprinkle with the lemon juice. Top with the sliced red onion, egg slices, and coleslaw.

2. Spread the second pumpernickel slice lightly with mayonnaise, and place it on top of the coleslaw. Cover with the Swiss cheese, lettuce, and tomato.

3. Spread the remaining pumpernickel slice lightly with mayonnaise and invert it to cover the sandwich. Cut the sandwich in thirds. Place a toothpick in each section to hold it together and serve.

In 1956 I won third place in the National Restaurant Association's contest for the most unusual sandwich in America. The winner was the Reuben. A Hawaiian Delight took second. The centerfold of the New York Herald Tribune, and also Arlene Francis on her television program, proclaimed that the Jim Dandy was by far the most nutritious and well-balanced sandwich in the contest—that the Reuben was basically unhealthy because of its fat and salt content, and that the Hawaiian was too sweet and impractical. The two top winners were the chefs of the Waldorf and the Metropolitan Life Insurance Company. I was the chef-owner of a twenty-four-seat restaurant. Need I say more? (P.S. The Jim Dandy sold for 75¢ in those days!)

—BOB SELIGMAN

Norma and Bob Seligman at granddaughter Eva's Bat Mitzvah, 1996.

surprise!

vegetables

In no chapter is the difference between Mama Hinda's cuisine and that of today's generation more apparent than this one. When I think back to my grandmother's cooking, nothing green comes to mind. Beets, carrots, onions, radishes—those familiar vegetables of Eastern Europe graced her table in America as well. When I asked my mother if she could remember eating any vegetables when she was growing up, she said, "Sure. We had potatoes."

Oh, I suppose you could say my grandmother had a victory garden—if you can call winning the war against aphids a victory. She grew roses, not vegetables! Which is not to say she wasn't fiercely patriotic. For my

"Ahead of her time, my mother actually steamed a veggie or two."

Caught off guard for the big shocker. (If Papa Harry were alive, he'd spill the beans!) Who's who on page 613.

grandparents, proud to be American citizens, Election Day was a major event, requiring hours of preparation and wardrobe consultation. But my grandmother contributed to the war effort by rolling miles of bandages for the Red Cross, not by harvesting broccoli.

By the 1950s, when I was growing up, the Jolly Green Giant had cut a mighty swath across the land and convenience was in. My generation, however, remembers vegetables as a toll to be paid for crossing the bridge to the treasure on the other side, as in "Eat your vegetables and you can have dessert." Or so I'm told. No one had to coax us to eat *anything* in our house.

Ahead of her time, my mother actually steamed a veggie or two. For company she'd present a gorgeous display: a whole head of cauliflower surrounded by bursts of red, green, and orange. But in truth, she did it more for presentation than nutrition. And as for the vegetables she served for family dinners, I suspect she was more concerned about filling us up low-calorically than she was about our vitamin consumption.

Those grandmas of yore who did serve vegetables came from a long tradition of overcooking them. When I interviewed Joyce Goldstein for her cookbook *Cucina Ebraica*, she suggested a reason. "These are people that lived without ovens," she noted. "They brought things to the baker to be cooked and picked up later, and some things were cooked a very long time. Vegetables—in those days you never got a crunch in your life!"

One vegetable dish to emerge from the shtetl as the quintessential fare of Eastern Europe is tsimmes, or carrot stew, which actually benefits from long, slow cooking. You'll find here an easy slow-cooker version with sweet potatoes and prunes and a Southwestern rendition with chiles. There's a hearty meat tsimmes on page 139 and another, my mother's gontze tsimmes version, on page 547.

You want retro? Try the Spinach and Mushroom Casserole. And don't count on leftovers if you serve Triple Corn Pudding or Tomato Pie.

Not to be outdone, the Sephardim who have married into our family have contributed Mediterranean favorites such as Roasted Ratatouille, Fassoulias, and Baked Zucchini, Eggplant, and Potatoes. I love these warm as a side dish or at room temperature as part of the appetizer display the Greeks call *meze*.

If it's fresh and crisp you're after, you'll find asparagus, stir-fried with lemon and mustard or flash-roasted at a high temperature—other veggies get the same heat treatment as well.

With today's emphasis on health, often a vegetable dish becomes a satisfying meal: Try Greenhouse Vegetable Chili, Eggplant and Portobello Moussaka, or African Vegetable Stew.

Vegetables for dinner. Mama Hinda would be scratching her head.

Top: Jodi and Stew Mackoff.
Bottom: Brent Cohen's mom, Sharon, minds the corn.

greenhouse vegetable chili

from Phyllis Epstein

It's hard to believe this flavorful dish is spa food. I doubt Chef Gonzalez ever envisioned such a thing, but just try this chili with a knaidel topping (page 140). Talk about fusion! (Another serendipitous discovery that comes from testing two different recipes on the same day.) **SERVES 8** P

1 cup dried pinto beans

1 cup dried small navy beans

1 cup dried black beans

1¹/₂ teaspoons olive oil

2 cups finely diced carrots

1 cup finely diced celery

1 cup finely chopped onion

³/₄ cup finely chopped green bell pepper

2 medium-size cloves garlic, minced

3 tablespoons chili powder

1 tablespoon ground cumin

1 tablespoon sugar

1 teaspoon kosher (coarse) salt, or more
   to taste

¹/₄ teaspoon freshly ground black pepper

³/₄ teaspoon red pepper flakes

1 cup dried brown lentils, picked over

2 cans (8 ounces each) tomato sauce

1 can (28 ounces) whole peeled tomatoes,
   undrained, chopped

The Greenhouse is perhaps one of the most spectacular spas in the world. All the facilities are breathtaking, and the food is a gourmet's delight. Chef Leopoldo Gonzalez generously shared this recipe with [my daughter] Vicki and me. It's comfort food without the guilt. We make it at home—this is our latest version —and remember the time we spent together. With three daughters, it was nice to get away once in a while with one at a time for a special experience. —**PHYLLIS EPSTEIN**

1. Pick through the pinto, navy, and black beans, removing any stones and/or debris. Rinse them, and place them all in a large bowl. Cover generously with cold water and soak overnight.

2. Heat the oil in an 8-quart stockpot over medium heat, tilting the pot to coat the bottom with the oil. Add the carrots, celery, onion, bell pepper, and garlic. Stir in the chili powder, cumin, sugar, salt, black pepper, and red pepper flakes. Cook, stirring frequently, until the vegetables are quite soft, 13 to 15 minutes.

3. Drain the beans and rinse them. Add the beans and the lentils to the vegetables. Stir in 2 quarts water and the tomato sauce and tomatoes, and bring to a boil. Then reduce the heat and cook at a low, steady boil, uncovered, stirring occasionally, until the beans are very tender, about 4 hours.

4. Add salt to taste, and serve.

jeff lichtman's african vegetable stew

from The Second Wednesday Book Club

Our book club gathered for our Cooking Pleasures photo shoot (see page 201). From left: Ivy Johnson, Lois Goren, Barbara Klingsberg, me, Linda Gomberg, Judi Weisman.

Our book group meets monthly to dine and discuss the latest read, and we always try to match the menu to the book. This dish was a big hit on *Poisonwood Bible* night and has become a favorite even among those who prefer the Cliffs Notes. I sometimes substitute collard greens for the chard. It should be spicy, but add the hot sauce to your taste. **SERVES 10**　**P**

2 tablespoons vegetable oil

1 large onion, chopped

1 clove garlic, or more to taste, minced

1 bunch (12 ounces) red- or white-stemmed Swiss chard, stems and leaves chopped separately

1 can (15 ounces) garbanzo beans (chickpeas), drained

$^1/_2$ cup raisins

2 medium-size sweet potatoes, cut into $^1/_4$-inch-thick slices (see box, page 285)

1 can (28 ounces) crushed tomatoes

Kosher (coarse) salt and freshly ground black pepper to taste

$^1/_2$ cup rice

Tabasco sauce to taste

1. Heat the oil in a large saucepan or Dutch oven over medium heat. Add the onion, garlic, and chard stems, and cook until the onion begins to soften, about 7 minutes. Add the chard leaves and cook until they have wilted, about 2 minutes more. Then stir in the garbanzo beans, raisins, sweet potatoes, tomatoes, and salt and pepper. Cook for a minute or two to combine the flavors.

2. Make a well in the center of the vegetables, and place the rice in the well. Cover the rice completely with the vegetables. Simmer, covered, until the rice is tender, about 25 minutes.

3. Add Tabasco sauce to taste. Stir, ladle the stew into large bowls, and serve.

lasagna primavera

from Joyce Wolf

"Primavera" is Italian for "spring," a fitting name for this garden in a bowl. Often made with a cream sauce, Joyce's take is more like a meatless version of the classic. Using no-boil lasagna noodles and your favorite prepared spaghetti sauce cuts down the work, and there's plenty of leftover sauce for another day. **SERVES 8 TO 10** ▣

2 tablespoons olive oil

1 medium-size onion, chopped

4 cloves garlic, crushed

1 pound white mushrooms, sliced

2 jars (26 ounces each) spaghetti sauce

2 teaspoons Italian seasoning

1 bunch broccoli, thick stems discarded,
   florets sliced

1 red bell pepper, stemmed, seeded,
   and cut into 1/2-inch-wide slices

1 green bell pepper, stemmed, seeded,
   and cut into 1/2-inch-wide slices

1 box (10 ounces) frozen chopped spinach,
   thawed and well drained

2 cups ricotta cheese

2 large eggs, beaten

1 box (8 ounces) no-boil lasagna

1 package (8 ounces) shredded mozzarella
   cheese

1 cup grated Parmesan cheese
   (preferably Parmigiano-Reggiano)

1. Heat the oil in a large skillet over medium heat. Add the onion and cook until soft, about 8 minutes. Add the garlic and cook for 1 minute more. Add the mushrooms and cook until they are tender and have released their juice, about 5 minutes. Then stir in the spaghetti sauce and Italian seasoning. Cook, uncovered, stirring occasionally, for 20 minutes.

> " When Judy asked for our signature recipes, I asked Artie what he thinks I make best. His answer, as if you couldn't guess, was 'reservations.' My son Eric's Italian friends used to say I make the best lasagna, but what do they know? I would usually make between five and ten pans, depending on if the kids were having parties for fifty or a hundred! What a time-saver the no-boil lasagna is, and it tastes just as good. You can use your favorite spaghetti sauce. (We like sun-dried tomato.) —JOYCE WOLF "

2. Meanwhile, preheat the oven to 350°F.

3. Add the broccoli florets and bell peppers to the sauce, and simmer until they are tender but still crisp, about 5 minutes. Remove the skillet from the heat.

4. Combine the drained spinach, ricotta, and eggs in a medium-size bowl, and stir thoroughly.

5. Line a lasagna pan with just enough sauce to coat the bottom. Arrange half of the noodles on top. Using a slotted spoon, layer half of the vegetables, with the sauce clinging to them, over the noodles. Then add half of the ricotta mixture, half of the mozzarella, and half of the Parmesan cheese, in that order. Repeat the layers of noodles, vegetables, ricotta mixture, mozzarella, and Parmesan.

6. Cover the pan loosely with aluminum foil (so the cheese doesn't burn) and bake for 30 minutes. Then uncover it and continue baking until the cheese is melted, bubbly, and golden, about 15 minutes more.

7. Allow the lasagna to rest for about 10 minutes. Then cut it into portions and serve.

roasted portobello wrap

from Jill and Jonathan Lamstein

my cousins Jill and Jonathan Lamstein, proprietors of the strictly kosher Josh's Place in New York, serve a variety of lighter, healthier alternatives to traditional kosher food. In this satisfying meatless wrap sandwich, the vibrant dressing is a lively contrast to the robust and meaty portobello mushrooms. **SERVES 4**　　**D**

10 portobello mushrooms (4 inches in diameter),
　woody stems removed
5 tablespoons olive oil
4 shallots, or 4 cloves garlic, chopped
4 teaspoons fresh rosemary, finely chopped
4 teaspoons fresh thyme, finely chopped
4 teaspoons kosher (coarse) salt
4 teaspoons freshly ground black pepper
2 medium-size Spanish onions, chopped
4 whole-wheat tortilla wraps
　(12 inches in diameter)
12 tablespoons (³/₄ cup) Herbed Wrap Dressing
　(recipe follows)
4 handfuls (about 1¹/₂ cups) mesclun greens
³/₄ cup grated Swiss cheese

1. Preheat the oven to 400°F.
2. Arrange the portobellos on a baking sheet and brush them with 2 tablespoons of the olive oil. Sprinkle the shallots, rosemary, thyme, salt, and pepper over the mushrooms, and roast until soft, 10 to 15 minutes. Set aside to cool.
3. Heat the remaining 3 tablespoons oil in a large skillet over medium heat. Add the onions and cook, stirring often, until they are soft and caramelized, about 15 minutes. Set aside.
4. When the mushrooms have cooled, slice them into ¹/₂-inch-wide strips. Place one of the whole-wheat wraps on a work surface. Spread 2 tablespoons of the herb dressing over the wrap. Add layers (in this order) of one fourth of the mesclun greens, portobello slices, caramelized onions, and grated Swiss. Top with 1 tablespoon of the herb dressing. Roll the wrap up halfway, tuck in the edges, and continue to roll the wrap until closed. Slice the wrap diagonally, cutting it in half.
5. Repeat with the remaining wraps and filling, and serve.

herbed wrap dressing

jonathan and Jill's fresh herb dressing is a lively topper for salads too. Use light mayonnaise if you prefer. **MAKES 1¹/₄ CUPS**　　**P**

1 cup mayonnaise
2 tablespoons Dijon mustard
2 tablespoons fresh lemon juice
¹/₂ tablespoon finely chopped fresh rosemary
¹/₂ tablespoon finely chopped fresh thyme
Kosher (coarse) salt and freshly ground black
　pepper to taste

Whisk all the ingredients together thoroughly in a bowl. Cover and refrigerate for up to 2 weeks.

stir-fried lemon-mustard asparagus

from Leslie Robbins

When spring has sprung, Leslie likes to stir-fry asparagus with a jolt of garlic and mustard and a whisper of lemon. Sure, peeling asparagus is a little extra work, but it really enhances the presentation, especially in this delicious dish. Don't allow the garlic to turn brown or it will taste bitter. **SERVES 2 TO 3**   **P**

1 pound medium-size asparagus, woody ends snapped off
1 to 2 tablespoons fresh lemon juice
1¹/₂ teaspoons prepared mustard
2 tablespoons extra-virgin olive oil
2 cloves garlic, sliced
¹/₄ cup thinly sliced scallions, white and green parts
Kosher (coarse) salt and freshly ground black pepper to taste

1. Peel the asparagus spears and cut them diagonally into roughly 1-inch lengths.

2. Whisk the lemon juice and mustard together in a small bowl, and set it aside.

3. Heat the oil in a wok or a large skillet over medium-high heat. Add the garlic and cook, stirring constantly so it doesn't burn, for 10 to 15 seconds. Add the asparagus and continue to stir-fry until it is crisp-tender but still bright green, about 5 minutes. Stir in the scallions and stir-fry for another few seconds.

4. Stir in the lemon-mustard mixture, add salt and pepper to taste, and serve immediately.

Variation: Michelle Gullion makes a similar dish: She blanches the asparagus first by plunging them into boiling water for 2 minutes and then immediately into an ice-water bath, which stops the cooking process and sets the color. Then she stir-fries the asparagus whole. (Be sure to dry the asparagus well before stir-frying.) The asparagus will cook in about 3 minutes.

Leslie and Marvin Robbins at Harrison and Becca's wedding in Atlanta. All the Rabinowitzes go to every simcha.

roasted asparagus

from Tracey Barrett

My daughter-in-law Tracey introduced me to roasted asparagus, and now I roast one vegetable or another practically every day. Roasting in a really hot oven concentrates the sugars in the vegetables, sizzling them to a luscious brown on the outside with an almost creamy texture on the inside. But beware of overdoing it: at 500°F they can overcook fast and turn mushy. **SERVES 4 TO 6** **P**

1 to 2 tablespoons olive oil

1¹/₂ to 2 pounds asparagus, woody ends snapped off

¹/₂ teaspoon kosher (coarse) salt

Freshly ground black pepper to taste

1 to 2 tablespoons sesame seeds (optional)

1. Preheat the oven to 500°F. Line a baking sheet with heavy-duty aluminum foil, and coat the foil with the olive oil.

2. Dry the asparagus well with paper towels and roll them on the prepared baking sheet to coat them with the oil. Sprinkle with the salt, pepper, and sesame seeds if using. Roast until browned on the outside and crisp-tender, 7 to 8 minutes, depending on the thickness of the spears.

3. Remove the baking sheet from the oven and serve immediately.

roasting vegetables

Other vegetables can be roasted the same way as the asparagus on this page:

■ **Broccoli:** about 10 minutes (watch carefully—turns mushy quickly)

■ **Brussels sprouts** (my personal favorite), cut in half, cut side down: 10 minutes

■ **Cauliflower:** about 10 minutes

■ **Eggplant:** Cut into ¹/₄- to ¹/₂-inch-thick slices: 10 to 12 minutes on one side, 3 to 4 minutes on the other (watch carefully and remove the thinner slices before they burn)

■ **Green beans:** 10 to 12 minutes (stir once)

bonnie's baked beans

from Bonnie Robbins

All of Bonnie's recipes are oh so easy and oh so good. Pick five different varieties of canned beans—pinto, black beans, black-eyed peas, garbanzo, navy beans, to name a few—and choose your favorite bottled barbecue sauce. This is a perfect dish to bring to a barbecue potluck. It can be made ahead of time and kept warm without overcooking. **SERVES 12** **P**

5 cans (15 ounces each) beans of assorted varieties (see headnote), drained

¹/₄ cup cider vinegar

1 bottle (16 ounces) barbecue sauce

1. Combine the beans, vinegar, and barbecue sauce in a large saucepan and bring to a boil. Lower the heat, cover the pan, and simmer, stirring occasionally, for 1 hour.

2. Uncover the pan and continue simmering, stirring often, until the liquid has been absorbed, 30 minutes to 1 hour. Watch that it doesn't scorch. (If the mixture appears too thick, add boiling water, $^1/_4$ cup at a time, and continue simmering, covered.) Serve hot.

Cousin Bonnie relaxing in the basement, 1954.

sweet-and-sour red cabbage

from Esther Cohen

I never met Brent's Grandma Esther, but her Sweet-and-Sour Red Cabbage with apples and raisins has become one of my favorite side dishes. I like it equally hot or cold, and especially served with brisket. **SERVES 4 TO 6**

1 tablespoon chicken fat, solid vegetable shortening, or vegetable oil

1 red cabbage (about 1$^1/_2$ pounds), cored and shredded

2 large green apples, peeled, cored, and thinly sliced

$^1/_4$ cup raisins

$^1/_4$ cup red wine vinegar

1 to 4 tablespoons sugar

1 bay leaf

2 teaspoons kosher (coarse) salt, or to taste

Freshly ground black pepper to taste

2 tablespoons cornstarch

1. Heat the fat in a large skillet over medium-high heat. Add the cabbage and apples and cook until the cabbage wilts, about 10 minutes. Add the raisins, vinegar, sugar, bay leaf, salt, pepper, and 1 cup water.

" *Grandma Esther [here with husband, Joe] was known as the Hallmark grandma, because she always sounded like a greeting card. Her favorite expression was 'Well, darlings, it's always a holiday when we can all be together.' At the end of every phone call there would literally be five extra minutes of 'I love you,' 'I love you more,' 'No, I love you more,' 'No, I love you more.' She was a really great lady, and we miss her.*

—BRENT COHEN

Bring to a boil. Then reduce the heat, and simmer, stirring occasionally, until tender, 20 to 25 minutes.

2. Mix the cornstarch with 2 tablespoons cold water and stir into the cabbage mixture. Raise the heat to medium-high and cook, stirring, until the liquid has evaporated, 5 to 10 minutes.

3. Remove the bay leaf, and serve hot or at room temperature.

carrots and apricots

from Joan Kalish

This honey-toned dish is a favorite for Rosh Hashanah, when sweet carrots, symbolizing our wish for a sweet new year, grace the holiday table. Everything here is golden. May the New Year be prosperous too! **SERVES 6 TO 8**　**P**

1 cup dried apricots, snipped in half

$^1/_2$ cup golden raisins

1 cup orange juice

2 bags (16 ounces each) frozen crinkle-cut or sliced carrots

2 tablespoons honey

2 tablespoons sugar

1 teaspoon fresh lemon juice

$1^1/_2$ teaspoons kosher (coarse) salt, or to taste

$^1/_2$ teaspoon ground cinnamon

1. Combine all the ingredients in a large saucepan. Stir in $1^1/_2$ cups water and bring to a boil.

2. Reduce the heat to a gentle boil and cook, uncovered, until the carrots are tender and the liquid has formed a sauce, 30 to 40 minutes. If the carrots begin to stick to the pan, add about $^1/_4$ cup boiling water and continue cooking. Serve hot.

Mach nisht kein tsimmes

DON'T MAKE A BIG FUSS (LITERALLY, A SWEET CARROT CASSEROLE)

Cousin Joyce (right) and me, 1958.

"*Back in the sixties, Judy was pregnant with Stuie and I was pregnant with Eric at the same time—our first babies, and we were both kind of nervous. So we asked her mom, my Aunt Lil, 'How do you know when the bath water is the right temperature?'*

'Easy,' she said. 'You put the baby in the water. If he turns red it's too hot, if he turns blue it's too cold.'

But my favorite Aunt Lil story is the ultimate curse she would give to anyone who really ticked her off: 'I should eat and she should get fat!'　**—JOYCE WOLF**"

hal's easy tsimmes

from Lillian Bart

my mother never met a tsimmes (a sweet carrot casserole) she didn't like, but she really makes a *tsimmes* (a fuss) about this one, which requires minimal attention and is hardly a *gontzeh tsimmes* (a big fuss) to prepare at all using a slow cooker. She finds that by adding the prunes well into the cooking process, they are less likely to fall apart. She also likes to give the carrots a head start, since they take longer to cook than the sweet potatoes.

SERVES 10　　　　　　　　　**M**

2 cups boiling water

3/4 cup (packed) dark brown sugar

4 teaspoons beef bouillon powder

1 1/2 pounds carrots, cut into
  1/2-inch-thick slices

1 1/2 pounds sweet potatoes, cut into 1-inch
  cubes (see box, page 285)

12 ounces pitted prunes

1. Pour the boiling water into a heatproof measuring cup or bowl, and stir in the brown sugar and beef bouillon powder. Place the carrots in a slow cooker, and add the hot liquid. Cook on high for 2 hours, stirring once each hour.

2. Reduce the heat to medium (or low if your cooker does not have a medium setting) and cook for 1 hour more.

3. Add the sweet potatoes, stir, and cook on medium (or low) for 3 hours.

4. Stir in the prunes and continue cooking until the sweet potatoes and carrots are tender and most of the liquid has been absorbed, 1 to 3 hours. Serve hot.

Notes: Since slow cookers vary as to heat output, check the mixture occasionally. If it begins to stick, stir in boiling water, 1/4 cup at a time, to produce a thick texture.

Look for meat tsimmes on pages 139 and 547.

southwestern tsimmes

in chile pockets

from Judy Bart Kancigor

I've adapted this recipe from one I found in Joan Nathan's *Jewish Cooking in America*. I love tsimmes, but it *is* sweet. Here the tsimmes stuffing is packed in chiles, a playful collision of sweet and hot—albeit Anaheims are pretty mild. Don't like chiles? You can skip the packaging and bake the stuffing mixture in a greased 6-quart casserole in a preheated 350°F oven for about 25 minutes or until heated through. **SERVES 12**　　**P**

2 pounds sweet potatoes (see box, page 285), cut into 1¹/₂-inch chunks

1 pound carrots, cut into 1-inch chunks

1 medium-size onion, coarsely chopped

12 ounces pitted prunes

3 tablespoons olive oil, plus extra for greasing the pan

12 fresh Anaheim chiles

6 tablespoons dark brown sugar

1 teaspoon ground cinnamon

¹/₂ teaspoon ground nutmeg

3 tablespoons fresh lemon juice, or to taste

Grated zest of 1 orange

1 bunch cilantro, chopped (¹/₂ cup)

1¹/₂ teaspoons kosher (coarse) salt, or to taste

1. Preheat the oven to 425°F. Line a 13 × 9-inch baking pan with heavy-duty aluminum foil.

2. Combine the sweet potatoes, carrots, onion, and prunes in the foil-lined baking pan. Add the olive oil and toss to coat the vegetables and prunes in the oil. Roast, uncovered, stirring occasionally, until the vegetables are soft and browned, about 1 hour. Remove the roasted vegetables from the pan and set them aside.

3. Raise the oven temperature to 450°F.

4. Place the chiles on the foil-lined baking pan and roast them, turning them occasionally, until their skin is black, about 20 minutes. Transfer the chiles to a plastic or paper bag, close it, and set them aside to cool. When the chiles have cooled, peel off the skin. Slit each chile open lengthwise and gently scrape out the seeds and veins, keeping the chile in one piece. Set the chiles aside. Discard the foil, oil the pan, and set it aside.

5. Place half the roasted vegetables in a food processor and add the brown sugar, cinnamon, nutmeg, lemon juice, orange zest, cilantro, and salt. Pulse until combined, but do not overprocess. Transfer the mixture to a large bowl. Process the remaining roasted vegetables, add them to the vegetable mixture in the bowl, and combine well.

6. Pat the chiles dry and stuff them with the tsimmes, slightly overstuffing so the filling is exposed. Place the stuffed chiles in the oiled baking pan. (The tsimmes can be prepared up to this point a day or two ahead.)

7. Preheat the oven to 350°F.

8. Bake until hot, about 20 minutes (longer if the mixture was prepared ahead and refrigerated). Serve hot.

mary tenenbaum's corn pudding

from Linda Nathan

Linda's grandma Mary made this typical Southern corn pudding often. The green pepper was Linda's addition. Her mother, Shirley, made it frequently when she was growing up, and she did for her children too. It's a snap to prepare and take to a potluck. Just double it and put it in a larger casserole. **SERVES 4 TO 6** **D**

triple corn pudding

from Joyce Wolf

Butter or vegetable cooking spray, for greasing
   the baking dish

2 tablespoons flour

2 tablespoons butter, melted

1 can (16 ounces) corn, drained

1 can (16 ounces) creamed corn

1/2 cup chopped green bell pepper

2 large eggs, beaten

1/2 cup milk

2 teaspoons sugar

1 teaspoon kosher
   (coarse) salt

1. Preheat the oven to 350°F. Grease a 1½-quart baking dish.

2. Whisk the flour into the butter in a large bowl. Add the remaining ingredients and mix thoroughly. Pour the mixture into the prepared baking dish and bake until set and golden, about 1 hour. Serve hot.

Four generations carry on the corn pudding tradition: Linda Nathan, mom Shirley Robbins, grandma Mary Tenenbaum, and daughter Lauren, 1984.

There's a chain of restaurants in the West called El Torito Grill that serves a scoop of sweet, sinfully rich, dense corn pudding with every entree, and I have to admit it's the main reason I go there. I've never asked for the recipe, but I don't have to. Cousin Joyce's corn pudding is every bit as good—or better.

SERVES 10   D

Vegetable oil, solid vegetable shortening,
   or vegetable cooking spray, for greasing
   the baking pan

2 cans (16 ounces) corn kernels, drained

1 can (16 ounces) creamed corn, undrained

1 box (8½ ounces) corn muffin mix

1 large egg, beaten

1 cup sour cream

8 tablespoons (1 stick) butter, melted

1/4 cup sugar

Kosher (coarse) salt and freshly ground black
   pepper to taste

1. Preheat the oven to 350°F. Grease a 2½-quart baking pan.

2. Combine the corn, creamed corn, and all the remaining ingredients in a large bowl

> " My grandmother [Mary] was incredibly feisty for her generation. She wore the pants in the family! She had open heart surgery years before it was common. If she lay dying in her bed and there was a party, she was up and at 'em. My mother was seventeen when she got fixed up on a blind date with my father. Grandma was only twenty years older and when she opened the door, my father thought she was his date!
> —LINDA NATHAN "

and mix thoroughly. Transfer the mixture to the prepared baking pan and bake until set, about 50 minutes. Serve hot.

Variation: Shelly Kancigor adds 2 tablespoons minced onion and 2 tablespoons minced green bell pepper or jalapeño pepper.

eggplant and portobello moussaka

from Judy Bart Kancigor

irst let's clear it up once and for all: it's pronounced MOO-sa-ka. This beloved Greek dish, with its endless variations, usually consists of ground lamb or beef layered with eggplant slices smothered in a creamy, cheesy béchamel topping. Here dense, meaty portobellos stand in for the meat in this satisfying vegetarian version. Although that beloved green container is handy, be sure to use freshly grated Parmesan for this dish. **SERVES 8** **D**

Olive oil, for greasing the baking sheets
  and pan
2 eggplants (1 to 1¹/4 pounds each), unpeeled,
  cut into ³/8-inch-thick slices
4 tablespoons olive oil

1 large sweet onion, finely chopped
1 pound portobello mushrooms, gills and
  woody stems removed (see Note),
  finely chopped
2 cloves garlic, crushed
2 cans (14¹/2 ounces each) diced tomatoes,
  1 drained and 1 undrained
¹/4 cup dry white wine
1 teaspoon ground cinnamon
1 teaspoon ground cumin
Freshly grated nutmeg to taste
¹/2 teaspoon kosher (coarse) salt,
  or to taste
¹/4 teaspoon freshly ground black pepper,
  or to taste
¹/4 cup flat-leaf parsley leaves, finely
  chopped
1¹/2 cups (6 ounces) freshly grated Parmesan
  cheese

FOR THE TOPPING
4 large eggs, beaten
¹/2 cup all-purpose flour
2 cups plain yogurt (full-fat or low-fat)
1 cup grated cheese, such as white Cheddar

1. Preheat the oven to 450°F. Grease two large baking sheets generously, or line them with aluminum foil and then grease the foil. Lightly grease a 13 × 9-inch baking pan.

2. Arrange the eggplant slices on the prepared baking sheets and bake until brown on one side, 12 to 15 minutes. Turn them over and bake until brown on the other side, 5 to 10 minutes more. Remove the thinner slices as they brown. (You want the eggplant to give off some of its moisture, but you don't want it dry and cracking.)

3. Meanwhile, heat 2 tablespoons of the olive oil in a large skillet over medium heat. Add the onion and cook until soft, about 7 minutes. Add the mushrooms and garlic and cook, stirring occasionally and adding 1 to 2 tablespoons of the remaining oil if necessary, until the mushrooms are tender and the liquid has evaporated, about 8 minutes. Add the tomatoes, wine, cinnamon, cumin, nutmeg, salt, and pepper. Cover the skillet and simmer, stirring occasionally, until the tomatoes are tender and the sauce is thick, about 15 minutes. (If the sauce looks thin after 10 minutes, uncover the skillet and continue cooking until the excess liquid has evaporated.) Stir in the parsley and remove from the heat.

4. Reduce the oven temperature to 375°F.

5. Arrange half of the roasted eggplant in the prepared baking pan, overlapping the slices slightly. Cover with half of the mushroom mixture and half of the Parmesan cheese. Repeat with the remaining eggplant, mushroom mixture, and Parmesan.

6. To prepare the topping, mix the eggs, flour, and yogurt in a bowl. Spread this evenly over the top layer, and sprinkle with the grated cheese.

7. Bake until bubbling and golden brown, about 30 minutes. Allow the moussaka to rest for 5 minutes before cutting it into squares and serving.

Note: A serrated grapefruit spoon or a melon baller is ideal for removing the mushroom gills.

eggplant parmigiana "sandwiches"

from Heather Orlow-Choset

ousin Heather prepares this dish with angel hair pasta, which she sprinkles with Parmesan or Romano cheese and crushed red pepper flakes. She serves plenty of sauce to pass so that guests can add it to either the pasta or the eggplant if they wish. Although Heather cringes at the thought, I have made this dish with a good-quality marinara sauce from the jar with no complaints.

SERVES 6   D

1/3 cup all-purpose flour

3 large eggs, beaten

1 to 1 1/4 cups Italian-flavored dry
    bread crumbs

1 large eggplant, unpeeled, cut into
    1/2-inch-thick slices (12 pieces)

4 to 8 tablespoons olive oil

1 box (10 ounces) frozen chopped spinach,
    thawed, drained, and squeezed
    very dry

1 container (16 ounces) ricotta cheese

About 3 cups Homemade Marinara Sauce
    (see page 152) or your favorite

1 package (8 ounces) shredded
    mozzarella cheese

Carole Orlow with daughters Suzy and Heather at Elissa and Gene's wedding, 2003.

1. Preheat the oven to 350°F.

2. Place the flour, eggs, and bread crumbs in separate shallow bowls. Dip the eggplant slices in the flour and shake off any excess. Then dip them in the egg, and then in the bread crumbs.

3. Heat 1 tablespoon of the oil in a large skillet over medium heat. Add as many eggplant slices as will fit in the skillet, and sauté until brown and crisp on one side, about 3 1/2 minutes. Remove the eggplant and heat another tablespoon of the oil in the skillet (this may not be necessary if using a nonstick pan). Return the eggplant slices to the skillet, browned side up, and sauté on the other side until brown and crisp, about 3 minutes. Set the eggplant aside on a paper-towel-lined baking sheet. Repeat with the remaining eggplant slices, adding oil as needed.

4. Meanwhile, combine the spinach and ricotta cheese in a bowl, and mix well.

5. Arrange 6 fried eggplant slices in a single layer in an ungreased 13 × 9-inch glass baking dish. Cover each eggplant slice with the spinach/ricotta mixture. Arrange the remaining eggplant slices over the spinach/ricotta mixture to form 6 "sandwiches."

6. Heat the marinara sauce, if necessary, and spoon it over the eggplant "sandwiches." Sprinkle with the mozzarella. Bake until the cheese is melted and golden, about 20 minutes.

7. Use a spatula to remove each "sandwich," and serve.

roasted ratatouille

from Regine Jaffe

Born in Morocco, Regine favors the Mediterranean dishes she remembers from her childhood. Because the vegetables are sliced rather than chopped and the ratatouille is baked rather than cooked on top of the stove, the vegetables retain their individual shape and character. I drain and chop the leftovers as a fresh and sprightly stuffing for omelets.

SERVES 10 TO 12　　　　　　**P**

3 large ripe tomatoes, cut into 1/2-inch-thick slices

1 large eggplant, unpeeled, cut into 1/2-inch-thick slices

Kosher (coarse) salt

1 large onion, cut into 1/4-inch-thick slices

2 red or yellow bell peppers, or 1 of each,
 stemmed, seeded, and cut into
 1/2-inch-wide rings
6 cloves garlic, coarsely chopped
2 tablespoons minced fresh thyme or
 rosemary, or a combination
12 large fresh basil leaves, slivered
Freshly ground black pepper to taste
4 tablespoons olive oil

1. Sprinkle both sides of the tomato and eggplant slices with salt, and set them aside to drain on paper towels for 1 hour. (Because the tomatoes release a lot of water, you will need to change their towels once or twice.)

2. Wrap each eggplant slice in three layers of paper towels, place it on the counter, and press down with the palm of your hand to release as much water as possible. Then pat dry.

3. Preheat the oven to 350°F.

4. Arrange half of the onion slices in a 13 × 9-inch nonreactive baking pan. Cover them with half of the eggplant slices, half of the pepper slices, and half of the tomato slices, in that order. Sprinkle with half of the garlic, half of the thyme, half of the basil, and pepper to taste. Drizzle with 2 tablespoons of the olive oil. Repeat the layers of onions, eggplant, peppers, and tomatoes. Sprinkle with the remaining garlic, thyme, basil, pepper, and 2 tablespoons oil.

5. Bake until the vegetables are tender, 50 minutes to 1 hour. Serve hot or at room temperature.

fassoulias

from Ketty Moreno

I put off testing this recipe for the longest time because I'm a big roasted vegetables fan and love them crisp— but a woman's got to do what a woman's got to do. Was I ever surprised. The ketchup, though hardly authentic, adds just the right touch of sweetness, and although the green beans were done at twenty-five minutes, I went ahead and listened to Ketty and cooked them for the full hour. Surprisingly, the beans aren't mushy at all, but pick up the sweetness of the tomatoes. I really love this dish served at room temperature, as part of a *meze* display with a variety of Mediterranean salads, such as Baked Eggplant Salad (page 113) and Moroccan Carrot Salad (page 112). **SERVES 4** **P**

1 pound green beans
1 tablespoon olive oil
1 small onion, chopped
2 cloves garlic, minced
2 medium-size tomatoes, or 4 canned tomatoes,
 chopped and drained (juices reserved)
2 tablespoons ketchup
1/2 teaspoon kosher (coarse) salt, or to taste
Freshly ground black pepper to taste

1. Cut off the stem end of the green beans, and cut the beans diagonally in half or thirds. Set them aside.

2. Heat the oil in a large skillet over medium heat. Add the onion and cook until soft, about 4 minutes. Add the garlic and cook, stirring constantly, for about 1 minute more.

3. Add the tomatoes, ketchup, and the liquid from the tomatoes plus enough water to make 1 cup. Bring to a boil. Then reduce the heat, add the green beans, and cover the skillet. Simmer slowly until the beans have absorbed all the liquid, about 1 hour. (If the liquid evaporates too quickly, add a little water. In the more likely event that there is too much liquid, cook uncovered until the liquid evaporates.)

4. Season with the salt and pepper, and serve warm or at room temperature.

irene's molded spinach

from Irene Rosenthal

Aunt Irene got this recipe from cousin Marilyn and made it her own. The original called for onion flakes, but Aunt Irene added the sautéed onions, green bell pepper, and garlic. "That's what gives it such zip" is the note I found on her handwritten recipe. My mother swears she is the one who gave her the idea, but I don't want to get into it. Both of them are right, however, about one thing: This zippy creamed spinach makes a popular accompaniment to many dishes. It can be prepared ahead and then baked later. **SERVES 8**　　　　**D**

2 tablespoons olive oil

1 cup chopped onion

$1/4$ cup chopped green bell pepper

1 large clove garlic, crushed

2 tablespoons butter, plus more for greasing the pan

2 tablespoons all-purpose flour

1 cup whole or low-fat milk

2 boxes (10 ounces each) frozen chopped spinach, thawed, drained, and squeezed as dry as possible

3 large eggs, well beaten

$1/2$ cup plus 2 tablespoons regular or light mayonnaise

1 teaspoon kosher (coarse) salt, or to taste

$1/4$ to $1/2$ teaspoon freshly ground black pepper, or to taste

1. Heat the oil in a medium-size skillet over medium heat. Add the onion and bell pepper and cook, stirring often, until soft, about 5 minutes. Add the garlic and cook, stirring constantly, for about 30 seconds more. Remove from the heat and set aside.

2. Preheat the oven to 350°F. Grease a $1^1/2$-quart nonreactive baking pan with butter or margarine.

3. Melt the butter in a small saucepan over medium-low heat. Whisk in the flour and cook, whisking constantly, for about 30 seconds. Gradually add the milk and continue whisking until thick, about 4 minutes. Combine the white sauce and the spinach in a bowl, and mix well.

4. Transfer the onion mixture to a blender, add the eggs, and puree. Add this to the spinach mixture. Then add the mayonnaise and combine thoroughly. Season with the salt and pepper. (The mixture can be prepared to this point and then refrigerated, covered, for up to 1 day. Bring to room temperature before baking.)

5. Transfer the mixture to the prepared baking pan. Set the pan in a larger baking pan, and fill the larger pan with hot water to reach about halfway up the sides of the smaller pan. Bake until a knife inserted in the mold comes out clean, 50 minutes to 1 hour. Serve immediately.

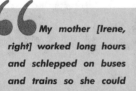

> *My mother [Irene, right] worked long hours and schlepped on buses and trains so she could give us the best and never, ever said she was tired. Yet there was always a home-cooked meal on the table, from soup to nuts, for us and even for our friends—and always a bag of leftovers for each guest to take home. Often she stayed up all night to type our papers, and our friends' too. At any age I could not match her energy. Nothing was too much for her. She always said that the only people who grow old are those who were born old to start with.*
>
> **—PHYLLIS EPSTEIN**

spinach-mushroom casserole

from Linda Nathan

L inda has been making this ever-popular casserole for company and bringing it to potlucks for decades. It's always a hit with adults and children alike, who don't seem to need any urging to eat these greens. Next to the cake mix, condensed soups probably did more to free up time for the '50s housewife than any other convenience food. I wonder what percentage of buyers over the years have actually bought cream of mushroom soup to make soup. **SERVES 10 TO 12 D**

Butter, for greasing the baking dish

2 large eggs

3 boxes (10 ounces each) frozen spinach, thawed, drained, and squeezed very dry

1 can (10 3/4 ounces) condensed cream of mushroom soup

1 cup regular or light mayonnaise

1 cup shredded Cheddar or Monterey Jack cheese, or a combination

1 medium-size onion, chopped

1/2 cup plain dry bread crumbs

4 tablespoons (1/2 stick) butter, melted

1. Preheat the oven to 350°F. Butter an 8 × 10-inch or a 7 × 11-inch nonreactive baking pan.

2. Using a fork, beat the eggs in a large bowl.

3. Add the spinach, soup, mayonnaise, cheese, and onion, and mix thoroughly. Then transfer the mixture to the prepared baking pan.

4. Mix the bread crumbs and melted butter in a bowl, and sprinkle this evenly over the spinach mixture. Bake until the mixture is set and the topping is golden brown and crisp, about 1 hour. Serve hot.

Variation: Bobbi Mackoff substitutes broccoli for the spinach and Ritz cracker crumbs for the bread crumbs.

Cousin Ronald gives his mom, Shirley, a smooch.

When Ronald and I were growing up, the neighborhood kids always hung out at our house for my mom's great snacks and my dad's tall tales. They couldn't get enough of the one about Daddy and his brothers playing for the Brooklyn Dodgers and remaining friends with the Babe, Gil Hodges, Duke Snider, and the rest. My favorite was his friendship with Brian Epstein, manager of the Beatles. We couldn't wait for the day that the Beatles would perform in our backyard!" **—LINDA NATHAN**

"My dad took life in stride. His passion was golf, but his heart was his grandchildren.
—RONALD ROBBINS

A few days before our wedding, Al [photo, right] told me that if I changed my mind about marrying his daughter, no problem. However, there would be three burly hoods waiting to break both my legs. The wedding went off without a hitch, but I never really knew how serious he was.
—FRANK NATHAN

spinach and wild mushroom medley

from Judy Bart Kancigor

developed this stuffing recipe to give my Turkey Breast Pinwheels that "wow" factor: a ribbon of bright green against the white turkey meat. This is not starchy like bread stuffings, but an elegant side dish—as creamy as creamed spinach but without the cream! Wild mushrooms lend a robust, earthy taste to the fresh spinach. I like to toast the bread crumbs for extra flavor. **MAKES ABOUT 5 CUPS; SERVES 8** **M** or **P** or **D**

5 tablespoons olive oil, or more if needed

2 large cloves garlic, chopped

16 to 18 ounces fresh spinach, well rinsed and
   squeezed dry

4 teaspoons toasted sesame oil, or more if needed

1 1/4 pounds fancy exotic mushrooms, cleaned
   and sliced (see Notes)

2 tablespoons nondairy margarine or butter

1 large leek, white part only, chopped
   (about 2 cups) and well rinsed

2 teaspoons herbes de Provence

2 1/2 cups fresh bread crumbs, toasted (see Notes)

1 cup pecans, toasted (see page 17) and
   chopped

1/2 to 1 cup homemade chicken stock (page 63)
   or vegetable stock, or low-sodium boxed or
   canned broth, or more if needed

1 1/2 teaspoons kosher (coarse) salt, or to taste

Freshly ground black pepper to taste

Vegetable oil, solid vegetable shortening,
   or vegetable cooking spray, for greasing
   the casserole (optional)

1. Heat 1 tablespoon of the oil in a wok or large saucepan over medium-high heat. Add the garlic and cook, stirring constantly, just until the color begins to change, about 15 seconds. Do not let it brown or it will become bitter. Add the spinach and cook just until wilted, 1 to 2 minutes. Remove the pan from the heat and drain the spinach, reserving the liquid. Chop the spinach. Wipe out the pan.

2. Heat 2 tablespoons of the olive oil and 2 teaspoons of the sesame oil in the same wok over medium-high heat. Add half the mushrooms and cook until they are tender and have released their juices, 3 to 5 minutes. Do not crowd the pan or the mushrooms will steam and not brown. (For portobellos add 2 minutes. For oyster mushrooms cook 2 minutes less.) Remove the mushrooms and set them aside in a single layer in a baking pan—again, so they will not steam. Repeat with the remaining oils and mushrooms. Wipe out the pan.

3. Melt the margarine in the same pan over medium-high heat. Add the leek and cook until it is soft and beginning to brown, about 5 minutes. Stir in the herbes de Provence and add the reserved liquid from the spinach. Cook, stirring constantly, until the liquid evaporates, about 5 minutes.

4. Transfer the leek to a large bowl. Add the spinach, mushrooms, bread crumbs, pecans, and stock. Toss all the ingredients together. If the mixture appears too dense, add more stock. Season with the salt and pepper. (The mixture can be made a day ahead and refrigerated, covered, up to this point.)

5. Use this mixture to stuff Turkey Breast Pinwheels (page 211). Or serve it as a side dish: Bring the mixture to room temperature if it was chilled. Preheat the oven to 350°F. Grease a 1 1/2-quart casserole with vegetable oil. Transfer the mixture to the prepared casserole and bake, uncovered, until piping hot, about 20 minutes.

Notes: Choose three or more varieties: shiitake, portobello, cremini, oyster, chanterelle, porcini, and so on. If using shiitake or oyster mushrooms, remove the stems and save them for stock. The amount of oil you need depends on the type of mushrooms used; some absorb more than others. If you need to add more oil, use the ratio of

1 to 3: 1 teaspoon sesame oil to 3 teaspoons (1 tablespoon) olive oil.

To toast the bread crumbs, spread them out on a baking sheet and bake in a preheated 350°F oven, shaking the baking sheet occasionally, until golden, 5 to 7 minutes. Watch carefully, as they burn easily.

spinach-stuffed squash

from Joan Kalish

Nature has provided acorn squash with a handy bowl just begging to be stuffed. Joan liked to fill the squash with a creamy spinach stuffing, crowned with Parmesan and bread crumbs. After baking the squash halves, if any of them wobble, cut a thin slice from the bottom so they can stand up straight. **SERVES 6**　**D**

3 small (1 to 1 1/4 pounds each) acorn squash

2 boxes (10 ounces each) frozen chopped spinach

Vegetable cooking spray, for greasing the baking pan

4 tablespoons (1/2 stick) butter

1 cup chopped onion

1 small package (3 ounces) cream cheese, cut into cubes

1 teaspoon garlic salt, or to taste

1/2 teaspoon freshly ground black pepper

1/8 teaspoon cayenne pepper

3 to 4 tablespoons grated Parmesan cheese

2 tablespoons plain dry bread crumbs

Mom (seated) with friends, Catskills, 1930s.

1. Preheat the oven to 400°F.

2. Cut each acorn squash in half. Remove the seeds and fiber. (I like to use a serrated grapefruit spoon or a melon baller for this.) Place the squash halves, cut side down, in a 13 × 9-inch baking pan, and add water to a depth of about 1/2 inch. Bake until the squash is tender and can be pierced with a fork, 30 to 35 minutes.

3. Meanwhile, cook the spinach according to the package directions, drain it well, and then squeeze it dry between paper towels.

4. Remove the squash from the baking pan, but leave the oven on. Wash the pan and lightly grease it with vegetable cooking spray. Place the squash halves, cut side up, in the prepared pan. Melt 1 tablespoon of the butter and brush it over the squash halves.

5. Melt the remaining 3 tablespoons butter in a large skillet over medium heat. When the foam subsides, add the onion and cook until soft, about 4 minutes. Then add the drained spinach, cream cheese, garlic salt, black pepper, and cayenne. Reduce the heat to low and stir until the cheese melts.

6. Divide the spinach mixture evenly among the squash shells. Sprinkle with the Parmesan cheese and bread crumbs. Bake until heated through and golden brown on top, about 20 minutes.

baked winter squash casserole

from Lillian Bart

My mother's fat-free, sugar-free squash casserole has satisfied many a craving on countless diets through the years, and she's been known to slip it to unknowing non-dieting guests with no complaints. **SERVES 8**　🅿

About 3¹/₂ pounds butternut squash

Vegetable cooking spray, for greasing
　the baking pan

¹/₃ cup sugar-free pancake syrup

4 to 5 packets artificial sweetener, or to taste

1 teaspoon pure vanilla extract

1 teaspoon ground cinnamon, plus more
　for sprinkling on top

1 teaspoon kosher (coarse) salt, or to taste

¹/₄ teaspoon ground nutmeg

¹/₄ teaspoon ground ginger

1 can (20 ounces) crushed pineapple,
　undrained

1. Preheat the oven to 350°F.

2. Pierce the squash in six places with a skewer (this keeps it from bursting) and microwave it on high power for 5 minutes. Rotate the squash and microwave it again on high power until it can be cut with a knife, 3 to 5 minutes more.

3. Slice the squash in half lengthwise and scoop out the seeds. Place the squash halves in a 13 × 9-inch baking pan, cut side down, and add water to a depth of 1 inch. Bake until it can be easily pierced with a fork, about 45 minutes. Remove the squash from the pan and allow it to cool.

4. Raise the oven temperature to 375°F. Wash and dry the baking pan, and grease it.

5. When the squash is cool enough to handle, scoop out the flesh and place it in a food processor. Add the syrup, sweetener, vanilla, cinnamon, salt, nutmeg, and ginger, and process until smooth. Stir in the pineapple and its juice, and transfer the mixture to the prepared baking pan. Smooth out the top, and sprinkle it lightly with cinnamon.

6. Bake, uncovered, until hot and slightly crusty, about 45 minutes. Serve immediately.

> *I never realized that when I married Marvin, I would acquire two mothers-in-law for the price of one. During the years Aunt Lil worked side by side sewing with my mother-in-law, Estelle (hating every minute of it and expressing her disdain by making nasty faces at the customers behind their backs), she adopted me as her daughter-in-law. How lucky could one girl be! Things that Estelle would never say or even think of saying came out of Aunt Lil's mouth. I feel very fortunate for having had both of them. As Aunt Lil says, 'More is better.' Now that Estelle and my own mother are gone, I always call Aunt Lil to tell her things I need to share with a mother and grandmother. I am truly glad to have her.*
> **—LESLIE ROBBINS**

aunt fanny's cabin baked yellow squash

from Linda Nathan

Aunt Fanny's was an Atlanta dining institution, and anyone who made it to Linda and Frank's wedding was there for the Friday night dinner given by her sister-in-law Samra and brother, Ronald, and her grandparents. Aunt Fanny's Cabin served authentic Southern food, family-style, while guests were serenaded by the staff gathered around an old piano. The menu was limited, and the baked squash was their signature side dish. Winter squash that has been baked and mashed may be substituted for the yellow squash. **SERVES 8 TO 10** **D** or **P**

Kosher (coarse) salt

3 pounds yellow summer squash, cut
   into 1-inch chunks

Solid vegetable shortening or
   vegetable cooking spray,
   for greasing the pan

1/2 cup chopped onion

2 large eggs, beaten

8 tablespoons (1 stick) butter or
   nondairy margarine, melted

1/2 cup cracker meal

1 tablespoon sugar

1/2 teaspoon freshly ground black pepper

> *I wanted to take my in-laws to Aunt Fanny's Cabin when they visited from Philadelphia, but my mother-in-law was kosher. Since she would eat fish outside the house, I called the restaurant and was assured by the owner, Mr. Hester, that although there was no fish on the menu, he would see to it that she had a fish meal. When we arrived, he was standing at the door in his white suit, Panama hat, and white shoes, and he said, 'I've got bad news for you. I sent Johnny to the creek early this afternoon to catch a trout. He didn't catch a thing, so he's just come back from the supermarket. Your dinner will be only slightly delayed.' Now that's Southern hospitality!*
> —MY FRIEND JUDY SOBEL

1. Bring 1 quart lightly salted water to a boil in a large saucepan. Add the squash and boil gently until tender (the skin can be easily pierced with a fork and the inside is soft but not falling apart), about 10 minutes. Drain the squash well in a fine-mesh strainer, transfer it to a large bowl, and mash it. The peels will not mash completely; they will give texture to the finished dish. Pour off any released moisture.

2. Preheat the oven to 375°F. Grease a 1 1/2-quart (preferably shallow) baking pan.

3. Add the onion, eggs, 1/4 cup of the melted butter, 1/4 cup of the cracker meal, the sugar, 1 teaspoon salt, and the pepper to the mashed squash. Mix thoroughly. Pour the mixture into the prepared baking pan. Top it with the remaining 1/4 cup melted butter, and sprinkle with the remaining 1/4 cup cracker meal. Bake until set and browned on top, about 1 hour. Serve hot.

carolyn dymond's tomato pie

from Marylyn Lamstein

arylyn's friend Carolyn says the best recipe for her homegrown tomatoes (she would never buy the supermarket variety) is to pick 'em and eat 'em. But she has been known to throw them into a pie, with fresh basil and chives from her herb garden and some sliced olives and mushrooms (at least she buys those), all smothered in a rich, cheesy topping. As I've never cultivated anything besides table manners myself, pardon me if I sound envious. **SERVES 6** **D**

1 unbaked 9-inch pastry shell

3 medium-size ripe tomatoes, peeled and
    cut into $1/2$-inch-thick slices

$1/2$ teaspoon kosher (coarse) salt

$1/4$ teaspoon freshly ground black pepper

10 fresh basil leaves

$1/4$ cup chopped fresh chives or scallions

$1/4$ cup sliced black olives

$1/4$ cup chopped white mushrooms

$1/4$ cup mayonnaise

1 cup grated Cheddar cheese

1. Preheat the oven to 425°F.

2. Bake the pie crust for 5 minutes. Then remove it from the oven and reduce the heat to 400°F.

3. Cover the bottom of the pie crust with the tomato slices. Sprinkle the salt, pepper, basil, and chives over them. Add the olives and chopped mushrooms.

4. Thoroughly combine the mayonnaise and cheese in a small bowl. Carefully spread the mixture evenly over the tomato slices, making sure it reaches the edges of the pie crust.

5. Bake until the crust is golden and the cheese has melted, about 35 minutes. (If the crust starts to brown too much, cover it with aluminum foil and finish baking.) Serve immediately or at room temperature.

Marylyn and daughter, Shari Nagy.

baked zucchini, eggplant, and potatoes

from Julie Gullion

ere garlic and rosemary infuse a trio of natural partners. This Mediterranean-style combo is lovely served hot with beef, chicken, or fish, but I like it even better at room temperature as part of a *meze* display. **SERVES 6** **P**

3 large zucchini, thinly sliced

3 large Japanese eggplants, unpeeled,
    thinly sliced

Kosher (coarse) salt

1/4 cup olive oil

3 medium-size russet potatoes,
    thinly sliced

6 cloves garlic, thinly sliced

2 teaspoons minced fresh rosemary

Freshly ground black pepper to taste

1. Place the zucchini and eggplant slices in a large bowl and sprinkle them generously with salt. Toss to coat all the slices with the salt. Then transfer them to a strainer set over the sink or a large bowl, and allow to stand for 1 hour.

2. Preheat the oven to 400°F. Pour the oil into a 13 × 9-inch baking pan and tilt to coat it completely.

3. Toss the potatoes, garlic, rosemary, and pepper in the oil and bake for 15 minutes.

4. Meanwhile, arrange the zucchini and eggplant slices in a single layer on three layers of paper towels. Place another triple layer of paper towels over them and press to absorb the released moisture.

5. Add the zucchini and eggplant slices to the potato mixture and combine well. (If you use a spatula, you will be less likely to break up the potatoes.) Bake, turning the vegetables once, until the potatoes are tender, about 25 minutes. Taste, and add salt if needed. (If you prefer crisper potatoes, turn on the broiler, place the baking pan 8 inches from the heat source, and broil until the potatoes are crisp and golden, 3 to 5 minutes.) Serve hot or at room temperature.

"miracle" latkes

from Judy Bart Kancigor

my friend Joanne Rocklin took this recipe to use in her novel for young readers, *The Very Best Hanukkah Gift*. She calls them "Miracle Latkes" because they use hardly any oil. Okay, so they're not exactly up there with a drop of oil lasting eight days, but they're a great kitchen project for the kids—so easy they can practically do it themselves. **MAKES 18 TO 20 SMALL LATKES** 🅟

2 tablespoons vegetable oil

5 medium-size zucchini, unpeeled

3 scallions, white part only,
    thinly sliced

2 large eggs, beaten

2/3 to 1 cup Italian-flavored dry
    bread crumbs

Kosher (coarse) salt and freshly ground
    black pepper to taste

1. Preheat the oven to 425°F. Coat two baking sheets with 1 tablespoon oil each.

2. Scrub the zucchini and pat them dry. Grate them by hand, or in batches in a food processor (do not overprocess—they should be shredded). Spread the grated zucchini out on paper towels and allow to drain for 30 minutes.

sukkot

Sukkot, also known as the Feast of Tabernacles, is the harvest festival mentioned in the Torah (Leviticus 23:34-39). Immediately following the fast of Yom Kippur, Jews the world over begin constructing sukkot (booths) in preparation for the joyous feast that begins four days later.

The sages of the Talmud prescribed the measurements and method of erecting the sukkah, within which people would eat and sleep during the week of Sukkot. How our forefathers must have rejoiced to enjoy the fruits of their labors as the growing season culminated in bushels of plenty.

Because the "dining room" of the sukkah is a distance away from the area of food preparation, traditional dishes for this holiday are easily transportable one-dish stews and casseroles like tsimmes, borscht, stuffed cabbage, and kibbeh.

The Kancigor family sukkah, 1981.

Stuffed vegetables are a popular choice, particularly in Israel, where every Sephardic and Asian culture has a favorite recipe.

Before we put on a room addition, we used to have a screened-in porch. Every year we would have a sukkah party. Barry would string up palm branches, and the kids would hang fruits and vegetables from them. But our most memorable Sukkot we spent in Israel in the fall of 1992. We could not have picked a better season to be there. Leaving Los Angeles the day after Yom Kippur, we found Jerusalem bustling with preparations for Sukkot. The terrace of every apartment sported a sukkah, and we ate breakfast each day under fruit-laden branches, our lavish Israeli buffet feast mirrored in the sukkah above. Truly we had reached the Promised Land at its lushest and most bountiful season.

3. Place the drained zucchini in a bowl and mix in the scallions, eggs, $2/3$ cup of the bread crumbs, and salt and pepper. Use your hands to form a "dough," adding up to $1/3$ cup more bread crumbs if necessary for it to stick together.

4. Using a soupspoon, mound the zucchini mixture on the prepared baking sheets. Press down with a fork to form pancakes about $2^1/2$ inches wide. Bake until the pancakes turn brown on the bottom, about 12 minutes. Turn the pancakes over and bake until they are brown on the other side, 5 minutes more. Serve immediately.

Note: The batter for these latkes can be fried in hot oil. Maybe not as miraculous but decidedly yummy.

the newest generation

potatoes, noodles, rice, and grains

Dr. Atkins would never have made it in the shtetl. If our ancestors went low-carb, they would starve. With meat unaffordable and fresh vegetables rarely available, the Jews of Eastern Europe relied on starches for survival.

For impoverished shtetl Jews, potatoes were a staple. In fact, John Cooper, in *Eat and Be Satisfied*, asserts that the population explosion among Eastern European Jews between 1825 and 1897 can be directly attributed to their consumption of this cheap and readily available food.

What is it about potatoes, that culinary chameleon, whether served plain and homey

"Once an auntie settled on a recipe, she rarely changed kugels in midstream."

Mama Hinda and Papa Harry's twenty-seven great-great-grandchildren (as of this writing!). Who's who on page 613.

or fussy and elegant, that is so, well, comforting? In this chapter we dig up and spice up the goods on the spud.

Cousin Carole's Potato Kugel is the real deal, from Grandma's kitchen to yours with just one whiff. You want latkes? Try my *splat!* method for the crispiest pancakes ever. Or for something really different, how about *Cookin' for Love* Malaysian Latkes with cashews, mint, and chopped jalapeno pepper. And why wait for Hanukkah to wow your guests with a Giant Stuffed Potato Latke Galette with Wild Mushrooms.

potato pointers

- Store potatoes in a cool, dark place, but never in the refrigerator, which will cause the starches to convert to sugar and sabotage your recipes.

- When boiling potatoes, think "steady simmer" rather than violent boiling. And here's a great tip I learned from Roy Finamore *(One Potato, Two Potato)*: Instead of throwing the cooked potatoes into a colander (and don't we all?), which crushes those on the bottom and causes them to continue to steam, Finamore suggests spreading the potatoes out in a single layer on a wire rack or basket that fits over the sink. This is especially important in making potato salad (see page 107).

- When mashing potatoes, for optimum results, says Finamore, use a ricer. Second-best is a hand masher, but forget the food mill, which overworks the potatoes and renders them gluey. A hand-held mixer will whip the potatoes, not mash them; if you use one, make certain the potatoes are lump-free before adding the butter or liquid.

Our family chefs bring you dishes from near and far: Paprikas Krumpli (fried potatoes with lots of sweet paprika) and Shlishkes (potato dough dumplings with buttered bread crumbs) from Hungary; from Germany, Hot Potatoes with Cucumber Cream; and rich, oniony potato blintzes that harken to our Russian past—but could any shtetl mama have envisioned our Potato Blintz Soufflé?

You'll find sweet potato dishes here as well (and, no, these are not yams; see page 285) from Mama Hinda's Sweet Potato Casserole (with marshmallows—but of course, *dahlink*) to a light and elegant Apricot Sweet Potato Pudding to cousin Bonnie's irresistible Cajun oven fries to cousin Laura's spectacular layered Yummy "Yam" Tart.

All the wonderful dishes we think of as typical Ashkenazic fare—noodles, kugels, kreplach, varenikas, pirogen, farfel, kasha, kishka—were Mama and Papa's comfort foods long before it became fashionable to use that term.

Noodles (lokshen in Yiddish) were filling and inexpensive to prepare and had the added advantage of being pareve (neutral), so they could be eaten at both meat and dairy meals. Monday and Thursday was *milchig* (dairy) night when my mother was a child. Sometimes they had fish, sometimes not, but always there were Mama's homemade noodles with pot cheese and sour cream.

Nowadays we're less likely to make our own noodles from scratch, except for dishes like pirogen, but we serve up store-bought versions in every possible shape and size. Kugels, of course, come first to mind. In this chapter I've limited them to lokshen kugels. For a delicious potato kugel, see page 279. Passover kugels, using matzoh or matzoh farfel, may be found on pages 554 to 558.

Top: Man can cook. My daughter-in-law Tracey's brother Tyler. Bottom: My mother's table set for Marylyn and Ben's machatunim dinner, 1959.

Not surprisingly—have you noticed the length of the dessert section?—most of the kugels found here are sweet, because those are my family's preference. These can be served as dessert, although in my family they are usually a side dish. (Happily, a few savory kugels did come my way: a sweet but peppery Jerusalem kugel, and a Romanian salt and pepper kugel.)

With so many kugels submitted, choosing among them was an impossible task better left to King Solomon. You add cheese, butter, and/or cream to noodles and fruit—well, to quote my mother, "What could be bad?"

Rita's Special Kugel with pears and cream. Aunt Sally's Ultra-Extra-Special Noodle Pudding (for *machatunim*) with cream, farmer cheese, pot cheese, and sour cream. Whether topped with fruit, glazed pecans, Frosted Flakes, or my personal favorite, Tam Tam crackers—or even baked bare, turning the top layer of noodles into irresistible crisps—every kugel seemed to say, "Choose me!" "No, me!"

With so little animal protein in their diet, shtetl Jews survived on nutritious grains that were ground into flour for noodles, dumplings, and bread; made into porridge; or mixed with fat and stuffed into casings for kishka. Kasha (buckwheat groats) and other grains were an essential part of daily meals—the varnishkas (bowties) came later. In Romania cornmeal became the national dish mamaliga (polenta to Italians). My husband recalls Grandma Becky serving it often, stirring and stirring for what seemed like hours—under her watchful eye there was never a lump. For our Sephardic cousins, rice is the staple of choice. Israelis combine it with lentils and fried onions to make majadra.

In this tummy-warming chapter you'll find stuffings as well: I use challah; cousin Samra, true to her Southern roots, favors corn bread; and my daughter-in-law Shelly's Minnesota family prefers wild rice. And if Dr. Atkins had not already taken his place at the big table in the sky, this chapter would kill him!

shirley's company potatoes

from Shirley Robbins

After four girls, Mama and Papa finally got their long-awaited son, Uncle Al, followed by, miracle of miracles, twin boys, Morris and Lou. How ironic that while in the service during World War II, two out of the three married Southern gals, left home, and moved to faraway Georgia. Mama and Papa would take the overnight train to visit them, Mama carrying her kosher chicken and other goodies for the long ride. When they would return from visiting y'all in Atlanta, Papa would say to Mama, "You call me *shoogah*, and I'll call you *sveetie*!"

> " Al was in the army during World War II for four out of the first five years of our marriage. When he finally came home, I wanted to surprise him, so I consulted a neighbor and got some recipes and worked all day making the dishes of his childhood: borscht, brisket, tsimmes, etc. Al took one look at the tsimmes and said, 'What is this___??!!! (expletive deleted).' I said, 'But Al, I was just trying to make you a dinner like your Mama used to make,' to which he replied, 'Who ever told you I liked my mother's cooking?'
>
> Anyway, I never made tsimmes again, so if you want the recipe, ask Sally. Here's something Al did like (and believe me, his mother never made it!) —**SHIRLEY ROBBINS** "

Aunt Shirley's favorite company side dish was her irresistibly creamy potatoes. While they take hours to cook, they're a snap to prepare. They're done when most of the creamy sauce has been absorbed, turning the tender potatoes into pure comfort food. If you like, you can roughly mash the potatoes for a more rustic feel. **SERVES 6 TO 8** 🅳

Butter or solid vegetable shortening,
    for greasing the baking pan
1 pint sour cream
1 can (10³/₄ ounces) condensed cream of
    mushroom soup
2 teaspoons kosher (coarse) salt
¹/₂ teaspoon freshly ground black pepper
3 pounds baking potatoes, peeled and
    cut into ³/₈-inch-thick slices
2 medium-size onions, sliced and separated
    into rings

1. Preheat the oven to 350°F. Grease a 3-quart baking pan.

2. Combine the sour cream, soup, salt, and pepper in a large bowl and stir well. Add the potatoes and onions and combine thoroughly. Transfer the mixture to the prepared baking pan and bake, covered, until the potatoes are quite

Papa and Mama took the train to Atlanta for Aunt Shirley and Uncle Al's wedding, 1941.

soft and have absorbed most of the sauce, $2^1/_2$ to 3 hours.

3. Toss gently to distribute the remaining sauce, and serve.

grilled baked potatoes

from Heather Orlow-Choset

Cousin Heather and her new hubby, Ian, enjoy grilled potatoes for dinner. In fact, more grilling takes place on the eleventh-floor terrace of their New York apartment, says Heather, than in the kitchen. On the terrace they can relax, have a glass of wine, and enjoy the view while the potatoes cook . . . or so she said before Wyneth was born! **SERVES 2** **P**

2 Idaho baking potatoes (10 to 12 ounces each), unpeeled
1 tablespoon olive oil
Garlic powder to taste
Kosher (coarse) salt and freshly ground black pepper to taste

1. Preheat a barbecue grill, set up for indirect cooking (see Note). Cut two pieces of aluminum foil that are large enough to wrap around the potatoes.

2. Prick the potatoes all over with a fork or skewer, and place each potato on a square of foil. Rub the potatoes all over with the olive oil, and sprinkle generously with garlic powder, salt, and pepper.

3. Wrap the potatoes tightly in the foil and place them on the top grate away from the coals (or over the unlit burner). Grill over indirect heat until the potatoes are soft when tested with a skewer, about 1 hour. Serve immediately.

Note: To set up a grill for indirect grilling, pile all of the coals on one half of the lower grate, leaving the other half empty. If you have a gas grill with two burners, light only one.

Variation: Try topping these grilled potatoes with chili (see page 241) for a hearty main dish or with sour cream and chives.

paprikas krumpli
(hungarian paprika potatoes)

from Barbara Nagy Itzkowitz

Hungarians love their paprika. Barbara, my cousin Shari's mother-in-law, prefers sweet to hot. But be sure to get imported Hungarian paprika, she says, for this dish, which she learned from her mother, who lived with Barbara and her family until her death in 1982. Avoid stirring the potatoes as they cook so they keep their shape, and do not mash them. **SERVES 6 TO 8** **P**

3 tablespoons solid vegetable shortening
or vegetable oil

1 large onion, chopped

2 tablespoons sweet Hungarian paprika

2 teaspoons kosher (coarse) salt, or to taste

$^1/_4$ teaspoon freshly ground black pepper,
or to taste

$2^1/_2$ pounds boiling potatoes, cut into $^1/_2$-inch-
thick slices

1. Melt the shortening in a large skillet over medium heat. Add the onion and cook until it is soft and lightly browned, about 10 minutes.

2. Stir in 1 tablespoon of the paprika, 1 teaspoon of the salt, and the pepper. Add the potatoes, and stir to distribute the onions and seasonings. Add $^1/_4$ cup water, cover the skillet, and simmer, gradually adding more water (up to $^2/_3$ cup in all), until the potatoes are tender, 20 to 30 minutes (or even longer if you like them as soft as my husband does). As they cook, add more paprika, salt, and pepper to taste. You will need to turn the potatoes occasionally, but try not to break them up. Serve immediately.

> **My mother, Barbara Bedo, was called nagymama, Hungarian for 'grandma,' by my children. (Nagy, pronounced 'nodj,' means 'grand' or 'large' and is a very common Hungarian name.) She came to America at the age of sixteen in 1928. She was the oldest of seven children and really raised her five brothers while her parents were busy working on the farm. The family was very poor. Her father, Albert, was a soldier during World War I, fighting for Austria-Hungary, as the country was known then. He was captured by the Russians and imprisoned in Siberia. After the war he walked home across Europe—it took him seven years! My mother used to tell the story that when she first sighted this bedraggled man with a long beard coming down the road, she ran to tell her mother that a hobo was coming. She did not recognize her own father.**
>
> **—BARBARA NAGY ITZKOWITZ**

hot potatoes
with cucumber cream
from Ilo Riebe

This is a traditional German dish that my daughter-in-law Shelly's Grandma Ilo prepares with potatoes and cucumbers from her garden. The cucumbers and onions must be sliced as thin as possible, says Ilo. They are added to a creamy sauce, enough to be thor-

Shelly's grandma Ilo and my mom really hit it off on Stu and Shelly's wedding weekend, 1988.

oughly covered with dressing and still be "saucy." This is a do-it-yourself dish: Each person smashes a hot potato and pours on the cucumbers and cream. **SERVES 5 TO 7**　　　　　　　　　　　**D**

Kosher (coarse) salt

3 cucumbers, peeled and very thinly sliced

5 to 7 large boiling potatoes

1 cup heavy (whipping) cream

7 tablespoons sugar

5 tablespoons distilled white vinegar

¹/₂ medium-size onion, very thinly sliced

Freshly ground black pepper to taste

1. Bring a large pot of lightly salted water to a boil.

2. While the water is heating, place the cucumber slices in a colander and set it over a bowl or in the sink. Sprinkle the cucumbers generously with salt, and allow to stand for 15 to 20 minutes.

3. Meanwhile, as soon as the water comes to a boil, add the potatoes and cook at a gentle boil until tender, about 20 minutes. Drain, and keep hot.

4. Rinse the salt off the cucumbers and drain them. Pat them dry with several changes of paper towels.

5. Combine the cream, sugar, and vinegar in a large bowl, and mix well. Add the cucumbers and onion, and mix thoroughly. Add salt if necessary and pepper to taste.

6. Serve each person a hot boiled potato, and pass the cucumber mixture. Using a fork, smash the potato flat on your plate. Spoon the cool cucumber mixture over the smashed potato, and dig in.

cheesy garlic mashed potato casserole

from Diane Podratz

R oasting tames garlic's pungent bite to a mellow, perfumed sweetness. Pair it with cheesy mashed potatoes and the combination is irresistible. This casserole is a favorite at Podratz family gatherings. It can be assembled ahead of time, refrigerated, and then baked before serving. **SERVES 10 TO 12**　　　　**D**

1 head garlic

1 tablespoon olive oil

Kosher (coarse) salt

5 pounds baking potatoes, cut into quarters

Butter or solid vegetable shortening,
*   for greasing the baking pan*

1 package (8 ounces) cream cheese,
*   at room temperature*

1 cup half-and-half

8 tablespoons (1 stick) butter, at room
*   temperature*

2 teaspoons onion salt, or to taste

2 teaspoons seasoned salt, or to taste

¹/₄ teaspoon freshly ground black pepper,
*   or to taste*

FOR THE TOPPING

2 tablespoons butter, melted

¹/₂ cup grated Parmesan cheese

Paprika to taste

1. Preheat the oven to 400°F.

2. Slice off the top one fourth of the garlic head to expose the cloves. Place the head on a piece of aluminum foil, or in a garlic roaster if you have one, and drizzle the olive oil over the exposed cloves. Wrap the foil tightly around the garlic, and bake for 40 minutes. Then unwrap the garlic and set it aside to cool. Reduce the oven temperature to 350°F.

3. Meanwhile, bring a pot of lightly salted water to a boil. Add the potatoes and cook until tender, about 20 minutes (test with a thin skewer or cake tester rather than a fork, and you won't break the potatoes apart.) Drain the potatoes and put them through a ricer or mash them well in a large bowl.

4. Grease a 13 × 9-inch nonreactive baking pan.

5. Place the cream cheese in the bowl of an electric mixer (either a standing mixer or a handheld one). Squeeze the roasted cloves of garlic over the cream cheese. Beat at medium speed until fluffy and combined, 5 to 10 seconds.

6. Add the cream cheese mixture, half-and-half, butter, onion salt, seasoned salt, and pepper to the potatoes, and mash. Transfer the mixture to the prepared baking pan.

7. Brush the top of the potatoes with the melted butter. Sprinkle with the Parmesan cheese and lightly with paprika. Bake until hot and lightly crusted, about 35 minutes. Serve hot.

Note: When reheating, allow the casserole to come to room temperature before placing in the oven.

eleanor's molded mashed potatoes

from Elaine Appelbaum

ousins Bonnie and Jackie's cousin Elaine loves to serve her friend Eleanor Freedman's specialty to guests at their vacation home on Cape Cod, and no one can guess that she uses instant potatoes. Your guests won't either. These cheesy, creamy mashed potatoes look elegant when unmolded, but you can also serve them right from the casserole.

SERVES 6 TO 8

7 tablespoons butter, at room temperature

1 to 2 tablespoons plain dry bread crumbs

4 cups instant potatoes

3/4 cup grated Swiss cheese

1/2 cup heavy (whipping) cream

1 1/2 to 2 1/2 teaspoons kosher (coarse) salt, or to taste

1/8 teaspoon freshly ground black pepper

Pinch of ground nutmeg

Yolks of 3 large eggs

1. Preheat the oven to 375°F. Grease a 6-cup mold or round baking dish with 1 tablespoon of the butter. Cut a round of cooking parchment to fit the bottom of the mold. Butter the paper, place it in the mold, and sprinkle the bottom and sides of the

mold with the bread crumbs. Shake out the excess.

2. Bring 3 cups water to a boil in a medium-size saucepan. Remove the pan from the heat and stir in the instant potatoes until smooth. Stir in the remaining butter and the cheese, cream, salt, pepper, and nutmeg. Add the egg yolks and mix thoroughly.

3. Transfer the mixture to the prepared mold and smooth out the top. Bake until golden, about 1 hour.

4. Loosen the potatoes by running a knife around the sides of the mold. To unmold, invert a serving platter over the mold and flip them over together. Peel off the parchment. Slice the potato mold into wedges, and serve.

Note: This dish can also be served straight from the casserole without creating a mold. To do so, eliminate the parchment in Step 1, and instead of sprinkling the bread crumbs in the mold, sprinkle them on top of the casserole before baking.

Elaine Appelbaum (below) and her parents, Nellie and Louis Jaffee (Aunt Hilda's aunt and uncle).

not-your-store-bought
potato blintzes

from Sally Bower

שhy limit rich, oniony potato knish filling to knishes? For some reason the first blintz never comes out right, so don't get discouraged. It does take a little practice to tilt the pan quickly enough so that the batter spreads over the whole pan before it cooks (think crepes). It helps to have a two-tablespoon measuring spoon. (Most coffee measures are two tablespoons, but check yours.) To make these blintzes pareve (neutral), substitute rice milk, soy milk, or nondairy creamer for the milk.

You can use this recipe for cheese blintzes (page 355) or apple blintzes too (page 357). **MAKES 30 BLINTZES** **D**

FOR THE BLINTZ PANCAKE
5 large eggs
1¹/₄ cups whole or 2% milk
1¹/₄ teaspoons kosher (coarse) salt
1¹/₄ cups all-purpose flour
Solid vegetable shortening or
vegetable oil,
for greasing the skillet

FOR THE POTATO FILLING
1 recipe Potato Knish filling (page 25)

Butter or margarine, for cooking
the blintzes

1. Prepare the pancake batter: Whisk the eggs, milk, salt, and 10 tablespoons ($^1/_2$ cup plus 2 tablespoons) water in a medium-size bowl. Gradually add the flour, whisking until smooth. Allow to rest for 15 minutes.

2. Lightly grease a 6-inch skillet, and heat it over medium-high heat. Pour in 2 tablespoons of the batter, taking the skillet off the heat momentarily as you quickly tilt the pan to cover the bottom with the batter. Cook the pancake on one side until it blisters—it takes only a few seconds. Slip the finished pancake (no, you don't cook the other side) onto a plate or paper towel. Repeat until all the batter is used, sandwiching the finished pancakes between sheets of waxed paper or paper towels to keep them separated. (You probably will need to grease the skillet lightly after every third or fourth pancake—possibly more often if you are not using a nonstick pan.)

3. To assemble the blintzes, form $^1/_3$ cup of the potato filling into a small log and place it on the lower half of the fried side of each pancake. Roll the pancake, folding the ends in as you go.

4. The blintzes can be either fried or baked. *To fry the blintzes*, melt about 1 tablespoon butter, margarine, or shortening in a large skillet over medium-low heat. Add as many blintzes as will fit, seam side down, and fry on all four sides until golden brown and crisp, about 10 minutes altogether. Drain the blintzes on paper towels. Repeat with the remaining blintzes.

To bake the blintzes, preheat the oven to 350°F. Grease a nonreactive baking pan (a 13 × 9-inch pan will hold about 15 blintzes) with butter, margarine, or shortening. Place the blintzes, seam side down, in the prepared baking pan and dot with butter, margarine, or shortening. Bake until golden brown, about 30 minutes. Serve hot.

Note: If you wish to freeze them, arrange the uncooked blintzes in a single layer on a baking sheet, cover with aluminum foil, and freeze. When they are frozen solid, transfer the blintzes to resealable freezer bags, so you can later retrieve as many as you like. Let them thaw completely before frying or baking.

rose rosenblum's shlishkes

from Alice Weiss

my husband Barry's Grandma Becky was born in Odessa and was of Romanian descent, but she had a Hungarian neighbor who taught her how to make shlishkes, tender potato pillows— think Italian gnocchi—boiled and then coated in buttery bread crumbs. Alas, my mother-in-law never got the recipe, so I was delighted when Aunt Sylvia's cousin Alice sent me her mother Rose's version. Be sure to use starchy baking potatoes for these dumplings, and cook them in their skins. The amount of flour needed will depend on the starchiness of the potatoes and their moisture content. If you peel the potatoes while they are still quite hot, the excess moisture will evaporate as the potatoes are cooling, so you won't have to add a lot of flour to be able to handle the dough.

Alice's mother also used this dough to make szilvas gomboc (plum dumplings). A small pitted Hungarian plum—an Italian plum can be substituted—is sprinkled with sugar and pressed into the shlishkes dough. (My friend Carolyn Gilboa remembers her mother using a cube of sugar to replace the plum pit. "Even the memory is luscious," she warbled.) Like shlishkes, these are boiled and then rolled in buttered bread crumbs.

SERVES 6 TO 8　　　　**D** or **P**

Kosher (coarse) salt

3 pounds baking potatoes, unpeeled,
*　　and well scrubbed*

1 egg, lightly beaten

Yolk of 1 egg, lightly beaten

1 cup sifted all-purpose flour, plus more
*　　as needed*

8 tablespoons (1 stick) butter or nondairy
*　　margarine*

1 cup fine dry plain bread crumbs

1. Bring a large pot of lightly salted water to a boil. Add the potatoes and cook, covered, over medium heat until they are soft when pierced with a skewer, about 30 minutes. (Don't use a fork, as it will break up the potatoes, making them watery.)

2. Drain the potatoes, transfer them to a bowl, and set them aside

> " *My mother's family was Romanian, and my father's family was Hungarian, and there was a constant battle as to which was better. I was Daddy's girl, and I always sided with my father. The music was better. The food was better. One day my mother said, 'I'll show him,' and she learned to make shlishkes. That night my father decided that maybe Romanian cooks were not so bad after all.*　**—ALICE WEISS** "

until they are just cool enough to handle. Then peel the hot potatoes and mash them in a large bowl. Add the egg, egg yolk, and 1 tablespoon salt, and mix well. Add enough of the flour, gradually, to make a soft dough.

3. Transfer the dough to a well-floured surface and knead until smooth. The dough should be firm but not sticky. Break off walnut-size pieces of dough. Flour your hands and roll each piece of dough between the palms of your hands to form a long cylinder about ³/₄ inch in diameter. Cut it into 1¹/₂-inch lengths. Repeat, using up all the dough. (The uncooked dumplings can be prepared up to this point and frozen.)

4. Bring a large pot of water to a rolling boil. Drop the dumplings, a few at a time, into the boiling water. As soon as they come to the surface (4 to 5 minutes), remove them with a slotted spoon and drain

Grandma Becky, my husband, Barry, and his mother, Edie.

them well. Keep them warm while you cook the rest.

5. Melt the butter in a large skillet. Stir in the bread crumbs and mix well. Roll the dumplings in the crumb mixture, and serve immediately.

potato blintz soufflé

from Judy Bart Kancigor

irth of a recipe: If cheese blintzes can be baked in a sweet egg batter for the ever-popular Cheese Blintz Soufflé (page 358), I reasoned, why couldn't I fashion a savory batter and do the same with potato blintzes? Any number of accents can be added, according to your taste and imagination. **SERVES 10 TO 15** 🄳 or 🄿

Butter, margarine, or solid vegetable
   shortening, for greasing the baking pan
12 to 15 potato blintzes, homemade
   (page 275) or store-bought,
   thawed if frozen
¹/₄ cup vegetable oil
1 medium-size onion, diced
6 large eggs
1¹/₄ teaspoons kosher (coarse) salt
¹/₄ teaspoon white pepper
2 cups regular or nondairy
   sour cream
¹/₄ cup chopped flat-leaf parsley

1. Preheat the oven to 350°F. Grease a 13 × 9-inch baking pan.

2. Arrange the blintzes in a single layer in the prepared pan.

3. Heat the oil in a medium-size saucepan over medium heat. Add the onion and cook until soft and golden, about 10 minutes.

4. Transfer the sautéed onion to a blender and add the eggs, salt, and white pepper. Blend until smooth. Add the sour cream and blend briefly, just until smooth. Stir in the parsley. Pour this mixture over the blintzes. Bake until set in the middle and golden brown, 45 to 50 minutes. Serve immediately.

Variations: Instead of (or in addition to) the parsley, try any of the following, in combination or alone:

- 3 cloves garlic, crushed, sautéed with the onions
- 1 head garlic, roasted (page 18), cloves squeezed into the mixture before blending
- ¹/₂ cup grated Parmesan cheese, stirred in after blending
- Chopped fresh dill, mixed with or in place of the parsley
- 1 can (4¹/₂ ounces) diced chiles, drained, stirred in after blending

My talented cousin Carole designed and sewed her own prom dress.

crusty potato kugel

from Carole Orlow

ousin Carole adapted this recipe from *A Treasure for My Daughter*, which was given by our synagogue's sisterhood to new brides. Sadly out of print, it was our bible in the '60s, not only for its recipes but also for its explanation of the Jewish traditions, told as a dialogue between a fictional mother and her (inquisitive, and, even for that era, unnaturally agreeable) daughter, Hadassah. It was everything a new bride needed to begin married life as a *balabusteh* (excellent homemaker). It starts with Proverbs 31:10: *A Woman of Valor* ("She looketh well to the ways of her household . . ."), traditionally recited at the Shabbat table, which has fallen into disuse of late, primarily in Reform Jewish homes. (I guess we're too liberated now to be put on a pedestal, thank you very much.)

Over the years Hadassah's endless questions have worn thin, but this recipe is definitely a keeper. As the kugel bakes, the aroma of oniony potatoes wafting through the house will draw all manner of otherwise occupied adults, and even Game Boy–playing children, into the kitchen, kvetching in unison, "Is it done yet?" **SERVES 8**   **P** or **M**

Vegetable oil or solid vegetable shortening, for greasing the baking pan

4 large eggs

1/3 cup matzoh meal

1/2 cup vegetable oil or chicken fat

2 1/2 teaspoons kosher (coarse) salt, or to taste (see Note, page 283)

1/4 to 1/2 teaspoon pepper, preferably white

2 teaspoons baking powder (see second Note, page 281)

3 pounds russet or baking potatoes, unpeeled

1 large onion, cut lengthwise into eighths

1. Preheat the oven to 400°F. Generously grease a 13 × 9-inch baking pan. Fit a food processor with the grating disk.

2. Beat the eggs in a large bowl. Add the matzoh meal, oil, salt, pepper, and baking powder, and mix well. Set aside.

3. Fill a large bowl with water, and as you peel the potatoes, drop them into the water. Cut each potato lengthwise into quarters or slivers no wider than your food processor's feed tube. (The idea is to have the potatoes exposed to the air as little as possible, to avoid having them turn dark.)

4. Feed the onions and potatoes together into the processor, and grate them.

5. Remove the grated onion/potato mixture from the processor and squeeze it between several changes of paper towels, extracting as much liquid as possible. Add the potato/onion mixture to the egg mixture and combine thoroughly.

6. Spoon the mixture into the prepared baking pan and bake until crusty and brown, about 1 hour.

7. Cut into squares and serve.

I'm manning the grill for my splat! latkes, early '80s.

potato latkes

from Judy Bart Kancigor

I have noticed through the years that there is a tendency among latke illuminati to view with disdain those who blend. "Oh, no," they tsk-tsk when they see my recipe, just a touch of feigned sympathy in their eyes. "I use a food processor. I like texture."

Texture? You want texture? I'll give you texture. Use my *splat!* method and you'll get all the texture you want with these crunchy babies. They're all crispy outsides, with practically no insides. My family hovers over the pan to fight over the thinnest ones, which are so full of holes you can practically see through them. Cathy Thomas, food editor of *The Orange County Register*, called them "crunchy wonders" and "crispy-brown snowflakes" . . . but I don't like to brag.

MAKES ABOUT 3 DOZEN LATKES P or D

2 pounds baking potatoes

2 large eggs

¹/₂ medium-size onion, coarsely chopped

¹/₂ medium-size firm apple, peeled and coarsely chopped

1¹/₂ teaspoons kosher (coarse) salt, or to taste (see Note, page 283)

¹/₈ teaspoon white pepper

1 teaspoon baking powder (see Notes)

¹/₄ to ¹/₂ cup all-purpose flour or matzoh meal

Peanut or canola oil, for frying

Applesauce and/or sour cream, for serving

1. Peel the potatoes and cut them into 1-inch cubes. To keep them white and release some of the starch, submerge them in a bowl of water while you're preparing the remaining ingredients.

2. Place the eggs in a blender. Add the onion, apple, salt, white pepper, and baking powder. Drain the potatoes and squeeze them dry in paper towels. Add enough of the potatoes to fill the blender (all 2 pounds may not fit). Turn on the blender, and pushing down on the sides with a rubber spatula (careful you don't blend the spatula—there is no rubber in this recipe), blend until the potatoes just move around. Add the remaining potatoes as you're blending, but do not overprocess or make it too smooth. The texture should resemble applesauce. (This takes about 6 seconds in my Osterizer.)

3. Transfer the batter to a large bowl and add the flour. The batter should be flowing, but not too thin.

4. Now for the real secret of my very crisp latkes: Pour enough oil into a large skillet to coat the bottom. Heat the oil over medium-high heat until it is quite hot but not smoking. Use a serving spoon to scoop up the batter (about 2 tablespoons per scoop), hold the spoon about 8 inches above the pan, and spill it all at once. *Splat!* Remove your hand quickly so you don't burn yourself. (Like tennis, it's all in the wrist.) The batter will splatter, forming holes . . . the better to hold the sour cream or applesauce. Repeat with as many as will fit in the skillet without crowding. Cook until browned, about 1 minute. Then flip them over and cook the other side for 1 minute.

5. Drain the latkes well on paper towels, and keep them warm while you cook the remainder, adding more oil as needed.

6. Serve immediately, with applesauce and/or sour cream.

Notes: *If you want to make the batter ahead,* to cook later or the next day, prepare it through Step 2 (do not add the flour), and pour the mixture into a tight-fitting glass jar (do not use plastic ware). Tap the jar on the counter to release any air bubbles, cover the batter well with a thick layer of flour, and refrigerate for up to 24 hours. When you are ready to use it, remove and discard the flour with the black layer that has formed beneath it. Transfer the batter to a large bowl, stir in the flour, and proceed with Step 4 using fresh flour.

During Passover, use kosher-for-Passover baking powder. If it is unavailable, the baking powder can be omitted.

For something different, serve the latkes with the optional dipping sauce in the Cherry Chili Chicken recipe (page 186).

Low-Fat Version: As we all know, we eat latkes at Hanukkah to commemorate the miracle of the rededication of the Temple, when a single cruse of oil burned for eight days, so we celebrate this significant event in our history by consuming eight days' worth of

hanukkah

* * *

Hanukkah (Hebrew for "dedication") is all about the oil. In 165 B.C.E., against great odds, Judah Maccabee and his tiny band of soldiers defeated Antiochus and the Syrian-Greek army. Wishing to rededicate the Temple, they found only enough oil to last one day. As every Jewish school child knows, that tiny flask of oil miraculously lasted eight days. But who knew it would set off a frying frenzy that would last for centuries!

Jews of Eastern European descent (Ashkenazim) commemorate the holiday with latkes. But who says potato pancakes are the only fritters fit to fry? Israelis celebrate Hanukkah with sufganiyot (jelly doughnuts, page 432), and every Jewish community the world over sets oil to bubbling to fry a traditional pastry.

Another lesser-known Hanukkah tradition involves the story from the Apochypha of Judith, a beautiful Jewish widow, who was asked to dine with the enemy general Holofernes. She plied him with cheese to make him thirsty for wine, and when he fell into a drunken stupor, she beheaded him with his own sword. Because her bravery is said to have inspired the Maccabees, some communities remember Judith by eating cheese during this holiday.

oil in one sitting! Where's the miracle in that? Wouldn't it be more in the spirit of Hanukkah to use a tiny drop of oil and feed crispy latkes to eight hungry people? Here's how:

Preheat the oven to 400°F. Spray a baking sheet (not nonstick) generously with vegetable cooking spray. Prepare the batter as described, and "fry" the latkes in a nonstick skillet coated with vegetable cooking spray. They will be limp as dishrags, but here's the trick: After they are "fried," dip each pancake in beaten egg white. Place the egg-white-coated latkes on the prepared baking sheet and bake until crisp on both sides, 3 to 5 minutes per side. Now, *that's* a miracle!

cookin' for love malaysian latkes

from Judy Bart Kancigor

I don't often adapt recipes from novels, but Sharon Boorstin's fun romp *Cookin' for Love* sent me straight to the kitchen. Heroine Miriam's thoughts seldom stray from food, and when she awakens from a dream about Grandma's latkes to find her Malaysian cleaver-toting captor frying curried onions, it's an "aha" moment of the kitchen kind. Cashews! Ginger! This is a latke with pizzazz! **MAKES 16 LATKES** **P**

$1/2$ **cup chopped unsalted cashews or peanuts**

$1/4$ **cup chopped mint or flat-leaf parsley, or a combination**

$1/4$ **cup finely chopped red bell pepper**

2 tablespoons finely chopped jalapeño pepper, seeded and deveined

2 teaspoons grated fresh ginger

$1 1/2$ **to 2 teaspoons kosher (coarse) salt, or to taste**

1 teaspoon curry powder

2 large eggs, beaten

2 large baking potatoes (12 ounces each), cut into wedges

1 medium-size onion, coarsely chopped

$1/4$ **cup all-purpose flour**

Vegetable oil, for frying

Cacik (page 114), adding 1 teaspoon toasted cumin seeds

1. Combine the cashews, mint, bell pepper, jalapeño, ginger, salt, curry powder, and eggs in a large bowl, and mix well. Set it aside.

2. Shred the potatoes and onion together in a food processor fitted with the shredding disk. Squeeze the potato/onion mixture between several changes of paper towels to release as much liquid as possible. Add the potato/onion mixture to the egg mixture, and combine well. Stir in the flour.

3. Pour enough oil into a large, heavy skillet to cover the bottom, and heat it over medium-high heat. When the oil is quite hot but not smoking, add a scant $1/4$ cup batter per latke and flatten them with a fork. Fry only as many latkes as will fit in the skillet

without crowding. Cook on one side until crisp and brown, 2 to 3 minutes. Turn over and cook until the other side is crisp and brown, 2 to 3 minutes. Transfer the latkes to paper towels to drain. Keep the latkes warm while frying the remainder. Serve immediately, with the Cacik.

Note: To taste the potato mixture, or any mixture containing raw eggs, microwave a tablespoon or so until cooked, 5 to 15 seconds, depending on the size and strength of your microwave; then taste.

giant stuffed potato latke galette
with wild mushrooms

from Judy Bart Kancigor

Inspired by a stuffed potato galette I found in Roy Finamore's *One Potato, Two Potato*, I devised this recipe by enclosing stir-fried wild mushrooms in a crispy potato pancake for a Hanukkah latke with attitude. It is a little tricky to turn, however. That's why I suggest browning it briefly on one side and then baking it. Depending upon your oven, you

> Lighting the candles, I am transported to the Hanukkahs of my youth. For the Rabinowitz cousins, raised together practically as siblings, our childhood was the New York version of the movie Avalon (without the fire, thankfully). Our parents were so close, we were always together: cousins Carole and Phyllis, Joyce and Marvin, Bonnie and Jackie, my brother, Gary, and I, and of course cousin Marilyn, who luxuriated for nine years as the only grandchild before the rest of us appeared. Ellen and Leslie, Ronald and Linda, our Atlanta cousins, made occasional appearances to round out the festivities. Uncle Al, in his gold slippers and yachting cap, would regale us wide-eyed kids about his submarine, and the identical twins, Uncle Morris from Atlanta and Uncle Lou from New York, would exchange their jackets, scaring their daughters, who suddenly saw two daddies. There were so many of us that Papa Harry even put a board in the children's table. The highlight, of course, was our Hanukkah party. The pile of latkes! The mountain of presents! The noise! The excitement! The squabbles! Then when we cousins started producing the great-grandchildren, Aunt Sally's basement bulged with four generations of Rabinowitzes, each bringing gifts for all the others. —JUDY BART KANCIGOR

Photo above: Barry and me with Brad and Stu on the first night of Hanukkah, 1970.

may not need to brown the other side after it has baked. **SERVES 8** 🅿

FOR THE MUSHROOM FILLING
About 2 tablespoons olive oil (see Notes)

About 2 teaspoons toasted sesame oil

8 ounces (total) of 3 or more varieties of mushroom, such as shiitake, portobello, oyster, chanterelle, cremini, and/or porcini, cleaned and sliced (see Notes)

¹/₂ teaspoon kosher (coarse) salt

FOR THE GALETTE
12 ounces large red-skinned potatoes, unpeeled

1 zucchini

¹/₂ medium-size onion

2 to 4 tablespoons finely chopped flat-leaf parsley

2 large eggs, lightly beaten

1 tablespoon all-purpose flour

¹/₂ teaspoon kosher (coarse) salt, or to taste

¹/₈ teaspoon freshly ground black pepper

Grated nutmeg to taste

¹/₂ teaspoon baking powder

Vegetable oil, for frying

1. Prepare the filling: Heat the olive and sesame oils in a large skillet over medium-high heat. Add the mushrooms, season with salt, and cook until they are tender and the juices have been released, about 5 minutes. (Do not crowd, or the mushrooms will steam and not brown.) *If using portobellos*, cook them by themselves for about 7 minutes before adding the other mushrooms. *If using oyster mushrooms*, cook them by themselves for about 3 minutes. Spread the cooked mushrooms out on a platter or baking sheet, rather than piling them in a bowl—again, so they do not steam—and set them aside.

2. Fill a medium-size saucepan with cold water, add the potatoes, and bring to a boil. Boil for 5 minutes. Then drain the potatoes, place them in a bowl, cover with cold water, and drain again. Cover with cold water again and allow to sit for 5 minutes. Drain the potatoes and pat them dry.

3. Using a box grater, shred the potatoes (with skins on) on the large holes. If you do not turn the potato as you are grating, you will be left with most of the peel—very convenient, because the ungrated peel will protect your knuckles. Discard the peel, but it is okay if some shreds of peel remain in the grated potatoes.

4. Rinse the zucchini well, pat it dry, and cut it crosswise into thirds. Grate the zucchini skins only (reserve the interiors for another use). Spread the shredded zucchini skin on a clean dish towel or paper towels, and let it drain for 15 minutes.

5. Using a box grater, shred the onion on the large holes until it is finely chopped but not mushy. Drain on a clean dish towel or paper towels for 15 minutes.

6. Preheat the oven to 375°F.

7. Combine the shredded potato and zucchini in a large bowl. Stir in the shredded onion along with the parsley, eggs, flour, salt, pepper, nutmeg, and baking powder.

8. Pour enough oil into a 10-inch oven-proof skillet to cover the bottom, and heat it over medium-high heat until it is very hot but not smoking. Carefully spread half of the potato mixture evenly in the skillet. Cover it evenly with the mushrooms. Cover with the remaining potato mixture. Press down with the back of a metal spatula, and fry just until a crust starts to form on the bottom, about 4 minutes.

9. Transfer the skillet to the oven and bake until the galette is set and very crisp on the bottom, about 40 minutes.

10. Remove the skillet from the oven (careful: the handle will be *hot*!). If the top is not brown, hold the galette in place with a spatula, and very carefully drain the excess oil into a bowl. Invert a dinner plate over the skillet and holding the two together (wear oven mitts, please), turn the galette over. Pour the drained oil back into the skillet and heat it until it is very hot but not smoking. Slide the galette back into the skillet, unbrowned side down. Fry until a crust forms, about 4 minutes.

11. Carefully drain the oil from the skillet as before, and slide the galette onto a serving plate. Slice into wedges and serve.

Notes: Different mushrooms absorb different amounts of oil, so use more or less oil as needed, maintaining a ratio of 1 part toasted sesame oil to 3 parts olive oil.

Before slicing them, remove the stems from shiitake and oyster mushrooms (save them for stock).

yams or sweet potatoes?

Is it a yam or a sweet potato? Another question that could drive you crazy.

When I need to know about potatoes, I consult Roy Finamore, whose *One Potato, Two Potato* is my potato bible. Sweet potatoes are often mislabeled 'yams,' says Finamore, and come from different plant species. The true yam is more like the potato and not nearly as sweet as the sweet potato.

Finamore credits vegetable authority Elizabeth Schneider for tracing the mix-up to African slaves, who may have begun calling the American sweet potato 'yams' because of their resemblance to the tubers they remembered back home.

True yams are ordinarily used in savory dishes. If it's sweet you're going for in your 'yam' dish, even if the sign in the market—or the ingredient list in your recipe—says 'yams,' what you want is that dark-skinned, orange-flesh beauty you look for every Thanksgiving: a sweet potato.

In the interest of accuracy, therefore, I'm using the term 'sweet potatoes' rather than 'yams' for the recipes in this book. Just don't believe everything you read in the market.

Variation: This potato batter makes tasty individual latkes as well, even without the mushroom stuffing: Prepare the batter, following Steps 2 through 7, without heating the oven. Then heat vegetable oil in a large skillet over medium-high heat until it is quite hot but not smoking. Drop the batter into the hot oil and press with the back of a spatula to flatten. Fry until crisp, 2 to 3 minutes. Turn and fry the other side, 2 to 3 minutes more. Drain on paper towels, and serve hot.

cajun sweet potatoes

from Bonnie Robbins

Sweet potatoes make oven fries with a wonderfully chewy texture that you don't get from white potatoes. These are sweet with a moderate kick, but feel free to add more Cajun seasoning if you prefer more heat. Most of the slices will seem soft at first, but they will crisp up in the time it takes to get them to the table. Some will remain soft but seductively chewy nonetheless. They're best served immediately but are irresistible even from the refrigerator, especially late at night when everyone is sleeping. **SERVES 6** P

Vegetable cooking spray, for greasing
  the baking sheets
3 pounds sweet potatoes (see box, page 285),
  cut into ¹/₄-inch-thick slices
3 tablespoons vegetable oil
1 tablespoon dark brown sugar
1¹/₂ teaspoons Cajun seasoning
¹/₂ teaspoon onion powder
¹/₂ teaspoon paprika
¹/₂ teaspoon kosher (coarse) salt
¹/₄ teaspoon garlic powder

1. Preheat the oven to 350°F. Spray two baking sheets.

2. Toss the potato slices with the oil in a large bowl.

3. Combine all the remaining ingredients in a small bowl, and mix well. Toss with the potato slices until thoroughly combined. (I find it easiest, although messy, to use my hands.) Arrange the potato slices in a single layer on the prepared baking sheets.

4. Bake, rotating the sheets once between oven racks and front to back, until brown, about 1 hour. Remove the thinner slices as they turn brown. Serve immediately.

Bonnie and Papa Harry, about 1952.

candied sweet potatoes

from Irene Rosenthal

Aunt Irene made her Candied Sweet Potatoes (although she called them Candied Yams; see box, page 285) as often as she made her Sweet Potatoes on Pineapple Rings (see page 291)—and sometimes she made both just to be sure she had everyone's favorites covered. She had an incredible memory for all her guests' preferences and dietary restrictions and a boundless capacity to please. **SERVES 8 TO 10** D or P

Butter or nondairy margarine, for greasing
   the baking pan
1 cup (packed) dark brown sugar
$^1/_4$ cup light corn syrup
$^1/_4$ cup orange juice
1 tablespoon fresh lemon juice
1 tablespoon pure vanilla or almond extract
$^1/_2$ teaspoon kosher (coarse) salt, or to taste
4 pounds sweet potatoes (see box, page 285),
   cut into 1$^1/_2$-inch chunks
3 tablespoons butter or nondairy margarine,
   cut into slivers

1. Preheat the oven to 375°F. Grease a
13 × 9-inch nonreactive baking pan.

2. Stir the brown sugar, corn syrup,
both juices, vanilla, and salt together in a
bowl. Stir in the sweet potatoes.

3. Arrange the sweet potato chunks,
with all the sugar mixture, in the prepared
baking pan. Dot with the butter. Cover with
aluminum foil, and bake for 30 minutes.

4. Uncover the pan and continue baking, basting and turning the sweet potatoes
occasionally, until they are tender and
glazed, about 1 hour. Serve hot.

yummy "yam" tart

from Laura Seligman

Okay, I lied. You'll be using sweet
potatoes for this dish, but I just
had to retain cousin Laura's recipe
title, because Yummy Sweet Potato Tart
wouldn't be quite as alliterative. (Strictly
speaking it's not really a tart either, but
trust me, it's yummy!) Overlapping slices
of sweet potatoes roast in a heavenly,
honey-thick, citrus-ginger sauce until
brown and crisp on the outside and
meltingly soft and custardy within.
SERVES 10 TO 12   **D** or **P**

Butter or margarine, for greasing the
   baking pan
4 pounds sweet potatoes (see box, page 285),
   cut into $^3/_8$-inch-thick slices (see Note)
$^1/_2$ cup all-purpose flour
$^1/_2$ cup orange juice
8 tablespoons (1 stick) butter or nondairy
   margarine
$^3/_4$ cup (packed) dark brown sugar
$^1/_4$ cup honey
2 tablespoons fresh lemon juice
1 tablespoon grated fresh ginger
Grated zest of 1 orange
1 to 2 tablespoons chopped candied ginger
   (optional)
2 teaspoons kosher (coarse) salt
1 teaspoon ground cinnamon

1. Preheat the oven to 375°F. Grease a
13 × 9-inch nonreactive baking pan.

2. Toss the potato slices with the flour in
a very large bowl. Set it aside.

3. Combine all the remaining ingredients in a small saucepan over medium heat.
Heat, stirring constantly, until the butter has
melted and the sugar has dissolved.

4. Arrange the sweet potato slices
in neat rows in the prepared baking pan,

Radiant parents of the Bat Mitzvah Katya, Laura and Jeremy Seligman, 1999.

overlapping the slices. Pour the sauce evenly over the potatoes. Cover, and bake for 45 minutes.

5. Press the potatoes into the sauce with the back of a spatula. Continue baking, uncovered, until the potatoes are tender and browned, about 45 minutes.

6. Allow the sizzling to stop and the tart to cool for a few minutes. Then use a slotted spoon to serve.

Note: For Laura's lovely presentation, look for slender sweet potatoes of approximately the same diameter.

apricot sweet potato pudding

from Claire Smolen

ho doesn't love apricots? Combine them with sweet potatoes and you have a real crowd-pleaser. The lemon and subtle apricot liqueur enhance the natural sweetness of the potatoes without overpowering them. **SERVES 8 TO 10**

D or **P**

5$^1/_3$ tablespoons ($^1/_3$ cup) butter or nondairy margarine, plus extra for greasing the baking pan

$^1/_3$ cup (packed) light brown sugar

3 pounds sweet potatoes (see box, page 285), baked, peeled, and mashed

$^3/_4$ cup dried apricots, diced

3 tablespoons apricot liqueur

4 teaspoons fresh lemon juice

1 teaspoon grated lemon zest

$^1/_4$ teaspoon kosher (coarse) salt, or to taste

1. Preheat the oven to 350°F. Grease a 1$^1/_2$-quart baking pan.

2. Bring $^2/_3$ cup water to a boil in a large saucepan. Add the butter and brown sugar, and stir until the butter has melted and the sugar has dissolved. Add the potatoes, dried apricots, liqueur, lemon juice, lemon zest, and salt. Mix thoroughly.

3. Transfer the mixture to the prepared baking pan and bake until heated through, about 30 minutes. Serve hot.

Claire Smolen (right) with daughter Samra at granddaughter Staci's Bat Mitzvah, 1994.

praline sweet potato bake

from Diane Podratz

For as long as my daughter-in-law Shelly can remember, her mom's sweet potato casserole has been the highlight of fall and winter celebrations as well as holiday dinners . . . amazing to me, because Shelly doesn't even like nuts! She makes an exception, however, for this dish: fluffy sweet potatoes, rich and buttery—a comforting foil for the irresistibly crisp praline topping. **SERVES 8** ▣ or ▣

FOR THE POTATOES

Butter, solid vegetable shortening, or vegetable cooking spray, for greasing the baking pan

2¹/₂ pounds sweet potatoes (see box, page 285), baked

8 tablespoons (1 stick) butter or nondairy margarine, at room temperature

2 large eggs, beaten

³/₄ cup (packed) dark brown sugar

1 teaspoon pure vanilla extract

FOR THE TOPPING

1 cup (packed) dark brown sugar

¹/₃ cup all-purpose flour

5¹/₃ tablespoons (¹/₃ cup) butter or nondairy margarine, at room temperature

1 cup pecans, chopped

1. Preheat the oven to 350°F. Grease a 13 × 9-inch nonreactive baking pan.

2. Mash the sweet potatoes in a large bowl, using a hand masher or a fork. Add the melted butter, eggs, brown sugar, and vanilla, and combine well. Spread this mixture evenly in the prepared baking pan.

3. Combine all the topping ingredients in a small bowl, and using a fork or your fingers, mix until it resembles coarse crumbs. Sprinkle this mixture over the potatoes and bake until set, golden brown, and crispy, about 40 minutes. Serve hot.

mama hinda's sweet potato casserole

from Carole Orlow

Cousin Carole has been making Mama Hinda's marshmallow-topped sweet potato casserole for decades. I adore it, but it has been a secret indulgence of late. I've somehow come to think of this dish as the stepchild of Thanksgivings past, like some old frock at the back of the closet ("that old thing?"), or as Rodney Dangerfield might have put it, "It ain't got no respect." That is, until I heard Julia Child interviewed on the radio one year right before the holiday. When asked what Thanksgiving dish she was most

The whole family gathered for Aunt Hilda's sister Flo's wedding to Al Lechter in 1952 . . . except for Aunt Sylvia and Uncle Morris (right).

anticipating, she said mashed sweet potato casserole with marshmallows! Ah, sweet vindication. **SERVES 12** 🅓 or 🅟

**Butter, nondairy margarine, or solid vegetable
shortening for greasing the baking pan**

FOR THE FILLING

3 cans (29 ounces each) sweet potatoes

1/3 cup (packed) dark brown sugar

**8 tablespoons (1 stick) unsalted butter
or nondairy margarine**

1/4 cup honey

1 teaspoon pure vanilla extract

**2 to 4 teaspoons kosher (coarse) salt,
or to taste**

FOR THE TOPPING

3 cups mini marshmallows

1 cup maraschino cherries (optional)

1. Preheat the oven to 375°F. Grease two

9- or 10-inch pie plates or one 13 × 9-inch nonreactive baking pan.

2. Drain the sweet potatoes, reserving 1/2 cup of the syrup. Using a potato masher or a fork, mash the potatoes in a large bowl.

3. Combine the reserved liquid with the brown sugar and butter in a small saucepan over medium heat. Heat, stirring often, until the butter has melted and the brown sugar has dissolved. Remove the pan from the heat and add the honey, vanilla, and 2 teaspoons of the salt; stir well. Add this mixture to the mashed sweet potatoes, and combine thoroughly. Taste, and add salt if needed.

4. Divide the mixture between the prepared pie plates, or place it all in the prepared baking pan, and bake for 20 minutes.

5. Sprinkle the mini marshmallows, and the cherries if using, over the mixture and press them into the surface. Continue baking until the marshmallows turn golden brown, about 10 minutes. Serve immediately.

stuffed orange sweet potato cups

from Sally Bower

ש hile Helen May's mother's recipe has not survived (see box, facing page), I have used Mama Hinda's sweet potato pie filling for these orange cups for my kids' cooking classes with great success. It's a terrific project that kids can do practically by themselves—they just love scooping out the oranges and filling the little cups. Marshmallows, cherries, chopped nuts, sprinkles, and all sorts of edible decorations are served buffet-style for topping.

SERVES 12   **D** or **P**

6 navel oranges, sliced in half crosswise
Mama Hinda's Sweet Potato Casserole filling
    (page 289)

FOR THE TOPPINGS
Mini marshmallows and/or
    Maraschino cherries
Chopped pecans or walnuts, toasted
    (see box, page 17)
Colored sprinkles, and assorted edible
    decorations (optional)

1. Preheat the oven to 350°F.
2. Scoop the flesh out of each orange half (reserve it for another use, such as in a fruit salad). A serrated grapefruit spoon is perfect for this purpose. Make sure each orange half can stand up straight. If any are wobbly, cut a thin slice off the bottom.

> " When Marilyn was a little girl, she loved to visit her friend Helen May, where a maid served the meals and everything was so elegant. One day she came home really impressed with little orange cups stuffed with sweet potatoes, and she insisted I call Helen's mother for the recipe.
> —SALLY BOWER "

3. Spoon the sweet potato filling into the scooped-out orange halves. Top with marshmallows, cherries, and nuts, as desired. Arrange the filled orange cups in an ungreased baking pan and bake until the filling is hot and the marshmallows are melted and golden brown, 15 to 20 minutes.
4. Top with sprinkles if using, and serve.

mama irene's sweet potatoes
on pineapple rings

from Vicki Miller

ᴎ ot to be outdone, Aunt Irene had her own version of Mama Hinda's concoction, which cousin Vicki has resurrected, much to the delight of her little boys, Max and Miles, who manage to finagle everyone else's marshmallows, too.

SERVES 12   **D** or **P**

Vegetable oil or vegetable cooking spray,
    for greasing the baking sheet
Mama Hinda's Sweet Potato Casserole filling
    (page 289; see Step 2)
1 can (20 ounces) crushed pineapple,
    well drained
12 pineapple rings (from two 20-ounce cans),
    drained
3 cups mini marshmallows
12 maraschino cherries

Max and Miles Miller taking cooking classes at the Ritz-Carlton Key Biscayne, Thanksgiving, 2004.

rita's special kugel

from Rita Miller

There's no contest: This is the king of kugels. It is sinfully rich, yet lighter in texture than others we have tried. How generous of cousin Vicki's mother-in-law, Rita, a retired kosher caterer in New Jersey, to share this treasure with us! Slice the wider pear and peach slices in half for a more elegant presentation, says Rita. And if sliced pears are unavailable, buy pear halves and slice them yourself.

SERVES ABOUT 24   **D**

Butter or solid vegetable shortening,
*   for greasing the baking pan*
Kosher (coarse) salt
12 ounces wide egg noodles
1 dozen large eggs, beaten
3 cups heavy (whipping) cream
1¹/₂ tablespoons pure vanilla extract
¹/₂ cup granulated sugar
¹/₂ cup (packed) light brown sugar
1 can (29 ounces) sliced pears or halves
*   in heavy syrup, drained and thinly*
*   sliced*
1 can (29 ounces) sliced peaches in
*   heavy syrup, drained and thinly*
*   sliced*
2 cans (11 ounces each) mandarin oranges,
*   drained*
³/₄ cup golden raisins

1. Preheat the oven to 350°F. Lightly grease a rimmed baking sheet or a shallow baking pan.

2. Prepare Mama Hinda's Sweet Potato Casserole filling, adding the drained crushed pineapple when you add the honey.

3. Arrange the pineapple rings in a single layer on an ungreased baking sheet. Using an ice cream scoop or a spoon, scoop the sweet potato mixture onto the pineapple slices, forming a mound. Bake for 10 minutes.

4. Press the marshmallows on top of the potato mounds, and set a cherry on top. Continue baking until the marshmallows get nicely brown, 10 to 15 minutes. Serve immediately.

> **When David and I got engaged, I cooked my first Thanksgiving dinner and served this family favorite that my grandmother always used to make for us.** —VICKI MILLER

the kugel wars

● ● ●

In a perfect world, every recipe I received from my family would fit into a cookbook the average person could lift without hiring a personal trainer. Alas, choices had to be made. What if someone dropped my cookbook on her toe and sued me? I could lose my home! My bonus miles! My 16-quart stockpot!

In some cases the decision was easy. My mother's chicken soup left all contenders in the dust. In other cases—kreplach comes to mind—I combined two recipes to produce what I felt was a better version than either of the originals, a case in which one plus one equaled more than two.

Then came the kugels. "Take mine!" "No, mine!" they all pleaded. It got ugly. Otherwise perfectly agreeable cousins came practically to blows extolling the virtues of . . . what? We're talking a noodle concoction here.

What is a kugel, and why does one's particular family recipe inspire such fierce loyalty?

A kugel is a baked pudding with a starchy base—potatoes or noodles are most common—bound with eggs, enriched with fat (butter, margarine, chicken fat, or oil) and peppered with an endless variety of colorful and tasty additions, such as vegetables, fruit, and/or cheese.

While today a kugel is usually served as a side dish, in the shtetls of Eastern Europe, where meat was rare and expensive, a starchy kugel could become a filling meal.

Some assembly required—true for swing sets and true for kugels—but for the most part, kugels are a snap to prepare. Once you've cooked and drained the noodles, you simply stir in the other ingredients and bake.

According to tradition, the kugel is Sabbath fare, imbuing it with almost mystical qualities. Its origins can be traced to the Middle Ages when it was cooked along with the cholent (Sabbath stew, pages 135 to 137). In a paper entitled "Holy Kugel: The Sanctification of Ashkenazic Ethnic Foods in Hasidism,"* Professor Allan Nadler discusses the symbolism attributed to this humble pudding by the Hasidic rabbis. While I doubt Aunt Sally had the rabbis in mind as she shopped for pot cheese, could some deeper, subconscious meaning have evolved through the centuries by osmosis?

Once an auntie settled on a recipe, she rarely changed kugels in midstream. She may try a new rice dish or potato pie, but her kugel was her badge of honor. The phrase "if it ain't broke, don't fix it" comes to mind. (Apparently my mother is a bit more fickle, flitting merrily, as is her wont, from kugel to kugel.)

As I tasted my way through this chapter, a version of that old song kept playing in my head: "When I'm not near the kugel I love, I love the kugel I'm near!"

I suggest you embark on your own kugel taste test. Who knows? Perhaps one of my relatives' signature kugels might just become your signature, too . . . if you're willing to replace your badge of honor.

Cutting the kugel for our Sukkot party, 1982.

*From *Food & Judaism*, edited by Leonard Greenspoon, Ronald A. Simkins, and Gerald Shapiro (Lincoln, Nebraska; Creighton University Press, 2005)

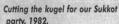
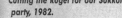

1. Preheat the oven to 375°F. Grease a 13 × 9 × 2-inch baking pan (see Notes, page 296).

2. Bring a large pot of lightly salted water to a boil. Add the noodles and cook until al dente, 5 to 7 minutes.

3. Meanwhile, combine the eggs, cream, vanilla, both sugars, and 1 teaspoon salt in a very large bowl. Stir well. Stir in the drained pears, peaches, mandarin oranges, and the raisins.

4. When the noodles are done, drain them well and stir them into the fruit mixture. Transfer it to the prepared baking pan and bake for 1 hour. Cover the kugel with aluminum foil and continue baking until golden and set, about 20 minutes more. (Test by inserting a butter knife in the center. It should come out clean.)

5. Cut into squares, and serve hot or at room temperature.

> " I created this recipe about thirty years ago, after six months of experimentation to try to make the best and most unusual dessert kugel possible. Since then it has been my carefully guarded secret. The first time I gave out the recipe was to my son, David, and his new bride, Vicki, so they could make it for their first Yom Kippur break-the-fast in San Francisco. Please bear in mind that this recipe was created long before cholesterol became a household watchword. Enjoy!
>
> —RITA MILLER "

grandma reila's incredible noodle pudding

from Ellen Gardner

Cousin Ellen's mother-in-law, Reila Katzelnik, makes this scrumptious kugel, which came from the now out-of-print *Plain Jane's Thrill of Very Fattening Foods Cookbook* by Linda Sunshine. That says it all, doesn't it? Linda credits her mother, Norma Sunshine, with her heirloom recipe, as valuable a family treasure as her nona's hand-crocheted tablecloth. **SERVES 12 TO 16**   **D**

Butter or margarine, for greasing the
   baking pan
Kosher (coarse) salt
1 pound wide egg noodles
8 tablespoons (1 stick) butter, melted
1 cup sugar
4 large eggs
1 cup pot-style cottage cheese
2 cups sour cream
2 cups whole milk
1 teaspoon pure vanilla extract
2 medium-size sweet firm apples, such as
   Gala or Fuji, peeled, cored, and chopped
1 can (16 ounces) sliced peaches,
   drained
$^1/_2$ cup orange marmalade
$^1/_2$ cup raisins

FOR THE TOPPING

¹/₂ cup crushed cornflakes

4 tablespoons (¹/₂ stick) butter

Cinnamon sugar: 2 teaspoons ground
  cinnamon mixed with 4 teaspoons sugar

1. Preheat the oven to 350°F. Lightly grease a 13 × 9 × 2-inch baking pan (see Notes, page 296).

2. Bring 4 quarts salted water to a boil in a large saucepan. Add the noodles and boil for 5 minutes. Drain well, and transfer to a large bowl. Pour the melted butter over the hot noodles, making sure that all the noodles are drenched in butter.

3. Mix the sugar and eggs in a blender until combined. Add the cottage cheese, sour cream, milk, and vanilla, and blend until smooth. Add this mixture to the noodles. Fold in the apples, peaches, marmalade, and raisins. Combine well. Transfer the noodle mixture to the prepared baking pan.

4. Lightly sprinkle the crushed cornflakes over the top of the pudding. Dot with the butter, then sprinkle with the cinnamon sugar. Bake until set, about 1 hour.

5. Cut into squares, and serve hot or at room temperature.

Reila Katzelnik, 1952.

aunt sally's ultra-extra-special noodle pudding
(for machatunim)

from Lillian Bart

This is the actual title in my mother's handwritten recipe book, followed by the comment, I kid you not: "If this won't give them a gall bladder attack, nothing will." I can only ask, are you trying to impress them or kill them?

The following recipe is half the original. What did she mix it in, a cauldron? Like so many of my mother's and aunts' recipes, the quantities were huge. *Machatunim* dinners were grand events, and everyone was invited—not just the parents, but sisters and brothers, their families, and so on. Anyone marrying into the Rabinowitz clan was treated to a dizzying round of dinners and brunches, as every aunt fêted the new families, welcoming them to the clan. It's amazing to me how they cooked for these crowds.

machatunim
**YOUR CHILDREN'S IN-LAWS
(THERE IS NO ENGLISH WORD
TO DESCRIBE THIS. TELLS YOU SOMETHING
ABOUT JEWISH CULTURE, DOESN'T IT?)**

Most of them had only a single oven and of course no microwave, and yet everything was always hot and delicious.

With all that cheese and sour cream (not to mention butter), this kugel is wickedly rich, yet not overly sweet. Although Aunt Sally didn't, I prefer to use the blender for a creamier texture. **SERVES 12 TO 16** D

Butter or solid vegetable shortening,
for greasing the baking pan
Kosher (coarse) salt
1 pound wide egg noodles
8 large eggs
8 ounces cream cheese, at room temperature
8 ounces farmer cheese
8 ounces pot cheese (see Notes)
³/4 cup sugar
1 cup sour cream
8 tablespoons (1 stick) butter, melted and
cooled
1¹/4 cups golden raisins

1. Preheat the oven to 350°F. Grease a 13 × 9 × 2-inch baking pan (see Notes).

2. Bring a large pot of lightly salted water to a boil. Add the noodles and cook until al dente, 5 to 7 minutes.

3. Meanwhile, mix the eggs, cream cheese, farmer cheese, pot cheese, sugar, and ¹/2 teaspoon salt in a blender until smooth. Pour the mixture into a large bowl, and stir in the sour cream, cooled melted butter, and raisins.

4. When the noodles are done, drain them well and stir them into the cheese mixture. Pour the mixture into the prepared baking pan and bake until set, about 1 hour.

5. Cut into squares, and serve hot or at room temperature.

Notes: If your baking pan isn't 2 inches deep, place any extra batter in a smaller casserole to be baked separately. You may need to reduce the baking time.

Pot cheese is like cottage cheese that has drained longer and is therefore drier. (If it is unavailable, drain cottage cheese in a cheesecloth-lined strainer in the refrigerator overnight.) Farmer cheese is pot cheese that has been pressed to release even more liquid, making it even drier and more crumbly.

mama irene's noodle pudding soufflé

from Suzy Orlow Solomonic

Aunt Irene's original handwritten recipe called for ³/4 pound cream cheese *and* a pint of sour cream. Perhaps by the time she gave it to her granddaughter Suzy, she was trying to cut down? (I'm kidding, I'm kidding.) Either way it's yummy. Assemble the kugel the night before and refrigerate it. While you sleep the sleep of the innocent, the noodles are soaking up all that, um, flavor. **SERVES 12 TO 16** D

Butter or solid vegetable shortening,
   for greasing the baking pan
Kosher (coarse) salt
1 pound medium-wide egg noodles
10 large eggs
$^3/_4$ cup sugar
1 cup (2 sticks) butter, melted and
   cooled
8 ounces cream cheese, at room
   temperature
1 can (20 ounces) crushed pineapple,
   undrained
1 can (16 ounces) fruit cocktail, drained
$^1/_2$ cup heavy (whipping) cream
2 cups crushed Frosted Flakes cereal

1. Butter a 13 × 9 × 2-inch baking pan (see Notes, facing page).

2. Bring a large pot of lightly salted water to a boil. Add the noodles and cook until al dente, 5 to 7 minutes.

3. Meanwhile, beat the eggs very well in a blender. Add the sugar, cooled butter, and cream cheese, and blend until thoroughly combined. Pour the mixture into a large bowl and add the pineapple with its juice, the fruit cocktail, and the cream.

4. When the noodles are done, drain them well and stir them into the egg mixture. Pour the mixture into the prepared baking pan and cover with the Frosted Flakes. Cover, and refrigerate overnight.

5. The next day, preheat the oven to 325°F.

6. Bake the pudding, uncovered, until set, $1^1/_4$ to $1^1/_2$ hours.

7. Cut into squares, and serve hot or at room temperature.

carol cohen's luscious noodle kugel

from Lillian Bart

These days my mom's signature kugel is one she got from her friend Carol Cohen, the lovely wife of our cantor (both, alas, no longer with us). Made with milk, it's lighter than most, but it is still devastatingly rich and sweet. The cherry pie filling is my mother's idea for a picture-perfect presentation. Mom likes to bake the kugel the day before serving, and then when she's ready to reheat it, she spreads the cherry pie filling on top.

SERVES 12 TO 16 D

Butter or solid vegetable shortening,
   for greasing the baking pan
Kosher (coarse) salt
1 pound medium-wide noodles
8 ounces cream cheese, at room temperature
2 cups sour cream
8 large eggs
4 cups whole milk
$^3/_4$ cup sugar
2 teaspoons pure vanilla extract
8 tablespoons (1 stick) butter, melted and
   cooled
$1^1/_4$ cups golden raisins
1 can (20 ounces) cherry pie filling
   (not plain cherries)

1. The day before serving, preheat the oven to 350°F. Grease a 13 × 9 × 2-inch baking pan (see Notes, page 296).

2. Bring a large pot of lightly salted water to a boil. Add the noodles and cook until al dente, 5 to 7 minutes.

3. Meanwhile, combine the cream cheese, sour cream, eggs, 2 cups of the milk, the sugar, vanilla, and 1 teaspoon salt in a blender. Blend until smooth. Pour the mixture into a large bowl.

Mom at work at my brother Gary's Weight Watchers office doing what she does best, meeting and greeting, 1980s.

4. When the noodles are done, drain them well and add them to the egg mixture. Stir in the butter, raisins, and remaining 2 cups milk.

5. Transfer the mixture to the prepared baking pan and bake until set, about 1½ hours.

6. Allow the kugel to cool; then cover and refrigerate overnight.

7. A few hours before serving, remove the kugel from the refrigerator and set it aside to come to room temperature.

8. Preheat the oven to 350°F.

9. Spread the cherry pie filling evenly over the kugel. Cover, and bake until heated through, about 30 minutes.

10. Cut into squares and serve hot.

Note: The kugel can also be frozen for up to 1 month. Thaw, spread with the filling, cover, and bake as directed.

aunt belle robbins's apple noodle kugel

from Bunny Lauer

Bunny, Uncle Willy's sister, provided me with details about Slonim, the town where Mama Hinda and Papa Harry were born—details that she gleaned from her own father's stories. Aunt Belle was another sister, but she was doubly related to us because she married Mama Hinda's brother, Sam. Mama's mother died young, so Mama really raised Uncle Sam, whom she brought to America with her as a child. Our Stuart is named for him.

> " My mother [Bunny] was afraid to drive, but when my kids were small she wanted to help out. Somehow she would manage to drive the five miles to my house without ever making a left turn. She'd go miles out of her way just so she could only turn right. All I know is I miss her terribly. What I wouldn't give to be able to pick up the phone and call her. **—HOLLY GRIPPO** "

Aunt Belle's kugel is a thing of beauty: puffy and golden, not overly sweet, at once light and creamy. Be sure to slice the apples really thin for the loveliest presentation.

SERVES 12 TO 16 🄳

Butter or solid vegetable shortening,
* for greasing the baking pan*
Kosher (coarse) salt
1 pound wide egg noodles
1 dozen large eggs
1 pound cottage cheese
1 cup sugar
2 cups sour cream
8 tablespoons (1 stick) butter, melted
* and cooled*
3 medium-size firm sweet apples,
* such as Gala or Fuji, peeled*
* and thinly sliced*

1. Preheat the oven to 350°F. Grease a 13 × 9 × 2-inch baking pan (see Notes, page 296).

2. Bring a large pot of lightly salted water to a boil. Add the noodles and cook until al dente, 5 to 7 minutes.

3. Meanwhile, combine the eggs, cottage cheese, sugar, and ³/₄ teaspoon salt in a blender and blend until smooth. Transfer the mixture to a large bowl, and stir in the sour cream and butter.

4. When the noodles are done, drain them well and stir them, along with the apples, into the egg mixture.

5. Transfer the mixture to the prepared baking pan and bake until set and golden, 1¹/₄ to 1¹/₂ hours. The kugel will puff up and then deflate slightly on cooling.

6. Cut into squares, and serve hot or at room temperature.

tam tam noodle pudding

from Debbie Levine

my sister-in-law Debbie got this recipe from a fellow teacher eons ago, and it has been a staple on her holiday table ever since. It's more like a dessert than a side dish, with its apple pie filling, heavy dose of raisins, and irresistibly crunchy topping made from—what else—Tam Tam crackers. I remember both my grandmas always having on hand a box of these not-too-rich, not-too-dry, habit-forming munchies—still my first choice as a chopped liver scoop. Manischewitz, which began in 1888 as

From top left clockwise: Aunt Belle, Papa Harry, Aunt Anna, Uncle Sam, Aunt Estelle, and Uncle Charlie.

a small matzoh factory, started producing Tam Tams in 1940, its first venture away from its matzoh product line, and they've been a staple in Jewish homes ever since.

Debbie says you'll get neater servings if you make the kugel a day ahead, refrigerate it, and then cut it into squares when it's cold. The next day, allow the kugel to come to room temperature and then reheat it, covered, in a preheated 350°F oven for about 25 minutes. This works for her Tam Tam pudding—and for all other kugels too.

SERVES 16 **D**

Butter or solid vegetable shortening, for greasing the baking pan

Kosher (coarse) salt

1 pound wide egg noodles

8 large eggs, beaten

2 cups sour cream

$^1/_2$ cup orange juice

$^1/_2$ cup sugar

$1^1/_2$ teaspoons pure vanilla extract

1 box (15 ounces) golden raisins

1 can (20 ounces) apple pie filling

FOR THE TOPPING

4 ounces ($^1/_2$ box) Tam Tam crackers

1 cup (2 sticks) butter, melted

$^3/_4$ cup sugar

$1^1/_2$ teaspoons ground cinnamon

1. Preheat the oven to 350°F. Generously grease a 13 × 9 × 2-inch baking pan (see Notes, page 296).

Tracy and Sam, me, Jessica, and Debbie doing "New York, New York" (the Rockettes have no worries). My in-laws' 65th anniversary, 2001.

2. Bring a large pot of lightly salted water to a boil. Add the noodles and cook until al dente, 5 to 7 minutes.

3. Meanwhile, combine the eggs, sour cream, orange juice, sugar, and vanilla in a large bowl. Mix well.

4. When the noodles are done, drain them well and stir them, along with the raisins and apple pie filling, into the egg mixture. Transfer the mixture to the prepared baking pan.

5. Prepare the topping: Crush the Tam Tam crackers by hand and sprinkle them over the noodle mixture. Stir the melted butter, sugar, and cinnamon together in a bowl, and sprinkle the mixture over the crackers.

6. Bake until set, $1^1/_2$ hours.

7. Serve hot, or allow to cool and then refrigerate to serve later (see headnote).

Debbie and Ronnie Levine, proud aunt and uncle, at Brad and Tracey's wedding, 1995.

janette goldberg's buttermilk noodle kugel

from Lillian Bart

m y mother makes friends wherever she goes. While we were shopping at the Museum of Tolerance gift shop one day, I walked out with a lovely engagement gift for my niece and my mother walked out with a kugel recipe from the saleswoman (her new best friend). Janette had gotten the recipe when she married in 1951 from her then mother-in-law, who was a caterer in Passaic, New Jersey. Its claim to fame was that it was a favorite of columnist Walter Winchell, a frequent customer. It's lovely for company, with its bright orange and apricot flavor and tang of buttermilk. It's easy, too, because you prepare it the day before, refrigerate it, and then just pop it in the oven the next day. **SERVES 12 TO 16** D

8 tablespoons (1 stick) butter or margarine

Kosher (coarse) salt

1 pound medium-wide egg noodles

5 large eggs, well beaten

1 quart buttermilk

Grated zest of 1 orange

3 tablespoons frozen orange juice concentrate, thawed

$3/4$ cup sugar

2 teaspoons ground cinnamon

12 ounces dried apricots, snipped

FOR THE TOPPING

2 cups lightly crushed (by hand) corn flakes

2 tablespoons sugar

1 teaspoon ground cinnamon

4 tablespoons ($1/2$ stick) butter or margarine, melted

1. Place the butter in a 13 × 9 × 2-inch microwave-safe glass baking dish, and melt it in the microwave. Tilt the dish to coat the bottom and sides with the melted butter.

2. Bring a large pot of lightly salted water to a boil. Add the noodles and cook until al dente, 5 to 7 minutes.

3. Meanwhile, whisk the eggs, buttermilk, orange zest, orange juice concentrate, sugar, $3/4$ teaspoon salt, and cinnamon in a large bowl until thoroughly combined. Pour in the excess butter from the baking pan, and stir.

4. When the noodles are done, drain them well and stir them, along with the apricots, into the buttermilk mixture. Transfer the mixture to the prepared baking pan and refrigerate, covered, overnight.

5. When you are ready to bake the kugel, you may notice that the noodles on top appear to be naked, as the sauce has settled. Not to worry—just stir the mixture to distribute the liquid evenly. Preheat the oven to 350°F.

6. Prepare the topping: Mix the corn flakes, sugar, cinnamon, and melted butter in a bowl. Sprinkle the topping evenly over the kugel.

7. Bake until set, about 1 hour.

8. Cut into squares, and serve hot or at room temperature.

mother bower's sweet-and-sour kugel

from Sally Bower

Aunt Sally's mother-in-law, Mirtza Bower, had been a caterer in Russia. No offense to Mama Hinda, but she's the one who really taught Aunt Sally to cook. This unusual kugel (reproduced, below, from her handwritten cookbook) was considered quite a delicacy in its time: hamantaschen-shaped kreplach filled with challah boiled in a sweet-and-sour mixture of oil, sugar, and lemon juice—sounds like a bread sandwich, doesn't it?—and then layered with oil and baked.

Aunt Sally met her future mother-in-law for the very first time when Uncle Lou brought her home for their Passover seder in 1931. That night Mirtza made a version of this kugel with Passover noodle dough, using prunes stuffed with a little sugar instead of the challah filling and, of course, her homemade sour cherry jam. That was the night Uncle Lou, with an armful of flowers, asked Aunt Sally to marry him in front of his whole family. Good thing she said yes! **P**

Aunt Sally and Uncle Lou's wedding. That's Lou's mother, Mirtza Bower (right), and his sister Sarah (left), 1931.

30

Mother Bowers Sweet + Sour Kugal
① white chollf - boil with lemon
juice sugar + pinch salt +
½ cup of oil . then add a little
Jam for color.
make a strudel dough with about
3 eggs salt + warm water flour little oil
pinch baking powder fill with above
ingredients. Roll dough + then fill +
make them look like small homstash
grease a deep pot with about ½ glass
oil a little sugar + lemon juice
+ a little honey (optional)
place each triangle in pot one on
top of another (layers) oil in between layers. and bake for about
2 hours. each piece should look like this
make this by making a ▽ long strip of dough
put in piece of filling + fold to form shape.
this is a delicacy!

> **My parents met at a dance. My father [Lou] was there with another girl, and when he saw my mother [Sally], it was love at first sight. He wanted to take her home, but his car only had a rumble seat, so he and his date sat in the front seat and my mother had to sit in the rumble seat. After that night he dropped that other girl, and my mother never took a back seat to anyone again. Within a few months they were engaged. That August they were married, and I was born the following May.** —MARILYN DUBIN

pecan kugel ring

from Joan Kalish

Follow me down Memory Lane for a moment. It's holiday time at Grandma's house, and her kugel has just come out of the oven. You and your cousins keep sneaking into the kitchen to pull off the little crispy bits of noodles peeking through the top. (In my family we call this progressive consumption of teeny bites "chipping.") Now fast forward, and Grandma's crispy bits are all grown up, glazed with sticky pecans and oozing with caramel, just begging to be "chipped." Trust me, this kugel is more crisp than kugel. If you were the kid waiting at the table for a nice, tender slice denuded of all those pesky, overdone noodle crisps, better bake this one covered or move on.

SERVES 12　　　　　　**D** or **P**

Butter, nondairy margarine, or solid vegetable
　　shortening, for greasing the bundt pan

FOR THE TOPPING
8 tablespoons (1 stick) unsalted butter or
　　nondairy margarine
1 cup (packed) dark brown sugar
1 cup pecan halves

FOR THE KUGEL
Kosher (coarse) salt
1 pound wide egg noodles
4 large eggs, lightly beaten
8 tablespoons (1 stick) butter or nondairy
　　margarine, melted and cooled
2/3 cup sugar
1 teaspoon ground cinnamon

1. Preheat the oven to 350°F. Generously grease a 10-inch bundt pan.

2. Prepare the topping: Melt the butter and brown sugar together in a small saucepan over medium heat, and stir until smooth. Pour the mixture into the prepared bundt pan. Arrange the pecans on top of the sugar mixture, rounded side down, in a decorative pattern. (Do not press them into the caramel too firmly, or they will fall off when the baked kugel is turned upside down and released from the pan.)

3. Bring a large pot of lightly salted water to a boil. Add the noodles and cook until al dente, 5 to 7 minutes.

4. Meanwhile, combine the eggs, cooled

melted butter, sugar, cinnamon, and $3/4$ teaspoon salt in a large bowl and mix well.

5. When the noodles are done, drain them well and stir them into the egg mixture. Transfer the mixture to the prepared pan and bake—uncovered if you're a "chipper," covered with aluminum foil for a softer texture—until set, about 1 hour.

6. Allow the kugel to rest, covered, for 5 minutes. Then run a knife around the edge of the bundt pan. Invert a serving plate over the pan, and holding the two together, carefully turn them over. Lift off the bundt pan, and let the "chipping" begin.

jerusalem kugel

from Nehama Hashman

This traditional kugel comes from my second cousin Nehama, who lives in Israel. Known there as *Kugel Yerushalmi*, Jerusalem Kugel is an altogether different animal from the sweet, often cheesy kugels my family is used to. It is very dense and both savory, from its heavy dose of pepper, and sweet, from caramelized sugar. It is traditionally served for the Sabbath kiddush and therefore is prepared by the observant before sundown on Friday and cooked in a slow oven overnight. Typically it is accompanied by pickles, so all four taste sensations—sour, salty, bitter (well, at least peppery), and sweet—collide at once. Israelis use a lot of pepper—I've seen recipes calling for 2 teaspoons or more—but $3/4$ teaspoon was all I could handle. Let your palate be your guide.

Preparing the caramel can be a little tricky. The sugar caramelizes in the oil, but the oil and sugar never come together. As soon as the sugar turns deep amber in color, remove it from the heat and pour the mixture into the noodles. Cook it any longer and your kugel will taste burnt. **SERVES 10 TO 12**   ℗

Vegetable oil, for greasing the tube pan

Kosher (coarse) salt

1 pound fine egg noodles

4 large eggs

$3/4$ cup sugar, or more to taste

$3/4$ teaspoon freshly ground black pepper, or more to taste

1 teaspoon ground cinnamon

$1/2$ cup vegetable oil

$3/4$ cup raisins (optional)

1. Preheat the oven to 300°F. Grease a tube pan with removable bottom.

2. Bring a large pot of lightly salted water to a boil. Add the noodles and cook until al dente, about 5 minutes.

3. Meanwhile, beat the eggs, $1/4$ cup of the sugar, $1^1/2$ teaspoons salt, $1/2$ teaspoon of the pepper, and the cinnamon in a large bowl.

4. Drain the noodles well and place them in another large bowl.

5. Prepare the caramel: Heat the remaining $1/2$ cup sugar and the oil in a small saucepan over medium heat, stirring occa-

survivors

● ● ● ● ●

My dad, Jan Bart, came to America as a child of eleven in 1930. (He was Avraham Shulim Strausser then.) Almost his entire family remained back in Sambor, Poland. Nehama, his cousin Salka's daughter, was just five years old when the Nazis swept through Sambor on August 4, 1942. Only twenty Jews in the entire town were saved, among them little Nehama and her mother and father, who were hidden in a railway station for sixteen months by the gentile manager of a restaurant. After the war the family emigrated to Israel, to build a new life. There, Nehama's sister was born. For many years Nehama corresponded with the righteous gentile who protected them, and she recently gave testimony to these events through Steven Spielberg's Shoah project.

sionally, until the sugar starts to clump, about 9 minutes. During this process, do not answer the phone or doorbell. Start stirring constantly. The clumps will recombine and the sugar will start turning from white to tan to amber in a matter of seconds. (At no time will the sugar and oil combine.) The moment the sugar turns deep amber, remove the pan from the heat and pour the caramel and oil into the noodles, stirring constantly until thoroughly combined.

6. Stir the hot noodle mixture, a spoonful at a time at first, into the egg mixture. As the eggs adjust to the heat of the noodles, you can incorporate larger and larger amounts of the noodles until all are thoroughly combined. Add $1/2$ teaspoon salt and the remaining $1/4$ teaspoon pepper, or to taste (see Note). Add more sugar if needed. Stir in the raisins, if using.

7. Transfer the mixture to the prepared tube pan, cover it tightly with aluminum foil, and bake for 2 hours.

8. To serve, *very carefully* remove the foil. (Maybe it's the pepper, but this fiery kugel really spews steam! Ouch!) Allow the kugel to cool in the pan for a few moments. Then run a flat knife around the side of the pan and around the tube (this may be unnecessary if your tube pan is nonstick). Grasp the tube with a towel or pot holder and lift it out of the pan. Loosen the bottom of the kugel with a flat knife.

9. Slice the kugel with a serrated knife and serve, crusty side up.

Note: To taste the mixture, or any mixture containing raw eggs, microwave a tablespoonful or so until the egg is cooked, 5 to 15 seconds; then taste.

romanian salt and pepper lokshen kugel

from Becky Green

my husband's Grandma Becky was of Romanian descent, and this peppery kugel was typical of the recipes her family brought to America. Grandpa Ben died before Barry was born (ironically while playing cards)—in fact,

Barry is named for him—and Grandma Becky lived with Barry's family. She did most of the cooking, and there was always a full-course, home-cooked meal every evening. Her peppery kugel was served often. My mother's friend Dorothy Rubin claims her Romanian Grandma Rosie made a similar kugel and would place a square of the kugel in the bottom of a bowl of chicken soup, which she says made it taste just like homemade noodles.

SERVES 10   **M** or **P**

Chicken fat or solid vegetable shortening,
*   for greasing the baking pan*
Kosher (coarse) salt
1 pound fine egg noodles
¹/₄ cup chicken fat or vegetable oil
1 large onion, grated
5 large eggs, beaten
³/₄ teaspoon freshly ground black pepper,
*   or more to taste (Romanians use a lot!)*

1. Preheat the oven to 350°F. Grease a 7 × 11- or 8 × 12-inch baking pan.

2. Bring a large pot of lightly salted water to a boil. Add the noodles and cook until al dente, about 5 minutes.

3. Meanwhile, heat the oil in a large skillet over medium heat. Add the onion and cook, stirring occasionally, until soft, about 5 minutes.

4. Drain the noodles and transfer them to a large bowl. Add the onion, with the oil, and the eggs, 2 teaspoons salt, and the pepper. Combine thoroughly.

5. Pour the noodle mixture into the prepared baking pan and bake until it is set

Grandma Becky was a phenomenal cook, but betting on the horses was her life. I can picture her still, all dressed up in her pin-striped suit, lace gloves, and hat, her hair pulled back in a stylish bun, as she would run to catch the bus to Jamaica Race Track. When she returned she wore her poker face, and we never knew if she won or lost. She usually went alone, unless her brother was in town—our disappearing Uncle Max, who was famous for going out to buy a paper and not coming back for five or six years. There were always racing forms in the house, and she would study them by the hour, and if Uncle Max was there, they would talk about the horses throughout dinner. Grandma Becky played cards too . . . with the men! My mother inherited the gambling gene and loved to follow the horses, making 'mind bets' when she couldn't get to the OTB and checking the results later. She would go by the horses' names (Bradley Deb was a favorite—what are the odds of that, her grandson and her daughter in one horse?)—a 'system' that paid off for her many times over the years"

—DEBBIE (KANCIGOR) LEVINE

"When I was in high school, my friends loved to come to our house for Grandma Becky's cooking and for tips on the horses. They'd visit even if I wasn't home! By the time off-track betting began in New York, Grandma Becky was already in a nursing home. She had a hard time believing that you could go to a local store to place a bet without having to go to the race track or to a bookie.

—BARRY KANCIGOR

and the edges are crispy and golden, about 45 minutes.

6. Cut into squares and serve hot.

potato pirogen

from Blanche Altman

Pirogen, varenikas, kreplach, piroshki, ravioli, wontons . . . The world loves a dumpling. Be sure to roll the dough quite thin, about $1/16$ inch, so the pirogen don't get gummy. Pirogen can be served boiled, straight from the pot, or boiled and then fried, which is, alas, infinitely more delicious. **MAKES ABOUT 6 DOZEN** **D** or **P**

FOR THE FILLING

3 medium-size russet or Idaho potatoes
   (1 pound total), unpeeled, well scrubbed
Kosher (coarse) salt
$1/4$ cup vegetable oil
1 large onion, chopped
Dash of white pepper, or to taste

FOR THE DOUGH

3 cups all-purpose flour, or more if needed
1 teaspoon kosher (coarse) salt
6 tablespoons ($3/4$ stick) butter or nondairy
   margarine, melted and cooled

About 8 tablespoons (1 stick) butter or nondairy
   margarine, for pan-frying (optional)

1. Prepare the filling: Place the potatoes in a pot of lightly salted water and bring to a boil. Cook until they are soft when pierced with a skewer, about 30 minutes. (Don't use a fork—it will break up the potatoes.)

2. Meanwhile, heat the oil in a large skillet over medium-low heat. Add the onion and

> *No matter how sick she was, Grandma Blanche never complained. When I would ask her why not, she would say, 'Dahlink, vat's the point? My friends, I vouldn't vant to bother them, and my enemies? I vouldn't vant them to know.'* —WENDY ALTMAN COHEN

cook slowly, stirring occasionally, until very soft and golden, about 20 minutes. Set the skillet aside.

3. Drain the potatoes and place them in a bowl. Set them aside to cool somewhat.

4. When they are cool enough to handle, peel the potatoes and either rice them (the ideal way) or mash them in a large bowl. Add the sautéed onion (with the oil), about 1 teaspoon salt, and the white pepper, and mash well. Allow to cool.

5. Prepare the dough: Stir the flour and salt together in a large bowl, using a wooden spoon. Slowly add the melted butter and $1/2$ cup water, and stir until well combined. (At some point you will need to start using your hands.) Gradually add another $1/4$ cup water until a moist, slightly sticky dough is formed. (If the dough is too dry, add water, 1 tablespoon at a time. If the dough is too sticky, add flour, 1 tablespoon at a time.) Knead the dough in the bowl, or on a lightly floured surface if that's easier, until it is smooth and elastic, 2 to 3 minutes. Allow the dough to rest, covered with plastic wrap, for 30 minutes.

6. Bring a large, wide saucepan of lightly salted water to a boil.

7. To assemble the pirogen, divide the dough into four portions and work on one

cooking pirogen—a shtetl tale

While my Aunt Isabelle's instructions for potato pirogen were vague—"Shape, then boil and fry them in butter until crisp, topping with sour cream. Cholesterol 100 percent!"—her memories of cooking pirogen as a child are priceless:

"Today I am twelve years old. I can't wait to go home after school. Mama is making potato pirogies for supper. It's a cold day in our little town of Sambor, Poland. I rush in, help myself to hot cocoa, which is kept for us on the back of the tall tile stove. The pungent smell of fried onions greets me. They'll go into the mashed potatoes. I help Mom with filling the prepared rounds of dough. I count ninety of them! After all, we are six children, Mama, Papa, Grandpa and Grandma. Mom puts two huge pots of water on the stove when a neighbor's daughter comes in crying. Her mother is very sick and needs Mama's help. She reaches for her coat and hesitates, but I assure her that I know what to do and tell her to go and help her friend. I do not know that the water must come to a boil before you drop the pirogies in to cook. I place every pirogi carefully in the pot and then turn up the heat and watch it come to a boil, and to my horror they all meld into a huge mass of dough and potato! Disaster and embarrassment! I took a lot of teasing from my brothers and cried, but Mom was very supportive, saying that she was sure I would turn into a very good cook and housewife, complimenting me on my courage and willingness to learn."

—ISABELLE FRANKEL

portion at a time, keeping the remaining dough covered so it does not dry out. Flour your work surface and rolling pin, and roll the dough out very thin. Cut out rounds of dough, using about a 3-inch-wide glass or cookie cutter. Place about $1/2$ tablespoon of the filling in the center of each round. Dip your finger in water and moisten half the outer edge of the round (this will help the dough to stick). Bring the unmoistened half over to form a semicircle, and pinch the edges together well (this is important so the pirogen will not fall apart in the boiling water). Place the filled pirogen on a lightly floured baking sheet and keep them covered as you work. (The pirogen may be frozen at this point, or you can freeze them once they are cooked.)

8. When the water has come to a rolling boil, drop some of the pirogen in, one at a time so the boiling does not stop. Do not crowd the pan—depending on the size and width of your pot, 8 to 10 is probably a good number. Cook at a steady, but not rapid, boil for 10 to 15 minutes. (The dough should be tender; to test, remove one and gently pierce an unfilled part with a fork.) Remove the pirogen with a slotted spoon and drain them well. Repeat with the remaining pirogen. Toss them in melted butter to keep them from sticking together and serve.

Note: Grandma Blanche, of course, was of the pan-frying school. To pan-fry the pirogen, melt the butter in a large skillet over medium heat. Add the pirogen and fry until golden brown, 3 to 4 minutes per side. Serve immediately.

To bake the pirogen, preheat the oven to 375°F. Butter a baking pan and fill it with as many pirogen as you wish to serve. Drizzle lightly with melted butter and bake, turning them occasionally, until light golden, about 15 minutes. Serve immediately.

sophie boyko's cheese pirogen

from Robin Kancigor Boyko

These slide-into-your-tummy cheese-filled dumplings become a satisfying side dish, a nosh right out of the pan, or the featured event, with sour cream and butter, as the Boykos prefer.

MAKES ABOUT 3½ DOZEN D

Above: Robin (second from left), her sister Lilly (left), mom, Roz, and Edie and Nat (my in-laws), 1991.

Right: Sophie Boyko gives daughter-in-law Robin a tutorial in the fine art of pirogen making.

FOR THE DOUGH

6 tablespoons (³/₄ stick) butter, melted and cooled

2 large eggs

White of 1 large egg

¹/₄ cup sour cream

1 teaspoon kosher (coarse) salt

3 cups all-purpose flour, or more if needed

FOR THE FILLING

1 package (7.5 or 8 ounces) farmer cheese

Yolk of 1 large egg, beaten

1 tablespoon butter, melted

2 teaspoons sugar

¹/₄ teaspoon ground cinnamon (optional)

Pinch of kosher (coarse) salt

Kosher (coarse) salt

Melted butter, for tossing and for baking

4 to 6 tablespoons butter, for pan-frying

1. Prepare the dough: Combine the cooled butter, eggs, egg white, sour cream, and salt in a bowl. Stir well.

2. Place the flour in a separate large bowl and make a well in the center. Pour the liquid ingredients into the well, and stir to incorporate the flour gradually. At some point you will need to start using your hands. Knead the dough gently on a board (lightly floured if necessary) until a moist, slightly sticky dough is formed. (If the dough is too dry, add water, 1 tablespoon at a time. If the dough is too sticky, add flour, 1 tablespoon at a time.) Knead the dough until it is smooth and elastic, 2 to 3 minutes.

Alternatively, although Sophie would probably disapprove, prepare the dough using a food processor: Place the flour and salt in the bowl of the processor. Whisk the melted butter, eggs, egg white, and sour cream in a measuring cup with a spout. Pulse the flour two or three times; then turn the processor on and slowly add the egg mixture through the feed tube. Process just until the

> The first time I asked my mother-in-law, Sophie, to teach me to make pirogen, she came over with bags of groceries as well as two rolling pins. I guess she thought I was totally ill-equipped for the job. When I told her I had a KitchenAid mixer, she looked at me in horror. 'No way! You have to feel the dough.' With great patience, she showed me the technique, literally making it with me hand-over-hand.
>
> Sophie doesn't need a special occasion to make pirogen. She'll just whip them up like magic and serve them as a main dish with sour cream and drizzled butter. She also likes to fry them before serving. Me, I'm happy just to eat them right out of the boiling water, but she makes sure that she and I eat only a couple so there'll be enough for Ron for a few days.
>
> Sophie told me she was glad I was making them, because she was afraid the recipe would die out with her. Apparently no one else in the family wants to try. When I make them myself, however, they never come out quite as good as hers. She told me I just need practice and have to learn to get a feel for the dough. Ron really loves them. He's quite proud of me when I make them and makes every effort not to compare them to his mother's. Bless his heart. That's also a good way to get me to make them again.
>
> —ROBIN KANCIGOR BOYKO

dough comes together and pulls away from the sides of the bowl.

Either way, allow the dough to rest, covered with plastic wrap, for 30 minutes. The dough should feel smooth, elastic, and slightly tacky.

3. While the dough is resting, prepare the filling: Mash the farmer cheese and egg yolk together in a small bowl, using a fork. Add the melted butter, sugar, cinnamon if using, and salt. Mix well.

4. Bring a large, wide saucepan of lightly salted water to a boil.

5. To assemble the pirogen, divide the dough into four portions and work on one portion at a time, keeping the remaining dough covered so it does not dry out. Flour your work surface and rolling pin, and roll the dough out very thin. Cut out rounds of dough, using about a 3-inch-wide glass or cookie cutter. Place about 1/2 tablespoon of the filling in the center of each round. Dip your finger in water and moisten half the outer edge of the round. Bring the unmoistened half over to form a semicircle, and pinch the edges together well (so the pirogen will not fall apart in the boiling water). Place the filled pirogen on a lightly floured baking sheet and keep them covered with plastic wrap as you work. (The pirogen can be frozen at this point, or you can freeze them once they are cooked.)

6. When the water has come to a rolling boil, drop some of the pirogen in, one at a time so the boiling does not stop. Do not crowd the pan—depending on the size and width of your pot, 8 to 10 is probably a good number. Cook at a steady, but not rapid, boil

until the pirogen float to the surface. Then cover the pan and boil gently until the dough is tender, 6 to 10 minutes in all. Remove with a slotted spoon and drain well. Using a slotted spoon, transfer the pirogen to a plate. Toss them in melted butter to keep them from sticking together and serve.

Note: To pan-fry the pirogen, melt the butter in a large skillet over medium heat, add the pirogen, and fry until golden brown, 3 to 4 minutes per side. Serve immediately.

To bake the pirogen, preheat the oven to 375°F. Butter a baking pan and fill it with as many pirogen as you wish to serve. Drizzle lightly with melted butter and bake, turning them occasionally, until light golden, about 15 minutes. Serve immediately.

farfel

• • • • •

Tiny farfel is a crumb-like noodle, which is dried and then toasted in the oven. So pervasive was its use among Eastern European Jews that in *The Shtetl Book,* Diane K. Roskies and David G. Roskies illustrate the distinction between Polish Yiddish and Lithuanian Yiddish with a map divided according to the way farfel was prepared. Jews west of the imaginary border they call the "gefilte fish line" cut farfel dough from flat sheets, ate sweetened gefilte fish, and spoke a different Yiddish dialect than their eastern neighbors, who ate spicy fish and chopped farfel dough into pellets. (In the far northeastern and southwestern reaches, farfel was grated from a hardened ball of dough.)

grandma blanche's farfel

from Wendy Altman Cohen

Although called egg barley, there is no such grain as farfel (just as, contrary to popular belief, there is no such fish as a gefilte). Farfel is actually a tiny egg noodle used in soups and in side dishes like this one—pure Jewish comfort food swaddled in sautéed onions and peppers. Perhaps it's the alliteration, but the word seems to bring a smile, especially to those who remember Farfel the dog, a wooden puppet that attained fame and fortune delivering the closing line ("chaaaaw-clit") in a Nestlé's Quik commercial during the 1950s and '60s. Not to be outdone, when Jerry Seinfeld becomes caretaker of an impossibly ill-behaved dog whose alcoholic owner has an attack of Bell's palsy on a plane, who's the dog? Farfel. (Not to be confused with farfalle, the Italian bowtie pasta that, despite its use as varnishkes in our kasha, has no dog named after it.) **SERVES 6 TO 8 M or P**

Wendy's grandma, Blanche Altman.

> *Before I met my husband, Brent, I was engaged for a time to someone else. My family was underwhelmed. Grandma Blanche took me aside and said, 'Dahlink, love may be blind, but marriage? It's a real eye-opener.'*
>
> **—WENDY ALTMAN COHEN**

3 to 4 tablespoons chicken fat, vegetable oil,
    solid vegetable shortening, or nondairy
    margarine, or any combination

1 large onion, finely chopped

1 green or red bell pepper, stemmed,
    seeded, and cut into ¼-inch dice

2 cloves garlic, crushed

8 ounces white mushrooms, sliced

3 cups homemade chicken stock (page 63) or
    low-sodium boxed or canned broth

1 bag (12 ounces) farfel (egg barley)

1 teaspoon kosher (coarse) salt, or to taste

¼ teaspoon freshly ground black pepper,
    or to taste

1. Heat the chicken fat in a large saucepan over medium-low heat. Add the onion, bell pepper, and garlic, and cook slowly until quite soft (and your kitchen smells like your grandma's), 20 to 25 minutes. Add the mushrooms and cook until they are tender and have

Debbie and Ronnie Levine at their surprise 25th anniversary party, 1995.

released their juice, about 5 minutes more.

2. Add the stock and bring to a boil. Stir in the farfel, salt, and pepper. Lower the heat and simmer, covered, until all the liquid has been absorbed, 20 to 25 minutes.

3. Taste, and add salt and pepper if needed. Serve hot.

A meichel in beichel
A TASTY TREAT IN YOUR BELLY

rice and vermicelli pilaf
from Debbie Levine

hen Debbie sent me this recipe, I smiled, because I used to make it all the time when my kids were growing up. My friend Beth Gershon gave me the recipe, and my kids called it "The Gershon Rice." Later, when I began writing about food, I interviewed an Armenian woman and learned that it is a popular Armenian dish. Indeed the commercial equivalent, Rice-A-Roni, was inspired by a similar dish from an Armenian neighbor of the founding DeDomenico family. I've since adopted a suggestion from the Armenian woman I interviewed, adding toasted pine nuts to the finished dish.

SERVES 6 TO 8　　Ⓜ or Ⓟ or Ⓓ

4 chicken or vegetable bouillon cubes,
   or 4 teaspoons chicken or vegetable
   bouillon powder

4 cups boiling water

4 tablespoons ($^1/_2$ stick) nondairy margarine
   or butter

1 cup crushed vermicelli

2 cups rice

$^3/_4$ cup pine nuts, toasted (see box,
   page 17; optional)

1. Dissolve the chicken bouillon in the boiling water and set aside.

2. Melt the margarine in a large saucepan over medium heat. Add the vermicelli and cook, stirring constantly, until the noodles are beginning to brown, about 4 minutes. (Watch carefully, as they burn easily.) Stir in the rice, coating it with the margarine, and sauté for 30 seconds to 1 minute. Then stir in the dissolved bouillon and bring to a boil.

3. Reduce the heat and simmer, covered, until the liquid has been absorbed, about 20 minutes. Stir lightly with a fork. Allow the pilaf to rest, covered, for 15 minutes or so.

4. Toss with the toasted pine nuts, if using, and serve.

Variation: For an Asian version, Bonnie Robbins substitutes toasted sliced almonds for the pine nuts. While the rice is resting, she adds one 10-ounce box of frozen snow peas, thawed; one 8-ounce can of whole water chestnuts, drained and thinly sliced; and one 4-ounce can of mushrooms, drained and sliced.

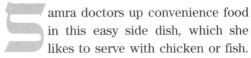

wild rice casserole

from Samra Robbins

Samra doctors up convenience food in this easy side dish, which she likes to serve with chicken or fish.

SERVES 6   **D** or **P**

Butter, nondairy margarine, or solid
   vegetable shortening, for greasing
   the baking pan

1 box (6 ounces) long-grain and wild rice mix

8 tablespoons (1 stick) butter or nondairy
   margarine

1 medium-size onion, finely chopped

1 rib celery, chopped

1 can (7 ounces) sliced mushrooms, drained

1 can (8 ounces) sliced water chestnuts,
   drained

2 tablespoons soy sauce

$^1/_2$ cup slivered almonds, toasted
   (see box, page 17)

1. Preheat the oven to 350°F. Grease a $1^1/_2$-quart baking pan.

2. Cook the rice mix according to the package directions.

3. Melt the butter in a medium-size skillet over medium heat. Add the onion and celery, and cook until soft and golden, about 10 minutes. Stir in the mushrooms and water chestnuts, and cook a minute or so just to heat through. Stir the mixture into the rice, along with the soy sauce and almonds.

4. Pour the mixture into the prepared baking pan and bake until browned and heated through, about 20 minutes. Serve hot.

susan nachawati's
kharouf mahshi
(syrian lamb and rice stuffing)

from Judy Bart Kancigor

In September 2001, I was working on a Thanksgiving story for *The Orange County Register*. I planned to visit three Orange County families from different ethnic backgrounds to show how each group incorporates its native foods into this most American of holidays. Given the population of Orange County, interviewing Mexican and Asian families was a no-brainer, but I was undecided about the third. Then came September 11, and my choice was clear: I had to find a Muslim-American family.

The Nachawatis then owned a Syrian restaurant in Anaheim, barely a mile from one that had been burned to the ground in the crazy backlash aftermath of 9/11. The whole family assembled at the restaurant to meet me for the interview: Susan and her husband, Isam; their two teenage children; and Susan's mother, who was visiting from Syria and spoke no English. As the interview progressed, these people

opened their hearts to me, speaking of their hopes in coming to America and the fear that now gripped them. Every once in a while, Susan's mother would whisper something to her grandson, and he would run into the kitchen to bring me more food. It all felt so familiar, just like being in a Jewish home. I gave them a copy of *Melting Pot Memories*, and I don't know if Susan ever made tsimmes or kasha, but her lamb stuffing has become a staple in my house, where it makes frequent appearances as a side dish, rather than as a stuffing.

Middle Eastern turkey, she explained, is typically split into pieces and simmered in a fragrant broth until it is three-quarters done, then roasted in a hot oven (550°F) until crisp, and served over kharouf mahshi. Susan uses the broth from cooking the turkey when she cooks the rice. For Thanksgiving they are as likely to stuff a leg of lamb as a turkey. Either way, the meat is certified halal in accordance with Islamic rites, similar in some ways to kashrut. "When we fly, we order a kosher meal," Susan told me, "and in the supermarket, if the product is marked 'kosher,' I don't even have to check the ingredients. I will buy it while I'm closing my eyes."

SERVES 6 TO 8　　　　　　　　　　Ⓜ

1/4 *cup olive oil*

1/2 *pound ground lamb*

2 *cups basmati rice, well rinsed*

2 *teaspoons kosher (coarse) salt*

2 *teaspoons Seven Spices (see Note)*

1/2 *cup pine nuts, toasted (see box, page 17)*

1. Heat the oil in a large saucepan over medium heat. Add the ground lamb and cook, breaking it up with a fork or the back of a spoon, until it is browned, about 8 minutes.

2. Stir in the rice, salt, Seven Spices, and 3½ cups water. Bring to a boil. Then lower the heat, cover the pan, and simmer until the liquid has been absorbed, 20 to 25 minutes.

3. Stir in the pine nuts. Fluff with a fork and serve.

Note: Seven Spices is a blend that varies by manufacturer but generally includes cumin, cinnamon, cloves, black pepper, white pepper, allspice, and nutmeg or cardamom. It is available in Middle Eastern markets.

malca's israeli majadra

from Wendy Altman Cohen

My husband Barry's cousin Wendy has picked up so many Israeli recipes from her friend Malca that she is beginning to think of herself as a *sabra* (native Israeli). Wendy's idea of fusion cooking is Grandma Blanche's brisket accompanied by Israeli majadra. She usually doubles the caramelized onion topping because husband Brent can't get enough. Wendy says she prefers to serve it in a shallow baking dish, rather than a

> " When we were first married, I knew Harold liked Spanish rice, so I got a recipe and made it for him. He said, 'This is good, but not as good as my mother's.' So I called my mother-in-law for the recipe and she said, 'What recipe? I open a can!' —MARILYN DUBIN "

bowl, in order to spread out the onions so everyone has a chance to get some.

SERVES 6 TO 8   P or D

1 cup dried lentils, rinsed and picked over

2 medium-size onions, diced

2 tablespoons olive oil

2 cups basmati rice, rinsed well and drained, or 2 cups long-grain white rice

1 tablespoon kosher (coarse) salt, or to taste

½ teaspoon ground cumin (optional)

½ teaspoon freshly ground black pepper

FOR THE TOPPING

3 tablespoons olive oil

3 medium-size onions, thinly sliced into rings

Plain yogurt, for serving (optional)

1. Place the lentils in a large saucepan, add 2 cups water, and bring to a boil. Then reduce the heat, cover the pan, and simmer until the lentils begin to soften, about 20 minutes. Pour the lentils and water into a strainer set over a 4-cup measuring cup. Set the drained lentils aside. Add enough water to the measuring cup to equal 4 cups, and set aside. Wash and dry the saucepan.

2. Heat the oil in the same large saucepan over medium heat. Add the onions and cook, stirring occasionally, until they are soft and golden, about 10 minutes. Add the rice, salt, cumin if using, pepper, lentils, and the reserved 4 cups liquid. Bring to a boil. Then reduce the heat and simmer, covered, until the water has been absorbed and the rice is tender, about 20 minutes.

3. Meanwhile, prepare the topping: Heat the oil in a large skillet over medium-low heat. Add the onion rings and cook, stirring occasionally, until they are very soft and caramel in color, about 20 minutes.

4. When the lentil/rice mixture is cooked, fluff it with a fork and transfer it to a serving bowl. Arrange the caramelized onion rings on top, and serve plain or with yogurt alongside.

kasha
with or without the varnishkes

from Lillian Bart

Say "kasha" and you get a smile. This Jewish staple—buckwheat groats (a health food really, it's so packed with vitamins and nourishment)—is yet another butt of endless jokes. Seinfeld's friend Elaine doesn't say that George's mother's house smells of lentils. What does it smell like? You got it: kasha.

Another controversy: A few apostates in the family—and I won't embarrass them by naming them, they are so wrong—are not varnishkes devotees. They like their kasha plain and simple. To me, kasha is not kasha without the bowties, their soft texture against the nutty kasha, a perfect marriage in an imperfect world.

My mother dresses it up with sautéed onions and green pepper. While most people use medium groats, Mom likes the extra nuttiness of the whole, which she toasts in the oven, despite the fact that the directions on the box do not say to—but then, that would involve reading the directions. **SERVES 12**   **M**

3 tablespoons vegetable oil

1 large onion, chopped

1 green bell pepper, stemmed, seeded, and chopped

1 large egg

1 box (13 ounces) whole buckwheat groats

4 cups homemade chicken stock (page 63) or low-sodium boxed or canned broth, plus more if needed

Kosher (coarse) salt and freshly ground black pepper

8 ounces bowtie pasta

1. Preheat the oven to 350°F.

2. Heat the oil in a large saucepan over medium heat. Add the onion and bell pepper and cook, stirring often, until soft and the onions are golden, 10 to 12 minutes.

3. Meanwhile, beat the egg in a medium-size bowl and stir in the groats, mixing until all the grains are coated. (This will help prevent the granules from sticking, but you will still need to break them up when toasting.) Spread the egg-coated groats on

Kasha: Something I learned at (or on) my mother's knee.

a baking sheet or in a shallow pan. Place it in the oven and bake, stirring often to separate the grains and prevent burning, until all the grains are dry, about 5 minutes. Remove the pan from the oven and separate the groats.

4. Add the stock to the onion mixture, and stir in the toasted groats. Season with salt and pepper to taste, and bring to a boil. Then reduce the heat to a simmer, cover the pan, and cook until the groats are tender and the water has been absorbed, 10 to 15 minutes. (If the groats are tender after 10 minutes, uncover the pan and continue cooking.)

5. Meanwhile, bring a large pot of lightly salted water to a boil. Add the bowtie pasta and cook until al dente, 10 to 12 minutes.

6. Drain the pasta and stir it into the kasha. Serve immediately.

In my family we use the word "kasha" to describe an impossible imbroglio, i.e., cousin A calls cousin B and repeats something cousin C said about cousin D. Now if cousin B shuts her mouth or has a senior moment and forgets about it, this is not a kasha. But if cousin B calls____(and you can fill in the blank with anyone at this point), now *that's* a kasha.

becky green's mamaliga
(jewish polenta)

from Edith Kancigor

I was feeling trendy one day and made polenta. Barry looked at it and gasped, "Mamaliga? You made me mamaliga?" I said, "What the heck is mamaliga?" Seems Grandma Becky used to make this traditional Romanian dish—what did she know from trendy—and Barry hadn't seen it in decades. Polenta and mamaliga sound so much better than "cornmeal mush," yet that's what it is. Some Romanian cooks mix the cooked mamaliga with 1/4 cup melted unsalted butter and 1 cup cottage cheese, drained and sieved, but Grandma Becky made it plain. **SERVES 4** **D** or **P**

1 teaspoon kosher (coarse) salt
1 cup medium-grain yellow cornmeal
1 tablespoon butter or nondairy margarine
Regular or nondairy sour cream, for serving
(optional)

1. Bring 4 cups water to a boil in a heavy saucepan. Stir in the salt. Very gradually sprinkle in the cornmeal, whisking constantly to prevent lumps.

2. Reduce the heat to a gentle boil and cook, stirring frequently, until the mixture has the consistency of thick cereal, 20 to 30 minutes.

3. Stir in the butter and serve immediately, with a dollop of sour cream if you like.

My husband, Barry, with his mom and Uncle Henry, who was so much younger than Barry's dad, he was more like a big brother.

> The mamaliga would stick to the pot, and my mother had to soak it for days. (But what don't you do for the children.) Today they sell instant polenta and nonstick pots, so it doesn't have to be such a job. My mother would serve it as a side dish with stew or brisket, and it would soak up all the delicious flavors of the meat. The next morning, if there was any left over, she would cut it into wedges and fry it, and we'd have it for breakfast with syrup.
>
> **—EDITH KANCIGOR**

kishka
(stuffed derma)

from Hinda Rabinowitz

Some of the most delicious Jewish dishes were born out of poverty. How're you going to feed a family, not to mention boarders, when you just got off the boat and haven't a pot to, um, cook in? With what the butcher throws away, that's how. In the days before the government pulled the plug on the casings (read intestines—let's call a spade a spade), Mama Hinda would stuff 'em, boil 'em, and brown 'em in the oven.

Purely in the interests of science, I actually tested this dish (I hope you appreciate this). Two pounds of fat! No wonder the stuff is so good. When my mother the sous-chef saw what I brought home from the butcher, she said I was nuts. "Can't you just throw that recipe out? Do you have to be so obsessive?" A real nostalgia freak, my mother.

Obsessive? *Moi?* If I were obsessive I would have bought a sausage attachment for my mixer and found kosher casings. I didn't do that, did I? Sorry, that's where I draw the line: I listened to Aunt Sally and baked them in foil.

Then we tasted the kishka, and my mother ate her words. That's not all she ate, but who's counting. I had to break that rule about letting things cool before you put them in the freezer or I could have eaten them all. You think potatoes are comfort food? Hah! How can I describe kishka? Picture the moistest stuffing you've ever had, at once fluffy and dense.

If any of you actually make this, please e-mail me. I have a little bet going with my mother. **SERVES ABOUT 18 . . . but only**

> **Mama Hinda used to get the casing for the derma from the kosher butcher. Cleaning it was some job. I don't think you can get them any more, even if you wanted to. You could also stuff a helzel [chicken neck] or just roll it up and bake it by itself.** —SALLY BOWER

if the ingredients are a secret. You'll have far fewer takers if you mention that little 2-pound "gift" from the butcher. What a shame. Then there will be all those leftovers calling to you from the fridge in the middle of the night.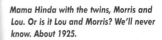

6 cups all-purpose flour

3 tablespoons instant oatmeal

3 tablespoons farina, Cream of Wheat, or Cream of Rice

2 tablespoons matzoh meal

2 tablespoons paprika

2 tablespoons kosher (coarse) salt

1 1/2 teaspoons freshly ground black pepper

1 large russet potato (12 ounces), shredded

1 large onion, grated

1 1/2 cups grated carrots

2 pounds beef fat, ground

1. Preheat the oven to 325°F. Line two rimmed baking sheets with heavy-duty aluminum foil (the derma logs will leak no matter how well you wrap them).

2. Mix the flour, oatmeal, farina, matzoh meal, paprika, salt, and pepper together in a large bowl. Add the potato, onion, and carrots, and mix thoroughly.

3. Add the ground beef fat and combine well. (Those disposable plastic gloves that food handlers wear are a godsend here.)

4. Divide the mixture into six equal portions and wrap each one in a large square of plastic wrap. Squeeze and roll each ball to form a log measuring 1 1/2 inches in diameter and 9 to 10 inches in length. Open the plastic wrap and roll each log onto a large square of aluminum foil (discard the plastic wrap). Roll up the foil, twisting the ends tightly to secure them. Place the wrapped logs on the prepared baking sheets. Bake, turning the logs and alternating their position on the baking sheets every 20 minutes or so, until cooked through, 1 1/4 to 1 1/2 hours. (To test for doneness, very carefully open a foil packet and cut down the middle—which won't hurt its appearance, since you will be serving the derma sliced. They will be quite soft, but there should be no raw spots in the middle.)

5. Allow the logs to rest in the foil for 5 to 10 minutes. Then unwrap them, carefully slice them with a serrated knife (see Note), and serve.

Note: Because there is no casing, these are a little soft for slicing. If you like, you can allow the logs to cool and then refrigerate them until they are

Mama Hinda with the twins, Morris and Lou. Or is it Lou and Morris? We'll never know. About 1925.

cold and firm, at least 2 hours. Then use a serrated knife to cut them into ³/₄-inch-thick slices. Reheat the slices in a preheated 350°F oven until sizzling hot, 12 to 15 minutes. Cover any unused slices to prevent them from drying out.

Mama Hinda and my brother, Gary, Florida, 1947.

mock kishka

from Sally Bower

Aunt Sally never owned a food processor, and she and I had many, shall we say, discussions about the value of grating by hand. Cousin Marilyn says that only in her old age did her mother relent and let her use one for making gefilte fish. It does save your knuckles in preparing this dish, and I don't think Aunt Sally would mind. I'm not going to pretend that this is the stuff that memories of 1950s Bar Mitzvahs are made of, but it's delicious nonetheless, moist and reminiscent of the real thing. (And you don't have to ask the butcher for 2 pounds of beef fat either.) **SERVES 8 TO 10**   **P** or **D**

1 large carrot, very coarsely chopped

1 medium-size onion, very coarsely chopped

1 large rib celery, very coarsely chopped

4 tablespoons (¹/₂ stick) nondairy margarine or butter, melted

70 Ritz or similar crackers, processed into crumbs (3 cups)

1 teaspoon kosher (coarse) salt, or to taste

¹/₂ teaspoon freshly ground black pepper, or to taste

1. Preheat the oven to 350°F. Line a rimmed baking sheet with aluminum foil.

2. Combine the carrot, onion, and celery in a food processor and process until ground, stopping and scraping down the sides of the bowl a few times to obtain a uniform consistency.

3. Stir the melted margarine into the cracker crumbs in a large bowl. Add the ground vegetables, salt, and pepper, and combine thoroughly.

4. Divide the mixture in half and wrap each half in a large square of plastic wrap. Squeeze and roll the dough to form a log measuring 1¹/₂ inches in diameter and about 10 inches in length. Open the plastic wrap and roll each log onto a piece of aluminum foil. Roll up the foil, twisting the ends tightly to secure them. Place the wrapped logs on the prepared baking sheet and bake, turning the logs and alternating their position on the baking sheet after 20 minutes, until cooked through, about 40 minutes.

5. Remove the logs from the oven and allow to cool in the foil. (Do not peek!) Refrigerate until cold and firm, at least 2 hours. When they are firm, unwrap them

and use a serrated knife to cut them into $3/4$-inch-thick slices.

6. Preheat the oven to 350°F.

7. Place the slices on an ungreased baking sheet and bake until sizzling hot, 12 to 15 minutes. Serve immediately.

challah dressing

from Judy Bart Kancigor

my M.O. at Thanksgiving is to serve new side dishes every year. The year I concocted this dressing, my daughter-in-law Tracey asked, "Would you mind breaking with tradition and making this entire meal next year?" No one believes that there are only two tablespoons of fat in the whole thing. I use this reduction method for my gravy too (page 210). Homemade chicken stock, my mother's especially, is the secret.

SERVES 8 TO 10　　　　　　　　**M**

$1/2$ cup dried cranberries

About $1/2$ cup orange juice

Vegetable cooking spray, for greasing
　the casserole

1 tablespoon nondairy margarine

1 tablespoon vegetable oil

3 leeks, white part only, chopped

1 bulb fennel, chopped

1 pound white mushrooms, thinly sliced

$2^1/2$ to $3^1/2$ cups homemade chicken stock (page
　63) or low-sodium boxed or canned broth

$1/2$ cup dry white wine

1 pound challah, crusts removed (see Notes),
　cut into $1/2$-inch cubes

1 tablespoon minced fresh rosemary (see Notes)

1 tablespoon minced fresh sage

1 to 2 teaspoons minced fresh thyme

$1/4$ cup chopped flat-leaf parsley

1 teaspoon poultry seasoning

1 teaspoon kosher (coarse) salt, or to taste

$1/2$ teaspoon freshly ground black pepper,
　or to taste

1. Combine the cranberries and orange juice in a small bowl, and set it aside.

2. Preheat the oven to 350°F. Grease a 2-quart casserole.

3. Heat the margarine and oil in a saucepan over medium-high heat. When the foam subsides, add the leeks, fennel, and mushrooms. Cook, stirring often, until the vegetables start to stick to the pan, about 10 minutes. Pour in $1/2$ cup of the chicken stock and continue cooking and stirring until the liquid evaporates and the vegetables stick to the pan again, about 5 minutes. Repeat this process twice more, adding $1/2$ cup stock each time and cooking until the liquid evaporates and the vegetables start to stick to the pan. (You will have used $1^1/2$ cups of stock so far, which concentrates the salt, so wait for the very end to correct the seasonings.) Remove the pan from the heat and stir in the wine. Deglaze the pan, scraping up all the crusty brown bits. Most of the alcohol will evaporate. Set the pan aside.

4. Drain the cranberries and transfer them to a large bowl. Reserve the orange juice for another use . . . such as drinking

it (with or without vodka). Add the sautéed vegetables, challah, rosemary, sage, thyme, parsley, and poultry seasoning. Toss to mix. Then stir in 1 to 1½ cups of the remaining stock if you like a fairly stiff dressing, more for a moister dressing. Season with the salt and pepper.

5. Transfer the dressing to the prepared casserole and bake for 45 to 60 minutes. (Cover the casserole if the dressing starts to dry out.)

Notes: The amount of chicken stock you add depends on how much challah is left after you trim the crusts. I prepare the challah in my bread machine, baking it in the machine rather than braiding and baking it in the oven, so the crusts are easy to slice off. Of course I save the crusts for challah chips (see Note, page 160; no one can believe there's so little fat in those chips, either!)

Some supermarkets carry a fresh herb mixture called "poultry blend" that contains rosemary, sage, and thyme. One package will save you money and be plenty for this dish.

corn bread dressing

from Samra Robbins

Samra's dressing, made with her own Buttermilk Corn Bread, is a family favorite, especially loved by her girls, who expect it whenever they come home to visit. Samra says she developed this recipe using three fourths of the baked corn bread, because as soon as her family smells the corn bread baking, they start hovering, and next thing you know there are lots of fingers in the pan. If you can't fight 'em, join 'em, she says, so she cuts off a portion of the corn bread to leave out for the tasters. **SERVES 8** **D**

FOR THE DRESSING

Butter, for greasing the baking pan
1 recipe Buttermilk Corn Bread (page 338),
*   still warm from the oven*
4 medium-size firm apples, peeled, cored,
*   and grated, with their juice*
½ cup chopped onion
½ cup chopped celery
½ cup whole milk
8 tablespoons (1 stick) butter, melted
2 large eggs, beaten
1 teaspoon poultry seasoning, or to taste
1 teaspoon kosher (coarse) salt, or to taste
¼ teaspoon freshly ground black pepper,
*   or to taste*
Dash of ground nutmeg
1 can (7 ounces) sliced mushrooms, drained
About 1 cup apple juice, if needed

FOR THE TOP

2 tablespoons butter, melted
Paprika

1. Preheat the oven to 350°F. Butter a 13 × 9-inch baking pan.

2. Crumble three fourths of the warm cornbread into a large bowl. Add all the remaining ingredients except the 1 cup apple

juice. Toss to mix, and then add enough apple juice to obtain a soft, wet consistency. (If the grated apples have given off enough juice, this extra juice may not be needed.)

3. Spread the mixture out in the prepared baking pan. Brush with the 2 tablespoons melted butter and sprinkle with paprika. Bake until set and golden brown, about 1 hour.

vi's wild rice stuffing

from Tom Frank

Tom likes to make his mom's stuffing for holiday dinners. Wild rice, Minnesota's state grain, is not really a rice but a grass. It is still harvested by the traditional American Indian methods— at least in Minnesota, where *wild* wild (as opposed to cultivated) rice comes from.

SERVES 8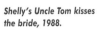

Vegetable oil, solid vegetable shortening,
   or vegetable cooking spray, for greasing
   the baking dish
1 cup wild rice
6 tablespoons (³/₄ stick) nondairy margarine
2 large onions, chopped
2 ribs celery, chopped
8 ounces white mushrooms, sliced
1 cup long-grain white rice
2 cups homemade chicken stock (page 63) or
   low-sodium boxed or canned broth

¹/₄ cup chopped parsley
2 teaspoons celery seeds
2 teaspoons poultry seasoning
1 cup chopped pecans, toasted
   (see box, page 17)
1 teaspoon kosher (coarse) salt

1. If you are not stuffing a bird, preheat the oven to 350°F. Grease a 1¹/₂-quart baking pan.

2. Rinse the wild rice thoroughly in a strainer under cold running water.

3. Combine the rice and 2 quarts water in a large saucepan and bring to a boil. Reduce the heat, cover, and simmer for 25 minutes. Drain the rice and set aside. (It will be only partially cooked.)

4. Melt the margarine in a large saucepan over medium heat. Add the onions and celery and cook until soft and golden, about 10 minutes. Add the mushrooms and cook, stirring constantly, for 5 minutes more. Then add the white rice, drained wild rice, stock, parsley, celery seeds, and poultry seasoning. Bring to a boil. Reduce the heat, cover, and simmer until the rice is tender, 15 to 20 minutes. Stir in the pecans and salt. (Adding salt after cooking ensures that the wild rice will be puffier and more flavorful.)

5. Use to stuff a bird, or transfer to the prepared baking dish and bake, covered, for 30 minutes.

Shelly's Uncle Tom kisses the bride, 1988.

mom & dad at work

breads

In re-creating old recipes, none was a greater challenge—or meant more to me—than Mama Hinda's challah. My childhood memories are filled with it. I had to get it right.

More than twenty years had passed since my mother had scribbled it down, at my behest, at Mama Hinda's hospital bedside just days before she died at age ninety-one. "Add a little sugar. Mix with warm water," she had written. Measurements, where given at all, are in "glasses," not cups. But which glass?

Somewhere between my third and fourth disastrous attempts, it occurred to me that perhaps asking someone for a recipe when she

"If it was to be done with a yarmulke, Papa was there."

—GARY BART

Our house was filled with song; their office was the stage. Who's who—well, what's what—on page 613.

is on her deathbed may not be the most opportune moment to do so. It was time for a little help from my friends. Okay—a lot of help! I e-mailed Faye Levy, author of *1,000 Jewish Recipes*. She generously clarified the measurements, but cautioned: "Is your grandmother's challah gaining the rosy glow of childhood memories, impossible to duplicate? Recalling the warm family atmosphere in which your loving grandmother served you challah may have something to do with how good it tasted."

Could Faye be right? I've never had a good memory for people—names *or* faces—but food? Ask me what I ate at cousin Marvin's Bar Mitzvah in 1957 and I can tell you. (Also how much I weighed . . . but that's another story.)

"Oh, Judy, why don't you just go to Poul's Bakery and buy a challah," suggested my mother. No one can ever accuse my mother of being overly sentimental.

But I was on a mission. So I consulted Fred Hyde, owner of Poul's in Orange, California, supplier of Friday challahs to the synagogues in the area. "My challah is too crusty," I

whined. Fred looked at my recipe: "Bake for 10 to 15 minutes in slow oven. Then raise heat," instructed Mama Hinda. Fred disagreed. "If the temperature is too cold, it takes longer to bake the inside, so it's drying on the outside. Most home ovens are about 25 degrees off, so bake it at 375 degrees for 20 to 25 minutes, never more than 30.

"And it's really hard to make bread at home if you're kneading by hand," he added. "Use your mixer, with the paddle if your machine can take it, or use the hook."

Mama Hinda kneaded by hand. And trust me, she had no personal trainer or ever saw the inside of a gym. But those were the arms that carried a nine-month-old baby on a ship across the Atlantic in 1907. Those arms held, dressed, fed, sewed for, and cleaned up after seven children, through the Depression, with no conveniences. No bicep curls would ever give me her strength.

Guiltily eying my KitchenAid, I told myself, hey, I'm not driving around in Papa Harry's '51 Pontiac. This is the twenty-first century. I'm sure Mama Hinda, who had witnessed the horse and buggy give way to *Sputnik*, would understand.

Miraculously, after a few more adjustments, there it was, lucky number thirteen. It wasn't Mama Hinda's recipe exactly, but it was Mama Hinda's challah, just as I remembered it. Thomas Wolfe was wrong, I thought. You *can* go home again. You just may have to take a different path to get there.

While I get a lump in my throat remembering Mama Hinda's challah, Papa Harry would get a teary, wistful look in his eyes when talking about the coarse black bread he remembered from the Old Country—so heavy, so dense, a "meal by itself," he'd say. My mother remembers that when she was growing up, Mama Hinda served a dark bread she called "health bread," perhaps her attempt to re-create the loaf *she* remembered from the shtetl. (No one complained about it except Uncle Lou, who detested it, and who to this day will not eat dark bread of any kind.)

Because man lives not by challah alone—even Mama Hinda's—you'll find a tempting variety of breads in this chapter, including old favorites like onion pletzlach, soft and seductive Bread Machine Pita (it'll spoil you for store-bought), garlic-infused breadsticks, mouth-watering buttermilk biscuits, picture-perfect popovers, even homemade Philadelphia Pretzels. Included here too are sweet pumpkin, banana, cranberry, and zucchini breads that double nicely as dessert, and a variety of English scones—perfect for tea or just plain noshing.

Bread is so basic, it stands for food itself. Our prayer before meals praises God for bringing forth bread from the earth. It's the stuff memories are made of. Perhaps someday a grandchild will get teary-eyed over mine.

shabbat

It's no secret that we Jews like to party! Shabbat, the only holiday mentioned in the Torah, is celebrated every week. On Friday evening, as sundown ripples across the time zones, observant Jews from Moscow to Madrid to Milwaukee put aside the cares of the week, gather with family, and welcome the Sabbath queen.

Shabbat begins with the lighting of candles and ends an hour after sundown on Saturday with the *Havdalah* ceremony: We recite a blessing over the wine, pass a spice box for all to inhale, and light a braided candle. Between those two events the observant do no work, as God rested on the seventh day of creation. Shabbat is a day of peace.

Some of the foods we associate with Shabbat were borne of Shabbat restrictions, such as gefilte fish (page 51) and cholent (pages 135 and 136). The meals are festive, befitting a holiday.

Every Shabbat eve of my childhood, my brother and I ran upstairs to Mama and Papa's tiny apartment. Mama would cover her eyes and recite the blessing over the candles. Then two loaves of challah would be blessed, and Papa would say the Kiddush over the wine. Finally, he'd place his hands on our heads and bless us too.

Celebrating Havdalah with Rabbi Asa (left), Stu, Barry, me, and Brad during Brad's Bar Mitzvah weekend, August 1980.

mama hinda's challah

from Hinda Rabinowitz

No food reminds me more of Mama than her challah, and no Jewish food is more wrought with symbolism. The poppy seeds recall the manna that fell from heaven, feeding the Israelites as they wandered for forty years in the desert. Mama always baked two golden loaves, to remember the double portion of manna God gave the Jews for the Sabbath, so that they would not work on that day.

The traditional braiding of the Sabbath challah was actually adopted by Jews from their German neighbors during the Middle Ages. As they did with so many other customs, Jews living in the Diaspora absorbed traditions from the surrounding culture. The rabbis then debated the symbolic meanings of these customs. Could the braiding signify God's plaiting Eve's hair for her wedding to Adam? The interlocked arms of lovers? Perhaps the triple concepts of the Creation, Exodus, and Messianic Age? As Maggie Glezer, author of *A Blessing of Bread*, told me when I interviewed her, "Jews admired [the Germans'] Sunday loaf. It looks beautiful, they thought. Obviously we want our Sabbath loaf to look as beautiful. We mix our traditions with the local traditions and create new ones."

As was the custom, Mama would always remove a little piece of dough, say a prayer, and bake it alongside the challah until it burned, a practice that harkens back to Numbers 15:17–21, a passage that calls for the separation of a portion of bread to be given to the priests—which, according to Aunt Sally, was Mama's way of showing that you don't keep everything for yourself. During summer, when it was too hot to light the stove, Mama would bring the dough to the local bakery to be baked.

With my grandparents living right upstairs, my brother, Gary, and I never needed coaxing to run up and light the Shabbat candles with them each Friday night. From the time we arrived home from school, the aroma of baking challahs sent intoxicating drifts through every room in our house. And on Rosh Hashanah, the traditional braided loaf gave way to a majestic spiral, signifying the circle of life. Only on this holiday would Mama Hinda fold in raisins for extra sweetness. We'd tear off chunks to dip in honey and wish each other a sweet New Year.

This recipe is adapted from one that Mama dictated to my mother during her final stay in intensive care. (She also, during the same hospitalization, asked the cleaning lady for the name of the product she was using to polish the metal bed!)

MAKES ONE 1½-POUND CHALLAH

No family celebration could begin without Papa making the blessing and cutting the challah.

3¹/₂ cups bread flour

¹/₂ cup warm water (100° to 110°F)

2³/₄ teaspoons (1 package plus 2 teaspoons)
    active dry yeast

1 teaspoon plus ¹/₄ cup sugar

2 large eggs, at room temperature

¹/₄ cup vegetable oil, plus extra for oiling
    the bowl

1¹/₂ teaspoons kosher (coarse) salt

¹/₃ cup raisins (optional)

Vegetable oil or vegetable cooking spray,
    for greasing the baking sheet
    (or parchment paper)

Egg wash: 1 egg yolk mixed with
    1 tablespoon water

Poppy seeds (optional)

1. Set aside 2 tablespoons of the flour. Place the remaining flour in the large bowl of an electric mixer fitted with a flat paddle or a dough hook. Make a well in the center of the flour and pour in ¹/₄ cup of the warm water. Sprinkle the yeast over the water and add 1 teaspoon of the sugar. Using a fork, stir the water, yeast, and sugar together gently, keeping the mixture in the well (don't worry if a little flour becomes incorporated). Let stand until bubbly, about 10 minutes.

2. In a separate bowl, beat the eggs, the ¹/₄ cup oil, the remaining ¹/₄ cup sugar, and the salt together with a fork. Add the egg mixture and the remaining ¹/₄ cup warm water to the flour mixture, and beat on

challah tips

■ To measure the flour, spoon it *lightly* into a cup and level it off with a knife.

■ Remember that the amount of flour you need will vary from day to day, even using the same recipe in the same kitchen. Aim for a slightly tacky dough that does not stick to your hands.

■ To eliminate air pockets and produce even strands, do as Maggie Glezer suggests in *A Blessing of Bread*: For best results, use a kitchen scale to weigh the dough and divide it evenly. Before braiding, roll each portion out as thin as possible, using a rolling pin, to form a round. Then roll the thin round up tightly, forming a strand. To lengthen the strand, do not pull; instead, push down, using the fleshy part of your palms, which allows the dough to extend itself. Then braid the strands.

■ When braiding challah, if you start from the middle and work out to both ends, you will get a neater loaf.

■ Don't overbraid, or your loaf will be flat. Five twists should be plenty.

■ When you have finished braiding, squeeze the ends of the loaf slightly toward the middle to make for a higher loaf. An 8- to 9-inch-long loaf should rise to a grand size.

■ To avoid deflating the loaf, use a pastry brush with soft bristles to glaze it with the egg wash.

■ The dough can be prepared through Step 2 a day ahead: Place the ball of dough in a large oiled bowl, turning the dough so it is oiled all over, and cover and refrigerate. When ready to bake, bring the dough to room temperature, set it aside to rise as described in Step 3, and continue with the recipe. Alternatively, you can refrigerate the shaped loaf, covered. As it returns to room temperature, the dough will continue to rise. Once the loaf has risen, continue with Step 7.

low speed until incorporated. Then beat on medium speed until smooth and silky, 5 to 10 minutes. The dough should feel slightly sticky and, to quote Jeffrey Nathan in *Adventures in Jewish Cooking*, "like a baby's tush." If it is too sticky, add the reserved 2 tablespoons flour (or more if necessary), 1 tablespoon at a time, and continue to mix for a few more minutes.

3. Oil a large bowl and place the ball of dough in it, turning the dough so it is oiled all over. Cover with a kitchen towel and set aside in a warm place until the dough has almost doubled in bulk, at least 1 hour. (Now to find a warm place: Mama Hinda used the top of her stove, but she had a pilot light. My garage on a summer's day does the trick for me, but I have also used my oven, preheated at the lowest setting and then turned off.)

4. When the dough has almost doubled, punch it down and knead it by hand for 1 to 2 minutes, incorporating the raisins, if using.

5. *For a braided challah*, separate the dough into three equal portions and roll each portion out to form a strand $1^{1}/_{4}$ to $1^{1}/_{2}$ inches wide and about 12 inches long (lightly flour your work surface only if necessary). Braid the strands (see Challah Tips, page 329).

using a bread machine

● ● ●

Some years ago I was inspired to buy a bread machine after staying with cousin Phyllis on a visit to New York and waking to the aroma of freshly baking bread. I could hardly wait to get home and try it! Since then I've used my bread machine often, much to my guests' delight as well as mine.

In converting bread recipes for use in the bread machine, it is important to note that different brands of machines work differently. Some call for placing the wet ingredients in the pan first, while others call for the dry ingredients first. Follow the manufacturer's directions.

You may have to adjust the proportion of flour to liquid to obtain the proper consistency. Here's what I suggest: Before you try other recipes, use the ones provided by the manufacturer of your machine. As the dough is kneading, pinch it to familiarize yourself with how it should feel. Then go ahead and experiment with other recipes. Feel the dough in the initial kneading stage, and if it feels too sticky, add flour, a tablespoon at a time, as it is kneading. If it feels too dry, add water (or other liquid called for in the recipe, such as milk or juice), also a tablespoon at a time, until you get the right consistency for your machine. It is not uncommon for recipes to vary by $1/_{2}$ cup of flour or more from machine to machine.

Peter and Phyllis on the day I awakened, as a guest in their house, to the aromas from their bread machine. I bought one as soon as I got home.

For a spiral Rosh Hashanah challah, roll the dough into a single rope about 34 inches long. Beginning at one end, wind the rope from the center of the spiral outward, keeping the center slightly elevated, like a turban. Tuck the end under.

6. Lightly grease a baking sheet or, better yet, line it with parchment paper. Place the shaped dough on the prepared baking sheet, cover it with a slightly dampened cloth, and allow it to rise in a warm place for 1 hour.

7. Preheat the oven to 375°F.

8. Brush the top of the loaf with the egg wash, and sprinkle it with poppy seeds, if using. Bake until the top is brown and the bottom sounds hollow when tapped with your fingers, 25 to 30 minutes.

9. Transfer the loaf to a wire rack and allow it to cool completely.

Notes: Made without preservatives, home-baked bread is an ephemeral pleasure, best eaten the day it's baked. After that it makes wonderful toast; or you can save thick slices for any of the French toast casseroles (pages 362 to 363). Use leftover challah to make your own bread crumbs or challah chips (see Note, page 160).

I like to leave the cut challah, cut side down, on a breadboard for the day. You can refrigerate it, wrapped well in plastic wrap and then in a resealable plastic bag, for up to a week, but I prefer to freeze it after the first day: Slice the loaf, placing plastic wrap between the slices and around the loaf, wrap it in a resealable plastic bag, and freeze for up to 1 month.

dorothy rubin's bread machine challah rolls

from Lillian Bart

My mother's friend Dorothy is famous for her honey-sweet rolls, which she bakes for every holiday. The raisins, mandatory in Dorothy's kitchen, are optional in ours because my family almost comes to blows on the raisins-versus-no-raisins issue. Fortunately, with rolls it's easy to please everyone. For the raisin-lovers among us (and Mom and I are at the top of *that* list), my mother divides the dough: one batch for the plain-challah purists (what do *they* know?) and a double dose of raisins in the other batch for us.

MAKES 20   P

2 large eggs, at room temperature

1/2 cup plus 2 tablespoons warm water

3 to 3 1/2 cups bread flour

1/2 teaspoon salt

1/3 cup vegetable oil

1/4 cup honey

1 tablespoon yeast for bread machines

1 cup raisins (optional)

Vegetable oil or vegetable cooking spray,
*   for greasing the baking sheet*
*   (or parchment paper)*

Egg wash: 1 large egg mixed with
*   1 tablespoon water*

1. Whisk the eggs and all the warm water together in a small bowl. Following the order suggested by the manufacturer, place the egg mixture, 3 cups of the bread flour, salt, oil, honey, and yeast in the bread machine bowl. Set the machine on the dough mode.

2. As the dough kneads, pinch it: It should feel tacky but should not stick to your fingers. If it is too sticky, add the remaining flour, a tablespoon at a time, until it is no longer sticky.

3. After the first kneading, add the raisins, if using.

4. Preheat the oven to 250°F for at least 3 minutes; then turn it off. Grease a baking sheet, or better yet, line it with parchment paper.

5. When the cycle has completed, remove the dough from the machine and divide it into 20 balls. Dorothy likes to keep them irregular and not handle them too much, but if you prefer a rounder roll, pull the outer edges of the dough into the center and fold them under. Place the dough balls on the prepared baking sheet.

6. Cover the rolls with a slightly dampened cloth, place the baking sheet in the oven (be sure the heat is turned off), and allow the rolls to rise until they have doubled in size, about 1 hour. Remove the baking sheet from the oven.

7. Preheat the oven to 350°F.

8. Brush the top of the rolls with the egg wash, and bake until they are golden brown, 14 to 15 minutes. Let the rolls cool on the baking sheet.

9. Store the rolls, covered with plastic wrap, at room temperature for 1 day. After that, wrap them individually in plastic wrap, place them in a resealable plastic bag, and refrigerate for up to 1 week or freeze for up to 2 months.

Note: The dough can be prepared 1 to 2 days ahead: Remove the dough from the bread machine and shape it into rolls. Cover them with plastic wrap and refrigerate on the baking sheet. When you are ready to bake them, bring the rolls to room temperature and proceed with Step 6.

onion pletzlach (rolls)

from Fanny Vitner

This is a cut-down version of Fanny's original recipe, which called for $3^1/_2$ pounds of flour and yielded a huge quantity of rolls. According to Aunt Sylvia, her mother would bake them by the hundreds and then give them away to grateful neighbors and friends. You can also make an onion board by rolling the dough flat before the second rise. (The board is like a flatbread, not spongy like focaccia.) These tender rolls, with their delicate onion flavor, are especially delicious warm from the oven. **MAKES 30 ROLLS OR 2 ONION BOARDS** D

FOR THE DOUGH

1 package active dry yeast

^{1}/$_2$ cup warm water (100° to 105°F)

^{3}/$_4$ cup milk

6 tablespoons sugar

1^1/$_2$ teaspoons salt

^{1}/$_4$ cup canola or vegetable oil, plus extra for oiling the bowl

1 large egg, beaten

4 to 4^3/$_4$ cups all-purpose flour

FOR THE TOPPING

1 tablespoon olive oil

1 cup finely chopped onion

Vegetable oil or vegetable cooking spray, or parchment paper for the baking sheets

1 egg, beaten

1. Sprinkle the yeast over the warm water in a large bowl and set it aside until foamy, about 5 minutes.

2. Heat the milk in a medium-size saucepan over medium heat just until bubbles form around the edge. Remove the pan from the heat and add the sugar, salt, and oil. Stir until the sugar has dissolved.

3. Add the milk mixture to the proofed yeast. Stir in the beaten egg and about 3^1/$_2$ cups flour, enough to make a soft dough. Knead the dough with your hands, adding more flour in ^{1}/$_4$-cup increments until the dough cleans the sides of the bowl and is only slightly sticky, about 4 minutes. Oil the bowl, and use the dough to spread the oil around the sides. Turn the

dough oiled side up, cover it with a kitchen towel, and set it aside in a warm place until doubled in bulk, about 1 hour.

4. Punch the dough down and set it aside to rise again in the same bowl, covered, until doubled, about 1 hour more.

5. Meanwhile, prepare the topping: Heat the olive oil in a small skillet over medium-high heat. Add the onion and cook, stirring frequently, until it is caramelized, about 10 minutes. Set aside.

6. Lightly grease two baking sheets, or better yet, line them with parchment paper.

7. After the dough has completed the second rise, punch it down and turn it out onto a lightly floured surface. Pull off golf-ball-size pieces, roll them into balls, and flatten them slightly between the palms of your hands so each looks like a flying saucer. (For onion boards, divide the dough in half and shape each half into a rectangle measuring about 12 × 8 inches.) Place the rolls or boards on the prepared baking sheets, cover with a kitchen towel, and set aside to rise for 30 minutes.

8. Meanwhile, preheat the oven to 350°F.

9. Uncover the baking sheets and brush the rolls (or boards) with the beaten egg. Sprinkle the onion topping evenly over them, and bake until golden brown, about 20 minutes for rolls, 25 minutes for boards.

10. Serve immediately, or allow to cool on a wire rack.

Fanny Vitner, Aunt Sylvia's mother, 1927.

toast

from Essie Korn Strausser Perlman King Friedman

• • • •

My father's oldest sister, Essie, didn't cook, but I couldn't leave her out of this book. She had no children of her own, so she spread her endless supply of love among her nieces and nephews.

Essie and her first husband, Uncle Sam (the sweetest guy, who used to call me "button nose"), lived with Grandma Ruchel in a two-bedroom walk-up off Prospect Park in Brooklyn. Grandma, of course, did all the cooking. When my parents went out of town, they would often leave me with them. (My brother, Gary, was considered too much for Aunt Essie to handle and was shipped off to Aunt Estelle, who had the strength for him!)

Tragically, a few weeks before my wedding, Uncle Sam suddenly had a heart attack and died. But Aunt Essie wouldn't miss seeing her niece get married for the world. She put on her pale blue frock and a happy face and came to my wedding. In her younger days Aunt Essie had been quite the babe, with lots of beaus. She couldn't bear to be alone, and soon married her second husband, Irving. Her *mazel* (luck): The wedding reception for the family was the weekend after John F. Kennedy's assassination—a bittersweet occasion. We breathed a sigh of relief that Aunt Essie was taken care of—and she was, for about twenty years, until Irving had a heart attack and died.

Aunt Essie was wretched, inconsolable, and lonely. Then she met Robert. Again we breathed a sigh of relief. Robert was ten years younger than she—or so she said—so surely she would not end her days alone. (I later learned that Robert was not ten, but actually *twenty* years younger than Essie.) Here's the story: Back in Poland, Grandma Ruchel had been divorced—another story altogether! Aunt Essie was her child from her first marriage. Then Grandma married Osias Moses Strausser, a man with four children whom she raised as her own. (My father was their child together.) When the family emigrated to America, Essie had to pretend to be Osias's daughter, and therefore on her papers her age was listed as ten years younger than she actually was. She kept up this fabrication all her life, believing until the day she died that if the government found out she had come here under false pretenses, she would be deported back to Poland.

So Aunt Essie and Robert lived in wedded bliss, and again we breathed an even deeper sigh of relief. But wouldn't you know it, after a few years, Robert had a heart attack and died (leading my son Stuart to reflect, "Whatever you do, don't marry Aunt Essie!").

All her life Aunt Essie fairly burst with love. Every phone call and birthday card ended with "I love you with all my heart and soul." She never cooked a thing in her life. Grandma and Essie's three husbands took care of that. (Between husbands she was too distraught to eat.) But when people would visit, she would get so excited she would make toast, one slice after the other, until the whole toasted loaf of bread was perched precariously on Grandma Ruchel's bone china. I can't look at a piece of toast today without smiling and thinking of her.

Left: Essie's passport photo when she was 27 but claimed to be 17; Gary, Grandma Ruchel, Essie, and me in Prospect Park, Brooklyn.
Top: Miriam Strausser, Osias's first wife, who died at 25; Osias Moses Strausser.

11. Store the rolls, covered with plastic wrap, at room temperature for 1 day. After that, wrap them individually in plastic wrap, place them in a resealable plastic bag, and refrigerate for up to 1 week or freeze for up to 1 month.

bread machine pita

from Judy Bart Kancigor

For my daughter-in-law Tracey's divine hummus (page 18), I wanted something more special than store-bought pita, so I experimented until I came up with this recipe. This pita is so bewitchingly soft on the inside, chewy on the outside, and with just the right hint of tang, that it can even stand alone. Betcha can't eat just one! **MAKES ABOUT 22** D

3³/₄ *cups bread flour*

1 *teaspoon baking powder*

1 *teaspoon salt*

²/₃ *cup milk*

²/₃ *cup plain yogurt*

2 *tablespoons olive oil*

1 *large egg*

1¹/₂ *tablespoons honey or sugar*

2 *teaspoons yeast for bread machines*

Vegetable cooking spray, for greasing the baking sheet

1. Place all the ingredients except the cooking spray in the bread machine bowl, following the order suggested by the manufacturer. Set the machine on the dough mode. (See box, page 330.)

2. Lightly grease a baking sheet.

3. When the cycle has completed, remove the dough and shape it into golf-ball-size balls. Place the balls on the prepared baking sheet, cover with a kitchen towel, and allow to rise in a warm place for 30 minutes. (An oven preheated to the lowest setting and then turned off works for me.)

4. Place an empty, ungreased baking sheet in the oven and preheat the oven to 500°F.

5. Roll the balls of dough to form flat rounds and place them on another ungreased baking sheet. When you have 7 or 8 rounds, remove the hot baking sheet from the oven (with a mitt, please!), spray it quickly with vegetable cooking spray, and quickly throw the flattened rounds onto the hot sheet. Bake until brown on one side, 2 minutes. Turn them over with tongs, and bake until brown on the other side, 1 minute more. Quickly remove the pitas from the baking sheet and place them in a single layer on another baking sheet. Respray the hot baking sheet, and repeat this process until all the dough has been flattened and baked.

6. The pitas will puff up on baking and will be easy to split if you don't cover them or seal them in a plastic bag. To serve, split the pitas and fill them for sandwiches, or cut or tear them into eighths for dipping. I like to serve them in a straw basket lined with a linen napkin.

rachel's garlic breadsticks

from Samantha Kancigor

W hen my boys were small and we lived on Long Island, my dear friend and neighbor, Babette Cohen, was an invaluable source of recipes. Her three daughters were like built-in mother's helpers, a godsend to me with my babies. Norma, the oldest, would ring my bell and ask if she could take them for a walk or help feed them. It was heaven! Babette's garlic breadsticks were dearly loved by both families, and although they have never met, her granddaughter Rachel (Norma's daughter), in upstate New York, and my granddaughter Samantha, in California, bake them with their grandmas, carrying on the tradition. **MAKES ABOUT 18** **D** OR **P**

1 pound pizza dough (see Notes)

1/4 cup extra virgin olive oil,
   plus extra for
   oiling the dough

4 to 5 large cloves garlic,
   finely minced

Cornmeal, for sprinkling
   on the baking sheet

All-purpose flour,
   for sprinkling on
   the work surface

Kosher (coarse) salt

1. Coat the ball of dough lightly with olive oil and place it in a bowl that is large enough for the dough to expand to twice its size. Cover the bowl with plastic wrap and set it aside in a warm spot until the dough has doubled in size, about 1 hour.

2. Meanwhile, toss the 1/4 cup olive oil with the garlic in a small bowl. Cover and refrigerate it (see Notes).

3. Preheat the oven to 425°F. Lightly sprinkle a baking sheet (not nonstick) with cornmeal.

4. Place the dough on a lightly floured surface and punch it down. Turn the dough over so both sides are lightly covered with flour. Lightly flour a rolling pin, and roll the dough out to form a rectangle—do not be concerned with perfection here. Transfer the dough to the prepared baking sheet and pull and stretch it to measure approximately 11 × 9 inches.

5. Strain about 2 tablespoons of the oil-garlic mixture, and cover and refrigerate it. Brush the remaining oil-garlic mixture over the surface of the dough, and sprinkle it lightly with salt. Using a pizza wheel, trace a rectangle about 3/4 inch in from the edges of the dough, creating a border. Then score vertical strips, about 3/4 inch apart, within that border. (Your rectangle of dough will look like a jail cell with a frame around it.) Be sure to score each slice all the way through to the baking sheet, but don't separate the strips.

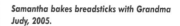

Samantha bakes breadsticks with Grandma Judy, 2005.

Immediately place it in the oven and bake until lightly browned, about 20 minutes.

6. Brush the breadsticks with as much of the reserved oil as you wish, and serve them as they come out of the oven. By now the aroma of baking garlic-scented bread will have summoned your guests—no need to ring the dinner bell. Watch as they fall all over themselves, tearing away the strips of garlic bread.

Notes: Use frozen or refrigerated pizza dough or homemade. If using frozen dough, let it come to room temperature before setting it aside to rise.

Don't count on having any leftovers. But if you do, wrap the breadsticks well in plastic wrap and then in resealable plastic bags, so the garlic smell doesn't permeate your refrigerator. Refrigerate or freeze. Reheat, thawed or still frozen, in a preheated 375°F oven for 5 to 7 minutes, or until hot.

Never leave garlic submerged in oil at room temperature without any acid present. Dangerous toxins may form.

buttermilk biscuits

from Zena Kaplan

One secret to baking biscuits—well, it's hardly a secret—is to handle the dough as little as possible. Southerners, who have elevated biscuit making to a high art form, have another secret: They will tell you it's all in the flour. Theirs is milled from soft red winter wheat, which contains less gluten than regular all-purpose flour and produces the lightest, tenderest biscuits. One brand is White Lily, available retail mostly in the South. My family gobbled these up even when they were baked with Gold Medal—we're from New York, so what do we know—but you can "import" White Lily by going to www.whitelily.com. **MAKES 10 TO 11** [D]

2 cups White Lily or all-purpose flour
1 tablespoon baking powder
$1/2$ teaspoon baking soda
$1/2$ teaspoon salt
$1/4$ cup solid vegetable shortening
1 cup buttermilk

1. Preheat the oven to 450°F. Line a baking sheet with parchment paper or leave it ungreased.

2. Sift the flour, baking powder, baking soda, and salt together into a bowl.

3. Using a pastry cutter or two knives, cut the shortening into the flour mixture until uniformly blended. Add the buttermilk and stir with a large spoon just until a soft, moist dough comes together.

4. Transfer the dough to a lightly floured surface. Turn the edges of the dough inward toward the center and turn the dough over. With floured hands or a floured rolling pin, pat or roll the dough out until it is $3/8$ inch thick. Cut out rounds with a 3-inch biscuit

cutter. (Cut down straight without twisting for a truly tender biscuit.)

5. Place the rounds of dough ¹/₂ inch apart on the baking sheet and bake until golden, about 12 minutes. Transfer the biscuits to a wire rack to cool. These are best served warm the day they're made, but leftovers are nice toasted the next day.

bullock's popovers

from Wendy Altman Cohen

Bullock's, in Los Angeles, was more than a department store; it was an institution—and one especially adored by ladies who lunch. The popovers were the biggest draw in the store's restaurant. Alas, Bullock's is gone, but the popovers live on. Wendy, always on the lookout for an easier way, streamlined the method by throwing all the ingredients in her blender. The popovers puff up big and brown and beautiful and are best served hot from the oven. **MAKES 8** D

Me, Ronald, Samra, and Eric at David Robbins's Bar Mitzvah, 1988.

Butter, for greasing the cups
2 cups all-purpose flour
³/₄ teaspoon salt
6 large eggs
2 cups milk
6 tablespoons (³/₄ stick) butter or margarine, cut into small pieces

1. Preheat the oven to 400°F. Generously butter 8 custard cups and place them on a baking sheet.

2. Place the flour, salt, eggs, milk, and butter in a blender and process until very smooth.

3. Pour the mixture into the prepared custard cups, filling them evenly. Bake until golden brown and puffy, about 1 hour. Serve immediately.

buttermilk corn bread

from Samra Robbins

Buttermilk makes Samra's corn bread mouthwateringly moist and is the secret of her corn bread dressing (page 322). But don't wait for something to stuff—this corn bread perks up Sunday breakfast too. **SERVES 6** D

Butter, for greasing the baking pan
1¹/₂ cups all-purpose flour
1¹/₂ cups yellow cornmeal

1/2 cup sugar

2 tablespoons baking powder

1 teaspoon salt

1/2 teaspoon baking soda

2 cups buttermilk

2 large eggs, well beaten

4 tablespoons (1/2 stick) butter,
   melted

1. Preheat the oven to 400°F. Generously butter a 13 × 9-inch baking pan.

2. Sift the flour, cornmeal, sugar, baking powder, salt, and baking soda together into a large bowl.

3. Add the buttermilk, eggs, and melted butter, and mix well.

4. Transfer the mixture to the prepared baking pan and bake until it is just beginning to brown around the edges and the center springs back when touched, 20 to 25 minutes.

5. Let the corn bread cool completely in the pan. Then cut it into squares and serve. It will keep, covered, at room temperature for up to 3 days.

buttermilk scones

from Claire Smolen

arm scones—sweetened versions of their biscuit cousins—are perfect right from the oven for tea or breakfast, and so easy that my grand-children can practically make them by themselves. Cousin Samra's mom, Claire, a true Southerner, says the secret to her seductive scones, as with her biscuits, is the buttermilk. Split the scones and use them as shortcakes mounded with summer berries or peaches and fresh whipped cream. **MAKES 16**   **D**

2 cups all-purpose flour

2 teaspoons baking powder

1/4 teaspoon baking soda

3 tablespoons sugar

1/2 teaspoon salt

8 tablespoons (1 stick) cold
   unsalted butter, cut into
   small pieces

1/2 cup buttermilk

1 large egg, lightly beaten

1 tablespoon milk

1. Preheat the oven to 425°F. Line a baking sheet with parchment paper or leave ungreased.

2. Combine the flour, baking powder, baking soda, 2 tablespoons of the sugar, and the salt in a bowl, and mix well. Using a pastry cutter or two knives, cut in the butter until the mixture resembles coarse crumbs. Add the buttermilk and egg, stirring until just moistened. Turn the dough out onto a floured surface and knead it gently about 5 times. Do not overwork it.

3. Divide the dough in half and pat each piece out to form a 6-inch round. Cut each round into 8 wedges and place the wedges 1 inch apart on the baking sheet. Brush with the milk and sprinkle with the remaining

1 tablespoon sugar. Bake until golden, 12 to 14 minutes.

4. Transfer the scones to a wire rack to cool. These are best eaten the day they're baked.

variations

. . .

LEMON-POPPY SEED SCONES: Combine 2 teaspoons grated lemon zest, 2 teaspoons poppy seeds, and $1/2$ teaspoon pure lemon extract with the buttermilk in Step 2.

Omit the milk-and-sugar topping. Instead, combine $1^1/2$ tablespoons fresh lemon juice and 1 cup confectioners' sugar, sifted, in a small bowl, and drizzle this mixture evenly over the warm scones.

ORANGE HAZELNUT SCONES: Combine 2 teaspoons grated orange zest, $1/2$ teaspoon pure orange extract, and $1/2$ cup toasted hazelnuts, chopped, with the buttermilk in Step 2.

Omit the milk-and-sugar topping. Instead, combine 3 to 4 tablespoons defrosted frozen orange concentrate and 1 cup confectioners' sugar, sifted, in a small bowl, and drizzle this mixture evenly over the warm scones.

CHOCOLATE CHIP SCONES: Combine $1/2$ cup mini chocolate chips and 1 teaspoon pure vanilla extract with the buttermilk in Step 2.

philadelphia pretzels

from Wendy Epstein

endy brought this recipe home from a third-grade school trip to the Greenkill Outdoor Education Center in upstate New York. As they grew up, she and her sisters, Vicki and Marcy, would bake them often, producing all sorts of shapes and sizes as well as the traditional pretzel ring. Delicious and easy to make, they're a great project to do with kids. Philadelphia pretzels are softer than the New York variety and are best eaten warm from the oven. You can sprinkle the pretzels with sesame seeds in addition to or instead of the salt, if you like. **MAKES 14**   **P**

1¹/2 cups warm water (105° to 110°F)
1 tablespoon active dry yeast
1 teaspoon sugar or honey
3¹/2 to 4 cups all-purpose flour,
    or 3 cups all-purpose flour and
    ¹/2 to 1 cup whole-wheat flour
1 teaspoon salt
Vegetable oil, for oiling the bowl
Egg wash: 1 large egg, beaten with
    1 tablespoon water
Kosher (coarse) salt

1. Pour the warm water into a bowl, and sprinkle the yeast, then the sugar, over it. Set it aside until bubbly, 5 to 10 minutes.

2. Mix 3^1/$_2$ cups of the flour with the salt in a large bowl, and add the yeast mixture. Stir, and then knead on a lightly floured surface until the dough is smooth and elastic, about 10 minutes. If it is too sticky, gradually add more flour.

3. Oil a mixing bowl and transfer the dough to it. Turn the dough so the oiled side is up. Cover with a clean kitchen towel and set aside in a warm place until doubled in bulk, about 1 hour.

4. Punch down the dough and turn it out onto a lightly floured surface. Pull off golf-ball-size pieces of dough and roll each one to form a rope about ^{1}/$_2$ inch wide and 20 inches long. Fold and twist the dough into bow shapes and place them on ungreased baking sheets. Once all the pretzels are shaped, cover the sheets with kitchen towels and allow them to rise until almost doubled in bulk, 30 minutes.

5. Meanwhile, preheat the oven to 425°F.

6. Brush each pretzel with some of the egg wash, and sprinkle with salt. Bake until pale golden, 10 to 15 minutes. These are best eaten warm.

Vicki, Marcy, and Wendy at the United Nations Ambassadors' Ball. Mom Phyllis chaired the event for about eight years.

To store sweet bread loaves, wrap in plastic wrap and then in aluminum foil and keep at room temperature for up to 3 days. Or freeze them, well wrapped in plastic wrap and then in foil, for up to 2 months. Thaw completely before removing the plastic wrap.

pumpkin bread

from Judy Bart Kancigor

This recipe was given to me eons ago by the first friend I made when we moved to California. My father had just died, I was 3,000 miles away from everyone I knew, and she was my rock. Somehow we lost touch and I've been looking for her for years. (D.A., if you're reading this, call me!) This pumpkin bread was an old family recipe that her grandmother baked in those large metal cans that juice used to come in before they went to plastic. I've always used loaf pans, but out of curiosity I decided to try it Grandma's way. I bought a large can of pineapple juice to use as my cooking vessel, so I substituted pineapple juice for the water in the original recipe. Well, I won't be baking it in a juice can again (and I don't suggest you do either), but the pineapple juice stays! This moist, spicy loaf, chock-full of crunchy nuts and bursting with dates and raisins, perfumes the house with the pungent aromas of fall. **MAKES 2 LOAVES** P

Solid vegetable shortening, for greasing
   the pans
3¹/₃ cups all-purpose flour
2 teaspoons baking soda
1¹/₂ teaspoons salt
¹/₂ teaspoon baking powder
1 teaspoon ground cinnamon
¹/₂ teaspoon nutmeg, preferably
   freshly grated
¹/₂ teaspoon ground cloves
2 cups canned pumpkin
   (not pumpkin pie filling)
²/₃ cup pineapple juice, orange juice,
   or water
²/₃ cup solid vegetable shortening
2²/₃ cups sugar
4 large eggs
1¹/₂ cups walnuts, toasted (see box, page 17)
   and chopped
³/₄ cup raisins
³/₄ cup snipped dates (or more raisins,
   if you prefer; see Note)

1. Preheat the oven to 350°F. Grease two standard loaf pans.

2. Sift the flour, baking soda, salt, baking powder, cinnamon, nutmeg, and cloves together into a large bowl, and set it aside.

3. Combine the pumpkin and pineapple juice in another bowl, and set it aside.

4. Cream the shortening and sugar with an electric mixer on medium speed until well combined, about 2 minutes. Add the eggs, one at a time, beating well after each addition.

5. Reduce the speed to medium-low and add the flour mixture in three additions, alternating with the pumpkin mixture in two additions, beginning and ending with the flour mixture and scraping down the bowl as necessary. Fold in the walnuts, raisins, and dates.

6. Divide the batter between the prepared loaf pans and bake until a toothpick or cake tester inserted into the center comes out clean, 1 hour and 10 to 20 minutes.

7. Transfer the pans to a wire rack and cool for 10 minutes. Then loosen the loaves by running a knife around the edges, remove them from the pans, and transfer them to the rack to cool completely.

Note: When cutting dates (or any dried fruit), poultry shears work better than a knife. Snip them to the size of raisins.

zucchini bread

from Tracey Barrett

When my daughter-in-law Tracey's garden overfloweth with zucchini, it's time to get out the loaf pans. This moist bread is rich enough to be called a cake, and in fact Tracey sometimes substitutes mini chocolate chips for the raisins, just for fun. **MAKES 2 LOAVES** P

Vegetable oil or vegetable cooking spray,
    for greasing the pans

3 cups all-purpose flour

2 teaspoons baking soda

1 teaspoon salt

$^{1}/_{2}$ teaspoon baking powder

1 teaspoon ground cinnamon

3 large eggs

1 cup vegetable oil

2 cups sugar

2 teaspoons pure vanilla extract

2 cups (about 12 ounces) shredded
    unpeeled zucchini

1 can (8 ounces) crushed pineapple,
    well drained

1 cup chopped pecans or walnuts
    (optional)

1 cup raisins (optional)

1. Preheat the oven to 350°F. Grease two standard loaf pans.

2. Sift the flour, baking soda, salt, baking powder, and cinnamon together into a bowl. Set it aside.

3. Whisk the eggs, oil, sugar, and vanilla together in a large bowl. Stir in the zucchini and pineapple. Add the flour mixture and mix until thoroughly combined. Stir in the pecans and raisins, if using.

4. Transfer the batter to the prepared loaf pans, and bake until a toothpick or cake tester inserted in the center comes out clean, about 1 hour.

5. Transfer the pans to a wire rack, and cool for 10 minutes. Then loosen the loaves by running a knife around the edges, remove them from the pans, and transfer them to the rack to cool completely.

sgt. x's cranberry orange bread

from Lillian Bart

my mother, a serial recipe collector (an actual recipe *trier*? not so much), volunteers every Tuesday afternoon at the local library. One day shortly before Thanksgiving, a policeman brought in a recipe and asked her to give it to someone who would be coming in later. Of course she had to copy it—her daughter was writing a cookbook, you know—and even mentioned that said daughter would put his name in her book. He declined the attribution (perhaps he was baking undercover?) but was happy to share the recipe. It was my mother's idea to chop the cranberries, which can be disconcertingly sour if you happen to bite down

Mom and Dad at a wedding, early '50s. Of course they were asked to sing.

on a whole one. In the summer blueberries make a nice substitute, although we take advantage of the pre-Thanksgiving cranberry price wars and freeze bags for any off-season cranberry bread cravings.

MAKES 1 LOAF　　　**D** or **P**

Butter or vegetable cooking spray,
    for greasing the pan
2 cups all-purpose flour
1 cup sugar
1¹/₂ teaspoons baking powder
1 teaspoon baking soda
¹/₂ teaspoon salt
1 large egg
¹/₂ cup orange juice
Grated zest of 1 orange
2 tablespoons butter or nondairy margarine,
    melted
2 tablespoons hot water
1 cup cranberries, coarsely
    chopped
1 cup chopped walnuts, toasted
    (see box, page 17)

Mom and Dad en route to Israel, 1952. So monumental was a trans-Atlantic flight that the whole family saw them off.

1. Preheat the oven to 350°F. Grease a standard glass loaf pan.

2. Sift the flour, sugar, baking powder, baking soda, and salt together into a bowl, and set it aside.

3. Using a fork, beat the egg in a large bowl. Stir in the orange juice, orange zest, melted butter, and hot water. Fold in the flour mixture just until blended. Do not beat. Gently fold in the cranberries and walnuts.

4. Transfer the batter to the prepared loaf pan, and bake until a cake tester inserted into the center comes out clean, about 1 hour.

5. Transfer the pan to a wire rack, and cool for 10 minutes. Then loosen the loaf by running a knife around the edges, remove it from the pan, and transfer it to the rack to cool completely.

Bon Voyage JAN & LIL

banana pecan bread

from Selma Zuckerman

If life gives you lemons, you make lemonade (but you already know that!) and if life gives you mushy bananas, you make banana bread. This dense, moist loaf was cousin Leslie's mom Selma's specialty, but if she was making it for Leslie, she'd leave out the nuts. **MAKES 1 LOAF**　　　**P**

Butter or vegetable cooking spray,
    for greasing the pan

3 cups all-purpose flour, plus extra
    for flouring the pan

1 teaspoon ground cinnamon

1 teaspoon baking powder

1 teaspoon baking soda

Pinch of salt

²/₃ cup (10 tablespoons plus 2 teaspoons)
    butter, at room temperature

1¹/₃ cups sugar

1 large egg, at room temperature

Yolk of 1 large egg, at room temperature

1¹/₂ cups mashed ripe bananas
    (3 medium-size bananas)

1 teaspoon pure vanilla extract

1 teaspoon pure almond extract

¹/₃ cup sour cream or buttermilk

³/₄ cup chopped pecans

³/₄ cup golden raisins (optional)

"My mother didn't cook much—she was real big on restaurants and takeout. The whole six years I was dating Marvin, before I married into the Rabinowitz clan, every time he came over for dinner she made the same meal: roast beef, baked potato, and green bean casserole. Gefilte fish she served from the jar, or if she was really in a mood to fuss, she doctored it up in the oven. The first time I tasted my future mother-in-law Estelle's homemade gefilte fish, I thought it tasted funny. It's what you're used to, I guess. The one thing my mother did make from scratch was banana bread, although that was more out of her sense of thrift than any love of baking. She just couldn't throw overripe bananas away."

—LESLIE (ZUCKERMAN) ROBBINS

Above right: Selma, 1940s.

1. Preheat the oven to 350°F. Grease and flour a large (10-inch) loaf pan.

2. Sift the flour, cinnamon, baking powder, baking soda, and salt together into a medium-size bowl. Set it aside.

3. Cream the butter and sugar with an electric mixer on medium-high speed until light, about 2 minutes. Add the egg and egg yolk, one at a time, beating well and scraping the bowl down after each addition. Blend in the mashed bananas, vanilla extract, and almond extract. Reduce the speed to low and add the flour mixture in three additions, alternating with the sour cream in two additions, beginning and ending with the flour mixture. Stir in the pecans, and the raisins if using.

4. Transfer the mixture to the prepared loaf pan and bake until it is golden brown and a cake tester inserted in the center comes out clean, about 1¹/₄ hours.

5. Transfer the pan to a wire rack, and cool for 10 minutes. Then loosen the loaf by running a knife around the edges, remove it from the pan, and transfer it to the rack to cool completely.

the barts

breakfast

Jews know all about fasting. Tishu B'Av, Yom Kippur, not to mention intermittent poverty-induced starvation. We also know all about breaking fasts. So when it comes to breakfast, we're all over it. Did we not invent the bagel?* (See next page.)

Okay, we didn't invent brunch. The notion of arising late and dining leisurely on a sumptuous breakfast at noon could hardly have occurred to our ancestors in the shtetl. But we sure do know how to take an idea and run with it.

They say breakfast is the most important meal of the day. To my mind, it can also be the most fun. Pancakes, French toast, egg dishes, blintzes . . . what a great way to start the day,

"Got lox? But of course!"

Three generations of Barts. (The great-grandkids came later.) Who's who on page 613.

even if your day begins at noon.

No offense to Aunt Jemima, but here you'll find three more creative (and infinitely more delicious) pancake choices: my son Stu's ethereal puff of a German Pancake, cousin Peter's homage to his mom's Apple-Cinnamon Pancakes (think apple latkes), and cousin Laura's why-tell-them-it's-good-for-them Oat Pancakes with banana, yogurt, and pecans.

When you think of breakfast, you think of eggs. When I was growing up, that meant Salami and Eggs. Cousin Axel's mom Mady's Hoppel-Poppel takes salami and eggs to a whole other level: a hearty scramble adding crispy potatoes and sautéed onions and peppers. Baked Eggs Provençal features eggs poached in tomato shells flavored with basil, parsley, and Parmesan cheese.

So we're talking breakfast and you're thinking: Got lox? But of course! Gerry's Leo is the ultimate Lox, Eggs, and Onions. Just thinking about them you can practically smell the slow-cooked, gloriously browned, caramelized onions. Or try cousin Samra's Lox Quiche with Swiss cheese and a hint of sherry and nutmeg.

Aunt Sally was the Rabinowitz resident blintz-maker. We love her Cheese Blintzes with their whisper of lemon topped with cousin Samra's Aunt Joan's Raspberry

Top: David and Kari Robbins. Bottom: Harry and Sally Cohen, about 1965.

Sauce. Or turn store-bought blintzes into Aunt Hilda's Cheese Blintz Soufflé.

Our family's variations on the French toast theme leave the humble white bread dipped in egg and fried in the proverbial dust. Caramel French Toast Casserole is like an oozy breakfast crème caramel. Or try Apple and Cheese–Stuffed French Toast layered with raspberry jam. There is even a savory version in cousin Vicki's mother-in-law Rita's Cheese Strata with scallions, parsley, and Dijon mustard.

With apologies to O'Neill, this chapter shows you how to break the fast of Long Night's Journey into Day—a good reason to go to sleep in the first place. Pleasant dreams!

*All right. Hold the calls and letters. Jews didn't exactly invent the bagel. Some say the first bagel was baked in 1683 by a Viennese baker, who shaped the circle of dough into a stirrup to pay tribute to the King of Poland, an avid horseman, for driving out the Turks. Others say the Uygurs of Eastern Turkestan have been eating a similar roll for 1800 years. But bagels came into their lovable own in the shtetl. And who put them on every breakfast table in America, the Uygurs?

salami and eggs

from Lillian Bart

hen I was growing up, there was always a salami in the house for sandwiches or salami and eggs, our all-time favorite lunch. When Gary and I were at sleep-away camp, on visiting day our parents would bring a whole salami and fresh rye bread, and we and our bunk-mates would have a feast. **SERVES 1** **M**

1 teaspoon vegetable oil

5 slices salami

2 large eggs

1. Heat the oil in a medium-size skillet over medium-high heat. Add the salami and cook on both sides until browned, about 2 minutes altogether.

2. Meanwhile, whisk the eggs in a bowl.

" When Joyce and I were growing up and it was time to buy an anniversary or birthday present for our parents, Aunt Lil would help with the shopping. She would ask us how much we wanted to spend, which was usually a dollar or two. Somehow Aunt Lil always found a 'bargain,' like a sterling silver bowl or a crystal dish. When I went to college, Aunt Lil was afraid that I would lose my Jewish heritage, so she started me in the salami-of-the-month club, enrolling me as the first and only member. I had the best-smelling room on campus. **—MARVIN ROBBINS** "

" When Mama and Papa went out, I was usually in charge of my brothers. My sisters were older and closer in age to each other, so they were always busy. (That meant I had to schlep the boys everywhere I went—even to the movies. That's the part I really hated!) One time—I must have been about twelve years old—Mama and Papa were gone and left me in charge. I wanted to make salami and eggs, so I sent my brother Al to get salami. While he was out, instead of waiting, I started to heat some oil, and the curtains caught on fire. I grabbed a coat from the closet near the kitchen and smothered the fire, but the curtains were completely burnt. Mama was so glad no one was hurt that she didn't even make a fuss about the ash all over her stove and white tile. She even collected on the insurance for the curtains. I don't think she ever liked them anyway. **—LILLIAN BART** "

3. Pour the eggs over the browned salami, reduce the heat to medium, and cook until they are golden brown on the bottom, about 2 minutes. Turn with a spatula and brown on the other side, about 2 minutes more. Serve immediately.

hoppel-poppel

from Mady Orlow

ousin Axel remembers his mother, Mady, preparing this traditional German dish when he was a child:

scrambled eggs tossed with browned potato chunks, sizzling salami, and fried onions and peppers. You can serve it as an omelet—cut it into wedges—but we prefer the more rustic scramble. For best results boil the potatoes ahead and refrigerate them; then cube them. **SERVES 4** **M**

2 medium-size boiling potatoes

Kosher (coarse) salt

1 cup (4 ounces) diced salami

$1/4$ cup plus 1 tablespoon vegetable oil

1 medium-size onion, chopped

$1/2$ green or red bell pepper,

   stemmed, seeded, and cut into

   $1/4$-inch dice

8 large eggs

Freshly ground black pepper, to taste

1. Place the potatoes in a medium-size saucepan, add water to cover, and bring to a boil. Lightly salt the water. Reduce the heat and simmer until the potatoes are barely tender, about 20 minutes. Do not overcook. Drain the potatoes and set them aside to cool. Then cut them into $3/4$-inch cubes.

2. Heat a large skillet over medium-high heat. Add the salami and cook, stirring often, until browned on all sides, about 3 minutes. Remove the salami and set it aside.

3. Heat the $1/4$ cup oil in the same skillet over medium-high heat, and add the potatoes. Cook, stirring often, until they are browned on all sides, about 8 minutes. While the potatoes are browning, sprinkle them with $1/2$ teaspoon salt. Remove the potatoes with a slotted spoon, leaving as much of the oil as possible in the skillet.

4. Heat the remaining 1 tablespoon oil in the same skillet over medium heat, and add the onion and bell pepper. Cook, stirring occasionally, until soft, about 6 minutes.

5. Meanwhile, whisk the eggs in a bowl.

6. Return the salami and potatoes to the pan, and stir. Pour the eggs over the salami mixture. Reduce the heat to low and cook, stirring occasionally with a spatula, until the eggs are set, about 3 minutes. Add salt, if needed, and pepper, and serve immediately.

> "*Oma [Grandma] is still a tough lady at ninety-five. She was diagnosed with leukemia at least twenty years ago, and the doctors gave her five years. Now they can't find any sign of the disease. She was a gymnast as a kid, and she swears that has saved her from injuries. She has fallen down her stairs at home a number of times, but thankfully she was fine, just bruised.*
>
> *Our Oma has always been a party animal. She loved to play cards nightly, but unfortunately all her card partners have died. Now she has a woman who drives her to get her nails and hair done and takes her to Hadassah luncheons and shopping. She won't leave the house unless her hair and nails are perfect.*
>
> *My fond memories as a child include Oma's famous grape cutter. You may not know this, but grapes should only be served attached to their stems and cut with a grape cutter, not pulled. If you tried grabbing a grape, she would go crazy. She gave me her sterling silver grape cutter about five years ago. Of course the first time I used it, it broke! Oma said she had it for seventy years and it never broke. She is trying to find a place to get it fixed for me.* —JODI ORLOW MACKOFF"

baked eggs provençal

from Rita Miller

These herb-flavored poached eggs nestled in tomato shells make a lovely brunch dish and are easy enough to serve for family breakfasts too. My recipe tester Beth Weisman said her six-year-old son, Benny, suggested putting the tomato tops, with their stems, back on for decoration. If you do this, put them in the oven for the last 10 minutes of baking. To make this dish pareve (neutral), substitute margarine for the butter and Italian-flavored bread crumbs for the Parmesan cheese. **MAKES 8**   D

8 medium-size ripe tomatoes

2 tablespoons butter, cut into small
    pieces, plus extra for greasing
    the baking pan

8 basil leaves, slivered

Garlic salt

Kosher (coarse) salt

Freshly ground black pepper

8 large eggs

About 3 tablespoons chopped parsley

About 2 tablespoons grated Parmesan cheese

1. Cut a thin slice from the stem end of each tomato. Scoop out the seeds and pulp, using a grapefruit spoon or melon baller, leaving the shell intact. Invert the tomatoes over paper towels and let them drain thoroughly.

Rita Miller with son David (cousin Vicki's husband) at their wedding rehearsal dinner, 1997.

(In a hurry? Wipe out the insides well with paper towels.)

2. Preheat the oven to 375°F. Butter a 13 × 9-inch nonreactive baking pan.

3. Place the tomato shells in the prepared baking pan. Sprinkle each tomato with slivered basil and a pinch each of garlic salt, kosher salt, and pepper.

4. Break 1 egg into each tomato shell. Dot the butter over the eggs, and sprinkle with the parsley. Bake for 10 minutes. Then sprinkle the Parmesan cheese over the eggs and continue baking until the egg whites are completely set and the cheese is beginning to brown, about 12 minutes for runny yolks, 14 to 15 minutes for firm but golden yolks. Serve immediately.

"leo"
(lox, eggs, and onions)

from Gerry Nelson

When I became obsessed with genealogy in the early 1980s, I learned that my husband, Barry, was descended on his Grandma Rose's side from a long line of famous rabbis dating back to Rashi in

Gerry Nelson and wife, Joanne Rocklin, with me "roasting"Joanne at her 50th birthday party with a riff on "These Are a Few of Her Favorite Things." (All guts, no talent.)

the 11th century! The day I made this discovery I called him at the office, very excited, to tell him that his great-great-great (etc., to the 13th power) grandfather was Saul Wahl, who in 1587 was king of Poland for a night. (Barry was underwhelmed, but when he came home from the office that night he said I could kiss his ring.) By now there are probably millions of descendants such as Gerry, making him Barry's, oh, probably 87th cousin, 35 times removed. (Other notable family members include Karl Marx, Helena Rubenstein, and Felix Mendelssohn—and believe me, if they were alive I'd be asking them for recipes too.)

This recipe originated with a French chef who during the 1940s and '50s worked at Rosenhein's Restaurant on Fordham Road and the Grand Concourse in the Bronx, partly owned by Gerry's father. The secret is in the very slow cooking of the onions and lox. Gerry advises that the quantities of onions and lox can be modified to taste, but I think his proportions are perfect. Since the lox breaks down into tiny pieces, there's no need to purchase fancy slices—the cheaper lox "ends" will do. On occasion Gerry has used vegetable oil for the health conscious, but butter is always, unfortunately, more delicious. (You can double or triple the recipe for a crowd.)

SERVES 4   D

4 tablespoons (¹/₂ stick) butter

4 large onions, thinly sliced

6 ounces lox ends

8 large eggs, beaten

1. Melt the butter in a large skillet over very low heat. Add the onions and cook *very* slowly, stirring occasionally, until they are browned and caramelized (do not let them burn), 30 minutes to 1 hour. This takes a long time, but it is an important step. (If you want, you can caramelize the onions the night before, but do not refrigerate them; just cover the skillet.)

2. Add the lox to the caramelized onions and cook over low heat until the lox breaks up into very small pieces. This also takes some time, perhaps 10 to 15 minutes. Incorporate the lox into the onions, using a fork.

3. When you are ready to serve the dish, raise the heat to high and add the eggs. Scramble vigorously with a fork, incorporating the eggs into the lox/onion mixture as they cook. You don't want the egg mixture to dry out, so while it is still rather liquid, quickly reduce the heat to low and continue stirring until it reaches the desired consistency. Serve immediately.

cheese strata

from Rita Miller

For many years cousin Vicki's mother-in-law, Rita, was a kosher caterer in New Jersey. This was a popular brunch selection, and it scored high marks at one of my recipe-testing potlucks as well. All the prep work is done a day ahead. Then the dish comes out of the oven all puffy and golden and looking like something out of *Alien*, but it settles down while cooling. **SERVES 10 TO 12**　D

12 slices white bread, crusts removed

8 tablespoons (1 stick) butter, melted

10 ounces Swiss or Cheddar cheese, shredded (2¹/₂ cups)

1 bunch (6 to 8) scallions, white and green parts, chopped

1 bunch flat-leaf parsley, chopped (¹/₂ cup)

Dried minced onions

6 large eggs

1 teaspoon salt

1 teaspoon Dijon mustard

1 cup sour cream

3 cups whole milk

1. Cut the bread slices in half diagonally. Pour the melted butter into a 13 × 9-inch nonreactive baking pan. Dip the bread into the butter, coating the slices on both sides. Arrange half the slices in a single layer in the baking pan. Sprinkle with half the cheese, half the scallions, and half the parsley. Sprinkle generously with onion flakes. Repeat with the remaining bread, cheese, scallions, parsley, and onion flakes.

2. Whisk the eggs, salt, and mustard together in a bowl. Beat in the sour cream until smooth, followed by the milk. Pour the egg mixture evenly over the layers in the baking pan. Cover, and refrigerate overnight.

3. When you are ready to bake the strata, preheat the oven to 350°F.

4. Bake until it is puffed and golden, 40 to 45 minutes. Cut into squares and serve immediately.

judi weisman's salvadoran cheese casserole

from Lillian Bart

Here's a twist on our blintz soufflé that my friend Judi got from a fellow teacher from El Salvador. When she brought it to a potluck, my mom had to have the recipe—which is so easy that she likes to bring it to potlucks too. It's sweet and quite rich, almost like a cake, so small servings will do. **SERVES 18**　D

Butter or vegetable cooking spray,
    for greasing the pan

6 large eggs

1 cup plus 2 tablespoons sugar

12 tablespoons (1¹/₂ sticks) unsalted butter
    or margarine, melted

2 cups small-curd cottage cheese

2 cups sour cream

2 tablespoons grated Parmesan cheese

1¹/₂ cups buttermilk baking mix,
    such as Bisquick

1. Preheat the oven to 300°F. Grease a 13 × 9-inch baking pan.

2. Beat the eggs in a large bowl. Add the sugar, melted butter, cottage cheese, sour cream, Parmesan cheese, and baking mix. Beat well.

3. Pour the mixture into the prepared baking pan and bake for 30 minutes.

4. Raise the oven temperature to 325°F and continue baking until the top is golden brown, 30 minutes.

5. Serve warm or at room temperature, cut into small squares.

judy kolodkin's lox quiche

from Samra Robbins

Samra's kitchen bible is "... *And It Was Good*," a cookbook put out by the Ahavath Achim Sisterhood of Atlanta. (The fact that she figures promi-nently in the book—as do her mother, Claire Smolen, and her aunt, Joan Kalish, with cameos by her cousin Lisa Comei, who all appear in these pages as well—has nothing to do with it, I'm sure.) This wonderful quiche from the daughter of a Temple member has become a brunch favorite with the frequent guests at Samra and Ronald's Savannah home, which Ronald lovingly refers to as the Robbins Marriott. I have had equal success making it with smoked salmon.

SERVES 8 TO 10   **D**

FOR THE CRUST

1 cup all-purpose flour

¹/₄ teaspoon salt

8 tablespoons (1 stick) cold unsalted butter,
    cut into small even pieces

¹/₂ cup small-curd cottage cheese

FOR THE FILLING

8 ounces Swiss cheese, shredded (2 cups)

4 ounces lox, finely chopped

1 tablespoon all-purpose flour

4 large eggs

2 cups half-and-half

2 tablespoons dry sherry

¹/₂ teaspoon kosher (coarse) salt

¹/₄ teaspoon ground nutmeg

2 tablespoons butter, melted and cooled

1. Prepare the dough: Stir the flour and salt together in a bowl. Using a pastry cutter or your fingers, cut the butter into the flour until the mixture resembles coarse meal. (You can also do this in a food processor.) Add the cottage cheese and blend

it in with your fingers (or in the processor) until the mixture forms a dough. Wrap the dough in plastic wrap and refrigerate it for 2 hours.

2. Roll out the dough on a well-floured surface to form a 12-inch round. Carefully fit it into a 9½- or 10-inch deep-dish pie plate. Turn the excess dough under and crimp the edge, using your thumb and forefinger.

3. Preheat the oven to 425°F.

4. Combine the Swiss cheese and the lox pieces in a medium-size bowl. Add the flour and toss to combine well.

5. Whisk the eggs in a large bowl. Add the half-and-half, sherry, salt, and nutmeg, and whisk to combine well. Stir in the Swiss cheese mixture, followed by the melted butter.

6. Pour the mixture into the pie crust and bake for 15 minutes. Then reduce the temperature to 350°F and continue baking until a knife inserted in the center comes out clean, 30 to 40 minutes.

7. Cut the quiche into wedges and serve hot or at room temperature.

cheese blintzes

from Sally Bower

Delicious year-round, cheese blintzes are traditionally served on Shavuot (see page 430), the holiday that commemorates the giving of the Torah on Mount Sinai, the wheat harvest, and the ripening of fruit. We eat dairy products because of the abundance of milk at this time as well as the association of the Torah with "milk and honey." Uncle Lou loved to top Aunt Sally's blintzes with a big dollop of sour cream. You can also serve them with fresh raspberry sauce (recipe follows). **MAKES 30 BLINTZES** **D**

FOR THE FILLING

1 package (8 ounces) cream cheese,
*   at room temperature*
2 large eggs, at room temperature
6 tablespoons sugar
2 teaspoons grated lemon zest
2 packages (8 ounces each) farmer cheese
2 cups cottage cheese

Not-Your-Store-Bought Potato Blintzes
*   (page 275, prepared through Step 2)*
Butter, vegetable oil, margarine, and/or
*   solid vegetable shortening, for cooking*

Samra (second from right) with new hubby, Ronald (left), Aunt Shirley, Linda (Ronald's sister), and Uncle Al on their way to a "hot" party at Atlanta's Progressive Club, 1969.

1. Prepare the filling: Place the cream cheese in the bowl of an electric mixer fitted with the paddle, and beat on medium speed until it is fluffy, about 30 seconds. Add the eggs, sugar, and lemon zest, and continue beating just until combined, 30 seconds more. Then beat in the farmer cheese. Stir in the cottage cheese and combine thoroughly.

2. To assemble the blintzes, place about 2 tablespoons of the filling on the lower half of the fried side of each crêpe. Roll the crêpe around the filling, folding the ends in as you go.

3. The blintzes can either be fried or baked. *To fry the blintzes*, melt about 1^1/$_2$ teaspoons

butter and 1^1/$_2$ teaspoons oil in a large skillet over medium-high heat. Add as many blintzes as will fit, seam side down, and fry them on all sides until golden brown and crispy, about 4 minutes altogether. Drain the blintzes on paper towels. Repeat with the remaining blintzes.

To bake the blintzes, preheat the oven to 375°F. Grease a nonreactive baking pan (a 13 × 9-inch pan will hold about 15) with

Aunt Sally with Marilyn, 1935. Marilyn was the first darling of the Rabinowitz clan—Mama and Papa's first grandchild, a title she held for nine years, until cousin Carole came along.

the great blintz experiment

Aunt Sally's recipe ended with "Fry or bake"—but how? I polled some family members, and as with so many other recipes, people expressed strongly held but contradictory opinions. Feeling like Christopher Kimball, the host of PBS's *America's Test Kitchen,* I embarked on The Great Blintz Experiment and fried the blintzes both before and after freezing, at medium-low, medium, and medium-high heat, covered and uncovered, in butter and in a combination of butter and oil.

I found that frying them, unfrozen, at medium-high heat, uncovered, in a butter/oil combination yielded the best results: blintzes that were crisp and golden on the outside with a piping hot, seductively oozy filling. This takes about 4 minutes, turning the blintzes to brown on all sides. There was no significant difference in using previously frozen (properly wrapped) thawed blintzes instead of never-frozen blintzes.

To fry frozen blintzes, I obtained the best results using medium heat with a covered pan in order to cook the filling thoroughly without burning the crust. It helps that my saucepan covers are glass, so I can see what's going on. This took 8 minutes. While these blintzes were more than satisfactory—no complaints from my husband or my neighbors, who just love it when I work in the "lab"—I still preferred the unfrozen blintzes, which seemed to be crisper.

When baked, there was no discernible difference between the frozen and unfrozen blintzes, except for the baking time.

The foregoing is my personal opinion and not necessarily that of the other members of the Rabinowitz clan, their agents, or affiliates.

butter, margarine, or shortening. Place the blintzes, seam side down, in the prepared baking pan and dot with more butter, margarine, or shortening. Bake until golden brown, about 40 minutes. Serve immediately.

Note: The assembled blintzes can be frozen for up to 1 month: Arrange them in a single layer on a baking sheet, cover with aluminum foil, and freeze. When they are frozen solid, transfer the blintzes to resealable freezer bags so you can later retrieve as many as you like. Fry the blintzes thawed (see Step 3) or if frozen, over medium heat, covered, for about 8 minutes. Or bake the frozen blintzes as described in Step 3, extending the time to 50 to 60 minutes.

raspberry sauce

from Joan Kalish

❛ ❛ ❛

1 package (10 ounces) unsweetened
    frozen raspberries, thawed
1/4 cup sugar, or to taste
1 tablespoon cornstarch
1 teaspoon grated lemon zest

Combine the raspberries, sugar, cornstarch, and lemon zest in a medium-size saucepan. Stir in 1/4 cup water, place over medium heat, and cook until the sauce thickens, about 1 minute. Remove from the heat and keep warm.

apple blintzes

from Stu Kancigor

Yes, you read right. I credit my son Stu for this dish. He brought home a recipe for French Apple Pancakes from his seventh-grade cooking class, and when he said they looked like "fat blintzes," a light bulb went on over my head. **MAKES 16**　　　　D

Butter, for greasing the baking pan

FOR THE FILLING
3 cups shredded peeled apples
    (about 5 medium-size apples)
3/4 cup sugar
1 teaspoon ground cinnamon

FOR THE BATTER
3 large eggs
1 tablespoon sugar
1 1/2 teaspoons vegetable oil
1/3 cup all-purpose flour
1/2 teaspoon salt
3/4 cup milk

Solid vegetable shortening or vegetable oil,
    for greasing the skillet

FOR THE TOPPING
4 tablespoons (1/2 stick) unsalted butter,
    melted
Cinnamon-sugar (see Note, page 478),
    for garnish

1. Preheat the oven to 400°F. Butter a 13 × 9-inch baking pan, and set it aside.

2. Prepare the filling: Mix the apples, sugar, and cinnamon together in a medium-size bowl, and set it aside.

3. Prepare the batter: Combine all the batter ingredients in a blender and process until smooth.

4. Lightly grease a 6-inch skillet and heat it over medium-high heat. When the skillet is hot, pour in just 2 tablespoons of the batter, holding the skillet off the heat momentarily as you quickly tilt the pan to spread the batter out. Cook until set—it takes only a few seconds—and then turn and fry on the other side for just a moment, just to set it. Slip the crêpe onto a plate or a paper towel. Repeat until all the batter is used, sandwiching the finished crêpes between sheets of waxed paper or paper towels to keep them separated. (You will probably need to grease the pan only after every third or fourth crêpe, especially if using a nonstick skillet.)

5. To assemble the blintzes, place 2 tablespoons of the filling on the bottom third of each blintz. Roll them up, tucking the sides in as you go.

6. Place the blintzes, seam side down, in the prepared baking pan. Drizzle the melted butter over them, and sprinkle with cinnamon-sugar. Bake until golden brown, about 15 minutes. Serve immediately.

cheese blintz soufflé

from Hilda Robbins

My daughter-in-law Shelly, a fast study, helps with the blintz assembly line, 1989. Is it just me, or do you also find it hysterical that she is wearing my Weight Watchers apron?

Aunt Hilda's cheese blintz soufflé made frequent appearances at her fabulous brunches. Okay, strictly speaking, it's not a true soufflé, that tour de force of the '50s housewife, an airy creation involving whipping the egg yolks and whites separately before baking and then praying no one slams a door. Here you can use store-bought cheese blintzes, or your own homemade, and doctor them up with a rich soufflé-*like* topping that does rise and fall somewhat in homage to its namesake. This popular dish from that long-gone era still never fails to please, no matter what you call it. **SERVES 12** D

Ma Hilda was not only our grandmother and best friend but our heart and soul. From her we all learned never to quit, because, as we all know, Ma never did. We will live each day loving and remembering Ma for her strong and caring heart, her tough spirit, and her kind-hearted mind. —ELISSA BISHINS KOMISHOCK, RANDI BISHINS, AND CHAD ROBBINS

8 tablespoons (1 stick) butter, melted

6 large eggs

³/₄ cup sugar

2 cups sour cream

2 tablespoons frozen orange juice
   concentrate

1 tablespoon pure vanilla extract

1¹/₂ teaspoons pure orange extract

12 frozen cheese blintzes, store-bought or
   homemade (page 355)

Ground cinnamon

1. Preheat the oven to 350°F.

2. Pour the melted butter into a 13 × 9-inch baking pan and spread it out to coat the bottom and sides.

3. Combine the eggs, sugar, sour cream, orange juice concentrate, and vanilla and orange extracts in a blender and process until smooth. Stir in the excess melted butter from the baking pan.

4. Arrange the blintzes in the prepared pan and sprinkle them liberally with cinnamon. Then pour the egg batter over the blintzes. Bake until puffy and browned, about 45 minutes. Serve immediately.

oat pancakes

from Laura Seligman

aura and hubby Jeremy met at a pantomime workshop in what they refer to as their "nuts and oats" days, the glorious (though not particularly stylish) '70s, when they embraced vegetarianism and a healthy lifestyle. Jeremy's sideburns are long gone and Laura now sports a stylish short do, but this recipe from that era is still a favorite. Serve some maple syrup alongside. **MAKES 8** D

1 cup oat bran, or 1¹/₄ cups rolled oats,
   whirled to a powder in a blender

1 cup all-purpose flour

1 tablespoon sugar

2 teaspoons baking soda

1¹/₂ cups plain yogurt

¹/₂ cup mashed ripe banana (1 medium-size
   banana)

2 large eggs, or whites of 4 large eggs

2 teaspoons pure vanilla extract

2 tablespoons butter or margarine

Pecan halves, for garnish

1. Combine the oat bran, flour, sugar, and baking soda in a large bowl. Stir well.

2. Whisk the yogurt, banana, eggs, and vanilla together in another bowl. Add the yogurt mixture to the flour mixture and combine well. The batter will be thick.

3. Melt the butter in a large skillet, and when the foam subsides, drop in the batter by the scant ¹/₄ cup. Spread the batter

with the back of a spoon to about 4 inches in diameter, and cook until light brown on both sides, about 2 minutes per side. The pancakes will puff up.

4. Garnish with the pecans and serve immediately, or keep warm in a preheated 200°F oven for up to 15 minutes.

Laura and Jeremy Seligman in their "nuts and oats" days. Oh, the '70s were good to them!

german pancake

from Stu Kancigor, Carole Orlow

The most amazing thing about this recipe, which comes from my son Stu's junior high school cooking class, is that I knew where to find it. (Nothing wrong with my long-term memory!) The second most amazing thing is that they let kids handle pans in a 450°F oven, but that was before people dreamed of suing McDonald's for burning themselves with hot coffee. Cousin Carole submitted the

> *When I was growing up, my mother worked, and after school my sister and I would go to Mama Hinda and Papa Harry's house. Since they lived upstairs from Aunt Lil and Uncle Jan, Aunt Lil was always available if I had a problem. When I was in sixth grade, my teacher threatened to flunk me in sewing. I had lost my apron, and she told me I wouldn't graduate. Aunt Lil made me an apron in one hour and I passed. Without Aunt Lil I never would have made it out of sixth grade!* —CAROLE ORLOW

same recipe, which her German in-laws have always enjoyed. The pancake is puffy and golden with a custard-like center, and so easy to make that there's no need to wait for company. But I'd leave handling the pan to the adults. **SERVES 6 TO 8** **D**

4 large eggs
¹/₂ cup whole milk
2 tablespoons sugar
6 tablespoons all-purpose flour
4 tablespoons (¹/₂ stick) butter or margarine
Cinnamon-sugar (see Note, page 478) or confectioners' sugar, for garnish

1. Place a heavy ovenproof skillet or a 9-inch round cake pan in the oven, and preheat the oven to 450°F.

2. Place the eggs, milk, sugar, and flour in a blender, and process until smooth.

3. When the oven has reached 450°F, carefully place the butter in the hot skillet and let it melt until it is hot and sizzling. Then

carefully pour the egg mixture into the skillet. Reduce the oven temperature to 425°F, and bake for 8 minutes. Then reduce the temperature to 375°F and bake until set, 7 minutes more. The edges of the pancake will be puffy and brown.

4. Remove the pancake from the oven, sprinkle it with cinnamon-sugar or confectioners' sugar, and serve immediately.

trude's german apple-cinnamon pancakes

from Peter Epstein

After many attempts to duplicate his mother's delicious German specialty, Peter nailed these crispy wonders that look and crunch like latkes. Peter prefers firm, tart apples such as Granny Smith for this dish. Be sure to get the oil really hot and fry the pancakes quickly on each side. **MAKES 24** **P**

2 large eggs
¹/₄ cup sugar
2 teaspoons ground cinnamon
¹/₂ teaspoon kosher (coarse) salt
1 teaspoon baking powder
1 teaspoon pure vanilla extract
¹/₂ cup orange juice
³/₄ cup all-purpose flour
3 cups chopped peeled tart apples
    (about 6 medium-size apples; see Note)
Vegetable oil, for frying
Cinnamon-sugar (see Note, page 478),
    for garnish

1. Beat the eggs with an electric mixer on high speed until light and lemon-colored, about 2 minutes. Reduce the speed to medium-high and blend in the sugar, cinnamon, salt, baking powder, and vanilla. Beat in the orange juice. Then beat in the flour until blended. Stir in the apples.

2. Pour oil to a depth of about ¹/₂ inch in a large skillet, and heat it over medium-high heat until very hot but not smoking. Drop the batter, about 2 tablespoons at a time, into the hot oil. Fry until golden, about 2 minutes for the first side, 1 minute for the second side. Do not crowd the skillet, and be sure the oil is very hot when you add the batter so the pancakes don't get soggy.

3. Sprinkle cinnamon-sugar over the pancakes and serve immediately, or keep them warm in a preheated 200°F oven for up to 15 minutes.

Note: Peter likes to slice the apples thin and then chop them.

Trude and Felix, Palm Springs, about 1960.

eric silverberg's caramel french toast casserole

from Shelly Kancigor

A s with so many dishes, the origins of French toast, which some say is neither French nor toast, are buried in legend. As one story goes, in 1724 Joseph French, the owner of a roadside tavern near Albany, New York, named the dish after himself. Others claim the dish has at least Belgian, if not French, roots. But what's in a name? This version is nice for brunch because it is prepared the night before. After baking, you flip it over to reveal the luscious, gooey, oozy caramel topping. Serve it warm to keep the lava flowing. **SERVES 8**　　　　　**D**

5 tablespoons butter, plus extra for
　　greasing the pan

1 cup (packed) light or dark brown sugar

2 tablespoons light corn syrup

2 tablespoons molasses

1 loaf (1 pound) challah, brioche,
　　or other rich bread, thickly sliced

5 large eggs

1¹/₂ cups whole milk

2 teaspoons pure vanilla extract

1. Butter a 13 × 9-inch baking pan.
2. Combine the butter, brown sugar, corn syrup, and molasses in a medium-size saucepan over medium heat, and heat until bubbly. Pour the mixture into the prepared baking pan. Arrange the bread slices over the syrupy mixture in two layers, breaking the bread apart if necessary to fill all the spaces. (You may not need to use all of the bread.)

3. Beat the eggs, milk, and vanilla together in a bowl, and pour the mixture over the bread. Cover the pan with plastic wrap and refrigerate overnight.

4. When you are ready to bake the casserole, preheat the oven to 350°F.

5. Bake, uncovered, until puffy and golden brown, about 45 minutes. (When it is removed from the oven, the top will settle down.)

6. To serve, loosen the sides well with a spatula or knife, invert a large platter over the baking dish, and flip the two over together. The top, which was the bottom, will be caramelized. Spoon any hot caramel remaining in the pan over the casserole, and serve immediately. The casserole can be kept in a preheated 200°F oven for up to 15 minutes before serving.

other brunch ideas

● ◗ ●

Check out the Appetizers chapter for Smoked Salmon Cheesecake (page 8) or Salmon Mouse (page 58). Cut larger squares of the Chiles Rellenos Quiche (page 32), Spinach and Cheese Frittata (page 33), Eggplant Frittata (page 34), or Greek Spinach Pie (page 31).

apple and cheese-stuffed french toast

from Arlyne Choset

Every new bride in our family knows the rule: You get engaged, you get a recipe from the *machatunim* for my cookbook. No sooner had Ian plunked that ring on cousin Heather's finger than she extracted this awesome brunch recipe from his mother. (You want something done? Ask Heather!) Her French toast is stuffed with cream cheese and jam and served on a bed of cinnamony apples. It's a good thing I had to get into that black dress for Heather's wedding or I would have eaten the whole thing! **SERVES 8**   **D**

1¹/₂ tablespoons fresh lemon juice

1¹/₂ tablespoons cornstarch

8 tablespoons (1 stick) butter, plus extra for greasing the baking pan

³/₄ cup (packed) light brown sugar

1 teaspoon ground cinnamon

¹/₄ teaspoon kosher (coarse) salt

4 large green apples, such as Granny Smiths, peeled, cored, and sliced

6 ounces cream cheese, at room temperature

1 loaf (1 pound) challah, thickly sliced (see Note)

About ¹/₂ cup raspberry or apricot jam

6 large eggs

³/₄ cup whole milk

1 cup half-and-half

1 tablespoon pure vanilla extract

Cinnamon-sugar (see Note, page 478), for sprinkling

1. Combine the lemon juice and cornstarch in a small bowl, stir well, and set aside.

2. Melt the butter in a large skillet over medium heat. Add the brown sugar, cinnamon, and salt, and stir until the sugar has dissolved. Add the apples and cook, turning them constantly, until they are beginning to soften, about 4 minutes. Stir in the lemon juice mixture and cook until thickened, about 30 seconds more. Set the skillet aside.

3. Spread the cream cheese over the challah slices, and set aside.

4. Butter a 13 × 9-inch baking pan.

5. When the apples have cooled, arrange them evenly in the prepared baking pan. Cover with half of the challah slices, cream cheese side up; if necessary, cut or tear the challah to fill all the spaces. Spread the jam evenly over the challah. Cover with the remaining challah slices, cream cheese side down, again cutting or tearing the challah as needed to fill all the spaces.

6. Whisk the eggs, milk, half-and-half, and vanilla in a bowl. Pour this

Arlyne Choset with her new daughter-in-law Heather, Hanukkah 2005.

mixture over the challah. Cover with plastic wrap and refrigerate overnight.

7. When you are ready to bake the French toast, preheat the oven to 350°F.

8. Sprinkle the casserole with cinnamon-sugar and bake, covered, for 40 minutes. Uncover and continue baking until it is puffy and golden, about 20 minutes more. Allow it to rest for 5 minutes. Then cut the French toast into squares, and serve.

Note: If you freeze the challah slices for an hour first, it will be easier to spread the cream cheese without squishing the bread flat.

easy cream cheese danishes

from Michelle and Ariel Wolf

ousin Michelle and (as of this writing) nine-year-old daughter Ariel like to bake these easy cheese Danishes together, as a surprise for daddy Eric and brother Justin. Ariel loves to bake, but (and I'm not sure how she got into our family) only as long as it's not chocolate. Ariel was Aunt Estelle's first great-grandchild. Ironically, after sewing for me and cousin Joyce, both my mother and Aunt Estelle, with all their talent, had seven grandsons between them. Then came a girl, Ariel, who used to call Aunt Estelle "Grandma Cupcake." **MAKES 8 LARGE OR 24 SMALL PASTRIES** D

Vegetable cooking spray, for greasing the pan

2 packages (8 ounces each) refrigerated crescent rolls

2 packages (8 ounces each) cream cheese, at room temperature

2 large eggs, separated, at room temperature

³/₄ cup sugar

1 teaspoon pure vanilla extract

1 teaspoon fresh lemon juice

Confectioners' sugar

1. Preheat the oven to 350°F. Grease a 13 × 9-inch baking pan.

2. Separate one package of the crescent rolls into 8 triangles, and arrange them, without letting them touch, in the prepared baking pan.

3. Blend the cream cheese, egg yolks, sugar, vanilla, and lemon juice with an electric mixer on medium speed, scraping the bowl several times, until smooth and creamy, about 1¹/₂ minutes. Spoon the mixture onto each triangle, dividing it evenly.

4. Separate the remaining package of crescent rolls and place 1 triangle over each filled triangle. Press the edges together to seal

Ariel, grandma Joyce, mom Michelle on an American Girl outing (read shopping spree), 2005.

in the filling. Whisk the egg whites until foamy, and brush egg white over each triangle.

5. Bake on the center oven rack until golden brown, 18 to 22 minutes. Transfer the Danishes to a wire rack and let them cool.

6. Dust the pastries with confectioners' sugar just before serving. Serve whole, or cut into thirds for mini Danish.

mrs. quast's applesauce muffins

from Jason Kancigor

When my grandson Jason was in kindergarten, I had the pleasure of assisting in his class for a few days when I was visiting. I helped the kids cut out magazine pictures of things beginning with the letter "L." His teacher, Mrs. Quast, sent me a certificate of appreciation along with her family recipe for applesauce muffins. They are sweet and welcoming, just like Mrs. Quast herself, with a moist, cakey texture. And so easy even a kindergartener can make them. Leave it to Mrs. Quast to know just what kids love. **MAKES 12** **D**

FOR THE MUFFINS

2 cups baking mix, such as Bisquick
$^1/_2$ cup sugar
1 teaspoon ground cinnamon
$^1/_2$ cup milk
$^1/_2$ cup unsweetened applesauce
2 tablespoons vegetable oil
1 large egg

FOR THE TOPPING

4 tablespoons ($^1/_2$ stick) unsalted butter
$^1/_3$ cup sugar
1 teaspoon ground cinnamon

1. Preheat the oven to 375°F. Fill 12 muffin cups with paper liners.

2. Mix all the muffin ingredients together in a bowl, and fill the cups two-thirds full with the batter. Bake on the center oven rack until a cake tester inserted in the center comes out dry, 12 minutes. Let the muffins cool completely in the pan set on a wire rack.

3. Prepare the topping: Melt the butter in a saucepan over medium heat, and pour it into a flat dish. Mix the sugar and cinnamon in another flat dish. Dip the muffin tops in the butter, then in the cinnamon-sugar.

4. The glazed muffins are best eaten the day they're made.

Even as a kindergartner, Jason liked to help with the baking.

banana chocolate chip muffins

from Suzy Orlow Solomonic

This is a simple recipe. Suzy's kids (Danielle, Jordan, and Michael) love to mash the bananas and help measure and pour the ingredients, and are very happy to eat the results of their labors, especially because they made them. **MAKES 12 STANDARD MUFFINS OR 24 MINI MUFFINS** [D]

3 very ripe medium-size bananas, mashed (1¹/₂ cups)

1¹/₂ cups all-purpose flour

¹/₂ cup sugar

1 large egg

4 tablespoons (¹/₂ stick) unsalted butter, melted

1 teaspoon baking soda

¹/₂ teaspoon pure vanilla extract

1 cup (6 ounces) chocolate chips

1. Preheat the oven to 375°F. Fill 12 muffin cups or 24 mini muffin cups with paper liners.

2. Combine the mashed bananas, flour, sugar, egg, melted butter, baking soda, and vanilla in a large bowl and mix thoroughly. Stir in the chocolate chips.

3. Spoon the batter into the cups, filling them about two-thirds full. Bake on the center oven rack until the muffins are brown and a cake tester comes out clean, about 25 minutes for standard muffins, 15 minutes for mini muffins. Let the muffins cool in the pan on a wire rack.

apricot pineapple conserve

from Sally Bower

A conserve is a thick mixture of fruits, nuts, and sugar that is used as a spread. Take away the nuts and you have preserves. Omit the nuts and cut the fruit into smaller pieces, and you have jam. Cook the jam for a shorter time and you have a glorious, fruity sauce with a punch of citrus, begging to be poured over ice cream or cake.

I had never made conserve (or jam or preserves, for that matter) before I tried Aunt Sally's recipe. It became such a favorite that I included it in my Rosh Hashanah cooking classes as a sauce for my mother's Nova Scotia Honey Orange Sponge Cake (page 413). Talk about easy! I would begin the class by asking for a show of hands: "How many of you have never made jam?" followed by "How many of you can open a can?" **MAKES ABOUT 2 PINTS** [P]

1 pound dried apricots, halved
  (cut larger ones in thirds)
1 can (20 ounces) crushed pineapple,
  undrained
3¹/₂ cups sugar
Grated zest of 1 orange
1 cup orange juice
¹/₂ teaspoon salt
³/₄ cup broken walnuts (optional)

1. Place the apricots in a medium-size saucepan, add water to barely cover, and bring to a boil. Boil until almost all the water has evaporated, 8 to 10 minutes.

2. Stir in the pineapple, sugar, orange zest, orange juice, and salt, and bring to a boil. Then reduce the heat to a steady, but not hard, boil and cook, stirring often, until there is almost no free liquid when a spoonful is placed on a saucer, about 50 minutes. As the liquid evaporates, you will need to stir more often to make sure the mixture does not scorch. Stir in the walnuts, if using, during the last 5 minutes of cooking.

3. Spoon the conserve into sterile canning jars and seal according to the manufacturer's directions. Or allow to cool to room temperature, and spoon it into clean glass jars, filling them three-fourths full. Freeze.

Variation: For a tasty topping for ice cream or cake, snip the apricots to the size of raisins. Proceed as described in Steps 1 and 2, but stop cooking when the apricot-pineapple mixture is fairly loose (looser than you would like to serve it, as it will congeal as it cools), about 30 minutes. Omit the nuts. Serve warm over cake or ice cream.

to make butter

· · ● · ·

This is from the first Jewish cookbook in America, *Mrs. Esther Levy's Jewish Cookery Book,* published in Philadelphia in 1871. It has everything a Jewish wife needed to know to run her household.

"In summertime skim the milk before the sun has heated the dairy; at this season it should stand, for butter, twenty-four hours without skimming, and forty-eight hours in winter; deposit the cream in a very cold cellar. If you cannot churn daily, change the cream into fresh scalded pots, but never omit churning twice a week. Keep the churn in the air, and if not a barrel one, set in a tub of water two feet deep, which will make the butter firm. When the butter is come, pour off the buttermilk and put the butter into a fresh scalded pan or tube which have been in cold water. Pour water on it, and let it lie to get hard before you work it. Then change the water and beat the butter with flat boards, so that not a particle of the buttermilk will remain; change the water until it ceases to become colored by the milk; then work some salt into the butter and make it into forms; put them into earthenware pans, filled with water, and cover them. You will then have very nice cool butter in the warmest weather."

under the chuppah

cakes

It's 1962: My mother resumes her singing career, Marilyn Monroe "allegedly" commits suicide, and presifted flour becomes widely available. (Maybe Marilyn never got the memo.)

Where once our *tantas* and *bubbes* had to sift flour before using, comes the revolution and now that laborious step is no longer necessary. A pamphlet I found in my mother's recipe pile, dated 1962, instructed housewives that the proper way to measure the new *presifted* flour is to stir, then spoon the flour lightly into a measuring cup and level it off. But remember that road paved with good intentions?

"For Mama Hinda and the aunties, baking a cake was second nature, in short, well . . . a piece of cake!"

Every Jewish parent's dream—to stand under the chuppah (canopy), symbol of a Jewish home, and see their children wed. Who's who on page 613.

Alas, one generation's revolution is another's distant memory, and before long, even stirring and spooning lightly became too burdensome for some, and people started scooping that measuring cup right into that sack of compacted (albeit presifted) flour before leveling it off—a technique bakers call "dip and sweep"—adding as much as 20 percent more flour than the recipe calls for. Before long the dippers and sweepers had taken over. You'd see them on TV. Recipes were written just for them, although purists still caution: To measure flour, stir, then spoon lightly into a measuring cup and level it off. The recipes in this book were tested using this method. Dip and sweep at your peril. (To add to the confusion, some recipes ask you to sift flour before measuring for further aeration. "One cup sifted flour" means you sift first and then measure. "One cup flour, sifted" means you measure and then sift.)

For Mama Hinda and the aunties, baking a cake was second nature, in short, well . . . a piece of cake! Typical for their era, they used 13 × 9-inch baking pans, standard issue for brides of the 1930s and '40s. Cakes were frosted and served right from the pan, or one could line the pan with waxed paper for removal before frosting. Today parchment paper is preferred, as experts advise us that waxed paper may burn. (This never stopped them, however. They didn't worry about cutting meat on wooden chopping boards

or tasting frosting containing raw eggs either. It must have been a less phobic era.)

In 1950 Nordic Ware released the first Bundt pan, which by the '60s had become the top-selling cake pan in the U.S. Mama Hinda never owned one, but the homespun 13 × 9-inch cakes offered here may be baked in a Bundt pan for a more festive appearance. Because this pan is deeper, they will take a bit longer to bake, however. One word of caution: If your Bundt pan has a dark nonstick lining, some bakers suggest lowering the baking temperature by 25 degrees.

Mama's Maple Walnut Cake is one of the oldest recipes in this chapter, handed down from mother to daughters. To this day the aroma of walnuts toasting signals that giddy anticipation of "company's coming!" as that cake was my mother's usual dessert for guests.

Aunt Sally's claim to fame was her Red, White, and Blue Cake, her tricolored marble beauty. She might serve her orange cake as well, but she'd always unfurl the Red, White, and Blue.

While Aunt Irene was most renowned for her bakery cookies, her exquisite, many-layered Budapest Coffee Cake and dense, dark traditional Rosh Hashanah Honey Cake were always expected at family gatherings.

Aunt Estelle was a sucker for chocolate. We especially adore her Chocolate

Top: My mother-in-law, Edie, with Stu and Brad, early '70s. Bottom: Frosting my in-laws' 35th anniversary cake, 1971.

baking: a piece of cake

In November 2001 *Gourmet* magazine ran a story about an angel food cake experiment. Sixty professional bakers were given the same recipe. When they brought in their cakes, no two were alike! Apparently, more than a measuring anomaly was going on here. For starters, no two ovens work quite the same way. A professional baker I interviewed told me that the average home oven is off by 25 degrees. Even a calibrated oven has hotter and cooler spots and may work differently from day to day. Therefore consider the baking times as suggestions, and it's best to rely on the visual cues and tests for doneness given.

If measuring flour is an inexact science, imagine how different people might whip egg whites differently! So many factors affect baking: altitude, humidity, temperature, quality of ingredients, equipment. I used a heavy-duty KitchenAid mixer to test these recipes. You may have another. The moral of the story? Individual (though still scrumptious) results may vary.

Here are some additional pointers to keep in mind:

■ Read through the entire recipe and measure out all your ingredients before beginning to bake.

■ Check the expiration dates of ingredients such as baking powder, baking soda, and yeast. When in doubt, throw it out.

■ Be sure all ingredients that are marked at room temperature actually are at room temperature. This is especially true for cheesecakes.

■ Separate eggs while they are cold. Then cover them with plastic wrap and allow them to come to room temperature.

■ For proper whipping of egg whites, be sure the bowl and beaters are spotlessly clean and that not even a speck of yolk gets into the whites. Drop each white separately into a small bowl before pouring it in with the others, so that if one yolk breaks, you don't have to start over.

That being said, baking is not quite the delicate chemistry experiment requiring a Ph.D that some hold it out to be, so don't be intimidated. The *Gourmet* article ended with some bakers' tips from the experts. The last, deemed the most important discovery, was that there is no one right way to obtain good results— so relax!

Chocolate Chip Cake, a rich sour cream cake studded with chips and smothered in Mocha Frosting, and her unusual Chocolate Cream Cheese Cake in which the creamy frosting is made from part of the batter.

But can you ever have enough chocolate? Cousin Samra supplied her grandmother's irresistible signature chocolate cake . . . her secret: The batter is refrigerated overnight before baking. Not to be outdone, Samra's mom Claire parted with both her decadent Sour Cream Chocolate Cake and her show-stopper of a White Chocolate Layer Cake.

Heirloom recipes like Mama Hinda's Bitter Almond Cake and Tanta Esther Gittel's Husband's Second Wife Lena's Nut Cake got a twenty-first century makeover. You'll find classics here like Boston Cream Pie and sliced rolled cakes as pretty to look at as they are yummy to eat. Our extended family contributed coffee cakes, sponge cakes, apple cakes, cheesecakes galore, and so many more—so sit yourself down and slice yourself the kindest cut of all.

sour cream chocolate cake

from Claire Smolen

This is your little black dress of cakes—always reliable, never goes out of style, equally appropriate for informal occasions with a simple sprinkling of confectioners' sugar or all dolled up for dressier affairs with a to-die-for chocolate buttercream frosting. Claire's stylish beauty has a delicate, soft crumb—an incredible texture. **SERVES 10 TO 12** **D**

Butter or unflavored vegetable cooking spray, for greasing the pan(s)

Parchment paper, if using two cake pans

4 ounces unsweetened chocolate

2 cups all-purpose flour, plus extra for dusting the pan(s)

1/2 teaspoon salt

8 tablespoons (1 stick) unsalted butter, at room temperature

2 cups sugar

1 teaspoon pure vanilla extract

2 large eggs, at room temperature

1 cup sour cream, at room temperature

1 1/4 teaspoons baking soda

1 tablespoon cider vinegar

1 cup boiling water

Chocolate Buttercream Frosting (optional; recipe follows)

1. Preheat the oven to 325°F. Grease a 10-inch tube pan with removable bottom, a 13 × 9-inch baking pan, or two 9-inch round cake pans. If using two pans, line them with parchment paper and grease again. Dust the pan(s) with flour and tap out the excess.

2. Melt the chocolate in the top of a double boiler set over simmering water, and set it aside to cool.

3. Sift the flour and salt together into a bowl. Set it aside.

4. Cream the butter and sugar with an electric mixer on medium speed, scraping the bowl several times, until light and fluffy, about 3 minutes. Add the cooled chocolate and the vanilla, and continue beating until smooth, about 2 minutes. Add the eggs, one at a time, beating well after each addition. Raise the speed to high and beat for 2 to 3 minutes to emulsify the mix. Reduce the speed to low and add the flour mixture in three additions, alternating with the sour cream in two additions, beginning and ending with the flour. Scrape the bowl after each addition and beat just until blended.

5. Dissolve the baking soda in the vinegar in a small dish, and add this to the batter. Mix well on low speed until blended. Slowly add the boiling water and continue beating until thoroughly combined, about 1 1/2 minutes.

6. Pour the batter into the prepared pan(s) and bake on the center oven rack until a cake tester inserted in the center comes out slightly moist, about 55 minutes for the tube pan, 45 minutes for the 13 × 9-inch pan, or 30 to 40 minutes for the 9-inch round cake pans.

7. Let the cake(s) cool in the pan(s) set on a wire rack for 10 minutes for the tube

general instructions for baking a cake
from Rita Miller

● ● ●

This was Rita's contribution to her B'nai B'rith cookbook over thirty years ago. David is now a daddy himself and loves to cook, even with little Max and Miles underfoot. As they say, what goes around comes around.

1. Light oven. Get out ingredients and utensils. Remove blocks and toys from table. Grease pan, crack nuts.

2. Measure flour; remove David's hands from flour, wash flour off him. Remeasure flour. Put flour, baking powder, and salt in sifter. Get dustpan and brush up

pieces of bowl David knocked on floor. Get another bowl.

3. Answer doorbell. Return to kitchen and remove David's hands from bowl. Wash and punish David. Answer phone. Return. Remove nutshells from newly greased bowl. Head for David, who flees, knocking bowl off table.

4. Wash kitchen floor, walls, sink, dishes.

5. Open a can of fruit for dessert.

---

pan, 5 minutes for the round cake pans. *If you used a tube pan*, run a knife around the center tube and the side of the pan, and lift the tube from the outer pan. Gently slide the knife between the bottom of the cake and the pan, and lift the cake off the pan. Return it to the rack to cool completely. *If you used two round cake pans*, turn the layers out and return them to the rack to cool completely. *If you used a 13 × 9-inch pan*, let the cake cool completely in the pan on the rack.

8. Place a sheet of waxed paper under the wire rack. *If you used two round cake pans*, spread some of the frosting over the top of one layer. Top it with the second layer, and cover the top and sides with frosting. Cut the cake into slices, and serve. *If you used the tube pan*, spread the frosting over the top and sides. Cut into slices and serve. *If you used the 13 × 9-inch pan*, spread

the frosting over the top. Cut the cake into squares, and serve.

chocolate buttercream frosting

● ● ●

This thick buttercream is sinfully rich and is made without the usual raw egg. **MAKES 2½ CUPS**　　**D**

8 tablespoons (1 stick) unsalted butter,
   at room temperature
2 cups confectioners' sugar, sifted
3 ounces unsweetened chocolate,
   melted and cooled
1 tablespoon strong brewed coffee
1 teaspoon pure vanilla extract

1. Cream the butter and confectioners' sugar with an electric mixer on medium speed until completely smooth, about 3 minutes.

2. Add the cooled chocolate and continue to beat until smooth, about 1 minute. Lower the speed, add the coffee and vanilla, and mix for 15 seconds. Raise the speed to medium-high and beat until light and fluffy, about 5 minutes.

grandma leah cahn's chocolate cake

from Samra Robbins

The secret to Grandma Leah's moist and fudgy cake—see Samra's comments on the facing page. **SERVES 8 TO 10** **D**

4 ounces unsweetened chocolate, coarsely chopped

2 cups all-purpose flour

2 cups sugar

$^1/_8$ teaspoon salt

8 tablespoons (1 stick) unsalted butter, at room temperature

Unsalted butter or unflavored vegetable cooking spray, for greasing the pan(s)

Parchment paper, if using two cake pans

3 large eggs, at room temperature

1 teaspoon pure vanilla extract

2 teaspoons baking powder

Chocolate Buttercream Frosting (page 373; optional)

1. Combine the chocolate and $1^1/_4$ cups water in a small saucepan, and cook over medium heat, stirring occasionally, until the chocolate has melted. Transfer the mixture to a medium-size bowl and set it aside to cool to room temperature.

Samra's daughter Hillary's pre–Bat Mitzvah Mexican Fiesta, 1991. Left: Samra with cousins Joyce and Leslie. Right: Hillary, Samra, and dad, Ronald.

2. Sift the flour, sugar, and salt together into the bowl of an electric mixer fitted with the paddle attachment. Add the butter and mix on medium speed until it has the consistency of coarse cornmeal, about 2 minutes.

3. Add the cooled chocolate mixture and beat on medium speed, scraping the bowl several times, until the batter is very thick and the chocolate is fully incorporated, 2 to 3 minutes. Cover and refrigerate overnight.

4. When you are ready to bake, preheat the oven to 325°F. Lightly grease a 9-inch tube pan with removable bottom or two 9-inch round cake pans. If you are using the cake pans, line them with parchment paper and grease them again.

5. With an electric mixer on medium speed, add the eggs, one at a time, to the batter, beating well after each addition and scraping the bowl several times. Beat in the vanilla, and then fold in the baking powder.

> *My grandma was always baking and would serve a different dessert every night. Her chocolate cake she thought of as a 'nosh' cake rather than a 'company' cake, and it really needs no frosting, as it is especially moist and fudgy. You can 'glam' it up, though, by baking it in layers and frosting it. Her secret is to put the batter in the refrigerator overnight, although I'm sure the original recipe said 'icebox' . . . it's that old. I remember hearing about their old house in Bishopville, South Carolina, which not only had an icebox but was the first in the neighborhood with indoor plumbing. People used to come by just to see their toilet.*
>
> —SAMRA ROBBINS

6. Scrape the batter into the prepared pan(s) and bake on the center oven rack until the cake springs back when lightly touched, about 1 hour for the tube pan, 35 to 40 minutes for the cake pans. Let the cake(s)

wrap it up!

Cool all cakes thoroughly before storing them. Generally speaking, most cakes taste best the day they are made, but you can store plain cakes, without frosting, under a cake dome, in an airtight plastic container, or wrapped well in plastic wrap at room temperature for 2 or 3 days.

For frosted cakes, press plastic wrap against each cut surface and store under a cake dome at room temperature for a day or two.

Cheesecakes and cakes with perishable fillings and frostings, such as custard or whipped cream, must be refrigerated. Cheesecakes will keep for up to 5 days and filled cakes for up to 3 days.

To freeze a plain cake without frosting, leave the parchment paper on the bottom if you have used it. Wrap the cake in plastic wrap and then in aluminum foil. Place a frosted cake, uncovered, in the freezer just until it's firm. Wrap the chilled cake well in plastic wrap and then in aluminum foil. Well-wrapped frosted or unfrosted cakes can be frozen for 1 to 2 months.

Thaw cakes that need to be refrigerated, loosely wrapped, in the refrigerator. Thaw other cakes in their wrapping at room temperature.

Looking for a flourless chocolate cake? Don't miss cousin Vicki's Too Good to Call Passover Cake Bête Noire on page 573.

cool completely in the pan(s) set on a wire rack.

7. If you plan to frost the cake, place a sheet of waxed paper beneath the wire rack. *If you used a tube pan*, run a knife around the center tube and the sides of the pan, and lift the tube from the outer pan. Gently slide the knife between the bottom of the cake and the pan, and lift the cake off the pan. Set it on the wire rack, and either frost it or serve it plain. *If you used two round cake pans*, carefully remove the layers from the pans. Place one of the layers on the wire rack and spread some of the frosting over the top. Top it with the second layer, and cover the top and sides with frosting.

8. Cut the cake into slices, and serve.

chocolate chocolate chip cake
with mocha frosting

from Estelle Robbins

Coffee and chocolate: a wickedly sinful combination. If you're going to sin, might as well combine your vices! Aunt Estelle got this from yet another customer, and her handwritten equations for doubling and tripling the recipe tell me it must have been a favorite. **SERVES 12 TO 16** **D**

FOR THE CAKE
Butter or unflavored vegetable cooking spray, for greasing the pan
2 cups all-purpose flour, plus extra for dusting the pan
2 teaspoons baking powder
2 teaspoons baking soda
1/4 cup unsweetened cocoa powder
8 tablespoons (1 stick) butter, at room temperature
1 1/4 cups sugar
2 large eggs, at room temperature
2 cups sour cream, at room temperature
2 teaspoons pure vanilla extract
2 cups (12 ounces) semisweet chocolate chips

FOR THE MOCHA FROSTING
8 tablespoons (1 stick) unsalted butter, at room temperature
1/4 cup unsweetened cocoa powder
1 teaspoon instant coffee granules
1 teaspoon pure vanilla extract
1/4 teaspoon salt
1 box (16 ounces) confectioners' sugar, sifted
1/2 cup milk, warmed

1. Preheat the oven to 350°F. Grease a 13 × 9-inch pan, dust it with flour, and tap out the excess.

2. Mix the flour, baking powder, baking soda, and cocoa powder in a bowl, and set it aside.

3. Cream the butter and sugar with an electric mixer on medium speed until light and fluffy, about 2 minutes. Add the eggs, one at a time, beating well and scraping the bowl after each addition. Reduce the speed to low and add the flour mixture in three additions, alternating with the sour cream in two additions, beginning and ending with the flour. Beat in the vanilla. Stir in the chocolate chips.

4. Scrape the batter into the prepared baking pan, and bake on the center oven rack until a cake tester inserted in the center comes out clean, 40 to 45 minutes. Let the cake cool completely in the pan set on a wire rack.

5. Prepare the frosting: Combine the butter, cocoa powder, coffee granules, vanilla, salt, confectioners' sugar, and *all but 1 tablespoon* of the hot milk in a mixer bowl and beat on low speed until well blended. Raise the speed to medium-high and continue to beat, adding the remaining 1 tablespoon milk if necessary, until the frosting has a spreading consistency.

6. Spread the frosting over the cake (an offset spatula is perfect for this). Cut into squares and serve.

a grain of salt

● ◗ ●

I follow cookbook author Rose Levy Beranbaum's advice (she writes bibles, after all) and use fine sea salt, rather than kosher salt, in baking. Because kosher salt is coarse, it dissolves more slowly and is hard to sift. Noniodized table salt is second best.

marilyn schnee's chocolate chip ripple

from Bonnie Robbins

This is a variation of the Sock-It-To-Me cake that was all the rage in the '60s and '70s, when even the most inexperienced of bakers could take a cake mix and "doctor it up." These cakes are foolproof and ever so moist. Use any flavor cake mix and pudding for your own combination. **SERVES 12**   **D**

Vegetable oil or unflavored vegetable cooking spray, for greasing the pan
All-purpose flour, for dusting the pan

FOR THE FILLING
3 tablespoons instant cocoa powder
3 tablespoons sugar
1 cup (6 ounces) semisweet chocolate chips

FOR THE CAKE
1 box (18.25 ounces) yellow cake mix
1 box (3.4 ounces) vanilla instant pudding mix
4 large eggs, at room temperature
3/4 cup vegetable oil
1 cup sour cream, at room temperature

1. Preheat the oven to 350°F. Grease a 10-inch tube pan with removable bottom, dust it with flour, and tap out the excess.

2. Prepare the filling: Mix the cocoa powder, sugar, and chocolate chips together in a bowl, and set it aside.

3. Prepare the cake: Combine all the cake ingredients in the bowl of an electric mixer and beat on low speed for 30 seconds just to combine. Scrape the bowl, then beat at high speed for 2 minutes.

4. Scrape half of the batter into the prepared tube pan, and sprinkle half of the filling mixture over it. Top with the remaining batter, and sprinkle with the remaining filling mixture. Swirl a knife through the batter to create a marble effect.

5. Bake on the center oven rack until the cake springs back when touched and a cake tester inserted in the center comes out clean, 45 to 55 minutes. Let the cake cool in the pan set on a wire rack for 10 to 20 minutes. Then run a knife around the center tube and the sides of the pan, and lift the tube from the outer pan. Gently slide the knife between the bottom of the cake and the pan, and lift the cake off the pan. Return the cake to the wire rack to cool completely. Cut the cake into slices, and serve.

> **When I bake my friend Marilyn's cake, my son Chad, daughter-in-law Emily, and I usually have a piece each and then—this is no joke—sit there and pick the rest of it apart. Does that remind you of my mother [Hilda]? To my mother there was only one way to eat cake. You never cut a slice; you picked off the chips and crumbs. My sister Jackie and I still either pick a cake apart or take little slivers. I guess my mother thought that you ate less if you just 'picked.' No wonder where Chad and I got that from, and Emily fits right in.**
> **—BONNIE ROBBINS**

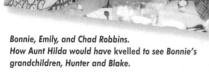

Bonnie, Emily, and Chad Robbins.
How Aunt Hilda would have kvelled to see Bonnie's grandchildren, Hunter and Blake.

leslie graham's chocolate-pistachio bundt cake

from Stacy Graham

The chocolate batter tunnels into the light green pistachio cake, creating pretty, colorful slices. For a more pronounced pistachio flavor, add 1/2 cup toasted chopped pistachios to the lighter batter. A few drops of green food coloring may be added as well. With only half a cup of oil, this is a lighter cake that is still wonderfully moist. **SERVES 12** Ⅾ

Vegetable oil or unflavored vegetable cooking spray, for greasing the pan

All-purpose flour, for dusting the pan

1 box (18.25 ounces) white or yellow cake mix

1 box (3.4 ounces) pistachio instant pudding mix

4 large eggs, at room temperature

¹/₂ cup vegetable oil

1 cup orange juice

³/₄ cup chocolate syrup

1. Preheat the oven to 350°F. Generously grease a 12-cup Bundt pan, dust it with flour, and tap out the excess.

2. Combine the cake mix, pudding mix, eggs, oil, and juice in the bowl of an electric mixer and beat on low speed for 1 minute. Scrape the bowl and beat on high speed until well blended, 3 minutes.

3. Scrape two thirds of the batter into the prepared Bundt pan. Add the chocolate syrup to the remaining batter, and beat on medium speed until combined. Scrape the chocolate batter evenly over the pistachio batter in the pan.

4. Bake on the center oven rack until the cake springs back when touched and a

> " *When I was first married, I couldn't boil water. Aunt Hilda appeared at my house one day and brought me a dozen little square pans of lasagna for the freezer, just to get me started. I've never forgotten it.* **—JOYCE WOLF** "

cake tester inserted in the center comes out clean, about 50 minutes. Allow the cake to cool in the pan set on a wire rack for 10 to 20 minutes. Then run a knife around the center and the edge of the cake, and turn it out on the rack to cool completely. Cut the cake into slices, and serve.

Leslie Graham and daughter Stacy, Rome, 2005.

chocolate cream cheese cake

from Estelle Robbins

m y two favorite *ch*'s, cheese and chocolate, combine in this light, tender cake in which the smooth, soft frosting is made with part of the batter. Decorate the cake with grated chocolate for an added fillip. **SERVES 10 TO 12** Ⅾ

Unsalted butter or unflavored vegetable
   cooking spray, for greasing
   the pan(s)
Parchment paper, if using two cake pans
2¹/₄ cups all-purpose flour, plus extra
   for dusting the pan(s)
1 teaspoon baking powder
1 teaspoon baking soda
1 teaspoon salt
6 ounces cream cheese, at room
   temperature
12 tablespoons (1¹/₂ sticks) unsalted butter,
   at room temperature
1 teaspoon pure vanilla extract
6¹/₂ cups (1¹/₂ pounds) confectioners'
   sugar, sifted
¹/₃ cup plus 1¹/₄ cups whole milk,
   at room temperature
4 ounces unsweetened chocolate,
   melted and cooled
3 large eggs, at room temperature

Aunt Estelle, 1940s.

1. Preheat the oven to 350°F. Grease the bottom and sides of two 9-inch round cake pans or one 13 × 9-inch baking pan. If using two pans, line them with parchment paper and grease again. Dust the pan(s) with flour, and tap out the excess.

2. Sift the flour, baking powder, baking soda, and salt together into a bowl, and set it aside.

3. Cream the cream cheese, 8 tablespoons (1 stick) of the butter, and the vanilla with an electric mixer on medium speed until light and fluffy, about 1 minute. Add the confectioners' sugar in three additions, alternating with the ¹/₃ cup milk in two additions, beginning and ending with the sugar. Beat in the melted chocolate. Measure out 2 cups of the mixture (for the frosting), cover with plastic wrap, and refrigerate.

4. Beat the remaining 4 tablespoons (¹/₂ stick) butter into the remaining batter on medium speed until incorporated, about 30 seconds. Beat in the eggs, one at a time, beating well and scraping the bowl after each addition. Reduce the speed to low and add the flour mixture in three additions, alternating with the 1¹/₄ cups milk in two additions, beginning and ending with the flour.

5. Scrape the batter into the prepared cake pan(s). Bake on the center oven rack until a cake tester inserted in the center comes out clean, about 30 minutes for the 9-inch round pans, 45 to 60 minutes for the 13 × 9-inch pan.

6. *If you used the 9-inch cake pans*, allow the layers to cool in the pans set on a wire rack for 10 minutes. Then unmold the layers and let them cool completely on the rack. *If you used a 13 × 9-inch pan*, let the cake cool completely in the pan set on a wire rack.

7. Remove the reserved frosting from the refrigerator 15 to 20 minutes before frosting the cake.

8. *If you used two round cake pans*, place a sheet of waxed paper under the wire

rack. Spread some of the frosting over the top of one layer. Top it with the second layer, and cover the top and sides with frosting. Cut the cake into slices, and serve. *If you used the 13 × 9-inch pan*, simply spread the frosting over the top. Cut the cake into squares, and serve.

aunt edye's chocolate loaf cake

from Allison Miller Solomon

A professional chef, Allison once worked for Gloria Vanderbilt and Anne Ford. Her Aunt Edye's loaf cake is devilishly moist and chocolatey. The recipe makes two: one loaf for now and one to freeze for unexpected company. (That's assuming the second loaf makes it to the freezer!) **MAKES 2 LOAVES**　**D**

❝ *Gloria entertained royalty. Irish housemaids would bring breakfast on lace-covered trays, and each bedroom suite had a different china pattern to complement the room.*

—ALLISON MILLER SOLOMON ❞

Parchment paper, for the pans
Unsalted butter or unflavored vegetable
　cooking spray, for greasing the pans
All-purpose flour, for dusting the pans
1 cup self-rising flour
2 tablespoons unsweetened cocoa powder
8 tablespoons (1 stick) unsalted butter,
　at room temperature
1 cup sugar
4 large eggs, separated
2 cups chocolate syrup, preferably Hershey's
2 teaspoons pure vanilla extract

1. Preheat the oven to 350°F. Line two 9 × 5-inch loaf pans with parchment paper. Grease the pans, dust them with flour, and tap out the excess.

2. Sift the flour and the cocoa powder together into a bowl, and set it aside.

3. Cream the butter and sugar with an electric mixer on medium speed until light and fluffy, about 2 minutes. Add the egg yolks, one at a time, beating well after each addition. Reduce the speed to low and add the flour mixture in three additions, alternating with the syrup in two additions, beginning and ending with the flour. Then beat in the vanilla.

4. Using a clean, dry bowl and beaters, beat the egg whites on medium-high speed until stiff peaks form, about 1¹/₂ minutes. Stir one fourth of the egg whites into the batter to lighten it. Then add the remaining whites in three additions, folding them in until incorporated.

5. Scrape the batter into the prepared loaf pans, and bake on the center oven rack until a cake tester inserted in the center

comes out clean, about 50 minutes. Allow the loaves to cool in the pans set on a wire rack for 10 minutes. Then run a knife around the edges and turn the loaves out. Return them to the rack to cool completely. Cut one or both loaves into slices, and serve.

white chocolate layer cake

from Claire Smolen

ש hite chocolate is not chocolate, but a sweetened cocoa butter product. Use the best quality for this festive company stunner. **SERVES 12 TO 14** **D**

Butter or unflavored vegetable cooking spray,
for greasing the pans
Parchment paper, for the pans
All-purpose or cake flour, for dusting
the pans
¹/₂ cup boiling water
4 ounces best-quality white chocolate
2¹/₂ cups cake flour, sifted
1 teaspoon baking soda
¹/₂ teaspoon salt
¹/₂ pound (2 sticks) unsalted butter,
at room temperature
2 cups sugar
4 large eggs, separated
1 teaspoon pure vanilla extract
1 cup buttermilk

1 cup walnut halves and/or pieces,
toasted (see box, page 17) and
chopped (optional)
Rich White Chocolate Frosting
(recipe follows)

1. Preheat the oven to 350°F. Grease three 8- or 9-inch round cake pans and line them with parchment paper. Grease the pans again, dust them with flour, and tap out the excess.

2. Pour the boiling water into a small bowl, add the white chocolate, and stir to melt the chocolate. Set it aside to cool.

3. Sift the flour, baking soda, and salt together into a bowl. Set it aside.

4. Cream the butter and sugar with an electric mixer on medium-high speed until light and fluffy, about 2 minutes. Add the egg yolks, one at a time, beating well and scraping the bowl after each addition. Add the melted chocolate and the vanilla, and mix well. Reduce the speed to low and add the flour mixture in three additions, alternating with the buttermilk in two additions, beginning and ending with the flour. Beat just until smooth.

5. Using a clean, dry bowl and beaters, beat the egg whites on medium-high speed until stiff peaks form, about 1¹/₂ minutes. Stir one fourth of the beaten egg whites into the batter to lighten it. Then add the remaining whites in three additions, folding them in until incorporated. Fold in the walnuts, if using.

6. Divide the batter evenly among the prepared cake pans, and bake on the center oven rack until the cake springs back when touched and a cake tester inserted in the center comes out clean, 25 to 35 minutes. (If

your center rack won't hold three pans, bake one in the center on the highest rack, but watch it closely.) Let the cakes cool in the pans set on wire racks for 10 minutes. Then run a knife around the edge of the cakes, turn them out, and return them to the rack to cool completely.

7. When the cakes are cool, frost one cake layer with the Rich White Chocolate Frosting and top with the second layer. Frost the second layer, and top with the third. Frost just the top of the third layer. Cut the cake into slices, and serve.

rich white chocolate frosting

This frosting, spread only on top of the cake and between the layers, is just enough to enhance the richness of the cake without overpowering it. If you prefer a thinner consistency, beat in additional cream a teaspoon at a time. If you prefer

it thicker, beat in additional confectioners' sugar a tablespoon at a time. **MAKES ABOUT 2 CUPS**

7 ounces best-quality white chocolate
4 tablespoons (1/2 stick) unsalted butter, at room temperature
1/4 cup heavy (whipping) cream
Pinch of salt
2 cups confectioners' sugar, sifted
1 teaspoon pure vanilla extract

Warm the white chocolate, butter, and cream in the top of a double boiler set over simmering water until the chocolate is barely melted. Remove the pan from the heat and stir until smooth. Beat in the confectioners' sugar and salt. Stir in the vanilla.

red, white, and blue cake

from Sally Bower

When Harold was courting cousin Marilyn, Aunt Sally offered him an assortment of her cakes. He took one look at her chocolate, vanilla, and cherry marble cake and said, "Do I eat it or salute it?" They've been calling it Red, White, and Blue Cake ever since. This tender cake was always Aunt Sally's signature cake, and we kids loved the colors. **SERVES 12 TO 16**   D

FOR THE CAKE

Unsalted butter or vegetable oil spray,
*   for greasing the pan*
All-purpose flour, for dusting the pan
Parchment paper, for the pan
1½ ounces unsweetened chocolate
½ pound (2 sticks) unsalted butter,
*   at room temperature*
2 cups granulated sugar
4 large eggs, separated
3 cups self-rising flour
1 cup milk
1 teaspoon pure vanilla extract
10 maraschino cherries, chopped
4 drops red food coloring

FOR THE FROSTING

2 tablespoons unsalted butter,
*   at room temperature*
3 tablespoons unsweetened cocoa powder
2 cups confectioners' sugar
¼ cup hot brewed coffee or hot water
2 teaspoons pure vanilla extract

1. Preheat the oven to 350°F. Grease a 13 × 9-inch baking pan, dust it with flour, and tap out the excess. Line the bottom with parchment paper.

2. Melt the chocolate in the top of a double boiler set over simmering water. Set it aside to cool slightly.

3. Set aside ⅔ cup of the flour.

4. Combine the milk and vanilla in a bowl, and set it aside.

5. Cream the butter and 1¾ cups of the granulated sugar with an electric mixer on medium speed, scraping the bowl several times, until light and fluffy, 3 to 4 minutes. Add the egg yolks, one at a time, beating well after each addition. With the mixer on low speed, add the remaining flour in three additions, alternating with the milk mixture in two additions, beginning and ending with the flour. Set the batter aside.

6. Using a clean, dry bowl and beaters, beat the egg whites on medium-high speed until soft peaks form. Add the remaining ¼ cup granulated sugar, a tablespoon at a time, beating for 10 seconds after each addition. Then raise the speed to high and beat until stiff peaks form, about 3 minutes total. Stir one fourth of the beaten egg whites into the batter to lighten it. Then add the remaining whites in three additions, folding them in until incorporated.

7. Place two bowls on your work surface. Place one third of the batter in one of the bowls, stir in the melted chocolate, and set it aside. Sift the reserved ⅔ cup flour over the remaining batter, and fold gently until it is well blended. Place half

Aunt Sally and Uncle Lou (right) with Harold and Marilyn (center) and Harold's parents, Ed and Anne Dubin (left), 1960s.

of this batter in the remaining empty bowl, and stir in the maraschino cherries and red food coloring. You now have three flavored batters.

8. Spoon the batters, using about a third of the batter per spoonful and alternating the flavors, into the prepared baking pan, forming nine dollops. Then, using a knife, swirl the batters to create a marble effect. Bake on the center oven rack until the top is lightly golden, the cake springs back when gently touched, and a cake tester inserted in the center comes out clean, 40 to 45 minutes. Let the cake cool in the pan set on a wire rack.

9. To unmold it, run a thin knife around the edges to loosen the cake from the baking pan. Turn the pan over onto a baking sheet, lift it off, remove the parchment paper, and then turn the cake right side up onto a serving plate. (Of course you could serve the cake straight from the pan as well.)

10. Prepare the frosting: Beat the butter, cocoa powder, confectioners' sugar, hot coffee, and vanilla with an electric mixer on medium speed until well blended and smooth, 1 to 2 minutes.

11. Spread the frosting over the cake with an offset spatula or the back of a spoon. Cut the cake into squares, and serve.

> " I know that all of us in the Rabinowitz blood line love food. No doubt some have been known to marry into our tribe after being courted by family delicacies. Like my father.
> —LAURA SELIGMAN "

paul's chocolate chip sour cream pound cake

from Marilyn Dubin

In days of yore, pound cake recipes called for a pound of flour, a pound of sugar, a pound of butter, and a pound of eggs—hence the name. The ratios have changed through the years, with pastry chefs adding their own little twists. As a student at Brooklyn College, I used to stop after class on the way to the bus for a slice of Wolfie's delicious pound cake. (The "Freshman 15" continued way past a year. Good thing I graduated early.) This cake is everything I remember from my detours to Wolfie's: buttery, dense, and ultra moist, and to boot it's got chocolate chips. Even better. **SERVES 12 TO 16**   **D**

Unsalted butter or unflavored vegetable cooking spray, for greasing the pan

3 cups all-purpose flour, plus extra for dusting the pan

1/4 teaspoon baking soda

1/2 pound (2 sticks) unsalted butter, at room temperature

2 cups sugar

6 large eggs, at room temperature

1 teaspoon pure vanilla extract

1 cup sour cream, at room temperature

1 1/2 cups (9 ounces) semisweet chocolate chips

Mama Hinda, Aunt Sally, and Uncle Lou with Marilyn, about 1936.

1. Preheat the oven to 325°F. Grease a 10-inch tube pan with removable bottom, dust it with flour, and tap out the excess.

2. Combine the flour and baking soda in a bowl. Stir well, and set it aside.

3. Cream the butter and sugar with an electric mixer on medium-high speed until light and fluffy, 2 to 3 minutes. Add the eggs, one at a time, beating well and scraping the bowl after each addition. Then beat in the vanilla until smooth.

4. Reduce the speed to low and add the flour mixture in four additions, alternating with the sour cream in three additions, beginning and ending with the flour. Fold in the chocolate chips.

5. Scrape the batter into the prepared tube pan, and bake on the center oven rack until a cake tester inserted into the center comes out clean, 1¼ to 1½ hours. Allow the cake to cool completely in the pan set on a wire rack.

6. Run a knife around the center tube and the sides of the pan, and lift the tube from the outer pan. Gently slide the knife between the bottom of the cake and the pan, and lift the cake off the pan. Cut the cake into slices, and serve.

old-fashioned apple cake

from Sally Bower

Every one of my "tasters" said Aunt Sally's apple cake was just like their *bubbe* or *tanta* used to make.

SERVES 6 TO 8

1¼ cups all-purpose flour

1 teaspoon baking powder

½ teaspoon salt

4 medium McIntosh apples, peeled
  and thinly sliced

½ cup apricot jam

Juice of ½ lemon

3 large eggs, at room temperature

1 cup sugar

½ cup vegetable oil

1 teaspoon pure vanilla extract

1. Preheat the oven to 350°F. Grease an 8-inch square baking pan.

2. Stir the flour, baking powder, and salt together in a bowl and set aside.

3. Combine the apple slices, jam, and lemon juice in a bowl and set aside.

4. Beat the eggs well with an electric mixer at medium speed. Gradually add the sugar, beating until light and fluffy, about 2 minutes, followed by the oil and vanilla, scraping the bowl several times. Reduce the speed to low and blend in the flour mixture.

5. Spread half the batter evenly into the prepared pan and cover with the apple

mixture. Top with the remaining batter and bake on the center oven rack until golden, about 1 hour. Cool the cake completely in the pan set on a wire rack. Cut into squares and serve.

bubbe rose's apple cake

from Sharon Mann

When cousin Linda's son Harrison married Rebecca, his mother-in-law, Sharon, instantly became my e-mail pal, as eager to share her own family's heirloom recipes as we were to welcome her family into the clan. With its streusel topping and strong cinnamon flavor, you've got a winner. The night I tested it on my *chavurah* (we are six couples who eat and laugh more than we do any serious discussing), this cake was the only nonchocolate offering in a sea of cacao. If an apple cake stands up to chocolate, you know it has to be good! Our friend Cole

Bubbe Rose Capler with Becca at Becca's Bat Mitzvah, 1992.

Sachs, who eats no chocolate (yes, there are a few of those out there), loved it so much he wound up schlepping the leftovers for the next day's seven-hour drive to his kids' home in Palo Alto. **SERVES 12**
D or **P**

Vegetable oil or unflavored vegetable cooking spray, for greasing the pan

FOR THE APPLE FILLING
4 large tart apples, peeled, cored, and sliced
1 tablespoon ground cinnamon
¹/₃ cup (packed) light brown sugar
1 tablespoon fresh lemon juice

FOR THE CAKE
2¹/₂ cups all-purpose flour
1 teaspoon baking powder
4 large eggs, separated
1 cup granulated sugar
1 cup vegetable oil
¹/₂ cup orange juice, preferably fresh
1 teaspoon pure vanilla extract
Pinch of salt
Ground cinnamon, for sprinkling
¹/₃ cup (packed) light brown sugar

FOR THE TOPPING
¹/₂ cup all-purpose flour
¹/₄ cup (packed) light brown sugar
1 teaspoon ground cinnamon
7 tablespoons unsalted butter or nondairy margarine, at room temperature

1. Preheat the oven to 350°F. Grease a 13 × 9-inch glass baking dish.

2. Prepare the filling: Combine the apples, cinnamon, brown sugar, and lemon juice in a bowl. Toss well and set it aside.

3. Prepare the cake: Combine the flour and baking powder in a bowl, and set it aside.

4. Beat the egg yolks and granulated sugar with an electric mixer on medium speed until the mixture is lemon-yellow, about 2 minutes. Add the oil, orange juice, and vanilla, and beat until well mixed. Reduce the speed to low and blend in the flour mixture. Scrape the sides of the bowl, and beat on medium speed just until combined.

5. Using a clean, dry bowl and beaters, beat the egg whites on medium-high speed until foamy, about 30 seconds. Add the salt and continue beating until stiff peaks form, about 1 1/2 minutes total. Stir one fourth of the beaten egg whites into the batter to lighten it. Add the remaining whites in three additions, folding them in until incorporated.

6. Scrape half of the batter into the prepared baking pan, level it, and sprinkle it lightly with cinnamon. Distribute the apple filling evenly over the batter, and sprinkle with the brown sugar and more cinnamon.

> *Rosh Hashanah was sure to bring my grandmother's delicious cake to the table. The apples in Toronto were just coming into season, and it was common to use a Spy apple, which you cannot even find here in the South. Any tart apple will do. My daughter, Rebecca, loved this cake as a special treat for breakfast on crisp fall days.*
>
> **—SHARON MANN**

Carefully spread the remaining batter over the apple layer.

7. Combine all the topping ingredients in a bowl, and mix with a fork until well blended and crumbly. Sprinkle the topping over the batter.

8. Bake on the center oven rack until golden brown on the top and the bottom, about 1 hour. Let the cake cool in the pan set on a wire rack. Cut the cake into squares, and serve warm or at room temperature.

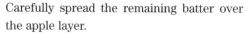

barbara horenstein's
banana chocolate chip cake

from Jessica Levine Levy

For my niece Jessica's bridal shower, we were all asked to bring a recipe. This moist cake, from her mother's friend Barbara, is studded with flecks of chocolate. Bananas and chocolate are made for each other, perhaps recalling their former proximity in tropical climes where shade-giving banana trees, sweetly termed "cocoa mothers," are planted close to cacao plants to protect them from the sun. Frost with your favorite chocolate frosting or the Chocolate Buttercream on page 373, or leave plain. **SERVES 12**

Butter, for greasing the pan

3 cups all-purpose flour

$^1/_2$ teaspoon salt

2 teaspoons baking soda

$^1/_2$ cup sour cream, at room temperature

1 cup (2 sticks) unsalted butter,
    at room temperature

$2^1/_2$ cups sugar

4 large eggs, at room temperature

2 cups mashed bananas
    (4 to 5 medium-size bananas)

2 teaspoons pure vanilla extract

$1^1/_2$ cups semisweet chocolate chips

1. Preheat the oven to 350°F. Grease a 13 × 9-inch baking pan.

2. Sift the flour and the salt together into a bowl, and set it aside.

3. Combine the baking soda and sour cream in another bowl. Stir well, and allow to stand for 5 minutes.

4. Cream the butter and sugar with an electric mixer on medium-high speed until light and fluffy, about 3 minutes. Reduce the speed to medium and blend in the eggs, one at a time, blending well and scraping the bowl after each addition. Reduce the speed to low and add the flour mixture in three additions, alternating with the sour cream mixture in two additions, beginning and ending with the flour. Blend in the mashed bananas, followed by the vanilla. Stir in the chocolate chips.

5. Scrape the batter into the prepared baking pan, and bake on the center oven rack until the cake springs back when touched and a cake tester inserted in the center comes out clean, 45 to 55 minutes. Allow the cake to cool in the pan set on a wire rack.

banana-pineapple bundt cake

from Sylvia Robbins

maybe it's just me, but after seeing *My Big Fat Greek Wedding*, I can't think about a *boont* cake without laughing, and it's all I can do to keep from serving it with a plant plopped in the center. Plant or no plant, Aunt Sylvia's *boont* cake is supermoist, a (tropical) breeze to throw together, and always fit for any occasion . . . even meeting the *machatunim!*

SERVES 12   P

Vegetable oil or unflavored vegetable
    cooking spray, for greasing the pan

3 cups all-purpose flour

2 cups sugar

1 teaspoon baking soda

1 teaspoon ground cinnamon

1 teaspoon salt

2 cups mashed bananas
    (4 or 5 medium-size bananas)

1 can (8 ounces) crushed pineapple, undrained

$1^1/_2$ cups vegetable oil

1 teaspoon pure vanilla extract

$^1/_2$ teaspoon pure almond extract

3 large eggs, lightly beaten

1. Preheat the oven to 350°F. Grease a 12-cup Bundt pan.

2. Sift the flour, sugar, baking soda, cinnamon, and salt together into a large bowl. Stir in the mashed bananas, pineapple with its juice, oil, both extracts, and the eggs.

3. Scrape the batter into the prepared Bundt pan, and bake on the center oven rack until it is golden brown and a cake tester inserted in the center comes out clean, about 1 hour and 5 to 10 minutes. Let the cake cool in the pan set on a wire rack for 10 to 20 minutes. Then run a knife around the center and the edge of the cake, and turn it out on the rack to cool completely. Cut the cake into slices, and serve.

> " Somewhere between printings of Melting Pot Memories, we lost Aunt Sylvia. She and Uncle Morris had a beautiful love affair that lasted until his death in 1995. How I miss her phone calls from Atlanta, when she'd say she needed her 'Judy fix.' Like Aunt Shirley and Aunt Hilda, she was always a Rabinowitz sister rather than a sister-in-law, and as children, we so looked forward to the visits of our Atlanta branch, with their exotic Southern accents. The more cousins to play with, the merrier! —JUDY BART KANCIGOR "

carrot cake

from Phyllis Epstein

A devout chocoholic, Cousin Phyllis makes only one exception to her chocolate-only repertoire, and that's her carrot cake. This lighter version of the classic is a moist and majestic-looking layer cake with a billowy cream cheese frosting. **SERVES 10 TO 12**　**D**

FOR THE CAKE

Vegetable oil or unflavored vegetable
　cooking spray, for greasing the pans
Parchment paper, for the pans
2 cups all-purpose flour, plus extra for
　dusting the pans
2 teaspoons baking soda
1 tablespoon ground cinnamon
1 tablespoon ground allspice
Dash of ground nutmeg
4 large eggs, at room temperature
2 cups sugar
1 1/2 cups vegetable oil
　1 tablespoon pure vanilla extract
　3 cups grated carrots
　　(about 1 pound carrots)
　1/4 cup sweetened flaked or
　　　shredded coconut (optional)

Boy, was I mad when this photo surfaced of Aunt Sylvia and Uncle Morris's wedding in Atlanta, 1949. Notice cousins Joyce and Marvin got to go and Gary and I got to stay home!

FOR THE CREAM CHEESE FROSTING

12 ounces cream cheese, at room
    temperature
8 tablespoons (1 stick) unsalted butter,
    at room temperature
1 cup confectioners' sugar, sifted
2 1/2 to 3 tablespoons frozen orange
    juice concentrate, thawed

FOR THE TOPPING (OPTIONAL)

3/4 cup walnut halves and/or pieces,
    toasted (see box, page 17) and
    chopped

Phyllis and me at a high school formal. I've cropped out our (very forgettable) dates.

1. Preheat the oven to 350°F. Grease two 9- or 10-inch round cake pans and line them with parchment paper. Grease again, dust them with flour, and tap out the excess.

2. Sift the flour, baking soda, cinnamon, allspice, and nutmeg together into a medium-size bowl, and set it aside.

3. Beat the eggs with an electric mixer on medium speed. Gradually add the sugar, beating thoroughly until light and fluffy, about 2 minutes. Slowly add the oil, followed by the vanilla. Using a rubber spatula, fold in the flour mixture, followed by the grated carrots and the coconut if using.

4. Divide the batter evenly between the prepared cake pans, and bake on the center oven rack until the cakes spring back when touched and a cake tester inserted in the center comes out clean, 30 to 40 minutes. Cool the cakes in the pans set on a wire rack for 5 minutes. Then run a thin knife around the edges of the pans, invert the pans, and remove the cakes. Return the cakes to the rack to cool completely.

5. Meanwhile, prepare the frosting: Beat the cream cheese, butter, confectioners' sugar, and 2 tablespoons of the orange juice concentrate with an electric mixer on medium speed until fluffy and smooth, about 3 minutes. Add the remaining orange juice concentrate by the teaspoon, beating until the frosting is of spreading consistency.

6. Frost the top of one cake layer with the cream cheese frosting, and top it with the second layer. Cover the top and sides with frosting, and sprinkle with the walnuts if using. Cut the cake into slices, and serve.

coconut date nut cake

from Joan Kalish

ait a minute! Not so fast! Don't turn that page! I've heard it a dozen times: You don't like coconut and/or you don't like dates. When did you make that decision—when you were nine? As a former English teacher, I'm calling upon a willing suspension of disbelief here. This is a wonderful old-fashioned dessert, the tenderest of cakes smothered in a molten buttery, crunchy topping. The alchemy between the two is irresistible. (Of course, if you do like dates and coconut, you'll need no prodding.) **SERVES 12** ⬛**D**

FOR THE CAKE

1 cup boiling water

1 teaspoon baking soda

1 cup pitted dates, cut into thirds

Butter or unflavored vegetable
cooking spray, for greasing the pan

8 tablespoons (1 stick) unsalted butter,
at room temperature

1 cup sugar

1 large egg, at room temperature

1 teaspoon pure vanilla extract

1¹/₂ cups cake flour, sifted

¹/₂ cup chopped walnuts

FOR THE COCONUT TOPPING

5 tablespoons unsalted butter

³/₄ cup (packed) dark brown sugar

5 tablespoons half-and-half

1¹/₂ cups sweetened flaked or
shredded coconut

1. Pour the boiling water into a small bowl, add the baking soda, and stir until it has dissolved. Place the dates in a 4-cup measuring cup or a bowl with a spout, and pour the baking soda mixture over them. Set aside to cool.

2. Preheat the oven to 350°F. Grease a 13 × 9-inch baking pan.

3. Cream the butter with an electric mixer on medium-high speed. Gradually add the sugar and beat until light and fluffy, about 2 minutes. Scrape the bowl and beat in the egg, followed by the vanilla. Reduce the speed to low and add the flour in three additions, alternating with the date mixture in two additions, beginning and ending with the flour. Stir in the walnuts.

4. Scrape the batter into the prepared baking pan, and bake on the center oven rack until the top is golden brown and the cake is beginning to pull away from the edges, about 25 minutes.

5. Meanwhile, prepare the topping: Melt the butter in a small saucepan. Stir in the brown sugar and half-and-half. Add the coconut and mix well. Simmer, stirring occasionally, for about 10 minutes.

6. As soon as the cake is done, remove it from the oven and turn on the broiler. Immediately spread the topping evenly over the hot cake. Place the cake under the broiler, setting it about 8 inches from the heat source, and broil until the topping bubbles and glazes, 1 to 1¹/₂ minutes. Watch carefully, as coconut burns easily. Let the cake cool completely in the pan set on a wire rack. Cut the cake into squares, and serve.

Murray and Joan Kalish
at cousin Daryl's
Bat Mitzvah, 1987.

coconut graham cracker cake

from Samra Robbins

Another entry from Ahavath Achim sisterhood's . . . *And It was Good*, this is a beautiful triple-layer marvel, moist and dense with the texture of a carrot cake, crowned with a luscious pineapple frosting. If you like, pour rum instead of pineapple juice over the baked layers and call it a Piña Colada Cake. In keeping with the tropical theme, you could substitute macadamia nuts for the walnuts. And, no, it's not a typo: there's only a third of a cup of flour in this cake.

SERVES 12 TO 14   **D** or **P**

FOR THE CAKE

Butter, solid vegetable shortening, or
    unflavored vegetable cooking spray,
    for greasing the pans
Parchment paper, for the pans
All-purpose flour, for dusting the pans
3/4 pound (3 sticks) unsalted butter or
    nondairy margarine, at room temperature,
    or 1 1/2 cups solid vegetable shortening
2 cups sugar
5 large eggs
1 pound graham cracker crumbs
    (see Note)
1 cup whole milk, soy milk, or nondairy milk
    substitute

1 teaspoon pure vanilla extract
1 1/2 cups sweetened flaked or shredded
    coconut
1 cup walnut halves and/or pieces, toasted
    (see box, page 17), chopped, and tossed
    with 1/3 cup all-purpose flour
Juice from crushed pineapple (see below)

FOR THE FILLING AND FROSTING

8 tablespoons (1 stick) butter or nondairy
    margarine, at room temperature,
    or 1/2 cup solid vegetable shortening
1 box (16 ounces) confectioners' sugar, sifted
1 can (8 ounces) crushed pineapple, drained,
    juice reserved

1. Preheat the oven to 350°F. Grease three 8-inch round cake pans and line the bottoms with parchment paper. Grease the lined pans, dust with flour, and tap out the excess.

2. Cream the butter and sugar with an electric mixer on medium speed, scraping the bowl several times, until light and fluffy, about 3 minutes. Add the eggs, one at a time, beating well and scraping the bowl after each addition. Reduce the speed to low and add the graham cracker crumbs in three additions, alternating with the milk in two additions, beginning and ending with the crumbs. Beat in the vanilla. Fold in the coconut and the walnut mixture.

3. Divide the batter evenly among the prepared cake pans, and bake on the center oven rack until they are golden brown and a cake tester inserted in the center comes out clean, 35 to 40 minutes. (If your center rack won't hold three pans, bake one in the center

of the highest rack, but watch it closely.) The cake will appear moist on top. Set the cake pans on a wire rack. While they are still warm, brush some of the reserved pineapple juice over the layers. Let them cool completely before removing them from the pans.

4. Prepare the filling and frosting: Blend the butter, confectioners' sugar, and drained pineapple with an electric mixer on medium speed. Raise the speed to high and blend until fluffy, just a few seconds. If the mixture is too thick, blend in some of the reserved pineapple juice, a teaspoon at a time, until the mixture is of spreading consistency.

5. Frost one cake layer with the frosting, and top with the second layer. Frost the second layer, and top with the third. Cover the top and sides with frosting.

Note: First it was the 1-pound can of coffee that shrank to 12 ounces. Have you noticed that the 1-pound box of graham cracker crumbs is now 13.5 ounces? If you don't want to buy two boxes of crumbs, crush 8 graham cracker squares in a food processor and add that to the 13.5-ounce box of crumbs. Then you'll get a pound . . . and have graham crackers left over to enjoy with your 12 ounces of coffee.

Aunt Sally, 1929.

tanta bayla's fruit cake crumble

from Sally Bower

Tanta Bayla Hyman was Uncle Lou Bower's aunt from Russia. Uncle Lou's family was so large, so spread out in Russia, the United States, and Cuba, that we used to say he had five hundred cousins (the most illustrious of whom, I might add, is Mitch Leigh, composer of *Man of La Mancha*.) Many of the five hundred never left Russia, and it was just Aunt Sally and Uncle Lou's luck to be visiting them in 1960 during the U-2 incident. We had quite a scare, but thankfully they returned safely.

Say "fruitcake" and most people conjure up that stepchild of the Christmas table, immortalized in a haiku I stumbled upon on CNN's website:

Not edible, yet
Durable when thrown under
A fast-moving car.

Jews have no such prejudice, however, about anything they call fruit cake (two words, as in a cake that happens to have fruit in it). We have our own hockey pucks to contend with.

For this easy cake with a nutty crumb topping, use cherry, apple, or blueberry filling or any flavor you like. Aunt Sally made it often for unexpected guests—like my mother, who would "drop in" on weekday evenings when she just had to escape. She would tell us she was going out to mail a letter. I grew up thinking that post offices were open at night and must have been very crowded, because she would be gone for hours. **SERVES 6 TO 8** **D**

Marilyn (second from right) at her Sweet 16 with her parents and her dad's family, 1948.

Unsalted butter or unflavored vegetable
cooking spray, for greasing the pan

FOR THE TOPPING

2 tablespoons unsalted butter,
at room temperature
¹/₄ cup sugar
¹/₄ cup all-purpose flour
¹/₂ cup walnut or pecan pieces, chopped

FOR THE CAKE

2 cups all-purpose flour
2 teaspoons baking powder
¹/₂ teaspoon salt
8 tablespoons (1 stick) unsalted butter,
at room temperature
1 cup sugar
3 large eggs, at room temperature
1 teaspoon pure vanilla extract
1 can (21 ounces) fruit pie filling

1. Preheat the oven to 350°F. Grease an 8-inch square cake pan.

2. Prepare the topping: Combine the butter, sugar, and flour in a bowl, and blend with a fork or your fingers until thoroughly combined. Stir in the walnuts and set aside.

3. Prepare the cake: Sift the flour, baking powder, and salt together into a medium-size bowl. Set it aside.

4. Cream the butter and sugar with an electric mixer on medium speed, scraping the bowl several times, until light and fluffy, about 2 minutes. Blend in the eggs, one at a time, scraping the bowl after each addition. Then blend in the vanilla. Reduce the speed to low and blend in the flour mixture until combined.

5. Scrape three fourths of the batter into the prepared cake pan and level it off. Cover it evenly with the pie filling. (If you're using apple, it's a good idea to cut the thicker slices in half for more coverage.) Drop the remaining batter on top of the pie filling and spread it out as much as you can. (You won't be able to cover it all, so don't even try. Just do your Jackson Pollock imitation—the crumb topping will cover it up anyway.) Sprinkle the crumb topping evenly over the top.

6. Bake on the center oven rack until lightly browned, about 1 hour. Let the cake cool in the pan set on a wire rack. Cut the cake into squares, and serve it warm or at room temperature.

orange cake

from Sally Bower

For her orange cake, the original sunny delight, Aunt Sally used fresh orange juice from the oranges Uncle Lou brought home from his fruit and vegetable concession. I'm sure she baked it in her 13 × 9-inch pan, but with its bright citrus glaze, this cake just screams for a Bundt. I don't think Aunt Sally would mind the update. Even at ninety-four, she was always open to new ideas. **SERVES 12** **D**

FOR THE CAKE

Butter or unflavored vegetable cooking spray,
for greasing the pan
All-purpose or cake flour, for dusting the pan
3 cups cake flour, sifted
1 teaspoon baking powder
1 cup orange juice, preferably fresh,
at room temperature
1 teaspoon grated orange zest
2 teaspoons pure orange extract
1/2 pound (2 sticks) unsalted butter,
at room temperature
2 cups sugar
4 large eggs, separated, at room temperature
Red and yellow food coloring (optional)

FOR THE ORANGE GLAZE

2 cups confectioners' sugar, sifted
3 to 4 tablespoons orange juice
1 tablespoon unsalted butter, at room
temperature
1 1/2 teaspoons grated orange zest

1. Preheat the oven to 325°F. Grease a 12-cup Bundt pan, dust it with flour, and tap out the excess.

2. Stir the flour and baking powder together in a medium-size bowl, and set it aside.

3. Combine the orange juice, zest, and orange extract in a small bowl, and set it aside.

4. Cream the butter and 1¾ cups of the sugar with an electric mixer on medium speed, scraping the bowl several times, until light and fluffy, 3 to 4 minutes. Add the egg yolks, one at a time, beating well and scraping the bowl after each addition. Reduce the mixer speed to low and add the flour mixture in three additions, alternating with the orange juice mixture in two additions, beginning and ending with the flour. Set the batter aside.

5. Using a clean, dry bowl and beaters, beat the egg whites on medium-high speed until soft peaks form. Add the remaining ¼ cup sugar, a tablespoon at a time, beating for 10 seconds after each addition. Then raise the speed to high and beat until stiff peaks form, about 3 minutes total. Stir one fourth of the beaten egg whites into the batter to lighten it. Then add the remaining whites in three additions, folding them in until incorporated. As you fold in the whites, add a few drops of red and yellow food coloring if you want a more orange-colored cake; be generous, as the color will fade during baking.

> *Cooking and baking was my mother's greatest pleasure. She never used 'lite' anything. She always said it's better to have just a taste of the real thing.* **—MARILYN DUBIN**

> *My mom [Sally, with Marilyn, right] and dad were on a three-month vacation touring Europe and Russia. When I think now of the chance they took, smuggling in prayer books and tallisim to their relatives . . . They couldn't talk freely to their family in their apartments and had to go outside to have discussions about their situation there. One family finally got out in the '60s. When my parents drove them around New York, the most amazing thing to them was seeing kosher butchers with Hebrew writing on the windows right out in the open.*
> —MARILYN DUBIN

6. Scrape the batter into the prepared Bundt pan, and bake on the center oven rack until the cake is lightly golden, the top springs back when gently touched, and a cake tester inserted in the center comes out clean, about 1 hour. Let the cake cool in the pan set on a wire rack for 10 to 20 minutes. Then run a knife around the center and the edge of the cake, and turn it out on the rack to cool completely.

7. Prepare the glaze: Combine all the glaze ingredients in a bowl. Place a sheet of waxed paper under the cake rack to catch the spills.

8. Drizzle the glaze over the cooled cake, allowing some to run down the center and the sides. Refrigerate the cake, uncovered, for about 30 minutes to allow the glaze to set completely. Cut the cake into slices, and serve.

fresh peach cake

from Sally Bower

Summer brought Aunt Sally's peach cake, always a special treat, because Uncle Lou, who had the fruit and vegetable concession at the local grocery, saved the most luscious peaches to bring home. But in our house we never had to go any farther than our own postage-stamp-size backyard, where Mama Hinda's "orchard" consisted of a peach tree, an apple tree, and a cherry tree. The peach tree bore fruit every other year (alternating with the apples). My parents used to bring the most humongous peaches to camp on visiting day—along with a three-foot salami and bags of rye bread. I was very popular.

SERVES 6 TO 8   **D** or **P**

Aunt Sally, Aunt Anna (Mama Hinda's sister), Aunt Irene, and Uncle Charlie vacationing in the Catskills, 1920s.

Unsalted butter or unflavored vegetable cooking spray, for greasing the pan

FOR THE TOPPING

2 tablespoons all-purpose flour

2 tablespoons sugar

1 tablespoon unsalted butter or nondairy margarine

FOR THE CAKE

1 cup all-purpose flour

1 teaspoon baking powder

Pinch of salt

8 tablespoons (1 stick) unsalted butter or nondairy margarine, at room temperature

¹/₂ cup sugar

2 large eggs, at room temperature

¹/₂ teaspoon pure vanilla extract

4 large fresh peaches (about 1¹/₂ pounds), unpeeled or peeled, pitted, and sliced

1. Preheat the oven to 350°F. Grease an 8-inch square cake pan.

2. Prepare the topping: Combine the flour, sugar, and butter in a bowl, and blend with a fork or your fingers until thoroughly combined. Set it aside.

3. Prepare the cake: Sift the flour, baking powder, and salt together into a bowl. Set it aside.

> " My mother [Sally] was very Zen, although she didn't know it. When she cooked, she was very focused into where she was and what she was doing at that moment. She had a love affair with her pots and her ingredients and her utensils. **—MARILYN DUBIN** "

4. Cream the butter and sugar with an electric mixer on medium speed, scraping the bowl several times, until light and fluffy, about 2 minutes. Blend in the eggs, one at a time, scraping the bowl after each addition. Then blend in the vanilla. Reduce the speed to low, add the flour mixture, and mix until just combined.

5. Remove 1 tablespoon of the batter and mix it with the peach slices. Scrape the remaining batter into the prepared cake pan, and arrange the peach slices on top. Sprinkle the topping over the peaches.

6. Bake on the center oven rack until lightly browned, about 45 minutes. Let the cake cool in the pan set on a wire rack. Cut the cake into squares, and serve warm or at room temperature. (A scoop of vanilla ice cream would be a nice accompaniment.)

buttermilk prune spice cake

from Irene Rosenthal

Americans are a resourceful lot. It's amazing how whole new industries spring up seemingly overnight. Take prunes (as an example, not a prescription). One day there they are on supermarket shelves and the next day they're gone, replaced by a revolutionary new crop: dried plums. And no farmers had to be retrained, no manufacturing equipment had to be modified . . . ah, American ingenuity. Where once the lowly prune conjured visions of stooped octogenarians with lower digestive dysfunction, the dried plum appeals to everyone, as universally lovable as the raisin. Aunt Irene used prunes for this moist, spicy cake packed with crunchy toasted pecans and dressed with a buttermilk glaze—but feel free to substitute dried plums, if you prefer. **SERVES 12**

D

Aunt Irene kvelling with her six granddaughters at Suzy's Bat Mitzvah, 1976.

FOR THE GLAZE

¹/₂ cup buttermilk

1 cup sugar

4 tablespoons (¹/₂ stick) unsalted butter, at room temperature

¹/₄ teaspoon baking soda

FOR THE CAKE

Vegetable oil or unflavored vegetable cooking spray, for greasing the pan

Parchment paper, for the pan

1 cup buttermilk, at room temperature

1 teaspoon baking soda

2 cups all-purpose flour, plus extra for dusting the pan

2 teaspoons ground cloves

2 teaspoons ground cinnamon

2 teaspoons ground allspice

2 teaspoons ground nutmeg

³/₄ teaspoon salt

1 cup vegetable oil, plus extra for greasing the pan

2 cups sugar

2 teaspoons pure vanilla extract

3 large eggs, at room temperature

1 cup pitted prunes, snipped into thirds

1 cup pecan pieces, toasted (see box, page 17) and chopped

1. Preheat the oven to 350°F. Grease a 13 × 9-inch baking pan, line the bottom with parchment paper, then grease the paper. Dust the pan with flour and tap out the excess.

2. Prepare the cake: Combine the buttermilk with the baking soda in a small bowl, and set it aside.

3. Sift the flour, cloves, cinnamon, allspice, nutmeg, and salt together into a bowl, and set it aside.

4. Blend the oil, sugar, and vanilla with an electric mixer on medium speed until well combined. Add the eggs, one at a time, beating well after each addition. Add the flour mixture in three additions, alternating with the buttermilk mixture in two additions, beginning and ending with the flour. Stir in the prunes and pecans.

5. Scrape the batter into the prepared baking pan, and bake on the center oven rack until the cake springs back when touched and a cake tester inserted in the center comes out clean, 50 to 60 minutes.

6. Place the baking pan on a wire rack set over a sheet of waxed paper, and immediately prepare the glaze: Combine the

buttermilk, sugar, butter, and baking soda in a small saucepan. Bring to a boil and boil for 5 minutes, stirring constantly with a wooden spoon. Then pour the glaze over the warm cake, and let the cake cool completely in the pan. Cut the cake into squares, and serve.

caramel apple crunch dessert

from Tracey Barrett

Tracey brought this dessert to a holiday celebration at our house. Someone else brought a chocolate mousse torte from a famous Beverly Hills bakery. By the end of the evening, Tracey's dessert was all gone. I wound up giving most of the torte to my neighbors. This rustic crumbled pecan-studded apple cake is scooped into dessert dishes and smothered in molten caramel. Ta-ta to you, torte.

SERVES 12 TO 15   D

FOR THE CAKE

Unsalted butter or unflavored vegetable cooking
    spray, for greasing the pan
2 cups all-purpose flour, plus extra for dusting
    the pan
2 teaspoons baking soda
2 teaspoons ground cinnamon
$^1/_2$ teaspoon ground nutmeg
1 teaspoon salt
8 tablespoons (1 stick) unsalted butter,
    at room temperature
2 cups granulated sugar
2 large eggs
2 teaspoons pure vanilla extract
4 cups chopped, peeled, firm, sweet apples
1 cup pecan or walnut pieces, toasted
    (see box, page 17) and chopped

FOR THE CARAMEL SAUCE

8 tablespoons (1 stick) unsalted butter
$^1/_2$ cup granulated sugar
$^1/_2$ cup (packed) dark brown sugar
$^3/_4$ cup half-and-half

1. Preheat the oven to 350°F. Grease a 13 × 9-inch baking pan, dust it with flour, and tap out the excess.

2. Sift the flour, baking soda, cinnamon, nutmeg, and salt together into a medium-size bowl. Set it aside.

3. Cream the butter and sugar with an electric mixer on medium speed until well combined, about 2 minutes. Add the eggs, one at a time, scraping the bowl and beating well after each addition. Beat until light. Beat in the vanilla. Reduce the speed to low and blend in the flour mixture just until incorporated. The batter will be quite stiff. Stir in the apples and pecans.

4. Scrape the mixture evenly into the prepared baking pan, and bake on the center oven rack until the cake is brown around the edges and the center is barely set, 40 to 45 minutes.

5. Meanwhile, prepare the sauce: Combine the butter, both sugars, and the half-and-half in the top of a double boiler set over simmering water. Cook, stirring, until thick and golden, about 10 minutes.

6. Crumble the cake into individual dessert dishes. Pour the warm sauce over the cake, and serve immediately.

not-so-bitter almond cake

from Hinda Rabinowitz

In her younger days Mama Hinda was famous for her Bitter Almond Cake, but alas, years later, bitter almonds were found to be mildly toxic if eaten raw (as if someone would) and became virtually unavailable to the home baker. Although experts advise you to use almonds plus some almond extract or oil of bitter almonds (if you can find it), something gets lost in the translation. The original recipe, so flavorful with the bitter almonds, proved a bit blah without them. Adding some almond extract helped, but I found that introducing grated chocolate produced a lovely blend of flavors. I think Mama Hinda, a great pragmatist, accustomed as she was to making do with what she had, would have approved. The chocolate stays in tiny dark specks—very subtle, until you taste it. Dust the cake with confectioners' sugar for a "special occasion" appearance. **SERVES 12** **P**

Vegetable oil or unflavored vegetable cooking spray, for greasing the pan

2 cups sifted all-purpose flour, plus extra for dusting the pan

1¹/2 cups whole almonds (with skin), toasted (see box, page 17)

2 teaspoons baking powder

2 ounces semisweet chocolate, grated

6 large eggs, separated

1¹/2 cups sugar

Finely grated zest of 1 orange

Finely grated zest of 1 lemon

¹/2 cup vegetable oil

³/4 cup orange juice (preferably fresh)

¹/4 teaspoon pure almond extract

1. Preheat the oven to 325°F. Grease a 10-inch tube pan with removable bottom, dust it with flour, and tap out the excess.

2. Combine ¹/2 cup of the flour and the almonds in a food processor, and process until the almonds are very finely ground. Transfer the mixture to a medium-size bowl and whisk in the remaining flour, the baking powder, and the grated chocolate.

3. Beat the egg yolks and ³/4 cup of the sugar with an electric mixer on high speed until thick and light, 3 to 4 minutes. Add both zests and the oil, orange juice, and almond extract. Beat on low speed until well blended. Add the flour mixture and beat on medium speed just until well blended.

4. Using a clean, dry bowl and beaters, beat the egg whites on medium-high speed

until soft peaks form. Add the remaining $^3/_4$ cup sugar, a tablespoon at a time, beating for 10 seconds after each addition. Then raise the speed to high and beat until stiff peaks form, about 6 minutes total. Stir one fourth of the beaten egg whites into the batter to lighten it. Then add the remaining whites in three additions, folding them in until incorporated.

5. Scrape the batter into the prepared tube pan, and bake on the center oven rack until the top springs back when touched and a cake tester inserted in the center comes out clean, 55 to 65 minutes. Let the cake cool in the pan set on a wire rack for 15 minutes. Then run a knife around the center tube and the side of the pan, and lift the tube from the outer pan. Gently slide the knife between the bottom of the cake and the pan, and lift the cake off the pan. Return the cake to the wire rack to cool completely. Cut the cake into slices, and serve.

tanta esther gittel's husband's second wife lena's nut cake

from Estelle Robbins

sther Gittel, who died in her fifties, was Papa Harry's sister from Atlanta, and my brother, Gary,

was named for her. (His legal name is Earl Gary, but my mother says Papa Harry called him "Oil-a-la," so out went the "Earl.")

The toasted hazelnuts give this moist, dense cake a lovely earthy flavor, playing nicely against a delicate accent of orange. It would be smashing with a chocolate glaze dripping down the sides for a special occasion (try the Chocolate Glaze on page 423), but is excellent on its own for snacking, tea, or more informal gatherings.

SERVES 10 ▪ **D**

Unsalted butter or unflavored vegetable cooking spray, for greasing the pan

1¹/₂ cups sugar

¹/₂ pound (2 sticks) unsalted butter, at room temperature

4 large eggs, separated

1¹/₂ teaspoons pure vanilla extract

1 teaspoon pure orange extract

Finely grated zest of 1 orange

1¹/₂ cups sifted all-purpose flour, plus extra for dusting the pan

1¹/₂ cups chopped hazelnuts, toasted (see Note)

1¹/₂ teaspoons baking powder

¹/₄ teaspoon salt

¹/₂ cup whole milk

1. Preheat the oven to 350°F. Grease a 9-cup Bundt pan, dust it with flour, and tap out the excess.

2. Remove 2 tablespoons of the sugar and set it aside. Cream the butter and the remaining sugar with an electric mixer on medium speed, scraping the bowl several

times, until light and fluffy, 3 to 4 minutes. Add the egg yolks, one at a time, beating well after each addition. Then beat in the extracts and the orange zest.

3. Combine $1/2$ cup of the flour and the hazelnuts in a food processor and process until the nuts are very finely ground, about 45 seconds. Transfer to a bowl and whisk in the remaining 1 cup flour, the baking powder, and the salt.

4. With the mixer on low speed, add the flour mixture in three additions, alternating with the milk in two additions, beginning and ending with the flour. Transfer the batter to a large bowl.

5. Using a clean, dry bowl and beaters, beat the egg whites on medium-high speed until soft peaks form. Add the reserved 2 tablespoons sugar, a tablespoon at a time, beating for 10 seconds after each addition. Then raise the speed to high and beat until stiff peaks form, about $2^1/2$ minutes total. Stir one fourth of the beaten egg whites into the batter to lighten it. Then add the remaining whites in three additions, folding them in until incorporated.

6. Scrape the batter into the prepared Bundt pan and smooth the top. Bake on the center oven rack until the top is golden brown, the cake springs back when lightly touched, and a cake tester comes out clean, 55 to 65 minutes. Let the cake cool in the pan set on a wire rack for 15 minutes. Then run a knife around the center and the edge of the cake, and turn it out on the rack to cool completely. Cut the cake into slices, and serve.

Note: I don't know about you, but I find skinning hazelnuts to be one of those thankless, dreary tasks that makes me want to run screaming out of the kitchen. Blessedly, some stores (such as Trader Joe's) now carry chopped, shelled, and skinned hazelnuts. Lena's recipe just called for "nuts," so feel free to substitute your favorite, although I find that hazelnuts combined with citrus is a perfect partnership.

If you can't find skinned hazelnuts or prefer to skin your own, here's what you do: Toast the shelled hazelnuts first (see box, page 17). Then, a handful at a time, place the warm nuts in a dish towel and rub them in the towel to remove as much of the skin as possible.

> It's hard for me now to recall childhood memories of my mom without thinking of my aunts too. I really had four mothers. My mother and Aunt Estelle, especially, were inseparable. And always so busy! Sewing and pinning and draping . . . and ripping, covering mistakes with laces and bows. Joyce and I never even suspected that we had problem figures. Everything we wore fit her lithe frame or my more, ahem, ample one. Did I appreciate that I had not one, but two personal couturiers? Probably not. I thought of my wardrobe as homemade, not handmade. It sounded so poor! Glamour to me was a store-bought dress. Oh, childhood memories. They're so selective!
>
> —JUDY BART KANCIGOR

mama hinda's maple walnut cake

from Irene, Sally, Estelle, Lil

My mother and her sisters all made Mama's maple walnut cake. It was their company special—even for each other! Soft and spongy, it reminds me of fall, with its sweet maple flavor. My mother probably hasn't made it in forty years, and Aunt Irene, Aunt Sally, and Aunt Estelle are gone, but I can still smell the aroma of walnuts toasting. **SERVES 12** P

Vegetable oil or unflavored vegetable cooking
   spray, for greasing the pan
2 cups sifted all-purpose flour, plus extra for
   dusting the pan
2 teaspoons baking powder
$^1/_2$ cup vegetable oil
$^3/_4$ cup cold brewed coffee
$2^1/_2$ teaspoons pure maple extract
7 large eggs, separated, at room temperature
1 cup (packed) light brown sugar
$^3/_4$ cup granulated sugar
$1^1/_4$ cups walnut halves and/or pieces,
   toasted (see box, page 17) and finely
   chopped

1. Preheat the oven to 350°F. Grease a 13 × 9-inch baking pan, dust it with flour, and tap out the excess.

2. Stir the flour and baking powder together in a bowl, and set it aside.

3. Combine the oil, coffee, and maple extract in another bowl, and set it aside.

4. Beat the egg yolks and brown sugar with an electric mixer on high speed, scraping the bowl several times, until very light and thick, 3 to 4 minutes. Reduce the speed to low and add the flour mixture in three additions, alternating with the oil mixture in two additions, beginning and ending with the flour.

5. Using a clean, dry bowl and beaters, beat the egg whites on medium-high speed until soft peaks form. Add the granulated sugar, a tablespoon at a time, beating for 10 seconds after each addition. Then raise the speed to high and beat until stiff peaks form, about 6 minutes total. Stir one fourth of the beaten egg whites into the batter to lighten it. Then add the remaining whites in three additions, folding them in until incorporated. Fold in the chopped walnuts.

6. Scrape the batter into the prepared baking pan and smooth the top. Bake on the center oven rack until the top is golden brown, the cake springs back when lightly touched, and a cake tester comes out clean, 55 to 65 minutes. Let the cake cool in the pan set on a wire rack. Cut the cake into squares, and serve it warm or at room temperature.

The four inseparable sisters: (Top) Aunt Estelle and my mom, Lillian. (Bottom) Aunt Sally and Aunt Irene, late '80s.

gesundheit kuchen
("good health cake")

from Herta Heidingsfelder

Herta Heidingsfelder, ninety as of this writing, still bakes her Gesundheit Kuchen for family and friends.

Herta remembers that in prewar Germany, it was customary to bring this cake to the sick or bereaved. She serves it often at family gatherings as, she says, the ingredients are pure and delicious and sure to bring good health to all who sit at the *kaffee klatsch* and enjoy it. Sometimes she tops this moist cake with a lemon glaze, at other times just a dusting of confectioners' sugar.

(There is a touching handwritten version of Gesundheit Kuchen from Mina Pächter in *In Memory's Kitchen*, edited by Cara De Silva, the tribute to the women of Terezín concentration camp who recorded their recipes from memory.) **SERVES 10 🄳**

¹/₂ pound (2 sticks) unsalted butter, at room temperature, plus extra for greasing the pan

2 cups sugar

5 large eggs, separated, at room temperature

2³/₄ cups self-rising flour

1 cup whole milk, heated to lukewarm

1 teaspoon pure vanilla extract

Grated zest of 1 lemon

Pinch of salt

Lemon Glaze (recipe follows) or confectioners' sugar

1. Preheat the oven to 350°F. Grease a 12-cup Bundt pan.

2. Blend the butter and sugar with an electric mixer on medium speed until smooth, about 2 minutes. Add the egg yolks and beat until light and fluffy, 5 minutes more. Then reduce the speed to low and add the flour in three additions, alternating with the warm milk in two additions, beginning and ending with the flour. Scrape the bowl, and blend in the vanilla and lemon zest.

3. Using a clean, dry bowl and beaters, beat the egg whites on medium-high speed until foamy, about 30 seconds. Add the salt and continue beating until stiff peaks form, 1¹/₂ to 2 minutes total. Stir one fourth of the beaten egg whites into the batter to lighten it. Then add the remaining whites in three additions, folding them in until incorporated.

4. Scrape the batter into the prepared Bundt pan, and bake on the center oven rack until a cake tester inserted in the center comes out clean, about 45 minutes. Let the cake cool in the pan set on a wire rack for 10 minutes. Then run a knife around the center and edges of the cake, and turn it out. Return it to the rack to cool completely. Place a sheet of waxed paper under the rack to catch the spills of the glaze, if using.

5. Drizzle the cooled cake with Lemon Glaze, if you like, or just before serving, sprinkle it with confectioners' sugar.

lemon glaze

MAKES ⅓ CUP **P**

1 cup confectioners' sugar, sifted
1 to 2 tablespoons fresh lemon juice

Combine the confectioners' sugar and 1 tablespoon of the lemon juice in a small bowl, and stir until smooth. Stir in additional lemon juice, a teaspoon at a time, until the glaze is of drizzling consistency. Use immediately.

cinnamon-nut sour cream coffee cake

from Robin Kancigor Boyko

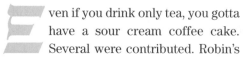

Even if you drink only tea, you gotta have a sour cream coffee cake. Several were contributed. Robin's took the cake! **SERVES 10 TO 12** **D**

Unsalted butter, at room temperature,
*   for greasing the pan*

FOR THE FILLING
½ cup (packed) dark brown sugar
6 tablespoons granulated sugar
½ teaspoon pure vanilla extract
1½ teaspoons ground cinnamon
1½ cups walnut halves and/or pieces, toasted
*   (see box, page 17) and chopped*
1 tablespoon unsalted butter, melted

FOR THE CAKE
2 cups sifted all-purpose flour
1½ teaspoons baking powder
1½ teaspoons baking soda
½ teaspoon salt
12 tablespoons (1½ sticks) unsalted butter,
*   at room temperature*
1½ cups granulated sugar
2¼ teaspoons pure vanilla extract
3 large eggs, at room temperature
1¼ cups sour cream, at room temperature

1. Preheat the oven to 350°F. Liberally grease a 10-inch tube pan with removable bottom.

2. Prepare the filling: Combine all the filling ingredients in a bowl. Mix well and set it aside.

3. Prepare the cake: Sift the flour, baking powder, baking soda, and salt together into a bowl. Set it aside.

4. Cream the butter with an electric mixer on medium speed. Add the sugar and vanilla, and beat until light and fluffy, about 2 minutes. Add the eggs, one at a time, beating well and scraping the bowl after each addition.

Reduce the speed to low and add the flour mixture in three additions, alternating with the sour cream in two additions, beginning and ending with the flour. Scrape the bowl and beat until smooth after each addition.

5. Pack 1 cup of the filling evenly over the bottom of the prepared tube pan. Cover with half of the batter. Spread 1¹⁄₄ cups of the filling evenly over the batter, and cover with the remaining batter. Top with the remaining filling.

6. Bake on the center oven rack until a cake tester inserted in the center comes out clean, about 1 hour. Let the cake cool in the pan set on a wire rack for 10 minutes. Then run a knife around the center tube and the sides of the pan, and lift the tube from the outer pan. Gently slide the knife between the bottom of the cake and the pan, and lift the cake off the pan. Return the cake to the rack to cool completely. Cut the cake into slices, and serve.

budapest coffee cake

from Irene Rosenthal

Aunt Irene once had a Hungarian neighbor who shared her family's coffee cake recipe. Leave it to Aunt Irene, who would work painstakingly on her decorated butter cookies, to have the patience to spread the filling between the four very thin layers of batter. I've given instructions for four layers, but cheating with three layers will still give you a delicious, robust cake with a homey cinnamon-flavored chocolate, raisin, and walnut filling. **SERVES 10 TO 12**

FOR THE FILLING AND TOPPING

³⁄₄ cup (packed) dark brown sugar

1 tablespoon ground cinnamon

1 tablespoon unsweetened cocoa powder

¹⁄₄ cup raisins, chopped

1 cup walnut halves and/or pieces, toasted
  (see box, page 17) and finely chopped

FOR THE CAKE

3 cups all-purpose flour

1¹⁄₂ teaspoons baking powder

1¹⁄₂ teaspoons baking soda

¹⁄₂ teaspoon salt

12 tablespoons (1¹⁄₂ sticks) unsalted butter,
  at room temperature, plus extra for
  greasing the pan

1¹⁄₂ cups granulated sugar

2 teaspoons pure vanilla extract

3 large eggs, at room temperature

2 cups sour cream, at room temperature

1. Prepare the filling/topping: Combine the brown sugar, cinnamon, and cocoa powder in a bowl, and mix thoroughly. Stir in the raisins and walnuts, and set it aside.

2. Preheat the oven to 375°F. Very generously butter a 10-inch tube pan with removable bottom.

3. Prepare the cake: Sift the flour, baking powder, baking soda, and salt together into a bowl, and set it aside.

4. Cream the butter with an electric mixer on medium speed. Add the sugar and vanilla, and beat until light and fluffy, about 2 minutes. Add the eggs, one at a time, beating well and scraping the bowl after each addition. Raise the speed to high, and beat until the mixture is light and creamy, about 1 minute. Then reduce the speed to low and add the flour mixture in three additions, alternating with the sour cream in two additions, beginning and ending with the flour. Scrape the bowl and beat until smooth after each addition.

5. Spread a thin layer of the batter in the prepared tube pan. (To spread the batter thin, drop it by tiny spoonfuls and then spread it out with the back of a spoon.) Sprinkle with about one third of the filling. Repeat, making four layers of batter and three layers of filling, ending with batter.

6. Bake on the center oven rack until a cake tester inserted in the center comes out clean, 50 to 60 minutes. Let the cake cool in the pan set on a wire rack for 10 minutes. Then run a knife around the center tube and the sides of the pan, and lift the tube from the outer pan. Gently slide the knife between the bottom of the cake and the pan, and lift the cake off the pan. Return the cake to the rack to cool completely.

Aunt Irene, 1939.

melissa hakim's pecan streusel coffee cake

from Arlene Feltingoff

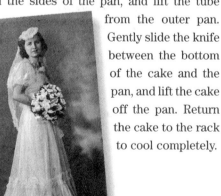

When Arlene's daughter Melissa and hubby Harvey stayed at the Whitehall Inn, a bed and breakfast in New Hope, Pennsylvania, Melissa brought home this recipe, which has become her signature and always brings back fond memories of a delightful weekend in that rustic stone farmhouse. This cake is especially wonderful for breakfast, as you can assemble it the night before and pop it in the oven in the morning. Melissa prefers pecans to the walnuts in the original recipe. **SERVES 12**　　**D**

FOR THE CAKE

Unsalted butter or unflavored vegetable cooking spray, for greasing the pan

2 cups all-purpose flour

1 teaspoon baking powder

1 teaspoon baking soda

1 teaspoon ground cinnamon

$1/2$ teaspoon salt

$2/3$ cup (10 tablespoons plus 2 teaspoons) unsalted butter, at room temperature

$1/2$ cup (packed) light brown sugar

1 cup granulated sugar

2 large eggs, at room temperature

1 cup buttermilk, at room temperature

FOR THE STREUSEL TOPPING

1 cup (packed) light brown sugar

1 teaspoon ground cinnamon

1 teaspoon ground nutmeg

¹/₂ cup chopped pecans

1. Generously grease a 13 × 9-inch baking pan.

2. Combine the flour, baking powder, baking soda, cinnamon, and salt in a bowl. Stir well, and set it aside.

3. Cream the butter and both sugars with an electric mixer on medium speed until light and fluffy, about 2 minutes. Add the eggs, one at a time, beating well after each addition. Reduce the speed to low and add the flour mixture in three additions, alternating with the buttermilk in two additions, beginning and ending with the flour. Scrape the batter into the prepared baking pan.

4. Mix all the topping ingredients together in a bowl. Sprinkle the topping evenly over the batter and pat it lightly

> *When I was dating, my mother [Irene] would be very upset if I was seeing too many different boys. She was always worried about what the neighbors would think, seeing different cars parked in front of our home. She also didn't like what she called the 'porch people.' Carole and I were not allowed to entertain on the porch. All guests had to come inside or go in the backyard. Only yentas congregated on the porch!*
>
> **—PHYLLIS EPSTEIN**

into the surface. Refrigerate, covered, overnight.

5. When you are ready to bake, preheat the oven to 350°F.

6. Bake the coffee cake on the center oven rack until a cake tester inserted in the center comes out clean, about 45 minutes. Transfer the pan to a wire rack to cool.

7. Cut the coffee cake into squares, and serve it warm or at room temperature.

grandma ethel jaffee's yeast cake

from Janice Einsbruch

This cake is huge and will serve quite a crowd—it takes up a whole sheet pan. The original recipe was even larger, calling for 4 cents yeast! The half version here is very impressive and works well in a bread machine. The glaze adds a bit of sweetness, but you could eliminate it if you want to serve the cake warm. To partially prepare it ahead, shape the cake and let it rise about halfway. Then cover it with plastic wrap and refrigerate it overnight. (It will continue rising in the refrigerator.) The next morning, simply pop it straight into a preheated oven. **SERVES 16 TO 24**

Parchment paper, for the baking sheet

FOR THE DOUGH

2¹/₄ teaspoons (1 package) active
    dry yeast

¹/₄ cup lukewarm water

¹/₂ cup sugar

1 large egg, at room temperature

Yolk of 1 large egg, at room temperature

¹/₂ cup sour cream, at room temperature

8 tablespoons (1 stick) unsalted butter,
    melted and cooled

3¹/₄ cups all-purpose flour, plus more
    as needed

¹/₂ teaspoon salt

FOR THE FILLING

8 tablespoons (1 stick) unsalted butter,
    at room temperature

²/₃ cup plus 2 tablespoons sugar

¹/₂ cup all-purpose flour

2 cups walnut halves and/or pieces,
    toasted (see box, page 17) and
    chopped

1 cup raisins

1¹/₂ tablespoons ground cinnamon

FOR THE TOP AND GLAZE

2 tablespoons unsalted butter, melted

1¹/₂ cups confectioners' sugar

1. Line a baking sheet with parchment paper, and set it aside.

2. Prepare the dough: Stir the yeast into the lukewarm water in a small bowl. Add 1 teaspoon of the sugar and blend well. Set it aside until the mixture looks foamy, about 5 minutes.

Jack and Ethel Jaffee, Aunt Sally and Uncle Lou, 1946. Sally and Ethel were dear friends and coconspirators. They arranged the shidduch (match) between Sally's brother Lou and Ethel's daughter Hilda.

3. Beat the remaining sugar, the egg, and the yolk with an electric mixer on medium speed just until well blended, about 1 minute. Blend in the yeast mixture. Then add the sour cream and melted butter, and beat for 1 minute. Reduce the speed to low and blend in the flour and salt until the dough comes together. Switch to the dough hook and knead on low speed until the dough is smooth and elastic, about 4 minutes. Add additional flour by the handful if the dough is too sticky. (Alternatively, turn the dough onto a lightly floured work surface and knead it by hand for 5 to 6 minutes.)

4. Lightly oil a bowl, and turn the dough in it so that it is covered with oil. Cover the bowl with a clean dish towel or plastic wrap. Let the dough rise in a warm place until doubled in size, 1¹/₂ to 2 hours.

5. Dust your work surface with flour. Turn the risen dough out of the bowl, dust the top of it with flour, and roll it out to form a thin rectangle, about 22 × 15 inches, with the long side parallel to the edge of your work surface.

6. Prepare the filling: Beat the butter, the 2/3 cup sugar, and the flour with an electric mixer on medium-low speed until smooth. Spread the mixture evenly over the dough, leaving a 1-inch border along the far long edge. Stir the nuts, raisins, cinnamon, and the remaining 2 tablespoons sugar together in a small bowl. Sprinkle this evenly over the butter mixture.

7. Brush the border lightly with water. Begin rolling the dough from the edge closest to you, tucking and straightening the dough as you roll it into a long, tight log. Pinch the seam to seal it. Shape the log into a large horseshoe and transfer it to the prepared baking sheet. Brush the top with the 2 tablespoons melted butter.

8. Preheat the oven to the lowest possible setting for 5 minutes; then turn the oven off. Cover the cake with a lint-free kitchen towel and place it in the turned-off oven. Let it rise until nearly doubled in size, about 1 1/2 hours. Remove the cake from the oven, and remove the towel.

9. Preheat the oven to 350°F.

10. Return the cake to the oven and bake it on the center oven rack until firm and golden brown, 35 to 40 minutes. Let the cake cool on the baking sheet set on a wire rack for 15 minutes. Then slide it off the sheet onto the rack and let it cool completely.

11. Prepare the glaze: Stir the confectioners' sugar with 2 to 2 1/2 tablespoons water in a small bowl until the mixture is smooth and thick. Place a sheet of waxed paper under the wire rack, and spread the glaze evenly over the top of the cake, allowing it to drip down the sides.

12. This cake is best eaten the same day it is baked, though it is still quite tasty the second day. Once the cake is cut, cover it with plastic wrap to keep it from going stale.

> " When Marilyn was a little girl, we went to Cuba to visit Lou's relatives, and Mama and Papa babysat. Mama made yeast cake, and when she wasn't looking, Marilyn stuck her little fingers in the cake and pulled out the nuts and raisins. When we came home, Mama told us to get an exterminator because there was a mouse in the house. **—SALLY BOWER** "

old-fashioned honey cake

from Irene Rosenthal

This is the dark, dense honey loaf, fragrant with spices, that we all recall from Rosh Hashanahs past. One bite and you can hear shofars blowing. **MAKES 1 LOAF** **P**

¹/₂ *cup raisins*

¹/₂ *cup orange juice*

2¹/₂ *cups plus 1 teaspoon all-purpose flour,*
plus extra for dusting the pan

2 *teaspoons baking powder*

¹/₂ *teaspoon baking soda*

1 *teaspoon ground cinnamon*

¹/₂ *teaspoon ground ginger*

¹/₂ *teaspoon ground cloves*

¹/₂ *teaspoon salt*

¹/₄ *cup vegetable oil, plus extra for*
greasing the pan

1 *cup sugar*

1 *cup honey*

2 *large eggs, separated, at room temperature*

Grated zest of 1 lemon

Grated zest of 1 orange

1 *cup strong brewed coffee, at room temperature*

¹/₂ *cup walnut pieces, toasted (see box, page 17)*
and chopped

1. Preheat the oven to 325°F. Grease a 9 × 5-inch loaf pan, dust it with flour, and tap out the excess.

2. Combine the raisins and orange juice in a small bowl, and set it aside until the raisins have plumped, 15 minutes.

3. Meanwhile, sift the 2¹/₂ cups flour and the baking powder, baking soda, cinnamon, ginger, cloves, and salt together into a bowl. Set it aside.

4. Blend the oil, sugar, honey, egg yolks, and both zests with an electric mixer on medium speed until thick and well blended, about 3 minutes. Reduce the speed to low and add the flour mixture in three additions, alternating with the coffee in two additions, beginning and ending with the flour.

5. Drain the raisins and discard (or drink) the orange juice. Dry the raisins with a paper towel. Mix the walnuts and raisins with the remaining 1 teaspoon flour, and stir them into the batter.

6. Using a clean, dry bowl and beaters, beat the egg whites on medium-high speed until stiff peaks form, 1 to 1¹/₂ minutes. Stir one fourth of the beaten egg whites into the batter to lighten it. Then add the remaining whites in three additions, folding them in until incorporated.

7. Scrape the batter into the prepared loaf pan, and bake on the center oven rack until the cake springs back when lightly touched and a cake tester inserted in the center comes out clean, 1 hour and 5 to 15 minutes. Allow the cake to cool in the pan set on a wire rack for 15 minutes. Then run a knife around the edges and turn the loaf out. Return it to the rack to cool completely. Cut the cake into slices, and serve.

Aunt Irene inspecting
my crocheting, 1995.

Our family was so large and Mama was so busy that my sister Irene was my second mother. She wanted me to amount to something and paid for my singing lessons and made sure I studied. She took me to concerts at Lewisohn Stadium in the Bronx when I was just a child. If I was in a bind, Irene was always there.

—LILLIAN BART

nova scotia honey orange sponge cake

from Lillian Bart

y mother got this recipe from her friend Corinne in Nova Scotia. We visited with them the summer before I turned fourteen, when I refused to go to sleep-away camp anymore. I traveled with my parents as they sang their way through the Catskills and Berkshires and then ferried up to Nova Scotia. Most memorable for me was the arrival of Princess Margaret, who almost killed herself stepping out of her shoe as she exited the helicopter. For my mother, most impressive was Corinne sending her mother out back to dig up potatoes for our dinner.

Through the years Corinne and my mom shared recipes before they lost touch (and if we could remember her last name, we'd tell you!). We've always loved this one, a light honey cake, really a honey sponge. Serve thick slices with Aunt Sally's Apricot Pineapple Conserve (the variation, page 367) and start a new tradition.

SERVES 12　　**P**

Parchment paper, for the pan

1 cup cake flour

1³/₄ cups all-purpose flour

1 teaspoon baking powder

1 teaspoon baking soda

1 teaspoon ground cinnamon

1 teaspoon ground allspice

1 teaspoon ground ginger

1 teaspoon salt

1 cup sugar

6 large eggs, separated, at room temperature

1 cup corn oil

1 cup honey

2 tablespoons orange juice

2 tablespoons orange liqueur or brandy

Grated zest of 1 orange

1 teaspoon pure orange extract

1. Preheat the oven to 325°F. Line a 10-inch tube pan with removable bottom with a circle of parchment paper cut slightly larger than the bottom. Press the extra paper against the sides of the pan.

2. Sift both flours and the baking powder, baking soda, cinnamon, allspice, ginger, and salt together into a bowl. Set it aside.

The choir rehearsing (Dad, the cantor in the background) for their gig at Stevensville Hotel in the Catskills (Mom, second from left, Seymour Brenner conducting), 1950s.

3. Set aside $^1/_4$ cup of the sugar.

4. Beat the egg yolks very well with an electric mixer on medium-high speed. Gradually add the remaining $^3/_4$ cup sugar, and continue blending until the mixture is thick and lemon-colored, about 3 minutes. Reduce the speed to medium and blend in the oil and honey. Then blend in the orange juice, liqueur, zest, and extract. Reduce the speed to low and gradually blend in the flour mixture.

5. Using a clean, dry bowl and beaters, beat the egg whites on medium-high speed until soft peaks form. Add the reserved $^1/_4$ cup sugar, a tablespoon at a time, beating for 10 seconds after each addition. Then raise the speed to high and beat until stiff peaks form, 4 minutes total. Stir one fourth of the egg whites into the batter to lighten it. Then add the remaining egg whites in three additions, folding them in until incorporated.

6. Scrape the batter into the prepared tube pan and bake on the center oven rack for 30 minutes. Reduce the temperature to 300°F and continue baking until the top of the cake springs back when touched, about 45 minutes more.

7. Let the cake rest in the pan for 30 to 45 seconds. Then invert the pan on its little feet (if your tube pan has them) or over a soda bottle (making sure it sits level) and let the cake cool completely.

8. Run a knife around the center tube and the side of the pan, and lift the tube from the outer pan. Gently slide the knife between the bottom of the cake and the pan, and lift the cake off the pan. Cut the cake into slices, and serve.

coffee cloud sponge cake

from Fanny Vitner

Cousin Ellen's Grandma Fanny was known for her baking, and indeed I found her recipes all over Aunt Estelle's and Aunt Sally's handwritten cookbooks. When I posted her Coffee Cloud Sponge Cake recipe on the Jewish Food List on the Internet, Judy Sennesh of New York wrote that she adds Coffee-Rum Syrup and Coffee Whipped Cream to her own version. I thought, what could be bad? Billowy cumulous mounds of cream swirled atop Fanny's ethereal coffee cloud. Heavenly! Ellen says her grandma would have wished she had thought of it. **SERVES 10 P or D**

2 cups all-purpose flour

1$^1/_2$ teaspoons baking powder

$^1/_2$ teaspoon salt

6 large eggs, separated

1$^1/_2$ cups sugar

1 tablespoon instant coffee granules
   dissolved in $^1/_2$ cup hot water,
   cooled

1 teaspoon pure vanilla extract

1 cup walnut pieces, toasted (see box, page 17)
   and chopped (optional)

$^1/_2$ teaspoon cream of tartar

Coffee-Rum Syrup (optional; recipe follows)

Coffee Whipped Cream (optional;
   recipe page 417)

1. Preheat the oven to 350°F. Have ready an ungreased 10-inch tube pan with removable bottom.

2. Sift the flour, baking powder, and salt together into a bowl, and set it aside.

3. Beat the egg yolks with an electric mixer on medium-high speed, and gradually add ³/₄ cup of the sugar. Scrape the bowl, and beat until lemon-yellow and thick, about 5 minutes. Reduce the speed to low and add the flour mixture in three additions, alternating with the coffee in two additions, beginning and ending with the flour. Beat in the vanilla. Fold in the nuts, if using.

4. Using a clean, dry bowl and beaters, beat the egg whites on medium-high speed until foamy, about 30 seconds. Add the cream of tartar and continue beating until soft peaks form. Add the remaining ³/₄ cup sugar, a tablespoon at a time, beating for 10 seconds after each addition. Then raise the speed to high and beat until stiff peaks form, about 5 minutes total. Stir one fourth of the beaten egg whites into the batter to lighten it. Then add the remaining whites in three additions, folding them in until incorporated.

5. Scrape the batter into the tube pan and bake on the center oven rack until the top is golden brown, the cake springs back when lightly touched, and a cake tester comes out clean, 60 to 65 minutes.

6. Remove the pan from the oven and allow the cake to rest for 30 to

45 seconds. Then invert the cake on its little feet (if your tube pan has them) or over a soda bottle (making sure it sits level). Let it cool for 30 minutes if using the Coffee-Rum Syrup, or let it cool completely if not.

7. Run a knife around the center tube and the side of the pan, and lift the tube from the outer pan. Gently slide the knife between the bottom of the cake and the pan, and lift the cake off the pan. Top the cake with the syrup and/or Coffee Whipped Cream, as desired, or serve it plain, as Fanny did.

coffee-rum syrup

MAKES ABOUT 1 CUP   **P**

¹/₂ cup sugar
2 teaspoons instant coffee granules
¹/₄ cup rum

1. Combine the sugar, coffee granules, and ¹/₂ cup water in a small saucepan and bring to a boil. Reduce the heat and simmer for 2 minutes. Remove the pan from the heat and add the rum.

2. Place the lukewarm cake on a serving plate. Prick the top and sides of the cake with a skewer. Slowly spoon the syrup over the top and sides of the cake until all the liquid has been absorbed.

Cousin Ellen with Grandma Fanny, mid '60s.

rosh hashanah/yom kippur

With the first crisp breeze at summer's close, I am filled with memories. Color War and the end of camp. The smell of newly sharpened pencils. New school clothes, and for the High Holidays: new hat, new gloves, new dress for each service. The haunting wail of the *shofar* (ram's horn) wafting up from the basement as my dad practices. *"Tekiah . . ."*

Because my father was a part-time cantor, we spent the High Holidays not with Mama and Papa and the family, but at various Catskills resorts and later at the Riverside Plaza Hotel in Manhattan, where my father performed for a congregation that had lost its building in a fire and never rebuilt. His Yemenite rendition of part of the service I have never heard since. And the chanting of *Kol Nidre* makes me wistful to this day. Alas, we never recorded his version.

According to *The Essential Book of Jewish Festival Cooking,* by sisters Miriyam Glazer and Phyllis Glazer (who coincidentally were practically my neighbors in Belle Harbor), there is no holiday called Rosh Hashanah in the Bible, only Yom Tru'ah, and the day of the blowing of the *shofar.* The destruction of the Second Temple in 70 C.E. changed forever the way we worship, conduct our daily life, and celebrate. The holidays, once markers of the agricultural seasons, were remolded by the rabbis and sages in the Diaspora. Rosh Hashanah evolved because, although our New Year had been in the spring, our ancestors adapted to the culture they were living in, which celebrated the New Year in the fall.

Over the centuries, as the Jewish people dispersed across the globe, traditions were added to the observance of the festivals. Jews of Eastern European descent dip apple slices in honey to wish each other a sweet year and eat carrots because the Yiddish word for carrots, *merren,* also means "increased," so we wish for "increased" health and prosperity at this time. No sour or bitter dishes appear on the Rosh Hashanah table. Some communities will not eat nuts at this time because the Hebrew word for "nut" has the same numerical value as the word for "sin."

The traditional challah (page 328) is baked into a majestic round spiral rather than the usual braid, symbolizing the cycle of life. (Mama Hinda included raisins for extra sweetness only at this time.)

Because Rosh Hashanah comes at the beginning of the lunar month, when the moon is hidden, some eat "hidden" or stuffed foods, such as kreplach (page 67). It is customary to serve the head of a fish, so we may be like the head and not the tail.

As we ready for the holiday, the expression "busy as a bee" comes to mind, and let's hope the bees really have been busy, because the quintessential ingredient of this festival table is honey. For Ashkenazim the holiday feast begins by dipping apples in honey and ends with honey cake and taiglach (page 485), little balls of dough boiled in honey syrup. Sephardim might enjoy baklava and will serve dates, quinces, or many-seeded pomegranates, symbolizing the wish that our people be numerous. Moroccans often eat vegetables sprinkled with sugar.

Traditionally on Rosh Hashanah we serve new fruits of the season. When she was a child, my cousin Lorraine knew that Rosh Hashanah was approaching when tiny Italian plums came into season for her mother Herta's Plum "Cake" (page 438).

The climax of the season is Yom Kippur, the Day of Atonement, the holiest day of the year, a time to repent and make amends. Aunt Sally remembered, from her childhood, the ritual of *kapores*—a live chicken waved over their heads to absorb their sins.

After the day of prayer and fasting, we enjoy a festive Break-the-Fast, usually a dairy meal, much like a brunch menu: fish, salads, kugels, bagels and lox, fruit, and of course honey cake, a sweet ending as we look forward to the sweet year ahead and wish each other *L'Shana Tova!*

coffee whipped cream

● ● ●

MAKES ABOUT 2 CUPS 🄳

1 cup heavy (whipping) cream
2¹/₂ teaspoons instant coffee granules
¹/₄ cup sugar
¹/₂ teaspoon pure vanilla extract

Whip the cream, coffee granules, sugar, and vanilla with an electric mixer on high speed until stiff peaks form, about 1¹/₄ minutes. Cover the top and sides of the cooled cake with the Coffee Whipped Cream. Refrigerate until ready to serve.

grandma fanny vitner's sponge cake

from Ellen Gardner

Ellen learned how to make sponge cake at her grandma's knee. Well, not her knee exactly, but from a precious letter sent to her when Ellen and Richard were newlyweds. **SERVES 10** 🄿

❝ *I used to love spending the night at my Grandma Fanny's. She taught me to drink coffee when I was little by filling the cup with more milk than coffee and giving me sugar cubes that I would hold in my mouth and suck on to make the coffee sweet.* —**ELLEN GARDNER** ❞

1¹/₂ cups all-purpose flour
1 teaspoon baking powder
6 large eggs, separated
1¹/₂ cups sugar
¹/₂ cup orange or pineapple juice
Pinch of salt

1. Preheat the oven to 350°F. Have ready an ungreased 10-inch tube pan with removable bottom.

2. Sift the flour and baking powder together into a bowl, and set it aside.

3. Beat the egg yolks with an electric mixer on medium-high speed, and gradually add ³/₄ cup of the sugar. Scrape the bowl and beat until the mixture is lemon-yellow and thick, about 5 minutes. Reduce the speed to low and add the flour mixture in three additions, alternating with the juice in two additions, beginning and ending with the flour.

4. Using a clean, dry bowl and beaters, beat the egg whites on medium-high speed until foamy, about 30 seconds. Add the salt and continue beating until soft peaks form. Add the remaining ³/₄ cup sugar, a tablespoon at a time, beating for 10 seconds after each addition. Then raise the speed to high and beat until stiff peaks form, about 5 minutes total. Stir one fourth of the beaten egg whites into the batter to lighten it. Then add

the remaining whites in three additions, folding them in until incorporated.

5. Scrape the batter into the tube pan, and bake on the center oven rack until the top is golden brown, the cake springs back when lightly touched, and a cake tester comes out clean, 60 to 70 minutes. Remove the pan from the oven and allow the cake to rest for 30 to 45 seconds. Then invert the pan on its little feet (if your tube pan has them) or over a soda bottle (making sure it sits level), and let it cool completely.

6. Run a knife around the center tube and the sides of the pan, and lift the tube from the outer pan. Gently slide the knife between the bottom of the cake and the pan, and lift the cake off the pan. Slice the cake with a serrated knife, and serve.

strawberry jelly roll

from Sally Bower

ho knows how many jelly rolls came out of Aunt Sally's kitchen. This golden yellow roll with its pleasing eggy flavor and spongy texture rises quite high, so it's best to roll it lengthwise. The flavor of the jam really comes

Cousin Ellen cooling off in Las Vegas.

"As Ellen's aunt, I was delighted to host Richard and Ellen's rehearsal dinner the night before their wedding. All the Rabinowitz relatives had come to Atlanta from New York for the occasion, and as usual, Ellen's father, Morris, from Atlanta and his identical twin, Lou, from New York were up to their old tricks of switching jackets to fool the kids. My son Michael, who was just a child at the time, got very upset that the New Yorkers wouldn't stand in line at the buffet and complained, 'Those Northerners!' He thought he was talking to Morris, but he was talking to Lou! Then we ran out of fried chicken, and when I asked Nellie, our housekeeper, why there wasn't enough food, she said, 'You didn't tell me that Northerners were coming!'

—JOANNE VITNER"

Sponge Cake Recipe

6 Eggs
1 1/2 Cups Flour
1 Teaspoon Baking Powder
Pinch of Salt.
1/2 Cup (either O Juice or Pinea
1 1/2 Cup Sugar.

Seperate the Whites of the
beat them good until s
beating them add 3/4 cup s
until its good & foamy (also i
Now get to the yellow of the 6
beat them until good & stiff
don't forget the 3/4 cup of th
which its left from the 1/2
after the yellow is nice
the flour which
Baking Pow

through, so try to use one of good quality.

SERVES 10 🅿 or 🅳

Vegetable oil, for greasing the pan

1¹/₃ cups cake flour, sifted

2¹/₄ teaspoons baking powder

¹/₄ teaspoon salt

4 large eggs

6 tablespoons cold water

1¹/₃ cups sugar

1 teaspoon pure vanilla extract

1 cup strawberry jam

Whipped cream, for garnish (optional)

1. Preheat the oven to 400°F. Line a 15-inch jelly roll pan with waxed paper, and grease the waxed paper lightly.

2. Sift the flour, baking powder, and salt together into a bowl, and set it aside.

3. Beat the eggs with an electric mixer on medium-high speed until light and frothy, about 2 minutes. Add the cold water, a little at a time, continuing to beat. Then gradually add the sugar. Reduce the speed to low and gradually add the flour mixture, mixing just until blended, followed by the vanilla.

4. Spread the batter evenly in the prepared pan and level it (an offset spatula works best for this). Bake on the center oven rack until the cake springs back when pressed lightly with a finger, 12 to 15 minutes.

5. Meanwhile, lightly dampen a lint-free kitchen towel, and spread it out on a work surface.

6. When the cake is done, immediately invert it onto the dampened towel and peel off the waxed paper. Spread the jam over the cake, and starting at one long side, roll

the cake, using the towel as a guide, to form a long log. Let the cake cool completely on a wire rack, covered with the towel.

7. Slice the roll with a serrated knife. Serve garnished with whipped cream, if you like.

> " *Some of my fondest memories are of spending summer days in Belle Harbor at the beach and then going back to Grandma Sally's for a barbecue. Papa Lou would burn every piece of meat to a crisp. I loved to raid the raspberry bush, and Grandma Sally would yell at me for picking them before they were ripe."*
>
> **—NEIL DUBIN**

> *"Neil didn't like strawberries, so for him I would fill the jelly roll with a soft chocolate filling. We used to have a raspberry bush. When they were in season I'd use raspberries. That Neil liked.*
>
> **—SALLY BOWER** "

chocolate cream roll

from Estelle Robbins

I f Aunt Sally's Strawberry Jelly Roll was the June Allyson of the dessert table—bright and cheery and all-American—Aunt Estelle's Chocolate Cream Roll was the Jane Russell: dark and seductive on the outside, soft-hearted within. The richness of the cream filling nicely complements the chocolate flavor of this fluffy dark roll, further enhanced by bits of shaved chocolate. **SERVES 10** **D**

FOR THE CAKE

1¹/₂ tablespoons vegetable oil

6 large eggs, separated

¹/₂ teaspoon cream of tartar

1 cup granulated sugar

¹/₂ cup Dutch-process unsweetened
    cocoa powder, such as Droste, sifted,
      plus extra for dusting the towel

1 teaspoon pure vanilla extract

¹/₂ cup self-rising flour, sifted

Confectioners' sugar, for dusting the towel

FOR THE FILLING AND GARNISH

1 cup very cold heavy (whipping) cream

1 tablespoon sugar

1 teaspoon pure vanilla extract

2 cups shaved semisweet chocolate

1. Preheat the oven to 350°F. Grease the bottom of a 17-inch jelly roll pan with about 1¹/₂ teaspoons of the oil. Line the pan with waxed paper, extending it about 1 inch over the ends, and grease the waxed paper with the remaining oil.

2. Beat the egg whites with an electric mixer on medium-high speed until foamy, about 1 minute. Add the cream of tartar and continue beating until soft peaks form. Add the sugar, a tablespoon at a time, beating for 10 seconds after each addition. Then raise the speed to high and beat until stiff peaks form, about 6 minutes total.

3. Add the egg yolks, cocoa powder, and vanilla, and beat with a wooden spoon until

Aunt Estelle's home was not only the site of her thriving dressmaking business; it was a meeting place. As a hem was raised, a waist nipped in, recipes were exchanged along with the gossip and glitz. She heard it all; nothing could faze her. But a new cake recipe would always raise an eyebrow.

—JUDY BART KANCIGOR

light and creamy. Very gently fold in the flour, a little at a time. Spread the batter evenly in the prepared pan and level it (an offset spatula works best for this). Bake on the center oven rack until the surface springs back when touched lightly with a finger, about 15 minutes.

4. Meanwhile, spread a lint-free kitchen towel on a work surface, and dust it lightly with cocoa powder and confectioners' sugar.

5. When the cake is done, immediately invert it onto the dusted towel and peel off the waxed paper. Trim the crusty edges with a sharp knife. Starting at one long side, roll the cake, using the towel as a guide to form a log. Let the cake cool completely, covered with the towel, on a wire rack.

6. Prepare the filling: Whip the cream, sugar, and vanilla together with an electric mixer on high speed until stiff, about 1¹/₂ minutes.

7. Carefully unroll the cake, and spread the sweetened whipped cream over it. Sprinkle with 1¹/₂ cups of the shaved chocolate, and reroll.

8. Slice the roll with a serrated knife. Serve garnished with the remaining shaved chocolate.

joyce simpson's pumpkin nut roll

from Randy Bart

my nephew Randy is better known for his photography than for his baking, but this pumpkin roll is his specialty, especially appreciated by his bride, Isabelle, a transplant from France, for whom Thanksgiving is an exotic new tradition. **SERVES 10** □

FOR THE CAKE

Vegetable oil, for greasing the pan

³/4 cup all-purpose flour, plus extra
for dusting the pan

1 teaspoon baking powder

2 teaspoons ground cinnamon

1 teaspoon ground ginger

¹/2 teaspoon ground nutmeg

¹/2 teaspoon salt

3 large eggs, at room temperature

1 cup granulated sugar

²/3 cup canned pumpkin
(not pumpkin pie mix)

1 teaspoon fresh lemon juice

1 cup walnut halves and/or pieces,
finely chopped

Confectioners' sugar,
for dusting the towel

FOR THE FILLING

6 ounces cream cheese, at room
temperature

4 tablespoons (¹/2 stick) unsalted butter,
at room temperature

1 cup confectioners' sugar, sifted

¹/2 teaspoon pure vanilla extract

1. Preheat the oven to 375°F. Grease a 15-inch jelly roll pan, dust it with flour, and tap out the excess.

2. Stir the flour, baking powder, cinnamon, ginger, nutmeg, and salt together in a bowl. Set it aside.

3. Beat the eggs with an electric mixer on high speed for 5 minutes. Gradually beat in the sugar. Stir in the pumpkin and lemon juice. Fold the flour mixture into the pumpkin mixture.

4. Spread the batter evenly in the prepared pan and level it (an offset spatula works best for this). Sprinkle with the walnuts, and bake on the center oven rack until the cake springs back when lightly touched, 15 to 20 minutes.

5. Meanwhile, spread a lint-free kitchen towel on a work surface and dust it lightly with confectioners' sugar.

6. When the cake is done, immediately invert it onto the dusted towel. Starting at a narrow end, roll the cake, using the towel as a guide to form a log. Let the cake cool completely, covered with the towel, on a wire rack.

My nephew Randy Bart and bride Isabelle on their honeymoon in Brazil.

7. Meanwhile, prepare the filling: Combine all the filling ingredients in a mixing bowl and beat with an electric mixer on medium speed until smooth.

8. Carefully unroll the cooled cake, spread the filling over it, and reroll it. Chill it for at least 2 hours. Slice the cake with a serrated knife, and serve.

> " Every fall around Halloween or Thanksgiving, my mom [Joyce] and I used to make this pumpkin cake together. We'd make several and freeze a couple for the holidays. We hadn't made it in a few years, and one year I surprised her by making it myself. —RANDY BART "

boston cream pie

from Judy Bart Kancigor

When I married Barry, he told me his favorite cake was Boston cream pie. Shame on me: I never made it for him! Until a few years ago, that is, when Becca Essenstein, a sous-chef at Sur La Table, where I was teaching, was raving about the Boston cream pie demonstrated by chef Carolyn Thacker the week before. The original was created in the Parker House Hotel in Boston, which also brought us Parker House rolls. Not a pie, it's actually a double-layer cake—and this one is lovely—with a rich custard filling and a silky chocolate glaze. **SERVES 8** **D**

Parchment paper, for the pans
2¹/₄ cups sifted cake flour
³/₄ teaspoon baking powder
³/₄ teaspoon baking soda
¹/₄ teaspoon salt
12 tablespoons (1¹/₂ sticks) unsalted butter, at room temperature, plus extra for greasing the pans
1¹/₂ cups sugar
2 large eggs, at room temperature
Seeds from 1 vanilla bean, or 1 teaspoon pure vanilla extract
1 cup buttermilk, at room temperature
Custard Filling (recipe follows)
Chocolate Glaze (recipe follows)

1. Preheat the oven to 375°F. Butter two 9-inch round cake pans, line the bottoms with parchment paper, and grease the parchment.

2. Sift the flour, baking powder, baking soda, and salt together into a bowl, and set it aside.

3. Cream the butter and sugar with an electric mixer on medium-high speed until light and fluffy, 2 minutes. Add the eggs, one at a time, beating for 1 minute and scraping the bowl after each addition. Beat in the vanilla seeds or extract. Reduce the speed to low and add the flour mixture in three additions, alternating with the buttermilk

in two additions, beginning and ending with the flour.

4. Pour the batter into the prepared cake pans and bake on the center oven rack until a cake tester inserted in the center comes out clean, about 20 minutes. Let the layers cool in the pans set on a wire rack for 15 minutes. Then remove them from the pans, peel off the parchment, and let them cool completely on the rack.

5. To assemble the cake, place one layer, top down, on a serving plate. Spread with the custard filling. Cover with the second layer, top up. Wrap in plastic wrap and chill thoroughly.

6. Glaze the chilled cake with the warm chocolate glaze. Refrigerate, uncovered, for 30 minutes to set the glaze. Cut the cake into slices, and serve.

custard filling

This creamy custard filling can be made up to 24 hours ahead.

6 tablespoons sugar
3 tablespoons all-purpose flour
3 tablespoons cornstarch
Yolks of 6 large eggs
2 cups whole milk
1 teaspoon pure vanilla extract

1. Sift the sugar, flour, and cornstarch together into the bowl of an electric mixer. Add the egg yolks and beat on medium speed

until the mixture is pale and light, about 2 minutes.

2. Bring the milk just to a boil in a medium-size heavy-bottomed saucepan. Very gradually add the milk to the egg mixture, whisking constantly by hand. Return the mixture to the saucepan and cook over medium heat, whisking or stirring constantly, until it is very thick, about 1 minute. Immediately strain the custard into a clean bowl, and stir in the vanilla. Cover with plastic wrap and refrigerate for 4 to 6 hours for the custard to set (you can make the custard up to 24 hours ahead).

chocolate glaze

When melting chocolate, don't overdo it. Remove the pan from the heat when the chocolate is not quite fully melted, and then stir it off the heat until smooth.

6 ounces semisweet or bittersweet chocolate, chopped
1/2 cup heavy (whipping) cream
1 teaspoon light corn syrup

1. Combine the chopped chocolate, cream, and corn syrup in the top of a double boiler set over simmering water. Stir frequently until the chocolate has almost melted (about 120°F). Do not overheat.

2. Remove the pan from the heat and stir

gently with a spatula until the glaze is completely smooth. Do not whisk or beat. Allow it to cool slightly (to 90° to 92°F) before glazing the cake.

sylvia's caramel toffee freezer cheesecake

from Marylyn Lamstein

Sylvia Aaron calls this recipe her "ice cream cake without the ice cream." Remove the cake from the freezer and leave it out just long enough so you can get a knife through it, she advises, for the ice-cream-cake texture.

Marylyn Lamstein (second from left) held by my mom, 1942, with her brother Michael, mom, Isabelle, Aunt Essie, and Aunt Anda.

We find the caramel flavor more intense when served straight from the refrigerator, but it's delicious either way. Few can resist the luscious appeal of caramel, especially when paired with rich, creamy cheesecake. For the best flavor, use a premium brand of caramel sauce. **SERVES 12** **D**

Unflavored vegetable cooking spray, for greasing the pan

FOR THE CRUST
3/4 cup finely ground graham cracker crumbs
3 tablespoons sugar
3 tablespoons unsalted butter, melted

FOR THE FILLING
2 packages (8 ounces each) cream cheese, at room temperature
3/4 cup sugar
3 large eggs, at room temperature
1 tablespoon pure vanilla extract
2 tablespoons all-purpose flour
1 cup sour cream, at room temperature
1/2 cup bottled caramel sauce or topping
1 bag (8 ounces) English toffee-flavored candy bits, such as Heath Bits 'O Brickle

1. Preheat the oven to 450°F. Grease a 9-inch springform pan.

2. Prepare the crust: Combine the graham cracker crumbs and sugar in a medium-size bowl, and stir to blend. Add the melted butter, stirring until the crumbs are evenly moistened.

3. Use the flat bottom of a glass to press the mixture evenly and firmly over the bottom of the prepared springform pan. Chill

> **Sylvia and I met in 1958, when we were both in college. She was going to Wayne State, and I was attending the University of Michigan. She had come to my school with some friends for a football game. It was a freezing cold day, and someone threw her up to her neck into a pile of snow. Sylvia, who is four foot eleven tops, was soaked to the skin. She ran into my dorm and was going from floor to floor crying, 'Help! Help!' Since I had no interest in football, I was probably the only one on campus remaining in the dorm. I brought her into my room, gave her my (too-long) flannel nightshirt, put her soaking clothes on the radiator, and made hot chocolate on my little hot plate. We've been friends ever since. Every time I make her freezer cheesecake I think of that freezing day that brought us together and thank heavens I never liked football.**
>
> **—MARYLYN LAMSTEIN**

until firm, about 30 minutes in the refrigerator or 15 minutes in the freezer.

4. While the crust is chilling, prepare the filling: Beat the cream cheese and sugar with an electric mixer on medium speed, scraping the bowl several times, just until smooth. Beat in the eggs, one at a time, scraping the bowl as needed. Then beat in the vanilla. Blend in the flour and then the sour cream. Do not overbeat. Beat in the caramel sauce just until blended. Stir in the toffee bits.

5. Scrape the batter over the chilled crust, and bake on the center oven rack for 10 minutes. Reduce the oven temperature to 250°F and continue baking until the top is pale golden brown and the center of the cheesecake seems barely set when shaken, 30 to 40 minutes. Let the cheesecake cool in the pan set on a wire rack for 2 hours. Then wrap it tightly in plastic wrap and freeze it overnight.

6. To serve the cheesecake, remove it from the freezer about 15 minutes before serving—just long enough so it can be sliced with a knife. Use a flexible spatula or a thin knife to loosen the cheesecake from the sides of the pan, and then release the springform. Cut it into wedges to serve.

Note: To serve the cheesecake without freezing it, wrap the cooled cheesecake tightly in plastic wrap and refrigerate it overnight. Use a flexible spatula or thin knife to loosen the chilled cheesecake from the sides of the pan, release the springform, and cut into wedges.

"lindy's" cheesecake

from Phyllis Epstein

This recipe has been passed off for years as coming from Lindy's, the famous New York restaurant and Broadway hangout immortalized as Mindy's in *Guys and Dolls*. Is it really their recipe? Who knows and who cares? If it's New York cheesecake you're after—the really dense, rich variety that sticks to the roof of your mouth—this is the real deal. I've even won two cooking contests with it. (Well, in truth, one was at my friend Joanne's house party where I gleefully beat out her husband, Gerry, and the other was an office party, but still . . .) I have greatly simplified the traditional crust preparation—there's really no need to roll it out. I usually whip the leftover heavy cream with a tablespoon of sugar and pipe it around the cake for even more dazzle. **SERVES 16 TO 20** D

Butter, for greasing the pan

FOR THE COOKIE CRUST
1 cup all-purpose flour
$^1/_4$ cup sugar
1 teaspoon grated lemon zest
$^1/_2$ teaspoon pure vanilla extract
Yolk of 1 large egg
4 tablespoons ($^1/_2$ stick) unsalted butter,
*   at room temperature*

FOR THE CAKE
5 packages (8 ounces each) cream cheese,
*   at room temperature*
1$^3/_4$ cups sugar
3 tablespoons all-purpose flour
1$^1/_2$ teaspoons grated lemon zest
1$^1/_2$ teaspoons grated orange zest
$^1/_4$ teaspoon pure vanilla extract
5 large eggs, at room temperature
Yolks of 2 large eggs, at room
*   temperature*
$^1/_4$ cup heavy (whipping) cream,
*   at room temperature*

> *The highlight of my wedding rehearsal dinner was Aunt Lil and Uncle Jan introducing the Rosenthal and Epstein families to the music of a new Broadway show, Fiddler on the Roof. They used the occasion to try out 'Sunrise, Sunset,' which was to be sung at our reception and ceremony. Tears filled the eyes of my German in-laws-to-be as I watched their reaction without really hearing the lyrics. Aunt Lil looked around at all the tears and said, 'Why is everyone crying? Was it that bad?'*
>
> **—PHYLLIS EPSTEIN**

FOR THE GLAZED STRAWBERRIES
1$^1/_2$ to 2 pints fresh strawberries
$^1/_2$ cup apricot jam
2 tablespoons brandy or water

1. Preheat the oven to 400°F. Butter the bottom and sides of a 9-inch springform pan. Separate the sides from the bottom of the pan and set the sides aside.

2. Prepare the crust: Combine all the crust ingredients in a food processor and process until the mixture forms a ball. Press one third of the dough evenly over the bottom of the prepared springform pan. Bake until golden, 8 to 10 minutes. Remove the bottom crust from the oven and set it aside. Raise the oven temperature to 500°F.

3. Press the remaining two thirds of the dough evenly over the sides of the springform, reaching about three fourths of the way up. Reattach the sides to the crust-lined bottom. Place the pan in the refrigerator.

4. Prepare the cake: Beat the cream cheese, sugar, flour, both zests, and the vanilla

with an electric mixer on high speed, just to blend. Reduce the speed to medium and beat in the eggs and egg yolks, one at a time, beating well and scraping the bowl well after each addition. Reduce the speed to low and add the cream, beating just until combined.

5. Scrape the batter into the prepared crust and bake for 10 minutes. Reduce the oven temperature to 250°F and bake for 1 hour. Let the cheesecake cool in the pan set on a wire rack.

6. While the cheesecake is cooling, prepare the strawberries: Rinse and hull the berries, and thoroughly pat them dry; set them aside. Combine the jam and the brandy in a small, heavy saucepan over medium heat, and heat until the preserves melt. Force the mixture through a sieve, and set it aside to cool.

7. When the cheesecake has completely cooled, arrange the strawberries in concentric circles on top, beginning at the outside edge. Brush the glaze over the berries. Refrigerate, covered, overnight.

8. Just before serving, remove the springform sides.

chocolate chunk cheesecake

from Joyce Wolf

ver since 1930, when Ruth Wakefield, of the Toll House Inn, discovered that little bits of choco-

late baked in her cookies kept their shape, the world's been in love with the chocolate chip. But that's a mere schoolgirl crush compared to the torrid affair we have when Joyce throws mega-size chips into her cheesecake. Here's a rare instance where my mother's cooking advice rings true: "If some is good, more is better."

Garnish the cheesecake with sliced strawberries and/or additional melted chocolate and mint leaves, if you like.

SERVES 12 D

FOR THE CRUST
1 cup crushed cream-filled vanilla cookies (about 12)
2 tablespoons unsalted butter, melted

FOR THE FILLING
3 packages (8 ounces each) cream cheese, at room temperature
1/2 cup (packed) light brown sugar
1 teaspoon pure vanilla extract
4 large eggs, at room temperature
1 package (8 to 10 ounces) large chocolate chips

1. Preheat the oven to 350°F. Have ready an ungreased 9-inch springform pan.

2. Prepare the crust: Combine the crushed cookies and the butter in a small bowl, and mix well. Press the mixture over the bottom of the springform pan. Bake on the center oven rack until golden, 10 minutes. Remove the pan from the oven and set it on a wire rack to cool while you prepare the filling.

3. Prepare the filling: Cream the cream cheese, brown sugar, and vanilla with an

electric mixer on medium speed, scraping the bowl several times, until well blended. Add the eggs, one at a time, beating well and scraping the bowl after each addition. Stir in the chocolate chips.

4. Scrape the mixture into the prepared crust and bake on the center oven rack for 45 minutes.

5. Run a knife around the edge of the cheesecake to loosen it from the pan, but do not remove the sides yet. Let the cake cool completely on a wire rack. Then wrap it in plastic wrap and refrigerate it overnight.

6. Remove the springform sides, cut the cheesecake into wedges, and serve.

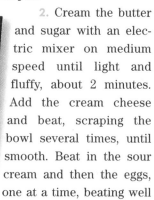

Artie and Joyce Wolf at son Eric's wedding to Michelle, 1993.

creamy cheesecake

from Debbie Levine

Debbie, my sister-in-law, says, "A lighter cheesecake, our family's favorite." Even husband, Ronnie, with his iron-man willpower, makes an exception for this one. **SERVES 12** **D**

Unflavored vegetable cooking spray, for greasing the pan

8 tablespoons (1 stick) unsalted butter, at room temperature

1¹/₂ cups sugar

3 containers (12 ounces each) whipped cream cheese, at room temperature

1 pint sour cream, at room temperature

5 large eggs, at room temperature

3 tablespoons cornstarch

1 tablespoon pure vanilla extract

1. Preheat the oven to 350°F. Spray a 9-inch springform pan.

2. Cream the butter and sugar with an electric mixer on medium speed until light and fluffy, about 2 minutes. Add the cream cheese and beat, scraping the bowl several times, until smooth. Beat in the sour cream and then the eggs, one at a time, beating well and scraping the bowl after each addition. Beat in the cornstarch and vanilla.

3. Scrape the batter into the prepared springform pan and place the pan in a larger pan. Add warm water to reach at least halfway up the sides of the springform. Bake for 1¹/₂ hours. Then turn off the heat and allow the cheesecake to cool in the oven for 3 hours (no peeking).

4. Wrap the cheesecake in plastic wrap, and refrigerate it overnight.

5. Release the springform, cut the cheesecake into wedges, and serve.

> **When Ronnie was growing up, his father, Harry, owned a fruit and vegetable store, and Ronnie would work there every weekend. Even as a child he knew the difference between collard greens and kale and how to pick an orange-fleshed melon at its sweetest, juiciest best. All of these fruits and vegetables are in his blood. No cookies or pastries for dessert for him, just melon—that's why everyone calls him 'the melon man.' Snacks? Not chips or candy, just vegetables. We laugh when dinner is at its end and everyone is eating those rich and wonderful desserts, and then there's Ronnie, the 'melon man,' enjoying his juicy, sweet melon.**
>
> **—DEBBIE LEVINE**

bavarian apple cheese torte

from Jackie Bishins

ousin Jackie says this delicious dessert is like a reliable friend. She's been making it for as long as she can remember, and it always brings the requisite ooh's and aah's with its buttery, cookie-like crust, cheesecake filling (and who doesn't like cheesecake?), and cinnamony apple crown. It would be smashing with warm caramel sauce dripping down the side and a dollop of whipped cream, but it is fine on its own too. And in case you're wondering, no, Jackie has no

Bavarian blood. I've never known her to yodel, and to my recollection, she's never worn braids. **SERVES 8 TO 10**

FOR THE CRUST

8 tablespoons (1 stick) unsalted butter, at room temperature

$^1/_3$ cup sugar

$^1/_4$ teaspoon pure vanilla extract

1 cup all-purpose flour

FOR THE FILLING

2 packages (8 ounces each) cream cheese, at room temperature

$^1/_2$ cup sugar

2 large eggs, at room temperature

1 teaspoon pure vanilla extract

FOR THE TOPPING

$^1/_3$ cup sugar

$^1/_2$ teaspoon ground cinnamon

4 cups thinly sliced peeled crisp, sweet apples (5 or 6 apples)

$^1/_4$ cup sliced almonds

1. Preheat the oven to 450°F. Have ready an ungreased 9-inch springform pan.

2. Prepare the crust: Cream the butter, sugar, and vanilla with an electric mixer on medium speed until blended. Beat in the flour just until combined. Use your fingers to spread the dough over the bottom and 1$^1/_2$ inches up the sides of the springform pan.

3. Prepare the filling: Beat the cream cheese and sugar with an electric mixer on medium speed until thoroughly combined. Add the eggs and vanilla, and mix well. Scrape the cheese mixture into the prepared crust.

4. Prepare the topping: Mix the sugar and cinnamon together in a small bowl. Place the apples in a large bowl, add the cinnamon-sugar, and toss. Arrange the apples on top of the batter, and sprinkle with the almonds. Bake on the center oven rack for 10 minutes. Reduce the heat to 400°F and continue baking until set, 25 to 35 minutes more.

5. Let the cake cool completely in the pan on a wire rack. Then wrap it in plastic wrap and refrigerate it overnight.

6. Remove the springform sides, cut the cake into wedges, and serve.

shavuot

● ● ● ● ●

Shavuot is known as the "cheese holiday." For Ashkenazim it's bring on the blintzes, while Sephardim enjoy cheese-filled borekas. But do we even need a holiday to enjoy cheesecake? And why do we eat dairy on this holiday?

For answers I consulted Rabbi Gil Marks, author of *Olive Trees and Honey* and *The World of Jewish Cooking*. "The use of dairy to celebrate this holiday is not a biblical injunction, nor is it mentioned in the Talmud," Marks told me. "Shavuot falls when the animals are weaning away from the mother, so you have a surplus of milk and therefore cheese, yogurt, and dairy products at this time. Once you have a tradition, you find meaningful reasons for it. Even in pagan pre-Christian and post-Christian holidays you will find dairy products traditional at this time of year because they were so abundant. Throughout most of history, dairy products were primarily consumed in the form of cheese."

Herdsmen of almost 6,000 years ago stored milk in the waterproof stomachs of animals (the first "bottles"), Marks said. The ancients discovered that when the milk separated, it coagulated into curds—the first fresh cheese—which not only tasted good, but lasted longer, especially when salted, than milk. (Blintzes and cheesecake would come much later!)

"For most of history people didn't drink milk straight," Marks explained, "because, until pasteurization, it was dangerous unless it came straight from the animal. So fermented forms like yogurt, cheese, and butter, which have a longer shelf life, are what people ate."

More important, Shavuot commemorates the giving of the Torah at Mt. Sinai. "No Jews existed before the giving of the Torah," Marks said. "Technically speaking, Israelites before then were not Jews. One of the new laws concerned keeping kosher, and since their utensils and any meat products they had produced before were no longer kosher, for the first Shavuot they had to eat dairy products. In addition, a tradition exists that when the Israelites returned to camp after receiving the Torah, their milk had curdled into cheese. So you have a variety of practical, mystical, and somewhat biblical reasons that developed for the association with dairy."

The only food that is actually connected biblically to the holiday is leavened wheat bread, Marks noted. "Leavening was allowed in the Temple only on two occasions: for the Thanksgiving offering and Shavuot, when two special loaves of raised wheat bread were brought before the altar and literally raised up. In the Bible, Shavuot is also known as the 'Festival of the Grain Harvest,' marking the end of the barley harvest and the beginning of the wheat harvest. As a result, many communities make special breads. A lot of traditional foods evolved reflecting the historical and nature angles of the festivals."

black bottom cheese cuplets

from Sally Bower

ש hen Aunt Sally met Uncle Lou at a dance long ago, chances are they were doing the Black Bottom, that crazy footwork that gave the Charleston a run for its money (and of which it has been said that your right hip doesn't know what your left hip is doing). Nothing crazy about these Black Bottoms, however— just a really easy dessert combining the world's most popular flavors, chocolate and cheese. **MAKES 4 TO 4¼ DOZEN MINI CHEESECAKES** ◻D

FOR THE CHEESE LAYER

8 ounces cream cheese, at room
   temperature
1 large egg, at room temperature
¹/₂ cup sugar
¹/₈ teaspoon salt
1 cup (6 ounces) chocolate chips

FOR THE CHOCOLATE LAYER

1¹/₂ cups all-purpose flour
¹/₄ cup unsweetened cocoa powder
1 teaspoon baking soda
¹/₂ teaspoon salt
1 large egg, at room temperature
1 cup sugar
¹/₂ cup vegetable oil
1 tablespoon distilled white vinegar
1 teaspoon pure vanilla extract

1. Preheat the oven to 350°F. Line 1³/₄-inch mini muffin cups with paper liners.

2. Prepare the cheese layer: Beat the cream cheese, egg, sugar, and salt with an electric mixer on medium speed, scraping the bowl several times, until light and smooth, about 2 minutes. Stir in the chocolate chips. Scrape the batter into another bowl and set it aside. (No need to rinse the mixing bowl or beaters.)

3. Prepare the chocolate layer: Stir the flour, cocoa powder, baking soda, and salt together in a small bowl.

4. Beat the egg, sugar, oil, vinegar, vanilla, and 1 cup water with the electric mixer on medium-low speed until well combined, about 1 minute. With the mixer on, gradually add the chocolate-flour mixture and continue beating until thoroughly combined, another minute or so. The batter will be thin.

5. Fill the mini muffin cups halfway with the chocolate batter, and top each one with about 1 teaspoon of the cheese batter. Do not overfill. While you are spooning it out, stir the chocolate batter occasionally.

6. Bake on the center oven rack until the edges begin to brown and a cake tester inserted into the chocolate layer comes out dry, 18 to 25 minutes. Let the cakes cool in the pans set on a wire rack for 10 minutes. Then remove the cakes from the pans and let them cool completely on the rack. Cover and refrigerate until chilled, at least 3 hours.

pnina shichor's sufganiyot (jelly doughnuts)

from Judy Bart Kancigor

m y friend Pnina makes her mother-in-law's sufganiyot every Hanukkah, when, in Israeli tradition, she and hubby David host a huge open house. She stands by the electric frying pan (her implement of choice, so dig yours out of the attic), whipping the doughnuts out by the dozen. They disappear as quickly as they are filled.

A few years ago, determined to learn her technique, I asked Pnina for a lesson. Busy at work, she invited me to bring all my equipment and ingredients to her travel agency, and between reservations, with phones ringing and faxes faxing, we made doughnuts.

These are the answer to Krispy Kreme in Israel, where jelly doughnuts are as popular as latkes for Hanukkah. Instead of injecting the jam into the cakes, a depression is formed in the dough and filled with jam after frying, making them as pretty to look at as they are impossibly irresistible to eat. These are very light doughnuts, reminiscent of beignets. Use different colored jams for an even showier display. **MAKES ABOUT 3¹/₂ DOZEN DOUGHNUTS** **P**

¹/₂ cup plus scant 1 cup warm water (105° to 110°F)

3 packages active dry yeast

¹/₂ **cup sugar**

¹/₂ **teaspoon salt**

¹/₂ **cup vegetable oil**

4 large eggs, beaten

5 to 6 cups all-purpose flour

Canola or corn oil, for frying

Jam (any flavor)

Confectioners' sugar

1. Preheat the oven on the lowest setting for 15 minutes, and turn it off.

2. Pour the ¹/₂ cup warm water into a very large (at least 6-quart) bowl. Add the yeast and stir to dissolve it. Then add 1 teaspoon of the sugar, stir, and set the mixture aside until bubbly, 5 to 10 minutes.

3. Stir the scant 1 cup warm water, salt, oil, remaining sugar, and eggs into the yeast mixture. Add 3 cups of the flour, and mix. Gradually knead in the remaining flour until the dough is spongy and elastic but still feels slightly tacky. Remove the dough and oil the bowl (no need to wash it). Turn the dough in the bowl to coat it all over with oil, and loosely cover the bowl with plastic wrap.

4. Let the dough rise in the turned-off oven until it nearly reaches the top of the bowl, about 2 hours.

5. Punch down the dough and roll it out on a lightly floured surface until it is ¹/₄-inch thick. Using a 3-inch biscuit cutter or glass, cut out rounds of dough. Place the rounds on a baking sheet and set them aside to rise, uncovered, for 30 minutes.

6. Pour oil to a depth of 1 inch into an

electric frying pan (preferred), deep fryer, or large, heavy skillet and heat it to 365°F.

7. Dip your fingers in flour, and lift up a round of dough. Move it back and forth between your two middle fingers to stretch the center of the round quite thin without tearing it. This will be the depression for the jam.

8. Quickly drop the rounds into the hot oil, depression side down—a few at a time, without crowding. Cover the pan and fry until the doughnuts are golden brown but not dark, about 30 seconds. Quickly turn them, cover the pan, and fry until the other side is golden brown, 30 seconds more. Drain the doughnuts on both sides on paper towels. Repeat with the remaining rounds of dough.

9. Fill the depressions with jam, and dust the doughnuts with confectioners' sugar. These are best when eaten warm. They don't keep well, but no matter. You won't have any leftovers.

blessing of the children

May your heart grow as wide as the ocean.

May you trust and value what you know, what you think, and what you feel.

May you discover your gifts, ones that make your heart sing, and offer them to the world.

What the world needs is more hearts singing.

May you love the world as you love yourself, and may you love yourself as you love the world.

May your capacity to forgive and be resilient open the gates for others to follow.

When trust is broken, repair it.

Where there is conflict, resolve it.

May you always treasure and have faith in the Three Jewels:

The mystery of life we know as G-d and the Shechina, the indwelling presence of the Divine.

The Jewish people, all your ancestors, your family, this community here today, and all who love you.

The Torah and all wisdom texts that touch your heart.

May your life unfold with insight, wisdom, and compassion.

May you be well, peaceful, and at ease.

May you know true happiness.

May your life be a blessing.

May you be blessed.

Danielle, Jordon, and Michael Solomanic with mom, Suzy, at Jordan's Bar Mitzvah, 2005.

Excerpt from original prayers by Laura Seligman given to Eva on the occasion of her Bat Mitzvah, June 1, 1996, and to Katya on the occasion of her Bat Mitzvah, May 8, 1999.

cousins . . . then & now

pies and pastries

ש hen Billy Boy returns from seeking a wife, his mother gives him the third degree. "Can she bake a cherry pie?" she sneers. One can just picture her: lips pursed, arms folded tightly across her chest, eyes narrowed into slits. She's about to lose Charming Billy to what?—some airhead with a dimple on her chin who cannot leave her mother? When he assures her that the young thing can not only bake a cherry pie, but she can do it quick as a cat can wink an eye, the marriage is sealed!

"Pie baking I thought of as a magical gift bestowed from birth on some."

Mama Hinda and Papa Harry's thirteen grandchildren. All of us cousins were raised together. Who's who on page 613.

As a young bride—and I do mean young ... eighteen! (I got my driver's license and my marriage license in the same year)—nothing epitomized consummate homemaking skills as much as the baking of pies, something I would not even attempt for decades.

I have already admitted to you previously that I lived for many years with a dough phobia, the result of a kitchen disaster I'll call the "kreplach incident." Although in the ensuing years I rolled cookie dough and turned out homemade knishes by the hundreds with ease, somehow pie baking I thought of as a magical gift bestowed from birth on some, but never to be attained by others. Genetics, perhaps?

Then in 1996 I decided to write a family cookbook. Recipes needed to be tested. I cooked. I baked. I learned to make borekas. I even perfected the dreaded kreplach! The pies I left for last.

Finally, in an "Aha!" moment of the kitchen kind, I realized . . . I roll cookie dough, I roll knish dough. Now I even roll kreplach dough! Surely I can roll pie dough.

My daughter-in-law Tracey's recipe for the luscious Pecan Pie we look forward to each Thanksgiving, complete with pie-making tips from her cooking class instructor, put that last notch in my belt.

I don't come from a long line of pie makers. I don't think Mama Hinda ever baked one—I know my mother never did. Aunt Estelle would bake an apple pie occasionally, a towering giant of a pie, quite tart, with a sweet, almost cookie-like crust. When her grandson Eric bought his first house with his wife, Michelle, he would bring her the apples from his tree. I found the crust recipe in her handwritten cookbook and happily offer it here.

So this would have been a really short chapter if not for the in-laws of in-laws!

My daughter-in-law Shelly *does* come from a family of pie makers. I've included her Lemon Meringue Pie as well as her mom's decadent chocolate cream, her grandma's tart, custardy rhubarb, and her aunt Barb's Swedish Kringler, not a pie actually, but a pastry, perfect for breakfast or snacking.

Does the mere mention of whipped cream set your taste buds atingling? Try the Key Lime Pie, a tart beauty piled high with billowy clouds. Aunt Sally's Apple Strudel with its multilayered crust bursts with fruit—an ambitious project that does take some practice. Barry had that look in his eye when I mastered it. I just thank goodness his mother never asked him when he met me years ago, "Can she bake an apple strudel?"

Top: My nephew, Ross Levine, learns pie baking at the Institute of Culinary Education. Bottom: Rolling dough with my niece Jessica (Stu looking on), about 1980.

joyce taback's fish market apple pie

from Judy Bart Kancigor

my friend Joyce got this recipe from a friend in Philadelphia, where the Fish Market Restaurant was considered a landmark. Their apple pie was legendary, with its creamy filling and crunchy walnut topping—the collision of flavors and textures will make your mouth sing. My trusty recipe tester Sandy Glazier substitutes pecans and loves the topping so much that she uses it when she makes an apple betty, too. The combination of cinnamon and cider in the dough makes this an ideal crust for fall pies, like apple, pear, or pumpkin, and the amount of dough is generous enough to allow you to make a thick fluted rim around the edge of the pie shell. **SERVES 8** **D**

FOR THE CRUST

1³/4 cups all-purpose flour

¹/4 cup granulated sugar

1 teaspoon ground cinnamon

¹/2 teaspoon salt

²/3 cup (10 tablespoons plus 2 teaspoons) cold unsalted butter, cut into small pieces

4 tablespoons apple cider or water, chilled

FOR THE FILLING

1¹/2 cups sour cream

1 large egg, beaten

1 cup granulated sugar

¹/4 cup all-purpose flour

2 teaspoons pure vanilla extract

¹/2 teaspoon salt

2¹/2 pounds McIntosh apples, peeled, cored, and sliced (about 7 cups)

FOR THE CRUNCHY WALNUT TOPPING

¹/2 cup all-purpose flour

¹/3 cup (packed) dark brown sugar

¹/3 cup granulated sugar

1 tablespoon ground cinnamon

¹/4 teaspoon salt

8 tablespoons (1 stick) unsalted butter, at room temperature

1 cup chopped walnuts

1. Prepare the crust: Combine the flour, sugar, cinnamon, and salt in a large bowl, and whisk to combine. Add the butter and mix together with a pastry blender, a fork, or your fingertips until the mixture has the consistency of coarse cornmeal.

2. Add just enough cider, a tablespoon and then a teaspoon at a time, until the flour is evenly moistened and the dough holds together when pressed into a ball. Do not overmix the dough or the crust will be tough. Form the dough into a flat disk, wrap it in plastic wrap, and refrigerate it for at least 1 hour or as long as overnight.

3. Preheat the oven to 450°F.

4. Lightly flour a work surface, and roll out the dough to form a round about 2 inches wider than the top of a 10-inch pie plate.

Carefully place the dough in the pie plate and press it into the bottom and sides. (Folding the dough loosely into quarters makes it easier to transfer.) Turn the overhanging pastry under and flute it to make a stand-up rim. Refrigerate for 20 minutes.

5. Prepare the filling: Combine the sour cream, egg, sugar, flour, vanilla, and salt in a large bowl and mix well. Add the apples and toss to coat them with the mixture.

6. Scrape the filling into the pie shell and immediately place it in the oven. Bake for 10 minutes. Reduce the temperature to 350°F, and bake for 35 minutes more.

7. While the pie is baking, prepare the topping: Combine the flour, both sugars, cinnamon, salt, and butter in a bowl, and mix thoroughly. Add the walnuts and combine well.

8. Remove the pie from the oven (leave the oven on) and set it on a baking sheet (to catch the topping crumbles). Stir the filling in the crust, gently but thoroughly. Then sprinkle the topping evenly over the filling. (The heat from the pie will soften the topping and help to spread it.)

9. Return the pie to the oven and bake for 15 minutes more. Let the pie cool on a wire rack before slicing it.

10. Store the pie, loosely covered in plastic wrap, at room temperature—do not reheat.

german plum "cake"

from Herta Heidingsfelder

The German plum cake called Zwetchgenkuchen is typical of the classic German dishes Herta learned from her mother-in-law. Although called a cake, it's really a tart with a rich, sweet cookie crust. In fact, Herta uses the same dough for her butter cookies. Typically plum cake is made with small Italian purple plums, which ripen at the end of summer, making it a traditional Rosh Hashanah dish. Earlier in the summer Herta uses fresh peaches, cut in quarters. The fruit must be tightly packed so very little dough is exposed. Sugar isn't sprinkled over the fruit until right before serving. Any earlier, Herta says, and the cake will be too juicy.

SERVES 6 TO 8 D

8 tablespoons (1 stick) unsalted butter, at room temperature, plus extra for greasing the pie plate
1/2 cup plus 2 tablespoons sugar
Yolk of 1 large egg, at room temperature
1 cup all-purpose flour, plus 1 to 3 tablespoons if needed
2 to 2 1/4 pounds fresh Italian plums, halved and pitted

Lorraine (Herta's daughter) with husband Michael, 1993.

> *My mother, Herta Lowenstein Heidings-felder, was born to Orthodox parents in Frankfurt am Main in 1915. She was the youngest of eight children, and her life was idyllic until Hitler's rise to power. My mom had met and dated my dad briefly in Germany. When he left for America with his family in 1934, he told her that if he was successful, he would send for her. In 1937 the situation in Germany became untenable, and thankfully my father and his parents sent for her and welcomed her into their apartment in Queens, where she lived until she found work as a nanny at the Louise Wise Adoption Agency. My folks married in 1939. My mother was so thankful to be given the opportunity to begin a new life in America that she devoted her life to making a home for my father and her in-laws, who lived with us until they died many years later. During those years she learned her cooking and baking skills from her mother-in-law.*
>
> **—LORRAINE GOLD**

1. Preheat the oven to 350°F. Butter a 9-inch pie plate, or the bottom and 1 inch up the sides of a 9-inch springform pan.

2. Be sure the butter and egg yolk are at room temperature. Combine the butter, the 1/2 cup sugar, and the egg yolk in a bowl and mix by hand until thoroughly combined. Gradually add the 1 cup flour. If it is too sticky, add the extra flour, 1 tablespoon at a time. Press the dough onto the bottom and barely up to the rim of the prepared pie plate, or over the bottom and 1 inch up the sides of the springform pan.

3. Cut two slits in each plum half, slicing it two thirds of the way down, so it fans out into three sections. Stand the plums upright in the pie plate, packed tightly in circles with the skin facing out and the uncut ends pressed into the dough. There should be very little dough exposed. Bake until the dough is lightly browned, about 45 minutes. The tart will seem juicy when it comes out of the oven. Let the tart cool on a wire rack.

4. If you will be serving the tart the same day, store it at room temperature. Otherwise store it, covered with plastic wrap, in the refrigerator for up to 2 days; allow it to come to room temperature before serving.

5. If you used a springform pan, remove the sides before serving. Immediately before serving, sprinkle the remaining 2 tablespoons sugar over the fruit.

ilo's rhubarb pie

from Barb Frank

my daughter-in-law Shelly's Grandma Ilo grows her own rhubarb for pie, but Ilo's daughter Barb, known as the pie maker in the family, is the one who usually bakes it. Ilo's old family recipe is the perfect blend of sweet and tart with a creamy, almost custard-like filling.

SERVES 8

Shelly and her father-in-law, Barry, at Brad and Tracey's wedding, 1995.

4 cups diced rhubarb (about 1¹/₃ pounds)

1¹/₄ cups sugar

5 tablespoons all-purpose flour

¹/₂ cup heavy (whipping) cream

1 large egg, well beaten

¹/₄ teaspoon ground nutmeg

Pinch of salt

One 9-inch unbaked pie shell, store-bought or
    homemade (pages 454 and 455)

Whipped cream, for serving (optional)

1. Preheat the oven to 400°F.

2. Combine the rhubarb, sugar, flour, cream, egg, nutmeg, and salt in a bowl and mix thoroughly.

3. Pour the mixture into the pie shell and bake for 15 minutes. Reduce the temperature to 350°F and bake until set, about 45 minutes more. (Wrap the edges of the crust with aluminum foil if they begin to darken too fast.)

4. Serve with whipped cream, if you like.

5. Store the pie, loosely covered in plastic wrap or under a glass dome, at room temperature overnight.

lemon meringue pie

from Shelly Kancigor

ש hen my daughter-in-law Shelly found out that lemon meringue was my husband's favorite pie, she dusted off this recipe from her seventh-grade home ec class and made it for his birthday every year while she and Stu lived in California. Since they've moved to Minnesota, Barry's birthdays have never been the same. (But not just because of the pie. After living close by for ten years, they left when our grandson Jason was only seven months old. When I told my mother they were moving, she said, "Are they taking the baby too?") Well, we had a good cry, but unfortunately so did the pie . . . until Shelly read a great tip to prevent "weeping" of the meringue: spoon it atop *hot* filling. Therefore, prepare the meringue first. The sugar stabilizes it so it can stand while you prepare the filling.

SERVES 6 TO 8   **D** or **P**

FOR THE MERINGUE

Whites of 3 large eggs, at room
    temperature

¹/₄ teaspoon cream of tartar

6 tablespoons sugar

FOR THE FILLING

Yolks of 3 large eggs, at room temperature

1¹/₂ cups sugar

¹/₃ cup cornstarch

**3 tablespoons unsalted butter or nondairy
margarine**

¹/₄ cup fresh lemon juice

1 tablespoon grated lemon zest

Generous pinch of salt

**One 9-inch pie shell, store-bought or
homemade (pages 454 and 455),
partially prebaked (see box, page 444)**

1. Preheat the oven to 350°F.

2. Prepare the meringue: Beat the egg whites with an electric mixer on medium-high speed until foamy, about 30 seconds. Add the cream of tartar and continue beating until soft peaks form. Add the sugar, 1 tablespoon at a time, beating for 10 seconds after each addition. Then raise the speed to high and beat until stiff peaks form, about 2¹/₂ minutes total. Set the meringue aside.

3. Prepare the filling: Lightly beat the egg yolks in a medium-size bowl. Set the bowl on a dish towel and set it aside.

4. Combine the sugar and cornstarch in a medium-size saucepan. Gradually stir in 1¹/₂ cups water and cook over medium heat, stirring constantly, until the mixture thickens and comes to a boil. Then boil for 1 minute. Remove the pan from the heat and *very* gradually (a tablespoon at a time at first) whisk at least half the hot mixture into the egg yolks (this is where that dish towel comes in handy—it keeps the bowl from swiveling around while you're busy whisking). Then

spoon the yolk mixture to the remaining hot mixture in the saucepan, bring it back to a boil, stirring constantly, and boil for 1 minute more. Remove the pan from the heat and stir in the butter, followed by the lemon juice, lemon zest, and salt. Mix thoroughly. Scrape the lemon filling into the baked pie shell.

5. Pile the meringue onto the hot pie filling, making sure it is sealed to the crust and using the back of a spoon to swirl it into peaks. Bake until the meringue is delicately browned, about 15 minutes.

6. To prevent shrinkage, cool the pie completely on a wire rack before refrigerating it. Chill it for at least 1 hour before serving. This is best eaten the day it's made.

diane bukatman's key lime pie

from Judy Bart Kancigor

my friend and baking guru, Diane Bukatman, makes a mean Key lime pie, one of the most popular recipes at her cooking school, aptly named For the Love of Food, in Reiserstown, Maryland. Light and lovely, the creamy lime filling is lots tarter than most, and the pie is smothered with billows of sweetened whipped cream. Use the greenest limes you can find for the zest. To prevent "melting" of the whipped cream, make sure the pie is completely cool before refrigerating it, and that it is well chilled before topping it. And you want Key lime juice for the filling, not regular lime juice. This is a large and generous pie—be sure to use a 10-inch *deep-dish* pie plate. **SERVES 10**　D

FOR THE CRUST

20 honey graham or cinnamon graham cracker
　　squares
4 tablespoons (¹/₂ stick) unsalted butter, melted

FOR THE FILLING

2 cans (14 ounces each) sweetened
　　condensed milk
Yolks of 8 large eggs
1¹/₂ cups Key lime juice, such as Nelli & Joe's
2 tablespoons grated lime zest
Pinch of salt
Vegetable cooking spray

FOR THE TOPPING

2 to 3 cups heavy (whipping) cream
¹/₂ to ³/₄ cup sugar, to taste
2 teaspoons pure vanilla extract

1. Preheat the oven to 350°F.
2. Prepare the crust: Crumble the graham crackers into the bowl of a food processor and pulse seven or eight times to form crumbs. Add the melted butter and pulse three or four times, until the butter and crumbs are well mixed. Transfer the crumbs to a 10-inch deep-dish glass pie plate, and using the heel of your hand, gently press them to form a crust on the bottom and up the sides of the plate. Place the

melted butter

● ● ●

When a recipe calls for melted butter, melt the butter until it is no longer solid, but do not heat it to the point of separating (into fat and milk solids). Be sure that the melted butter is well combined with the mixture to which it is being added. Let the butter cool slightly if it is being added to a mixture containing raw eggs.

pie plate on a cookie sheet and bake on the center oven rack until lightly browned, about 10 minutes. Let the crust cool completely on a wire rack. (Leave the oven on.)

3. Prepare the filling: Combine the condensed milk and the egg yolks in a medium-size bowl and whisk gently, without creating bubbles, until combined. Slowly pour in the lime juice while whisking continuously. Stir in the lime zest and salt.

4. Pour the filling into the cooled graham cracker crust and bake on the center oven rack until the filling is almost set, 30 minutes. (It should jiggle just slightly when the pie plate is moved.) Remove the pie from the oven and let it cool *completely* on a wire rack.

5. Lightly spray a sheet of plastic wrap with vegetable cooking spray. Cover the pie with the plastic wrap, oiled side down. (This will prevent the wrap from sticking to the pie. If you don't cover it, you will get a hard, rubbery crust on the lime custard.) Refrigerate the pie until it is thoroughly chilled, 2 to 6 hours.

6. Prepare the topping: Pour the cream into the bowl of an electric mixer and place

it and the beaters in the freezer to chill for about 2 minutes. Then add the sugar and vanilla and whip on high speed until the cream begins to hold medium-firm peaks but is not dry, about 3½ minutes.

7. Top the chilled pie with the whipped cream. Cover the pie lightly with plastic wrap and keep it refrigerated until ready to serve. Theoretically the pie will keep for 2 days, but this theory has never been tested at my house.

home chef pecan pie

from Tracey Barrett

If there's one dessert my daughter-in-law Tracey is known for, it's her pecan pie. She got the recipe and tips from chef Barbara Shenson, who was teaching for Home Chef, a cooking school and store in San Francisco (later sold to Viking), where the focus was on basic skills and

pie dough tips

To avoid shrinkage, refrigerate a pie shell for at least 30 minutes before baking.

The edge of the crust can overbake if it is too thin. When placing the round of dough in the pie plate, leave an extra ½-inch overhang of pastry, and then fold it under itself along the edge of the pie plate.

techniques for the home cook. This is her fail-safe crust, Tracey tells me, which can be used for savory pies as well—just omit the sugar. **SERVES 8** **D**

FOR THE CRUST
2 cups (10 ounces) all-purpose flour

1 teaspoon granulated sugar

1 teaspoon fine sea salt (preferred) or table salt

8 tablespoons (1 stick) unsalted butter, chilled and cut into small, even cubes

5 tablespoons solid vegetable shortening, chilled

5 to 6 tablespoons ice water

FOR THE FILLING
3 large eggs

1 cup plus 2 tablespoons (packed) dark brown sugar

¼ cup light corn syrup

¼ cup dark rum, or 2 tablespoons pure vanilla extract

¼ teaspoon fine sea salt (preferred) or table salt

4 tablespoons (½ stick) unsalted butter, melted

1⅓ cups (5 ounces) pecans, toasted (see box, page 17) and coarsely chopped

1. *To prepare the crust by hand:* Combine the flour, sugar, and salt in a large bowl. Using a pastry blender, cut in the butter and shortening until the mixture is crumbly. Add the ice water, 1 tablespoon at a time, until the dough begins to come together. Handle the dough as little as possible.

To prepare the crust in a food processor: Place the flour, sugar, and salt in the processor bowl and process for 5 seconds to combine. Scatter the butter and shortening

blind baking

● ● ●

Some recipes call for a prebaked pie shell. Blind baking, as it is called, is used for pies with fillings that do not get baked, such as puddings, or for pies such as those with custard fillings that are baked further but will benefit from prebaking so that the bottom crust does not become soggy.

To partially bake a pie shell that will be filled and baked further, roll out the dough and fit it into the pie plate. Prick the bottom lightly with a fork and line it with parchment paper. Fill the shell to the brim with pie weights, beans, or rice. Bake the shell in a preheated 375°F oven for 10 minutes. Remove the shell from the oven, remove the weights and parchment, and return it to the oven for 5 minutes more. The pie shell will finish baking when the shell is filled and returned to the oven.

For a filling that does not require baking, the shell must be baked completely. Follow the instructions above, but bake the shell in a preheated 375°F oven for 20 minutes. Remove the shell from the oven, remove the weights and parchment, and return it to the oven and bake until the shell is evenly golden, 5 to 7 minutes more.

evenly over the flour and process until the mixture looks like coarse meal, about 10 seconds. Drizzle 3 tablespoons ice water evenly over the mixture. Process again, adding water through the feed tube, 1 tablespoon at a time, until the mixture just begins to come together, about 45 seconds.

2. Gather the dough into a ball and flatten it slightly to form a disk. Wrap it in plastic wrap and refrigerate it for at least 30 minutes; or wrap it in plastic wrap and then in aluminum foil or a resealable plastic bag, and refrigerate it for up to 1 week or freeze it for up to 1 month.

3. On a lightly floured surface, roll the dough out to form an 11-inch round that is 1/4 inch thick. Roll the pastry around the rolling pin and then unroll it into a 9-inch pie plate, gently easing it in with your knuckles (to avoid tearing holes with your fingernails and to give a nice even press to the dough). Use a paring knife to trim the edge of the dough 1/2 inch wider than the outside edge of the pie plate, and turn the excess under. Crimp the edge, using your thumb and forefinger, or gently press it with the tines of a fork. Use any leftover dough for decorations (see box, page 447). Cover the crust with plastic wrap and refrigerate it for at least 30 minutes before filling and baking. (You can refrigerate it for up to 1 week or freeze it for up to 1 month. If frozen, thaw the crust overnight in the refrigerator, not at room temperature.)

4. Preheat the oven to 375°F.

5. Prepare the filling: Using a fork, whisk the eggs in a large mixing bowl until light colored and fluffy. Add the brown sugar, corn syrup, rum, and salt. Stir until the ingredients are thoroughly mixed and the sugar is completely dissolved. Add the melted butter and combine well. Stir in the pecans.

6. Pour the filling into the unbaked pie shell and bake until a cake tester inserted into the filling comes out clean, 40 to 45 minutes. Don't panic if the top appears cracked; it will settle down on cooling (see Notes). Let the pie cool on a wire rack.

7. Let the cooled pie set up, covered with plastic wrap, for at least 6 hours before serving. The pie can be baked up to 1 day ahead; store it, covered, at room temperature.

Notes: Use a fork to blend the eggs, not a hand mixer. Overbeating the eggs may cause the top of the baked pie to crack.

If you don't care to decorate the unbaked shell, the extra dough will keep—wrapped in plastic wrap and then in aluminum foil or a resealable plastic bag—for up to 1 week in the refrigerator or up to 1 month in the freezer. Use it to top a turkey pot pie (killing two leftovers with one rolling pin!).

sarah nodiff's pineapple cream cheese pie

from Sally Cohen

Sally Cohen was Papa Harry's niece from St. Louis. This cream cheese pie with the surprise pineapple filling was a specialty of her friend Sarah. To prevent the crust from becoming soggy, be sure the pineapple layer is completely cool and the cream cheese layer ready to go before spreading them in the crust and baking. Either Aunt Estelle's (page 455) or Mom's (page 454) will work fine—and so will the crust for Home Chef Pecan Pie (page 443). **SERVES 6 TO 8**　　**D**

FOR THE PINEAPPLE LAYER

1/3 **cup sugar**

1 **tablespoon cornstarch**

1 **can (8 ounces) crushed pineapple, undrained**

FOR THE CREAM CHEESE LAYER

1 **package (8 ounces) cream cheese, at room temperature**

1/2 **cup sugar**

1/2 **teaspoon salt**

2 **large eggs, at room temperature**

1/2 **cup milk**

1 **teaspoon pure vanilla extract**

One 9-inch **unbaked pie shell, store-bought or homemade (see headnote))**

1/2 **cup chopped pecans**

1. Preheat the oven to 400°F.

2. Prepare the pineapple layer: Combine the sugar and cornstarch in a small saucepan. Add the pineapple and cook, stirring constantly, over medium heat until the mixture is thick and clear, about 12 minutes. Pour the mixture into a bowl and allow it to cool completely.

3. Prepare the cream cheese layer: Combine the cream cheese, sugar, and salt in the bowl of an electric mixer and blend on medium speed, scraping the bowl several times, until smooth, about 1 minute. Add the eggs, one at a time, beating well after each addition. Then blend in the milk and vanilla.

4. Spread the cooled pineapple mixture in the unbaked pie shell. Spread the cream cheese mixture over the pineapple, and

sprinkle with the chopped pecans. Bake for 10 minutes. Then reduce the temperature to 325°F and bake until the crust is golden brown and the filling is set, 50 minutes more. Let the pie cool in the pan set on a wire rack. Then refrigerate it, covered, for at least 2 hours before serving.

5. Store the pie, covered with plastic wrap and then with aluminum foil, in the refrigerator for up to 2 days.

postcards chocolate silk pie

from Gary Bart

Kauai is my brother Gary's spiritual home and frequent vacation destination. His favorite dining spot is Postcards in Hanalei, a gourmet vegetarian restaurant set in a plantation cottage between the taro fields and the mountains. He convinced owner Marti Paskal to share the restaurant's recipe for its beloved Chocolate Silk Pie, a vegan dessert (no dairy or eggs), which I've adapted here. Tofu, a welcome ingredient in

Gary and wife, Karina, at Postcards.

the kosher kitchen, is perfect for creating creamy pareve desserts without the artificial flavors of some nondairy products.
SERVES 12 🅿

FOR THE GRAHAM CRACKER CRUST
24 to 28 graham cracker squares
6 tablespoons soy margarine, melted

FOR THE FILLING
4 cups (24 ounces) semisweet chocolate chips
1 cup (packed) light brown sugar
2 packages (12.3 ounces each)
 silken-style tofu
3 tablespoons pure vanilla extract

1. Preheat the oven to 350°F.

2. Prepare the crust: Grind the graham crackers in a food processor until very fine; you should have 2 cups. Add the melted margarine and process to combine. Transfer the mixture to a 9-inch springform pan and press it firmly over the bottom, using your fingers or the back of a spoon. Bake until the crust is just brown around the edges, about 7 minutes. Set it aside to cool completely.

3. Prepare the filling: Melt the chocolate chips in the top of a double boiler set over simmering water. Transfer the melted chocolate to the bowl of a food processor, and add the brown sugar and the tofu. Process until very smooth, scraping the bowl several times. Add the vanilla and process again.

4. Pour the chocolate mixture into the cooled crust, cover, and refrigerate until chilled and set, at least 3 hours. Remove the springform sides and serve chilled.

5. Store the pie, covered with plastic wrap and then wrapped in aluminum foil, in the refrigerator for up to 5 days.

Note: In the interest of full disclosure, I should note that Postcards, ever mindful of healthy ingredients, uses barley malt chips and turbinado sugar. (I am so bad!)

decorating a pie shell

● ● ●

Leftover dough can be used to decorate the top of a pie crust rim. Gather the scraps and either reroll the dough to ¹/₄-inch thickness or just use an available piece. With a paring knife or a cookie cutter, cut out leaf patterns or other shapes measuring about 1 inch wide and 2 inches long. Whisk 1 tablespoon water with 1 egg yolk in a small bowl. Lightly brush the back side of the leaves with this egg wash, and attach them to the horizontal edge of the pie shell. Refrigerate the entire pie shell for 30 minutes before filling and baking.

You can also bake some leaves separately and use them to decorate the top of the baked pie. Bake them along with the pie on an ungreased baking sheet until lightly browned, 10 to 15 minutes. Then just place them on top of the filling before serving.

For a two-crust pie, "glue" the (unbaked) shapes to the top crust with the egg wash, and then bake the pie. If you like, you can give the entire top crust a light coating of the egg wash for added shine.

german chocolate cream pie

from Diane Podratz

This easy freezer pie is my son Stu's favorite, reports my *machatenista*, Diane, from the frozen north. I'm not surprised. **SERVES 6 TO 8**   **D**

4 ounces Baker's German sweet chocolate,
   broken into large pieces
¹/₃ cup whole milk
1 small package (3 ounces) cream cheese,
   at room temperature
2 tablespoons sugar
1 container (8 ounces) Cool Whip, thawed
One store-bought 9-inch graham cracker crust

1. Combine the chocolate and 2 tablespoons of the milk in a saucepan and heat over low heat, stirring constantly, until the chocolate melts. Remove from the heat.

2. Beat the cream cheese and sugar with an electric mixer on medium speed, until smooth and free of lumps, scraping down the sides of the bowl several times, 1 to 2 minutes. Add the remaining milk and the chocolate mixture, and beat until smooth. Fold in the Cool Whip.

3. Spoon the mixture into the crust, cover it, and freeze for at least 4 hours or up to 1 day. Remove the pie from the freezer about 30 minutes before serving.

apple strudel

from Sally Bower

Aunt Sally notes, "There is no sugar in this dough. For strudel the sweetness is in the filling. Also, you sprinkle it with confectioners' sugar when done."

Alas, that was the extent of Aunt Sally's advice before she died. Fortunately my friend Sandy Calin, who learned the fine art of strudel making at her mother's knee, came to the rescue. "Your dough was too thick," she instructed when I whined about my disastrous first attempt. Veteran strudel makers like to brag that their dough is so thin they can read a newspaper through it. This takes practice. I remember as a child watching as my father's mother, Grandma Ruchel, stretched the dough as she circled a card table spread with tea towels and pulled it until it was paper-thin.

Sandy gave me a great tip about my filling too. She grates the apples, rather than slices them, and then squeezes out the moisture, ending up with about an 8-ounce glass of apple juice when she's finished. When she was a child, this was her favorite part of the process. She and her brother would fight over the wonderful fresh juice. **SERVES 12 TO 14**

FOR THE DOUGH
2 cups all-purpose flour
Pinch of salt
1 large egg, beaten
6 tablespoons warm water
1 tablespoon vegetable oil, plus
    extra for brushing the dough

FOR THE FILLING
7 medium-size firm, tart apples,
    such as Granny Smith, peeled
    and cored
1 tablespoon fresh lemon juice
3/4 cup sugar
2 teaspoons ground cinnamon
1 cup slivered almonds, toasted
    (see box, page 17)
1 cup chopped walnuts, toasted
    (see box, page 17)

Parchment paper or vegetable oil,
    for the baking sheet
All-purpose flour, for dusting the cloth
Vegetable oil, for brushing the dough
1/2 cup plain dry bread crumbs

1. *To prepare the dough by hand,* combine the flour and salt in a large bowl. In a separate bowl, whisk the egg, warm water, and oil until well mixed. Make a

> *I started collecting recipes at the age of thirteen. By the time I graduated from high school, my desk was packed with yellowed, stained pages. I wonder now if anyone else had this secret habit. Perhaps it was the flip side of sneaking food, or the continuum of dreaming of Grandma Sally's strudel and her Red, White, and Blue Cake.*
>
> **—LAURA SELIGMAN**

well in the center of the flour mixture, add the egg mixture, and mix with a fork or your hands until the dough comes together. Transfer the dough to a lightly floured work surface and knead until it is smooth and elastic, about 5 minutes.

To prepare the dough in a food processor, place the flour and salt in the processor bowl. In a separate bowl, or in a measuring cup with a spout, whisk the egg, warm water, and oil until well mixed. Pulse the flour in the food processor two or three times. Then with the machine running, slowly add the egg mixture through the feed tube. Process just until the dough comes together and pulls away from the sides of the bowl.

2. Form the dough into a flattened ball and brush it all over with oil. Wrap the dough in plastic wrap. Pour hot water into a metal or ceramic bowl and let it sit for a minute to warm the bowl. Then pour the water out and dry the bowl thoroughly. Invert the warmed bowl over the dough and set it aside for at least 30 minutes.

3. Meanwhile, prepare the filling: Shred the apples in a food processor fitted with the shredding disk. Squeeze the shredded apples with your hands until they are very dry. (Drink the apple juice or divide it evenly among your children to avoid conflict.) Combine the shredded apples, lemon juice, sugar, and cinnamon in a bowl and mix well. Stir in the almonds and walnuts. Set the filling aside.

Aunt Sally with granddaughter Eva in 1985. The dough must be stretched on the back of your hands for Aunt Sally's super-flaky, many-layered pastry, bursting with apples and nuts. A challenge for a three-year-old, but Aunt Sally believed in starting them young!

4. Preheat the oven to 350°F. Line a baking sheet with parchment paper, or grease it.

5. Cover a table with a lint-free cloth (or your grandma's tea towels, if you have any) and dust it lightly with flour. Place the dough on a lightly floured work surface and roll it out to about 8 inches square. Then, with both hands closed in a fist, palms down, loosen and stretch the dough over the back of your hands until it is about 14 inches in diameter. Place the dough in the center of the floured cloth, and using your fingertips, gently stretch it from the middle outward, until it is paper-thin. When it is thin enough, it will be white all over; any yellow areas are not thin enough and will be tough when baked. The thinner the dough gets, the more easily it tears, so patch the tears when they are small to prevent major rents. When finished, the dough will measure at least 36 × 36 inches.

6. Trim off the thicker edges of the dough, and brush the dough lightly with oil. Sprinkle the bread crumbs in a 2-inch-wide strip about 3 inches in from the edge closest

to you. (This will absorb any excess moisture and help to prevent leaking.) Scrape the filling over the bread crumbs, and cover with the 3-inch edge of dough. Fold in the sides and continue rolling, using the cloth to hold the strudel together and folding in the sides as you roll it to form a long log. As you fold the dough, brush each dry surface with oil. Transfer the strudel to the prepared baking sheet, carefully bending it to form a horseshoe shape. Brush it with oil and bake until golden, 40 to 45 minutes. Let the strudel cool completely on the baking sheet set on a wire rack. Then slice it diagonally into 2-inch-wide pieces.

7. Store the strudel on a platter, loosely covered with waxed paper or plastic wrap, at room temperature for up to 3 days.

8. Take the rest of the day off. You deserve it.

Note: The unbaked strudel can be frozen, wrapped in plastic wrap and then in aluminum foil, for up to 6 months. Do not thaw it; brush the frozen strudel with oil and bake it, adding about 15 minutes to the baking time.

> " My mother [Claire] is a gourmet cook and always uses butter. I never even heard of margarine until I met Ronald and was introduced to the Rabinowitz family. I thought it tasted like yellow Crisco. When I substitute shortening or Nyafat instead of chicken fat in my mother's recipes, she just cringes! —SAMRA ROBBINS "

ice-cream strudel

from Claire Smolen

Yes, you're reading it right. The secret of this incredibly rich dough is ice cream—the higher the premium, the richer the dough. I happened to mention to my friend Gail Hara that I was testing Claire's recipe and she said that she has been making this dessert for years. She invited me to her house one day for a demonstration (tit for tart, shall we say, after she came to mine to watch me make kreplach). **MAKES 4 DOZEN PIECES** D

FOR THE DOUGH

1 pound (4 sticks) cold unsalted butter,
   cut into small pieces
4 cups all-purpose flour
1 pint vanilla ice cream, softened

FOR THE FILLING

$1/2$ cup sugar
1 teaspoon ground cinnamon
1 large jar (18 ounces, $1^2/3$ cups) apricot,
   strawberry, peach, or other preserves
2 cups pecan halves, toasted (see box, page 17)
   and chopped
1 cup raisins

1. Combine the butter and flour in a large bowl. Using a pastry blender, a fork, or your fingertips, blend until the mixture

has the consistency of coarse cornmeal. Add the softened ice cream and mix to form a dough. Divide the dough into four portions, wrap each portion in plastic wrap, and chill until the dough can be handled, 1 hour in the refrigerator or 30 minutes in the freezer (or as long as overnight in the refrigerator).

2. Preheat the oven to 350°F. Line a rimless cookie sheet (preferred) or a rimmed baking sheet with parchment paper.

3. Combine the sugar and cinnamon in a small bowl.

4. Using a lightly floured rolling pin, roll out one portion of the dough on a lightly floured work surface to form a rectangle about 14 inches long, 8 inches wide, and $1/4$ inch thick (Alternatively, roll it out between two sheets of waxed or parchment paper.) Spread one fourth of the preserves over the dough, leaving a $1/2$-inch border along the edges. Sprinkle with $1/2$ cup of the pecans and $1/4$ cup of the raisins. Then sprinkle lightly with some of the cinnamon-sugar. Roll the rectangle up jelly-roll fashion, forming a 14-inch-long log, and place it on the prepared cookie sheet. Repeat with the remaining dough and filling.

5. Sprinkle the strudels with cinnamon-sugar, and bake until they are lightly browned, about 45 minutes.

6. If you used a rimless cookie sheet, slide the strudels onto a cutting board. Otherwise, use two spatulas to transfer them carefully. Using a sharp serrated knife, slice each roll, while still hot, into 12 pieces. Serve them warm or at room temperature.

swedish kringler

from Barb Frank

This traditional pastry, from my daughter-in-law Shelly's Aunt Barb, is easy to make and has a pleasant almond flavor without being overpowering or overly sweet. It is usually served for breakfast, but if the mood hits you at noon, go for it! You can also cut the pastries diagonally into 1-inch bars and serve them as cookies, or serve thicker slices topped with whipped cream for dessert. **SERVES 8 TO 10**　D

FOR THE CRUST
**8 tablespoons (1 stick) cold unsalted butter,
 cut into 24 pieces**
$1/2$ cup all-purpose flour
2 tablespoons ice water

FOR THE SECOND LAYER
8 tablespoons (1 stick) unsalted butter
1 cup all-purpose flour
3 large eggs
$1/2$ teaspoon pure almond extract

FOR THE FROSTING
1 teaspoon unsalted butter, melted
1 cup confectioners' sugar, sifted
1 teaspoon pure almond extract
$1^1/2$ tablespoons milk
**$1/2$ cup sliced almonds (optional), toasted,
 if using (see box, page 17)**

1. Preheat the oven to 375°F.

2. Prepare the crust: Combine the butter and flour in a medium-size bowl. Using a pastry blender or a fork, cut the butter into the flour until the pieces of butter are the size of small peas. Stir in the ice water with a fork, mixing just until combined. Divide the dough in half and spread each piece out on a 15-inch baking sheet, making the dough 4 to 5 inches wide and the length of the baking sheet.

3. Prepare the second layer: Combine the butter and 1/2 cup water in a medium-size saucepan and bring to a boil. As soon as the butter melts, remove the pan from the heat and pour the mixture into a bowl. Let it stand for about 5 minutes to cool a bit. Then, using a fork, stir in the flour until smooth. Add the eggs, one at a time, whisking vigorously after each addition. Stir in the almond extract.

4. Spread the second layer over the two strips of dough, spreading it to the edges. Bake until golden brown and puffed up a bit, about 45 minutes. Let the strips cool completely on the cookie sheet set on a wire rack.

5. Prepare the frosting: Combine the melted butter, confectioners' sugar, almond extract, and milk in a bowl and mix until smooth.

6. Spread the frosting over the cooled kringler, and garnish with the sliced almonds if using. Cut into 3-inch-wide slices to serve. These taste best the day they are baked.

gladys rousso's baklava

from Judy Bart Kancigor

My friend Betty Sackler tells me her mother, Gladys, originally from the Isle of Rhodes, made baklava with her own filo dough prepared from scratch. Betty would come home from school on Friday afternoons to find her mother, her aunts, and several close friends busily preparing for Shabbat. Friday was baking day, when everything was prepared for the whole week: potato borekas, biscochos (cookies), and of course baklava. The dining room table, the kitchen table, and five or six card tables, all spread with white cloths, held the delicate sheets of homemade filo. Like coming home to a bakery, she said.

One day when Betty was feeling especially nostalgic, I invited her over to bake. We felt Gladys's presence all afternoon as the smell of toasting almonds and walnuts permeated my kitchen. Of course, with good-quality prepared frozen filo dough available now, we opted for that shortcut. The toasted bread crumbs blend well with the nuts, adding a little bulk, and help sop up the delicious syrup. **MAKES 44 TO 48 PIESES** P

Gladys and grandson Steven Sackler, of blessed memory, at his Bar Mitzvah, 1978.

452

Vegetable oil, for the baking pan

FOR THE FILLING

2 cups walnut halves or pieces, toasted
  (see box, page 17)
2 cups whole almonds (with skins), toasted
  (see box, page 17)
¹/₃ cup sugar
¹/₃ cup sesame seeds
3 slices (about 1 ounce each) white bread,
  toasted and cut or torn into pieces
1 teaspoon ground cinnamon
Pinch of ground cloves

FOR THE DOUGH

1 box (1 pound, about 32 sheets) frozen
  filo dough, thawed according to the
  package directions
1 cup vegetable oil

FOR THE SYRUP

3 cups sugar
¹/₂ cup honey
1 teaspoon fresh lemon juice

1. Grease a 13 × 9 × 2-inch baking pan.

2. Prepare the filling: Combine all the filling ingredients in a food processor and pulse, scraping down the sides of the bowl as needed, until the nuts are finely chopped. Set it aside.

3. Cut the stack of filo sheets in half, forming two stacks measuring approximately 13 × 9 inches each. Cover the stacks of dough with plastic wrap and then a lightly moistened towel to prevent the dough from drying out as you work. Place 3 sheets of filo dough in the prepared baking pan and brush the top layer with oil. Sprinkle 1 to 2 tablespoons of the filling evenly over the top layer of dough. Add another sheet of filo (or two—don't be concerned if a couple of sheets happen to stick together), brush it with oil, and sprinkle with another 1 to 2 tablespoons of the filling. Repeat the layers until all the filo sheets are used, ending with 3 sheets of filo on top. Brush the top with oil and cover tightly with plastic wrap, gently pressing the layers together. Set it aside to set up (for easy slicing later) while you prepare the syrup.

4. Preheat the oven to 350°F.

5. While the oven is heating, prepare the syrup: Combine the sugar and 3 cups water in a medium-size saucepan over medium-high heat. Bring to a boil, stirring occasionally and using a brush dipped in water to remove any sugar crystals that cling to the sides of the pan. Reduce the heat to medium and boil, without stirring, until the sugar has dissolved and the mixture has reduced by almost half, 5 to 10 minutes. Carefully stir in the honey and cook over medium heat until bubbles appear around the sides of the pan. Remove from the heat and stir in the lemon juice. Set the syrup aside while you bake the baklava.

6. Discard the plastic wrap and using a long, sharp knife, cut the baklava diagonally into strips about 1¹/₂ inches wide. (Take care to cut straight down until the tip of the knife penetrates all the layers and touches the bottom of the pan.) Turn the pan and repeat the diagonal cuts in the opposite direction, forming diamond shapes. Bake on the center oven rack until the pastry is crisp and golden on top, 35 to 45 minutes. Transfer the baking pan to a wire rack, and slowly pour

the syrup evenly over the top (the syrup should be warm to pour easily—rewarm it if necessary). Allow the baklava to cool completely at room temperature, at least 4 hours.

7. Using the same long, sharp knife, recut the diamond shapes. Carefully remove each piece of baklava from the pan with a thin metal spatula. Serve at once, or store between layers of parchment paper in an airtight container at room temperature for up to 1 week.

mom's best pie crust

from Samra Robbins

Orange juice makes a wonderful dough for this very flaky crust. For a more pronounced orange taste, add some grated orange zest. Or try lemon juice for an even tangier flavor. This versatile crust can be used for savory as well as sweet pies. As a savory crust, its citrus flavor would be especially lovely for a chicken or lamb pie. **MAKES CRUST FOR 1 DOUBLE-CRUST PIE OR 2 INDIVIDUAL PIE SHELLS** **P**

2¹/₂ cups all-purpose flour

1 teaspoon salt

³/₄ cup solid vegetable shortening, chilled, cut into small pieces

6 to 7 tablespoons orange juice, chilled

1. Place the flour and salt in a large bowl and whisk to combine. Add the shortening and mix together with a pastry blender or fork until the mixture resembles coarse meal.

2. Sprinkle the orange juice over the mixture, 1 tablespoon at a time, mixing lightly with a fork until the flour is moistened and the dough holds together when pressed into a ball. Do not overmix the dough or the crust will be tough. The dough should barely hold together but not be crumbly.

3. Divide the dough in two pieces: one piece slightly larger than the other for a two-crust pie, equal halves for two individual pie shells. Form the dough into two flat disks, wrap each disk in waxed paper, and refrigerate them for at least 1 hour or as long as overnight.(For rolling instructions, see box, facing page.)

High school sweethearts Samra and Ronald going to the prom, 1965 (Ron's sister Linda at right).

aunt estelle's pie crust

from Estelle Robbins

This is a sweet, cookie-like crust that can be made with either butter or shortening. While some prefer a butterier flavor, baking with shortening produces a slightly flakier crust that can be served with both meat and dairy meals. This is a versatile crust for any sweet filling.

MAKES CRUST FOR 1 DOUBLE-CRUST PIE OR 2 INDIVIDUAL PIE SHELLS **D** or **P**

2¹/₄ *cups all-purpose flour*

1 *cup sugar*

1 *teaspoon baking powder*

¹/₂ *pound (2 sticks) cold unsalted butter or chilled solid vegetable shortening, cut into small pieces*

1 *large egg, well beaten*

1. Combine the flour, sugar, and baking powder in a large bowl and whisk to combine. Add the butter (or shortening) and mix together with a pastry blender, a fork, or your fingertips until the mixture resembles coarse meal.

2. Add the beaten egg to the dough, mixing lightly with a fork until the dough holds together when pressed into a ball. Do not overmix the dough or the crust will be tough.

3. Divide the dough in two pieces: one piece slightly larger than the other for a two-crust pie, equal halves for two individual pie shells. Form the dough into two flat disks, wrap each disk in waxed paper, and refrigerate them for at least 1 hour or as long as overnight. (For rolling instructions, see box this page.)

rolling out pie shells

TO MAKE INDIVIDUAL PIE SHELLS, place a disk of dough on a lightly floured work surface, cover it with a piece of waxed paper, and roll it out to form a round about 2 inches larger than the top of a 9- or 10-inch pie plate. Transfer the dough to the pie plate and use your fingers to fit it into the bottom and up the sides of the plate. Trim the overhang to ¹/₂ inch, and then fold it under itself along the edge of the pie plate. Repeat with the remaining disk of dough. Sprinkle the pie shells lightly with flour, cover with plastic wrap, and chill for at least 1 hour. Fill and bake as instructed in the pie recipe; or prebake, partially or fully (see box, page 444).

TO MAKE A TWO-CRUST PIE, roll out the disks as instructed above, making sure the larger disk rolls out to a round that is a full 2 inches larger than the top of the pie plate. Transfer the bottom pie shell to the pie plate and fit as directed above. Fill the shell, top it with the second crust, and pierce the top in several places with a fork. Crimp the edges, and bake as instructed in the pie recipe.

bubbes

cookies

There's a little bit of the Cookie Monster in all of us. "ME WANT COOKIE!" Who can't relate to that?

Cookie love is almost instinctive, maybe because they're our earliest treats. Give a baby her first cookie, and she looks at you as if to say, "I've been eating strained squash and spinach, and all this time you had *these*?"

We learn to bake by making cookies. There's the traditional image: Mom in her organdy apron, pumps, and pearls, guiding your plump little hands as you sift, stir, and roll. She lets you lick the bowl . . . or at least she did before the raw egg police came

"The gift of love in just one bite."

Bubbes are for loving! (My friend Rhoda Friedman says grandchildren are the only reason to have children in the first place!) Who's who on page 613.

this is the way the cookie crumbles

- Please read the baking tips on page 371.
- Nag, nag, nag. I've said it before, but I'll say it again. To measure flour: First stir it, then spoon lightly into a measuring cup and level it off.
- Line your cookie sheets with parchment paper. If you don't have any, go out and get some! Greasing the pan makes for burnt bottoms and overspread cookies. (Of course silicone liners are fine too.)
- Not all ovens bake the same, so adjust baking times accordingly. Cookies bake for such a short time that even a minute can make the difference between a delectable bite and a burnt offering.
- For rolled cookies, roll the dough between sheets of parchment or waxed paper while it is soft. Then refrigerate or freeze before cutting them out.
- Do yourself a favor and invest in several large baking sheets. Some people prefer to bake cookies one sheet at a time on the middle oven rack, and some like to save time by baking two sheets at a time, which involves rotation. Either way is fine. I don't like to take sides.
- To avoid overspreading, don't overbeat when creaming the butter and sugar.
- Wait until cookies have completely cooled before storing. Store most baked cookies in a plastic airtight container for up to 3 days or freeze them for up to 2 months. Place parchment or waxed paper between the layers. For best results, wrap cookies in plastic wrap—one or several at a time—before freezing. Most unbaked cookie doughs (except for soft cookies) may be frozen for up to 1 month. Take out as much or as little as you like and create your own memories!

along to spoil the fun . . . sigh. This is the stuff of which memories are made . . . well, maybe *your* memories. My mother never baked cookies when we were growing up. She didn't buy them either. Dad was a diabetic and we were supposed to be on diets. But when no one was home, one could always sneak upstairs to Mama Hinda and Papa Harry's apartment. They weren't diabetic and they didn't diet either, so don't cry for me, Argentina.

Somehow between the organdy apron and the feminist movement, cookie baking got a bad rap, as in the expression "staying home and baking cookies," like you have to "stay home" to bake cookies! Hah! That's the beauty of cookies. Baking them doesn't have to be a complicated, all-day project. Working moms can create memories too.

Family get-togethers brought Aunt Irene's decorated bakery cookies and cinnamon mandelbrot (and she was a working mom long before it was fashionable to be one), Aunt Estelle's Rugelach and chocolate chip nuggets, Aunt Hilda's chocolate-studded sour cream mandelbrot, and Aunt Sally's thumbprint jam cookies, which, according to my grandchildren, have assured me forever a place in the grandmas' hall of fame. Holidays brought Aunt Sally's Rosh Hashanah taiglach and Aunt Hilda's mom Ethel's hamantaschen for Purim.

As I baked my way through this chapter, I learned to make Rugelach, buttery Greek Kourabiedes, sand nuggets, and kichel and fashioned a cookie puzzle from Grandma Ethel's sturdy Crisco cookies. I felt the loving arms of others' *bubbes* and *tantas* as they passed down their signature poppy seed cookies and Cream-Filled Hanukkah Stars. I got homesick for New York over my daughter-in-law Shelly's Black & Whites and nostalgic for the days when my sons and their friends seemed to inhale my Lemon Snowcaps.

From Israel came chocolate-filled yeast rugelach; from Antwerp, honey cookies; from Minnesota, Ilo's generations-old cherry bars; Sweet Smooches from Atlanta; delicate Chocolate Bohemian Cookies from Michigan; and from everywhere in between, the gift of love in just a bite.

When Mama Hinda died, I took the things that would remind me most of her: a wooden bowl and hand chopper for cracking nuts, a few old stirring spoons, her latke frying pan, the covered glass candy jar she kept on the coffee table for broken chunks of Hershey's chocolate (talk about returning to the scene of the crime!), and the white enamel soup pot she kept in the linen closet that held the cookies.

Mama Hinda baked only one type of cookie. It was a plain drop cookie with an almost crumbly texture that she and Papa enjoyed with their evening tea. No one had the recipe. If truth be told, I'm not sure they were even that good! But I must have eaten a million of them in my forays upstairs. I've tried countless recipes without success. It's been decades since I've tasted them, but I'll know them when I find them. The search goes on. Stay tuned!

mama irene's fancy bakery butter cookies

from Jodi Orlow Mackoff

Aunt Irene's decorated cookies were as professional as a baker's and expected at every party. Although my daughter-in-law Shelly met her only a few times—and by then her baking days were long gone—these cookies have become Shelly's favorite for rolling, and it tickles me to know that my grandchildren in Minnesota, who never knew Aunt Irene, feast on these treats from my childhood.

Aunt Irene's granddaughter Jodi now makes them with her own children, who love to decorate them with M&M's and sprinkles. When Samantha and Jenna were little, they used to feed as many to their shih tzu, Oreo (may he rest in peace)—this *is* a cookie-conscious household—as they did to themselves. **MAKES ABOUT 4 DOZEN** 🄳

3 cups all-purpose flour

¹/₂ teaspoon baking powder

¹/₂ teaspoon salt

¹/₂ pound (2 sticks) butter, at room temperature

¹/₂ cup sugar

1 large egg, at room temperature

1 tablespoon pure vanilla extract

> As a child I often watched and helped my mother [Irene] create these treats. Later my girls and their friends joined me in producing many renditions of this recipe. Visiting day at sleepaway camp in Maine always meant packing three full cans of Mama Irene's butter cookies in various shapes, colors, and decorations. We also would use them as place cards for the children's parties, rolling them 1/8 inch thick and cutting the dough into 2- x 3-inch oblong shapes, then writing each name on the cooled cookie with melted chocolate or colored icing. Sometimes we would substitute peppermint, almond, or lemon extract for some of the vanilla just for variety.
>
> **—PHYLLIS EPSTEIN**

1. Sift the flour, baking powder, and salt together into a bowl, and set it aside.

2. Cream the butter and sugar with an electric mixer on medium speed, scraping the bowl once or twice, until smooth and creamy, about 1 minute. Beat in the egg until combined, followed by the vanilla. Reduce the speed to low and gradually beat in the flour mixture.

3. Roll the dough out between two pieces of waxed or parchment paper until it is 1/8 to 1/16 inch thick, making as many sheets of dough as are comfortable to handle. Without removing the paper, pile the sheets of dough onto a baking sheet and freeze them until firm, about 30 minutes.

4. Preheat the oven to 400°F. Line several baking sheets with parchment paper.

5. Remove a sheet of dough from the freezer, remove the paper, and cut it into shapes with cookie cutters. Reroll and cut out the scraps, cutting out as many cookies as will fit on two baking sheets.

6. Bake, two sheets at a time, on the bottom third and top third oven racks, rotating the sheets from top to bottom and front to back halfway through, until delicately brown, about 6 minutes. Let the cookies cool on the baking sheets set on wire racks.

7. Repeat with the remaining dough.

Note: To decorate the cookies, use chocolate chips, dried cherries, or your choice of nuts, either stirred into the dough or pressed into the cut-out shapes; or add food coloring to the dough after the flour is incorporated. If you like them glazed, mix 1 egg yolk with 2 tablespoons water and brush this over the cookies before baking.

grandma ethel's famous crisco cookies

from Hilda Robbins

thel Jaffee and Aunt Sally were great friends and matchmakers (they brought Ethel's daughter—Aunt Hilda—and Sally's brother—Uncle Lou—together). I'm sure Ethel made these cookies by hand a million times, and you can too. I like to use the machine with a paddle just to save time (but hey, my mother the sous-chef is doing the dishes!), but it isn't really necessary. Give the youngest child a wooden spoon and they will come out just as good.

These sturdy cookies are extremely versatile. Roll them and cut them out with your favorite cookie cutters. Form the dough into cylinders and slice them for "icebox" cookies. Roll the dough into balls and flatten them with a sugar-dipped glass for sugar cookies. Make a giant cookie puzzle (see box, page 462). Add chocolate chips, nuts, raisins, poppy seeds . . . the possibilities are endless. (And as an added benefit for the observant, they can be served with meat or dairy meals.) **MAKES ABOUT 8 DOZEN** 🅿

Aunt Hilda (top center) with Uncles Morris and Lou and her mom, Ethel Jaffee, seated, 1940s.

2 cups solid vegetable shortening

1¹/₂ cups sugar

3 large eggs, at room temperature

2 teaspoons pure vanilla extract, or

1 teaspoon pure vanilla extract

and 1 teaspoon almond extract

or maple or peppermint or

you name it!

5 cups all-purpose flour

¹/₂ teaspoon salt

1. Cream the shortening and sugar with an electric mixer on medium speed, scraping the bowl several times, until smooth and creamy, about 1 minute. Add the eggs, one at a time, beating until combined. Then add the vanilla. Scrape the bowl and beat just to combine.

2. Stir the flour and salt together in a bowl, and stir the flour mixture into the wet ingredients with a wooden spoon. (If you try to beat it in, you'll be wearing it.) Beat on medium-low speed just to combine.

3. Roll the dough out between two pieces of waxed or parchment paper until it is ¹/₈ to ¹/₄ inch thick, making as many sheets of dough as are comfortable to handle. Without removing the paper, pile the sheets of dough onto a baking sheet and freeze them until firm, about 30 minutes.

4. Preheat the oven to 350°F. Line several baking sheets with parchment paper.

5. Remove a sheet of dough from the freezer, remove the paper, and cut it into shapes with cookie cutters. Reroll and cut out the scraps, cutting out as many cookies as will fit on two baking sheets.

6. Bake, two sheets at a time, on the bottom third and top third oven racks, rotating the sheets from top to bottom and front to back halfway through, until the cookies

are beginning to brown at the edges, 10 to 15 minutes. Let the cookies cool on the baking sheets set on wire racks.

7. Repeat with the remaining dough.

Variation: Aunt Sally added 1 cup chopped walnuts and/or 2 cups (12 ounces) chocolate chips.

cookie puzzle

If your cable service provides the Fine Living channel (and if you didn't sneeze), you might have caught me demonstrating this cookie puzzle in a 1-minute spot during the last several Hanukkah seasons. This is a great project for kids for holidays, birthday parties, rainy days, or any time. **Makes two puzzles.**

1. Prepare the Crisco Cookies dough as described in Steps 1 and 2 (page 461).

2. Line two 13 x 9-inch baking pans with parchment or waxed paper, leaving a few inches overhanging on opposite sides for easy removal later. Pat half the dough evenly into each pan. Cover with another sheet of parchment or waxed paper, cover the pan with aluminum foil, and freeze for several hours or overnight, until quite firm.

3. Remove the baking pans from the freezer and release the dough by pulling the overhanging paper. Smooth out the dough with a rolling pin, and using a ruler and a sharp knife, cut each piece of dough into an even rectangle. (You can use the scraps to make cut-out cookies.)

4. Preheat the oven to 350°F. Line two baking sheets with parchment paper.

5. Transfer each rectangle of dough to a prepared baking sheet. Using a sharp knife, cut the rectangles into puzzle shapes, using a curving motion, being careful not to separate the pieces. (If you bake the pieces separated, they will spread, and you won't be able to put the puzzle back together.) Bake, one pan at a time, on the center oven rack until browned along the edges, 16 to 20 minutes.

6. While the cookies are still warm, recut along the puzzle lines with a sharp knife, and separate the pieces. (If some of the internal puzzle pieces look a little underbaked, pop them back in the oven for another minute or two.) Let the puzzle pieces cool on a wire rack.

7. When the pieces are cool, put the puzzle back together on a baking sheet and decorate it with Royal Icing (see Note) and assorted edible decorations (sprinkles, balls, colored sugar, etc.).

Note: Royal icing dries hard and is perfect for decorating cookies. I prefer to prepare it with meringue powder (available at cake decorating stores or hobby shops) rather than fresh egg whites: Follow the directions on the meringue powder package. Use an assortment of colors and turn your junior Picassos loose. Transfer the colored icing to 12-inch disposable pastry bags fitted with a tip and decorate away.

Baking with my niece Jessica, early '80s.

kourabiedes

from Ketty Moreno

These Greek cookies are a cross between a butter cookie and shortbread and are so rich that they melt *on the way* to your mouth. Traditionally they are round or crescent-shaped, but Ketty sliced them diagonally into rhomboids (if I remember my geometry). She shaped them by rolling the dough into a cylinder, flattening the dough using her three middle fingers (as if extended in a Cub Scout salute), and then slicing the flattened dough. Her cookies were always perfectly uniform, as though machine-stamped, but when I tried the Cub Scout method (and despite the fact that I've done my time as a den mother), mine looked like an art project gone awry. Only by using a rolling pin could I ever hope to earn this merit badge. Salute if you prefer. Sloppy or neat, they taste heavenly. Be sure your butter is at room temperature so you don't overbeat the dough. **MAKES ABOUT 4 DOZEN** D

¹/₂ pound (2 sticks) unsalted butter,
   at room temperature
³/₄ cup sugar
Yolk of 1 large egg, at room temperature
¹/₂ teaspoon pure vanilla extract
¹/₄ teaspoon pure almond extract
2 cups all-purpose flour, plus more
   if necessary
Confectioners' sugar, for dusting

1. Cream the butter and sugar together with an electric mixer on medium speed just until blended, about 30 seconds. Don't overbeat. Scrape the bowl and blend in the egg yolk and both extracts. Reduce the speed to low and gradually add the flour, beating just until incorporated; add only enough flour to achieve a dough that barely sticks to your hand (see Note). Wrap the dough in plastic wrap and refrigerate it until it can be handled, several hours or as long as overnight.

2. Preheat the oven to 325°F. Line two baking sheets with parchment paper.

3. Divide the dough into four portions and work with one at a time, while keeping the remainder refrigerated. Roll the dough out between two sheets of waxed paper until it is ¹/₄ inch thick. Using a sharp knife, slice the dough into 1¹/₂-inch-wide strips. Slice the strips on the diagonal, making the cuts 1 inch apart. Reroll and reuse any scraps.

4. Place the pieces 1 inch apart on the prepared baking sheets. Bake, two sheets at a time, on the bottom third and top third oven racks, rotating the sheets from top to bottom and front to back halfway through, until the cookies are lightly browned at the edges, about 20 minutes. Let the cookies cool on the sheets set on wire racks until they can be lifted, about 30 seconds. Then transfer them to the rack to cool completely.

5. Repeat with the remaining dough.

6. When they are completely cool, dust the cookies with confectioners' sugar.

Note: I don't know about you, but I'd rather send the rolled dough back to the fridge to firm up than add more flour or roll it on a floured board. I think you get a richer cookie that way. This does require some juggling back and forth, however, as the heat of your hands quickly melts the butter and softens the dough.

cream-filled hanukkah stars

from Lauren Kancigor

my granddaughter Lauren, age seven at this writing, has taken over the baking of these itsy-bitsy, teeny-weenie Hanukkah cookies. Her little fingers are perfect for handling these delicate, almost puff-pastry-like stars. My daughter-in-law Shelly converted her aunt Mary Skolberg's round holiday cookie by using a tiny Star of David cookie cutter. They then sandwich them with pale blue filling. The smaller the better in Shelly's family. Aunt Mary used to cut these cookies out with a soda bottle cap. Lauren's cookie cutter measures an inch from tip to tip. My 1½-incher is as small as I can handle and is what I used for my cooking classes, but you can use any size (or even shape) you choose. **MAKES ABOUT 10 DOZEN 1½-INCH SANDWICHES OR 12 DOZEN 1-INCH SANDWICHES** **D**

¹/₂ pound (2 sticks) unsalted butter, at room temperature
¹/₃ cup heavy (whipping) cream
2 cups all-purpose flour
Sugar, for dipping the cookies
Buttercream Frosting (recipe follows)

1. Blend the butter and cream with an electric mixer on medium speed until well combined, about 1 minute. Reduce the speed to low, add the flour, and beat just until combined.

2. Divide the dough into four balls and roll each ball out between two pieces of waxed or parchment paper until it is ¹/₈ to ¹/₄ inch thick. Without removing the paper, pile the sheets of dough on a baking sheet and freeze until firm, about 30 minutes.

3. Preheat the oven to 350°F. Line a baking sheet with parchment paper (preferred) or leave it ungreased. Pour sugar into a shallow dish for dipping.

4. Remove a sheet of dough from the freezer, remove the paper, and cut out cookies with a small Star of David cookie cutter. Gather up the scraps, reroll, and cut out as many cookies as will fit on one baking sheet. Dip each cut-out cookie in the sugar, covering both sides, and place them close together on the baking sheet (they will not spread). Using a fork, prick each cookie four times to make sixteen holes (to prevent overpuffing), and bake one sheet at a time on the center oven rack until the cookies are barely starting to change color, 7 to 9 minutes. Let the cookies cool on the baking sheet set on a wire rack.

5. Repeat with the remaining dough.

6. Spread the frosting lightly over half the cookies, and press the other cookies on top to make a sandwich.

buttercream frosting

Shelly says the consistency of this frosting should be somewhere between mayonnaise and peanut butter. If it's too thin, add more confectioners' sugar. If too thick, add a little cream. Add only enough food coloring to make a very pale blue frosting. **MAKES 1¹/₂ CUPS**

8 tablespoons (1 stick) unsalted butter,
*   at room temperature*
2¹/₂ cups confectioners' sugar, sifted
2 tablespoons heavy (whipping) cream
1 teaspoon pure vanilla extract
2 to 3 drops blue food coloring

Cream the butter and confectioners' sugar with an electric mixer on medium speed, scraping the bowl occasionally, until the mixture is smooth, about 2 minutes. Beat in the cream and vanilla. Add blue food coloring, 1 drop at a time, mixing until combined and until you have the desired color. Use the frosting within 24 hours.

barbara klingsberg's linzer cookies

from Judy Bart Kancigor

Few can resist these jam-filled sandwich cookies, generously coated with powdered sugar, with a fetching bit of raspberry peeking through the center. My friend Barbara, who owns every kitchen tool known to man (or woman), uses a fancy-shmancy linzer cookie form for this heirloom recipe from her mother, Wanda Kellich—but another friend, Blossom Morris, gave me a great tip for cutting out the center holes: She uses the top of a lipstick tube! I use a scalloped-edge cookie cutter for the top cookie and a plain round one for the bottom. **MAKES ABOUT 2 DOZEN**　　　　**D**

1 cup all-purpose flour
¹/₃ cup confectioners' sugar, plus more for
*   sprinkling*
Pinch of salt
¹/₂ cup ground pecans or walnuts
1 teaspoon pure vanilla extract
8 tablespoons (1 stick) unsalted butter,
*   at room temperature*
About ³/₄ cup seedless raspberry jam

Lauren rolls the dough
for her Hanukkah stars.

1. Sift the flour, confectioners' sugar, and salt together into a medium-size bowl. Stir in the nuts and vanilla. Blend in the butter by hand until the mixture holds together and the flour is incorporated.

2. Roll out the dough between two pieces of waxed or parchment paper until it is 1/8 inch thick. Without removing the paper, place the sheet on a baking sheet and place it in the freezer until firm, about 30 minutes.

3. Preheat the oven to 350°F. Line two baking sheets with parchment paper.

4. Remove the top layer of waxed paper, and working quickly, use a round cookie cutter, biscuit cutter, or glass to cut out as many 2-inch rounds as possible. Place them on the prepared baking sheets. Cut out and remove a small round from the center of half of the cookies. Gather up the scraps, reroll, and cut out as many more cookies as possible. (If the dough becomes too soft to handle, chill it in the refrigerator for a few minutes.)

5. Bake the cookies on the center oven rack until they are light gold, 10 to 12 minutes. Let the cookies cool on the baking sheets set on wire racks.

6. Spread the flat side of the hole-less cookies with a scant teaspoon of jam. Top with the "holey" cookies and sprinkle generously with confectioners' sugar. With the tip of a knife, drop additional jam in the center hole.

grandma mollie weiser's/sally cohen's poppy seed cookies

from David Miller and Sheilah Cohen

Papa Harry's niece Sally, from St. Louis, and David Miller's grandmother, Molly Weiser, were both famous for their poppy seed cookies. The recipes David and Sheilah sent me were astonishingly similar, but frankly, neither one worked. Both were too soft to roll and pointed up the difficulty in trying to re-create those moments from the past. Our grandmas sifted flour— they had to! And what did they measure with? A *yahrzeit* glass, of course. Did they spoon lightly into a cup? I doubt it. I played with both recipes, made four versions, and sent a package with four samples each to David in New York and to Sally's daughter-in-law Sheilah in St.

Louis. Amazingly, each picked the recipe closest to the other's as the one they remember. The following is a composite of both.

This "cookie" is really more like a cracker, not overly sweet, but as habit-forming as a potato chip. If it's a rich poppy seed cookie you're after, add ground poppy seeds to Mama Irene's butter cookies (page 459) or Grandma Ethel's Hamantaschen (page 468). **MAKES ABOUT 8 DOZEN** Ⓟ

3 cups all-purpose flour

1 tablespoon baking powder

Pinch of salt

2 large eggs, at room temperature

$1/2$ cup plus 2 tablespoons peanut (Mollie's) or vegetable (Sally's) oil

$3/4$ cup sugar

$1/4$ cup poppy seeds

1 teaspoon pure vanilla extract

1. Stir the flour, baking powder, and salt together in a medium-size bowl. Set it aside.

Grandma Mollie Weiser, about 1920. Although she lived in a tenement on the Lower East Side, her sister Kate was an expert, self-taught seamstress and made sure her baby sister always looked like a fashion plate.

❝ *This is a favorite recipe that my Grandma Mollie used to make for the holidays. She knew that I loved them and would always make sure that I went home with a private stash. When I was away at summer camp or college, she would always send me a tin of them that would get devoured in seconds."* —DAVID MILLER

"Grandma Mollie was David's mother's mother. When David proposed to me, he gave me her engagement ring, which was given to her by her husband almost eighty years before. She was a very special woman, and she meant a lot to David." —VICKI MILLER

"I have my mother's [Mollie's] original scrap of paper that the recipe was scribbled on, and looking at it after all these years, I came to realize that she not only used a yahrzeit glass for a measuring cup, but for a tablespoon she used her soupspoon, which was an old-fashioned European-style spoon and is larger than a standard tablespoon measure. I also remember that she sometimes used peanut oil, and when I tried that, it definitely made a difference. —RITA MILLER ❞

2. Beat the eggs, oil, sugar, poppy seeds, and vanilla with an electric mixer on medium speed until thoroughly mixed, about 2 minutes. Reduce the speed to low and add the flour mixture, beating until it is fully incorporated. The dough will be very sticky.

3. Roll the dough out between two pieces of waxed or parchment paper until it is $1/8$ inch thick, making as many

sheets of dough as are comfortable to handle. Without removing the paper, pile the sheets onto a baking sheet and place them in the freezer until firm, about 30 minutes.

4. Preheat the oven to 350°F. Line several baking sheets with parchment paper.

5. Remove a sheet of dough from the freezer, remove the paper, and cut the dough into shapes with a 2-inch round cookie cutter. Gather up the scraps, reroll, and cut out as many cookies as will fit on two baking sheets. Place the cookies an inch apart on the prepared baking sheets and bake, two sheets at a time, on the bottom third and top third oven racks, rotating the sheets from top to bottom and front to back halfway through, until the cookies are nicely browned, 12 to 15 minutes. Remove the cookies with a spatula and let them cool on wire racks.

6. Repeat with the remaining dough.

> **When my daughter Elissa was about three, we were on our way to visit my parents [Hilda and Lou] in Florida. We had to stop in Atlanta, and Uncle Morris [Lou's identical twin] came to the airport to see us as we waited for the next flight. When Elissa saw Uncle Morris, she was so excited to see her Grandpa Lou. Then when we got to Fort Lauderdale, try explaining to a three-year-old how her grandpa, whom we just left in Atlanta, got to the gate before we did! She was traumatized! The twins did the same thing to my sister, Bonnie, when she was Elissa's age. How she cried to see two daddies. Some things never change.** —JACKIE BISHINS

ethel jaffee's hamantaschen

from Hilda Robbins

et your imagination run wild when filling these cookies. Substitute any nut, any dried fruit, any flavored jam, even any juice for your own combo. Use prunes instead of raisins and add 2 tablespoons ground poppy seeds for an update on the traditional mohn cookies (*mohn*, pronounced "mun," is the German and Yiddish word for poppy seed). Or how about aloha-taschen with macadamia nuts, dates, and pineapple jam and juice? Or for Aunt Estelle's personal preference: Add ½ cup chopped chocolate instead of or in addition to the nuts. For an adult version, substitute 1 tablespoon liqueur for 1 tablespoon of the orange juice. You can also use preserves (any flavor) or any of the wonderful commercial fillings put out by Solo (apricot is my favorite) or Love'n Bake, especially their Schmears (Chocolate, Almond, and Cinnamon) as well as their Prune Lekvar and Poppy Seed filling. Use this recipe for rolled-out butter cookies too. **MAKES ABOUT 9 DOZEN** D

4¼ cups all-purpose flour

2 teaspoons baking powder

½ teaspoon salt

8 tablespoons (1 stick) unsalted butter,
    at room temperature

1/2 cup solid vegetable shortening

1 cup plus 2 tablespoons sugar

3 large eggs, at room temperature

1/4 cup milk, half-and-half, or nondairy creamer,
   at room temperature

1 teaspoon pure vanilla extract

Raisin Nut Filling (recipe follows)

1. Stir the flour, baking powder, and salt together in a medium-size bowl, and set it aside.

2. Cream the butter, shortening, and sugar with an electric mixer on medium-low speed, scraping the bowl several times, until smooth and creamy, about 3 minutes. Add the eggs, one at a time, beating after each addition, and beat until combined, about 1 minute more. Then blend in the milk and vanilla. Don't be alarmed if the mixture appears grainy. Add the flour mixture, 1 cup at a time, and blend on low speed until incorporated.

3. Divide the dough into four balls, and roll each ball out between two pieces of waxed or parchment paper until it is 1/8 inch thick. Without removing the paper, pile the sheets of dough on a baking sheet and place them in the freezer until firm, about 30 minutes.

4. Preheat the oven to 350°F. Line several baking sheets with parchment paper.

5. Remove the sheets of dough from the freezer one at a time. Remove the paper and cut out the dough with a 2½-inch round cookie cutter, biscuit cutter, or glass. Gather up the scraps, reroll, and cut out as many cookies as will fit on two baking sheets. Spread a level ½ teaspoon of the filling over each cookie, and pinch the cookie tightly in three places to form a triangle shape. Place the cookies close together on the prepared sheets (they won't spread), though without touching. Bake, two sheets at a time, on the bottom third and top third oven racks, rotating the sheets from top to bottom and front to back halfway through, until the cookies are golden brown on the edges and bottoms, about 15 minutes. Let the cookies cool on the sheets set on wire racks.

6. Repeat with the remaining dough.

Notes: After Purim, make pretty bow cookies: Instead of pinching the filled cookies in three places, grab the edge of each cookie at 3 and 9 o'clock, and pinch.

raisin nut filling

thel didn't live to see the food processor, but I think it produces the best texture for her hamantaschen filling.

MAKES 1 CUP P

3/4 cup pecans or walnut halves and/or
   pieces, toasted (see box, page 17)

1 cup raisins

1/4 cup apricot jam

1/2 teaspoon grated lemon zest

1/2 teaspoon grated orange zest

2 tablespoons orange juice

1. Place the nuts in a food processor and pulse until finely chopped and uniform but not a paste. Remove the nuts and set aside.

2. Place the raisins, jam, lemon zest, orange zest, and orange juice in the food processor and process until the mixture forms a ball. Add the ground nuts and process just to combine.

chocolate hamantaschen

from Judy Bart Kancigor

ong ago, in my den mother days, a friend gave me her family's recipe for Polish kolacky. I shaped them as Haman's hats and made them for Purim. Because my family wouldn't touch poppy seed filling, preferring chocolate to any fruit, I created my own tradition.

Bulletin! This just in! *Taschen* means "pockets," and Haman never wore a three-cornered hat! (You just can't believe anything you hear these days.) Matthew Goodman, the "Food Maven" columnist of the *Forward*, points out in *Jewish Food: The World at Table* that these Purim sweets were originally called mohntaschen, meaning "poppy seed pockets." Over the years the word morphed into hamantaschen ("Haman's pockets"), referring to his coat pockets, which supposedly held the lots (*purim*) he cast in order to choose the date for the slaughter of the Jews in his kingdom. **MAKES ABOUT 4 DOZEN** **D**

purim

It has all the elements of pulp fiction: a foolish king (Ahasuerus), a spurned wife (Vashti), a wicked first minister (Haman), a beautiful maiden (Esther), and her honorable protector (Mordecai). Add: An assassination plot foiled + a people saved = millennia of rejoicing.

Fast forward 2,500 years, and some scholars assert that Purim, the holiday of merriment and trickery, may itself be a trick, casting doubt that the story ever happened! You tell that to those colorfully costumed kids, drowning out the name Haman with *graggers* (noisemakers) every time it is mentioned in the *Megillah* (Book of Esther). This is a day to party!

To celebrate our deliverance, sweets are the order of the day. Gifts of cakes and fruit *(shaloch manot)* are exchanged. Ashkenazim eat three-cornered hamantaschen (Haman's pockets), traditionally filled with poppy seeds. Sephardim enjoy honeyed pastries called oznei Haman (Haman's ears).

FOR THE DOUGH

1 package (8 ounces) cream cheese,
  at room temperature
¹/₂ pound (2 sticks) unsalted butter,
  at room temperature
3 tablespoons granulated sugar
2 cups all-purpose flour

FOR THE FILLING

3 ounces unsweetened chocolate
1 can (14 ounces) sweetened condensed milk
1 teaspoon pure vanilla extract

1 egg, lightly beaten
Confectioners' sugar

1. Prepare the dough: Cream the cream cheese, butter, and sugar with an electric mixer on medium speed until blended and smooth. Reduce the speed to low and gradually add the flour, beating until incorporated. Divide the dough into three portions, and roll each portion out between two pieces of waxed or parchment paper until it is $^1/_8$ inch thick. Without removing the paper, pile the sheets of dough onto a baking sheet and place them in the freezer until firm, about 30 minutes.

2. Prepare the filling: Combine the chocolate and the condensed milk in a small saucepan over low heat, and stir until smooth. Remove the pan from the heat and stir in the vanilla. Set the filling aside to cool to room temperature. (The filling can be covered and refrigerated for up to 3 days. Let it sit at room temperature until spreadable.)

3. Preheat the oven to 350°F. Line several baking sheets with parchment paper.

4. Remove the sheets of dough from the freezer one at a time. Remove the paper and cut out the dough with a 2½-inch round cookie cutter. Gather up the scraps, reroll, and cut out as many more cookies as possible. (If it becomes sticky, return the sheet of dough, in the waxed paper, to the refrigerator to firm up.)

My son Brad emcees as Ahasuerus at his synagogue's Purim party. (Costume designed and executed by his Grandma Lil, of course!)

Brush each round with the beaten egg, and drop 1 level teaspoon of the filling in the center. Pinch the cookies tightly in three places to form a triangle shape.

5. Place the cookies on the prepared baking sheets and bake, two sheets at a time, on the bottom third and top third oven racks, rotating the sheets from top to bottom and front to back halfway through, until the edges of the cookies are just beginning to brown, 18 to 22 minutes. Let the cookies cool on the baking sheets set on wire racks.

6. Repeat with the remaining dough and filling.

7. Sprinkle confectioners' sugar over the cookies just before serving.

anna wallach's viennese almond crescents

from Marylyn Lamstein

After innumerable taste testings by my neighbors, my mother's library squad, my husband's office staff, and the discriminating mavens at the temple, Marylyn's almond crescents took first place over several similar recipes that were contributed. The unmistakably heady flavor of almonds, the unabashedly rich, melt-in-your-mouth, buttery texture—it's easy to see why these were her family's favorite.

MAKES 2 DOZEN

^{1}/$_2$ **cup blanched almonds**

1^3/$_4$ **cups all-purpose flour**

^{1}/$_3$ **cup sugar**

14 tablespoons (1^3/$_4$ sticks) cold unsalted butter, cut into small pieces

Confectioners' sugar, sifted, for sprinkling

1. Combine the almonds, flour, and sugar in a food processor and process until the almonds are finely ground. Distribute the butter over the mixture and process until the dough just comes together. Form the dough into two 12-inch-long logs, cover them with plastic wrap, and refrigerate overnight.

2. Preheat the oven to 325°F. Line a baking sheet with parchment paper.

3. Cut the dough into 1-inch lengths. Bend each piece to form a crescent shape. Place them on the prepared baking sheet and bake on the center oven rack until the cookies are just beginning to turn yellow, about 25 minutes. Let the cookies cool slightly on the baking sheet set on a wire rack. While they are still slightly warm, sprinkle them generously with confectioners' sugar. Then carefully transfer the cookies to a wire rack to cool.

Anna and Anshel Wallach were not related to us, but they were like an aunt and uncle to me. My dad [Sol] ran away from home in Poland on foot at the age of twelve. He was disgusted with his father, who studied Torah all the time and never worked, leaving his mother to scrape together money to feed the three children. My dad worked in the coal mines in Belgium, cleaned public toilets in Paris, and finally, by age seventeen or eighteen, scraped together the fare for a ship bound for Canada. On board he met Anshel, and having no papers, they both jumped ship and snuck into the U.S.

My dad had the name and address of an uncle, Mendel Rothman, a dealer in dry goods, who gave him a job as a peddler. He met my mother [Isabelle] through her father, who was also working for Mendel. They fell instantly in love, but the family considered him a black sheep: He had left home and abandoned his family and had no prospects.

They married anyway, and when I was about six, my father had to go to Cuba with an attorney to enter the U.S. legally. I remember my mother crying when he was gone. (My dad certainly proved the family wrong, as he went on to achieve great success in the furniture and appliance business and was one of the most generous and charitable of men, bringing to the United States many refugees after World War II ended and helping many family, friends, and customers in financial need.)

Anshel and Anna and my parents remained good friends all their lives. Anna would send me recipes when I was first married and living in Kansas, where Ben was stationed in the Air Force. These rich almond cookies used to be a staple in my house. The kids loved them and I made them every week. I can't remember when I made them last, however, because of Ben's cholesterol. They're almost all butter!

—MARYLYN LAMSTEIN

rugelach

from Estelle Robbins

Years ago, when cousin Staci Robbins visited from Atlanta on a high school trip, she mentioned that when she makes rugelach, she does what her Grandma Claire taught her: She brushes them with melted butter before baking. This way they brown without overbaking, not to mention what it does for the taste. I adore cousin Marilyn Dubin's filling with these rich cookies—she got it from her friend Paul Morris. I like to use it for strudel, hamantaschen, and coffee cakes as well. **MAKES ABOUT 8 DOZEN** **D**

FOR THE DOUGH

1 pound (4 sticks) unsalted butter, at room
  temperature
2 packages (8 ounces each) cream cheese,
  at room temperature
4 cups all-purpose flour

MARILYN'S FILLING

1 cup sugar
1 tablespoon ground cinnamon
2 cups pecan halves and/or pieces, walnut
  halves and/or pieces, or slivered almonds,
  toasted (see box, page 17), and chopped
1 cup sweetened flaked or shredded coconut
1 cup raisins

About 1¹/₂ cups seedless raspberry or
  apricot jam
About 5 tablespoons unsalted butter, melted

> ❝ No matter how busy she was, my mother-in-law, Estelle, always found time to prepare the foods her family loved most—mandelbrot, rugelach, strudel—either to be served at her house with a cup of coffee, sent home to be enjoyed, or shipped to her grandsons' camp or college. Even during her illness she made sure that great-granddaughter Ariel had her own special treat from Grandma Cupcake. She wanted all of us to be friends as well as family, and through her wisdom and her chicken soup, her wish was granted.   **—LESLIE ROBBINS** ❞

1. Prepare the dough: Cream the butter and cream cheese with an electric mixer on medium speed until blended and smooth. Scrape the bowl, reduce the speed to low and gradually add the flour. Knead the dough lightly in the bowl until the flour is incorporated and the dough is smooth. Wrap it well with plastic wrap and refrigerate for 2 hours or as long as overnight.

2. Prepare the filling: Mix the sugar, cinnamon, nuts, coconut, and raisins together in a medium-size bowl, and set it aside.

3. Preheat the oven to 350°F. Line several baking sheets with parchment paper.

4. Divide the dough into eight portions and work with one at a time, while keeping the remainder refrigerated. Gently knead a portion of dough until it is soft enough to roll. Roll the dough out on a lightly floured board or between two sheets of waxed or parchment paper, and cut out a 10- to 12-inch round (I use a pot lid with a sharp edge). Spread a thin layer of jam over the dough,

and sprinkle about $^1/_2$ cup of the filling over it. Using a pizza wheel, cut the round into 12 wedges, as you would a pie. Roll up each triangle, starting at the large end. With the tip end down, bend each cookie slightly to form a crescent shape. Place the cookies on the prepared baking sheets and brush them with melted butter.

5. Bake, two sheets at a time, on the bottom third and top third oven racks, rotating the sheets from top to bottom and front to back halfway through, until the rugelach are lightly golden, 20 to 25 minutes. They will seem soft, but they will firm up on cooling. Carefully transfer them to a wire rack to cool.

Mama Hinda with Aunt Estelle, who is holding cousin Joyce, 1942.

salka's yeast rugelach

from Nehama Hashman

my Israeli cousin Nehama sent me her mother's recipe for rugelach. The yeast dough makes them softer than the more familiar cookie variety. As with breadsticks, the dough is refrigerated to allow the yeast to do its thing and let the dough develop some flavor. This is a puffy pastry with an irresistibly rich chocolate filling. **MAKES 4 DOZEN** D

FOR THE DOUGH
2 packages active dry yeast
$^3/_4$ cup whole milk, heated to lukewarm
1 tablespoon sugar
Yolks of 2 large eggs
2 teaspoons pure vanilla extract
Finely grated zest of 1 lemon
$^1/_2$ pound (2 sticks) unsalted butter, melted and cooled
$3^1/_2$ cups all-purpose flour, plus more as needed
Pinch of salt

FOR THE FILLING
1 cup sugar
$^1/_2$ cup slivered almonds, toasted (see box, page 17)
2 tablespoons unsweetened cocoa powder
$^1/_2$ cup semisweet chocolate chips
2 tablespoons unsalted butter, at room temperature
About $^3/_4$ cup seedless raspberry jam

FOR THE TOPPING
$^1/_3$ cup sugar
1 teaspoon unsweetened cocoa powder
2 tablespoons ground almonds
Whites of 2 large eggs

1. Prepare the dough: Stir the yeast into the lukewarm milk in the bowl of an electric mixer. Add the sugar and blend well. Set aside until the mixture looks foamy, 5 to 10 minutes.

2. Add the egg yolks, vanilla, lemon zest, and butter to the yeast mixture and beat on medium speed until well blended. Add the $3^{1}/_{2}$ cups flour and the salt, and mix on low speed until the dough comes together. Switch to the dough hook and knead on low speed until the dough smooths out, about 3 minutes; it will still have a rough, broken look where the hook breaks into the dough. (Alternatively, turn the dough out of the bowl onto a lightly floured work surface and knead it by hand for 4 to 5 minutes.) Add more flour by the handful only if the dough is too sticky. Transfer the dough to a resealable plastic bag, seal it, and refrigerate it for at least 2 hours or as long as overnight.

3. Prepare the filling: Combine the sugar, almonds, cocoa powder, chocolate chips, and butter in a food processor and process to a crumby paste. Set it aside. Set the jam aside separately.

4. Line several baking sheets with parchment paper.

5. Divide the dough into four portions and work with one at a time, while keeping the remainder refrigerated. Shape a portion of dough into a disk. Dust your work surface with flour. Roll the dough out to form a thin 12-inch round. Spread a thin layer of jam over the dough, leaving a $^{1}/_{2}$-inch border around the edge. Crumble one fourth of the filling with your fingers, and sprinkle it over the jam. Using a pizza wheel, cut the round into 12 equal triangles, as you would a pie. Roll up each triangle, starting at the large end. With the tip end down, bend each

our family legend

Nehama is related to us through my father's mother's side, the Breitbarts, the most illustrious of whom was Zishe Breitbart, a vaudeville and circus strongman in the 1920s. Son of an impoverished blacksmith from Lodz, Poland, Breitbart amazed the world with his feats of strength. Heralded as the modern Samson and the Iron King, he became a Jewish folk hero, twisting bars of iron, pulling trains with his teeth, and killing bulls with his fist. In pre-Holocaust Europe and America, he was a legend, defending his people and encouraging them to be strong. (Tragically, at 32 he died from blood poisoning, caused by driving a spike through boards with his bare hands, piercing his knee with a rusty nail.)

While other kids heard bedtime tales of princes, frogs, and giants, my brother, Gary, and I were weaned on the Circle of Death, a motordome balanced on the strongman's chest bearing two motorcycles chasing each other in a circle. The fact that a Jew had become famous for his strength was remarkable; the fact that he was a relative was riveting!

My brother—so fascinated with the strongman's heroic deeds that his friends actually called him "Zishe"—became obsessed, and after decades of research, in 2001 produced a movie based on his life, *Invincible*, written and directed by Werner Herzog (see page 142).

cookie slightly to form a crescent shape. Place the cookies on the prepared baking sheets, spacing them 3/4 to 1 inch apart, as they will rise somewhat. Repeat with the remaining dough and filling.

6. Prepare the topping: Mix the sugar, cocoa powder, and ground almonds in a small bowl. Using a fork, beat the egg whites in another small bowl until lightly foamy.

7. Brush the top of each cookie with egg white. Sprinkle the topping lightly over the cookies. Cover lightly with a lint-free kitchen towel, and set aside to rise for 20 minutes.

8. Preheat the oven to 375°F.

9. Bake the rugelach on the center oven rack until they are golden brown, about 15 minutes. Allow them to cool on the baking sheets set on wire racks. These are best eaten the same day they're baked.

abbe's amazing almond mandelbrot

from Abbe Dubin

mandlen is Yiddish for "almonds," so I guess these could be called Almond Almond Bread. Like Italian biscotti, mandelbrot are crunchy twice-baked cookies.

Cousin Neil's wife, Abbe, marches to a different drummer. Even her mandelbrot is unconventional. Instead of rolling the dough into logs (you couldn't anyway, it's so sticky), she spreads it out in a baking pan, bakes it, and then slices it. These are crisp and quite almondy, made even more so by the perfumy almond extract. **MAKES ABOUT 7 DOZEN**　Ⓟ

Unflavored vegetable cooking spray,
　for greasing the pan
3 cups all-purpose flour
2 teaspoons baking powder
3/4 teaspoon salt
1/2 cup vegetable oil
1 cup sugar
3 large eggs
1 teaspoon pure vanilla extract
1 teaspoon pure almond extract
1 cup chopped blanched, natural,
　or slivered almonds, toasted
　(see box, page 17)

1. Preheat the oven to 350°F. Spray a 13 × 9-inch baking pan.

2. Stir the flour, baking powder, and salt together in a medium-size bowl, and set it aside.

3. Combine the oil, sugar, eggs, and both extracts with an electric mixer on medium speed until well blended. Reduce the speed to low and blend in the flour mixture, followed by the almonds.

4. Spread the dough evenly in the prepared baking pan, and level it (an offset spatula works well for this purpose). Bake on the center oven rack until golden, 45 minutes.

5. Remove the baking pan but leave the oven on. Using a serrated knife, cut the baked dough into four equal lengthwise pieces. (If you drag the knife through in one motion rather than sawing back and forth, you'll get fewer crumbs.) Then cut the pieces into 1/2- to 3/4-inch-wide slices. Place the slices, cut side down, on a baking sheet and bake until they are as crisp as you like, 7 to 15 minutes. (You will need to do this in two batches or use a second baking sheet.) Turn the cookies over onto the unbaked side and bake for another 7 to 15 minutes. Let the cookies cool completely on the baking sheets set on wire racks.

mama irene's cinnamon mandelbrot

from Vicki Miller

These cookies are very crisp and dreadfully delicious and sweet— my favorite for dunking in coffee, but Mama Irene's granddaughters always preferred hot cocoa. **MAKES ABOUT 7 DOZEN** **P**

4 cups all-purpose flour
2 teaspoons baking powder
1/2 teaspoon salt
4 large eggs
1 1/2 cups sugar
1 cup vegetable oil

2 tablespoons pure vanilla extract
2 cups (12 ounces) semisweet chocolate chips
Cinnamon-sugar, for sprinkling (see Note)

1. Stir the flour, baking powder, and salt together in a medium-size bowl, and set it aside.

2. Whisk the eggs, sugar, oil, and vanilla in a large bowl. Gradually stir in the flour mixture, followed by the chocolate chips. The dough will be very sticky. Cover the bowl and refrigerate overnight.

3. Preheat the oven to 350°F. Line two baking sheets with parchment paper.

4. Divide the dough into four portions. On a floured board, pat one piece of dough into a rectangle the length of the baking sheet and about half the width. Sprinkle it generously with cinnamon-sugar (a shaker is handy for this). Fold the dough in half lengthwise and pat it down to form a narrow log. Repeat with the remaining dough.

5. Place 2 logs on each of the prepared baking sheets. Bake both sheets at the same time, on the bottom third and top third oven

> My fondest memory of Mama Irene is her signature mandelbrot cookies. With six granddaughters to please, she always made different batches for everyone's taste. (Mine was the extra-hard with chocolate and cinnamon.) She always had tins of them stashed away, and when I'd visit with a surprise hello, she'd pull one out for me to take home. Mama Irene was my grandmother, friend, and confidante and made me feel proud to be a part of this incredible, diverse family.
>
> **—VICKI MILLER**

racks, rotating the sheets from top to bottom and front to back halfway through, until the tops are firm to the touch, about 25 minutes.

6. Remove the baking sheets from the oven, but leave the oven on. Let the logs cool for 3 minutes on the baking sheets. Then, using a serrated knife, cut each log diagonally into ³/₄-inch-thick slices. Place the slices, cut side down, on the baking sheets and sprinkle them generously with additional cinnamon-sugar. Bake for 10 minutes. Turn the cookies over onto the unbaked side and sprinkle them liberally with cinnamon-sugar. Turn the oven off and leave the cookies in the oven for 1 hour.

7. Let the cookies cool completely on the baking sheets set on wire racks.

Note: To make cinnamon-sugar, stir 2 tablespoons ground cinnamon into 1 cup granulated sugar and blend well.

ma hilda's chocolate chip mandelbrot

from Randi Bishins; Elissa Komishock

Sure, they're Aunt Hilda's mandelbrot, but where I live they're called Judy's mandelbrot, as I've

Randi and Elissa, Aunt Hilda's granddaughters.

been making them, much to the delight of family, friends, and neighbors, for thirty years at least. Sour cream gives these cookies an incredible texture. And look who's making them now: Aunt Hilda's granddaughters Randi and Elissa. Consider the baton passed!

(Bonnie and I are having a little "debate," however, about forming the loaves. She swears—and I'm sure she wouldn't lie—that her mother would arrange the dough on the sheets immediately after mixing it. Maybe it's the California climate, but I've never been able to form that sticky dough. I find refrigerating or freezing the dough makes it much easier to handle, but if you can do it her way, my toque's off to you!) **MAKES 9 TO 10 DOZEN** D

6 cups all-purpose flour

2 teaspoons baking powder

2¹/₄ cups sugar

4 large eggs

1¹/₄ cups vegetable oil

1¹/₄ cups sour cream

1 tablespoon pure vanilla extract

2 to 3 packages (12 ounces each)
   semisweet chocolate chips

1 cup chopped walnuts, toasted
   (see box, page 17; optional)

> **My mother [Hilda] passed away between Rosh Hashanah and Yom Kippur. A few weeks before, she called and said we had to cook for the holidays. I got all the ingredients for her stuffed cabbage, mandelbrot, etc., and we worked, her in her walker and me running around the kitchen cooking with her. At one point she forgot about her walker and backed away from the sink and fell backwards. It was horrible at the time because I couldn't lift her. Thank heavens my dad came in. That was my mother, always thinking of the family and the holiday food. Because she was so sick, we never got to eat her goodies for the holidays, but when we did after she died, it was a wonderful memory of her. Today when I make my mother's mandelbrot, using her recipe exactly, my son, Chad, swears something's different. In his eyes it will never be the same.**
>
> **—BONNIE ROBBINS**

1. Whisk the flour, baking powder, and sugar together in a large bowl, and set it aside.

2. Whisk the eggs in another large bowl. Add the oil, sour cream, and vanilla, and whisk until smooth. Gradually stir in the flour mixture. Stir in the chocolate chips, and the walnuts if using. Cover the bowl and freeze or refrigerate (sorry, Bonnie) until the dough is firm enough to handle, at least 2 hours or as long as overnight.

3. Preheat the oven to 325°F. Line two baking sheets with parchment paper.

4. Working on a lightly floured board, form the dough into logs the length of the baking sheet and 2 to 3 inches wide. Arrange the logs on the baking sheets, spacing them evenly apart. Bake, two sheets at a time, on the bottom third and top third oven racks, rotating the sheets from top to bottom and front to back halfway through, until they are golden brown on the bottom and light brown on top, about 1 hour.

5. Remove the baking sheets from the oven (but leave the oven on, if you prefer crispier mandelbrot). Let the logs cool on the baking sheets for 3 minutes. Then, using a serrated knife, cut each log on the diagonal into $1/2$- to $3/4$-inch-wide slices. Optional: Place the slices, cut side down, on the baking sheets and bake until they are golden brown, 5 to 10 minutes. Turn the cookies over onto the unbaked side and bake for another 5 to 10 minutes. Let the cookies cool completely on the baking sheets set on wire racks.

jam cookies

from Sally Bower

The most popular of the *Melting Pot Memories* cookies I brought to Rochester for Katya's Bat Mitzvah weekend, Aunt Sally's Jam Cookies are now my signature "Grandma" cookie—just ask Jason and Lauren! My daughter-in-law Shelly tells me that Jason once selected a commercial jam cookie from a snack machine. She was surprised, because Jason is not a big sweets-eater. He took one bite and gave it back to her, saying, "I thought these were going to be like Grandma Judy's."

MAKES ABOUT 8 DOZEN D

**¹/₂ pound (2 sticks) unsalted butter,
  at room temperature**
**8 tablespoons (1 stick) margarine,
  at room temperature**
¹/₂ cup solid vegetable shortening
1¹/₄ cups sugar
Pinch of salt
Yolks of 4 large eggs, at room temperature
4 cups all-purpose flour
**About 1 cup strawberry jam (or any flavor
  that strikes your fancy)**

1. Preheat the oven to 350°F. Line several baking sheets with parchment paper.

2. Cream the butter, margarine, shortening, sugar, and salt with an electric mixer on medium speed, scraping the bowl several times, until smooth and creamy, about 1¹/₂ minutes. Add the egg yolks and beat until combined, about 1 minute more. Reduce the speed to low and blend in the flour just until incorporated.

3. Roll balls of dough about 1 inch in diameter and place them 1¹/₂ inches apart on the prepared baking sheets. Make a firm indentation in the middle of each ball with your thumb or index finger, and fill it with jam. Bake, two sheets at a time, on the bottom third and top third oven racks, rotating the sheets from top to bottom and front to back halfway through, until the cookies are just starting to brown at the edges, 12 to 16 minutes. Let the cookies cool on the baking sheets set on wire racks until they can be easily lifted, about 1 minute. Then transfer them to the rack to cool completely.

4. Repeat the process with the remaining dough and jam.

dori solomon's powdered nut cookies

from Tracey Barrett

my daughter-in-law Tracey's friend Dori brought these one summer afternoon when the two families got together for a "playdate." These rich cookies looked especially elegant when their little girls sat down to "tea" with the porcelain tea set Dori and Rob had given our Samantha at birth. Leah and Sam got the giggles when both their noses became covered in powdered sugar. Because these cookies are baked in a slow oven for a longer time, they don't have to be watched as closely as some. **MAKES ABOUT 4 DOZEN** 🄳

**¹/₂ pound (2 sticks) unsalted butter,
  at room temperature**
¹/₄ cup granulated sugar
2 teaspoons pure vanilla extract
Pinch of salt
2 cups all-purpose flour
1¹/₂ cups finely chopped pecans
³/₄ cup confectioners' sugar, sifted

1. Preheat the oven to 250°F. Line two baking sheets with parchment paper.

2. Cream the butter, granulated sugar, and vanilla with an electric mixer on medium speed, scraping the bowl several times, until

smooth and creamy, about 1 minute. Stir the salt into the flour. Reduce the speed to low and blend in the flour mixture just until incorporated. Stir in the chopped nuts.

3. Roll the dough into balls slightly larger than marbles and place them 2 inches apart on the prepared baking sheets. Flatten them slightly with the heel of your hand. Bake both sheets at the same time, on the bottom third and top third oven racks, rotating the sheets from top to bottom and front to back halfway through, for 45 minutes. The cookies are done when the underside has no "raw" spots.

4. Allow the cookies to cool for a minute or so on the baking sheets. Then, while they are still warm, gently roll them in the confectioners' sugar. Let them cool completely on the baking sheets set on wire racks.

5. Repeat with the remaining dough.

6. Just before serving, dust the cookies again with confectioners' sugar.

gloria kremer's chocolate bohemian cookies

from Laura Seligman

I'd love to say Laura had a bohemian grandmother who handed down this recipe, but she actually got it from a rather conventional friend. Too young to ever have been called "bohemian" herself, Laura did, however, go through a shoeless, long-haired phase. Even played the dulcimer. Does that count? Anyway, she loves making these for her friends and for daughter Katya, who appreciates taking a goodie package back to college. The cookies are very delicate and oh so pretty with their chocolate flecks. If you're handy with a cookie press or pastry tube, use a star tip for an even lovelier presentation.

MAKES ABOUT 5 DOZEN   D or P

1/2 pound (2 sticks) unsalted butter, at room temperature, or 1 cup solid vegetable shortening
1 1/4 cups confectioners' sugar
1 teaspoon pure vanilla extract
1/8 teaspoon salt
1 1/4 cups all-purpose flour
6 ounces milk or semisweet chocolate, ground in a food processor

1. Preheat the oven to 250°F. Line several baking sheets with parchment paper.

2. Cream the butter, confectioners' sugar, and vanilla with an electric mixer on medium speed, scraping the bowl several times, until smooth and creamy, about 1 minute. Stir the salt into the flour. Reduce the speed to low and blend in the flour mixture just until incorporated. Stir in the ground chocolate.

3. Drop the dough by the teaspoonful, 1 1/2 inches apart, onto the baking sheets. Bake, two sheets at a time, on the bottom third and top third oven racks, rotating the sheets from top to bottom and front to back

halfway through, for 40 minutes. These cookies do not brown, so very carefully—when warm these cookies are especially fragile—lift a few with a spatula and inspect the bottoms. If you see a raw spot in the middle, continue baking for another 5 minutes or until fully baked.

4. Let the cookies cool completely on the baking sheets set on wire racks.

5. Repeat with the remaining dough.

chris creighton's sand nuggets

from

Brad Kancigor and Tracey Barrett

When my son Brad and daughter-in-law Tracey moved into their new home, it came with practically an orchard: plum, orange, avocado, and apple trees, and a magnificent persimmon in the front yard. The first year, just as the persimmons were ripening, a woman knocked on the door and asked if she could pick some. Never having even tasted a persimmon, Brad was only too glad to have someone remove what he considered potential detritus about to drop and litter the yard. Chris showed up with a 15-foot picker and went to work. The next week, there she was with an assortment of persimmon goodies: cake, cookies, persimmon leather, even

ice cream. There was only one problem: Tracey and Brad soon discovered that they didn't like persimmons!

The following year, not wishing Chris to go to any unnecessary trouble, they mentioned that they really didn't care for persimmons and for her not to bother, just to take the darn things away. At harvest time, right on schedule, she arrived with her picker . . . and a tray of her chocolate-dipped Sand Nuggets, a family recipe from her native Switzerland.

El Niño took the plum tree; the oranges don't get enough sun, so they have no taste; the squirrels and birds get to the avocados before Brad and Tracey do; but heaven help them if lightning strikes the persimmon! Those Sand Nuggets have become an eagerly anticipated yearly ritual. **MAKES ABOUT 4 DOZEN** D

1/2 pound (2 sticks) unsalted butter,
    at room temperature
1 cup sugar
3 cups all-purpose flour
1 cup plain dry bread crumbs
1/8 teaspoon salt
2 1/2 tablespoons pure vanilla extract
1 1/3 cups (8 ounces) semisweet chocolate chips

1. Melt the butter in a small saucepan over high heat. As soon as it foams, remove it from the heat and stir. Pour the butter over the sugar in the bowl of an electric mixer, and beat briefly just to blend. Add 2 cups of the flour along with the bread crumbs, salt, and vanilla, and blend thoroughly on medium-high speed. Blend in the remaining

1 cup flour, and continue beating until the mixture is thoroughly blended, scraping down the sides and bottom of the bowl. It only takes a minute or so, but all the butter must be thoroughly absorbed or there will be white spots in your cookies where the butter didn't penetrate.

2. Preheat the oven to 350°F. Line a baking sheet with parchment paper.

3. Use a metal 1-tablespoon measuring spoon to form the cookies—preferably a deep spoon rather than a shallow one. The mixture is sandy—it is not a dough and cannot be formed into balls or rolled out. Pack some of the mixture firmly into the spoon by pressing hard against the side of the bowl. (This works best if the "sand" is still warm.) Level it off, turn the spoon upside down over the baking sheet (and close to it), and tap the spoon on the baking sheet. The cookie will fall out—just as it did, says Chris, when you dumped your pail in the sandbox so long ago. If the cookie does not hold its shape, you didn't press the "sand" firmly enough into the spoon, so try again. The cookies don't spread, so they can be placed close together, though without touching.

4. Bake on the center oven rack until the cookies are medium brown, 20 to 25 minutes, but watch the bottoms, because they burn easily. Allow the cookies to cool on the baking sheet set on a wire rack.

5. Repeat with the remaining cookie mixture.

When Tracey is baking, daughter Samantha can always be counted on to help.

6. Meanwhile, melt the chocolate chips in the top of a double boiler set over simmering water. When they are barely melted, remove the pan from the heat and stir to finish the melting.

7. Using an offset spatula, spread the melted chocolate over the bottom of each cookie. Set the cookies, chocolate side down, on waxed paper and refrigerate them for at least 30 minutes for the chocolate to set.

egg kichel

from Bunny Lauer

Kichel means "cookie" in Yiddish; the plural is *kichelach*. When playing with babies, Papa Harry used to sing, *"Potchie, potchie, kichelach,"* the equivalent of "Clap hands, clap hands, till Daddy comes home."

These kichelach from Uncle Willy's sister Bunny are light and airy, what some recipes refer to as "Nothings" (but in a good way!). Aunt Sally and Aunt Irene used a similar recipe. Both of them always had a separate stash made with sugar substitute if my father was coming.

MAKES ABOUT 8 DOZEN Ⓟ

1 1/2 cups all-purpose flour

3 large eggs

1/2 cup vegetable oil

2 teaspoons sugar

1/2 teaspoon baking powder

1/2 cup cinnamon-sugar (see Note, page 478),
    for sprinkling

1. Preheat the oven to 400°F. Line a baking sheet with parchment paper.

2. Blend the flour, eggs, oil, sugar, and baking powder with an electric mixer, preferably with the paddle attached, on medium speed for 5 minutes. Drop the dough by the 1/2 teaspoon, 2 inches apart, onto the prepared baking sheet. Sprinkle the cookies liberally with cinnamon-sugar.

3. Bake on the center oven rack for 10 minutes. Then reduce the heat to 300°F and bake until the cookies are puffed and brown, 15 minutes more.

4. Let the cookies cool on the baking sheet set on a wire rack.

5. Raise the heat to 400°F and repeat with the remaining dough. These are best eaten the day they're baked.

rosh hashanah honey cookies

from Ruchi Padwa

This cookie comes from Antwerp, Belgium, where my husband's distant cousin Ruchi managed to find the time to type up this heirloom family recipe in the midst of a new school year, Yom Tov and Bar Mitzvah preparations, not to mention caring for her then ten children (there are twelve now), sewing their dresses and outfits, and with baby Yanky on her lap. The recipe called for 2,400 grams of flour and a kilo of sugar. This is one-fifth of the original. (Oh, yes. Ruchi mentioned she was glad she already had two batches in the freezer!) Of all the tested cookies I sent my in-laws, these unadorned, toothsome little honey balls were their favorite to have with tea. Have a honey-sweet year, says Ruchi! **MAKES ABOUT 8 DOZEN** P

2 large eggs

1/3 cup honey

1 cup sugar

2/3 cup vegetable oil

1 1/2 teaspoons pure vanilla extract

1/2 teaspoon baking powder

1/2 teaspoon ground cinnamon

2 tablespoons seltzer or club soda

4 1/4 cups all-purpose flour

1. Fit an electric mixer with the dough hook, and beat the eggs, honey, sugar, oil, vanilla, baking powder, cinnamon, and seltzer on medium-low speed for 15 minutes. Add the flour and mix until incorporated. Cover the bowl and refrigerate for several hours or as long as overnight.

2. Preheat the oven to 350°F. Line several baking sheets with parchment paper.

3. With oiled hands, form the dough into walnut-size balls, and place them 1 inch apart

on the prepared baking sheets. Bake, two sheets at a time, on the bottom third and top third oven racks, rotating the sheets from top to bottom and front to back halfway through, until golden brown, 14 to 17 minutes. (Watch that the bottoms do not burn.)

4. Let the cookies cool on the baking sheets set on wire racks.

5. Repeat with the remaining dough.

taiglach

from Sally Bower

These sticky balls of dough are the quintessential Rosh Hashanah treat. "It's a lot of work," said Aunt Sally, "but if you feel like *potchking*, try it!" The secret is to boil the dough balls in the honey syrup very, very slowly so they cook all the way through without burning. Of course, the best way to know if they're cooked is to taste one—but please, be careful! Remove one with a slotted spoon and allow it to cool first, or you'll need a tongue transplant (and you'll start fasting way before Yom Kippur.) **MAKES ABOUT 6 DOZEN** **P**

Sally seated with Morris and Lou; Estelle behind, about 1927.

3 *large eggs*

2 *tablespoons vegetable oil*

2 *teaspoons Scotch whiskey*

$^1/_2$ *teaspoon baking powder*

$^1/_2$ *teaspoon ground ginger (optional)*

$1^1/_2$ *cups all-purpose flour, plus more as needed*

2 *cups honey*

$^1/_4$ *cup sugar*

$^1/_2$ *cup boiling water*

Juice of $^1/_2$ *lemon*

$^1/_2$ *cup finely chopped walnuts*

1. Beat the eggs, oil, and whiskey in a large bowl until well blended, about 1 minute. Stir in the baking powder and ginger. Gradually add the flour, first mixing with a wooden spoon, then kneading with floured hands to make a soft, sticky dough.

2. Transfer the dough to a floured board and knead until it is smooth and pliable, 2 to 3 minutes. Divide the dough into four portions, flouring your hands for easier handling. Roll the dough between your palms to make long ropes about $^1/_2$ inch in diameter. Cut them into $^1/_2$-inch pieces with a knife.

3. Combine the honey and sugar in a heavy 6-quart pot and mix well. Bring to a boil over medium heat. Once the syrup is boiling, reduce the heat and add the taiglach a few at a time, making sure the syrup continues to boil slowly. Cover and simmer gently, shaking the pot occasionally to prevent them from sticking, until the taiglach are golden brown, about 30 minutes. Turn the taiglach carefully with a wooden spoon. When done, they will sound hollow and will be dry and crisp inside. They should be a rich amber color.

4. Remove the pot from the heat. Immediately but gradually add the boiling water and the lemon juice. Be very careful—the syrup will bubble up as you add the liquid, so add it slowly and mix well.

5. Remove the taiglach from the hot syrup with a slotted spoon, and lay them out on waxed paper. When they are cool enough to handle, roll each one in the finely chopped walnuts. Serve them in paper candy cups.

6. Repeat with the remaining dough.

Variation: If you prefer to serve the taiglach in the syrup, add ¹/₂ cup coarsely chopped walnuts and ¹/₂ cup raisins to the syrup during the last 10 minutes of cooking. Spoon the cooked taiglach into a storage container, and pour the syrup, raisins, and walnuts over them.

> *My dieting stints are legendary: from Atkins to Stillman to nine months at Duke's Rice Clinic and finally Weight Watchers. (Surely I was born fifty pounds overweight.) I would watch cousin Marvin come home from school and polish off a double box of Mallomars and never gain an ounce. It wasn't the Mallomars that I lusted after, but Aunt Estelle's chocolate chip cookies. I still salivate just thinking about them.*
>
> *Our diet-conscious household was a cookie-free zone, but when no one was home, one could always sneak upstairs to Mama and Papa's apartment for a fistful of Mama Hinda's sugar cookies, which she kept in her big enamel soup pot in the linen closet or in a tin next to the refrigerator. Once I was helping myself to that tin and failed to notice Mama quietly reading the newspaper at the table. She looked over her glasses and said, 'Kum, Garylah, take just one.'*
>
> **—GARY BART**

the famous chocolate chip cookies

from Estelle Robbins

ℵ othin' said lovin' like a tin of Aunt Estelle's chocolate chip cookies. And she didn't confine her generosity to her own grandchildren. While other grandmas would store their wares in regulation-size cookie tins, Aunt Estelle always had three or four huge Charles Chips cans filled to the brim on the credenza in her living room. Her recipe notes (complete with batter stains) are for five times the original! It must have been an all-day project.

When I asked Aunt Estelle for the recipe, I was astounded when she said she just uses the one on the back of the bag of chocolate chips. Now, I've made Toll House cookies, and no way are these the same. Toll House cookies spread; Aunt Estelle's are little, crisp nuggets with a lot more crunch. Then I looked at her recipe book with her handwritten cross-outs. She had nixed the butter (which contains water) in favor of all shortening (pure fat), which explains why they spread less. Using all brown sugar with no granulated gives them a caramelized flavor. Even substituting milk, which has more sugar and a higher fat content, for the water in the original recipe changes the flavor. Oh, yes. She also doubled the amount of chocolate chips. No scientific explanation necessary for that one! **MAKES ABOUT 6 DOZEN** **D**

2¹/₄ cups all-purpose flour

1 teaspoon baking soda

¹/₂ teaspoon salt

1 cup solid vegetable shortening

1 cup (packed) light brown sugar

1 teaspoon pure vanilla extract

1¹/₂ teaspoons whole milk

2 large eggs

4 cups (two 12-ounce packages) semisweet chocolate chips

1. Preheat the oven to 375°F.

2. Sift the flour, baking soda, and salt together into a bowl, and set it aside.

3. Beat the shortening, brown sugar, vanilla, and milk with an electric mixer on medium-low speed just until combined, about 30 seconds. Beat in the eggs, one at a time, scraping the bowl as necessary, until combined. Reduce the speed to low and add the flour mixture, a little at a time, just until blended. Stir in the chocolate chips. (For grandsons David and Eric, substitute white chocolate chips.)

4. Drop the dough by heaping teaspoonfuls, spacing them about 1 inch apart, onto ungreased baking sheets. Bake, two sheets at a time, on the bottom third and top third oven racks, rotating the sheets from top to bottom and front to back halfway through, until the cookies are brown around the edges, about 9 minutes. (Watch that the bottoms don't burn.) Let the cookies cool on the baking sheet set on a wire rack until they can be easily lifted, 1 to 2 minutes. Then transfer them to the rack and let them cool completely.

5. Repeat with the remaining dough.

Great-niece Colby Dubin's letter to Aunt Estelle, 1996.

> Dear Aunt Estelle,
> How are you are you doing in the hospitol I herd that you broke your valve. do you fell better. I hope they fix your brochen heart. I love you. And when you get better come down to florida and bring cholate chip cookies with you.
> Lots of love hugs and kissis
> love, Colby

chocolate chip butter cookies

from Hillary Robbins

ousin Hillary, who lives in Chicago, brought her mom (Samra) to Stagman's, a chichi boutique in Glencoe, Illinois. Not the first place you'd think of for baking advice, but set on a plate for the customers were these outrageous, very buttery, melt-in-your-mouth cookies, and next to them, the recipe. They say you can never be too rich or too thin. These are just right: rich, thin, and crisp. **MAKES ABOUT 5¹/₂ DOZEN** D

My brother, Gary, with Aunt Estelle. She designed and made that dress for grandson Eric's wedding. When she died, Leslie gave it to me.

¹/₂ **pound (2 sticks) unsalted butter, at room temperature**
¹/₂ **pound (2 sticks) margarine, at room temperature**
1 cup (packed) light brown sugar
1 teaspoon pure vanilla extract
3 cups all-purpose flour, sifted
³/₄ **cup chopped pecans**
1 cup (6 ounces) semisweet chocolate chips

the magic cookie

Years ago I went to a fancy Italian restaurant, and after dinner they served a cookie wrapped in some sort of waxed paper. The maître d' came to the table and unraveled the cookie wrapping on his pinky, stood it up on the table, struck a match, and lit the top of it. When the flame hit the bottom of the wrapping, it just went up in the air and disappeared. I thought that was fabulous, so I took one of them and put it in my wallet and saved it. Years and years later I'm at Aunt Estelle's house and she asks, "Do you have any pictures of Randy?" I took out my wallet and there it was, the raveled-up cookie wrapping.

I said, "Aunt Estelle, do you have a match?"

She says, "Gary, you don't smoke."

"I know, I know, but just give me a match," and I unraveled it, and put it on the table and I lit it.

She says, "What are you doing?"

"Don't worry, don't worry. Watch," and the flame went right down and burned a hole in the table! I was shocked. I apologized profusely, and she stared at that burn and the hole, and she said, "Don't worry, Gary. Now I have something to remind me of you at every meal." **—GARY BART**

1. Preheat the oven to 350°F.

2. Cream the butter, margarine, brown sugar, and vanilla with an electric mixer on medium speed, scraping the bowl several times, until smooth and creamy, about 1 minute. Reduce the speed to low and blend in the flour just until incorporated. Then blend in the pecans. Stir in the chocolate chips.

3. Using a melon baller or a spoon, drop the dough onto ungreased baking sheets, spacing the cookies 1 inch apart. Bake, two sheets at a time, on the bottom third and top third oven racks, rotating the sheets from top to bottom and front to back halfway through, until they are golden brown around the edges, 15 to 20 minutes. Let the cookies cool completely on the baking sheets set on a wire rack.

4. Repeat with the remaining dough.

amaretto-apricot chews

from Shelly Kancigor

Some like 'em crisp; some like 'em chewy. My daughter-in-law Shelly belongs to the chewy camp, and these almond-flavored morsels bursting with apricots and laced with liqueur are her very favorite. Use kitchen shears to snip the apricots. **MAKES ABOUT 4½ DOZEN** **D** or **P**

FOR THE COOKIES

1 cup all-purpose flour

1 teaspoon baking soda

½ pound (2 sticks) unsalted butter or nondairy margarine, at room temperature

¾ cup (packed) light brown sugar

½ cup granulated sugar

1 large egg

1 tablespoon Amaretto liqueur

2½ cups rolled oats

1 cup snipped dried apricots (the size of raisins)

½ cup finely chopped natural, blanched, or slivered almonds

FOR THE ICING

2 cups sifted confectioners' sugar

2 to 3 tablespoons Amaretto liqueur

1. Preheat the oven to 375°F. Line two baking sheets with parchment paper.

2. Stir the flour and baking soda together in a bowl, and set it aside.

3. Cream the butter and both sugars with an electric mixer on medium speed, scraping the bowl several times, until smooth and creamy, about 1 minute. Add the egg and Amaretto, and beat until combined, about 1 minute more. Reduce the speed to low and blend in the flour mixture just until incorporated. Stir in the oats, apricots, and almonds.

4. Drop the dough by rounded teaspoons, 1 inch apart, onto the prepared baking sheets. Bake both sheets at the same time, on the bottom third and top third oven racks, rotating the sheets from top to bottom and front to back halfway through, until the cookies are just beginning to turn brown at the edges, about 9 minutes. The cookies will appear soft and golden on the bottom; do not overbake. Let the cookies cool on the baking sheet set on a wire rack until they can be safely moved, about 1 minute. Then transfer them to the rack and let them cool completely.

5. Repeat with the remaining dough.

6. Prepare the icing: In a medium-size bowl, stir the confectioners' sugar with enough of the Amaretto to make an icing of drizzling consistency. Drizzle the icing over the cooled cookies.

When Shelly is baking, you can bet Jason and Lauren will get into the act.

chocolate drops

from Leslie Graham

Cousin Leslie's chocolate cookies are cakey soft, and we love them dipped in my daughter-in-law Shelly's vanilla frosting. Using parchment paper keeps the bottoms from burning. Cut it so that it overhangs. Then when you take the pans from the oven, you can quickly remove the paper, with the cookies on it, from the hot pan. **MAKES ABOUT 5 DOZEN** D

4 ounces unsweetened chocolate

1 cup sour milk (see Note) or buttermilk

3 cups all-purpose flour

1 teaspoon baking soda

1/2 teaspoon salt

1/2 pound (2 sticks) unsalted butter,
    at room temperature

2 cups (packed) light brown sugar

2 large eggs, at room temperature

1 teaspoon pure vanilla extract

Hometown Vanilla Frosting (optional;
    recipe follows)

1. Preheat the oven to 375°F. Line several baking sheets with parchment paper.

2. Melt the chocolate in the top of a double boiler set over simmering water. When it is barely melted, remove it from the heat and stir to finish the melting. Stir in the sour milk, and set it aside to cool.

3. Stir the flour, baking soda, and salt together in a medium-size bowl, and set it aside.

4. Cream the butter and brown sugar with an electric mixer on medium-high speed, scraping the bowl several times, until light and fluffy, about 2 minutes. Add the eggs, one at a time, beating well after each addition. Reduce the speed to medium and blend in the chocolate mixture and the vanilla. Reduce the speed to low and blend in the flour mixture just until incorporated.

5. Drop the dough by rounded tablespoons, about 2 inches apart, onto the prepared baking sheets. Bake, two sheets at a time, on the bottom third and top third oven racks, rotating the sheets from top to bottom and front to back halfway through, until the center springs back when touched, about 10 minutes. (Watch carefully that the bottoms don't get hard or, worse, burn.) Cool on the baking sheets set on a wire rack.

6. Repeat with the remaining dough.

7. If you are using it, spread the vanilla frosting over the cooled cookies, or, for a showy presentation, dip each cookie halfway into the frosting so the chocolate peeks through. Set them on waxed paper until the frosting is firm.

Note: To make sour milk, stir 1 tablespoon distilled white vinegar or fresh lemon juice into 1 cup whole milk and let the mixture stand at room temperature for 10 to 15 minutes.

Do not store soft and crisp cookies together, to retain their respective textures.

hometown vanilla frosting

from Shelly Kancigor

MAKES A GENEROUS 1 1/2 CUPS **D**

5 tablespoons half-and-half or whole milk

2 tablespoons solid vegetable shortening

1 tablespoon unsalted butter, at room temperature

1 teaspoon pure vanilla extract

1/4 teaspoon salt

3 cups confectioners' sugar, sifted

1. Place the cream in a small saucepan over medium heat and heat just until it is steaming and bubbles are forming around the edge. Remove the pan from the heat.

2. Beat the shortening, butter, vanilla, and salt with an electric mixer on medium-high speed until thoroughly blended. Add the confectioners' sugar, 1 cup at a time, alternating with the hot cream, and beat until the frosting is of spreading consistency.

black & whites

from Shelly Kancigor

ew Yorkers know all about black & whites, the oversize cakelike confection prevalent in the city's bakeries and delis. Shelly came up with these quite by accident, when she tried a recipe that was mislabeled "Sugar Cookies." To her surprise, when they came out of the oven they were soft, reminding her of the black & whites Stu covets on every trip to the Big Apple—so she frosted them. Delish!

MAKES 2 TO 2 1/2 DOZEN **D**

4 1/2 cups all-purpose flour

2 teaspoons baking powder

1 teaspoon baking soda

1/2 teaspoon salt

2 cups sugar

1 1/4 cups solid vegetable shortening

2 large eggs

1 teaspoon pure vanilla extract

1 cup buttermilk or sour milk
    (see Note, page 490)

Black & White Icing (recipe follows)

1. Preheat the oven to 350°F. Line two baking sheets with parchment paper.

2. Combine the flour, baking powder, baking soda, and salt in a medium-size bowl. Whisk gently to blend, and set aside.

3. In a large bowl, beat the sugar and shortening with an electric mixer on medium speed until smooth and creamy, 2 to 3 minutes. Add the eggs and vanilla and beat, scraping the bowl several times, until well blended, 1 to 2 minutes. Reduce the speed to low and add the flour mixture in three additions, alternating with the buttermilk in two additions, beginning and ending with the flour. Beat just until blended.

4. Scoop the batter using a 2-inch ice cream scoop or a 1/4-cup measure, leveling it off across the top before dropping it onto the

prepared baking sheets, spacing the cookies about 2 inches apart. Bake, one sheet at a time, on the center oven rack until the bottoms are just golden and the centers spring back when lightly touched, 18 to 20 minutes. Let the cookies cool on the baking sheet set on a wire rack for 5 minutes. Then, using a spatula, place the cookies upside-down on the rack and let them cool completely.

5. Using a flexible spatula or a blunt knife, spread a thick layer of white icing on half of each flat surface; then quickly spread a thick layer of chocolate icing over the other half. (If the icing in the bowl begins to set up before you have finished, whisk it vigorously to soften it.) Allow the cookies to sit at room temperature until the icing is set, about 30 minutes.

black & white icing

. . .

MAKES 1²/₃ CUPS, HALF WHITE AND HALF CHOCOLATE

4 cups confectioners' sugar, sifted
6 tablespoons whole milk
1 teaspoon pure vanilla extract
3 tablespoons unsweetened cocoa powder

1. Combine the confectioners' sugar, milk, and vanilla in a large bowl and whisk until smooth.

2. Transfer half of the icing to a medium-size bowl, and add the cocoa powder and 2 teaspoons water. Whisk until smooth.

> *There are so many wonderful memories I have of my grandmother Estelle. We had definitely more than a typical grandmother-grandchild relationship. She was one of my best friends, my biggest fan and supporter. No matter what I needed, anything at all, she would always be there for me.*
>
> **—WARREN ROBBINS**

phyllis's chocolate nut meringue kisses

from Estelle Robbins

I don't know how Aunt Estelle baked in the apartment she moved into after Uncle Willy died. It certainly had no kitchen counter space, and her table was always piled high with fabric and used more as a cutting board than for baking.

Sure, you can make these cookies for Passover, but Aunt Estelle—who got the recipe from cousin Phyllis—made these lovely chocolate-glazed meringues year-round for all kinds of *simchas*, from Bar Mitzvahs to showers to birthday parties.

They make a beautiful gift as well—that is, if you know where to hide them from your family. **MAKES ABOUT 4 DOZEN**
D or **P**

Whites of 4 large eggs, at room
    temperature
1 cup sugar
1 teaspoon pure vanilla extract
2 ounces unsweetened chocolate, grated

FOR THE GLAZE AND TOPPING
1 cup (6 ounces) semisweet chocolate chips
$^1/_4$ cup light cream or soy or nondairy
    creamer
$1^1/_2$ cups walnuts, toasted (see box, page 17)
    and finely crushed

1. Preheat the oven to 275°F. Line several baking sheets with parchment paper.

2. Beat the egg whites with an electric mixer on medium-high speed until soft peaks form. Add $^2/_3$ cup of the sugar, a tablespoon at a time, beating for 10 seconds after each addition. Then raise the speed to high and beat until stiff peaks form, about 3 minutes total. Beat in the vanilla. Gradually fold in the remaining $^1/_3$ cup sugar and the grated chocolate.

3. Drop the meringue by heaping teaspoons (or use a pastry tube) onto the prepared baking sheets, and bake on the center oven rack until the cookies are dry to the touch, 45 to 50 minutes. Let the cookies

cool on the baking sheet set on a wire rack until they can be easily lifted, 1 to 2 minutes. Then transfer the cookies to the rack and let them cool completely.

4. Repeat with the remaining meringue.

5. Prepare the glaze: Combine the chocolate chips and the cream in the top of a double boiler, and heat over simmering water until the chocolate has melted. Stir well, and remove from the heat.

6. Dip the tips of the cooled cookies into the chocolate glaze and then into the crushed walnuts. Let them sit on a sheet of waxed paper until the glaze is set.

sweet smooches

from Staci Robbins

A fitting entry from Staci, who, while in high school, took fourth place in the Michigan State Forensics competition with her sales pitch for Hershey. These lovable cookies are best if not refrigerated or frozen, as the chocolate kiss in the center will become very hard. **MAKES 5 TO 6 DOZEN** **D**

$^1/_2$ pound (2 sticks) unsalted butter, at room
    temperature
$^1/_2$ cup sugar
1 teaspoon pure vanilla extract
1 cup pecans, finely chopped (about $3^1/_2$ ounces)
2 cups all-purpose flour
12 ounces unwrapped Hershey's Kisses

Y ou'll find more meringue cookies in the
Passover chapter, on pages 582 to 586.

1. Preheat the oven to 350°F. Line several baking sheets with parchment paper.

2. Mix the butter with a fork in a large bowl until light and fluffy. Add the sugar, vanilla, and pecans, and mix until well combined. Add the flour and stir just until incorporated.

3. Form the cookies with your hands, wrapping each kiss in a heaping tablespoon of dough, taking care to retain the shape of the kiss. Place the cookies on the prepared baking sheets. They won't spread, so they can be placed close together, though without touching.

4. Bake, two sheets at a time, on the bottom third and top third oven racks, rotating the sheets from top to bottom and front to back halfway through, until the cookies are lightly golden, 20 to 25 minutes. Let them cool on the baking sheets set on wire racks.

best brownies ever

from Estelle Robbins

If loving chocolate was a crime, most of us would be on death row. These fudgy-wudgy brownies are a chocoholic's dream. Got a yen? In no time you've got your fix. Don't overmix the batter or the brownies will be heavy, and underbake them a tad. **MAKES 12 TO 16** **P**

Unflavored vegetable cooking spray, for greasing the pan

2 ounces unsweetened chocolate

8 tablespoons (1 stick) unsalted butter

1 cup sugar

2 large eggs

1 teaspoon pure vanilla extract

Pinch of salt

1/2 cup all-purpose flour

1 cup (6 ounces) semisweet chocolate chips

Confectioners' sugar, for dusting (optional)

1. Preheat the oven to 350°F. Spray an 8-inch square cake pan.

2. Combine the chocolate and butter in a double boiler set over simmering water, and heat until melted. Set aside to cool for 5 minutes.

3. Transfer the chocolate mixture to a medium-size bowl and stir in the sugar. Add the eggs, one at a time, and beat until smooth. Beat in the vanilla and salt. Gradually fold in the flour. Do not overmix. Fold in the chocolate chips, and transfer the mixture to the prepared cake pan.

4. Bake on the center oven rack until the brownies are barely set in the middle and a cake tester comes out with moist crumbs attached, 20 to 25 minutes. With brownies, underbaking is better than overbaking.

5. Let the brownies cool completely in the pan set on a wire rack. Then dust with confectioners' sugar, if you like, and cut into squares.

Aunt Estelle, early 1950s.

blondies

from Daryl Robbins, Kari Robbins

I heard on the news that sales of brunette hair coloring have just overtaken blonde. (And they say blondes have more fun.) It's the eternal war: good against evil, ebony and ivory, chocolate and vanilla. Both cousins Daryl and Kari submitted the same recipe, and both prefer these butterscotch bars to their chocolate version. These blondies have brunette streaks, and like their darker counterparts, they mustn't be overbaked. **MAKES 12 TO 16**

D or **P**

Unflavored vegetable cooking spray,
 for greasing the pan
1 cup all-purpose flour, plus more for flouring
 the pan
$^1/_2$ teaspoon salt
8 tablespoons (1 stick) unsalted butter or
 nondairy margarine
1 cup (packed) light brown sugar
1 large egg
1 teaspoon pure vanilla extract
1 cup (6 ounces) semisweet chocolate chips
 (see Note)

1. Preheat the oven to 350°F. Spray and flour an 8-inch square cake pan.

2. Stir the flour and salt together in a small bowl.

3. Melt the butter in a small saucepan over low heat. Put the brown sugar in a mixing bowl, pour the melted butter over it, and beat with an electric mixer on medium speed until smooth, about 1 minute. Add the egg and vanilla and beat until combined, about 1 minute more. Gradually fold in the flour mixture, followed by the chocolate chips.

4. Spread the batter evenly in the prepared pan, and bake on the center oven rack until a toothpick inserted in the center comes out barely clean, 20 to 25 minutes. Do not overbake.

5. Let the blondies cool in the pan set on a wire rack; then cut them into squares.

Note: To make Pure Blondies, substitute white chocolate chips.

lili lamm's chocolate- cherry cake

from Susan and Frank Levy

My niece Jessica's in-laws contributed this Hungarian family favorite from Grandma Lili. Although it's called a cake, it's more like a chocolate cherry-covered brownie, a blissful marriage of sweet and tart.

Sour cherries, a common ingredient in Grandma's time, are harder to find these days. Occasionally you'll see them in farmers' markets, or frozen or canned in specialty stores and some supermarkets. Mama Hinda always had a tree (and, yes, it did grow in Brooklyn), but it's her sweet cherry tree in the postage-stamp backyard of my childhood home that I remember. Not that we would have known whether it was sour or sweet, because we never ate a single cherry. Every June, Papa Harry, on the watch for the opportune moment to pick, would play the waiting game, hoping to beat the birds to the luscious fruit. And every year it was Birds 1, Papa Harry 0. One day the cherries were almost ripe; the next morning there would be nothing but pits hanging from the branches. **MAKES 12 TO 16** 🄳

Unflavored vegetable cooking spray,
for greasing the pan
1 cup (6 ounces) semisweet chocolate chips
8 tablespoons (1 stick) unsalted butter,
at room temperature
1/2 cup sugar
3 large eggs, separated, at room temperature
1/2 cup all-purpose flour, plus extra for
flouring the pan
Pinch of salt
1 can (about 16 ounces)
pitted sour cherries,
or 1 1/2 cups pitted fresh
or frozen (thawed),
drained and patted dry

1. Preheat the oven to 350°F. Spray and flour an 8-inch square cake pan.

2. Heat the chocolate chips in a double boiler set over simmering water until barely melted. Remove the pan from the heat, and stir to finish the melting. Set it aside to cool.

3. Cream the butter and sugar with an electric mixer on medium-high speed, scraping the bowl as needed, until light and fluffy, about 1 1/2 minutes. Add the melted chocolate and beat until combined, 30 seconds more. Add the egg yolks, one at a time, beating well after each addition. Scrape the bowl. Reduce the speed to low and blend in the flour just until incorporated.

4. Using a clean bowl and beaters, beat the egg whites on medium-high speed until foamy, about 20 seconds. Add the salt and continue beating until stiff peaks form, 1 to 1 1/2 minutes total. Stir one fourth of the egg whites into the batter to lighten it. Then add the remaining whites in three additions, folding them in until incorporated.

5. Scrape the batter into the prepared cake pan and top it with the cherries. Bake on the center oven rack until the cake starts to pull away from the sides of the pan and a cake tester inserted in the center comes out barely clean, 35 to 40 minutes. Do not overbake.

Left: Susan and Frank Levy at son Josh's wedding to my niece Jessica, 2004. Right: Grandma Lili Lamm (seated), about 1987. Josh is to her right.

6. Let the cake cool completely in the pan set on a wire rack. Then cut it into squares.

loretta modelevsky's chocolate date squares

from Lillian Bart

ש hen my mother's friend Loretta brought her mother's signature squares to Heritage Pointe, the Jewish home for the aging (which Loretta helped found and where my mother volunteered), they were gone in seconds. Of course my mom grabbed the recipe. For those of you who think you don't like dates, think again: These squares are positively decadent. There's just so much going on in one little bar—the bits of chocolate chips, luscious fruit, the crunch of nuts, the moist cake. Dates and chocolate are a wonderfully unique and addictive combination. Don't say I didn't warn you.

MAKES 12 TO 16　　　　　　　　　P

FOR SOAKING THE DATES

1 1/2 cups boiling water

1 cup pitted dates, coarsely snipped (use kitchen shears)

1 teaspoon baking soda

FOR THE CAKE

Unflavored vegetable cooking spray, for greasing the pan

1 1/4 cups plus 3 tablespoons all-purpose flour

3/4 teaspoon baking soda

1/4 teaspoon salt

1/2 cup solid vegetable shortening

1 cup sugar

2 large eggs, lightly beaten

FOR THE TOPPING

2 cups (12 ounces) semisweet chocolate chips

1/2 cup chopped walnuts

1/2 cup sugar

1. Prepare the dates: Pour the boiling water over the dates in a medium-size bowl. Stir in the baking soda, and set it aside to cool.

2. Preheat the oven to 350°F. Spray a 9-inch square cake pan.

3. Make the batter: Sift the flour, baking soda, and salt together into a medium-size bowl, and set it aside.

4. Cream the shortening and sugar with an electric mixer on medium-low speed, scraping the bowl several times, until blended, light, and smooth, about 3 minutes. Add the eggs, one at a time, followed by the date mixture, and blend until incorporated. Reduce the speed to low and blend in the flour mixture just until incorporated. Scrape the batter into the prepared cake pan.

5. Prepare the topping: Combine the chocolate chips, walnuts, and sugar in a medium-size bowl.

6. Sprinkle the topping evenly over the batter, pressing the mixture lightly into the

batter with your fingers. Bake on the center oven rack until the edges are just starting to become firm and leave the sides of the pan, about 55 minutes.

7. Let the cake cool completely in the pan set on a wire rack; then cut it into squares. (It will be easier to cut if you freeze it, covered, for about 30 minutes to firm it up.)

tracy grob's
butter pecan chocolate caramel squares

from Shelly Kancigor

These crunchy, almost candy-like squares are wickedly addictive and will call to you, no matter how well hidden, even from a locked freezer. My daughter-in-law Shelly has a thing for milk chocolate, but if you prefer semisweet, they're great that way too. **MAKES 3 DOZEN** **D**

Shelly and my mom at my nephew Ross's Bar Mitzvah, 1991.

FOR THE CRUST

2 cups all-purpose flour

1 cup (packed) light brown sugar

8 tablespoons (1 stick) cold unsalted butter, cut into 8 pieces

1 cup pecans, toasted (see box, page 17) and coarsely chopped

FOR THE CHOCOLATE CARAMEL TOPPING

^{2}/$_3$ cup (10 tablespoons plus 2 teaspoons) unsalted butter

^{1}/$_2$ cup (packed) light brown sugar

1 cup (6 ounces) milk chocolate chips

1. Preheat the oven to 350°F. Have ready an ungreased 13 × 9-inch baking pan.

2. Prepare the crust: Place the flour and brown sugar in a food processor and pulse to combine. Distribute the butter over the mixture and process until the dough comes together. Press the dough over the bottom of the baking pan. Scatter the pecans over the dough, pressing them in gently.

3. Prepare the topping: Combine the butter and brown sugar in a small saucepan and bring to a boil. Boil for 1 minute, stirring constantly.

4. Pour the hot caramel over the crust and tilt the pan to distribute it evenly. Bake on the center oven rack until the entire surface is bubbly, 18 to 22 minutes.

5. Remove the baking pan from the oven and sprinkle the chocolate chips evenly over the surface. Allow the chips to melt for 2 to 3 minutes. Then spread the melted chocolate evenly over the surface, using an offset spatula. Refrigerate for the chocolate to set, 1 to 2 hours. Then cut into squares.

washington nut bars

from Vi Carlson

Shelly's great-aunt Vi (only she pronounces it "ahnt"), from Spokane, has been making these bars for decades. She remembers when margarine first came out: It was sold with a capsule of yellow food dye that you had to knead into the solid block of margarine (called "oleo" then) so that it would look more like butter. The filling for these bars reminds me of pecan pie. In fact, substitute pecans for the walnuts and you've got pecan pie squares. **MAKES 24 TO 36**   **P** or **D**

FOR THE CRUST

1 cup all-purpose flour

2 tablespoons (packed) light brown sugar

8 tablespoons (1 stick) cold nondairy
  margarine or unsalted butter,
  cut into 8 pieces

FOR THE FILLING

2 large eggs

²/₃ cup dark corn syrup

¹/₃ cup granulated sugar

3 tablespoons nondairy margarine or
  unsalted butter, melted

1 teaspoon pure vanilla extract

1 cup chopped walnuts

1. Preheat the oven to 350°F. Have ready an ungreased 8-inch square cake pan.

2. Prepare the crust: Place the flour and brown sugar in a food processor and pulse to combine. Distribute the margarine over the mixture, and process until the dough comes together. Press the dough over the bottom of the cake pan. Bake on the center oven rack until set and beginning to turn golden, about 20 minutes.

3. Meanwhile, prepare the filling: Beat the eggs in a medium-size bowl. Stir in the corn syrup, sugar, melted margarine, vanilla, and walnuts.

4. Pour the filling over the baked crust and return the pan to the oven. Bake until set and golden brown, about 30 minutes. Let the cake cool completely in the pan set on a wire rack. Then cut it into squares or bars.

cheesecake bars

from Shelly Kancigor

Sometimes there's just no time to bake a cheesecake when you want one. These bars are as creamy and delicious as cheesecake and can be thrown together in a few minutes. Unfortunately they can be murder to get out of the pan neatly. Here's a great tip: Freeze the baked bars in the pan, covered, just to firm them up a bit, and then slice them. **MAKES 32**   **D**

FOR THE CRUST

Unflavored vegetable cooking spray,
for greasing the pan

²/₃ cup (10 tablespoons plus 2 teaspoons)
unsalted butter, at room temperature

2 cups all-purpose flour

²/₃ cup (packed) light brown sugar

FOR THE FILLING

2 packages (8 ounces each) cream cheese,
at room temperature

1 cup sugar

¹/₄ cup whole milk

2 large eggs, at room temperature

2 tablespoons fresh lemon juice

1 teaspoon pure vanilla extract

1. Preheat the oven to 350°F. Spray a 13 × 9-inch baking pan.

2. Prepare the crust: Stir the butter, flour, and brown sugar together in a bowl. Reserve 1¹/₄ cups of the mixture for the topping, and press the remainder evenly over the bottom of the prepared baking pan. Bake on the center oven rack until the crust is set but not yet brown, about 12 minutes.

3. Meanwhile, prepare the filling: Beat the cream cheese, sugar, and milk with an electric mixer on medium speed, scraping the bowl several times, until light and fluffy, about 1 minute. Add the eggs, lemon juice, and vanilla, and beat, scraping the bowl several times, until blended, about 45 seconds.

4. Scrape the filling onto the crust, and sprinkle the reserved crumb mixture evenly over it. Bake until the filling is set and the topping is golden, about 25 minutes. (If it looks puffy and uneven, it will settle when cooled.)

Let it cool completely in the pan set on a wire rack. Then cover and freeze for 30 minutes before cutting into squares or bars.

raspberry pecan bars

from Nancy Miller Haas

ancy's delicate bars were the first tested cookies that I sent to my in-laws in Florida. They loved them so much, they froze them and doled out only two a day to make them last longer.

MAKES 6 TO 7 DOZEN D or P

FOR THE CRUST

Unflavored vegetable cooking spray,
for greasing the pan

12 tablespoons (1¹/₂ sticks) unsalted butter
or nondairy margarine, at room temperature

1 cup sugar

2 large eggs

1 teaspoon pure vanilla extract

3 cups all-purpose flour

About ³/₄ cup seedless raspberry jam

FOR THE TOPPING

Whites of 2 large eggs

Pinch of salt

1 cup sugar

1 tablespoon all-purpose flour

1 cup pecans, toasted (see box, page 17) and chopped

1. Preheat the oven to 375°F. Spray the bottom and sides of a 15-inch jelly-roll pan.

2. Prepare the crust: Cream the butter and sugar with an electric mixer on medium speed, scraping the bowl several times, until smooth and creamy, about 1 minute. Add the eggs and vanilla, and beat until combined, about 1 minute more. Reduce the speed to low and blend in the flour just until incorporated. Using your fingers, press the dough evenly over the bottom of the jelly-roll pan. Spread the jam over the dough, creating a thin layer (an offset spatula works well for this) and leaving a 1/2-inch border uncovered. Bake on the center oven rack until the crust is golden around the edges, 15 minutes.

3. Meanwhile, using a clean, dry bowl and beaters, prepare the topping: Beat the egg whites on medium-high speed until foamy, about 30 seconds. Add the salt and continue beating until soft peaks form. Add the sugar, a tablespoon at a time, beating for 10 seconds after each addition. Beat in the flour. Then raise the speed to high and beat until stiff peaks form, about 4 minutes total. Fold in the pecans.

4. Spread the topping over the crust and bake until the meringue is golden, 15 minutes. Let it cool completely in the pan set on a wire rack. Then cut into 1 1/2-inch squares. (It helps to dip a sharp knife in hot water, wipe it clean, and then cut.)

Variation: For Apricot Pecan Bars, substitute apricot jam for the raspberry.

cherry bars

from Ilo Riebe

Finally we met Ilo, my daughter-in-law Shelly's irrepressible grandma, at Stu and Shelly's wedding weekend in Minnesota. And finally we got to taste her famous Cherry Bars, an old family recipe, which she brought to the midnight pool party following the wedding. It was love at first sight . . . with Ilo as well as her bars! Both are cheery, irresistible, and chock-full of fun. **MAKES 30 TO 36** **D**

FOR THE CRUST
Unflavored vegetable cooking spray,
for greasing the pan
2 cups all-purpose flour
1/4 cup plus 1 tablespoon confectioners' sugar,
sifted
1/2 pound (2 sticks) unsalted butter, at room
temperature, each stick cut into 8 pieces

FOR THE FILLING
2 large eggs
1 cup sugar
About 10 maraschino cherries,
finely chopped (1/4 cup), juice reserved
1 teaspoon pure vanilla extract
1/2 cup chopped walnuts, toasted
(see box, page 17)
3/4 cup sweetened flaked or shredded
coconut

1. Preheat the oven to 350°F. Spray a 13 × 9-inch baking pan.

Shelly and Stu's midnight pool party after their wedding, 1988, when we first tasted Ilo's cherry bars—and pickles! (but not necessarily in that order).

lemon snowcap squares

from Judy Bart Kancigor

ong after I did my last stint as school snack mom, I would periodically get requests from Stu's and Brad's old classmates for the recipe for these tart, confectioners'-sugar-topped squares, my signature take-along to Little League games, Purim carnivals, Cub Scout meetings, and splash fests in our backyard pool. The only problem was that they were difficult to cut—not that anyone ever gave me demerit points on neatness. It turns out that as with the Cheesecake Bars, the trick is to cool them completely in the pan, then cover the pan with aluminum foil and freeze it for 30 minutes or so, just to firm them up a bit. Now cut, and voilà! Beautiful squares any bakery would be proud of. **MAKES 12 TO 16** **D**

2. Prepare the crust: Combine the flour, confectioners' sugar, and butter in a food processor and pulse just until crumbly. Set aside about one fourth of the crumbs. Continue processing the remaining crumbs until the mixture comes together in a ball. Press the dough over the bottom of the prepared baking pan, and bake on the center oven rack until the crust is just beginning to brown around the edges, 15 minutes.

3. Meanwhile, prepare the filling: Beat the eggs with an electric mixer on medium-high speed until frothy. Add the sugar and beat until thick, about 2 minutes. Add 2 tablespoons reserved maraschino cherry juice and the vanilla, and beat until combined. Stir in the cherries, walnuts, and coconut, and mix well.

4. Spread the filling over the baked crust, and sprinkle the reserved crumbs evenly over the top. Bake until the top is golden brown, 25 to 30 minutes. (Watch that the edges don't burn.) Let it cool completely in the pan set on a wire rack. Then cut it into squares.

FOR THE CRUST
8 tablespoons (1 stick) unsalted butter, at room temperature
1 1/3 cups all-purpose flour
1/4 cup sugar

FOR THE FILLING
2 large eggs
3/4 cup sugar
2 tablespoons all-purpose flour
1/4 teaspoon baking powder

3 tablespoons fresh lemon juice

1/2 teaspoon finely grated lemon zest

Confectioners' sugar, for sprinkling

1. Preheat the oven to 350°F. Have ready an ungreased 8-inch square cake pan.

2. Prepare the crust: Combine the butter, flour, and sugar in a bowl and beat with an electric mixer on medium-low speed until blended, about 1 minute. Pat the mixture over the bottom of the baking pan. Bake on the center oven rack until brown at the edges, 15 to 20 minutes.

3. Meanwhile, prepare the filling: Blend all the filling ingredients on medium speed (no need to wash the bowl or beaters) until thoroughly combined.

4. Pour the filling over the crust and bake until set, 18 to 20 minutes. Let it cool completely in the pan set on a wire rack. Then cut into squares and sprinkle with confectioners' sugar.

drop-dead cookies

from Estelle Robbins

Everyone's got a version of these easy, throw-together chewy bars. You just layer the ingredients and let the sweetened condensed milk do all the work. But why the title? Here's my theory: Aunt Estelle's home, the center of her dressmaking business, was filled at all hours with women in various stages of undress, swapping recipes and gossip while being pinned and corseted. I imagine "drop dead" was a common appellation, as in "drop-dead gorgeous" or "he should only," so why not the cookies!

MAKES 12 TO 16　　　　　　Ｄ

8 tablespoons (1 stick) unsalted butter or
 margarine

1 cup graham cracker crumbs

2 cups (12 ounces) semisweet chocolate chips

1 cup sweetened flaked or shredded coconut

1 can (14 ounces) sweetened condensed milk

1 cup chopped walnuts

1. Preheat the oven to 350°F.

2. Place the butter in a glass 8-inch square cake pan, put it in the oven, and let the butter melt. Tilt the pan to spread the butter evenly. Layer the remaining ingredients in the buttered pan in the order given.

3. Bake on the center oven rack until set and golden, 20 minutes. Let it cool in the pan set on a wire rack; then cut into squares.

Variation: Lorraine Gold and Robert Seligman add butterscotch chips, Lorraine uses pecans instead of walnuts.

Aunt Estelle (right) with my mom behind Uncle Al and Uncle Charlie (seated) holding the twins, 1920s.

barry's
family

desserts and candy

I once read that your food texture preferences may hold clues to your state of mind. Those that prefer crunchy, crusty, chewy foods are thought to harbor anger and aggression, while those who prefer soft, smooth, creamy foods are stuck in childhood, yearning for comfort.

I wonder. I would think my predilection for nuts, crusts, and all things crisp stems more from a desire for longer and more intimate contact with food than from any need to connect with my inner Genghis Kahn. Foods that slip quietly from the tongue to the belly

"Talk about comfort food!"

Barry's parents, the best in-laws anyone could wish for, married seventy years at this writing. Who's who on page 613.

Tracey Barrett—anyone for dessert?

fly beneath my radar. A tantalizing, brief moment and they're gone. The encounter just ends too quickly.

Then in *The Sex Life of Food: When Body and Soul Meet to Eat*, I read Bunny Crumpacker's astonishing notion that crunchiness replaces food's flavor: "Crunchy food makes a lot of noise as we chew it, and taste gets lost in the uproar . . . we are left with nothing but the sound and the fury."

Uh-oh. Not for nothing was I an English major. I remember the end of that Shakespearean allusion. It's ". . . the sound and the fury *signifying nothing*"! Has all that gnawing been a mere distraction? And more important, what have I been missing?

I resolved to wake up and taste the pudding, and if I should wind up swaddled in childhood comfort along the way, all the better.

As I tested recipes, I found this chapter perfect for this exercise with its wobbling custard, jiggling Jell-O, and quivering Coconut Flan. Hardly a crustus interruptus in sight! Creamy Chocolate Mousse, velvety Chocolate Soufflé, light and luscious Lemon Chiffon, meltingly sweet Crème

Caramel. Crumpacker may have something there. Flavors do seem more intense when accompanied by the sound of silence.

Talk about comfort food! I spent "quality time" with homey, folksy rice pudding and custard, razzle-dazzle showstoppers like English trifle and Tiramisù, a retro Baked Alaska, even Barry's grandma's Blueberry Varenikas: pillows of fruit-filled pasta that slide down the throat with barely a whisper.

Candy, the childhood treat we never outgrow, rounds out the chapter with homemade buttery caramels, Chocolate–Peanut Butter Balls, Candied Orange Peel, irresistible Chocolate Strawberries, and Chocolate Candy Bourbon Balls.

There are times you yearn to suck your thumb, but sometimes you want to smash a wall. When you've waited all day for that repairman who never showed, ice cream may be yummy, but I'll have mine with nuts!

Above: Kids in the kitchen, Jake and Jenna Mackoff. Below: My niece Jessica does the honors for her parents' 25th anniversary party, 1995.

hilda's chocolate soufflé

from Jackie Bishins

ℵ ext to the fondue set, the soufflé dish was one of the most popular engagement gifts (we didn't know from showers) when I got married in the early '60s. I never used either one. (But of course I still have them. I swear, I need a 12-step program.) Chalk it up to fear of falling. Aunt Hilda had no such phobias. Her soufflé is everything a chocolate soufflé should be: very light and airy with a strong chocolate flavor. The crusty top is nicely cracked, for a dramatic presentation.

SERVES 6 TO 8   **D**

³/₄ **cup sugar**

¹/₄ **cup all-purpose flour**

2 cups whole milk

2 tablespoons unsalted butter, plus extra
  for greasing the soufflé dish

4 ounces unsweetened chocolate

2 teaspoons pure vanilla extract

6 large eggs, separated

¹/₄ **teaspoon salt**

1. Combine the sugar and flour in a medium-size heavy saucepan. Blend in the milk. Then add the 2 tablespoons butter and the chocolate. Cook over low heat, stirring constantly until thick and smooth, about 10 minutes. Add the vanilla and set aside to cool.

2. Preheat the oven to 325°F. Grease the bottom only of a 2-quart soufflé dish (or other baking dish with a flat bottom and deep sides).

3. Beat the egg yolks with an electric mixer on low speed until very light and thick, about 2 minutes. Fold in the cooled chocolate mixture.

4. Using a clean bowl and beaters, beat the egg whites and salt with an electric mixer on high speed until the whites form peaks that are stiff but still moist, 3 to 4 minutes. Carefully fold one fourth of the beaten egg whites into the chocolate mixture to lighten it. Then carefully fold in the remaining whites, being careful not to overblend.

5. Transfer the mixture to the prepared soufflé dish and bake until the soufflé is puffed and the top has risen, 50 minutes. If you like a firmer soufflé, bake it for 5 minutes more. (But whatever you do, don't open that oven door.)

6. Soufflés collapse as they cool, so serve immediately.

chocolate mousse

from Judy Bart Kancigor

ⵟ his recipe from an eons old National Council of Jewish Women cookbook is rich and easy and, unlike most mousses, is made without raw eggs. It would be equally smashing in a graham cracker crust or on a meringue shell.

SERVES 6 TO 8   D

Yolks of 5 large eggs

¹/₂ cup plus 2 tablespoons sugar

1 cup whole milk

3 ounces semisweet chocolate

1 ounce unsweetened chocolate

1 envelope unflavored gelatin

1 tablespoon cold water

1 cup heavy (whipping) cream

Fresh raspberries, mint sprigs, or whipped
*   cream, for garnish (optional)*

1. Combine the egg yolks and the ¹/₂ cup sugar in a double boiler set over barely simmering water. Cook, stirring almost constantly, until quite thick, 10 to 12 minutes. Transfer the egg yolk mixture to a large bowl. Set it aside.

2. Combine the milk and both chocolates in a small, heavy-bottomed saucepan over medium-low heat. Heat, stirring often, until the chocolate has melted and the mixture is blended and smooth. Remove it from the heat.

3. Place the gelatin in the cold water in a small bowl, and let it sit for 2 minutes to soften. Stir the gelatin into the hot chocolate mixture until it is completely dissolved.

4. Fill a large bowl with ice cubes and set it aside. Now, while whisking the egg yolk mixture, very gradually add the hot chocolate mixture. Whisk until thoroughly blended. Place this bowl in the ice-cube-filled bowl, and stir the mixture with a rubber spatula until it starts to thicken, about 5 minutes.

5. Whip the cream and the remaining 2 tablespoons sugar with an electric mixer on medium-high speed until soft but firm peaks form, about 1 minute. Fold the whipped cream into the chocolate mixture. Spoon the mousse into your prettiest goblets, and refrigerate for at least 1 hour to set. (The mousse can be held in the refrigerator for up to 1 day.)

6. Top the mousse with raspberries, sprigs of mint, and/or additional whipped cream, if you like, and serve.

flo lechter's orange ring

from Bonnie Robbins

C ousin Bonnie gave me this recipe decades ago. (And if the name "Lechter" sounds familiar, yes, Bonnie's uncle Al Lechter founded the one-time mega housewares chain, so Aunt Flo must have known something about cooking!) Orange and pineapple are made for each other, but note: Both fresh and frozen pineapple contain an enzyme that prevents gelatin from setting, so use only canned. Serve this for dessert or as a side dish on a buffet table. **SERVES 8 TO 10**   P

Vegetable cooking spray, for greasing
the mold
1 can (11 ounces) mandarin oranges, drained,
juice reserved
1 can (8 ounces) crushed pineapple packed
in juice, drained, juice reserved
1 box (6 ounces) orange-flavored gelatin
1 pint orange sherbet (not sorbet),
softened

My cousin Bonnie and I were just reminiscing that when my mom [Flo] and her mom [Hilda] cooked, they always wore a 'cobbler' apron over their street clothes, whereas we always wear sweats. Something right out of Leave it to Beaver, although I don't think they wore their pearls.
—ROBIN FRANK

1. Spray a 5-cup ring mold (or other shape) with vegetable cooking spray.

2. Combine the juice from the mandarin oranges with the juice from the crushed pineapple in a 2-cup measuring cup, and add water to reach 1³/4 cups. Bring this mixture to a boil, either in a small saucepan or in the microwave.

3. Place the gelatin in a medium-size bowl and pour the boiling juice mixture over it, stirring until the gelatin dissolves. Add the sherbet and stir until it has melted and is thoroughly combined. Chill in the refrigerator until thickened (drawing a spoon through the gelatin leaves a definite impression), 1 to 1¹/2 hours.

4. Stir the mandarin oranges and pineapple into the thickened mixture, and spoon it into the prepared mold. Refrigerate, covered, overnight.

5. Unmold the dessert (see page 59, Step 5) immediately before serving.

Above: Lou and Sally Bower, Hilda and Lou Robbins, Flo with her date, Uncle Morris, 1940s.

Right: Flo and Al Lechter at nephew Chad and Emily's wedding, 1998.

paul's lemon chiffon

from Marilyn Dubin

This refreshing, light dessert looks so pretty, you'll hate to cut into it. The nonfat version is a satisfying, guiltless end to a meal. I like to chill my bowl and beaters, as well as the milk, in the freezer—it makes the milk whip up quickly. (I do this with whipping cream as well.) **SERVES 12**   **D**

1 can (12 ounces) evaporated milk

1 box (3 ounces) lemon-flavored gelatin

1 cup boiling water

Unsalted butter, for greasing the pan

About 40 ladyfingers

(from three 3-ounce packages)

3/4 cup sugar

Grated zest of 2 lemons

Juice of 2 lemons (6 tablespoons)

Pinch of salt

1 to 3 drops yellow food coloring

1. Pour the evaporated milk into an ice cube tray or an 8-inch glass or ceramic baking dish, and freeze it until crystals start to form, about 45 minutes.

2. Combine the gelatin and the boiling water in a small bowl, and stir until the gelatin has dissolved. Refrigerate until the mixture is cool and syrupy, about 45 minutes.

3. Butter the bottom and sides of a 9-inch springform pan, and line the bottom and sides with the ladyfingers.

4. Beat the evaporated milk with an electric mixer on high speed until it starts to thicken, about 1 minute. Add the sugar, lemon zest, lemon juice, salt, and the gelatin mixture, and beat until very thick, about 1 minute. Beat in the food coloring. Carefully pour the mixture into the prepared springform pan and refrigerate it overnight.

5. When you are ready to serve the dessert, slide a thin knife around the edges of the pan before releasing the sides. Cut the lemon chiffon into wedges, and serve.

Nonfat version: Use nonfat evaporated milk and slivers of nonfat pound cake or angel food cake instead of ladyfingers.

english trifle

from Claire Smolen

Trifle. Hardly! This layered dessert, an unabashed stunner with its multitude of flavors, textures, and colors, has been around for centuries and rates high on the *wow* meter. There are probably as many recipes floating around as there are those who use them. Any spirit can be used, such as a liqueur, rum, or even none at all. Sponge cake or pound cake can be substituted for the ladyfingers. This is no time for modesty: use a large, deep glass bowl to show off all the pretty layers. **SERVES 12 TO 16**   **D**

'trī-fəl, *n., something of little value or importance; a trivial thing, idea, etc.; a paltry matter. From Webster (that killjoy—obviously not a relative)*

1 quart whole milk or half-and-half, or a
    combination

³/₄ cup sugar

¹/₄ cup (packed) cornstarch

Pinch of salt

Yolks of 8 large eggs

2 teaspoons pure vanilla extract

3 packages (3 ounces each) ladyfingers

¹/₂ cup cream sherry, brandy, or Marsala wine

1 cup seedless black raspberry preserves

¹/₃ cup slivered almonds, toasted (see box,
    page 17)

¹/₃ cup crumbled almond or coconut macaroons

1 to 2 cans (16 ounces each) dark red pitted
    cherries, drained (optional)

2 cans (11 ounces each) mandarin oranges,
    drained (optional)

1¹/₂ cups heavy (whipping) cream

1. Pour the milk into a medium-size heavy saucepan and heat it over medium heat until it is steaming and small bubbles form around the edges. Remove the pan from the heat.

2. Meanwhile, whisk the sugar, cornstarch, and salt together in a medium-size bowl. Add the egg yolks and whisk until smooth.

3. Pour about 1 cup of the scalded milk into a measuring cup with a spout. Very slowly add the hot milk to the egg yolk mixture while whisking it vigorously. (Place a dish towel under the bowl to keep it steady.) Pour the yolk mixture into the remaining hot milk in the saucepan, and cook over medium heat, beating constantly with a wire whisk, until it almost reaches the boiling point, but do not let it boil. The mixture will have thick-

ened. Remove the pan from the heat and stir in the vanilla. Set it aside to cool completely, about 30 minutes.

4. Arrange the ladyfingers on the bottom and around the sides of a deep 2¹/₂-quart glass bowl. Sprinkle the sherry over the ladyfingers on the bottom. Spread one third of the preserves over the ladyfingers on the bottom of the bowl, then one third of the custard, one third of the almonds, one third of the crumbled macaroons, and one third of the cherries and mandarin oranges, if using. Repeat the layers. Then repeat them one more time, ending with the macaroons. (Save the remaining cherries and oranges, if you used them, for the top.)

5. Beat the cream with an electric mixer on medium-high speed until it holds soft peaks, 1 to 2 minutes. Spread the whipped cream over the top of the layers. Decorate with the remaining cherries and/or mandarin oranges, if using. Cover, and refrigerate for 8 to 24 hours for the flavors to mingle.

6. Spoon the trifle, going through all the layers, onto dessert dishes and serve . . . with a flourish, if desired.

tiramisù

from Lilly Kancigor Cohen

I t was an '80s thing . . . but it tastes just as good today. *Tiramisù* means "carry me up" in Italian—whether referring to the lightness of this cream-filled confection, the caffeine involved, or the ecstasy by which one is transported, having tasted it, is unknown. While Marsala wine is traditional, Lilly prefers coffee-flavored brandy for a double dose of java.

SERVES 12 TO 16   **D**

FOR THE ESPRESSO SYRUP

2 cups brewed espresso or very strong coffee,
    at room temperature

¹/₄ cup sugar

¹/₂ cup coffee-flavored brandy, coffee liqueur,
    brandy, or rum

FOR THE FILLING

Yolks of 3 large eggs

¹/₂ cup sugar

8 ounces mascarpone cheese

2 tablespoons coffee-flavored brandy,
    coffee liqueur, brandy, or rum

1 teaspoon instant espresso powder or
    instant coffee powder

²/₃ cup heavy (whipping) cream

1 package (14 to 16 ounces) crisp Italian
    ladyfingers (see Note)

8 ounces semisweet or bittersweet chocolate,
    grated

3 tablespoons unsweetened cocoa powder

FOR THE GARNISH

Maraschino cherries with stems
    (optional)

Confectioners' sugar

1. Prepare the syrup: Combine the brewed espresso, sugar, and brandy in a medium-size bowl. Stir to dissolve the sugar, and set aside.

2. Prepare the filling: Fill a very large bowl with ice and a little cold water, and set it aside.

3. Combine the egg yolks and ¹/₄ cup of the sugar in a large heatproof bowl, and beat with a handheld electric mixer on medium speed until pale yellow, 1 to 2 minutes. Place the bowl over a saucepan of simmering water (but not touching the water) and beat until the mixture is thick, quadrupled in volume, and hot to the touch (160°F on an instant-read thermometer), about 10 minutes. Then remove it from the heat and place it in the bowl of ice water. Beat on medium speed until the mixture is cool to the touch, about 10 minutes.

4. Combine the mascarpone, brandy, instant espresso powder, and the remaining ¹/₄ cup sugar in a bowl and beat on medium speed until light and fluffy, 1 to 2 minutes. Fold in the cooled egg yolk mixture.

5. In another bowl, beat the cream on medium-high speed until it holds soft peaks, 1 to 2 minutes. Fold the whipped cream into the mascarpone mixture, just until evenly distributed.

6. Working with one at a time, dip half of the ladyfingers into the espresso syrup and arrange them snugly over the bottom of an ungreased 13 × 9-inch or other shallow 2¹/₂-quart glass baking pan. Drizzle with about half of the remaining espresso syrup. Spread half of the mascarpone mixture evenly over the ladyfingers, and sprinkle with half of the grated chocolate. Place half of the cocoa powder in a fine-mesh sieve and sift it over the top. Repeat the layers: dipped ladyfingers, remaining espresso syrup, remaining mascarpone mixture, remaining chocolate,

and remaining cocoa powder. Cover tightly with plastic wrap and refrigerate for at least 8 hours or up to 2 days to blend the flavors.

7. To serve, garnish the top with maraschino cherries, if you like. Cut into squares, and dust each serving with confectioners' sugar.

Note: Regular ladyfingers are too soft and will become soggy. Italian ladyfingers (called savoiardi) are crisper and will absorb the syrup.

crème caramel

from Marcy Epstein

This golden, rich, caramel-flavored custard unmolds easily whether it's served hot or cold. "This was one of my favorite desserts that my mom would make when my father's parents came for dinner," says Marcy. "The caramelized top and sweet, creamy center always made it a special treat." **SERVES 6**　**D**

Marcy Epstein: chemist by day at First Spice, the family business; by night, formulates sumptuous sweets like this one.

Unsalted butter, at room temperature, for greasing the custard cups
¹/₂ cup plus ¹/₃ cup sugar
3 large eggs, or yolks of 6 large eggs
¹/₄ teaspoon salt
2 cups whole milk
¹/₄ teaspoon ground nutmeg, or to taste, plus extra for garnish
1¹/₂ teaspoons pure vanilla extract
Hot water

1. Preheat the oven to 350°F. Grease six 1-cup custard cups or a 1¹/₂-quart casserole.

2. Place the ¹/₂ cup sugar in a small, heavy saucepan over medium-low heat and cook, stirring constantly, until it has melted and caramelized (turned a medium amber color), about 15 minutes. Divide the caramelized sugar among the prepared cups, turning them so the caramel coats the sides. (Be very careful. Melted sugar really burns.) Set the cups aside so the caramel can cool and harden while you prepare the custard.

3. Combine the eggs, remaining ¹/₃ cup sugar, and salt in a large bowl and beat until combined.

4. Combine the milk, nutmeg, and vanilla in a medium-size saucepan over medium-high heat, and heat gently until bubbles form around the edge. Pour the milk mixture gradually into the egg mixture, whisking constantly. Strain the custard mixture into another bowl, and then divide it among the caramel-lined custard cups.

5. Place the cups (or casserole) in a large, shallow pan with sides 2 to 3 inches high. Pour enough hot water into the shallow pan to reach halfway up the sides of the

custard cups. Sprinkle a little nutmeg over the tops of the custards to garnish them. Bake just until a knife inserted into the custard comes out clean, 30 to 35 minutes.

6. To serve, run a knife around the sides of the custard(s), and invert them onto dessert plates. The caramel sauce will run down the sides of the custard.

Notes: To serve the Crème Caramel cold, refrigerate it, covered (still in the cups or casserole), for 2 hours or as long as 1 day. Then unmold and serve.

In the unlikely event that you encounter resistance getting the custard out of the casserole, place a warm cloth on top of the dish when you invert it.

monique lapisse-mauras's coconut flan

from Isabelle Mauras-Bart

my nephew Randy's new bride, Isabelle, makes her mother's Coconut Flan, a variation of the classic crème caramel, in a favorite pan brought from her native France, but a 9-inch deep-dish pie plate works just fine too. **SERVES 6** **D**

> **I grew up in the little French village of Panjas, about 100 miles south of Bordeaux, in the region called Gers, very famous for its good food (foie gras in particular) and for Armagnac (a liqueur similar to Cognac). In fact, my grandfather worked in Armagnac production, and he is an incredible wine and liqueur connoisseur. Like most French people, we always eat dessert at the end of each meal. Our closeness to Spain makes flan-like dishes very popular. Flan would be an easy dessert for more casual meals.**
>
> **—ISABELLE MAURAS-BART**

3/4 cup sugar

1 can (14 ounces) sweetened condensed milk

2 cups whole milk

3 large eggs

1 teaspoon pure vanilla extract

1 cup sweetened flaked or shredded coconut, toasted (see Note)

Hot water

1. Preheat the oven to 325°F.

2. Combine the sugar and 1/3 cup water in a small, heavy saucepan and cook over medium heat until the mixture is thick, bubbling, and just amber colored, 8 to 10 minutes. As it cooks, brush down any crystals forming on the sides of the pan with a wet pastry brush (or keep the pan covered for the first 5 minutes). The mixture will be very hot, so be careful. Immediately pour the caramel into a 9-inch deep-dish pie plate or other 2-quart nonreactive baking dish. Wearing pot holders or mitts and working quickly, swirl the dish to coat the bottom and halfway up

My niece Isabelle with her mom, Monique, on a recent visit from France. First stop: Vegas!

mom's berries and swedish cream

from Shelly Kancigor

the sides with caramel. Set the pie plate aside to cool while you prepare the custard.

3. Whisk the condensed milk, whole milk, eggs, and vanilla together in a medium-size bowl until smooth. Stir in the toasted coconut. Pour the mixture into the caramel-coated pie plate. Set the pie plate in a larger pan, and pour enough hot water into the larger pan to reach halfway up the sides of the pie plate.

4. Bake on the center rack of the oven until the custard is just set on top and a knife inserted near the center comes out clean, 45 to 50 minutes. Carefully remove the pie plate from the water and place it on a wire rack. Let the flan cool for 1 hour. Then refrigerate it, covered, for at least 4 hours or up to 2 days.

5. To serve, run a small spatula around the edge of the pie plate to loosen the flan. Invert a shallow bowl or rimmed serving platter over the pie plate. Turn the two over together, shaking gently to release the flan if necessary. Spoon some of the caramel sauce over each serving.

Note: To toast the coconut, scatter it on a baking sheet and bake in a preheated 350°F oven, stirring occasionally, until golden, 7 to 10 minutes.

When I was a kid, a typical lunch of berries and cream meant berries and sour cream. That's it. Oh, you wanted sugar? There you go.

This dessert takes berries and cream to a whole 'nother level, from kiddie lunch to elegant dessert. Swedish cream is a mixture of sour cream and heavy cream. Served with fresh berries, this dessert, similar to an Italian panna cotta, is pretty as a summer day and mighty yummy too.

SERVES 6 D

2 cups heavy (whipping) cream

1 cup sugar

1 envelope unflavored gelatin

2 cups sour cream

1¹/₂ teaspoons pure vanilla extract

About 6 cups fresh berries (blueberries, strawberries, raspberries . . .)

Semisweet chocolate, grated, for garnish (optional)

Fresh mint leaves, for garnish (optional)

1. Combine the cream, sugar, and gelatin in a medium-size saucepan and cook over medium heat until the gelatin dissolves and the mixture barely comes to a boil. Refrigerate until it thickens, 2¹/₂ to 3 hours.

2. Stir the sour cream and vanilla together, and add this to the gelatin mixture. Refrigerate until firm, 1 to 2 hours.

3. Spoon the Swedish Cream into sherbet dishes and top with the berries. Garnish with grated chocolate and mint leaves, if using.

baked custard

from Sally Bower

Writer Ambrose Bierce called custard "a vile concoction produced by a malevolent conspiracy of the hen, the cow, and the cook." Obviously he never had a Jewish mother to ease him through a childhood illness, a tussle with bullies, or a scraped knee with this most comforting of comfort foods. Before puddings came in a box, our tantas and bubbes made this simple dessert often. Aunt Sally said it can be served in the cup or unmolded. Sliced berries make a nice addition. **SERVES 6** **D**

**2 cups whole milk, or 1 cup whole milk plus
    1 cup heavy (whipping) cream**

3 large eggs

¹/₄ cup sugar

1 teaspoon pure vanilla extract

Pinch of salt

Ground nutmeg (optional)

Hot water

1. Preheat the oven to 300°F.

2. Place the milk in a medium-size sauce-pan and heat it over medium heat just until it is steaming and bubbles are forming around the edge.

3. While the milk is heating, beat the eggs in a 4-cup heatproof measuring cup or other container with a spout.

4. Then, very slowly, whisking constantly, pour the scalded milk mixture into the beaten eggs. Whisk in the sugar, vanilla, and salt.

5. Pour the mixture through a strainer into 6 custard cups. Sprinkle with nutmeg, if using. Set the cups in a larger pan and pour in hot water until it comes halfway up the sides of the custard cups. Bake until the custard is set and a knife inserted in the center comes out clean, about 50 minutes. Remove the cups from the water bath and let the custard cool to room temperature. Then refrigerate it, covered, for at least 2 hours before serving.

ilo's stovetop rice pudding

from Diane Podratz

Diane, Shelly's mom, remembers her mother, Ilo, having warm rice pudding waiting on the stove for the children when they came home from school on a cold winter's day. Now Diane makes it for those grandchildren we share, to bring to friends when they are sick, or just when the yen for ultimate comfort hits. This is the creamy, old-fashioned rice pudding grandmas used to be famous for before diners and manufacturers gave it a bad name by overcooking it into a solid mass . . . which you will do too if you're busy programming your new cell phone and forget about it, as I did the first time I tested it. **SERVES 6**   **D**

1 cup medium-grain rice

3 cups whole milk

1 cup half-and-half

³/₄ cup sugar

1 tablespoon butter

¹/₂ teaspoon salt

Ground cinnamon, for sprinkling

1. Combine the rice and 2 cups water in a medium-size heavy saucepan, and bring to a boil. Reduce the heat to a simmer and cook, covered, until the rice is tender and the liquid has been absorbed, about 20 minutes.

2. Remove the pan from the heat and add the milk, half-and-half, sugar, butter, and salt. Stir well. Return the pan to the stove and bring the mixture just to a boil. Reduce the heat to a simmer and cook, stirring occasionally, until most of the liquid has been absorbed, 45 minutes to 1 hour. Do not overcook; the mixture will thicken as it cools.

3. Serve warm, with a light sprinkling of cinnamon on each serving.

Note: Although Shelly's family doesn't, I like to add 1 cup raisins along with the milk in Step 2.

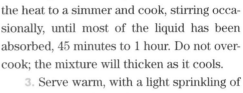

taylor's homeland holiday pavlova

from Shari Nagy

Shari spent the first years of her marriage in Australia, where she picked up this recipe. She named it for Taylor, her firstborn, who kicked happily away in utero as she tried it the first time in her cliff-top home overlooking the Pacific. Many Aussies prefer to top this crunchy-chewy meringue puff with passion fruit and kiwi, but just about any combination of seasonal fruits will do. It's best to eat this as soon as it's assembled, as the finished dessert becomes unpleasantly soft when it's kept in the refrigerator. For a low-fat dessert, substitute your favorite flavored yogurt for the whipped cream. **SERVES 4 TO 6**   **D** or **P**

> **My Grandma Ilo, one of seven children, grew up on a farm . . . several actually, because the family was always moving. They were very poor, and her dad would rent one farm after another. One day he would say, 'We have to leave,' and the next day they would hop on the wagon and go. It was Ilo's job to walk the cow for the long trek. On the way other farmers would take them in for the night and let them rest.**
> **—SHELLY KANCIGOR**

FOR THE MERINGUE

¹/₂ teaspoon plus 1 tablespoon cornstarch

Whites of 3 large eggs, at room temperature

³/₄ cup superfine or ultrafine sugar

1 teaspoon distilled white vinegar

1 teaspoon pure vanilla extract

FOR THE FILLING

1¹/₂ cups heavy (whipping) cream or nondairy
*   whipping cream*

1¹/₂ tablespoons confectioners' sugar

1 teaspoon pure vanilla extract

3 to 4 cups assorted fresh fruit, such as sliced
*   kiwi; sliced bananas; hulled, quartered*
*   strawberries; raspberries or other berries;*
*   pineapple chunks; or sliced pitted peaches*
*   or nectarines*

1. Preheat the oven to 375°F. Line a baking sheet with parchment paper.

2. Prepare the meringue: Draw an 8-inch circle on the parchment paper, using a metal cake pan as a guide. Dust the circle with the ¹/₂ teaspoon cornstarch.

3. Beat the egg whites with an electric mixer on medium speed until they form soft peaks, 1 to 2 minutes. Raise the speed to high and add the sugar, 1 tablespoon at a time, beating for at least 10 seconds after each addition. Beat until the whites stand in stiff, shiny peaks. Beat in the remaining 1 tablespoon cornstarch, the vinegar, and the vanilla, beating until fully incorporated. (This entire procedure will take 4 to 5 minutes.)

4. Mound the meringue on the prepared parchment, spreading it out within the 8-inch circle. Using the back of a spoon or the tip of a rubber spatula, swirl to make a slight depression in the center, forming a shallow nest. (To prevent breakage later, leave the meringue at least ³/₄ inch thick on the bottom and sides.)

5. Bake on the center rack of the oven for 10 minutes. Reduce the temperature to 200°F and bake until the outside of the meringue is dry, crisp, and barely beige, 1¹/₄ hours. Turn off the heat and allow the meringue to dry in the turned-off oven for 1 hour. Then remove the baking sheet, place it on a wire rack, and let the meringue cool completely, about 1 hour more. Carefully peel the parchment off the meringue, and set the meringue aside. (The baked meringue can be stored in an airtight container at room temperature for up to 1 week.)

6. No more than 1 hour before serving, prepare the filling: Beat the cream, confectioners' sugar, and vanilla with an electric mixer on medium speed until soft peaks form, 1 to 2 minutes. Cover and refrigerate. Gently toss the fruits together in a bowl. Cover and refrigerate, if desired.

7. Just before serving, place the meringue shell on a serving plate. Mound the whipped cream in the center. Using a slotted spoon, spoon the fruit over the top, allowing some of the fruit to fall over the sides. Serve immediately.

Baby Taylor with her Aunt Debbie, mom, Shari, and great-grandma, Isabelle, 1996.

banana wraps
with fat-free chocolate sauce

from Wendy Epstein

Filo has gotten a bad "wrap." In most desserts it's the butter, not the filo, that adds all the calories and fat. Go ahead and indulge in this luscious dessert; there are minimal calories in both the wrap and the sauce. The crispy exterior contrasts nicely with the smooth bananas and slightly chewy dried fruit inside. And the sauce can also be used on fruit, ice cream, or even as chocolate syrup in a mocha drink or for hot chocolate.

SERVES 6   **P**

3 large ripe but firm bananas

2 tablespoons orange liqueur or orange juice

2 tablespoons dried cranberries or other dried fruit

2 tablespoons raisins

1 tablespoon pure vanilla extract

1 teaspoon ground cinnamon, or to taste

Vegetable cooking spray

12 sheets frozen filo dough, thawed

Yolk of 1 egg, beaten

1/4 cup sliced almonds

FAT-FREE CHOCOLATE SAUCE

1/2 cup best-quality unsweetened cocoa powder, preferably Dutch-process

1/2 cup pure maple syrup

2 tablespoons apple juice

1 tablespoon orange liqueur or orange juice

1. Preheat the oven to 350°F. Line a baking sheet with parchment paper.

2. Cut each banana into 4 pieces, once horizontally and once vertically, and place them in a large bowl. Toss the banana quarters with the liqueur, dried cranberries, raisins, vanilla, and cinnamon. Set aside.

3. Spread a sheet of filo dough out on your work surface and spray it gently but thoroughly with vegetable cooking spray. Fold it in half to make a rectangle measuring about $8^1/2 \times 12^1/2$ inches. Repeat with the remaining 5 sheets of filo. Lay the rectangles side by side on your work surface, with the short sides nearest you, and again spray them lightly but thoroughly with vegetable cooking spray.

4. Place 2 banana quarters horizontally in the center of each rectangle near the bottom. Evenly distribute the dried fruit and soaking liquid on top of the bananas. Fold the filo two-thirds of the way up, over the filling (like folding a burrito); then fold in the sides and continue folding until you have a neat rectangular packet.

5. Place 6 more sheets of filo dough on the counter and spray them with vegetable cooking spray. Fold them in half, lay them side by side, and spray them again. Then place the filled packets horizontally in the center of each sheet, near the bottom, and wrap the filo around them as in Step 4.

6. Place the wraps, seam side down, on the prepared baking sheet. Brush them with the egg yolk. Slit the top of each wrap a couple of times on the diagonal, barely cutting through the filo dough. Sprinkle the sliced almonds over the top, and bake until golden brown, about 30 minutes.

7. Prepare the sauce: Combine the cocoa powder and maple syrup in a small saucepan and heat gently over medium heat, whisking to combine. Add the apple juice and orange liqueur, and whisk over low heat until smooth and warm. Bring the sauce to a boil and boil gently for 2 minutes to thicken it a bit. Then set it aside to cool.

8. Transfer the sauce to a plastic squeeze bottle and squeeze a design on each plate; place a wrap on each plate, and zigzag some sauce on top. (Or drizzle the sauce with a spoon.) Serve warm or at room temperature.

blueberry varenikas

from Rose Kancigor

my father-in-law's mother, Grandma Rose, had only sons, and alas, none of her recipes survived. But taste is a memory with no expiration date. After much trial and error—and feeling a little like Violet, the giant blueberry in *Willy Wonka*—I came up with a reasonable facsimile of the smooth, buttery, slippery, impossibly irresistible dumplings we all remember.

Varenikas are usually filled with fruit, although Grandma Rose often made them with potatoes and onions too. Her blueberry varenikas were her specialty, particularly beloved by my father-in-law. Be sure to seal

pop's orange bounty

● ● ●

There is no after-holiday letdown in our house: January is Honeybell season in Florida, and my father-in-law, Nat, is busy assembling packages for children, grandchildren, and great-grandchildren across the country. Our oranges arrive, right on schedule, each one lovingly wrapped, like jewels from Harry Winston. Honeybells are as sweet as Pop. Their season is short. We enjoy them while we can. **—JUDY BART KANCIGOR**

the dough well to prevent leakage: While it's pretty on the inside, blueberry filling seeping into the boiling water will turn the dumplings blue on the outside. Not attractive. (Won't affect the taste, however!) **MAKES 3½ TO 4 DOZEN** **D** or **P**

FOR THE FILLING

2 pints blueberries

1 cup sugar

2 teaspoons fresh lemon juice

2 tablespoons cornstarch

FOR THE DOUGH

3 cups all-purpose flour

½ teaspoon salt

2 large eggs

2 tablespoons vegetable oil

About 2 tablespoons butter or nondairy margarine, melted, for tossing (optional)

4 to 6 tablespoons (½ to ¾ stick) butter or nondairy margarine, for pan-frying (optional)

Regular or nondairy sour cream, for serving

1. Prepare the filling: Combine the blueberries, sugar, and lemon juice in a saucepan. Cook over low heat, stirring often, until the blueberries form a sauce, 10 minutes. Mix the cornstarch with 2 tablespoons water in a bowl, and stir this into the blueberry mixture. Continue cooking until thick, about 1 minute. Drain, reserving the blueberries and syrup separately. Set aside to cool.

2. *To prepare the dough by hand*, combine the flour and salt in a large bowl. Whisk the eggs, $1/2$ cup water, and the oil in a separate bowl until well mixed. Make a well in the center of the flour mixture, add the egg mixture, and mix with a fork (Grandma Rose used her hands, and you can too

My husband, Barry, and his dad, Nat, about 1945.

if you like) until the dough comes together. Remove the dough from the bowl and knead it on a lightly floured surface until it is smooth and elastic, about 5 minutes.

To prepare the dough using a food processor, place the flour and salt in a food processor. Whisk the eggs, $1/2$ cup water, and the oil in a separate bowl, or in a measuring cup with a spout, until well mixed. Pulse the flour in the food processor two to three times. Then turn the processor on and slowly add the egg mixture through the feed tube. Process just until the dough comes together and pulls away from the sides of the bowl.

3. Cut the dough in half. Shape each half into a disk, cover it with plastic wrap, and refrigerate for at least 30 minutes or as long as overnight.

4. To assemble the varenikas, divide each disk of dough in half and work on one portion at a time, keeping the remaining dough covered so it does not dry out. Flour your work surface and rolling pin, and roll the dough out very thin. Cut out rounds of dough, using a 3-inch-wide glass or cookie cutter. Place a teaspoon of the blueberries in the center of each round. Dip your finger in water and moisten half the outer edge of the round (this will help the dough to stick).

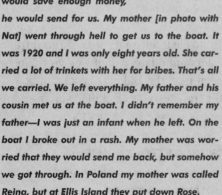

" *In Poland my grandfather dealt in horses and had a lot of land. I went to cheder (yeshiva). My father left for America in 1913: When he would save enough money, he would send for us. My mother [in photo with Nat] went through hell to get us to the boat. It was 1920 and I was only eight years old. She carried a lot of trinkets with her for bribes. That's all we carried. We left everything. My father and his cousin met us at the boat. I didn't remember my father—I was just an infant when he left. On the boat I broke out in a rash. My mother was worried that they would send me back, but somehow we got through. In Poland my mother was called Reina, but at Ellis Island they put down Rose.*

—NAT KANCIGOR "

Bring the unmoistened half over to form a semicircle, and pinch the edges together well (this is important so the varenikas will not fall apart in the boiling water). Place the filled varenikas on a baking pan and keep them covered as you work. (The varenikas can be frozen at this point. You don't need to thaw them before proceeding.)

5. Bring a large, wide saucepan of water to a boil.

6. When the water has come to a rolling boil, drop some of the varenikas in, one at a time so the boiling does not stop. Do not crowd the pan—depending on the size of your pot, 8 to 10 is probably a good number. Cook at a steady, but not rapid, boil for 10 to 15 minutes. Remove the varenikas with a slotted spoon and drain them well. Repeat with the remaining varenikas. Toss with melted butter, if using, and serve, or pan-fry.

7. To pan-fry the varenikas, melt 1 tablespoon of the butter in a large skillet over medium heat. Add as many varenikas as will fit comfortably in the pan and fry until golden, 3 to 4 minutes per side. Add more butter as needed to fry the remaining varenikas.

8. Serve immediately, with the blueberry syrup, topped with sour cream.

Helping Grandma Rose make varenikas for my boys, Stu and Brad, 1970.

baked alaska

from Joan Barrett

This extravagant finale conjures up visions of supper clubs and ocean-bound luxury liners. Actually Joan was inspired by the smashing dessert served at Crotched Mountain Inn, the mountain resort in Francestown, New Hampshire, where the family used to go skiing. The twist here is using marshmallow creme to add body and sweetness to the meringue, a trick she picked up from the owner. To enhance the showstopping presentation even further, Joan serves a spoonful of amaretto-laced strawberries on the side.

If your *batterie de cuisine* doesn't include a fancy ice cream mold, no problem: just use a 6-cup mixing bowl. And if you don't own a platter that will withstand extreme temperature changes, place the ice cream bombe on a baking sheet or a wooden cutting board covered with a double thickness of aluminum foil. (Just be sure to clear adequate space in your freezer to accommodate whichever you choose.) If you like, the Baked Alaska can be carefully transferred to a chilled serving platter just before serving. **SERVES 8** **D**

FOR THE ICE CREAM BOMBE
Vegetable oil, for greasing the mold
1 pint pistachio ice cream
1 pint vanilla ice cream
1 pint strawberry ice cream

FOR THE MARSHMALLOW MERINGUE
Whites of 6 large eggs, at room temperature
1 cup marshmallow creme, preferably
Marshmallow Fluff

FOR THE AMARETTO STRAWBERRIES
2 pints fresh strawberries, hulled and sliced
¹/₃ cup Amaretto liqueur
2 tablespoons sugar

1. Prepare the bombe: Lightly grease the inside of a 6-cup mold with vegetable oil. Freeze the mold until it is very cold, at least 30 minutes. Alternatively, line a 6-cup mixing bowl with plastic wrap (for easy removal), letting the plastic hang over the sides, and refrigerate until needed (rather than freeze, to avoid frost buildup on the plastic wrap).

2. Let the pistachio ice cream soften slightly (see Notes). Then spread it in an even layer over the bottom of the chilled mold, smoothing the top with a spatula. Cover with the plastic wrap, pressing it tightly against the ice cream to seal it. Freeze until firm, at least 2 hours.

3. Let the vanilla ice cream soften slightly (see Notes). Open up the plastic wrap and pack the vanilla ice cream in an even layer directly on top of the pistachio, smoothing the top with a spatula. Re-cover with plastic wrap, pressing it tightly against the ice cream, and freeze until firm, at least 2 hours.

4. Let the strawberry ice cream soften slightly (see Notes). Open up the plastic wrap and repeat the layering with the strawberry ice cream. Re-cover and freeze until very firm, at least 4 hours or as long as overnight.

5. If you used a mold, dip it into a bowl of very hot water for 2 seconds to loosen the ice cream, and then invert it onto a freezer-safe, ovenproof platter. If you used a mixing bowl as a mold, invert it onto the platter and peel off the plastic wrap. Freeze the ice cream bombe, uncovered, until it is firm to the touch, about 15 minutes.

6. Meanwhile, prepare the Marshmallow Meringue: Beat the egg whites with an electric mixer on high speed until they form soft peaks, 1 to 2 minutes. Continue beating, adding the marshmallow creme a spoonful at a time, until the whites form stiff, glossy peaks, 2 to 3 minutes. (Don't be alarmed if some bits of marshmallow creme have not blended in smoothly. They will soften when the meringue is heated.)

7. Remove the ice cream bombe from the freezer. Using a spatula or the back of a spoon, carefully and completely cover the top and sides of the ice cream with a thick layer of meringue, making swirl patterns as you work quickly. Return the bombe to the freezer, uncovered, and leave it until the meringue is firm, at least 2 hours. Then wrap it carefully in plastic wrap, cover with aluminum foil, and freeze it for up to 3 days.

8. The day you plan to serve the Baked Alaska, prepare the Amaretto Strawberries: Combine the strawberries, Amaretto, and sugar in a bowl. Toss gently to coat. Cover, and refrigerate until the sugar has dissolved and the flavors have blended, at least 30 minutes or up to 8 hours.

9. Just before serving, preheat the oven to 500°F.

10. Bake the frozen Alaska on the center rack of the oven, watching it carefully, just until the meringue begins to brown, 3 to 5 minutes.

11. Cut the Baked Alaska into thick slices or wedges with a sharp knife dipped in hot water, wiping it clean before making the next slice. Serve the slices on chilled dessert plates, with a spoonful of Amaretto Strawberries on the side.

Notes: To soften ice cream, let it stand for 5 to 10 minutes at room temperature, or heat it in the microwave on high power for 2 to 3 seconds. The ice cream should still be quite firm, but just spreadable. Don't allow the ice cream to become too soft or to melt, as ice crystals will form when it is refrozen, ruining the texture of your dessert.

Buy only farm-fresh eggs that have been kept under refrigeration.

Brad Kancigor and Tracey Barrett, engaged, 1994.

glass, topped with a scoop of vanilla ice cream with biscotti on the side. This recipe comes from Barbara Shenson, a renowned Bay Area chef who demonstrated this elegant dessert at a Wellesley alumnae event.

SERVES 6　　　　D

ice cream
with strawberries & red wine

from Tracey Barrett

I t's summer and strawberries are at their most voluptuous, perfumy best. Black pepper brings out the flavor of the berries, adding a subtle but intriguing bite. Tracey likes to serve them in a martini

1/4 cup sugar

1/3 cup dry red wine

1 cinnamon stick (3 inches long)

2 pints strawberries, hulled

1/8 teaspoon freshly ground black pepper

6 scoops vanilla ice cream

6 biscotti

1. Combine the sugar, wine, and cinnamon stick in a saucepan, and simmer over medium heat for about 5 minutes to dissolve the sugar, steep the cinnamon stick, and reduce the syrup somewhat. Set aside to cool to room temperature.

2. If the strawberries are large, cut them in quarters; if small, cut in half. Place the berries in a large bowl, and sprinkle the pepper over them.

3. Discard the cinnamon stick and pour the sauce over the berries. Divide the berries and sauce among six individual bowls. Top with the ice cream, and serve the biscotti on the side.

claire cappel's drunken fruit compote

from Lillian Bart

For years my mom's bring-along for holiday feasts has been her friend Claire's Drunken Fruit. She prefers the mixed dried fruit that includes dried pineapple, mango, apricots, apples, and prunes, but feel free to use any combination of fruit you prefer. Serve for dessert or as an accompaniment to turkey or other main course. **SERVES 12**　Ｐ

2 pounds mixed dried fruit, larger pieces
　　cut in half
1 can (20 ounces) pineapple chunks or
　　tidbits, undrained
1 cup dry sherry
1 tablespoon fresh lemon juice
1 can (20 ounces) regular or light cherry pie
　　filling

1. Preheat the oven to 350°F.

2. Combine the dried fruit, pineapple, sherry, and lemon juice in a 13 × 9-inch glass baking dish. Spread the cherry pie filling over the mixture.

3. Cover with aluminum foil and bake for 40 minutes. Uncover and bake until thickened, 15 minutes more. Serve warm or at room temperature.

homemade rhubarb sauce

from Ilo Riebe

My daughter-in-law Shelly's Grandma Ilo grows her own rhubarb for her sauce, especially beloved over vanilla ice cream (and yes, she cranks that herself too). My friend Carolyn Arnold, a California transplant who comes from Minnesota, as does Ilo, tells me her family makes rhubarb sauce exactly the same way. When she was growing up, everyone had a patch of rhubarb in their yard, and rhubarb sauce was a rite of spring and early summer. Use only the red part of the stem. Discard the leaves, which are poisonous. **MAKES ABOUT 2 CUPS**

Ｐ

Mom at the mike, 1950.

2 cups chopped rhubarb
　　(red part only, ³/₄-inch pieces)
¹/₂ cup sugar

1. Wash the rhubarb very well.

2. Combine the rhubarb and 1 cup water in a medium-size saucepan and bring to a boil. Cook, uncovered, over medium heat until the rhubarb is tender and beginning to break apart, 7 to 10 minutes. Don't cook it too long or it will lose its pink color. Add the sugar and stir until it dissolves. Set aside to cool.

3. Serve the rhubarb by itself or over ice cream. (The sauce will keep, covered and refrigerated, for 1 week.)

raya tarab's pomerantzen
(candied orange peel)

from Judy Bart Kancigor

This recipe was given to me by my Israeli friend Raya Tarab, whom I "met" on the Jewish Food List (see page XLVI) and its offshoot, Rinaslist. We began corresponding privately shortly after I joined, and soon she even offered to test recipes for me, carefully documenting the results with hilarious sidebars. When she mentioned that she and her family were coming to California, I invited her to dinner.

"What?" said Barry. "You invited someone you met on the Internet to come to our house? Are you crazy? What if she's an ax murderer?" I tried to convince him that I didn't think Raya, her husband Shlomo, and her then six-year-old daughter, Dana, were ax murderers. We had the most delightful visit, and Raya later confided that Shlomo had said in the car on the way to our house, "What? You met these people on the Internet? What if they're ax murderers?"

Tragically, almost a year ago at this writing, this young, vibrant, witty mother of three passed away, mourned by list members around the globe and never to be forgotten. Of all the recipes we shared, this is my favorite, given to Raya by her step-grandfather, Nathan Haneman. While Saba Nathan soaked the peels in changes of water for three days to remove some of the bitterness, we've streamlined the procedure by triple-boiling them. Sprinkling the chopped nuts on the chocolate-covered peels rather than dipping the peels into the nuts makes for a neater, clump-free presentation. Pomerantzen, which means "oranges" in Yiddish, are traditionally served for the festival of Sukkot. **MAKES ABOUT 10 DOZEN PIECES** P or D

6 thick-skinned medium-size navel or Valencia oranges

4 1/2 cups (2 pounds) sugar, plus about 3/4 cup for rolling

2 teaspoons ground ginger (optional)

8 ounces bittersweet, semisweet, or white chocolate, finely chopped (optional)

1 1/4 cups finely chopped toasted almonds (optional) (see box, page 17)

1. Scrub the oranges well to remove any chemical spray. Using a sharp knife, cut a thin

> **Saba [Grandpa] Nathan used to do the same recipe with other citrus peels. I remember the grapefruit, which were okay, and the pomelo, which were to die for. In Israel it is pretty customary to dip the sugared peels, when dry, into chocolate or white chocolate, or half-dip them—though my Saba never did this. Use your imagination. This is a very popular candy here.**
>
> **—RAYA TARAB**

slice off the top and bottom of each orange to expose the flesh. Score the rind of each orange into quarters, from stem end to the bottom, cutting through the white pith. Carefully cut the rind away from the fruit. Reserve the fruit for another use. Using the sharp edge of a spoon, scrape off any bits of membrane that are sticking to the rind. Scrape the white pith, if necessary, so that the pieces are no thicker than $1/4$ inch and no thinner than $1/8$ inch (so they will hold up to the repeated boiling). Cut each section of rind lengthwise into $1/4$-inch-wide strips. Trim the edges neatly, if desired.

2. Place the orange strips in a large, heavy-bottomed saucepan. Add cold water to cover by about 1 inch, and bring to a boil over medium-high heat. Cook at a steady boil for 5 minutes. Drain; then repeat this process two more times, each time beginning with fresh water. Drain the blanched strips in a sieve.

3. In the same pan, stir the $4^1/2$ cups sugar and the ginger, if using, to blend. Stir in $4^1/2$ cups water, and cook over medium-low heat, stirring frequently, until the sugar has dissolved and the mixture reaches the soft thread stage (230° to 234°F on a candy

thermometer—a drop of boiling syrup will form a soft 2-inch thread when immersed in a glass of cold water), 8 to 10 minutes.

4. Wash down the sides of the pan with a wet pastry brush to remove any sugar crystals. Add the orange strips, swirling the pan to coat them with syrup. (Do not stir, as this could cause the syrup to crystallize. Use a fork to separate the pieces, if necessary.) Cook, uncovered, adjusting the heat as needed to keep the syrup at a simmer, until the syrup has reduced to about 3 tablespoons and the strips are tender and translucent, 45 minutes to 1 hour. (Do not let the syrup reduce completely, as the strips could burn.) Drain the strips in a sieve, discarding the remaining syrup. (Alternatively, reserve the strained orange-ginger syrup to sweeten iced tea or other drinks. It will keep for weeks when stored airtight in the refrigerator.)

5. Set two to four (depending on size) wire racks over sheets of waxed paper or baking sheets to catch the drips. Using a fork or a slotted spoon, arrange the orange strips on one or two of the racks; do not let the pieces touch. Let them sit until cool enough to handle, about 30 minutes.

6. Place the remaining $3/4$ cup sugar in a small bowl. Add the orange strips, a few at a time, tossing and turning to coat them thoroughly; then place the sugar-coated strips on the clean wire rack(s). Let them sit until they are completely dry, 4 to 6 hours. Store the candied orange peel, layered between sheets of waxed paper or parchment in an airtight container, for up to 1 week at room temperature.

7. To make chocolate-dipped candied orange peel, set a small heatproof bowl over

a saucepan of barely simmering water, taking care that the water does not touch the bottom of the bowl. Add the chocolate and cook, stirring occasionally, just until melted and smooth, 5 to 10 minutes. Remove the bowl of melted chocolate from the heat. Working quickly, dip the dried candied orange strips, one piece at a time, into the chocolate, coating one half to three quarters of the strip and letting the excess chocolate drip back into the bowl. (If the chocolate becomes too firm, place the bowl over simmering water for a minute or two and stir until it is melted and smooth.) Arrange the chocolate-coated strips individually on a clean wire rack(s) set over waxed paper or a baking sheet. If desired, sprinkle the still-warm chocolate coating with the toasted almonds. Let sit until the chocolate has set, about 30 minutes in the refrigerator or 1 hour at cool room temperature. Store, layered between sheets of waxed paper or parchment in an airtight container, for up to 1 week at room temperature.

Libby Gordon (seated), Papa Harry's cousin from Canada, with her family.

8 ounces walnut halves, half finely chopped and half left whole

1 cup honey

1/2 cup plain dry bread crumbs, plus more for dusting

2 teaspoons unsweetened cocoa powder

1. Combine the walnuts, honey, and bread crumbs in a medium-size (preferably nonstick) saucepan and bring to a boil over medium heat. Reduce the heat to a simmer and cook, stirring often with a wooden spoon, until the mixture is quite thick, clings together, and leaves the sides of the pan, about 7 minutes. Stir in the cocoa powder.

2. Spread additional bread crumbs over a metal baking pan. Dump the honey goo onto the pan and set it aside to cool slightly. As soon as it is cool enough to handle (but still warm), roll it in the bread crumbs and shape it into a log about 11 inches long with tapered ends, in the shape of a salami. Roll it tightly in plastic wrap, cover it with aluminum foil, and refrigerate until firm, about 2 hours.

3. To serve, use a serrated knife to cut the "salami" into 3/8-inch-thick slices.

candy "salami"

from Libby Gordon

This candy really looks like slices of salami. The cocoa makes it look dark, and the nuts look like the little pebbles. Aunt Sally told me cousin Libby once served it on a *milchig* (dairy) plate as a joke to scare Mama Hinda.

MAKES ABOUT 2 DOZEN SLICES Ⓟ

chocolate–peanut butter balls

from Beth Pincus

Sometimes called "Buckeyes," these addictive candies couldn't be easier to make. To speed up the assembly, let the children—or grandchildren—help with the rolling and dipping. Eaten frozen, the flavor is reminiscent of ice cream bonbons. For a creamier treat, let them thaw in the refrigerator for 10 to 20 minutes before serving. Margarine works better than butter in this recipe because it doesn't freeze as hard, so the centers stay soft when frozen. **MAKES ABOUT 7 DOZEN** Ⓟ

1 jar (18 ounces) creamy peanut butter

1 cup (2 sticks) salted nondairy margarine,
at room temperature

1 pound (about 3³/₄ cups) confectioners'
sugar, sifted

3 cups (18 ounces) semisweet or other
dark chocolate morsels

3 tablespoons solid vegetable shortening

1. Line two baking sheets with parchment or waxed paper.

2. Beat the peanut butter and margarine with an electric mixer on medium speed until well blended, 1 to 2 minutes. Gradually add the confectioners' sugar, beating until the mixture is smooth, 1 to 2 minutes more. Cover and refrigerate until the mixture is firm but still moldable, about 30 minutes.

3. Scoop up the peanut butter mixture with a small spoon and form it into 1-inch balls by rolling it between the palms of your hands. Arrange the balls in a single layer on the prepared baking sheets and place in the freezer, uncovered, until cold and firm, about 20 minutes. (For longer storage, cover tightly with plastic wrap and freeze for up to 2 months.)

4. Combine the chocolate morsels and shortening in a double boiler or in a heatproof bowl set over a pot of barely simmering water (take care that the water does not touch the bottom of the bowl). Cook over low heat, stirring occasionally, until melted and smooth.

5. Using a fork or a small slotted spoon, dip the cold peanut butter balls, one at a time, into the melted chocolate, turning to coat them completely and allowing any excess chocolate to drip back into the bowl. (If the undipped peanut butter balls begin to soften, return them to the freezer until they firm up.)

6. Return the chocolate-dipped candies to the parchment-lined baking sheet and freeze, uncovered, until the chocolate is firm to the touch, about 20 minutes.

7. Refrigerate the candies, in layers separated by waxed paper, in an airtight container for up to 3 days. Or freeze them in airtight containers for up to 2 months. Serve them directly from the freezer, or thaw them in the refrigerator first, then serve.

homemade caramel candy

from Diane Schulte

Lauren Kancigor at age 7 in 2006. Because Lauren loves these caramels so much, Diane sends a box just for her at holiday time.

my then six-year-old granddaughter, Lauren, tasted these caramels—lovingly handmade and individually wrapped—at her Uncle Craig's wedding and adored them so much that she insisted I include them. Diane, Craig's new mother-in-law, says this old family recipe comes from her sister, Mary Hunt, a great cook and baker, who lives on a farm in South Dakota. Note that although they are not difficult to make, they do take 2 to 3 hours to cook and at least another 2 hours to cool. According to my trusty recipe tester Virginia Sauer, comparing these homemade confections to store-bought is like comparing filet mignon to hamburger. **MAKES ABOUT 8 DOZEN BITE-SIZE PIECES** ▣

¹/₂ **pound (2 sticks) unsalted butter, plus**
   extra for greasing the pans
4 cups heavy (whipping) cream
4 cups sugar
1¹/₂ cups light corn syrup
Pinch of salt (optional)
1 cup (4 ounces) chopped walnuts
   (optional)

1. Lightly grease the bottom and sides of a 15-inch jelly-roll pan with butter, and set it aside. Lightly butter the sides of a heavy 4- to 6-quart saucepan or Dutch oven.

2. Combine the butter, 2 cups of the cream, the sugar, corn syrup, and salt, if using, in the prepared saucepan. Cook over medium heat, stirring frequently with a wooden spoon, until the butter has melted and the sugar has completely dissolved. Then bring the mixture to a full, rolling boil, stirring frequently with the wooden spoon. Reduce the heat to a gentle simmer and cook, uncovered, stirring occasionally, until a candy thermometer registers 234°F (the start of the soft ball stage—a drop of boiling syrup will form a soft ball when immersed in a glass of cold water and flatten out when removed). This will take 1¹/₂ to 2 hours. Throughout this period, check frequently to ensure that the mixture continues to simmer gently.

3. When the thermometer registers 234°F, very slowly add the remaining 2 cups cream, a mere trickle at a time in order to keep the mixture at a gentle simmer. Stir gently with a clean wooden spoon.

4. Continue to cook, stirring occasionally, until the thermometer reaches 248°F (firm ball stage—a drop of boiling syrup will form a firm ball when immersed in a glass of cold water and not flatten out when removed), about 30 minutes. Watch

very carefully at this stage. As soon as the thermometer reaches 248°F, remove the pan from the heat and stir in the walnuts, if using. Immediately pour the caramel into the prepared jelly-roll pan. (Do not be tempted to scrape the saucepan, as the part that's left may be grainy. The caramel that is stuck to the pan can be transferred to a heatproof bowl to be enjoyed by the cook, or offered to any congregating kibbitzers in exchange for cleaning the pot.) Place the jelly-roll pan on a trivet or rack, and allow the caramel to cool for about 2 hours. Then cover it with plastic wrap and set it aside for at least 2 hours more before cutting it. (Overnight is fine.) If any puddles of butter accumulate on top of the caramel, wipe them off with paper towels.

5. Using a sharp knife, cut the caramel into the desired sizes and shapes. Wrap each piece in candy foil, plastic wrap, or waxed paper, and store in an airtight container. The caramels will remain fresh for up to 1 week at room temperature, for up to 2 weeks in the refrigerator, or for up to 1 month in the freezer.

Variation: For even softer caramels, stop the cooking process at 246°F.

Note: My recipe tester, Virginia, also alerted me to the importance of using a dependable candy thermometer. To check its accuracy, clip it to the side of a saucepan, fill the pan with water, and bring to a boil. The thermometer should register 212°F. If it does not, you will have to adjust the recipe accordingly. To read a candy thermometer accurately, your eye should be level with the mercury. Also, make sure that you can easily find 248°F. If necessary, use a dot of nail polish to mark the spot.

chocolate candy bourbon balls

from Marcy Epstein

Bourbon enhances these very chocolatey candy balls without overpowering them, though it might be strong for children (or those who can't tolerate alcohol.) It didn't dissuade the Epstein girls, apparently. **MAKES 6 DOZEN** Ⓟ

> *I remember this dessert not so much for the end product (which is delicious!) but rather for my family's group effort in preparing the ingredients and anticipating the fruits of our labor. It takes three to four days for the chocolate and bourbon to set. Mom would store them on top of the breakfront in the dining room, and of course my sisters and I would pass by day in and day out trying to figure out how to get to them before my mom was ready to take them down. Suffice it to say, by the time Mom did finally take them down, one or two had always managed to escape.*
> —MARCY EPSTEIN

8 ounces semisweet chocolate, coarsely
   chopped

65 vanilla wafers (about two thirds
   of a 12-ounce package), or more
   if needed

1 cup (about 4 ounces) pecans, finely
   chopped

2/3 cup plus 1/2 cup sugar

1/2 cup bourbon, plus extra for moistening
   the paper towels

1/4 cup light corn syrup

1. Melt the chocolate in a small, heavy saucepan over low heat, stirring it almost constantly. (Alternatively, melt it in a double boiler set over barely simmering water or in the microwave.) Remove the pan from the heat and let the chocolate cool to luke-warm.

2. Pulverize the vanilla wafers in a food processor until they resemble dry bread crumbs.

3. Combine the vanilla wafer crumbs, the pecans, and the 2/3 cup sugar in a large bowl. Pour in the chocolate mixture, bourbon, and corn syrup, and stir vigorously until well combined. Scoop up a rounded teaspoon of the mixture and pat it into a ball about 1 inch in diameter. If the batter appears too dry, add more bourbon. If the batter appears too wet, add more crumbs. Shape all the mixture into 1-inch balls. Roll the balls in the remaining 1/2 cup sugar, and when they are lightly coated all over, place them in a 2-quart jar or other container with a tight-fitting lid.

4. Cut four layers of paper towels to fit over the candy inside the jar. Lightly moisten the paper layers with bourbon, press the towels firmly over the bourbon balls, and secure the lid. Set the bourbon balls aside at room temperature for 3 to 4 days before serving. Tightly covered, they can be kept for 3 to 4 weeks at room temperature.

joanne's chocolate strawberries
with chocolate leaves

from Judy Bart Kancigor

Before my son Brad and daughter-in-law Tracey's wedding, my friend Joanne spent hours helping me decorate and fill welcome baskets for the out-of-towners. I was only too happy, then, when her son Michael married Rupa, to join the merry assembly line in her kitchen, dipping strawberries and painting leaves for the celebration. A few things to keep in mind: The berries must be completely dry before you dip them. As the chocolate is melting, be careful not to get any water in the chocolate or it will seize up. Joanne says you can also use the same technique to dip dried apricots or figs. **MAKES 16 LEAVES (THE NUMBER OF STRAWBERRIES DEPENDS ON THEIR SIZE)** **P**

FOR THE BERRIES

2 pints ripe but firm strawberries, preferably
with stems, at room temperature

8 ounces good-quality semisweet
chocolate, chopped

FOR THE LEAVES

3 ounces good-quality semisweet chocolate,
chopped

16 small nontoxic leaves, such as lemon,
camellia, or gardenia leaves, washed
and thoroughly dried

1. Line several baking sheets with waxed paper, and set them aside.

2. Rinse the berries and dry them thoroughly.

3. Melt the 8 ounces of chocolate in a double boiler set over barely simmering water just until shiny. Do not allow the chocolate to bubble or any water to get into the chocolate.

4. Dip each strawberry, holding it by the stem, into the melted chocolate, turning it to coat about three fourths of the berry and allowing any excess chocolate to drip back into the pan. Place the chocolate-covered berries on the prepared baking sheets. Refrigerate until set, about 30 minutes.

5. Prepare the leaves: Melt the 3 ounces of chocolate as described in Step 3. Using a small, clean paintbrush, paint a layer of chocolate over the back (vein side) of each leaf. Be careful not to paint the sides of the leaf or the chocolate will be difficult to peel off. Refrigerate, chocolate side up, until firm, at least 30 minutes.

6. When the chocolate is firm, hold each leaf by the stem end and gently peel the leaf away from the chocolate. (Use a toothpick to prevent leaving fingerprints.)

7. To serve, arrange the strawberries in a single layer in the center of a serving platter, surrounded by the leaves.

Sugar rationing ended just
in time for my brother, Gary,
to develop his sweet tooth.

passover

Ask most Jewish children, "What's your favorite holiday?" and you'd think "Hanukkah" would be the quick response. For me all the blue and gold beribboned gift boxes in the world can't hold a *shammos* to Passover. To my mind, you just can't beat the cuisine. Personally, I never did understand how eating those special holiday delicacies helps us remember the suffering of our ancestors.

Cousins, do you remember Papa Harry's wonderful Seders with the whole family gathered at the mile-long table whose boards had boards? Good for you. I was never there! We spent our Passovers in the

"Where leaven fears to tread, to the rescue comes the egg."

Purim, Pesach, Rosh Hashanah, Sukkot, and Hanukkah—we mark the seasons as we celebrate each holiday. Who's who on page 613.

Catskills: Youngs Gap, Brown's, then finally the Windsor Hotel, where my dad, Jan Bart, was working, conducting his magnificent Seders, complete with choir (including my mom Lillian's glorious contralto) for 850 people. How to describe the Catskills of the 1950s and '60s? Like a Jewish land cruise—the breeding ground for so many entertainers, glamorous, fun-packed, the buffet that never ended.

At my dad's last Seder, in 1970, he was so proud when grandson Stuart, age four, stepped up to the microphone to recite the Four Questions in perfect Hebrew. And how proud he would be to see grandson Bradley and wife Tracey's Seders today.

the bread of our affliction

The festival of Passover commemorates the exodus of the Hebrew slaves from Egypt. In their haste to depart they could not wait for their bread to rise, so the dough was baked in flat cakes. As a reminder of our passage to freedom, Jews throughout the world eat matzoh for the eight-day holiday (seven in Israel).

This poor bread that sustained our ancestors in the desert we call the "bread of

Dad conducts the Passover Seder at the Windsor Hotel in the Catskills, 1960.

affliction" to remember that once we were slaves in Egypt. But through the miracles of God, we were led into freedom, enabling us to use our ingenuity, skill, traditions, and collective memory to create a glorious celebration around it. To focus on what we do without for those eight days is to see the glass half empty.

During the Seder (the word means "order" in Hebrew), we eat matzoh with haroset (pages 540 to 542 and 544), the fruit and nut mixture resembling the mortar the ancient Hebrews used when they were slaves in Egypt—you'll find both Ashkenazic and Sephardic versions here. We combine it with bitter herbs—try Uncle Lou's horseradish, page 53—to remember the bitterness of slavery and the sweetness of freedom.

Imaginative Jewish cooks through the ages, like a million Iron Chefs all working with the same surprise ingredient, have molded,

tradition! tradition!

We have a lovely custom in our family. At the end of the Seder, each participant dates and signs the inside back cover of her or his Hagaddah. It's fun to look back and see the changing handwriting of the children, the divorced (and, alas, deceased) family members or friends, and guests whose names are a complete mystery. (Who *was* that masked man?) Some people, like our friend Sylvan Swartz, write little notes like "Nice Seder, but not enough food!" (Very funny, Sylvan.) Or my personal favorite from my friend Helaine's witty son, Max: "Nice tune, but can you dance to it?" And the food stains do lend a certain charm. *Chag Sameach!*

pesach: spring cleaning on steroids

Mama Hinda was a burier. No, not an undertaker. Okay, spell it *berye*—Yiddish for major-domo cleaner extraordinaire. As in white-glove test above the door frame. As in you could eat off the floor. As in using the basement oven to keep the upstairs kitchen clean. And if Mama was thorough during the year, before Passover she was a fanatic. Passover preparation is spring cleaning on steroids—a joyous frenzy to ready the house for the holiday and remove all *chometz* (bread or any food containing leaven). So stringent is the prohibition that Jews are forbidden not only to consume, but even to possess bread or leaven during the holiday.

Weeks before, she would scrub, scour, scald, polish, and shine. As the holiday approached, her Passover dishes—one set for *milchig* (dairy) and one set for *fleishig* (meat)—would be brought from the basement and washed. My Aunt Sally remembered that when she was a child in the 1920s, Mama would soak glasses for three days for use during the holiday. No closet, no shelf, no corner evaded her purification ritual.

On the night before Passover, Papa Harry and the children would search the already scoured home for any remaining crumbs of *chometz*, which would be swept up with a feather and burned.

Downstairs in the cold cellar, the earthen crock of russel (fermented beets) Mama had started weeks before stood ready to infuse her crimson borscht, and eggs by the crate awaited whisking by her practiced hand into ethereal sponge cakes and irresistible nut tortes.

Once the house was proclaimed *chometz*-free, the newly lined shelves would be filled with a dizzying array of Passover groceries, including matzoh meal for hundreds of knaidlach (page 65) soon to be floating in gallons of soup, farfel (crumbled matzoh) for her kugels, and, of course, boxes and boxes of matzoh.

crumbled, whipped, layered, fried, baked, infused, and combined matzoh with an astonishing variety of other ingredients to produce a tempting feast. The fact that we base a glorious celebration on the bread of affliction illustrates that we have the freedom to do so.

Passover is the most celebrated of all Jewish holidays, and even those who rarely step into a shul all year knock themselves out cooking for this one. We mix it up with dishes that honor our traditions and just enough new stuff to keep it interesting. Why else would you find Matzoh Brei and Goat Cheese and Pine Nut Mini Cheesecakes in the same chapter?

Many of the recipes throughout the other chapters can be used for Passover. I've selected two main dishes to include here: my mother's Ashkenazic Killer Brisket with Tsimmes and Sephardic Chicken with Olives and Honey. For Seder browse the many brisket, short ribs, lamb shanks, veal, chicken, Cornish hens, and turkey recipes (see Index). Omit the accompanying noodles, couscous, grains, and (for Ashkenazim) rice, and so on, and substitute:

- Matzoh meal for bread crumbs

- Potato starch for corn starch or flour

- Passover imitation Dijon mustard for mustard

- Nondairy creamer or soy milk for cream

- Honey for corn syrup

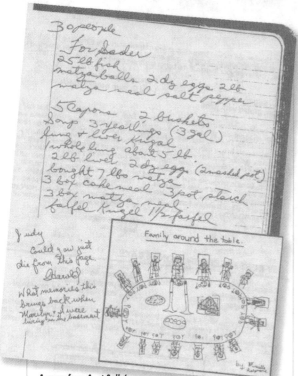

A page from Aunt Sally's recipe notebook with attached note from her son-in-law, Harold; drawing by Danielle Solomonic, 1996.

With most starchy sides off-limits, at least for Ashkenazim (see box, page 549), the matzoh kugel or schalat takes center stage. You'll find both a savory version—a veritable cornucopia of vegetables—and several sweet ones here. For a real showstopper, try the optional presentation of my Apple Matzoh Schalat. And Barry's cousin Barbara's Matzoh Stuffing is everything a stuffing should be: unadulterated comfort heaven and just too darn luscious to serve only once a year.

The exception to the starch ban is potatoes, permitted for both Ashkenazim and Sephardim. Oma's Bubbelach are irresistible, crunchilicious bites that somehow never make it to the table. Look for other potato dishes on pages 267 through 291.

Every year more and more Passover products are available commercially—cake mixes, cereals . . . even noodles. Mama Hinda, of course, made her own. My mother recalls her preparing her own *Pesachdicke* noodles, which she rolled into paper-thin sheets and then cut into strips *(bletlach)* on a lokshen *bret*, a wooden board that Papa Harry made for this purpose. All the aunties made them, but Aunt Irene preserved the recipe for us.

While the Seders get all the glory, this is an eight-day holiday, and our family has all the bases covered, from breakfast muffins, "rolls," and "bagels" to latkes, matzoh brei, and fritters, even a Spinach Lasagne for a dairy meal. Sephardics layer matzoh in lasagne-like strips for minas: You'll find a spinach-cheese version here.

Okay, you've eaten your spinach. Now you can have dessert! Sure, no flour is

klp:
kancigors love passover!

Well, of course, but it really stands for *Kosher L'Pesach* ("kosher for Passover"), meaning that a particular product has been certified by a rabbinic agency for use during Passover. While some foods do not require Passover certification, many do. As guidelines may change from year to year, it's best to consult your own rabbinic authority. Two websites have been especially helpful to me in this regard: www.kosherquest.org and www.kashrut.com.

In this chapter all ingredients listed—chocolate, cocoa powder, brown sugar, whipping cream, maple syrup, wine, liqueurs, even sprinkles—are available (at least as of this writing) and assumed to be KLP.

passover checklist

FOR THE SEDER PLATE

Maror: Bitter herbs (e.g., horseradish, page 53)

Haroset: Fruit and nut mixture
(pages 540 to 542 and 544)

Karpas: Green vegetable, such as parsley

Betzah: Roasted egg (see Notes)

Zeroah: Roasted shank bone (see Notes)

Some Seder plates contain a sixth cup for:

Hazeret: Bitter lettuce or Romaine

Orange: Optional (see Notes)

Notes: To roast an egg, hard-boil it first. Otherwise it tends to shatter in the oven, making a mess. Then roast the hard-boiled egg in the oven along with whatever you are roasting or baking until it turns dark and speckled, about 1 hour.

I've been using the same shank bone for my Seder plate for about thirty years. Right before the Seder it comes out of the freezer, and right afterwards it goes back in. *(It doesn't get eaten. Cheesh!)* We call it the Kancigor Family Shank Bone. Upon my demise my daughters-in-law will just have to fight over it.

Vegetarians, take heart: We are commanded to place two roasted elements on the Seder table: the roasted egg (symbol of the second offering brought to the Temple) and the shank bone (reminder of the paschal lamb). Some vegetarians substitute an avocado pit for the roasted egg and a roasted beet for the shank bone, leading to lively discussion.

And why an orange on the Seder plate, another recent innovation? A widely circulated myth has it that Dr. Susannah Heschel once addressed a convocation of Orthodox rabbis, one of whom supposedly commented, "A woman belongs on the *bimah* (podium) like an orange belongs on the Seder plate." Actually, Heschel began the tradition as a gesture of solidarity with gays and lesbians and other marginalized groups. Hardly traditional, but a great conversation starter.

AT THE TABLE

Candelabrum and candles

Haggadahs

Yarmulkes

Pitcher of water, bowl, and towel for Urchatz

Pillow on left arm of leader's chair

3 whole matzohs wrapped in matzoh cover

Extra matzoh for the table

Saltwater for dipping the karpas

Kosher wine

Wine goblets for each guest, plus extra goblet
for Elijah

Extra chair for Elijah

Extra dishes of haroset, bitter herbs, and karpas
for passing

Hard-boiled eggs (see Notes)

Miriam's cup and water pitcher (see Notes)

Notes: Hard-boiled eggs are passed because Passover celebrates spring and rebirth as well as freedom. But let's face it: With all that glorious food awaiting us, do we really want to start the meal filling up on a hard-boiled egg? My mother solves that problem neatly by using tiny quail eggs.

A new custom has developed of late: remembering Miriam, Moses' sister, a prophetess whom God honored for her bravery by bestowing upon her a miraculous well which sustained the Israelites in their forty years of wandering through the desert. Customs vary as to its use. In some homes, participants pour a little water from their own glasses into Miriam's cup. We fill Miriam's cup with water and pass it around, asking each guest to pour off some water into her or his own drinking glass. Everyone at the table, man or woman, then receives symbolically the life-giving force this brave woman gave our people.

permitted during the holiday, but Jews love a challenge. Where leaven fears to tread, to the rescue comes the incredible, edible egg!

When you think of Passover desserts, sponge cakes come first to mind. Whether served plain or accessorized—try Aunt Sally's Lemon Fluff or Aunt Estelle's Strawberry Cream Filling and Chocolate Frosting—you'll find two citrusy sponge cakes in this chapter as well as a banana and pecan-date. Two nut cakes are de rigueur on the Rabinowitz table: Mama Hinda's Passover Nut Cake, a grand walnut-laden beauty, and Aunt Sally's very dense chocolatey wonder.

But sponge cakes are just the beginning. A deep, dark, dreadfully decadent flourless chocolate cake we call Too Good To Be Called Passover Cake Bête Noire is super easy to prepare and steals the show. And if you just can't get enough chocolate, try cousin Ronna's chewy, gooey Chocolate Fudge Pecan Pie or cousin Heather's Chocolate Hazelnut Caramel Tart. Oh heck, it's Passover. Try them all!

A bountiful bevy of macaroons, lacy Farfel-Nut Thins, luscious squares and brownies, and—drum roll, please—a candy-like Chocolate Covered Matzoh Toffee . . . too bad Passover lasts only eight days!

ashkenazi haroset

from Judy Bart Kancigor

Haroset is a fruit and nut mixture that symbolizes the mortar used to bind the stones and bricks used by the ancient Hebrews when they were slaves in Egypt. I always made lots because my kids liked it on matzoh for breakfast, as a switch from matzoh brei. Every country makes its own from local fruits and nuts, and one year, bored with the Ashkenazi haroset we were all used to (and probably having way too much time on my hands), I made a variety of them and had everyone vote for their favorite. Guess which won? The Ashkenazi, of course! Old habits die hard.

What to do with leftover haroset? Add some to your matzoh brei, or freeze it, and after Passover try haroset instead of applesauce in breads and cakes.

Walnuts are traditional, but I take my cue from my Atlanta cousins and use pecans. But whichever you choose, please, please, toast thy nuts! (I've never seen this instruction on any haroset recipe anywhere, but trust me, you won't believe the difference!) **MAKES 2⅓ CUPS** **P**

Papa Harry presiding over the Seder in Aunt Sally's basement, about 1958. Notice—no Barts present. We were always in the Catskills for my parents' Passover gig.

3 medium-size crisp sweet or tart apples,
or a combination, peeled, cored and
cut into eighths
1 cup pecans or walnuts, or a combination,
toasted (see box, page 17)
2 tablespoons sweet red wine
3 tablespoons honey
1 teaspoon ground cinnamon

1. Place the apples in a food processor and process until chopped. Transfer them to a mixing bowl.

2. Place the pecans in the food processor and chop them. Add them to the apples, and stir in the wine, honey, and cinnamon.

3. This is best served the day it's made, but it will keep, covered, in the refrigerator for up to 5 days (the nuts will soften after the first day).

sephardic haroset

from Judy Bart Kancigor

According to Oded Schwartz (*In Search of Plenty: A History of Jewish Food*), there is no mention of bee-keeping in the Bible, and scholars believe the honey referred to (as in "the land flowing with milk and honey") must have been extracted from fruits such as dates.

My friend Janet Thaler's mom, Rachel Levy from the Isle of Rhodes, makes her traditional haroset with lots of dates. No added sweetener is necessary. Rachel uses a pressure cooker and then presses the mixture through a ricer to separate out the date skin. I believe I've already expressed my thoughts on the pressure cooker (page 139) and am afraid I lack Rachel's patience with the ricer. My food processor version gets chunked up with a generous dose of toasted pine nuts and pistachios. **MAKES 4 CUPS**　Ⓟ

2 medium-size crisp sweet apples,
peeled, cored, and cut into eighths
1 pound pitted dates
1 cup (6 ounces) raisins
1/2 cup (3 ounces) dried apricots
1/4 teaspoon ground cinnamon
1 cup pine nuts, toasted
(see box, page 17)
1 cup roasted unsalted pistachio nuts

1. Combine the apples, dates, raisins, apricots, and cinnamon in a medium-size saucepan and cover with 2 cups water. Bring to a boil, reduce the heat, and simmer, covered, stirring occasionally, until quite soft, about 45 minutes. Most of the liquid should have boiled away. If not, simmer uncovered for a few minutes more. Set aside to cool to lukewarm.

2. Transfer the mixture to a food processor and pulse until smooth. Stir in the toasted pine nuts and pistachios.

3. This is best served the day it's made, but it will keep, covered, in the refrigerator for up to 7 days (the nuts will soften after the first day).

yemenite haroset truffles

from Judy Bart Kancigor

Two recipes in Faye Levy's *1,000 Jewish Recipes*—her Yemenite Haroset and Haroset Truffles—inspired me to create these pretty little haroset balls. They are so sweet, spicy, and festive, they really belong on the dessert table, but I like to serve them during the Seder, where they won't get lost amidst that ostentatious display of sponge cakes, tortes, cookies, and pastries. (Ah yes, poor us. No bread for a week. Thus we remember the sufferings of our ancestors!) **MAKES 16 TO 20** Ⓟ

FOR THE TRUFFLES

1/3 cup (2 ounces) pitted dates
1/3 cup (2 ounces) dried figs
1/3 cup (2 ounces) raisins
1/3 cup (2 ounces) dried apricots
2 1/2 tablespoons honey
1 1/2 teaspoons ground cinnamon
1/2 teaspoon ground ginger
1/8 teaspoon ground cloves
1/8 teaspoon ground cumin
3/4 cup toasted coarsely chopped pecans
   (see box, page 17)
3/4 cup slivered almonds, toasted
   (see box, page 17)
1 1/2 tablespoons orange liqueur

FOR THE COATING

1/2 cup slivered almonds, toasted
   (see box, page 17) and finely ground

1. Combine the dried fruit, honey, and spices in a food processor and pulse until smooth. Add the pecans, slivered almonds, and orange liqueur, and process until just combined.

2. Form the mixture into balls 1 to 1 1/2 inches in diameter. Roll them in the ground almonds,

Seder at our house 2002. Note orange on the Seder plate (see page 539); first course: salmon gefilte fish (page 54).

and place them in individual fluted foil or paper candy cups. Refrigerate, covered, until firm, at least 3 hours. These will keep for up to 5 days in the refrigerator.

goat cheese and pine nut mini cheesecakes
with cranberry haroset

from Judy Bart Kancigor

These delicate mini cheesecake puffs can be served as an appetizer or atop a mixed green salad. The sweet-tart flash of cranberry stands in lively contrast to the tangy goat cheese resting on a bed of crunchy pine nuts—all in one delicious bite. **MAKES 24**   D

Vegetable cooking spray, for greasing the muffin cups

FOR THE CRUST
6 tablespoons matzoh meal
¹/₄ cup pine nuts, ground
2 tablespoons butter, melted
2 tablespoons freshly grated Parmesan cheese
¹/₄ teaspoon salt
¹/₈ teaspoon freshly ground black pepper

FOR THE FILLING
6 ounces cream cheese, at room temperature
5 ounces goat cheese, at room temperature
1 large egg, beaten
1¹/₂ teaspoons dried dill
¹/₄ teaspoon ground cumin
¹/₄ teaspoon salt
¹/₄ teaspoon freshly ground black pepper
About ¹/₂ cup Cranberry Haroset (recipe follows)

1. Preheat the oven to 350°F. Lightly grease 24 mini muffin cups (unnecessary if they are nonstick).

2. Prepare the crust: Combine all the crust ingredients in a bowl, add 1 tablespoon water, and mix thoroughly. Spoon 1 teaspoon of the crust mixture into each muffin cup, and press it down firmly.

3. Prepare the filling: Beat the cream cheese and goat cheese together with an electric mixer on medium speed until thoroughly combined. Scrape the bowl and beat in the egg, dill, cumin, salt, and pepper.

4. Divide the cheese mixture evenly among the prepared cups—about a heaping tablespoon each—and smooth the tops.

5. Bake on the center oven rack until the cheesecakes are rounded and puffy, about 15 minutes. Allow them to cool in the pan set on a wire rack for 10 minutes. Then run a thin knife around the edges (unnecessary if the cups are nonstick) and carefully guide each one out with a small spoon. Garnish with a tiny dollop of Cranberry Haroset, and serve warm or at room temperature.

cranberry haroset

I developed this haroset as a sweet garnish for my Goat Cheese and Pine Nut Mini Cheesecakes, but of course you can use it for your Seder as well. Omit the nuts and it makes a wonderfully thick, preserve-like spread. Great! Something new to slather on matzoh. And next time Purim rolls around, try it as a filling for hamantaschen. It makes a dynamite filling for rugelach too. **MAKES 2 3/4 CUPS** P

1 small sweet or tart apple, peeled, cored,
    and finely chopped
1 small pear, peeled, cored, and finely chopped
1/2 cup sweetened dried cranberries
1/4 cup pitted dates, chopped
1/4 cup golden raisins
1/2 cup sweet red wine
2 tablespoons honey
1 tablespoon fresh lemon juice
1/4 teaspoon ground cinnamon
1/4 teaspoon ground ginger
1/4 cup pine nuts, toasted (see box, page 17)
    and ground
1/4 cup slivered almonds, toasted
    (see box, page 17) and ground

1. Combine the apple, pear, cranberries, dates, raisins, wine, honey, lemon juice, cinnamon, and ginger in a medium-size saucepan. Bring to a boil, then reduce the heat, cover, and simmer, stirring occasionally, until the fruits are very soft and the liquid is reduced, about 1 hour.

2. Set the mixture aside to cool to room temperature. (The mixture can be prepared up to this point a day or two ahead and refrigerated, covered. When you are ready to serve it, bring the haroset to room temperature.)

3. Stir in the ground pine nuts and almonds, and serve.

> " Nothing meant more to my grandma, Mama 'Reen, than her family. Having a household to cook for made her happy, and the more place settings there were, the happier she was. No one left her house hungry, and having a large family, with guests always welcome, Mama 'Reen had many reasons for living a long and happy life. All she ever wanted was someone to cook for, crochet for, and love unconditionally.
> —MARCY EPSTEIN "

mama hinda's passover noodles

from Irene Rosenthal

Passover noodles. Sounds like an oxymoron, doesn't it? Walk down the Passover aisle in some big-city supermarkets today and one would hardly know it's Passover. "Faux" products—adaptations of all sorts of *chometz*—

abound, including noodles. Mama Hinda had no such conveniences. If you wanted noodles, you made your own, these from very thin matzoh meal pancakes. In her heyday Aunt Irene had the quickest wrist action in the West and made the thinnest pancakes, sliced into angel-hair-like shreds to float in her golden chicken soup. Those with less acute reflexes may find it difficult to tilt the pan quickly enough to obtain a uniform pancake from 2 tablespoons of batter. No matter. They get sliced up anyway. **MAKES ALMOST 2 CUPS** 🅿

1 tablespoon matzoh cake meal

1/4 cup cold water

4 large eggs, beaten

1/4 teaspoon salt

Vegetable oil or solid vegetable shortening, for greasing the skillet and for frying

1. Combine the cake meal and the cold water in a small bowl, and beat with a fork until smooth. Add the eggs and salt, and mix thoroughly.

2. Lightly grease an 8-inch skillet, and heat it over medium-high heat. Pour in 2 tablespoons of the batter and quickly tilt the skillet, taking it off the heat momentarily, to make a very thin pancake. Cook the pancake on one side until it sets—it takes only a few seconds—tipping the skillet in all directions so the batter spreads to fill the bottom. Slip the finished pancake onto a plate or paper towel. Repeat. You probably will need to grease the pan lightly only after every third or fourth pancake, especially if you are using a nonstick pan. Continue until all the batter is used, piling the finished pancakes on top of each other. Set them aside to cool.

3. When the pancakes are cool enough to handle, take half of them and roll them up tightly. Slice into thin shreds with a sharp knife. Repeat with the remaining pancakes. Serve the "noodles" in soup.

Aunt Sally making Mama Hinda's Pesach noodles for the soup, 1985.

where's the soup?

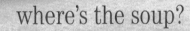

No, we didn't forget! You'll find chicken soup on page 63 and matzoh balls—both traditional and with shiitake mushrooms—on pages 65 and 66. For Passover, we serve them with mandlen (soup nuts).

In Yiddish the word *mandlen* means "almonds," and in Hebrew almonds are *shkedim*. Interestingly, both words also mean "tonsils," obviously referring more to form than to function. Mandlen was often used as generic word for nuts, not just for almonds in particular. No wonder we call those airy little balls "soup nuts."

beet eingemacht
(preserves)

from Rose Kancigor

Alas, Barry's Grandma Rose had only sons (whose wives weren't all that interested in her recipes, frankly), and no one wrote down her for- mula for this perennial Passover favorite. *Eingemacht* loosely means "worked in" in Yiddish (see Esrog Eingemacht, page 119), and this beet concoction was used like a jam and spread on matzoh through- out the holiday week. I consulted *bubbes* from coast to coast and experimented with different versions, trying to re-create the chunky texture and sweet, slightly tart flavor my then ninety-two-year-old father- in-law remembered. (Between this and Grandma Rose's blueberry varenikas, my kitchen tile needs regrouting!)

After much consultation with Pop in Florida, who was only too delighted to receive my FedExed samples, we settled on this adaptation of a recipe shared by my friend Diane Sachs. Her husband, Cole, says his grandmother, Ettie Hurvitz, in Rochester, New York, made it every Pesach in huge quantities so she could mail jars of the stuff to relatives. He remembers one Pesach in the 1950s when she mailed some to his mother, Elsie Sachs, in Yonkers, and the jar broke in the postman's bag. It was purple mail for everyone that day!

MAKES 6 CUPS   **P**

3 pounds fresh beets (weighed without
   greens)
3 cups sugar
Grated zest of 2 lemons
Juice of 2 lemons (6 tablespoons)
1/2 teaspoon kosher (coarse) salt
1 1/2 cups (6 ounces) slivered almonds
1/2 teaspoon ground ginger, or more to taste

1. Preheat the oven to 400°F.

russel borscht
from Hinda Rabinowitz

When the children were little, Mama Hinda used to make russel (fermented beet juice) for her borscht. She'd start weeks before Passover, and when she was done, she had a clear, bright red liquid that smelled like wine. Then when she wanted to make borscht, she would go down to the basement and ladle out some russel to use as a base, adding fresh beets and sugar. Aunt Sally didn't have a recipe, but she remembered the process. **P**

"You scrub some beets and peel them and cut them into quarters. Put them in a large jug—it was like pottery—with water almost to the top. Put the top back on the jug on an angle—you leave a little opening—and cover it with a clean cloth. In about ten days, there will be a white foam on the top. You skim it off carefully and stir it all up. Put the cover back on and leave it there for two or three weeks. It ferments like that. By Pesach it is sour, so you don't need lemons for the borscht."

—SALLY BOWER

2. Wrap each beet in aluminum foil and roast them until tender, about 1 hour. Set them aside to cool.

3. When the beets are cool enough to handle, peel and finely chop them. Place the chopped beets in a large pot and add the sugar, lemon zest, lemon juice, salt, and 3 cups water. Bring to a boil. Boil moderately (not a rolling boil, but more than a simmer), uncovered, stirring occasionally, for 1 hour. The mixture should still be somewhat soupy.

4. Add the almonds and boil gently, stirring often, until thick, 1 hour. (If the mixture starts to get too thick at any point, add boiling water, 1/4 cup at a time, and continue cooking, covered. If it seems too soupy, just cook it a little longer, uncovered.) Stir in the ginger. Let the mixture cool.

5. Spoon the Beet Eingemacht into clean glass jars, seal, and store in the refrigerator for up to 1 month or in the freezer for up to 6 months.

Note: I must admit to taking one liberty: Every recipe I looked at called for peeling raw beets, then slicing or chopping them. What a job! I didn't want to do that, and I figured you wouldn't want to either. Roasting makes the skins peel off easily, not to mention what it does for the flavor. (Roast some extra for your salad and see!) Then chopping is mere child's play.

Barry's Grandma Rose and Grandpa Ben, 1950s.

my mom's killer brisket
with tsimmes

from Lillian Bart

It's Passover again as we make our annual trek to Brad and Tracey's for their beautiful Seder. Airport security is *farklempt*. Setting off the metal detectors is my Apple Matzoh Schalat (page 556) in Mama Hinda's metal pan. Nestled between the toys for Samantha and Blake are tins of sweets. My mother is shlepping two huge jars of frozen chicken soup (page 63), a tray of matzoh balls (page 65), and of course her killer tsimmes. Cheesh! You'd think those airport officials never saw tsimmes before!

The Yiddish word *tsimmes* means "a big fuss," so little wonder this dish took that name. Tsimmes is my mother's favorite childhood dish, and every time she makes it, she makes more of a *tsimmes* out of it. It's never the same way twice, of course. Her latest twist is briefly broiling the sweet potatoes and carrots to crisp them up. Sometimes she adds pineapple chunks, sometimes parsnips. But always she's real heavy on the prunes, not only because she loves them but because she claims she can still hear Aunt Estelle complaining that Mama Hinda never added enough of them. Apricots or any other dried fruit can be substituted if you feel no similar compunction to make things up to Aunt Estelle. **SERVES 8 TO 10** Ⓜ

1 tablespoon vegetable oil

4 to 5 pounds first-cut beef brisket

2 large onions, sliced

2 cloves garlic, crushed

^{1}/2 cup sweet red wine or water

1 cup pineapple or orange juice

1 package dehydrated onion soup mix

2 to 3 teaspoons kosher (coarse) salt,
   or to taste

^{1}/2 teaspoon freshly ground black pepper

^{1}/4 cup honey

^{1}/4 cup plus 2 tablespoons (packed) light
   brown sugar

1 tablespoon fresh lemon juice

1^1/2 teaspoons grated fresh ginger

1^1/2 teaspoons ground cinnamon

Ground nutmeg to taste

3 cups (1^1/2 pounds) pitted prunes,
   dried apricots, or a combination

^{1}/2 cup raisins

3 pounds sweet potatoes (see box, page 285),
   cut into 1^1/2-inch chunks

1^1/2 pounds carrots,
   cut into ^{1}/2-inch-thick slices

Paprika, for sprinkling

1. The day before serving, heat the oil in a Dutch oven or other large, heavy pot over medium-high heat. Add the

> *I remember the Passover Seders in Mama and Papa's tiny apartment upstairs from Aunt Lil and Uncle Jan in their two-family house in Belle Harbor. We were hungry and Papa would let us eat while he finished the service. If you wanted salt, Mama would put kosher salt in a little dish near your plate. Papa never could keep a secret and always showed us where he hid the matzoh.*
> **—MARVIN ROBBINS**

meat (fat side down first), and brown it well on all sides, about 5 minutes per side. Transfer the meat to a plate.

2. Add the onions to the pot and cook, stirring often, until they are soft and brown, about 8 minutes. Add the garlic and cook for 1 minute more. Then stir in 3 cups water and the wine, juice, onion soup mix, 1 teaspoon of the salt, and ^{1}/4 teaspoon of the pepper. Bring to a boil. Reduce the heat, return the meat to the pot, cover, and simmer until a fork can pierce the meat but it is not quite

Okay, I lied. That's my brother, Gary (left), at Papa Harry's Seder, about 1960, so obviously my parents must have left him home! (Don't worry—years of therapy later, he's just fine.)

done, 1³/4 to 2¹/4 hours, depending on the thickness of the meat.

3. Remove the pot from the heat and allow it to cool somewhat. Then remove the meat and slice off all visible fat. Transfer the meat, with the gravy, to a large bowl or container and refrigerate it, covered, overnight.

4. The next day, preheat the oven to 350°F.

5. Remove the bowl from the refrigerator and skim off the congealed fat. Remove the meat and cut it into ¹/4- to ³/8-inch-thick slices. Set it aside.

6. Transfer the gravy to a Dutch oven or other large, heavy, ovenproof pot and bring it to a boil. Turn off the heat and stir in the honey, brown sugar, lemon juice, ginger, cinnamon, nutmeg, 1 teaspoon of the salt, or more to taste, and remaining ¹/4 teaspoon pepper. Return the sliced meat to the pot. Add the prunes and raisins. Arrange the sweet potatoes and carrots on top. Baste the meat and vegetables with the sauce and bring back to a boil.

7. Transfer the pot to the oven and bake, covered, for 30 minutes, basting after 15 minutes.

8. Sprinkle the potatoes and carrots lightly with paprika, and continue baking, uncovered this time, basting every 15 minutes, until the carrots and potatoes are very tender, about 30 minutes. If you like (and if your oven has a broiling mode), turn the oven setting to broil, place the pot on the lowest rack, and broil the potatoes and carrots briefly until crisp.

9. Serve hot.

sephardic chicken
with olives and honey

from Judy Bart Kancigor

This recipe was inspired by the Jaffa Orange–Ginger Chicken with Baharat in Joan Nathan's *Foods of Israel Today*, and it has become one of the most popular dishes in my cooking classes. Freshly ground spices add a heady aroma and exotic flavor. (Use a coffee grinder to do this. Just don't grind coffee in it.) Joan uses baharat, an Israeli spice mixture, during the year, which you can find in a Middle Eastern market, and you can use it too. But I love this Moroccan spice combination, which flavors the Spicy Apricot Lamb Shanks. **SERVES 4 TO 5** Ⓜ

different vibes for different tribes

Kitniyot refers to legumes (including beans, peas, soybeans, lentils, and peanuts), rice, corn, string beans, mustard, seeds (including sesame, poppy, coriander, and fennel), as well as certain spices, such as cumin. While observant Ashkenazi Jews do not eat them during Passover, Sephardim never adopted this prohibition and might enjoy this chicken dish for the holiday. Ashkenazim, however, would consider some of the spices in the Moroccan Spice Mix *kitniyot*.

FOR THE SAUTEED VEGETABLES

2 tablespoons olive oil

6 to 8 ounces shallots, chopped

2 cloves garlic, finely chopped

8 ounces white mushrooms, sliced

FOR THE CHICKEN

4 to 5 large boneless, skinless chicken
   breast halves

$^{1}/_{2}$ cup matzoh cake meal

1 tablespoon Moroccan Spice Mix
   (page 167)

1 teaspoon salt

1 teaspoon paprika

2 tablespoons olive oil, or more as needed

1 tablespoon nondairy margarine

FOR THE SAUCE

$1^{1}/_{4}$ cups homemade chicken stock
   (page 63) or low-sodium canned broth

$^{1}/_{2}$ cup dry white wine

2 tablespoons honey

1 tablespoon grated fresh ginger

2 tablespoons orange liqueur

2 tablespoons fresh lemon juice

Grated zest of 1 lemon

$^{1}/_{2}$ cup pitted small green olives

$^{1}/_{4}$ cup sliced oil-packed sun-dried tomatoes,
   drained

1 tablespoon capers, drained (optional)

1 teaspoon Moroccan Spice Mix (page 167),
   or to taste

Salt and freshly ground black pepper,
   to taste

1. Prepare the vegetables: Heat the olive oil in a large, heavy frying pan over medium heat. Add the shallots and cook, stirring often, until they are soft but not browned, about 3 minutes. Add the garlic and continue cooking, stirring constantly, for 1 minute more. Then add the mushrooms and cook, stirring often, until they are soft and reduced in size, about 5 minutes. Transfer the sautéed vegetables to a bowl and set it aside. No need to wash the pan.

2. Prepare the chicken: Pound the chicken breasts lightly in the thickest part, just to even them out somewhat. (I like to use a resealable plastic bag for this, but do as you wish.) Dry the chicken thoroughly with paper towels. On a dinner plate, combine the matzoh cake meal, Moroccan Spice Mix, salt, and paprika. Just before you cook it, coat the chicken thoroughly in the matzoh-spice mixture, shaking off the excess. Heat the oil and margarine in the same frying pan over medium-high heat. Add the chicken and sauté until browned, about 3 minutes. Turn the chicken over and brown the other side, about 2 minutes. Remove the chicken from the pan and set it aside. Drain any excess oil from the pan, being careful not to discard the brown bits.

3. Prepare the sauce: Add the chicken stock to the pan and bring it to a boil, scraping up the brown bits. Reduce the heat and add the sautéed vegetables, wine, honey, ginger, orange liqueur, lemon juice, and lemon zest. Bring to a boil. Reduce the heat and simmer, stirring occasionally, for about 10 minutes. Then add the olives, sun-dried tomatoes, capers, and Moroccan Spice Mix. Simmer for 5 minutes, stirring occasionally, for the flavors to blend. Add salt and pepper to taste.

4. Return the chicken to the pan, cover it with the sauce, and simmer, covered, for about 5 minutes. Turn the chicken over and continue simmering, covered, until it is cooked through, about 5 minutes more. Serve immediately.

Note: After Passover, 1 tablespoon light soy sauce can be added with the ginger.

mina de espinaka
(matzoh, spinach & cheese pie)

from Ketty Moreno

mina is a Sephardic layered savory pie. Ketty's Spinach and Cheese Frittata is so popular with her family that she created a mina for Passover, layering the filling between sheets of softened matzoh crowned with Cheddar cheese. This dish is lovely for a dairy lunch or brunch during the holiday week. **SERVES 8**　**D**

Vegetable cooking spray, for greasing the baking pan
5 boards matzoh
1 recipe Spinach and Cheese Frittata mixture (page 33), omitting the matzoh meal, uncooked
1 large egg, beaten
³/₄ cup grated Cheddar cheese

1. Preheat the oven to 350°F. Grease a 13 × 9-inch baking pan.

2. Soak the matzoh boards in cool water until it is flexible and thoroughly saturated, but not falling apart. If you can lift it easily, it's not soaked enough. Drain it on dish towels, covering the matzoh with more towels and squeezing gently to eliminate the moisture. Carefully transfer the moistened matzoh to the prepared baking pan, tearing it as necessary to line the bottom in a single layer. (The edges can overlap slightly.) Reserve the remaining matzoh.

3. Pour the frittata mixture over the matzoh, and top with another layer of soaked matzoh, overlapping the torn edges slightly (the matzoh will shrink somewhat during baking).

4. Brush the top generously with the beaten egg, sprinkle with the grated cheese, and bake on the center oven rack until the pie is set and golden, about 35 minutes. Cover the pan and allow the pie to rest for a few minutes. Then cut it into squares, and serve.

> *My daughter Julie was given an assignment in fifth grade to do a project using measurements. She decided to create a Passover cookbook, using eleven of my recipes. She helped prepare them all that year, using a grand total of fifty-two measurements. Although by now we know the recipes by heart, every year we bring it out, and that well-worn and well-loved cookbook always evokes memories of Passovers past. By the way, Julie got an A.*　**—BETH PINCUS**

elaine asa's spinach lasagna

from Lillian Bart

With the Seder dinners a beautiful memory, the six additional days of Passover would loom before us as arid as the Sinai itself if not for the creativity of Jewish cooks through the ages who have transformed that barren board into thousands of delicious permutations.

Our friend Elaine developed this recipe years ago, when three of her four children became vegetarians. For years she served a vegetarian Seder—she just had to get creative. (Now that the children are far away, she's back to brisket every year.) Elaine still serves this dish for Passover lunches, however, and when my mom was invited one year, of course she took the recipe.

SERVES 8   **D**

Vegetable cooking spray, for greasing the
*   baking pan*
2 boxes (10 ounces each) frozen chopped
*   spinach, thawed*
2 tablespoons butter
1 medium-size onion, chopped
5 boards matzoh
5 large eggs, separated
1 pint cottage cheese
1/4 cup sour cream
1/2 teaspoon plus a pinch of salt
8 ounces Cheddar or Monterey Jack cheese,
*   shredded (2 cups)*

1. Preheat the oven to 350°F. Grease a 13 × 9-inch nonreactive baking pan.

2. Drain the spinach very well. Then squeeze it in several changes of paper towels to remove as much liquid as possible. Break up the spinach with a fork.

3. Melt the butter in a medium-size skillet over medium heat. Add the onion and cook until soft and golden, about 7 minutes. Set aside.

4. Crumble the matzoh into a large bowl, add cold water to cover, and soak just until the matzoh is soft but not soggy. Drain the soaked matzoh thoroughly, wipe the bowl dry, and return the matzoh to the bowl. Add the spinach and sautéed onions, and combine well. Set the mixture aside.

5. Beat the egg yolks with a fork in a large bowl. Stir in the cottage cheese, sour cream, and the 1/2 teaspoon salt.

6. Beat the egg whites with an electric mixer on medium-high speed until foamy, about 30 seconds. Add the pinch of salt and beat until stiff peaks form, about 2 minutes total. Add the egg whites to the cottage cheese mixture in three additions, folding them in until incorporated after each addition.

7. Spread half the cottage cheese mixture in the prepared baking pan. Top with the spinach mixture, then half the shredded Cheddar. Spread the remaining cottage cheese mixture over that, and top with the remaining shredded Cheddar.

8. Bake on the center oven rack until set and golden, 40 to 45 minutes. Cut into squares and serve.

matzoh stuffing

from Barbara Musikar

Barry's distant cousin Barbara found us when researching our mutual Padwa family (Barry's Grandma Rose's *mishpucha*) on www.jewishgen. org. Through e-mails back and forth and shared research, we became pen pals (keyboard pals?) and finally met when I spoke at the National Jewish Genealogy Society conference in Washington, D.C. In a bizarre coincidence, guess who Barbara discovered was a witness to her relative's naturalization petition? Our Papa Harry!

Sorry, Aunties. Barbara's Matzoh Stuffing had yours beat by a mile. Comfort food in a casserole dish, it's springy and colorful, with cheerful flecks of orange and green. You can also bake it in individual muffin cups, if you wish. Of course you could stuff a chicken or turkey with it as well, although a *minhag* (custom) exists among certain observant Jewish communities not to roast anything on Passover except the shank bone and egg for the Seder plate. **SERVES 12** Ⓜ or Ⓟ

Nondairy margarine or vegetable cooking
    spray, for greasing the casserole
¹/₄ cup vegetable oil
2 tablespoons nondairy margarine,
    plus slivers for scattering on top
2 cups chopped onions

1 cup chopped celery
2 medium-size carrots,
    cut into ¹/₄-inch dice
10 boards matzoh
¹/₄ cup chopped flat-leaf parsley
1 cup homemade chicken stock
    (see page 63) or low-sodium
    boxed or canned chicken broth or
    vegetable stock
2 large eggs, lightly beaten
2 teaspoons salt, or more to taste
2 teaspoons good-quality paprika
1 teaspoon poultry seasoning
¹/₄ teaspoon freshly ground black pepper,
    or more to taste

1. Preheat the oven to 350°F. Grease a 2-quart casserole or 12 muffin cups.

2. Heat the oil and the 2 tablespoons margarine in a large skillet over medium-high heat. Add the onions, celery, and carrots, and cook, stirring often, until the onions are soft and translucent and the carrots are fork-tender, 10 to 12 minutes.

3. Meanwhile, crumble the matzoh into a large bowl, add cold water to cover, and soak a few seconds, just until it is soft but not soggy. Drain the soaked matzoh thoroughly, wipe the bowl dry, and return the matzoh to the bowl.

4. Add the sautéed vegetables to the softened matzoh. Stir in the parsley, chicken stock, eggs, 2 teaspoons salt, paprika, poultry seasoning, and ¹/₄ teaspoon pepper. Mix thoroughly, and add more salt and pepper to taste (see Note).

5. *To prepare a stuffing casserole,* transfer the mixture to the prepared

casserole dish, dot it lightly with thin slivers of margarine, and bake, uncovered, on the center oven rack until set and golden brown, 40 to 45 minutes.

To prepare stuffing muffins, place about ¹/₂ cup stuffing mixture in each prepared muffin cup. Dot them lightly with thin slivers of margarine, and bake on the center oven rack until set and golden brown, 20 to 25 minutes. Run a knife around each muffin if necessary, and remove them from the cups. Serve hot.

Note: Before tasting any mixture containing raw eggs, microwave a tablespoon or so until the egg is cooked, 5 to 15 seconds; then taste.

garden veggie matzoh schalat
(kugel)

from Judy Bart Kancigor

The word *schalat* derives from *cholent*, originally a pudding cooked like a kugel with the Sabbath stew, and is not even a poor relation of the "charlotte" pudding on fine French menus. This is another dish I created for my cooking classes, a savory version of the sweet Apple Matzoh Schalat (page 556) I've been making for years. **SERVES 16 TO 20** Ⓜ or Ⓟ

Olive oil, for greasing the baking sheet and baking pan

1 medium- to large-size eggplant, cut into ¹/₂-inch dice

3 bell peppers, different colors (I use red, yellow, and orange)

9 boards matzoh

¹/₄ cup olive oil

2 medium-size onions, chopped

1 to 1¹/₂ cups homemade chicken stock (page 63) or low-sodium boxed or canned chicken broth or vegetable stock

8 ounces white mushrooms, sliced

2 small jars marinated artichoke hearts, drained and sliced

1 box (10 ounces) frozen chopped spinach, thawed

8 leaves fresh sage, sliced and chopped

2 teaspoons fresh rosemary, minced

4 tablespoons (¹/₂ stick) nondairy margarine, melted and cooled

9 large eggs, separated

¹/₄ to ¹/₂ teaspoon ground nutmeg, preferably freshly grated

¹/₄ teaspoon red pepper flakes

1 to 3 teaspoons salt

Freshly ground black pepper, to taste

About 2 tablespoons nondairy margarine, cut into thin slivers

1. Preheat the oven to 375°F. Line a baking sheet with aluminum foil, and generously grease the foil.

2. Place the diced eggplant on the baking sheet and roast until it is starting to brown but still holds its shape, about 10 minutes. Set it aside.

3. Meanwhile, roast the peppers over a direct flame on top of the stove (or once the eggplant has finished cooking, in the oven with the temperature raised to 450°F, turning, until black all over, about 20 minutes). Place the blackened peppers in a paper or plastic bag, close the bag, and allow them to cool for about 15 minutes. When the peppers are cool, remove the black skin as well as the seeds and stems. Do not rinse them. Cut the peppers into $1/2$-inch pieces.

4. Meanwhile, crumble the matzoh into a very large bowl, add cold water to cover, and soak a few seconds, until the matzoh is soft but not soggy. Drain the soaked matzoh thoroughly, wipe the bowl dry, and return the matzoh to the bowl.

5. Heat the oil in a large skillet over medium heat. Add the onions and cook, stirring often, until soft, about 7 minutes. Add $1/2$ cup of the stock and cook the onions over high heat, stirring often, until the stock evaporates, about 10 minutes. Repeat this process twice more, using $1/2$ cup of the stock each time and scraping to release the browned bits, about 10 minutes total. Add the mushrooms and cook until their liquid has released and evaporated and they have reduced in size, about 5 minutes more. Stir in the artichokes and cook for 1 minute.

6. Add the sautéed vegetables to the soaked matzoh. Stir in the eggplant and roasted peppers.

7. Drain the spinach very well, and then squeeze it between paper towels to extract as much liquid as possible. Break up the spinach with a fork, and add it to the matzoh mixture. Stir in the sage, rosemary, and melted margarine. Mix well.

8. Beat the egg yolks with an electric mixer on medium-high speed until thick and lemon-colored, about 3 minutes. Blend in the nutmeg and red pepper flakes. Add this to the matzoh mixture.

9. Using a clean, dry bowl and beaters, beat the egg whites on medium-high speed until foamy, about 45 seconds. Add a pinch of the salt and beat until stiff peaks form, about 3 minutes total. Stir one fourth of the egg whites into the matzoh mixture to lighten it. Then add the remaining whites in three additions, folding them in until incorporated. Add the salt and pepper to taste (see Note).

10. Preheat the oven to 350°F degrees. Grease a 13×9-inch baking pan.

11. Pour the mixture into the prepared baking pan, and dot it lightly with thin slivers of margarine. Bake on the center oven rack until set and golden, 1 to $1^1/4$ hours.

12. Cut into squares and serve hot.

Note: Before tasting any mixture containing raw eggs, microwave a tablespoon or so until the egg is cooked, 5 to 15 seconds; then taste.

apple matzoh schalat
(kugel)

from Judy Bart Kancigor

I've been making this Passover schalat for as long as I can remember. I always baked it in a 13 × 9-inch pan, as I describe here. But several years ago Natalie Haughton, food editor of the *Los Angeles Daily News*, came to my home with a photographer to interview me for a Passover feature story. She suggested that I bake my schalat in a springform pan, and the result is amazing: Pineapple rings with strawberry centers encircle this fruity kugel, studded with blueberries and mandarin oranges for a rainbow of color too pretty to cut. If you want to try it, follow the instructions in the box on the facing page. **SERVES ABOUT 16**   **P** or **D**

Nondairy margarine or butter,
   for greasing the baking pan
1 cup (packed) dried apricots or
   golden raisins, or a combination
2 cans (20 ounces each) pineapple rings,
   drained, juice reserved
6 medium-size apples, peeled and
   thinly sliced
Juice of 1 lemon (about 3 tablespoons)
9 boards matzoh
9 large eggs, separated
1¹/₂ cups sugar

Grated zest of 1 lemon
1 tablespoon ground cinnamon,
   plus extra for sprinkling
1¹/₂ teaspoons vanilla
   (see box, page 564)
¹/₂ teaspoon salt
6 tablespoons (³/₄ stick) nondairy
   margarine or butter, melted
   and cooled
2 cups fresh or frozen strawberries
About 1 cup fresh or frozen blueberries
1 can (11 ounces) mandarin oranges
3 tablespoons nondairy margarine
   or butter, slivered

1. Preheat the oven to 350°F. Generously grease a 13 × 9-inch baking pan.

2. Snip the apricots to the size of raisins. (Kitchen shears work much better than a knife for this purpose.) Combine the snipped apricots and the reserved pineapple juice in a small bowl, and set it aside.

3. Toss the apple slices with the lemon juice in a bowl (to prevent browning), and set it aside.

4. Crumble the matzoh into a very large bowl, add cold water to cover, and soak a few seconds just to soften the matzoh. Drain the soaked matzoh thoroughly, wipe the bowl dry, and return the matzoh to the bowl.

5. Beat the egg yolks and ³/₄ cup of the sugar with an electric mixer on medium-high speed until thick and lemon-colored, about 3 minutes, scraping the bowl as necessary. Beat in the lemon zest, cinnamon, vanilla, and salt. Stir in the melted margarine.

6. Stir the egg yolk mixture into the soaked matzoh. Drain the apricots, and add

for a knock-their-socks-off schalat presentation

• ◆ ●

Instead of using the 13 x 9-inch baking pan, generously grease the bottom and sides of a 10-inch springform pan with shortening. (If you have only a 9-inch springform pan, you will have some batter left over, which you can bake separately in a small dish.) Dry the pineapple, berries, and mandarin oranges well with paper towels so they will stick. Press pineapple rings carefully onto the greased sides of the pan. Press the tips of some of the strawberries into the center of each pineapple ring, facing outward. Press mandarin oranges and blueberries artfully into the spaces between the pineapple rings. If any of the fruit refuses to stick, use a bit more shortening as "glue."

Slowly pour the matzoh mixture into the pan, being careful not to disturb the fruit sticking to the sides. Decorate the top with more fruit. Dot it with the slivers of margarine and sprinkle with cinnamon. Bake, uncovered, until the center is firm, 1¼ hours. Allow the schalat to rest, covered, for 10 minutes. Then carefully release the spring mechanism and slowly lift the sides away. Take bows!

Create your own knock-their-socks-off presentation of this matzoh schalat using a springform pan.

until soft peaks form. Add the remaining ¾ cup sugar a tablespoon at a time, beating for 10 seconds after each addition, until stiff peaks form, about 6 minutes total. Stir one fourth of the egg whites into the matzoh mixture to lighten it. Then add the remaining whites in three additions, folding them in until incorporated.

8. Pour the matzoh mixture into the prepared baking pan. Decorate the top with the pineapple rings, strawberries, blueberries, and mandarin oranges in a pretty design. Dot with the slivers of margarine, and sprinkle with cinnamon. Bake, uncovered, until firm, about 1 hour.

9. Cut into squares and serve hot.

apricot matzoh kugel

from Samra Robbins

Samra makes this kugel every Passover. What a hit! The caramelized farfel topping is so addictive that she always doubles it, she says, because the kids eat it like candy and she never has enough to put on the kugel. The topping also makes a great base for *Pesachdicke* granola. Just add raisins or other dried fruit and any nuts of your choice. **SERVES ABOUT 16**   D

them and the apples to the matzoh mixture. Combine well.

7. Using a clean, dry bowl and beaters, beat the egg whites on medium-high speed

FOR THE TOPPING

2 tablespoons butter

2 cups matzoh farfel

1/2 cup (packed) dark brown sugar

FOR THE KUGEL

Butter or vegetable cooking spray,
   for greasing the baking pan

3/4 cup raisins

2 cans (16 ounces each) apricot halves,
   drained, juice from 1 can reserved

3 cups matzoh farfel

5 large eggs

2 cups sour cream

8 tablespoons (1 stick) butter, melted
   and cooled

1/2 cup granulated sugar

1 medium-size apple, peeled and shredded

1. Prepare the topping: Melt the butter in a large skillet over medium heat. Add the farfel and the brown sugar and cook, stirring constantly, until the farfel caramelizes (gets brown and crunchy), 3 to 5 minutes. Set it aside to cool. (If you haven't doubled the topping recipe, have a fly swatter handy for sneaky fingers.)

2. Preheat the oven to 350°F. Grease a 13 × 9-inch baking pan.

3. Combine the raisins and the reserved apricot juice in a small bowl, and set it aside.

4. Place the farfel in a large bowl, add cold water to cover, and soak a few seconds just until the matzoh farfel is soft but not soggy. Drain the soaked farfel thoroughly, wipe the bowl dry, and return the farfel to the bowl. Set it aside.

5. Combine the eggs, sour cream, melted butter, and granulated sugar in a blender and whirl until smooth. Add the egg mixture to the soaked farfel. Stir in the shredded apple, along with the raisins and their soaking liquid. Pour this mixture into the prepared baking dish. Arrange the apricot halves on top, round side up. Sprinkle the topping evenly over the apricots, and bake on the center oven rack until set, about 1 hour.

6. Cut into squares and serve hot.

plan ahead

Schalats and kugels can be made a day or two ahead. On the day of serving, allow the dish to come to room temperature. Then heat it, covered, in a preheated 350°F oven until warm, 30 to 40 minutes.

oma's bubbelach

from Malka Engel-Padwa

Well, I don't know how old you have to be before you no longer qualify as a child (see box, facing page), but no matter—no one can resist these crispy potato puffs. Malka, related to Barry on Grandma Rose's side, is a food writer and cookbook author in Antwerp, Belgium, where she is a frequent contributor to the bi-monthly *Koopjes* magazine and others.

> *Bubbelach can be served alone, in soup, or as a snack, sprinkled with sugar. This was my mother-in-law's recipe, and on Pesach, Oma's Bubbelach are always a treat for the children.*
>
> **—MALKA ENGEL-PADWA**

This recipe is adapted from her cookbook, *Malka's Kosher Kitchen*, which contains recipes from her grandmothers, family, and friends. **MAKES ABOUT 32** **P**

2 pounds baking potatoes, cut into
    1¹/₂-inch cubes
1 teaspoon plus a pinch of kosher (coarse) salt
Pepper, preferably white, to taste
4 large eggs, separated
Vegetable oil, for frying

1. Bring a medium-size saucepan of lightly salted water to a boil. Add the potatoes and boil gently until they can be easily pierced with a skewer. (Don't use a fork, which will break them apart.) Drain the potatoes and put them through a ricer (preferred), or mash them by hand, in a bowl. Add the 1 teaspoon salt and the pepper, and stir in the egg yolks.

2. Beat the egg whites with an electric mixer on medium-high speed until foamy, about 30 seconds. Add the pinch of salt and beat until the whites form stiff peaks, about 1¹/₂ minutes total. Fold one fourth of the egg whites into the potato mixture to lighten it. Then fold in the remaining whites.

3. Pour oil to a depth of about 1 inch in a large skillet and heat it over medium-high heat. Drop the potato mixture by the rounded tablespoon into the hot oil (do not crowd the skillet). Fry on both sides until golden brown, 2 to 3 minutes per side. Drain the puffs on paper towels, and serve immediately.

passover bagels

from Sally Bower

For those who can't go even one week without cream cheese and lox, have a Passover bagel. Now there's an oxymoron for you. Reminds me of an e-mail I received from a reader commenting on a Passover story I wrote for *The Orange County Register* a few years back:

Aunt Sally in the Roaring Twenties.

> *Your mention of Passover bagels reminded me of my youth in the San Fernando Valley. Our local supermarket had a fresh bakery on site and always had challahs on Friday. It took three years before the bakers realized their annual mistake when just before Pesach each year they'd put up a sign reading: "Don't forget to order your Passover challah."* **—CHUCK ROSEN**

And, no, these bagels are not even remotely chewy—for that you *will* have to wait a week—but they'll hold up the cream cheese without crumbling like matzoh, and they do have a hole. **MAKES 18** 🅟

2¹/₂ *cups matzoh cake meal*

2 *tablespoons sugar*

2 *teaspoons potato starch*

1 *teaspoon salt*

1 *cup vegetable oil*

Parchment paper, vegetable oil, or vegetable cooking spray, for the baking sheet

1 *dozen large eggs*

1. Combine the cake meal, sugar, potato starch, and salt in the bowl of an electric mixer.

2. Combine the oil and 2 cups water in a small saucepan and bring to a boil. Pour the hot liquid over the cake meal mixture all at once. Stir to combine well, and set aside to cool.

3. Preheat the oven to 375°F. Grease a baking sheet, or better yet, line it with parchment paper.

4. After the mixture has cooled, beat in the eggs, a few at a time, with the electric mixer on medium speed, beating well and scraping the bowl occasionally. (You *can* do this with a wooden spoon, per Aunt Sally's directions, but using an electric mixer is much easier.)

5. Drop about ¹/₃ cup batter for each bagel onto the prepared baking sheet, spacing them about 1¹/₂ inches apart. Dip your finger in oil and form a 1-inch hole in the center of each one. (The hole will close somewhat during baking.) Bake on the center oven rack until golden brown, 50 to 55 minutes.

6. Remove the baking sheet from the oven and immediately poke the bagels with a skewer to allow steam to escape and the insides to dry. Transfer the bagels to a wire rack to cool.

7. Serve within a day, or wrap in plastic wrap and freeze. Reheat frozen bagels, uncovered, in a preheated 350°F oven until crisp, about 12 minutes.

matzoh meal rolls

from Hinda Rabinowitz

my mother remembers taking these muffins to school for lunch during Passover. Mama Hinda must have made hundreds for her seven hungry children.

These make great rolls too—a welcome change from matzoh, especially for the kids who'd rather take a sandwich to school for lunch. Fewer crumbs too. Janitors like that. **MAKES 8 SANDWICH ROLLS OR 16 DINNER ROLLS** 🅟

Papa Harry and Mama Hinda, Florida, 1946.

2 cups matzoh meal

1 tablespoon sugar

1 teaspoon salt

$^1/_2$ cup peanut oil, or 8 tablespoons (1 stick)
    nondairy margarine

Parchment paper, vegetable oil, or vegetable
    cooking spray, for the baking sheet

4 large eggs

1. Combine the matzoh meal, sugar, and salt in the bowl of an electric mixer.

2. Combine the oil with 1 cup water in a small saucepan, and bring to a boil. Pour the hot liquid over the matzoh meal mixture all at once. Set it aside to cool.

3. Preheat the oven to 375°F. Grease a baking sheet, or better yet, line it with parchment paper.

4. After the mixture has cooled, beat in the eggs, one at a time, with the electric mixer on medium speed, beating well and scraping the bowl after each addition.

5. With oiled hands, form each $^1/_3$ cup dough (for sandwich-size rolls) into a disk, flattening it slightly. Place them about $1^1/_2$ inches apart on the prepared baking sheet. (For dinner rolls, use about half as much dough.) Bake on the center oven rack until golden brown, 50 to 55 minutes.

6. Remove the baking sheet from the oven and immediately poke the rolls with a skewer to allow steam to escape and the insides to dry. Transfer the rolls to a wire rack to cool.

7. Use within a day, or wrap in plastic wrap and freeze. Reheat frozen rolls, uncovered, in a preheated 350°F oven until crisp, about 12 minutes.

passover fruity muffins

from Judy Bart Kancigor

שׁhen my boys were growing up, I used to make these every Passover as a healthy snack to tuck into a lunchbox or have with milk after school.

MAKES 3 DOZEN   P

Vegetable cooking spray,
    for greasing the muffin cups

1 cup mashed banana
    (from 2 large ripe bananas)

1 large apple, peeled and grated

1 large carrot, peeled and grated

$^1/_2$ cup apple juice

1 cup matzoh meal

1 cup raisins

1 cup pecan halves, chopped (optional)

$^2/_3$ cup sweetened flaked or shredded coconut

2 large eggs, beaten

$^1/_4$ teaspoon salt

" My mother [Irene] never kept cake in the house. For unexpected company, she would whip up matzoh meal pancakes, whether it was Passover or not. When [my husband] Peter brought me home from our first date, she served them, with a variety of jams, at midnight! Peter couldn't believe a table could be set up so quickly. Remember, my mother-in-law got raves for her beauty, not for being a domestic diva! "
—PHYLLIS EPSTEIN

1. Preheat the oven to 375°F. Grease 36 mini muffin cups.

2. Combine all the ingredients in a large bowl, and mix well. Fill the prepared muffin cups level with the top, and bake on the center oven rack until the muffins are puffed and golden brown, about 35 minutes. Let the muffins cool in the tin for 10 minutes. Then transfer them to a wire rack to cool completely before serving.

matzoh brei

from Lillian Bart

The world is divided into two camps: those who like their matzoh brei sweet and those who prefer it salty. I'm with Mom. We love it sweet. Until I married Barry, it never occurred to me that anyone would like it any other way. This recipe is a Passover breakfast staple. Want something really different? Try adding some leftover haroset for a special treat. **SERVES 1**   **D** or **P**

1 board matzoh

1 large egg

1 teaspoon sugar

$^1/_4$ teaspoon vanilla (see box, page 564)

Dash of ground cinnamon

About 2 tablespoons butter or
    nondairy margarine, for frying

Maple syrup, jam, or cinnamon-sugar
    (see Note, page 478), for serving

1. Crumble the matzoh into a small bowl, add cold water to cover, and let it soak a few seconds, just until the matzoh is soft but not soggy. Drain the soaked matzoh thoroughly, wipe the bowl dry, and return the matzoh to the bowl.

2. Beat the egg into the matzoh. Add the sugar, vanilla, and cinnamon.

3. Melt the butter in a medium-size frying pan over medium heat. When the foam has subsided, pour in the batter all at once. Spread it out with a fork, and cook until it is golden and set on one side, about 2 minutes. Turn it over and fry on the other side, about 2 minutes.

4. Serve with syrup, jam, or cinnamon-sugar.

Notes: You can even fry the Matzoh Brei using vegetable cooking spray instead of butter or margarine. (Yeah, right, diet during Passover. Ha!)

My favorite Passover story came several years ago from Gershon Padwa, Barry's distant cousin in Antwerp, Belgium, who then had nine children (at this writing there are 12), in an e-mail that began this way:

" Dear Judy –
I'm so sorry I haven't written in such a long time. My parents came to stay with us for Pesach and my in-laws too. We also had some cousins staying here with their children, but today everyone cleared out and I'm looking forward to a nice quiet evening with just the eleven of us. "

Salt-lovers: Replace the sugar, vanilla, and cinnamon with $1/2$ teaspoon salt. Sprinkle the fried pancake with additional salt, if desired (and Barry does!).

banana cheese chremslach
(fritters)

from Sylvia Robbins

Aunt Sylvia's antidote to the matzoh brei boredom blues were these crispy, delicious fritters, topped with a tiny dollop of sour cream and sprinkled with cinnamon-sugar. Jam, honey, or maple syrup would make equally great toppings. **SERVES 4 TO 6**　　　**D**

1 cup matzoh meal

1 cup milk

$1/2$ cup mashed banana (1 medium-size banana)

1 cup cottage cheese

1 teaspoon ground cinnamon

$1/2$ teaspoon salt

2 large eggs, lightly beaten

About 2 tablespoons butter, for frying

1. Place the matzoh meal in a large bowl and pour the milk over it. Stir, and allow to stand for 10 minutes. Then stir in the mashed banana, cottage cheese, cinnamon, and salt. Add the eggs and mix well.

2. Melt the butter in a large skillet over medium heat, and drop the batter by the tablespoon into the hot skillet. Fry until the fritters are crisp and brown on one side, about $2^{1}/_{2}$ minutes. Turn them over and fry on the other side, about 2 minutes.

3. Serve the chremslach immediately, or keep them warm in a preheated 200°F oven for up to 15 minutes.

Aunt Sylvia and Uncle Morris at my nephew Randy's Bar Mitzvah, 1983.

my best passover sponge cake

from Janice Einsbruch

What would Passover be without sponge cake? Whipped egg whites, trapping tiny air bubbles, expand to six or seven times their volume, creating an ethereal confection. Janice, cousin Bonnie and Jackie's cousin, has been making her version for decades. We like it topped with Aunt Sally's Lemon Fluff, but you can use a lemon glaze (page 406), or apricot-pineapple sauce (page 366), dust it with confectioners' sugar, or serve it unadorned. **SERVES 12**   **P** or **D**

9 large eggs, at room temperature, 7 separated
1¹/₂ cups sugar
¹/₂ cup matzoh cake meal

¹/₂ cup potato starch
Grated zest of 1 lemon or orange
Juice of 1 lemon, or 3 tablespoons orange juice
Pinch of salt
Lemon Fluff (recipe follows), for garnish
  (optional)

baking for passover

Challenge breeds creativity, and at no time of year is the challenge greater than at Passover, when for eight days (seven in Israel), Jews, forbidden to eat bread or other leaven, eat matzoh in remembrance of our ancestors' hasty departure from Egypt. And if cooking for Passover is a challenge, then creating Passover desserts is the decathlon.

Oh, to devise spectacular sweets without flour or leavening! For ingenious kosher cooks it's no problem! (Well, I can think of one problem—if you're allergic to eggs! And if you're allergic to eggs *and* nuts . . . you're in for a long week!)

Any lingering thoughts on the restrictions of Passover are quickly dispelled by dessert. The display following the Passover Seder is as elaborate as any you see all year—at least in my family. Cousins will try to outdo each other with their sponge cakes, tortes, pies, and bars, bringing a sweet ending to our sweet celebration.

While every year more and more kosher-for-Passover products are introduced for adding flavor and variety to desserts, several ingredients bear discussion:

VANILLA
Pure vanilla extract, made from grain alcohol, is not considered kosher for Passover (although the bean itself is), and the observant will not use it. In baking for Passover, you have several choices:

■ Kosher-for-Passover vanilla, which is not an extract, but rather artificial vanilla flavoring.

■ Vanilla sugar, a common ingredient in Europe but not as well known here, comes in little packets and is sugar that has been superinfused with the vanilla bean. Substitute 1 packet for each 1¹/₂ teaspoons vanilla extract; the small amount of sugar in it will not affect your recipe. You can find it in kosher markets, and I've even seen it in the Jewish food section in some supermarkets.

■ Vanilla sugar you make yourself: About 2 weeks before Passover, split 1 vanilla bean in half lengthwise and crosswise and bury the pieces in 2 cups sugar. Seal tightly and store it in a cool, dark place. Shake it occasionally. Replace the sugar as you use it. It will keep until next Pesach.

■ A kosher-for-Passover liqueur, such as Amaretto.

CONFECTIONERS' SUGAR
While kosher-for-Passover confectioners' sugar is available, it is expensive and easy enough to create yourself: To make your own, combine ¹/₂ cup minus 1¹/₂ teaspoons granulated sugar and 1¹/₂ teaspoons potato starch in a blender or mini food processor. Pulse until a fine powder is formed.

WRAP IT UP
For storing instructions, see page 375 for cakes and page 458 for cookies.

1. Preheat the oven to 350°F. Have ready an ungreased 10-inch tube pan with removable bottom.

2. Combine the 2 whole eggs and the 7 yolks in the bowl of an electric mixer and beat on medium-high speed. Gradually add the sugar and beat until light, about 4 minutes. Reduce the speed to low and add the cake meal and potato starch, followed by the zest and juice, and beat well to combine.

3. Using a clean, dry bowl and beaters, beat the egg whites on medium-high speed until foamy, about 45 seconds. Add the salt and continue beating until stiff peaks form, about 3 minutes total. Stir one fourth of the egg whites into the batter to lighten it. Then add the remaining whites in three additions, folding them in until incorporated.

4. Spoon the batter into the tube pan. Bake on the center oven rack until the cake springs back when lightly touched, 45 to 50 minutes.

5. Remove the pan from the oven and allow it to rest for 30 to 45 seconds. Then invert the pan on its little feet (if your tube pan has them) or over a soda or wine bottle (making sure it sits level), and set it aside until the cake is completely cool. Then run a knife around the center tube and the sides of the pan and lift the tube from the outer pan. Gently slide the knife between the bottom of the cake and the pan, and lift the cake off the pan.

6. Serve topped with Lemon Fluff, if desired.

lemon fluff
from Sally Bower

A unt Sally always served Passover sponge cake with a healthy dollop of her Lemon Fluff. You can use it as a refreshing topping for fresh berries—swirled in individual goblets, topped with a sprig of mint perhaps, or in your loveliest crystal bowl. **MAKES ABOUT 3 CUPS**　**P** or **D**

Yolks of 5 large eggs
1 cup plus 2 tablespoons sugar
Juice of 2 lemons (6 tablespoons)
Grated zest of 2 lemons (2 tablespoons)
1 cup nondairy whipping cream or heavy
　(whipping) cream

1. Combine the egg yolks, the 1 cup sugar, the lemon juice, and the lemon zest in a double boiler set over simmering water and cook, whisking constantly, until quite thick, 15 to 20 minutes. Transfer the mixture to a small bowl and set it aside to cool. (Do not refrigerate it.)

2. When the lemon mixture is cool, whip the cream with the remaining 2 tablespoons sugar, using an electric mixer on high speed, until it forms firm peaks, $1^{1}/_{4}$ minutes.

3. Whisk the cooled lemon custard. Stir one fourth of the whipped cream into the custard to lighten it. Then fold in the remaining whipped cream. Cover and refrigerate until serving time. The Lemon Fluff will keep for 1 day.

estelle's famous passover sponge cake

from Estelle Robbins

After my father died, my mom stayed in New York and worked side by side with Aunt Estelle in her dress-making business. It took me seven years to talk her into joining us in California, and when she finally did, Aunt Estelle was bereft. (Her sponge cake recipe sent by letter ended with: "I miss your mother very much," only hinting at the depth of her despair.)

Aunt Estelle was famous for her *Pesachdicke* sponge cake (nicknamed Aunt Estelle's Mile-High Sponge Cake by cousin Laura), which she made all year-round. The superinfusion of citrus is what her cake was known for.

SERVES 12   **P** or **D**

9 large eggs, separated, at room temperature

1¹/₄ cups sugar, sifted

Juice and grated zest of 1 lemon

Juice and grated zest of 1 orange

1¹/₂ tablespoons lemon extract

1 tablespoon orange extract

1 heaping cup (packed) Passover potato starch, sifted (see Note)

Sugar, for sprinkling (optional)

Strawberry Cream Filling (recipe follows; optional)

Chocolate Frosting (recipe follows; optional)

1. Preheat the oven to 325°F. Have ready an ungreased 10-inch tube pan with removable bottom.

2. Beat the egg yolks with an electric mixer on medium-high speed, very gradually adding 1 cup of the sugar until the mixture is very thick and very light yellow. Continue to beat until the sugar is completely dissolved. This may take 15 minutes or more. Scrape the bowl several times.

3. Meanwhile, combine the lemon and orange juices, zests, and extracts in a container with a spout, and set it aside.

4. Reduce the mixer speed to low and add the potato starch in three additions, alternating with the juice mixture in two additions, beginning and ending with the potato starch.

5. Using a clean, dry bowl and beaters, beat the egg whites on medium-high speed until soft peaks form. Add the remaining ¹/₄ cup sugar, a tablespoon at a time, beating for 10 seconds after each addition, until stiff peaks form, about 4 minutes total. Stir one fourth of the egg whites into the batter to lighten it. Then add the remaining whites in three additions, folding them in until incorporated.

6. Transfer the batter to the tube pan. If you want a crusty top, sprinkle a little sugar over the batter. (Eliminate this step if you prefer a soft top.) Bake on the center oven rack until the cake springs back when lightly touched, about 1 hour and 10 minutes.

7. Remove the pan from the oven and allow it to rest for 30 to 45 seconds. Then invert the pan on its little feet (if your tube pan has them) or over a soda or wine bottle

(making sure it sits level), and set it aside until it is completely cool.

8. Run a knife around the center tube and the side of the pan, and lift the tube from the outer pan. Gently slide the knife between the bottom of the cake and the pan, and lift the cake off the pan. If desired, split the cake into two layers, fill it with Strawberry Cream Filling, and/or top it with Chocolate Frosting.

Note: Some Orthodox communities observe the custom of not using matzoh meal, which when moistened, might become a leavener. They would bake this sponge cake, which calls for potato starch rather than the usual matzoh cake meal and potato starch mixture.

strawberry cream filling

I f life gives you lemons, make lemonade. If your sponge cake isn't a mile high, cut it in half and fill it! **P** or **D**

1 pint fresh strawberries, hulled,
    lightly rinsed, drained, and dried
1 cup nondairy whipping cream or
    heavy (whipping) cream
2 tablespoons confectioners' sugar
    (see box, page 564)

1. Using a serrated knife, cut the cooled cake in half horizontally.

2. Whip the cream and sugar in a chilled bowl until it holds stiff peaks, about 4 minutes, and spread it over the bottom layer. Cover with strawberries, reserving some for garnish. Cover with the top half of the cake and garnish with the reserved berries.

chocolate frosting

MAKES 1¼ CUPS　　**P** or **D**

1 cup semisweet chocolate chips
¼ cup nondairy whipping cream or
    heavy (whipping) cream
1 tablespoon nondairy margarine or butter
¼ cup slivered almonds, toasted
    (see box, page 17)

1. Combine the chocolate chips, whipping cream, and margarine in a 2-cup

> *When I was growing up, our Seders were more about the food than the ceremony. My mother was a spectacular cook, and the highlight of the evening was her incredible golden chicken soup with matzoh balls that were lighter than air. One year when we were very young we were invited to have Seder with friends. The ceremony seemed to go on forever, and we were starved. When the chicken soup was finally served, to us it looked like water. When we got home my mother said, 'It looked like the chicken ran through the soup!' I never forgot that crack.*
>
> **—NANCY GIMPEL SILBERMAN**

microwave-safe measuring cup or bowl. Heat in the microwave in 30-second bursts at 50% power, stirring until the chocolate is melted and the mixture is smooth. (Alternatively, heat the ingredients in a double boiler set over simmering water.)

2. Drizzle the warm glaze over the cake, allowing some to run down the center and the sides. Sprinkle the toasted almonds over the top of the cake. Refrigerate the cake for about 30 minutes, uncovered, to allow the glaze to set completely. Then slice the cake with a serrated knife.

> Passover was magical not only for the cooking, but also for the tall tales. One year when I was in grade school, Uncle Al came from Atlanta to Aunt Estelle's and Uncle Willy's for Passover. He promised [my brother] Barry and me a submarine. This prize was even better than the silver dollars we collected when we found the afikomen and the loving gazes we received for reciting the Four Questions in Hebrew. But the best prize of all was Uncle Al's check for $1 million signed 'Al the Great.' **—LAURA SELIGMAN**

Uncle Al, the kiddies' pal, with Aunt Shirley, 1950s.

passover banana sponge cake

from Barbara Musikar

SpongeBob meets Chiquita Banana: a marriage made in heaven. Here's a sponge cake that is dense and moist—delicious plain, or sliced in half and filled with banana slices and sweetened whipped cream. **SERVES 12** **P**

3/4 cup matzoh cake meal

1/4 cup potato starch

8 large eggs, separated

1 1/2 cups sugar, sifted

2 teaspoons grated lemon or orange zest

3 tablespoons fresh lemon or orange juice

1 cup mashed banana (from 2 large, very ripe bananas)

1 cup finely chopped pecans

1/4 teaspoon salt

1. Preheat the oven to 325°F. Have ready an ungreased 10-inch tube pan with removable bottom.

2. Sift the cake meal and potato starch together three times into a bowl, and set it aside.

3. Beat the egg yolks with an electric mixer on medium-high speed. Gradually add the sugar and beat until thick and lemon colored, about 5 minutes. Add the zest and juice, followed by the mashed bananas and nuts,

Aunt Sally holding my brother, Gary, and me, with cousin Marilyn (standing), 1946.

grandma sally's passover chocolate nut cake

from Laura Seligman

Cousins: Those of us who began married life in Aunt Sally's furnished basement apartment (and didn't we all?) will remember that we needed no calendar to tell us that Passover was coming. The sound from upstairs of Uncle Lou cracking walnuts for Aunt Sally's Passover Chocolate Nut Cake was a dead giveaway. She always made several for her huge Seder crowds and for noshing all week.

SERVES 8 TO 10　　　**P** or **D**

¹/₄ cup matzoh cake meal, plus extra for
　　dusting the tube pan
2 tablespoons potato starch
2 tablespoons nondairy margarine or
　　unsalted butter, at room temperature,
　　plus extra for greasing the tube pan
³/₄ cup sugar
8 large eggs, separated
Juice and grated zest of ¹/₂ lemon
Pinch of salt
2 cups (8 ounces) walnut halves or pieces,
　　finely chopped
¹/₂ cup semisweet chocolate chips,
　　ground
Chocolate Glaze (recipe follows; optional)

and beat until well combined. Reduce the speed to low and add the cake meal mixture just until incorporated.

4. Using a clean, dry bowl and beaters, beat the egg whites on medium-high speed until foamy, about 45 seconds. Add the salt and beat until stiff peaks form, about 3 minutes total. Stir one fourth of the egg whites into the batter to lighten it. Then add the remaining whites in three additions, folding them in until incorporated.

5. Scrape the batter into the tube pan, and bake on the center oven rack until the cake is golden brown, the top springs back when touched, and a cake tester comes out clean, 60 to 70 minutes. Remove the pan from the oven and allow the cake to rest for 30 to 45 seconds. Then invert the pan on its little feet (if your tube pan has them) or over a soda or wine bottle (making sure it sits level), and set it aside until the cake is completely cool.

6. Run a knife around the center tube and the side of the pan, and lift the tube from the outer pan. Gently slide the knife between the bottom of the cake and the pan, and lift the cake off the pan. Cut into slices and serve.

> **Every year before Passover I would call Grandma Sally in Florida to go over her special recipes. Having grown up with this cake since I was born, I knew that this taste of the Old World is delicious and moist and quite dense. (Just don't serve it next to Aunt Estelle's mile-high sponge cake!) She made it for so many years that she knew its ways intimately and reassured me every time I called until I no longer had to ask, but I loved to call her anyway to consult with her about my menu. She was an impresario in the kitchen: confident, directive, and no-nonsense. What a TV personality she might have been!**
>
> **—LAURA SELIGMAN**

1. Preheat the oven to 325°F. Lightly grease a 10-inch tube pan, dust it with matzoh cake meal, and tap out the excess.

2. Sift the cake meal and potato starch together into a small bowl, and set it aside.

3. Beat the margarine with an electric mixer on medium-high speed and gradually add $1/2$ cup of the sugar, scraping the bowl several times, until incorporated, about 2 minutes. Beat in the egg yolks, one at a time, scraping the bowl frequently, until smooth and light, about 3 minutes. Then beat in the lemon juice and zest. Reduce the speed to low and add the cake meal mixture.

4. Using a clean, dry bowl and beaters, beat the egg whites on medium-high speed until foamy, about 45 seconds. Add the salt and beat until soft peaks form. Add the remaining $1/4$ cup sugar, a tablespoon at a time, beating for 10 seconds after each addition. Continue beating until stiff peaks form, about 6 minutes total. Stir one fourth of the egg whites into the batter to lighten it. Then add the remaining whites in three additions, folding them in until incorporated. Fold in the walnuts and ground chocolate chips.

5. Scrape the batter into the prepared tube pan and bake on the center oven rack until a cake tester inserted in the center comes out clean, 60 to 65 minutes. The cake will be pale in color and just beginning to brown around the edges. Let the cake cool completely in the pan set on a wire rack. (Do not invert it.)

6. Run a knife around the center tube and the side of the pan, and lift the tube from the outer pan. Gently slide the knife between the bottom of the cake and the pan, and lift the cake off the pan.

7. Glaze the cooled cake, if you like: Place a sheet of waxed paper under a wire rack to catch the spills, and set the cake on the rack. Drizzle the glaze over the cake, allowing some to run down the center and the sides. Refrigerate, uncovered, until the glaze sets, about 30 minutes, then cut into slices and serve.

chocolate glaze

While neither Aunt Sally nor Laura ever adorned this cake, I've taken the liberty of suggesting this simple glaze. Make it right before glazing the cake.

MAKES ABOUT $1/2$ CUP   **P** or **D**

2 ounces semisweet chocolate

2 tablespoons nondairy margarine or
unsalted butter

Combine the chocolate and margarine in a microwavable bowl and microwave with 30-second bursts at 50% power until barely melted. (Or melt them in a double boiler set over simmering water.) Stir to finish the melting, and use immediately.

mama hinda's passover nut cake

from Sally Bower

This was the very first recipe I tested for my cookbook. My mother the sous-chef was on hand in what would become over the next few years her classic pose: chopping nuts, squeezing lemons, and cleaning behind me as I baked. My grandmother, Mama Hinda, died in 1975 at the age of ninety-one. Who knows when she had last baked her Passover Nut Cake? Yet I vividly remembered that moist, nutty cake. I could almost smell it and taste it after all those years.

I took the cake out of the oven, snipped off an edge, and said, "Mom, is this it?" pushing the cake into her mouth. For the

first time in her life my mother was speechless. Her eyes became saucers and filled with tears. No words were necessary. Thank you, Aunt Sally, for recording Mama's recipes in that notebook of yours. **SERVES 14 TO 16**　　　　　**P**

1 cup matzoh cake meal

1/2 cup potato starch

12 eggs, separated

2 cups sugar

1 cup vegetable oil

Juice and grated zest of 1 lemon

1/4 cup seltzer

1 cup chopped walnuts
(not too finely chopped)

1. Preheat the oven to 325°F. Have ready an ungreased 10-inch tube pan with a removable bottom.

2. Sift the cake meal and potato starch together into a bowl, and set it aside.

3. Beat the egg yolks with an electric mixer on medium-high speed until light, gradually adding 1 cup of the sugar. Beat until the mixture is thick and lemon-colored, 5 to 6 minutes. Reduce the speed to medium-low and gradually add the oil, lemon juice, lemon zest, and seltzer. Gradually blend in the cake meal mixture. Stir in the nuts.

4. Using a clean, dry bowl and beaters, beat the egg whites with an electric mixer on medium speed until soft peaks form. Raise the speed to medium-high and add the remaining 1 cup sugar, 1 tablespoon at a time, beating for 10 seconds after each addition, until stiff peaks form, about 9 minutes total. Stir one fourth of the egg whites into

the batter to lighten it. Then add the remaining whites in three additions, folding them in until incorporated.

5. Scrape the batter into the tube pan, and bake on the center oven rack until the cake is golden brown, the top springs back when touched, and a cake tester comes out clean, about $1^1/_2$ hours.

6. Remove the pan from the oven and allow the cake to rest for 30 to 45 seconds. Then invert the pan on its little feet (if your tube pan has them) or over a soda or wine bottle (making sure it sits level), and set it aside until the cake is completely cool.

7. Run a knife around the center tube and the sides of the pan, and lift the tube from the outer pan. Gently slide the knife between the bottom of the cake and the pan, and lift the cake off the pan. Cut into slices and serve.

Passover 1946. My mom, Lillian (left), pregnant with my brother, Gary, Mama Hinda, Papa Harry, Uncle Lou Robbins, and Aunt Hilda, pregnant with Bonnie.

passover pecan date torte

from Sally Bower

Dates and shredded apple make for a dense, moist cake. Dust it with confectioners' sugar for a regal look. Or top it with fresh strawberries, for a crowning touch. **SERVES 12 TO 14** **P**

1$^1/_3$ cups matzoh cake meal

2 tablespoons unsweetened
   cocoa powder

$^1/_2$ teaspoon ground cinnamon

$^1/_4$ teaspoon ground cloves

$^1/_4$ teaspoon ground allspice

Juice and grated zest of 1 lemon

Juice and grated zest of 1 orange

8 large eggs, separated

1$^3/_4$ cups plus 2 tablespoons sugar

25 pitted dried dates (6$^1/_2$ ounces),
   diced (see Note)

$^1/_2$ cup toasted chopped pecans
   (see box, page 17)

1 medium-size apple, peeled, cored, and
   finely chopped

Confectioners' sugar (see box, page 564),
   for dusting

1. Preheat the oven to 350°F. Line the bottom of a 9-inch springform pan with parchment paper.

2. Sift the cake meal, cocoa powder, cinnamon, cloves, and allspice together into a bowl. Set it aside.

3. Measure the lemon juice (up to 3 tablespoons) into a measuring cup. Add enough orange juice to equal $^1/_3$ cup altogether. Reserve the remainder of the orange juice for another use. (Got vodka?) Set the juice mixture aside.

4. Beat the egg yolks and the $1^3/_4$ cups sugar with an electric mixer on medium-high speed until the mixture is thick and pale yellow, 2 to 3 minutes. Beat in the lemon and orange zests. Reduce the speed to low and add the cake meal mixture in three additions, alternating with the juice in two additions, beginning and ending with the cake meal. Stir in the dates, pecans, and apples.

5. Using a clean, dry bowl and beaters, beat the egg whites on medium-high speed until soft peaks form. Add the remaining 2 tablespoons sugar, a tablespoon at a time, beating for 10 seconds after each addition, until stiff peaks form, about $5^1/_2$ minutes total. Stir one fourth of the egg whites into the batter to lighten it. Then add the remaining whites in three additions, folding them in until incorporated.

6. Transfer the batter to the lined springform pan, and bake on the center oven rack until the cake is golden brown and a tester comes out clean, about 1 hour. Let the cake cool in the pan set on a wire rack.

7. When the cake is cool, run a knife around the sides of the pan and release the side. Turn the cake upside down onto a platter and remove the parchment paper. Sprinkle the top with confectioners' sugar, and serve.

Note: While I usually wax poetic over Medjool dates, they are too soft for this recipe. Use ordinary dates, such as Noor.

too good to call passover cake bête noire
(flourless chocolate cake)

from Vicki Miller

Vicki brought this cake to Brad and Tracey's first Passover in their new home, when Vicki and David were living in San Francisco. She got the recipe from her sister-in-law, Allison Miller Solomon, a chef and caterer, who found it in Lora Brody's first book, *Growing Up on the Chocolate Diet*. Bête Noire means "black beast" in French—but how did this creamy, truffle-like slice of chocoholic heaven come by such an ominous name? When I contacted Lora for permission to use the recipe, she explained that it took her hundreds of tries to perfect it. (Her son, who serves it in his restaurant, The Night Kitchen, in Montague, Massachusetts, calls it The Heart of Darkness!) With all due respect to Conrad, testing it might have been brutal for Lora, but it was worth it—this super-easy recipe certainly is no beast for *us* to prepare. (It is a beast to walk off, however.)

SERVES 6 TO 8   D

8 ounces unsweetened chocolate,
very coarsely chopped

4 ounces semisweet chocolate,
very coarsely chopped

1 1/3 cups sugar

1/2 pound (2 sticks) unsalted butter,
at room temperature, cut into
small pieces

5 extra-large eggs

1. Preheat the oven to 350°F. Butter a 9-inch round cake pan (not a springform), line it with a round of parchment paper, and butter the paper.

2. Place both chocolates in a food processor and process until finely chopped.

3. Combine the sugar and 1/2 cup water in a saucepan and bring to a rolling boil. Stir to dissolve the sugar.

4. With the processor on, add the boiling sugar syrup to the chocolate through the feed tube. Add the butter, piece by piece, followed by the eggs. Process only until very smooth.

5. Pour the mixture into the prepared cake pan. Set the pan in a larger baking pan, and fill the larger pan with warm water to reach halfway up the side of the cake pan. Carefully transfer the pan to the oven, and bake on the center oven rack until a sharp knife inserted in the center comes out clean, 25 to 30 minutes. Remove the cake pan from the larger pan and transfer it to a wire rack to cool for 10 minutes.

6. Run a sharp knife around the edge of the pan. Cover the pan with plastic wrap, and invert it onto a baking sheet. Lift off the pan and peel off the parchment paper. Then invert a cake plate over the cake, and invert the plate and baking sheet together, so the cake is now right side up. Remove the plastic wrap.

7. Serve the cake warm, cold, or at room temperature.

chocolate fudge pecan pie

from Ronna Wolf

This gooey, fudgy brownie pie, baked in a chocolate cookie crust, is Ronna and Marc's favorite—so much so that they enjoy it during the rest of the year as well. It's very rich and very sweet, so delicate portions will do you. You may want to pair this with vanilla ice cream or whipped cream (or nondairy substitutes with a meat meal) to offset the intensity of the chocolate. (Like that's a bad thing!)

SERVES 10 TO 16   **D** or **P**

FOR THE CRUST

Vegetable cooking spray, for greasing the pan

1/2 cup potato starch

1/4 cup matzoh cake meal

1/4 cup sugar

1/4 cup unsweetened cocoa powder

1/4 teaspoon salt

Yolk of 1 large egg

6 tablespoons (3/4 stick) cold unsalted butter
or nondairy margarine, cut into 12 pieces

FOR THE FILLING

8 tablespoons (1 stick) unsalted butter or
    nondairy margarine

1 cup semisweet chocolate chips

2 large eggs

1 cup sugar

3 tablespoons matzoh cake meal

3 tablespoons potato starch

1 teaspoon vanilla (see box, page 564)

Pinch of salt

1 cup pecan halves, toasted (see box, page 17)
    and finely chopped

1. Preheat the oven to 350°F. Spray a 9- or 10-inch deep-dish pie plate.

2. Prepare the crust: Combine the potato starch, cake meal, sugar, cocoa powder, and salt in a food processor and process to mix. Add the egg yolk and cold butter, and process until the crust comes together. Press the crust onto the bottom and up the sides (but not on the rim) of the prepared pie plate. Bake until the surface appears dry and barely set, about 8 minutes. Set the pie plate on a wire rack to cool.

3. Prepare the filling: Warm the butter and $1/2$ cup of the chocolate chips in a small saucepan over medium-low heat until barely melted. Remove the pan from the heat and stir to finish melting. Set the mixture aside to cool for 5 to 10 minutes.

4. Whisk the eggs in a medium-size bowl. Add the sugar, cake meal, potato starch, vanilla, and salt, and combine well. Blend in the cooled chocolate mixture. Stir in the remaining $1/2$ cup chocolate chips and $1/2$ cup of the pecans.

5. Spoon the filling into the pie shell and press the remaining pecans lightly onto the surface. Bake on the center oven rack until set, 30 to 35 minutes. Don't be alarmed if it cracks a bit and puffs. Let the pie cool completely on a wire rack.

6. Cut the pie into thin wedges and serve at room temperature or chilled. (To chill, refrigerate it, covered, for at least 2 hours.)

Aunt Estelle, Joyce, me,
Uncle Willy holding Marvin, and Aunt Sally, 1946.

" I was having Seder in my house for thirty-six people and needed a side dish to feed the crowd. My mother-in-law Estelle was no longer here to advise me, so I went rummaging through her notebook (an eclectic collection of various-sized food-stained pages) and found her recipe for Matzoh Farfel Pudding. In looking it over, I noticed that it listed salt and sugar, but no amounts. So I called Aunt Sally, who instructed me to read her the ingredients and she would tell me how much salt and sugar to use. When I got to the part that said 'twenty-nine eggs,' she stopped me. I thought she was going to laugh that the pudding required twenty-nine eggs. Instead she said, 'What, was she so cheap, she couldn't use thirty?' **—LESLIE ROBBINS** "

chocolate hazelnut caramel tart

from Heather Orlow-Choset

I adapted this luscious Passover dessert from a tart recipe that Heather learned at a cooking class at De Gustibus in New York with chef John Schenk. I like to use Aunt Sally's Passover Mandelbrot variation for the crust, but any store-bought crisp Passover cookies will do.

SERVES 12   **P** or **D**

FOR THE CRUST

About 8 ounces crisp Passover cookies, store-bought or homemade (see Variation, page 579), processed into crumbs (1³/₄ cups)

¹/₃ cup (5¹/₃ tablespoons) nondairy margarine or unsalted butter, melted

2 tablespoons granulated sugar

FOR THE CHOCOLATE FILLING

3 ounces semisweet or bittersweet chocolate, chopped

5 tablespoons nondairy margarine or unsalted butter

1 large egg

Yolk of 1 large egg

6 tablespoons granulated sugar

¹/₄ teaspoon vanilla (see box, page 564)

1 tablespoon matzoh cake meal

FOR THE CARAMEL FILLING

¹/₃ cup (5 tablespoons plus 1 teaspoon) nondairy margarine or unsalted butter

¹/₃ cup (packed) light brown sugar

FOR THE NUT LAYER

¹/₂ cup chopped toasted hazelnuts (see box, page 17)

1. Preheat the oven to 375°F.

2. Prepare the crust: Combine all the crust ingredients in a bowl and stir until well mixed. Press the mixture onto the bottom and side of a 9-inch tart pan with removable bottom (or on the bottom and up about 1 inch on the side of a 9-inch springform pan). Place the tart pan in the refrigerator.

3. Prepare the chocolate filling: Melt the chocolate and margarine in a small sauce-pan, or in a double boiler set over simmering water, stirring to combine. (Or melt them in a microwave oven with 30-second bursts at 50% power.) Set the mixture aside to cool.

4. Stir the egg, egg yolk, sugar, and vanilla together in a medium-size stainless-steel bowl, and place the bowl over a pan of simmering water. (Warning: Do not set the bowl over the simmering water before adding the eggs or your eggs will cook.) Heat the mixture, stirring it constantly with a heatproof spatula (not a whisk), just until the sugar dissolves. Try not to incorporate any air into the mixture.

5. Remove the egg mixture from the heat and fold in the chocolate mixture. Sift the cake meal over the mixture and fold it in. The chocolate filling can be made up to

4 hours ahead and kept, covered, at room temperature.

6. Prepare the caramel filling: Combine the margarine and brown sugar in a small saucepan and cook over low heat, stirring frequently, until the mixture is thick and syrupy and coats a spoon or whisk, 3 to 5 minutes. Pour the caramel evenly over the bottom crust.

7. Sprinkle the hazelnuts evenly over the caramel. Pour the chocolate filling carefully over the hazelnuts.

8. Bake on the center oven rack until the edges of the filling puff up, 12 to14 minutes. The center will be slightly soft. Let the tart cool on a wire rack for at least 15 minutes before removing it from the pan. Serve warm or at room temperature.

lemon angel pie

from Shirley Robbins

A unt Shirley served her Lemon Angel Pie often for company dinners or family get-togethers, but I think it also makes a great Passover dessert, with its meringue shell and tart lemon filling. **SERVES 8**   **D** or **P**

Aunt Shirley and Uncle Al Robbins, 1950s.

FOR THE FILLING

Yolks of 4 large eggs
¹/₂ cup sugar
2 teaspoons grated lemon zest
¹/₂ cup fresh lemon juice
Pinch of salt

FOR THE PIE SHELL

Solid vegetable shortening, for greasing the pie plate
Whites of 4 large eggs
¹/₄ teaspoon salt
1 teaspoon distilled white vinegar
1 cup sugar

FOR THE TOPPING

1 cup heavy (whipping) cream or nondairy whipping cream
2 teaspoons sugar

1. Prepare the filling: Beat the egg yolks and sugar with an electric mixer on medium-high speed until thick and lemon colored, about $1^{1}/2$ minutes. Beat in the lemon zest, juice, and salt. Transfer the mixture to a double boiler set over simmering water and cook, stirring, until thick, about 6 minutes. Remove it from the heat and set it aside to cool. Cover and refrigerate until ready to serve.

2. Preheat the oven to 275°F. Generously grease a 9- or 10-inch deep-dish pie plate.

3. Prepare the pie shell: Using a clean bowl and beaters, beat the egg whites with an electric mixer on medium-high speed until foamy, about 30 seconds. Add the salt and vinegar,

and beat until soft peaks form. Add the sugar, a tablespoon at a time, beating for 10 seconds after each addition, until stiff peaks form, about 3 minutes total.

4. Spread the meringue in the prepared pie plate, mounding it up the sides to form a shell. Bake on the center oven rack until the outside is dry, crisp, and barely beige, $1^{1}/4$ hours. Set it aside to cool on a wire rack. The crust may be made several hours in advance, but do not refrigerate.

5. Prepare the topping: When ready to serve, beat the cream and sugar with an electric mixer on medium speed until soft peaks form, 1 to 2 minutes.

6. Spread half the whipped cream over the meringue shell. Cover it with the filling, and then top with the remaining whipped cream.

> " When I was little and the kids at school told me there wasn't a tooth fairy, I consulted my grandma [Shirley], 'You would never lie to me, right?' She said, 'Never.' So I asked her, 'Who's the tooth fairy?' to which she responded, hardly coming up from her soup, 'Your mother and father.' My parents' jaws dropped. They couldn't believe she would give up something like that so easily.
>
> I miss my grandmother. She was one of my best friends. We had so much in common even though we were fifty years apart. Although she couldn't be at my wedding, I am so happy she got to meet Beca. She left me with one last piece of advice I will always cherish: 'Don't let this one get away!' **—HARRISON NATHAN** "

passover chocolate chip mandelbrot

from Estelle Robbins

my friend Dede Ginter tested this recipe for me, and her husband Ed's AK *(alter kocker)* Poker Club gave these light and crispy cookies eight thumbs up. If a recipe called for chocolate chips, you could always count on Aunt Estelle to use lots. She should have named these Passover Downfall. Enough said. Mom says "ditto." **MAKES ABOUT 6 DOZEN**   **D** or **P**

Parchment paper or vegetable cooking
   spray, for the baking sheet
$^{1}/2$ pound (2 sticks) unsalted butter or
   nondairy margarine, at room temperature
2 cups sugar
6 large eggs, at room temperature
1 teaspoon vanilla (see box, page 564)
$2^{1}/2$ cups matzoh cake meal
$^{3}/4$ cup potato starch
4 cups (two 12-ounce bags) semisweet
   chocolate chips

1. Preheat the oven to 350°F. Line a baking sheet with parchment paper or spray it.

2. Cream the butter and sugar with an electric mixer on medium speed until

> *About three years ago, when our golden retriever died, we contacted the Golden Retriever Rescue Society to select another. I saw a dog I loved, but Samra thought he was a little wild. I wanted to bring him home right away, but it was right before Pesach, and Samra said, 'How can you bring a new dog into the house now? We have all these people coming!' but I didn't listen, and [my daughter] Staci and I went and got him. This 'wild' dog stayed in his kennel with the door open all evening during the Seder, and about 11:15, we're all sitting in the living room, and in walks the dog with the afikomen in his mouth! We had no little kids at that time, and we had just forgotten about it. He never even took a bite. We knew we had picked the right dog.*
>
> **—RONALD ROBBINS**

smooth and creamy, about 2 minutes. Beat in the eggs, one at a time, scraping the bowl several times. Then beat in the vanilla. Reduce the speed to low, and add the cake meal and potato starch. Scrape the bowl, and blend just until thoroughly combined. Stir in the chocolate chips. (If the dough feels too sticky to handle even with floured hands, cover it with plastic wrap and refrigerate until it is stiff, 30 minutes to several hours.)

3. Divide the dough into 4 portions. Flour your hands with cake meal, and form each portion into a log the length of the baking sheet. Space the logs evenly on the prepared baking sheet, and bake on the center oven rack until they are golden and the tops are firm to the touch, 30 minutes.

4. Remove the baking sheet from the oven and let the logs cool for 3 minutes. Then, using a serrated knife, cut each log on the diagonal into $3/4$-inch-thick slices. Place the slices, cut side down, on the baking sheet and bake on the center oven rack until golden brown, 10 minutes. Turn the cookies onto the unbaked side. Turn the oven off and put the baking sheet back in the oven. Leave it there for 15 to 30 minutes for softer mandelbrot, longer for crisper ones. (I leave them in until the oven has cooled completely, as we like them really crisp.) Let the mandelbrot cool completely on the sheet set on a wire rack before serving.

Note: If your baking sheet is smaller than 17 × 12 inches, you will need to use two. Position the racks in the upper and lower thirds of the oven, and rotate the sheets from top to bottom and front to back halfway through the baking and crisping in Step 4.

Variation: For Aunt Sally's version, use 1 cup vegetable oil instead of the butter, and substitute 2 cups chopped walnuts or almonds for the chocolate chips. This is the version I use to whiz into crumbs for Passover cookie crusts (see page 576).

white chocolate sprinkle cookies

from Taylor Nagy

my cousin Marylyn Lamstein's first grandchild, Taylor, age nine at this writing, is very creative, especially in the kitchen. She came up with this cookie for Seder this year, a variation on mom Shari's chocolate chip theme, a favorite with all the kids. **MAKES ABOUT 4 DOZEN** **P** or **D**

FOR THE COOKIE

1 cup matzoh cake meal

3/4 cup potato starch

1 teaspoon salt

1/2 pound (2 sticks) nondairy margarine or unsalted butter, at room temperature

3/4 cup (packed) dark brown sugar

3/4 cup granulated sugar

2 large eggs, at room temperature

*2 teaspoons vanilla
  (see box, page 564)*

FOR THE GLAZE

6 ounces white chocolate

1/4 cup nondairy creamer or light cream

Sprinkles, for decorating the tops

1. Preheat the oven to 375°F. Line several baking sheets with parchment paper or leave them ungreased.

2. Sift the cake meal, potato starch, and salt together into a bowl, and set it aside.

3. Cream the margarine and both sugars with an electric mixer on medium speed, just to combine. Add the eggs, one at a time, beating well and scraping the bowl after each addition. Beat in the vanilla. Reduce the speed to low and gradually add the cake meal mixture, blending just until combined.

4. Drop rounded teaspoonfuls of the dough, spacing them 1 1/2 inches apart, on the baking sheets. Bake on the center oven rack until the cookies are brown around the edges, 10 to 12 minutes. The centers will be golden and appear soft. Allow the cookies to cool on the baking sheet set on a wire rack until they can be safely moved, about 30 seconds. Then transfer them to the rack to cool completely.

5. Prepare the glaze: Combine the white chocolate and the creamer in the top of a double boiler set over simmering water, and heat until the chocolate has melted; stir

until the mixture is smooth. Spread the glaze over the cooled cookies, and top with the sprinkles. Let the glaze set for 30 minutes before serving.

judy zeidler's farfel-nut thins

from Tracey Barrett

I met cookbook author Judy Zeidler eons ago, when she was giving a Passover demonstration at Bristol Farms in Pasadena. Her lacy almond cookies became my daughter-in-law Tracey's favorite. She made her giant version for their first Passover in their new home and has been doing so every year since. But she has to make lots, because somehow they tend to disappear before the Seder. Tracey says to save the crumbs to sprinkle over ice cream. **MAKES ABOUT 18**

P or **D**

³/₄ **cup sliced almonds**

1 tablespoon matzoh cake meal

1 cup matzoh farfel

1 cup sugar

¹/₄ **teaspoon salt**

**8 tablespoons (1 stick) nondairy margarine or
    unsalted butter, melted**

1 large egg, beaten

1 teaspoon vanilla (see box, page 564)

1. Position the racks in the middle and upper thirds of the oven, and preheat the oven to 325°F. Line two baking sheets with aluminum foil or parchment paper.

2. Combine ¹/₂ cup of the almonds and the matzoh cake meal in a food processor, and grind. Set the mixture aside.

3. Combine the matzoh farfel, sugar, and salt in a medium-size mixing bowl, and mix well. Pour the melted margarine over the farfel mixture, and blend until the sugar dissolves. Stir in the egg and vanilla, followed by the remaining ¹/₄ cup almonds and the ground almond mixture, and combine thoroughly.

4. Drop tablespoonfuls of the mixture onto the prepared baking sheets, 4 to 6 to a sheet. (These really spread.) Bake until golden brown, 8 to 10 minutes, rotating the pans top to bottom and front to back after 5 minutes. Slide or lift the foil off the sheets, and let the cookies cool completely. Reline the baking sheets and repeat with the remaining dough. When they have cooled completely, lift them from the foil and serve.

Samantha Kancigor helps with Passover baking.

spago pistachio macaroon sandwiches
with chocolate ganache

from Judy Bart Kancigor

Y ou haven't been to a Seder till you attend the one at Spago—Wolfgang Puck's glitzy Beverly Hills hangout for the rich and famous—held each year to benefit Mazon, the international hunger relief organization. Family and friends joined me a few years ago when I covered the event for the *Jewish Journal of Greater Los Angeles*. (Some journalists cover the waterfront. I cover the matzoh.)

Pastry chef Sherry Yard, whose book *The Secrets of Baking: Simple Techniques for Sophisticated Desserts* took the cov-

eted James Beard Award in 2004, shared her recipe for what she calls her Menagerie of Macaroons. "At Spago our pasta is made with egg yolks," she told me, "so we are always challenged to create dishes with egg whites. If you could build a house out of meringue, I would!"

While Yard uses almonds, I opt for pistachios for these yummy green sandwich cookies with their rich chocolate filling. **MAKES ABOUT 20**   **D** or **P**

FOR THE CHOCOLATE GANACHE FILLING
8 ounces semisweet or bittersweet chocolate, chopped
$^1/_2$ cup heavy (whipping) cream or nondairy whipping cream

FOR THE COOKIE
2 cups (about 8 ounces) shelled, unsalted pistachio nuts, toasted (see box, page 17)
$^1/_2$ cup confectioners' sugar (see box, page 564)
$^1/_8$ teaspoon salt
Whites of 3 large eggs, at room temperature
$^1/_8$ teaspoon cream of tartar (see Note)
3 tablespoons granulated sugar
$^1/_4$ teaspoon almond extract
5 drops green food coloring

1. Prepare the chocolate ganache filling: Place the chocolate in a heatproof bowl. Bring the cream to a boil in a small saucepan over medium heat. Pour the hot cream over the chocolate, stirring gently until melted and smooth. Cover and refrigerate until the ganache is cool and thick but still spread-

> " Seder was always special because of the family hoopla, getting together, laughing, singing and of course the delicious food, coanchored by Mama Hinda and the aunts. We all stuffed ourselves into their tiny living room, candles lit, scents of holiday delicacies, the mountain of pots in the teeny kitchen—and of course Mama had no dishwasher—babies crying and cooing, Papa chanting, the Rabinowitz women serving and never, ever complaining that they were tired or anything was too much.
>
> —PHYLLIS EPSTEIN "

able, about 1 hour. (If made in advance, cover and refrigerate for up to 1 week. Let it sit at room temperature until it is spreadable but still cool.)

2. Meanwhile, preheat the oven to 325°F. Line two baking sheets with parchment paper.

3. Prepare the cookies: Combine the cooled pistachios, confectioners' sugar, and salt in a food processor, and pulse until the nuts are finely ground. Transfer the mixture to a large mixing bowl and set it aside.

4. Beat the egg whites with an electric mixer on medium-high speed until foamy, about 30 seconds. Add the cream of tartar, if using, and beat until soft peaks form. Add the granulated sugar, a tablespoon at a time, beating for 10 seconds after each addition, until stiff peaks form, about 3 minutes total. Add the almond extract and food coloring, and beat for 30 seconds more. The meringue will appear dark, but it will fade when baked.

5. Stir about one fourth of the meringue into the pistachio mixture until it is evenly moistened. Then add the remaining meringue in three additions, folding it in gently. Drop tablespoons of the mixture, 1 inch apart, onto the prepared baking sheets. Use the back of a spoon to spread them out to form 1- to 1^1/$_2$-inch-wide rounds.

6. Bake, one sheet at a time, on the center oven rack until the cookies are just firm to the touch and lightly browned at the edges, 20 to 25 minutes. Let the cookies cool completely on the baking sheets set on wire racks. Then carefully remove them from the parchment. (If made in advance, the cookies can be stored in an airtight plastic container at room temperature for up to 3 days.)

> " Passover always meant a huge family get-together. I sat at the kids' table until I got married. (That was the definition of not being a kid: getting married.) Everyone who wasn't married yet got a coin for the afikomen. In fact, I believe even [my sister] Heather got a coin at Marvin and Leslie's house last Passover, although she was thirty and engaged. As the years went on, the actual Seder got shorter and shorter and the food more and more elaborate as the traditional brisket and turkey, matzoh kugel and potato kugel, matzoh ball soup and gefilte fish—once made exclusively by Mama Irene in her tiny kitchen—were delivered by catering truck as our family grew. I remember Mama Irene in the old days always made green beans and almonds, her fancy vegetable, and cooked carrots in a sweet sauce (of course, using the leftover carrots from the soup—nothing should go to waste!).
> —JODI ORLOW MACKOFF "

7. Spread a scant tablespoon of the ganache filling over the flat sides of half of the cookies. Place the remaining cookies on top, flat side down, pressing gently to form a sandwich.

8. The cookies are best served the same day they are filled.

Note: If you can't find kosher-for-Passover cream of tartar, it may be omitted during Passover.

For another meringue-type cookie suitable for Passover, try Phyllis's Chocolate Nut Meringue Kisses, page 492.

chocolate macaroons

from Barbara Straus

I f your only experience with macaroons is those coconut pellets that come in a can, you're in for a big surprise. These are rich and chocolatey, with the coconut augmenting rather than overpowering the chocolate. **MAKES ABOUT 6 DOZEN** Ⓟ

2 cups (12 ounces) semisweet or
   bittersweet chocolate chips
Parchment paper or vegetable cooking
   spray, for the baking sheets
Whites of 4 large eggs
Pinch of salt
1 cup sugar
2 teaspoons vanilla (see box, page 564)
¹/₂ teaspoon fresh lemon juice
1¹/₂ cups sweetened flaked or
   shredded coconut

1. Melt the chocolate in a double boiler set over simmering (not boiling) water. Remove the pan from the heat and set it aside to cool.

2. Preheat the oven to 350°F. Line a baking sheet with parchment paper or lightly grease it. (If two baking sheets will fit side by side on your oven rack, use two.)

3. Beat the egg whites with an electric mixer on medium-high speed until foamy, about 30 seconds. Add the salt and beat until soft peaks form. Add the sugar, a tablespoon at a time, beating for 10 seconds after each addition, until stiff peaks form, about 3 minutes total. Beat in the vanilla and lemon juice. Fold in the coconut and melted chocolate until thoroughly blended.

4. Drop teaspoonfuls of the batter, 1 inch apart, on the prepared baking sheet (the batter will stiffen as it stands, but it's nothing to worry about). Bake on the center oven rack until the macaroons puff up, 10 to 13 minutes. Don't allow the edges to get brown or they will be overdone. Let the cookies cool on the baking sheet set on a wire rack until they can be safely moved, 1 to 2 minutes. Then transfer them to the rack to cool completely.

5. Repeat, baking and cooling the remaining macaroons. Once cooled, they are ready to serve.

“

Dear Judy—

I remember well Pesach with your family in the Catskills. [My brother] Marc would read Torah for your dad with his special Pesachdicke trop.* He recalls it well to this day. In fact, we're driving to New York tomorrow to spend the Seders with the family, and on Sunday morning Marc is layning in shul. I'm getting the third aliyah so I can bask in the music of the trop your father taught him for Pesach in the early 1950s.

—STEPHEN STRAUS

”

*Trop: Marks indicating musical notes for chanting the Torah, etc.

joan friedman's chocolate meringues

from Lillian Bart

‫ש‬hen my mom's friend Joan gave her this recipe, she assured her it would be easy. Maybe in Joan's family. Everyone in ours likes them a different way, from ooey-gooey (that would be me!), to barely set (my brother, Gary), to crisp and well-done (my husband, Barry, who faints at the sight of rare roast beef, so why should meringues be any different?). You'll never see place cards at Mom's table ("Oh, just sit where you want"), but *only* at Mom's are the meringues labeled!

MAKES AT LEAST 3 DOZEN　　　**P**

1 cup (6 ounces) chocolate chips

¹/₂ teaspoon vanilla (see box, page 564)

Parchment paper or vegetable cooking spray,
　for the baking sheets

Whites of 2 large eggs

¹/₈ teaspoon distilled white vinegar

¹/₂ cup sugar

³/₄ cup walnuts,
　chopped

1. Melt the chocolate in a double boiler set over simmering water. Stir in the vanilla, and set it aside to cool.

2. Preheat the oven to 350°F. Line a baking sheet with parchment paper or grease it. (If two baking sheets will fit side by side on your oven rack, use two.)

3. Beat the egg whites with an electric mixer on medium-high speed until foamy, about 30 seconds. Add the vinegar and beat until soft peaks form. Add the sugar, a tablespoon at a time, beating for 10 seconds after each addition, until stiff peaks form, about 2 minutes total. Gently fold in the

In the early '50s, Manischewitz, my dad's sponsor, sent a photographer to the house to take pictures of my brother, Gary, for their advertising. (Mom can't remember if they were ever used!)

melted chocolate, followed by the chopped walnuts.

4. Drop rounded teaspoonfuls of the batter, about 1 inch apart, on the prepared baking sheet (the batter will stiffen as it stands, but it's nothing to worry about). Bake on the center oven rack until the cookies are puffed, about 10 minutes for a gooey chocolate center, a minute or so longer for a crisper cookie. Let the cookies cool on the baking sheet set on a wire rack until they can be safely moved, 1 to 2 minutes. Then transfer them to the rack to cool completely.

5. Repeat, baking and cooling the remaining cookies. Once cooled, they are ready to serve.

pecan cookies

from Inez Swartz

Hard to believe that with no added fat, these crisp cookies from cousin Marilyn's sister-in-law taste so buttery, like a butterscotch crisp. **MAKES ABOUT 3 DOZEN** **P**

Parchment paper or vegetable cooking spray, for the baking sheet

2 cups pecans, plus about 3 dozen pecan halves for topping the cookies

1 cup (packed) light brown sugar

Pinch of salt

White of 1 large egg

1 teaspoon fresh lemon juice

Judy and I almost never got to sit at Mama and Papa's Seder table, because we were always with my folks in the Catskills, but I remember the preparations, as they lived upstairs from us. Mama Hinda took the commandment to clean all the chometz (non-Passover food crumbs) from her home literally. You would think she was preparing her apartment for a surgical operation, it was that clean. I remember Uncle Lou taking a clean white dish towel and checking the top of her door frames. Mama missed nothing. Her home sparkled like at no other time of the year.

—GARY BART

1. Preheat the oven to 375°F. Line a baking sheet with parchment paper or generously grease it.

2. Combine the 2 cups pecans and 2 tablespoons of the brown sugar in a food processor, and process until the nuts are finely chopped.

3. Combine the chopped pecans, remaining brown sugar, and salt in a bowl. Add the egg white (unbeaten) and lemon juice, and stir until thoroughly combined. Drop rounded teaspoonfuls of the mixture, about $1^1/2$ inches apart, on the prepared baking sheet. Press a pecan half into each cookie.

4. Bake on the center oven rack until the cookies are golden brown around the edges, 8 to 11 minutes. Watch the bottoms, as they burn easily. Let the cookies cool on the baking sheet set on a wire rack until they can be safely moved, 1 to 2 minutes. Then transfer them to the rack to cool completely.

5. Repeat, baking and cooling the remaining cookies, and serve.

rita berlin's mock oatmeal cookies

from Lillian Bart

Our friendship with Rita goes back more than thirty years. The night her husband, Stew, learned that my dad was Jan Bart, he unearthed a signed 8 × 10 glossy from his busboy days in the Catskills! Over the years we've shared more than recipes—the *simchas* and *tsurris* that bind a friendship. These cookies really remind you of oatmeal cookies, but crisper and with a whisper of cinnamon. They're great as is, but for fancy snacking, move them onto that doily with a chocolate (page 570) or white chocolate glaze (page 580). **MAKES ABOUT 4 DOZEN** Ⓟ

1. Preheat the oven to 350°F. Line a baking sheet with parchment paper or grease it. (If two baking sheets will fit side-by-side on your oven rack, use two.)

2. Combine the matzoh meal, farfel, sugar, cinnamon, and salt in a medium-size bowl.

3. Beat the eggs with a fork in a separate bowl until foamy, and then beat in the oil. Add the egg mixture to the matzoh meal mixture, and combine well. Fold in the nuts.

4. Drop rounded teaspoonfuls of the dough onto the prepared baking sheet, and flatten them slightly. They don't spread, so they can be placed close together, but without touching. Bake on the center oven rack until the cookies are golden brown on the bottom and edges, about 15 minutes. Let the cookies cool on the baking sheet set on a wire rack until they can be safely moved, about 1 minute. Then transfer them to the rack to cool completely.

5. Repeat, baking and cooling the remaining cookies. Once cooled, they are ready to serve.

Parchment paper, vegetable
   oil, or vegetable cooking
   spray, for the baking
   sheet
1 cup matzoh meal
1 cup matzoh farfel
1/2 cup sugar
1/2 teaspoon ground
   cinnamon
1/2 teaspoon salt
2 large eggs
1/2 cup vegetable oil
1/2 cup chopped walnuts

Rita and Barry at Brad and Tracey's wedding reception, 1995. At the wedding of the last child, the parents sit in the center of a circle and the guests dance the mazinka around them.

passover apricot squares

from Marlene Mutzman

These are easy cookies with a rich crust, gooey fruit filling, and nutty streusel topping. Marlene (cousin Joyce's *machatenista*) prefers apricot, but you can choose raspberry or any other flavor you like. Can't decide? Swirl two for squares as pretty to look at as they are delicious to eat. **MAKES 32**   **P** or **D**

¹/₂ **pound (2 sticks) unsalted nondairy**
  margarine or butter, at room temperature,
  plus extra for greasing the baking pan
1 **cup sugar**
Yolks of 2 large eggs
2 **teaspoons grated lemon zest**
1 **teaspoon vanilla (see box, page 564)**
¹/₄ **teaspoon salt**
2 **cups matzoh cake meal**
1 **jar (12 ounces) apricot preserves**
³/₄ **cup chopped walnuts**

1. Preheat the oven to 325°F. Grease a 13 × 9-inch glass baking pan.

2. Cream the margarine and sugar with an electric mixer on medium speed until light and fluffy, about 2 minutes. Add the egg yolks and continue beating until well combined, scraping the bowl as necessary. Then add the lemon zest, vanilla, and salt. Reduce the speed to medium-low and add the cake meal, beating until combined.

> " I remember taking turns reading and reciting the prayers around the Seder table. It was always very orderly until we got to the part where you read about the four sons. You could always count on cousin Marvin to call on Heather to read the 'wicked son.' It never failed. After a few years of this, Heather finally didn't wait to be called on. She would just read as soon as it got to 'her' part.
>
> **—SUZY ORLOW SOLOMONIC**

3. Press about two thirds of the mixture over the bottom of the prepared baking pan and bake on the center oven rack for 20 minutes. Remove the pan from the oven and spread the preserves evenly over the crust. Sprinkle the walnuts over the preserves, and crumble the remaining dough over the top. Bake until the topping feels set and is beginning to turn golden, 30 to 35 minutes. (Check the bottoms. They should be just beginning to turn golden too.) Cool in the baking pan set on a wire rack. Then cut into squares and serve.

helen rubin's brownies

from Holly Grippo

The highest compliment one can pay a Passover dessert is to say, "It's so good, I make it all year." That's exactly what Holly's note read. These are really fudgy brownies that those guys on Madison Avenue must have had in mind when they penned "Got milk?" **MAKES 16 TO 20** Ⓟ

Vegetable oil or vegetable cooking spray,
    for greasing the pan
$1/2$ cup plus 1 tablespoon unsweetened
    cocoa powder
1 cup vegetable oil
$1/4$ cup cold coffee or water
2 cups sugar
4 large eggs, lightly beaten
1 teaspoon almond-flavored liqueur
$1/4$ teaspoon salt
1 cup matzoh cake meal

1. Preheat the oven to 350°F. Grease an 8-inch square cake pan.

2. Whisk the cocoa powder with the oil and coffee in a medium-size bowl until smooth.

3. Add the sugar, eggs, liqueur, salt, and cake meal, *in that order*, incorporating each before adding the next. Stir until smooth.

4. Transfer the batter to the prepared pan and bake on the center oven rack until the cake begins to pull away from the edges of the pan and a toothpick inserted in the center comes out barely clean, 35 to 40 minutes. Let the brownies cool in the pan set on a wire rack before cutting.

Variation: My friend Barbara Queen substitutes $1/4$ cup ground almonds for $1/4$ cup of the matzoh cake meal.

linda gomberg's mocha nut bars

from Judy Bart Kancigor

My friends and I have been making Linda's bars every Passover since she submitted them to our Heritage Pointe cookbook a million years ago. These thin brownie-like bars, with a hint of coffee, are equally at home on your grand finale dessert buffet or at a coffee-and-gab fest with "the girls" (and we do!). **MAKES 32 TO 40** Ⓟ or Ⓓ

2 ounces semisweet chocolate
8 tablespoons (1 stick) nondairy margarine
    or unsalted butter, plus extra for
    greasing the cake pans
1 teaspoon instant coffee granules
$1/4$ teaspoon salt
2 large eggs, at room temperature
1 cup sugar
$1/2$ cup matzoh cake meal
$1/2$ cup chopped walnuts

1. Preheat the oven to 325°F. Generously grease two 9-inch square cake pans.

2. Melt the chocolate and margarine in a double boiler set over simmering water, or in a microwave oven in 30-second bursts at 50% power. Stir in the coffee granules and salt, and set the mixture aside to cool.

3. Beat the eggs and sugar together in a medium-size bowl. Blend in the cooled chocolate mixture. Gradually stir in the cake

meal. Divide the mixture between the prepared cake pans and level it evenly (yet another reason to buy that offset spatula). Sprinkle the walnuts over the top.

4. Bake on the center oven rack until the brownies are barely set in the middle and the edges are just beginning to pull away from the pan, 15 to 18 minutes. Immediately cut into squares. Then set the pan on a wire rack to cool before serving.

chocolate-covered matzoh toffee

from Robin Kancigor Boyko

n o matter how many other desserts I'm serving, I've got to make Robin's Matzoh Toffee. Sometimes the easiest is the best. You just heat butter and brown sugar, pour it over matzoh, and bake, then melt chocolate over the whole shebang. My daughter-in-law Shelly tells me her Grandma Ilo used to make the same thing on the farm, using saltines or graham crackers. **MAKES . . . NOT ENOUGH!** 🄳 or 🄿

About 4 boards matzoh

1 cup (2 sticks) unsalted butter or nondairy margarine

1 cup (packed) dark brown sugar

2 cups (12 ounces) semisweet chocolate chips

¹/₂ cup walnut pieces, toasted (see box, page 17) and chopped (optional)

1. Preheat the oven to 450°F. Line a 17 × 11-inch baking pan with aluminum foil or parchment paper.

2. Arrange the matzoh in the prepared pan in a single layer, breaking them, if necessary, to fill all the spaces.

3. Combine the butter and brown sugar in a small saucepan over medium heat, and bring to a boil, stirring constantly. Cook until thick and syrupy, about 3 minutes.

4. Pour the toffee mixture over the matzoh and spread it out evenly. Bake until bubbly, 4 minutes.

5. Remove the pan from the oven and sprinkle the chocolate chips over the toffee layer. Bake for 1 minute more. Then

My dad, Jan Bart, with the Barry Sisters, regulars on the American-Jewish Caravan of Stars radio show, 1950s.

remove the pan from the oven and set it aside until the chocolate has melted, about 5 minutes. Spread the melted chocolate out evenly. Sprinkle with the walnuts, if using. Refrigerate until the chocolate is firm, 30 minutes to 1 hour.

6. Cut or break into pieces. And don't throw away those leftover crumbs. My friend Joanne says they're awesome over ice cream.

grandma ruchel's pesach carrot candy

from Isabelle Frankel

Grandma Ruchel Strausser, who died when I was sixteen, was my dad's (and Aunt Isabelle's) mother. She was a very sweet lady, quite religious, a cook in the Galician tradition. In Poland she worked in her sister's bakery, and we can still taste her butter cookies, which melted in your mouth.

A few years ago my brother, Gary, and I made a pilgrimage to her old apartment in Brooklyn, which we hadn't seen since we were kids. Unbelievably, the present tenants let us in. I was flooded with memories of Grandma Ruchel, prayer book in hand, bowing and praying as she faced the Tam Tam cabinet, which I as a child assumed were holy crackers. (I did not know she was facing east.) In that very room she made her chicken soup, complete with chicken feet and little chick eggs. (Can you even buy them anymore?) There I watched her stretching strudel dough on a card table laid out with tea towels. The butter cookies are lost forever, but Aunt Isabelle remembered these (mainly because it was her job to shred the carrots). **MAKES ABOUT 6 DOZEN** 🅿

2 pounds carrots, finely shredded
2¹/₂ cups sugar
¹/₂ cup orange juice
Grated zest of 1 orange
1 to 2 teaspoons ground ginger, or to taste
¹/₂ teaspoon salt
2 cups whole natural almonds, toasted
    (see box, page 17) and chopped

1. Place the carrots, sugar, orange juice, orange zest, ginger, and salt in a medium-size, heavy-bottomed pot and bring to a steady simmer over medium heat. Simmer, uncovered, until the mixture is very thick, 1¹/4 to 1¹/2 hours. Stir the mixture occasionally during the first hour; then, during the last 15 to 30 minutes, stir often and watch carefully that the mixture does not scorch. As soon as the color changes from orange to reddish-brown, remove the pot from the heat and stir in the chopped almonds.

2. Grease a baking sheet with vegetable oil, or dampen a wooden cutting board. Spread the hot carrot-nut mixture about ¹/4-inch thick over the prepared baking sheet. Let it cool slightly, and then cut it into 1- to

$1^1/_2$-inch diamond shapes. Let them cool completely.

3. Store the candy, with waxed paper between the layers, in an airtight container at room temperature. It will keep until Shavuot!

imberlach
(ginger candy)
from Ruchel Strausser

*I*mber means "ginger" in Yiddish. I tried many recipes from old cookbooks, hoping to re-create Grandma Ruchel's spicy, distinctively Passover ginger candy. Finally, when I tried this one from my friend Wendy Baker, decades instantly dissolved, and once again I was a child of nine in Grandma Ruchel's kitchen, my tongue burning from the pungent ginger, jaws aching, but reaching for just one more piece. The recipe was brought from Russia by Wendy's great-grandmother, who passed it down to her grandmother, Sophie. **MAKES 3 DOZEN** P

FOR THE CANDY
2 pounds honey
$4^1/_2$ cups matzoh farfel
1 cup chopped hazelnuts, or more as needed
4 teaspoons ground ginger, or to taste

FOR THE TOPPING
$^1/_4$ cup chopped hazelnuts
About $^1/_4$ teaspoon ground ginger

1. Prepare the candy: Bring the honey to a boil in a large, heavy-bottomed saucepan over high heat. Gradually stir in the farfel. Add the hazelnuts and ginger, and stir until thick, about 3 minutes. Watch it like a hawk (Grandma Sophie's words) so it doesn't burn.

2. Reduce the heat to medium-low and very carefully add $^1/_4$ cup water. Stir constantly until the mixture is brown and almost too thick to stir. This can take 10 to 30 minutes, depending on the water content of the honey and how hard you want the finished product to be.

3. Dampen a wooden cutting board, and transfer the candy to it. Dip your hands in ice water, and using your palms, spread the

> *I don't remember the year, but we traveled from Cincinnati to Atlanta to have Seder with [my wife] Linda's family. During the whole Seder, we could hear this roaring wind, and it wasn't Elijah! Because Grandpa Paul liked to do the whole Haggadah, we couldn't interrupt the Seder to see what was going on. The lights kept flickering and we could hear this awful crash, but he never missed a beat. When the Seder was finally over, we rushed to the windows. A tornado had knocked down a tree, tearing a huge hole in the roof of the house across the street, turning it into a sukkah. "* —FRANK NATHAN
>
> Addendum: "Uncle Morris and Aunt Sylvia lived a few streets over, and a tree went through their house as well. That's how they got the beautiful addition to their home!
>
> —LINDA NATHAN

hot candy out $1/4$ inch thick. Sprinkle the hazelnuts and ginger on top, and cut it into diamond shapes.

4. The candy will keep for weeks in an airtight plastic container at room temperature.

stuffed prunes

from Irene Rosenthal

Passover, 1975. It seemed like a good idea: I'd introduce the subject of prayer to my religious school class by asking my eager, precocious teenagers to write a telegram to God. I expected thank-you's and gimme's. Imagine my reaction to this:

Dear God stop please send prunes stop
this matzoh is killing me!

I've never looked at a board of matzoh since (nor a prune, for that matter) without thinking of Michael Porter (of blessed memory).

What a lovely ending to a beautiful meal: stuffed purple prunes layered with sunny lemon slices and perfumed with cloves—a nice dessert anytime, but particularly welcome at Passover. It looks dazzling on the table in its own dish, or you can place two cooked prunes each into foil candy cups and garnish them with the lemon. **SERVES 8 TO 12** **P**

2 lemons, thinly sliced
3 whole cloves
1 pound large pitted prunes
About 1 cup walnut halves, toasted
  (see box, page 17)
1 cup sugar

1. Line the bottom of a large skillet with the lemon slices and cloves.

2. Fill the cavity of the prunes with 1 or 2 walnut halves, and arrange the stuffed prunes over the lemon slices.

3. Combine $1^{1}/2$ cups water and the sugar in a small saucepan, and bring to a boil. Pour this syrup over the prunes. Cover the skillet and boil gently for 10 to 12 minutes. Uncover and cook, basting often, until the liquid has almost evaporated, about 5 minutes more.

4. Arrange the cooked prunes and lemon slices in a single layer in an 11×7-inch glass dish, and allow to cool. (Discard the cloves.) Serve at room temperature.

let's par-tay!

drinks

Okay, you can stop laughing now. We have about one hundred and fifty sweets (and that's not including Passover) and twenty-five drinks, only eighteen of which are alcoholic. Need I remind you that this is a *Jewish* cookbook? I think Jackie Mason said it best (you provide the inflection):

You never see a Jew in a bar . . .
unless he got lost looking
for a piece of cake.
—THE WORLD ACCORDING TO ME!: JEWS AND GENTILES

Jackie of course is going for the laugh, and in the twenty-first century the notion that Jews don't drink seems more like an worn-out myth. And yet . . . one hundred fifty as opposed to eighteen. Maybe it's just my family, but I doubt it!

"A little Guggel-Muggel was Mama Hinda's wonder drug of choice."

All the Rabinowitzes attend every celebration. We sure do know how to party! Who's who on page 613.

kosher wine

Not so long ago, the words "kosher wine" brought to mind that syrupy sweet, almost cough-medicine-like concoction served as an accompaniment to prayers. Not anymore. Barely a generation ago, observant Jewish baby boomers, hipper and more sophisticated than their parents, demanded the same selection and quality found in the nonkosher world, and winemakers took notice. The result was an explosion of kosher wines onto the market from just about every winemaking region of the world, and the quality is virtually indistinguishable from their nonkosher counterparts.

What makes a wine kosher is the use of certified kosher yeast and filtering agents, the exclusive use of equipment under rabbinical supervision, and its handling by Sabbath observant Jews from the crush to the bottle. The most orthodox Jews require it be also served by Sabbath observant Jews. Some kosher wine undergoes flash pasteurization, rendering it mevushal (Hebrew for "cooked") with no sacrifice in quality or flavor. Mevushal wines may then be handled by anyone.

Wine is so central to the celebration of Jewish festivals that grapes are the only fruit that has its own special blessing. And now the selection is endless. Where once your choice was between blackberry and grape, kosher wines to suit every pocketbook are now garnering top awards.

"The biggest time of year for new releases is Passover," said Eitan Segal, Director of Public Relations for Royal Wine Corporation, the world's largest producer, importer, and distributor of kosher wines, in an interview. "Passover is the single most observed Jewish holiday of the year. Every adult is required to drink four cups of wine at each of the two Seders. This is the season when even the nonobservant are most interested in kosher wine."

The overwhelming majority of kosher wines are kosher for Passover, and a "P" or the words "kosher for Passover" will appear on the label. "What makes a wine kosher for Passover is the absence of any products which contain leavening or any other product prohibited during the Passover holiday," Segal noted.

But it's not just observant Jews who are buying kosher wine. So are millions of others who associate the word "kosher" with purity and high standards.

Our tradition from the earliest Biblical times sanctifies the drinking of wine, which has its own blessing and features prominently at life-cycle celebrations and bereavements, on Shabbat and the holidays. During the Passover Seder, we are commanded to drink four cups of wine. In fact, on Purim we are even encouraged to overindulge in alcohol. And with the proliferation of kosher wines, observant Jews have now joined their nonkosher counterparts in appreciating the dizzying array of choices from just about every wine-producing region of the world.

Papa Harry loved his schnapps, as he called whiskey, and continued his two-shot-per-day habit (as well as his two cigar-per-day habit) until the day he died at 89. He kept his bottle under the kitchen sink, and I can still see him now, standing there before lunch and before dinner, throwing his head back and belting that shot down in one gulp. "Ah, goot!"

In his younger days he made his own cherry vishnyek (cordial), a reasonable facsimile of which you'll find here. I don't ever remember seeing Mama Hinda drink more than a glass of ceremonial wine, but she would help herself now and again to Papa's schnapps in order to concoct a gugglemuggle: her instant cure for the children or anyone in the household who was ailing (if she could catch them!).

The twenty-five recipes in this chapter read like a stroll through the decades. Retro classics like Strawberry Daiquiri, Lynchburg Lemonade, and Cosmopolitan. Timeless favorites like Bloody Mary and Margarita.

Teetotalers take heart. Relax with a warming Turkish Coffee or Hot Vanilla. Enjoy a Strawberry Crush, Fruit Smoothie, or Cousin Phyllis's take on the Orange Julius, transporting you back to the streets of New York. And speaking of New York, this chapter wouldn't be complete without my husband Barry's Black and White Malted and New York Egg Cream, recalled from his teenage days working in his father's Brooklyn candy store.

And while we're waxing nostalgic, although they are not recipes, check out my excursuses on Two Cents Plain and A Glezel Tay (a cup of tea), the latter the perfect ending to a holiday repast and a fitting close to this walk down Memory Lane. *L'Chaim!*

guggel-muggel

from Hinda Rabinowitz

Before the advent of antibiotics, a little Guggel-Muggel was Mama Hinda's wonder drug of choice. According to Aunt Sally, she made it by adding warm milk to eggs and honey, then lacing it with some of Papa Harry's schnapps. Upon ingestion, the ailing were known to leap out of bed (whether cured or in avoidance of a second dose is unknown). Her exact recipe is lost forever, but my mother and I spent a delightful afternoon perfecting this recreational version. Try it as a warming toddy on a cold evening. You'll have sweet dreams. **SERVES 1** **D**

1 cup whole milk
1 large egg
3 tablespoons honey
2 to 3 tablespoons Scotch whiskey
1/4 teaspoon pure vanilla extract
Dash of ground nutmeg

1. Combine the milk, egg, and honey in a small saucepan. Whisk constantly over low heat until very hot and frothy. (Do not boil.)

2. Stir in the whiskey and vanilla. Serve immediately, sprinkled with nutmeg.

Note: My mother assures me that Mama Hinda never measured and probably just heated some milk and stirred in the honey, schnapps, and a raw egg, with nary a worry about salmonella. In fact, she would give the twins, Morris and Lou, raw eggs to take with them to the candy store to stir into their malteds to "build them up," a tastier alternative to the gallons of cod liver oil they were forced to consume.

champagne punch 1

from Marian Weiss

Fruit and sparkle jazz up this colorful champagne punch with its oranges, strawberries, and floating island of sherbet. Be sure all the ingredients are chilled, and prepare the punch close to serving time. **SERVES 24 TO 30** **P**

1 can (46 ounces) Hawaiian Punch, chilled
1 bottle (2 liters) ginger ale, chilled
1 bottle (750 milliliters) champagne, chilled
1 can (11 ounces) mandarin oranges, drained
1 pint fresh strawberries, rinsed, hulled and sliced
Ice ring or mold (see Note)
1 pint raspberry sherbet

1. Immediately before serving, combine the Hawaiian Punch, ginger ale, and champagne in a chilled punch bowl.
2. Stir in the mandarin oranges and strawberries. Carefully slide the ice ring into the bowl. Float the sherbet in one piece.

> " When my girls were young and we used to visit [my sister] Linda and [brother-in-law] Frank, she always made them a 'Blue Linda': ginger ale with blue food coloring and a cherry. This was a famous drink for the girls that they always looked forward to. **—RONALD ROBBINS** "

Note: To make an ice ring or mold, freeze water or orange juice in a small ring mold, the bottom of a Bundt pan, or even a small bowl. Additional oranges and strawberries can be frozen in the ice for even more pizzazz. Unmold the ring by briefly lowering the bottom of the mold into a bowl of hot water, then inverting the mold.

champagne punch 2

from Lillian Bart

You don't see punch bowls around as much today as in years past. My mother had a silver one for our huge family gatherings. I think the last time she made this festive punch was for my surprise graduation party from college. (Well, it was supposed to be a surprise, but Papa Harry never could keep a secret. My mother told me that all the preparations were for my father's birthday. That afternoon Papa came downstairs, took my face in both hands, and informed me, "Judelah, dah pahty's fah *you*, dahlink!") **SERVES 24** P

2 bottles (750 milliliters each) champagne, chilled

2 cups apricot brandy, chilled

1 cup vodka, frozen

1¹/₂ bottles (1 liter each) ginger ale, chilled

2 lemons, sliced

2 oranges, sliced

Ice ring or mold (see Note, facing page)

1. Immediately before serving, combine the champagne, brandy, vodka, and ginger ale in a chilled punch bowl.

2. Carefully slide the ice ring into the bowl, float the lemon and orange slices, and serve.

Plan: Mom to walk Gary down aisle.
Action: Gary takes off without her.
Mom (in her usual sotto voce): Gary, where are you going?
Gary: I'm getting married!
Mom: Aren't you forgetting something?

sangría

from Joyce Simpson

tandard party fare in the '60s, Sangría is now making a comeback. Serve this in a large pitcher, or for a showy display, freeze ice in a Jell-O mold and float it in a punch bowl. (That's assuming that you were around in the '60s and thus own a Jell-O mold—or a punch bowl, for that matter!) **SERVES 12 TO 15** P

1 lemon, thinly sliced

1 orange, thinly sliced

1 lime, thinly sliced

¹/₂ cup brandy

¹/₂ cup orange liqueur, such as Sabra

¹/₄ cup sugar

2 bottles (1 liter each) Spanish red wine, chilled

1 to 2 bottles (12 ounces each) club soda, chilled

2 trays ice cubes, or 1 ice ring (see Note, facing page)

1. Combine the lemon, orange, and lime slices in a large bowl or pitcher, and add the brandy and liqueur. Cover, and let the fruit macerate in the refrigerator for 30 minutes to 2 hours.

2. Combine the sugar and 1 cup of the wine in a bowl or a large glass, and stir to dissolve the sugar. Pour this over the macerated fruit. Add the remaining wine, cover, and refrigerate until chilled, at least 4 hours.

3. When you are ready to serve the sangría, either transfer it to a punch bowl and float the ice ring in it or serve from a pitcher filled with ice cubes.

strawberry daiquiri

from Syble Solomon

Syble says you can add ice if you want a less potent drink, and then this will serve more than four. Eliminate the rum and you've got a refreshing slurpy for the kids. **SERVES 4** 🅿

1 can (6 ounces) frozen limeade, undiluted

2 to 4 scoops lime sherbet

1 cup fresh or frozen strawberries, rinsed and
    hulled if fresh

Sugar to taste (optional)

¹/₄ to ¹/₂ cup rum

Whiz all the ingredients in a blender and pour into chilled cocktail glasses.

l'orange treat

from Ross Levine

my nephew's original cocktail is a cross between a Rum Screwdriver and a Rum Martini—a Rum Screwtini perhaps? **SERVES 1** 🅿

1¹/₂ ounces dark or golden rum

5 ounces fresh orange juice

¹/₄ teaspoon sweet vermouth

Pour the rum over ice cubes in a highball glass. Stir in the orange juice and vermouth, and serve.

Ross and bride Ariana take a cooking class together.

margarita

from Beverly Metzger-Kleinman

Barry's cousin Bev makes what she calls the perfect margarita. And she should know. An ardent Jimmy Buffett fan (read Parrot Head), Margaritaville is her spiritual home. But Parrot Heads do more than listen to music and sport tropical clothing. Parrot-Heads in Paradise Inc., a nonprofit humanitarian organization, raises money for many charitable, educational, and environmental concerns. So if, when celebrating with friends, she wants to raise a glass, I say, *"L'Chaim!"*
SERVES 1 🅿

Beverly (here with husband, Richard) has helped raise hundreds of thousands of dollars for Parrot-Heads in Paradise.

1 wedge lime

Kosher (coarse) salt

$1/2$ ounce triple sec

1 ounce lime juice

$1^1/2$ ounces tequila

3 ounces Sweet-and-Sour Mix
(recipe follows)

1 orange or pineapple slice, for garnish

1. Rub the outside rim of a cocktail glass with a lime wedge, and then dip the rim in kosher salt, coating it well.

2. Blend the triple sec, lime juice, tequila, and Sweet-and-Sour Mix in a blender. Pour over ice cubes in the salt-rimmed glass. Garnish with the orange slice, and serve.

Note: Bev likes to use orange or lime juice to make the ice cubes.

sweet-and-sour mix

MAKES 4 CUPS   P

$1^1/2$ cups sugar

1 cup fresh lemon juice

1 cup fresh lime juice

1. Combine $1^1/2$ cups water with the sugar in a medium-size saucepan and bring to a boil. Stir until the sugar dissolves. Set the syrup aside to cool.

2. Mix the cooled syrup, lemon juice, and lime juice in a pitcher, cover, and chill. The mix can be made up to 1 week ahead.

tequila sunrise

from Frank Nathan

The grenadine on top of this drink mimics the red and orange colors of a sunrise. "This is how I get my vitamin C," says Frank. **SERVES 1**   P

2 ounces tequila

6 ounces orange juice

1 ounce grenadine

1. Pour the tequila and orange juice over ice cubes in a 12-ounce glass, and stir.

2. Slowly pour in the grenadine, and serve.

lynchburg lemonade

from Frank Nathan

This sparkling bracer is named after Lynchburg, Tennessee, home of the Jack Daniel's distillery. A fitting entry from Frank, who grew up in Chattanooga. **SERVES 4**   P

> *I was the assistant administrator of The Jewish Home in Atlanta, but more importantly, I was in an Army Reserve unit. I was the only Jewish officer in the unit, where Ronald was a cook (if you can believe that). One day Ronald approached me about taking out his sister Linda. To get him off my back, I called her, saying, 'I'm Frank Nathan. You don't know me from Adam.' She thought my name was Adam. We went out that night to my apartment after grocery shopping for the dinner I fixed for us. That was August and we were married the following April.*
>
> **—FRANK NATHAN**

4 ounces Jack Daniel's Tennessee Whiskey
4 ounces Triple Sec
4 ounces Sweet-and-Sour Mix (page 601)
16 ounces lemon-lime soda
Lemon slices, for garnish

Combine the whiskey, triple sec, sour mix, and soda in a pitcher filled with ice. Float a few lemon slices for garnish, and serve.

Joyce and Artie Wolf and Marvin Robbins at Staci Robbbin's Bat Mitzvah, 1994.

ben morett's appletini
from Arthur Wolf

rtie's friend and accountant, Ben, says that vodka should always be kept in the freezer, making for a thicker and silkier drink. And use a good vodka, such as Absolut or Grey Goose. A real drinker can tell the difference between a bar vodka and a good one, he informs me. Despite the fact that James Bond says a martini must be shaken and not stirred, for this drink Ben prefers to do neither. **SERVES 1**   **P**

1¹/₂ ounces frozen vodka
1¹/₂ ounces apple-flavored schnapps, chilled
1 slice Granny Smith apple, for garnish

1. Pour the vodka into a chilled martini glass.
2. Add the schnapps, but do not stir. Garnish with the apple slice, and serve.

> *As you know, in order to become an attorney, I had to pass the bar. The drinks I'm contributing are the result of that long and arduous task. Personally, I prefer Scotch on the rocks or gin and tonic. However, everybody raves (until they fall down) about these.*
>
> **—MARVIN ROBBINS**

stoli ohranj martini

from Marvin Robbins

The less vermouth, the drier the martini. Winston Churchill's recipe is said to have called for a quick glance at the vermouth bottle from across the room. **SERVES 1** 🄿

3 ounces frozen Stolichnaya Ohranj
  vodka
Tiny drop of dry vermouth
1 orange slice, for garnish

1. Combine the vodka and some cracked ice in a martini shaker. Add a *very tiny* drop of vermouth, and shake.

2. Strain the contents into a chilled martini glass. Garnish with the slice of orange, and serve.

cosmopolitan

from Marvin Robbins

Marvin sometimes uses orange-flavored vodka for those who prefer an even more citrusy cocktail. **SERVES 1** 🄿

3 ounces vodka
1/2 ounce orange liqueur
1/2 ounce cranberry juice
2 teaspoons lime juice
1 lime slice, for garnish

Combine the vodka, liqueur, cranberry juice, and lime juice in a shaker filled with chipped ice. Shake, and strain into a chilled martini glass. Garnish with the lime slice, and serve.

sea breeze

from Marvin Robbins

No hard and fast rules here. Marv says you can also serve this in a martini glass by shaking it first in a shaker filled with chipped ice and then straining it into a chilled martini glass. **SERVES 1** 🄿

2 ounces vodka
2 ounces cranberry juice
2 ounces grapefruit juice
1 lime slice, for garnish

1. Fill a highball glass with ice. Add the vodka.

2. Stir in the cranberry and grapefruit juices. Garnish with the lime slice, and serve.

brett feltingoff's stoli cream

from Brad Kancigor

And I thought mandelbrot and kugels were controversial! Everyone has an opinion, it seems, on how to serve vodka. Brad's friend Brett is a James Bond fan too, but he feels this drink has to be stirred to even out the vodka taste. His Stoli Cream is like a Dr. Brown's cream soda with a kick. **SERVES 1** **P**

1¹/₂ ounces vanilla-flavored Stolichnaya vodka

4 to 5 ounces tonic water

Fill a glass with ice cubes, and pour the vodka over them. Add the tonic water and stir.

Bat Mitzvah Suzy with parents, Axel and Carol, 1976.

bloody mary

from Axel Orlow

myths abound as to the naming of this drink. The title is generally ascribed to Mary I of England, the sixteenth-century queen famous for much burning at the stake—but there are contenders. As legend has it, the drink originated in Harry's Bar in Paris in the 1920s, although comedian George Jessel claims to have invented it in the same decade. The ubiquitous celery stalk, so the story goes, was added in the 1960s by an unnamed celebrity who was served a Bloody Mary without a swizzle stick and grabbed a piece of celery from the relish tray to stir it. **SERVES 1** **P**

1¹/₂ ounces vodka

4 ounces V-8 or tomato juice

¹/₂ teaspoon prepared white horseradish

10 drops Worcestershire sauce

3 drops Tabasco sauce

1 teaspoon lime juice

1 lime wedge, for garnish

1 rib celery, for garnish

Combine the vodka, V-8, horseradish, Worcestershire, Tabasco, and lime juice in a cocktail shaker filled with crushed ice. Shake, and strain into a chilled highball glass. Garnish with the lime wedge and celery, and serve.

french 75

from Heather Orlow-Choset

Heather's cocktail of choice got its name from the 75-mm field gun used by the French army during World War I. Evidentally it packs a wallop!

SERVES 1 🅿

³/₄ ounce Bombay Sapphire gin

¹/₂ ounce fresh lemon juice

¹/₂ ounce simple syrup (see Note)

About 4 ounces champagne

1 lemon twist, for garnish

1. Combine the gin, lemon juice, and simple syrup in a shaker, add some chipped ice, and shake. Strain the mixture into a 6-ounce champagne flute.

2. Fill the flute with champagne, garnish with a lemon twist, and serve.

Note: To make simple syrup, combine 1 cup water and 1 cup sugar in a medium-size saucepan. Stir over medium heat until the sugar dissolves. Then bring to a boil, reduce the heat, and simmer for 3 minutes. Refrigerate until cold. This can be stored, covered, in the refrigerator for 1 month.

> " Papa Harry took me for my driving test. He sat in the back seat while I drove with the examiner beside me. I can still hear Papa's editorial comments: 'Oy!'—'Goot, dahlink!'— 'Oy vey!' When I found out I got my license, I ran to Mama and Papa's house to tell them first. Of course, Papa knew I would pass!
>
> **—PHYLLIS EPSTEIN** "

cherry vishnyek

from Harry Rabinowitz

Papa Harry used to make a cordial with the sour cherries from their trees. When Aunt Estelle was three years old, she uncorked the bottle when no one was looking and helped herself to the cherries. Fortunately they soon found her wobbling around, and except for her first hangover, no harm was done.

This recipe, from *Yiddish Cuisine: A Gourmet's Approach to Jewish Cooking* by Robert Sternberg, is probably pretty close to Papa Harry's, although Aunt Sally said he didn't measure any more accurately than Mama Hinda did. (Vishnyek is distinguished from slivovitz, which is made from plums.) **SERVES ABOUT 15** 🅿

1 pound sour cherries, pitted and cut in half

2¹/₂ cups sugar

1 liter vodka

1. Place the cherries in a large glass canning jug with a clamp-seal top. Add the sugar, and then pour in the vodka. Clamp the lid of the jug, and shake it vigorously to dissolve the sugar. Place the jug in a cool, dark

place and allow it to ferment for at least 6 to 8 weeks, shaking the jar once a day.

2. Uncover the jar and, through a funnel lined with cheesecloth, strain the liqueur into a decanter. Cork or cover the decanter, and serve the liqueur as you would any liqueur or cordial: on special occasions, or as an after-dinner drink, or as a palate cleanser after the fish course.

orange phyllis

from Phyllis Epstein

Beloved by millions, the Orange Julius had its humble beginnings at Julius Freed's fresh juice stand in the 1920s—thence to the sidewalks of New York and to every mall in America. The recipe of course is a trade secret, but there are copycats aplenty. This is Phyllis's version, adored by the kids as they were growing up. **SERVES 6**　　　**D**

1 quart orange juice
1 box (3⁵/₈ ounces) vanilla pudding mix
　　(not instant)
1 envelope whipped topping powder,
　　such as Dream Whip
Crushed ice

Combine all the ingredients in a blender and whirl for 15 to 20 seconds. Pour into glasses and serve.

strawberry crush

from Tracey Barrett

This refreshing summer cooler is a standout for company when it's served in fancy chilled glasses garnished with a mint, but it's easy enough to prepare for family enjoyment. In fact it tastes just as good in a sippy cup. Just ask my grandson Blake. **SERVES 5 TO 6**　　**P**

1 pint strawberries, rinsed, dried,
　　and hulled
2 cups ice cubes
Splash of lime juice
Sugar, to taste
5 or 6 mint sprigs, for garnish

Whirl the strawberries, ice, lime juice, and sugar in a blender. Pour into chilled wine or champagne glasses, garnish each glass with a sprig of mint, and serve.

Blake Kancigor shares his strawberry stash with his cousin Jason.

fruit smoothie

from Eva Seligman

Ripe, soft fruits work best for this drink. It's a great way to use up those overripe bananas that no one wants to eat, says Eva. A cup of strawberries, frozen or fresh, can be substituted for the peach or the banana. **SERVES 2** [D]

1 medium-size peach, peeled and
   pitted
1 small banana
1 cup vanilla yogurt
2 tablespoons frozen orange juice
   concentrate
6 ice cubes, slightly crushed
2 teaspoons fresh lemon juice,
   or to taste
1 tablespoon sugar, or to taste

Combine all the ingredients in a blender and whirl until smooth.

sleep. Here's his modern microwave version. The ultimate comfort food, he says. **SERVES 1** [D]

1 cup milk
1 teaspoon honey
1/4 teaspoon pure vanilla extract

1. Pour the milk into a mug. Stir in the honey and vanilla. Microwave on high power for 45 seconds.

2. Stir to dissolve the honey, and then microwave until hot, 30 seconds more. Stir again, and serve.

Jeremy flying high at daughter Eva's Bat Mitzvah.

hot vanilla

from Jeremy Seligman

This relaxing bedtime drink is a throwback to the days when mom Norma would make warm milk with honey when Jeremy was sick, to help him

new york egg cream

from Barry Kancigor

There's neither egg nor cream in the classic egg cream, which gets its name from its head of foam, said to resemble beaten egg whites (although one school of thought holds that the original 1890s version may indeed have used eggs and cream). My husband, the soda jerk, couldn't be pinned down to measurements, but in the privacy of our home (and in the interests of science) I held out the old measuring spoon as he displayed his finesse. He had lots of rules, however, for the preparation of this Big Apple legend. **SERVES 1** D

■ The milk must be ice-cold.

■ You've got to spritz with seltzer. Barry's father's Brooklyn candy store had a pull-down seltzer dispenser, ideal for making this concoction. Seltzer dispensed from a seltzer bottle with a siphon is second best (see box, below). Club soda is sloppy thirds, but it will work.

■ The chocolate syrup must be Fox's U-Bet—no substitutions. (Again, the store had a dispenser. "Two pushes" was Barry's measurement.)

■ Snappy comebacks to know-it-all customers: optional.
SERVES 1 D

2 tablespoons cold whole milk
About 1 cup seltzer
2 generous tablespoons Fox's U-Bet chocolate
  syrup

2 cents plain

● ● ● ● ● ●

Seltzer, the forerunner of what we now know as club soda, was called "2 cents plain" in the old days. Children would be sent to the corner store with a pitcher, and the soda man would fill it for 2 cents. Then, with inflation, 2 cents bought you a glass of seltzer in a restaurant. Later seltzer became available in glass squirt bottles, sold by the wooden crate and delivered by the seltzer man, who also supplied flavored syrups for those who didn't want their seltzer plain. (It was an enterprising New Yorker's memory of this do-it-yourself soft drink that inspired New York Seltzer, setting off an explosion of flavored seltzers and waters in the '80s.)

Seltzer became popular in Jewish homes because it is pareve (neutral) and could be served with meat meals. There was always a bottle with its squirt-it-yourself top on our table. The seltzer man would deliver the crates of seltzer, which were kept in the vestibule. My brother, Gary, four or five years old at the time, found the who-o-o-o-sh of squirting seltzer particularly fascinating and will never live down the day he decided to fill up his wagon with the bubbly stuff. (He also was mesmerized by the sound of air being let out of a car's tires, but that's another story altogether.)

In the 1967 film *The Graduate,* Mr. Robinson offers one word of advice to Benjamin, anticipating great future opportunity—the same word that sounded the death knell to the seltzer bottle: "Plastics." So much so that Molly O'Neill, in discussing seltzer in her *New York Cookbook,* refers to the years before and after plastic as B.P. and A.P. Enter the screw-top plastic bottle, exit the seltzer man. (At this writing there are a handful of companies left that home-deliver seltzer in glass bottles, among them: A-1 Seltzer and Beverage Company in North Hollywood, California; Gomberg Seltzer Works in Brooklyn, New York; Pittsburgh Seltzer Works in Pittsburgh, Pennsylvania; and Seltzer Sisters in the San Francisco Bay Area.)

1. Pour the milk into a 12-ounce glass.

2. Spritz with seltzer almost to the top.

3. Add the syrup, wait a moment for it to fall to the bottom, and then stir with a long spoon. If you get at least an inch of foam, you did it right.

Note: Barry's dad also served a vanilla egg cream made with Fox's U-Bet vanilla syrup.

authentic black and white malted

from Barry Kancigor

my husband, Barry, learned to make malteds as a youngster, helping his father in his candy store on Utica and Church in Brooklyn. The trick to making a great malted is to almost freeze the milk, he says. And you must use a malted machine, not a blender, which is too fast. Barry obtained his prehistoric, previously owned

My husband, Barry, the soda jerk, in his father's candy store, Brooklyn, early '50s.

Hamilton Beach model from a restaurant supply house. **MAKES 1 VERY GENEROUS SERVING** **D**

3 tablespoons Fox's U-Bet chocolate syrup
  (see bulleted list, facing page)
1 cup semi-frozen whole milk
  (freeze for about 1 hour)
2 scoops vanilla ice cream
2 teaspoons malted milk powder, or
  to taste (see Note)
Whipped cream, for garnish

1. Pour the syrup into the metal cup of a malted machine. (Barry says to avoid ridicule, put away the measuring spoon. It's about $1/2$ inch.) Add the milk, ice cream, and malt. Blend until whipped, almost smooth, and frothy, $1^1/2$ to 2 minutes.

2. Pour into a chilled glass and garnish with whipped cream around the rim. Serve the remainder in the metal cup.

Note: A malted without malt is not a malted, but a shake. You've got to use fresh malt, says Barry. The malted milk powder they sell in supermarkets? Fuggedaboudit. We get the real deal from CTL Foods (www.ctlcolfax.com). The amount you use is very subjective. I've seen recommendations ranging from 1 teaspoon to 2 rounded tablespoons. Barry says too much malt overpowers the taste, but you will have to experiment.

turkish coffee

from Ketty Moreno

To make Turkish coffee, Ketty told me, you must first pulverize the coffee into a very fine powder, preferably by hand-grinding it with a special Turkish brass mill rather than a commercial coffee grinder. Only the very powdery coffee can seal the water properly during the boiling process. The coffee is then made in a long-handled copper pot called an *ibrik*, narrow on top and wider at the bottom, and served in little cups. It is very important to get a froth on the top, and it is considered an insult if any guest does not get his share of froth. **SERVES ???**   **P**

Sugar, to taste (optional)
Water
Pulverized coffee

1. Place the desired amount of sugar in the *ibrik*. Fill the *ibrik* with water up to the neck, and then sprinkle the coffee powder on top, completely covering the water. It is important that you do not stir it—the coffee forms a seal over the water. The amount of coffee depends on the size of the *ibrik* (see Note). Turkish coffee is quite strong.

2. Heat the *ibrik* over medium-low heat just until the water begins to foam. You must watch it carefully. As soon as the water foams to the top of the *ibrik*, remove it from the heat (it boils over quickly). Do not stir or you will lose the froth.

3. When the foam has subsided, place the *ibrik* on the heat and repeat the process two more times, heating the water almost to a boil and then letting it subside.

4. To serve, spoon some froth into each cup, and then pour the coffee down the side of the cup so as not to disturb the froth. Let the coffee grounds settle for a minute before drinking.

Note: *Ibriks* come in different sizes. Generally most people use a heaping teaspoon of coffee to 1 cup of water, and sugar to taste.

decongestant tea

from Syble Solomon

Syble says this is an unusual drink she's used with her own children and shared with parents she's worked with whose infants had frequent respiratory problems. It works like a charm, she says. **SERVES 1**   **P**

4 parts dried mint

2 parts fennel seeds

2 parts dried rosemary

1 part ground ginger

Honey, for serving

1. Mix the mint, fennel seeds, rosemary, and ginger together in a jar. Tightly sealed, the mixture will keep for at least 1 year.

2. For 1 portion, use 1 tablespoon of the mixture to 1 cup of boiling water. Allow to sit for 1 minute, then strain and serve with honey to taste.

Note: For a young child who is congested, steep about ¼ cup of the mixture in 1 quart of hot water. Pour it through a strainer and add the strained liquid to the baby's bath water. Your baby (or child or *you*) will breathe much easier and sleep better!

a glezel tay

Coffee, plentiful in Budapest and Vienna, was scarce and expensive in the shtetls of Eastern Europe, where tea was the ubiquitous beverage. Our ancestors sipped tea from a glass, not a cup, usually with a lump of sugar between the teeth. Tea was brewed loose (not in bags, so the strength could be controlled), using a samovar, a Russian metal urn that was heated by its central tube filled with hot charcoal. Even the humblest shtetl homes had one, and I remember Mama Hinda speaking wistfully of the samovar she had to leave in Slonim to help pay for her ticket to America in 1907. In those days "Come in for a glass of tea" was the equivalent of our "Let's go for coffee"—another way of saying "Let's talk." Old habits die hard, and generations later, even with a Starbucks on every corner, tea just feels right after a holiday meal.

Left: Uncle Morris at Daryl's Bat Mitzvah, 1987. Right: Barry toasts Tracey and Brad—just married—1995.

conversion tables

approximate equivalents

1 STICK BUTTER = 8 tbs = 4 oz = ½ cup

1 CUP ALL-PURPOSE PRESIFTED FLOUR OR DRIED BREAD CRUMBS = 5 oz

1 CUP GRANULATED SUGAR = 8 oz

1 CUP (PACKED) BROWN SUGAR = 6 oz

1 CUP CONFECTIONERS' SUGAR = 4½ oz

1 CUP HONEY OR SYRUP = 12 oz

1 CUP GRATED CHEESE = 4 oz

1 CUP DRIED BEANS = 6 oz

1 LARGE EGG = about 2 oz or about 3 tbs

1 EGG YOLK = about 1 tbs

1 EGG WHITE = about 2 tbs

Please note that all conversions are approximate but close enough to be useful when converting from one system to another.

weight conversions

US/UK	METRIC	US/UK	METRIC
½ oz	15 g	7 oz	200 g
1 oz	30 g	8 oz	250 g
1½ oz	45 g	9 oz	275 g
2 oz	60 g	10 oz	300 g
2½ oz	75 g	11 oz	325 g
3 oz	90 g	12 oz	350 g
3½ oz	100 g	13 oz	375 g
4 oz	125 g	14 oz	400 g
5 oz	150 g	15 oz	450 g
6 oz	175 g	1 lb	500 g

liquid conversions

U.S.	IMPERIAL	METRIC
2 tbs	1 fl oz	30 ml
3 tbs	1½ fl oz	45 ml
¼ cup	2 fl oz	60 ml
⅓ cup	2½ fl oz	75 ml
⅓ cup + 1 tbs	3 fl oz	90 ml
⅓ cup + 2 tbs	3½ fl oz	100 ml
½ cup	4 fl oz	125 ml
⅔ cup	5 fl oz	150 ml
¾ cup	6 fl oz	175 ml
¾ cup + 2 tbs	7 fl oz	200 ml
1 cup	8 fl oz	250 ml
1 cup + 2 tbs	9 fl oz	275 ml
1¼ cups	10 fl oz	300 ml
1⅓ cups	11 fl oz	325 ml
1½ cups	12 fl oz	350 ml
1⅔ cups	13 fl oz	375 ml
1¾ cups	14 fl oz	400 ml
1¾ cups + 2 tbs	15 fl oz	450 ml
2 cups (1 pint)	16 fl oz	500 ml
2½ cups	20 fl oz (1 pint)	600 ml
3¾ cups	1½ pints	900 ml
4 cups	1¾ pints	1 liter

oven temperatures

F	GAS MARK	C	F	GAS MARK	C
250	½	120	400	6	200
275	1	140	425	7	220
300	2	150	450	8	230
325	3	160	475	9	240
350	4	180	500	10	260
375	5	190			

Note: Reduce the temperature by 20°C (68°F) for fan-assisted ovens.

who's who

about 1952. **Bottom:** *Josh and my niece Jessica Levine Levy; my sister-in-law Debbie, her son, Ross, Nat and Edie, Ronnie, and Jessica at Brad and Tracey's wedding, 1995; Barry's aunt and uncle, Roz and Henry Kancigor, 1949.*

holidays, page 534 **Top:** *My brother, Gary, and Dad, Cantor Jan Bart, Windsor Hotel, Passover, 1966; Yiddele, Yochanan, and Henoch Padwa, Purim, 2005, Antwerp, Belgium; the Solomonic and Mackoff kids (from upper left clockwise) Samantha, Jordan, Danielle, Jake, Jenna, and Michael, Hanukkah, 2006.* **Center:** *My grandson Jason's first Hanukkah (Grandma's my name, spoiling's my game), 1996; Tracey Barrett, Brad Kancigor, and Samantha, Hanukkah, 2004.* **Bottom:** *Stu, Barry, me, and Brad, Hanukkah, 1973; me and Barry, Sukkot, 1981; my friend Rita Berlin, Brad Kancigor, and Stew Berlin (being Stew), Rosh Hashanah, 1979.*

let's par-tay, page 594 **Top:** *Uncle Lou Robbins; Heather Orlow-Choset, Vicki and David Miller, and Marcy Epstein with Harrison Nathan and Wendy Epstein behind; my mom, Lillian.* **Center:** *My husband, Barry, held aloft by pals Barry Feltingoff and Al Deitch and cousin Marvin Robbins; Vicki and David Miller; Ronnie and Debbie Levine at their 25th anniversary party.* **Bottom:** *Leslie and Marvin Robbins; (standing) my daughter-in-law Tracey's brother, Tyler Barrett, Samantha Kancigor (waving), Kelly McGill-Barrett, Stu Kancigor, our dear friends the Solomons (Rob, holding Leah, and Dori); (seated) Tracey Barrett and Brad Kancigor; Leslie and Marvin Robbins.*

credits

Front cover: *Challah: Tetra Images/Jupiterimages; Matzoh ball soup: Jeff Shaffer/Dawn Smith and Larry Getz/Getty Images; Potato pancakes: Michael Brauner/Getty Images; Rugelach: Melanie Acevedo/Jupiterimages.*

Back cover: *Kasha varnishkes: Alison Miksch/Jupiterimages; Chicken: Susan C. Bourgoin/Jupiterimages; Michael Mahovlich/Masterfile; Author photo: Brad Kancigor.*

Dust jacket: *Front flap: Photo by Paul Poplis/Jupiterimages;* **Back flap:** *Photo by Ann Venegas reprinted by permission of The Orange County Register, copyright 2007.*

Page xxx: *Map of Jewish Eastern Europe 1830–1914 from The Shtetl Book by Diane K. Roskies and David G. Roskies, Ktav Pub. Inc., reprinted by permission of David K. Roskies.*

Page xxx: *Modern map of Eastern Europe from Russia, Eurasian States, and Eastern Europe 1998 by M. Wesley Shoemaker, 29th Edition, reprinted by permission of Stryker-Post Publications, Harpers Ferry, WV.*

Page xxxii: *Excerpt from The Destruction of Slonim Jewry by Nachum Alpert, copyright © 1989 by Nachum Alpert, English translation by Max Rosenfeld, is used with the permission of the U.S. Holocaust Memorial Museum, Washington, DC.*

Pages xxxi, xxxii, and xxxv: *Photos by Roman Vishniac reprinted by permission of Mara Vishniac Kohn, courtesy the International Center of Photography, New York, NY.*

Page xxxiv: *Photo of the S.S. Zeeland, reprinted by permission of The Mariners' Museum, Newport News, VA.*

Pages xviii and 63: *Photo by Ann Venegas reprinted by permission of The Orange County Register, copyright 2007.*

Pages 168 and 175: *Photos by Daniel Ottenstein reprinted by permission of Daniel Ottenstein, www.danielottenstein.com.*

Pages 172, 201, 202, and 242: *Photos by Nick Koon reprinted by permission of Nick Koon, www.nicholaskoonphotography.com.*

The author is grateful for permission to reprint the following recipes:

Page 8: *Sheilah Kaufman's Smoked Salmon Cheesecake ("Smoked Salmon Cheesecake"), from Simply Irrestible; Easy, Elegant, Fearless, Fussless Recipes by Sheilah Kaufman, © 2000 by Sheilah Kaufman. Used by permission of the author.*

Page 174: *Corrinne's Mock Schmaltz ("Mock Chicken Fat"), from The New International Goodwill Recipe Book, 6th Edition, published by The Johannesburg Women's Zionist League, © 1990 by the Women's Zionist Organization of South Africa. Used by permission of the organization.*

Page 225: *Rice Paper–Wrapped Sea Bass ("Haddock Steaks in Rice Paper with Shallot-and-Soy Sauce"), from Happy Cooking by Jacques Pepin, © 1994 by Jacques Pepin. Used by permission of the author.*

Page 294: *Grandma Reila's Incredible Noodle Pudding ("My Mom's Incredibly Fattening Noodle Pudding"), from Plain Jane's Thrill of Very Fattening Foods Cookbook by Linda Sunshine, © 1985 by Linda Sunshine. Used by permission of the author.*

Page 605: *Cherry Vishnyek ("Vishnyek"), from Yiddish Cuisine; A Gourmet's Approach to Jewish Cooking by Robert Sternberg, © 1998 by Robert Sternberg. Used by permission of Rowman & Littlefield Publishing Group.*

Page 573: *Too Good To Call Passover Cake Bête Noire (Flourless Chocolate Cake) ("Bête Noire") from Growing Up on the Chocolate Diet by Lora Brody, © 1990 by Lora Brody. Used by permission of the author.*

index